Architecture in Development

This extensive text investigates how architects, planners, and other related experts responded to the contexts and discourses of "development" after World War II. Development theory did not manifest itself in tracts of economic and political theory alone. It manifested itself in every sphere of expression where economic predicaments might be seen to impinge on cultural factors. Architecture appears in development discourse as a terrain between culture and economics, in that practitioners took on the mantle of modernist expression while also acquiring government contracts and immersing themselves in bureaucratic processes. This book considers how, for a brief period, architects, planners, structural engineers, and various practitioners of the built environment employed themselves in designing all the intimate spheres of life, but from a consolidated space of expertise. Seen in these terms, development was, to cite Arturo Escobar, an immense design project itself, one that requires radical disassembly and rethinking beyond the umbrella terms of "global modernism" and "colonial modernities," which risk erasing the sinews of conflict encountered in globalizing and modernizing architecture.

Encompassing countries as diverse as Israel, Ghana, Greece, Belgium, France, India, Mexico, the United States, Venezuela, the Philippines, South Korea, Sierra Leone, Singapore, Turkey, Cyprus, Iraq, Zambia, and Canada, the set of essays in this book cannot be considered exhaustive, nor a "field guide" in the traditional sense. Instead, it offers theoretical reflections "from the field," based on extensive archival research. This book sets out to examine the arrays of power, resources, technologies, networking, and knowledge that cluster around the term "development," and the manner in which architects and planners negotiated these thickets in their multiple capacities—as knowledge experts, as technicians, as negotiators, and as occasional authorities on settlements, space, domesticity, education, health, and every other field where arguments for development were made.

The Aggregate Architectural History Collaborative is dedicated to advancing research and education in the history and theory of architecture. Since 2006, Aggregate has held dozens of workshops and symposia throughout North America in partnership with major universities, exhibitions, and research centers. Aggregate presents innovative scholarship on its website *we-aggregate.org* and has published the collected volumes *Governing by Design: Architecture, Economy, and Politics in the Twentieth Century* (2012) and *Writing Architectural History: Evidence and Narrative in the Twenty-First Century* (2021).

Architecture in Development is edited for Aggregate by Arindam Dutta, Professor of Architectural History and Theory at the Massachusetts Institute of Technology; Ateya Khorakiwala, Assistant Professor of Architecture at the Columbia University; Ayala Levin, Associate Professor in the Department of Architecture and Urban Design at the University of California, Los Angeles; Fabiola López-Durán, Associate Professor of Art and Architectural History at Rice University; and Ijlal Muzaffar, Associate Professor of Modern Architectural History at the Rhode Island School of Design.

"Brilliantly questioning the figure of 'development' that haunts modernism, Aggregate gets down to the dirt of the Bretton-Woods world: the entanglement of architectural discourse in food insecurity and mining infrastructures, debt servicing and dictators, supply chains of materials and expertise. A must-read for architectural thinkers."

Swati Chattopadhyay, *University of California, Santa Barbara, USA*

"This timely book addresses a major blind spot in contemporary architectural scholarship: the central role of the design disciplines in the processes of modern, postcolonial development in creating the exclusions and inequalities of our time."

Fernando Lara, *Potter Rose Professorship, University of Texas at Austin, USA*

Architecture in Development
Systems and the Emergence of the Global South

Edited by Aggregate

LONDON AND NEW YORK

Cover Image: Gustavo Diaz, *Detalle de la cartografía hallada en la Abadía Benedictina de Ottobeuren*. Fechada y firmada: Siglo V a.C., Lotfi Asker Zadeh. (Papel incendiado rescatado del Segundo Gran Incendio. Actualmente conservado en el Museo de la Eterna.)

First published 2022
by Routledge
4 Park Square, Milton Park, Abingdon, Oxon OX14 4RN

and by Routledge
605 Third Avenue, New York, NY 10158

Routledge is an imprint of the Taylor & Francis Group, an informa business

© 2022 selection and editorial matter, Aggregate; individual chapters, the contributors

The right of Aggregate to be identified as the author of the editorial material, and of the authors for their individual chapters, has been asserted in accordance with sections 77 and 78 of the Copyright, Designs and Patents Act 1988.

All rights reserved. No part of this book may be reprinted or reproduced or utilised in any form or by any electronic, mechanical, or other means, now known or hereafter invented, including photocopying and recording, or in any information storage or retrieval system, without permission in writing from the publishers.

Trademark notice: Product or corporate names may be trademarks or registered trademarks, and are used only for identification and explanation without intent to infringe.

Every effort has been made to contact copyright-holders. Please advise the publisher of any errors or omissions, and these will be corrected in subsequent editions.

British Library Cataloguing-in-Publication Data
A catalogue record for this book is available from the British Library

Library of Congress Cataloging-in-Publication Data
Names: Aggregate (Group), editor.
Title: Architecture in development: systems and the emergence of the global South/edited by Aggregate.
Description: Abingdon, Oxon; New York: Routledge, 2022. | Includes bibliographical references and index.
Identifiers: LCCN 2021043472 (print) | LCCN 2021043473 (ebook) | ISBN 9781032045320 (hardback) | ISBN 9781032045337 (paperback) | ISBN 9781003193654 (ebook)
Subjects: LCSH: Architecture and society—History—20th century. | Architecture—Economic aspects—History—20th century. | Economic development—History—20th century.
Classification: LCC NA2543.S6 A63125 2022 (print) | LCC NA2543.S6 (ebook) | DDC 720.1/03—dc23
LC record available at https://lccn.loc.gov/2021043472
LC ebook record available at https://lccn.loc.gov/2021043473

ISBN: 978-1-032-04532-0 (hbk)
ISBN: 978-1-032-04533-7 (pbk)
ISBN: 978-1-003-19365-4 (ebk)

DOI: 10.4324/9781003193654

Typeset in Minion
by Apex CoVantage, LLC

Contents

Acknowledgments ix
List of contributors xi

    Introduction 1
    Arindam Dutta, Ateya Khorakiwala, Ayala Levin, Fabiola López-Durán, and Ijlal Muzaffar for Aggregate

Part I   Developmental time **23**

1 Incompletion: on more than a certain tendency in postwar architecture and planning 25
    Arindam Dutta

2 God's gamble: self-help architecture and the housing of risk 47
    Ijlal Muzaffar

Part II   Expertise **63**

3 Planning for an uncertain present: action planning in Singapore, India, Israel, and Sierra Leone 65
    Ayala Levin

4 To which revolution? The National School of Agriculture and the Center for the Improvement of Corn and Wheat in Texcoco and El Batán, Mexico, 1924–1968 85
    Nikki Moore

5 From rice research to coconut capital 105
    Diana Martinez

6   "The city as a housing project": training for human settlements at the Leuven PGCHS in the 1970s–1980s   123
Sebastiaan Loosen, Viviana d'Auria, and Hilde Heynen

Part III   Bureaucratic organization   141

7   Folders, patterns, and villages: pastoral technics and the Center for Environmental Structure   143
Ginger Nolan

8   The technical state: programs, positioning, and the integration of architects in political society in Mexico, 1945–1955   161
Albert José-Antonio López

9   "Foreigners in filmmaking"   179
Felicity D. Scott

Part IV   Technological transfer   195

10   The making of architectural design as *Sŏlgye*: integrating science, industry, and expertise in postwar Korea   197
Melany Sun-Min Park

11   Infrastructures of dependency: US Steel's architectural assemblages on Indigenous lands   217
Manuel Shvartzberg Carrió

12   Reinventing earth architecture in the age of development   237
Farhan Karim

Part V   Designing the rural   257

13   Globalizing the village: development media, Jaqueline Tyrwhitt, and the United Nations in India   259
Olga Touloumi

14   "Ruralizing" Zambia: Doxiadis Associates' systems-based planning and developmentalism in the nonindustrialized South   279
Petros Phokaides

15   Food capital: fantasies of abundance and Nelson Rockefeller's architectures of development in Venezuela, 1940s–1960s   303
Fabiola López-Durán

16	The Jewish Agency's open cowsheds: Israeli third way rural design, 1956–1968 *Martin Hershenzon*	323
17	Floors and ceilings: the architectonics of accumulation in the Green Revolution *Ateya Khorakiwala*	343

Part VI   Land   363

18	Policy regionalism and the limits of translation in land economics *Burak Erdim*	365
19	Leisure and geo-economics: the Hilton and other development regimes in the Mediterranean South *Panayiota Pyla*	381
20	Antiparochì and (its) architects: Greek architectures in failure *Konstantina Kalfa*	401

Index   417

Acknowledgments

The editors would like to thank the MIT Department of Architecture; Princeton Mellon Initiative in Architecture, Urbanism & the Humanities; Rice University School of Humanities; and UCLA School of the Arts and Architecture for generously supporting the publication of this book.

Contributors

Viviana d'Auria is an architect, urbanist, and associate professor in international urbanism at the Department of Architecture, KU Leuven, Belgium. Through her work she explores the epistemological contribution of development aid to the discipline of urbanism, within a more general interest in the transcultural construction of cities and their contested spaces.

Arindam Dutta is a professor of architectural history and theory at the Massachusetts Institute of Technology. He is the author of *Bureaucracy of Beauty: Design in the Age of its Global Reproducibility* (2007). His *The Liberal Arts after Liberalization: Sahmat, 1989–2019* is currently under preparation.

Burak Erdim is an associate professor of architectural history and design at North Carolina State University. His research traces the operations of transnational planning cultures, and his recent book, *Landed Internationals: Planning Cultures, the Academy, and the Making of the Modern Middle East*, was published by the University of Texas Press (2020).

Martin Hershenzon is trained as an architect and architectural historian (PhD University of Pennsylvania, 2016). He teaches at the Bezalel Academy of Arts and Design and at the Shenkar College of Engineering, Design and Art. His research focuses on civic representation, architectural knowledge, and agency in postwar architecture culture. In addition, Hershenzon leads projects in design education and new urban design methodologies.

Hilde Heynen is a professor of architectural theory at the Department of Architecture, KU Leuven, Belgium. Her research focuses on issues of modernity, modernism, and gender in architecture. She is the author of *Architecture and Modernity: A Critique* (MIT Press, 1999) and *Sibyl Moholy-Nagy: Architecture, Modernism and Its Discontents* (Bloomsbury, 2019).

Konstantina Kalfa is a research associate at the School of Architecture of the National Technical University of Athens and adjunct faculty at the Department of Art Theory and History of the Athens School of Fine Arts. Her research revolves around the study of architecture in postwar modernization and development, with a particular focus on informal housing practices and how these are intertwined with multiple types of politics and social conflicts. She is the author of the book *Self-Sheltering, Now! The Invisible Side of the American Aid to Greece* [in Greek] (Futura, 2019).

Farhan Karim is an associate professor of architecture at the University of Kansas. He is the author of *Of Greater Dignity Than Riches: Austerity and Housing Design in India*. He has edited the *Routledge Companion to Architecture and Social Engagement* and *Boundary, Flows and the Making of Modern Muslim Selves through Architecture*.

Ateya Khorakiwala is an assistant professor of architecture at Columbia University. She researches infrastructure, materiality, and aesthetics during India's developmental decades. Her book-in-progress, *Famine Landscapes*, investigates the intersections between architecture, infrastructure, and hunger in India in the twentieth century.

Ayala Levin is an associate professor in the Department of Architecture and Urban Design at the University of California, Los Angeles. She is the author of *Architecture and Development: Israeli Construction in Sub-Saharan Africa and the Settler Colonial Imagination* (Duke University Press, 2022).

Sebastiaan Loosen is a postdoctoral researcher and senior assistant at the Institute for the History and Theory of Architecture (gta), ETH Zürich. He completed a PhD on the history of architectural theory in Belgium (KU Leuven, 2019) and has recently initiated a project on architectural training programs established in the context of development aid.

Albert José-Antonio López is a historian of modern architecture and planning. He is a postdoctoral fellow at the University of New Mexico at Albuquerque and has previously taught at the University of California at Santa Barbara. He holds a PhD in history, theory, and criticism from the Massachusetts Institute of Technology.

Fabiola López-Durán is an associate professor of art and architectural history at Rice University. She earned her PhD in history, theory and criticism of architecture from MIT. Adopting a transnational and interdisciplinary perspective, López-Durán's research and teaching interrogates the cross-pollination of ideas and mediums—science, politics, and aesthetics—that ignited the process of modernization on both sides of the Atlantic, with an emphasis on Latin America. López-Durán's book, *Eugenics in the Garden: Transatlantic Architecture and the Crafting of Modernity*, investigates a particular strain of eugenics that, at the turn of the twentieth century, moved from the realms of medicine and law to design, architecture, and urban planning—becoming a critical instrument in the crafting of modernity. This book received a SAH/Mellon Author Award in 2018 and the Robert Motherwell Book Prize in 2019.

Diana Martinez is an assistant professor of architectural history and the director of architectural studies at Tufts University. She is completing a book manuscript, *Concrete Colonialism: Architecture, Infrastructure, Urbanism and the American Colonial Project in the Philippines*.

Nikki Moore is a postdoctoral fellow in global architecture at Wake Forest University. Her current research focuses on the industrialization of food-based commodities and concurrent development practices in modern Latin America, focusing on their symbiotic relationship to art, architectural practice, and social justice. Moore's research is supported by the Social Science Research Council, Mellon Foundation, Graham Foundation, Wagoner

Foundation, Rice University, University-Based Institute for Advanced Study, and Society of Architectural Historians.

Ijlal Muzaffar is an associate professor of modern architectural history and the Department Head of Theory and History of Art and Design at RISD, the Rhode Island School of Design. He received his PhD in architectural history from MIT and a master of architecture from Princeton University. His work has appeared widely in edited volumes, biennale catalogues, and peer-reviewed journals. He is a founding member of the architectural history research collaborative and publishing platform Aggregate. His first book, *The Periphery Within: Modern Architecture and the Making of the Third World*, slated to come out from the University of Texas Press in Spring 2022, looks at how modern architects and planners shaped the discourse on Third World development and its associated structures of power after the Second World War.

Ginger Nolan is an assistant professor of architectural history at the University of Southern California. Her work engages issues of social justice, media technologies, and governmentality. She has published *The Neocolonialism of the Global Village* (2018) and *Savage Mind to Savage Machine: Racial Science and Twentieth-Century Design* (2021), both by the University of Minnesota Press. Her work has also been published in scholarly journals including *Grey Room*, *Journal of Architecture*, and *Architecture Theory Review*.

Melany Sun-Min Park is a design and workplace strategist at Gensler. She holds a PhD in architecture from Harvard University. She was named the 2020 Korea Society Sherman Family Emerging Scholar. Melany's research has been supported by the D. Kim Foundation for History of Science and Technology in East Asia, Harvard Korea Institute, and Harvard Asia Center.

Petros Phokaides holds a PhD from the National Technical University of Athens and is currently an assistant professor at the University of Thessaly Greece. His research focuses on architecture, infrastructures, and broader landscape transformations across multiple spatial scales to understand postcolonial visions, geopolitics, political economy, and socio-environmental change in the Global South. He serves on the editorial board of *Architectural Histories*.

Panayiota Pyla is an architectural historian and theorist with a PhD from the Massachusetts Institute of Technology. She is currently associate professor of architecture at the University of Cyprus, having previously served on the faculty of the University of Illinois, Urbana-Champaign. Among her works is the edited book *Landscapes of Development: The Impact of Modernization Discourses on the Physical Environment of the Eastern Mediterranean* (Harvard University Press, 2013) and the book (coedited with Sibel Bozdogan and Petros Phokaides) *Coastal Architectures and the Politics of Tourism: Leisurescapes of the Global Sunbelt* (Routledge, forthcoming 2022).

Felicity D. Scott is a professor of architecture, director of the PhD program in Architecture (History and Theory), and codirector of the program in Critical, Curatorial and Conceptual Practices in Architecture (CCCP) at the Graduate School of Architecture, Planning and Preservation, Columbia University. Her books include *Architecture or Techno-Utopia:*

Politics After Modernism (MIT Press, 2007), *Ant Farm* (ACTAR, 2008), *Outlaw Territories: Environments of Insecurity/Architectures of Counter-Insurgency* (Zone Books, 2016), and *Disorientations: Bernard Rudofsky in the Empire of Signs* (Sternberg Press, 2016).

Manuel Shvartzberg Carrió is an assistant professor in urban studies and planning at the University of California, San Diego. An architect and architectural historian, he researches histories and theories of architecture and geopolitics, particularly how technologies and infrastructures mediate regimes of settler colonialism, racial capitalism, and processes of decolonization.

Olga Touloumi is assistant professor of architectural history at Bard College. Her forthcoming book *The Global Interior: United Nations and World Ordering* (University of Minnesota Press) examines the United Nations and the design of its platforms for liberal internationalism. Her research focuses on the intersection of buildings, media, and twentieth-century internationalist projects. She has coedited *Sound Modernities: Architecture, Media, and Design*; and *Computer Architectures: Constructing the Common Ground, 1945–1980* (Routledge, 2019). Her writing has appeared in the *Journal of the Society of Architectural Historians, Buildings & Landscapes, Journal of Architecture*, and *Harvard Design Magazine*. Her research has received fellowships from the National Endowment for the Humanities, the Max Planck Institute for the History of Science, the Alexander S. Onassis Foundation, and the Canadian Center for Architecture, among others.

Introduction

Arindam Dutta, Ateya Khorakiwala, Ayala Levin,
Fabiola López-Durán, and Ijlal Muzaffar for Aggregate

The chapters in this volume look at how architects, planners, and other related experts responded to the contexts and discourses of "development" after World War II. The discourses of development augured both an institutional shift and a cultural turn in the processes of modernization and capital formation around the world. They entailed an intensification and expansion of knowledge and expertise that accompanied the formation and transformation of new nation-states, transformed governmental mandates, and expanded franchises, along with the accompanying shifts in cultural and economic imaginaries. These chapters explore histories of architecture and urban planning that both participated in and were driven by these shifts. In large part, the discourses of development were not new. On the one hand, they referred back to ideas about transitions to modern forms of society from agrarian and "primitive" societies that had been prevalent since the eighteenth century, ideas that were given a statutory (and violent) mandate in the Soviet Union's New Economic Policy in the interwar years. On another level, they linked back to archaic arguments of pastoral power, often rehearsing classical arguments about the relationships of state, society, and sovereignty as well as the uses and place of knowledge in managing these relations. The Foucauldian themes of governmentality and biopolitics—knowledge forms revolving around the nature of wealth, population, territory, health, hygiene, consumption, and the disciplining of behavior—were central to these new deployments of expertise, often seeking to replace politics in the classic sense. Considerable areas of overlap lay between colonial and postcolonial regimes in this regard, not least the critical significance that colonizer and (ex-)colonized accorded to the realm of "culture," seen both as a wellspring but also as an obstruction in these discourses of freedom and emancipation. Consequently, development theory would not manifest itself in tracts of economic and political theory alone. It would manifest itself in song poetry, cinema, theater, literature and art, indeed in every sphere of expression where economic predicaments might be seen to impinge on cultural imaginaries.

Architecture and urban planning would appear in development discourse as a crucial terrain operating somewhere between culture and economics. Architects styled themselves both as aesthetic world-builders, styling the flurry of institution-building that took place in developing countries at this time in an array of modernist forms, and as mundane contractors, making claims on fiscal outlays and immersing themselves in bureaucratic and procurement processes. For a brief period of time, architects and planners found themselves at the deliberative table wherever projects were being conceptualized, tasked to undertake

DOI: 10.4324/9781003193654-1

buildings dedicated to political, biopolitical, or cultural functions, working alongside economists, doctors, researchers, politicians, and industrialists to design the very manner in which people ate, learned, worked, and produced. Development was, to cite Arturo Escobar, an "immense design project" itself,[1] one that today requires radical disassembly and rethinking beyond innocuous terms like "global modernism" and "colonial modernities" that risk erasing the sinews of conflict encountered in these globalizing and modernizing projects. This book seeks both to investigate and assemble ongoing scholarship on *architecture in development*, attending equally to the conflicting politics of knowledge and hierarchies of resource mobilization embedded in the resulting architectural forms.

If economic growth, defined by technological advances and industrialization, was seen as essential to support the newfound freedoms of the developing world, culture provided an alternative tent under which the philosopher-princes of development theory could gather the collective and individual drivers of motivation. What went by the name of development "theory," therefore, was not some unitary concept but as an unwieldy smorgasbord of themes, initiatives, and interventions. As such, these ideas would assume many avatars across the world, infusing the political language of wildly opposed, inconsistent, and unrelated views of savant and gangster alike, affording ideological shelter *both* for hegemonic regimes of different kinds *and* opposition to them. Utilized as a shared *lingua franca* by despots, Oxbridge and LSE-trained heresiarchs, social justice movements, militaries, bureaucrats, and guerrillas, by non-Marxists and Marxists alike, the rhetoric of development would also provide cover for umpteen private and public idiosyncrasies and hobbyhorses, enabling different cliques to establish little and large fiefdoms in bureaucracies, governments, and universities alike. Its keywords would be used to legitimate a vast variety of professions and pursuits, from the lowest tier of political bosses and fixers to large knowledge-institutional and fiscal networks composed of scientists, technicians, bureaucrats, and consultants, not to rule out expanding global cohorts of expertise-peddling hacks and charlatans.

Any timeline of development history that we may provide here must consequently only be a provisional one. Decolonization was not some singular, uniform, or even controlled process, given the myriad juridical and governmental norms as well as economic rationales with which various colonial regimes came to control large tracts of territory around the world. At the turn of the twentieth century, many Latin American and Asian countries, including China, were nominally independent even if their sovereign powers were strongly controlled by semicolonial domains of influence, many of which slid handily into neocolonial forms of dominance after the Second World War. Likewise, the premise of sovereignty in the newly independent countries of the mid-twentieth century were significantly complicated by the onset of the Cold War almost immediately after the war, leading to brutal counterinsurgency wars in Malaya, Kenya, Vietnam, and Algeria. If World War II ended centuries of warfare over national boundaries in Europe, the European exit from the colonies would, by contrast, instigate—and actively propagate—new waves of warfare among territories tentatively kept at peace by imperial détente in the metropole. The five years after the Second World War would see the largest population migrations ever in history, and state-formation in the Third World would be accompanied by equally unprecedented mass slaughter and genocide on unimaginable scales, establishing patterns that have yet to cease. The tropes of development would thereby come to be wholly entangled within and complicated by these histories, creating alibis for betterment and oppression often in the same breath, and creating as many new types of perpetrators and saviors as beneficiaries and victims. Like other discourses of freedom, the emancipatory rhetoric of development proves to be handy for the financialization and militarization of societies alike.

The term development remains just as powerful today. It is invoked as an alibi to legitimize a complete lockdown of movement and communication in Kashmir, extrajudicial murders in Indonesia, and state-aided razing of rainforests in the Amazon. The ambivalence within its postulates allows it to infect opposing agendas in electoral contests—to wit, United States President Donald Trump's pronouncement, "We're a developing nation, too"—but also new movements for social, economic, and environmental justice. At various levels, the discourses of development have conditioned everything from speech acts to, say, the diameter of a water pipe or the composition of cement or fertilizers. The oscillation between ambivalence and high specificity impact, in turn, countervailing practices of control and freedom, conditioning the manner in which these words are understood, defined, and voiced. What development (like similar such words as modernity) *means* or could mean, for the purposes of this book, would be a futile question; it receives as many definitions as the innumerable kinds of actors who see benefit in deploying some idiom of development in their own interest.

This book sets out to examine the arrays of power, resources, technologies, networking, and knowledge that cluster around this necessarily ambiguous realm, and the manner in which architects and planners negotiated these thickets in their multiple capacities, as epistemic authorities, as technicians, as negotiators, and as commentators and prognosticators on the future of government, settlements, space, domesticity, education, health, and every other field where arguments for development were invoked.

THE BRETTON WOODS SYSTEM IN THE DEVELOPING WORLD

Toward the end of the Second World War, the dominant consensus that emerged within economic and political circles was that the world economy requires managing. The conference of economists from Allied countries that took place in the Mount Washington Hotel in Bretton Woods, New Hampshire, of July 1–22, 1944, represented an opening gambit for laying out a new, cohesive, and globally encompassing monetary system for the postwar world. The principal core of the Bretton Woods system was its effort to abolish the plural but also clannish order of the old European empires in order to establish a coordinated monetary system for a world composed of a far larger number of sovereign nation-states. Uncertainty in global markets, the argument went, deepened when states and politics acted in contradictory directions or when states' traditional fiscal-monetary fecklessness in market intervention went contrary to economic logic. These at least were the primary reasons adduced by economists in the 1940s for the Great Depression, as well as for the many such prior depressions of the previous century. The singular instrument that the Bretton Woods system focused on to battle the uncertainty of the capitalist system as ordained by the pre-war imperial regimes was the money form. In creating the new system, money, along with its haphazard and ad hoc determinations of "price," was detached from its association with the "natural" world, that is, the metallic standard, and reposed instead in a new, self-fulfilling *social* construct, a single exchange system pegged to the clout of the American dollar.

By any measure, the "hero" at Bretton Woods was the ailing John Maynard Keynes, whose *General Theory of Employment, Interest and Money*, published in 1936, expounded on the key role that the money-form, as a crucial determinant of market expectations, could play under certain constraints in stimulating investment within an ever-looming landscape of risk. The state's strategic injection of money as an inflationary instrument within a finite range of underemployment, Keynes had argued, could have the effect of modulating wage prices and commodity prices as a way of stimulating demand, such that markets would not be subject to the *simultaneous* demand and supply crises as experienced during the Great Depression. This gambit aimed to "save capitalism from the capitalists" by curbing the worst tendencies of the market to swing in boom and bust cycles.

The institutions founded in the wake of the Bretton Woods systems had global repercussions in the norms that it stipulated for monetary convertibility between national markets. It is hard to underscore the extent to which this was based on an extraordinary international compact between its participating nations. At one fell swoop, the output of a small fruit orchard in the Himalayas, the supply of diamonds in Rhodesia, the wages of a policeman in Singapore, the cost of a highway on the outskirts of Paris, and countless such unrelated economic "transactions" across the globe became linked to each other through the mediation of the American dollar, which became the default global currency for settlements across the world's diverse market systems.

Yet this presumptive multilateralism still remained, as many noted at the time, an Anglo-American compact. The Soviet Union and its satellites stayed out of Bretton Woods, based on their very different reading of the money form and its relationship to the state. The Bretton Woods conference had also included, in the words of the Mount Washington hotel staff that served as the venue, a "gathering of Colombians, Poles, Liberians, Chinese, Ethiopians, Russians, Filipinos, Icelanders and other spectacular peoples" comprising a substantial portion of the 730 delegates present, late-colonial proxies and peripheral witnesses to a change in the armature of Empire.[2] Pushed to the fringe of these deliberations, representing by far the demographic majority of the planet but invited only on the say-so of their colonial masters of the time, they were little solicited for their views on the creation of a global arrangement that they correctly understood, and voiced concerns about, as radically poised to overwhelm their future.

This marginalization did not reflect their political marginalization alone: their sidelining also reflected a structural lacuna in the Keynesian economic universe and hence in the design of the Bretton Woods agreements. The *General Theory* goes to great lengths to stipulate the specific relations of wages (demand), levels of employment and output under which its arguments for monetary infusion by the state and the cost of money (inflation) hold true. Another way of putting this is to say that Keynesian tools only worked at near full-employment levels, a premise that assumes a fully industrialized society. To deploy this strategy in conditions other than full employment was, to use Keynes' famous phrase, like "pushing on a string," infusing money and technology into worlds that had little aptitude to (productively) employ it.

Evidently this begged the question of the "developing" world, defined as they were by minimal penetration by modern, mechanized industry. "Pump-priming" demand through inflation was pointedly out of place for a nonindustrial workforce with the low productivity outputs associated with non-mechanized economies, a condition that development economists promptly took to describing as "surplus," "underemployed," or "unemployed" labor. Nonetheless, the monetary norms laid down at Bretton Woods reflected the Keynesian calculus, thus subjecting the entire developing world to an institutional armature that deemed them, de facto, if not irrelevant, certainly "defective" in terms of the theory driving this arrangement. This institutional arrangement thus implicitly recreated a hierarchy where industrial (formerly colonial) powers would retain primacy over countries enmeshed in primary production and resource extraction. If the developing world was, by definition, that in which Keynesian monetary theory did not hold, then "development economics" and "development planning" would appear in the postwar period as fields driven precisely by the desire to bridge the epistemological gap between Keynesian assumptions and the large tracts of the planet where these assumptions did not hold.

The effect of the money form on exchanges in every other social sphere has long been the object of study, from some of the earliest theological texts to a slew of modern scholarship in almost every discipline, and the conceivers of the Bretton Woods arrangement understood well that their impact would go far beyond monetary-fiscal decisions alone. In addition to the International Monetary Fund and the World Bank, the two institutions designated to shore up global financial markets, the Bretton Woods Organizations also comprised, under the umbrella of the United Nations and outside it, multi-lateral arrangements and charters dedicated to health, education, culture, labor rights, the environment, housing, quality standards, scientific research and cooperation, statistics, to name some of the prominent areas. Biopolitics and technique took precedence in realms where previously *laissez faire* approaches and conventional politics had reigned before, under the premise that "disinterested" agreements could be reached sooner and easier amongst experts arguing about methodology than in the internecine, squabbling play of interests that comprised most societies and dispensations of power. Many of the authors in this volume interrogate the work done by these Bretton Woods Organizations to show how the combination of biopolitics and technique have been central to organizing the post-Bretton Woods built environments.

A corollary to the Bretton Woods international arrangements of a single exchange system pegged to the dollar was the primacy accorded to *sovereign* nation-states as the principal agency tasked with guiding this new international compact. With Washington holding the fiscal reins, it nonetheless devolved on nation-states to negotiate the fraught predicaments of socialization produced by this monetary system. In its own way, the emphasis placed by the Bretton Woods system on the centrality and importance of the state cannot be discounted here, tantamount to something like apostasy within the economic liberal privileging of the autonomy of markets that it was otherwise designed to propagate. The hobgoblin that haunted the proceedings of the Mount Washington Hotel conference and analyses of the worldwide depression that preceded it was the Soviet *Gosplan*. In the 1920s, the forced modernization undertaken by the Soviet New Economic Policy had entailed the active alteration, from on high, of the terms of trade between agriculture and industry, a process involving the state's intervention in determining prices all along the chain of commodities. While Keynes was none too taken with the ultimate viability of the Soviet system, the reasons behind the central role accorded to the state in the *General Theory* was as much political as economic, in that its theories were intended to defend political liberalism against the growing attractions of communism given the widespread despair of the Great Depression. Still, the *General Theory* restricted the state's role solely to monetary manipulation while defending a circumscribed chaos or "animal spirits" in capitalist markets as essential to their vitality. Although there was a world of difference between the so-called "developing" economies and the Keynesian model, the autonomy accorded within the Bretton Woods system to what Alain Badiou has termed the "metapolitical state"—the subsumption of all politics to the state as capitalist governor—was essential to the premise of development.[3]

Competing ideas as to the role of the state defined almost any polity or country within the postcolonial theatres of development, and certainly these differences became salient in geopolitical terms as well in the conception of the so-called three Worlds—First, Second, and Third—that charted or sought to chart differing ideological worldviews, or at least differing spheres of influence.[4] The state's role as primary caretaker of the economy, rather than the market, became an essential feature of the developing world, in itself marking a significant departure from prewar colonial regimes where an emphasis on *laissez faire* economics and low public spending represented the obverse coin of economic extraction and captive markets.

Correspondingly, in the Bretton Woods system, shoring up states' sovereignty represented the flipside of the protean technology that lay at its base: debt. To secure debt, essential in building and stabilizing "proper" capitalization of markets, it also became necessary to strengthen the monetary wherewithal of states. In this regard, the ideological conflicts of the Third World emerged, as in the First and Second, over the degree to which this interventional power in monetary affairs also extended to fiscal prerogatives. Further differences emerged around questions of the deficit. Newly sovereign countries often saw large deficits as essential to achieving modernization at a faster pace; conversely, international financial lending agencies were wary, as today, of the inflationary implications of enlarged deficits on the state's ability to honor its debts.

These differences, however, did not polarize the First and Third Worlds. If these two-stroke engines—sovereign debt and the management of deficits in fiscal initiative—aimed to heighten governmental prerogative in both developed and developing worlds, they also introduced a measure of homogeneity in the ways in which governments conceived of their subjects as economic entities, in both North and South. As the Pakistani economist Mahbub ul Haq introduced his study of economic planning, "All economic plans read alike. If one picks up the plans of India, Pakistan, Ghana, Egypt, Nepal or Ceylon, at random, what is surprising is not their apparent differences but their basic similarity."[5] This was mirrored across the developed world, where economists routinely pointed to the structural barriers posed by low productivity, surplus labor, and under-capitalization to returns on investment.

This double bind, of conceptualizing larger and larger projects to justify the contraction of larger and larger loans on one hand and of greater oversight over states by extra-statal lenders in defining the nature of projects on the other, made up the principal scaffold of what we could call "development time": a temporal extension between projects that would continue indefinitely in the service of so-called national development "goals." The "development decades" of the 1950s–1970s—on par with *les trentes glorieuses* in fully-industrialized countries—saw a profusion of state-initiated megaprojects launched throughout the world. A new form of instrument, the sovereign-backed loan, formed the lubricant for a profusion of technologies that flowed around the world, from condoms, civics lessons, and engineered rice to pozzolans, submachine guns, and antibiotics.[6]

THE NEW (DIS)BALANCE

In the early postwar era, development economics within the Bretton Woods institutions was initially characterized by a fixation on "balanced" growth. Proponents of balanced growth argued that in countries without "mature" capitalist market sectors and institutions, the path to economic growth was only possible by simultaneous investment on multiple fronts, from industrial and agricultural production to health, education, and social services. These investments required a carefully orchestrated combination of infrastructural development, tax incentives, urban and regional planning projects, government subsidies, and centralized administrative control. An independent and self-supporting system would emerge only when every aspect of capitalist production was ticking in sync with all the others. Established on a significant scale, such a system would independently attract further investment and would establish mutually supporting and self-aggregating market activity. In the "Big Push" model advanced by the Harvard economist Paul Rosenstein-Rodan, development planning was necessary to establish "economies of scale," the maximum quantity up to which the cost of producing a commodity could be reduced by producing it in greater quantities. The problem of development, so it was assumed, was only one of coordination, of setting the system in place, of turning gears and wheels in sync until the whole mechanism started to tick on its own accord, picking up speed and adding more parts to its movements.[7]

In order to reach this tipping point, what the MIT economist Walt Rostow, in line with the "modernization" theory brewing in American academic circles, called "take-off," large infusions of debt would necessarily capitalize on massive changes precipitating in undercapitalized countries, such that developing countries could rush past, at a fell swoop, the centuries of internecine struggle between tradition and modernity as witnessed in the capitalist countries of Europe.[8] In attempts to implement modernization theory, experts went beyond economic factors to identify elements within "tradition" that necessarily needed to be dismantled to arrive at the modern. Political elites within developing countries also essentially subscribed to these views, committing states to undertake massive efforts at socialization, often posed as the realization of the utopic premises of anti-colonial movements. Each free contraceptive pill, subsidized textbook, new strain of long-grained rice, liter of clean water bore within itself a little morsel of expanded state debt. In the event, as one "development handbook" put it:

> It has been said that the nation state has become too small for the big things, and too big for the small things. To the watchman's duty [i.e. the liberal model of non-intervention in economic affairs] of maintaining law and order have been added such responsibilities as maintaining price stability, ensuring high levels of employment and high growth rates; devising a population policy, regional policy, industrial policy and agricultural policy; responsibility for redistributing incomes and alleviating poverty through social services; protection of the environment, physical and human resources, and energy policy; as well as numerous others.[9]

The state thus came to embody two otherwise unrelated worlds or realms of time: the servicing of the debt on the one hand and the socialization of its "people" on the other. The former referred to a principle of contractual obligation, determined by an immutable and undifferentiable temporal order: the durational time of the debt or bond (the 1-year, 5-year, 10-year, 30-year loan). The latter referred to negotiation, an irreconcilable field of social contracts and types of contracts written and unwritten in multiple temporal worlds, which the state must force or coerce into a manageable "plurality" or communitarian ideal of "society" in order to survive.

In the financially bolstered—from elsewhere as it were—states of the postwar period, this juxtaposition of two temporal fields—of the scripted time of debt management on the one hand and the unscripted predicaments of socialization on the other—will find renewed commitment to theories of systems. Systems theory was first given shape in the knowledge frameworks and institutional strife of the eighteenth-century European "Enlightenment." Then too, it had comprised a similar confrontation between an order of truth and legitimacy manifested in a singular, monotheistic godhead, increasingly challenged by the expansion of markets and finance and the corresponding mercantilist-physiocratic emphasis on a "natural history" that reverted phenomenality to a field described by a dynamics of use and exchange. It is not coincidental that Noam Chomsky would look to the Port-Royal grammarians in elucidating his Cartesian linguistics (1966) or that Albert O. Hirschman would revisit eighteenth-century assertions on behavior as the basis for the creation of modern economics, as would be the case with Alexandre Koyré's arguments on closed and infinite universes, to name a few.[10] Michel Foucault's path-breaking *Les mots et les choses* (1966) implicitly mines this perceived continuum between the knowledge order of the postwar state and the knowledge order accompanying the inception of the modern, capitalist state.[11]

SYSTEMS AND EXPERTISE

In the postwar era, systems theories infused knowledge orders and institutional claims to legitimacy equally in First, Second, and Third Worlds. We could argue that the heterodoxy that systems theories sought to embody lent them the fungibility to apply to every context, whether characterized by adherents of liberal or socialist ideology. The ascendancy of systems theory across these ideological divides spoke particularly to its claims of bringing heterogeneous processes together and referencing conditions of complexity. In the process, systems theories emerged as overarching constructs that allowed mutually incoherent inputs and insights from multiple disciplines. Within this new theology, insights from psychoanalytic theories on Oedipal fixations, anthropologists' studies on fetishes, structural linguistics, thermodynamics in physics, and biological studies in genetics could be handily traded in for each other in the interest of novel, promising epistemological claims that portended to both study and orchestrate the processes of change. The mid-twentieth-century stance was thus markedly different from the "spirit of system" theories in the eighteenth century, which had all ultimately folded back into arguments for fixity in the universe.[12] Positing different system dynamics as partial wholes and parts, postwar theorists emphasized the incomplete understanding of phenomena as a *precondition* for the importance and truth claims of their work: one could only rely on partial knowledge to devise systems that were effectively a combination of different kinds of parts. Incompletion thus turned systems into arguments of scale. A system was a system only insofar as its parts were readable in the context of larger arrays or series of such parts and wholes: ultimately, systems theories were theories of relations. The economist Paul Krugman speaks of systems as an essential prerequisite to model any large-scale action, given any actor within the system would only have partial knowledge of its components:

> [Any] kind of model of a complex system . . . amounts to mak[ing] a set of clearly untrue simplifications to get the system down to something that you can handle; those simplifications are dictated partly by guesses about what is important, partly by the modeling techniques available. And the end result, if the model is a good one, it is an improved insight why the vastly more complex real system behaves the way it does.[13]

It is not hard to imagine the fascination that governmental bodies and firms had for this protean theory of theories that explicitly referred to "practice" as its goal ("something you can handle"), one that professed a liberalism premised on "rights" on the one hand and a conservative focus on productivity on the other. Systems offered a legitimacy that authority of any kind intrinsically craves: in portraying all decisions as premeditated, unifying the state's past and future actions as if cogently arrived at in a uniform series, it covered over the disordered, anarchic political and market surroundings. The claim to epistemic coherence, an affectation at best, would provide a key alibi for the expansion in the scale and conceptualization of projects, in essence putting in play a self-fulfilling process: a theory of system that leads to larger and larger systems being employed in the world.

Nowhere would this be more true than in the theaters of development. Hugh Keenleyside, the first director-general of the United Nations Technical Assistance Administration (UNTAA), described the agency as contributing to a

> great crusade for human progress [driven by] high purposes . . . based upon the assumption that it is possible and practical to transfer knowledge and techniques from one area to another for the purpose of advancing the economic and social development of the people of the world.[14]

In this systemic embrace, both metaphorical and literal, the transferability of "knowledge and techniques" would become the condition for the profusion of projects and would spell the heyday of the professional "expert."

If you were a teacher, doctor, social worker, film or television technician, statistician, nurse, agronomist, banker, engineer, architect, planner, economist, and so on, in this period, new state outlays and expanded ministerial and bureaucratic prerogatives promised you a secure career and benefits that were compounded with the cultural capital that came with your putatively "noble" professional contributions to nation-building. There would be more of you than ever before in the history of the planet. Should you have had the luck, from wealth or connection, to have studied in the Western metropole, chances were high that you would be precipitously hoisted to the apex of this or that governmental body or department. The youthful sojourn to the metropole established your immediate kinship with the developing world's political elite, most of whom had cut their political teeth on educational campuses of the Western world, reading Karl Marx, John Stuart Mill, Leon Trotsky, Harold Laski, John Dewey, Henri de Saint-Simon, John Ruskin, Auguste Comte, and Abraham Lincoln. Chances were equally high that an enormous quantity of projects would be laid on your table. When Habib Rahman arrived back in Calcutta in 1946 after having obtained two degrees at MIT and interning with Walter Gropius and Konrad Wachsmann in Cambridge, MA, he was immediately appointed Senior Architect of the West Bengal Public Works Department, where he completed nearly eighty projects in Bengal by 1953; upon his move to Delhi, he undertook another 150. Gropius's other Indian acolyte, Achyut Kanvinde, similarly completed close to a thousand buildings over his career, most of these being public commissions.

Tethered by the Bretton Woods system, expanded state fiscal prerogatives rained veritable manna on a roving global diaspora of experts—*soi-disant* and otherwise—and consultants, peddling a cornucopia of conceptual hi-jinks and epistemic wares. An example is the firm of Constantinos A. Doxiadis, whose suite of services in planning, design, and engineering garnered projects in 40 different countries, with an office on every continent. More corporate entities—such as Arup, Gensler, and SOM—were not far behind, all of whom affected some kind of theory of system while peddling their own proposals. Other "academic" actors, less-entangled in governmental domains but no less voluble in in terms of their publishing and mediatic footprints, found in the developing world bracing opportunities for new civilizing capers: Maxwell Fry and Jane Drew, Candilis, Josic, and Woods (CJW), Otto Koenigsberger, Charles Abrams, Jaqueline Tyrwhitt, Buckminster Fuller, Louis Kahn, and a sizeable legion of deracinated Bauhäuslers.

These forays closely shadowed neocolonial turf wars in different parts of the planet: British consultants capitalized on the abiding networks of the erstwhile British Empire, the French consultants in the Francophone globe, and American and Soviet missions faced off in diplomatic cocktail parties in tropical heat, angling for the next hydroelectric dam or industrial encampment. Schools, hospitals, housing, universities, laboratories, industrial plants, capitol complexes, transit and defense installations, commercial and bureaucratic offices, new settlements, infrastructure and city plans, and new structures and new spatial imaginaries were wrought in "modern" combinations of grids and curves. These projects also transformed the nature of material circulation and extraction, creating new supply chains of steel, cement, sand, plastic, and other building materials across the world.

The scale of operations, however, that architects were called on to answer should not be understood in itself as a sign of power for the profession. In the new statist domain, the terms of success of a profession could also be described as producing the terms of its ultimate weakness or subservience. Each claim on the instrumentality of buildings and spatial configurations to secure public goods or biopolitical benefits (as in the case of housing) involved fending off competing claims by other disciplines, professionals, suppliers, or consultants, all angling for control of the same packets of resources. Who should define the form of a health clinic, doctors, or architects? Should scarce resources in education be spent on better buildings, more textbooks, or better salaries for teachers? Who should weigh in on highway construction and new railway alignments—architect-planners, landed interests, engineers, or bankers? Is a house primarily a financial allotment or a roof and walls (or alternatively, first a roof, the initial investment, and then the walls)? Who should have primacy in devising the shape of bridges, large buildings, traffic patterns, etc.: engineers or architects? As these contests over expertise intensified, architects and planners found themselves stretched to make knowledge claims in fields as diverse as the "sectors" in which buildings or planning were required, which is to say everything. The expansion of domain control, in other words, may well have augured the attenuation or even evacuation of domain: to wit, Doxiadis's Ekistics, a "science" devoid of content if there ever was one.

What rendered these expanded state domains something of a fool's challenge was the impossibility of defining an even broker who could adjudicate sagely and in real time between these competing claims of expertise and necessity. Such had been the gist of Friedrich A. von Hayek's early excoriation of the figure of the "Central Planner" in his famed formulation of the "knowledge problem."[15] On many levels, the Central Planner was always something of a bogeyman, conjured up by opponents of *dirigisme* rather than an actual office or person possessed of any such executive powers. Indeed, the primary flaw of the Hayekian knowledge problem may have lain not in the "external" problem of marrying data to phenomena but in the *internal* psychodynamics of expert committees themselves. Even the most rudimentary scrutiny of the institutions and bureaucracies devoted to development work behind the Pecksniffian claims to systemic action revealed a world of competing clans, jealousies, and intellectual loyalties, along with confusions as to mandate, insufficient budgets, and inevitable wanting for competent personnel. This is a narrative that the accusations of neocolonial interventionism, routinely leveled at foreign experts by domestic political actors across the developing world, have inevitably missed: the inherent dysfunction and general incompetence within aid organizations themselves. First, there was the problem of recruitment. Since the UN's permanent staff was small, outside experts had to be solicited for each mission, who could only be paid through (usually measly) honorariums. This resulted in a constant struggle to obtain competent staff who had to leave their well-paid positions and family obligations and sally forth on development "missions" to face dysentery, mediocre wages, sketchy lodgings, and obdurate administrations. In this light, post hoc reflections by transient experts such as the housing expert Charles Abrams sent on UN development missions throughout the 1950s and 1960s make for both somber and comical reading:

> American experts were especially hard to enlist partly because of the small fees and partly because every candidate was subject to a rigorous search by the Federal Bureau of Investigation (particularly, in the context of 1950s McCarthyism) when they learned that investigators would visit their former landladies, employers, and disgruntled employees, scour their pasts, and compile all the hearsay into a file—all for a two- or three-month visit entailing a fee of $50 a day or less.[16]

Second, as Abrams further added, there was the problem of information management. Studies compiled by UN experts represented new literature on little-studied topics in the developing world but were not published and were interred in the "secret archives of the UN's basement."[17] Third, the focus on multilateral agreements meant that one could not encourage private enterprise for fear of inviting "Russian criticism, while any recommendations for socialization may alarm the capitalist nations."[18] The result was a "neutral" language, in Abrams's view, shorn of any confrontation of realities and therefore of no real use.

It was not just the UN that appeared at the crossroad of irreconcilable agendas; the same could be said of US aid agencies themselves. Abrams's account of the relationships between the Inter-American Development Bank (IDB), US Agency for International Development (USAID), and the International Cooperation Administration (ICA) provides us yet another snapshot of this imperceivable chaos transpiring behind bureaucratic screens:

> There was no identifiable policy concerning the relations between [US]AID and IDB. Both were operating in the same areas and in the same countries. In the absence of an effective liaison between [them], applications for loans were made to both, and neither knew much about what the other was doing. Both were in competition. . . . There was now no clear division of authority whatever, and both agencies made separate deals with the same Latin-American officials and in the same countries—a kind of interagency *laissez faire*. . . . Policies roved, crisscrossed, and intermingled. . . . For even had there been any constructive objectives written for the [US]AID program, there were no trained people to carry them out, and there was little data on which judgments were made.[19]

Given these dire descriptions, it can be argued that a further function of systems theories was to furnish governments, development agencies, experts and hacks alike with the patina of organization, the pretense that all was, and would be, well in the happy marriage of knowledge to power. Systems theory could be used to project coordination where in fact nothing was coordinated. It could also project newness where little had in fact changed in the functioning and interrelationships of states, capital, and their constitutive factions.

Indeed, some development experts even wised up to this fact, arguing that whether development occurred by chance or (policy) premeditation was in fact of little importance.

This was the brunt of Albert O. Hirschman's theory of "forward-backward linkages," who argued that the planning sequences that planners obsessed about—first building the highways, then setting up a car industry—were in effect a misspent use of intellectual energy.[20] In Hirschman's view, development did not follow the kind of linear modelling as propounded in the "Big Push" and take-off theories, or in the many Five Year Plans arrived at by different countries. For him, it was essentially a conglomerate enterprise, involving many changing actors, institutions, and interests, and leading to what in conventional economic terms would be called disequilibria and alternations. According to this view, development inevitably generated failures, setbacks, and conflicts. Capital and education—factors which conventional economics defined as prerequisites for development—did not preclude these tensions and conflicts, nor the unpredictability they entailed. No matter how well planned a project, it generated countervailing forces that would conspire to undermine it. In this environment, a development agency was to focus on allocating resources in a few key sectors of the economy without providing any "complementary" investments. The imbalances produced through such investment would produce political pressures for action on other fronts, resulting in the reallocation of resources over time. This shift would then create another imbalance, and consequently a new set of political demands, thereby repeating the cycle. For Hirschman, these forces were in fact critical lessons for people, teaching them to cope with currents of change by turning disappointments into learning experiences. Whenever a development project "failed" in conventional terms, it in fact generated unforeseen new opportunities. One thus needed to adopt a "learning-based" view of development. In the long run, investment firms would work this out in the "fast fail" logics of venture capital.

For Hirschman, it mattered little which part of a system was introduced first, over time the rest of the system would in any case catch up. What guaranteed that each project would indeed be carried forward to its proper *telos*, that the world would not come to be littered—as indeed it would—with the flotsam of countless half-realized projects, of holes dug in one place and pipes delivered somewhere else, of incomplete fragments of infrastructure and installations falling into ruin simply because at a given time a patron here and a patron there was able to secure a piece of funding of which he also got a piece? Here Hirschman's thinking expressly tips over into soteriology: in the end, he argued, development thinking had to be tethered by a "bias for hope." Perhaps this hope relied in the end on the agnosticism that Keynes had advocated so clearly on the selection of projects in the famous section in the General Theory on "digging holes." It mattered little, Keynes had argued, what kind of projects had been conceived and executed (or not) in a given quarter, whether people were simply paid money to dig holes and fill them up. Far more significant was the fact that money would be paid and eventually spent, beefing up demand for the wheels of supply to start turning again.[21]

It also helped that the more projects failed, the larger demand there was for economists. Indeed, if one form of expertise rose above this morass of discordant interests and barely concealed, conflicting sets of eyes on the main chance, this was the economist, a profession given signally new importance after the Second World War and whose cadres would undergo tremendous expansion in both their numbers and the prerogatives arrogated to them. The principal reason for this precipitous uptick in the economists' powers were the mechanisms of global debt itself, more institutionally coordinated than ever before and given sanction, at least for the time being, by multilateral agreements to which states were beholden to like never before. Economics thus became the *lingua franca* in which all manner of incompatible claims had to be brought to bear on the new institutional order. Stationed close to fiscal spigots and able to set the terms for project procurements, economists acquired the upper hand in determining what comprised or did not comprise a legitimate claim to both knowledge and practice, in fields as diverse as housing to animal husbandry to budgets for art. As Abrams put it, one of the principal challenges of housing in the developing world was precisely that "economics still ruled the aid program."[22]

Responding to this epistemic hierarchy, the language of architects and planners in this period showed a distinct shift toward making economistic claims in their efforts to establish professional legitimacy. This was not new, as we might recall the writing of Frederick Law Olmstead on what we would today call "value capture" from urban improvements, Karel Teige and Ludwig Hilberseimer's on housing, or Frank Lloyd Wright, who in his Broadacre City propositions composed large tracts of economic reflection to a degree unthinkable today. But in these earlier propositions, economics provided a tool to model their idealism; the idiosyncrasy of their economics mirrored the idiosyncrasy of their forms. By contrast, the economics professed by architects of the 1950s and 1960s can be compared to the postcolonial "mimic men" of V. S. Naipaul's memorable novel, imitating the language of epistemic dominance to get by in global development circuits. Architects, amongst others, *had to learn* to converse in the language of economists for their profession to qualify as legitimate knowledge.

ARCHITECTURE *IN* DEVELOPMENT

As an epistemological undertaking, development theory emerged from a hiatus or mismatch between the investment criteria in mainstream economic theory oriented toward fully industrialized contexts and the structurally different challenges faced by countries with the bulk of their population immersed in the unmodern realm. In that light, a debate flourished as to whether development economics in fact required a different economics with new presumptions and differing points of data about economic behavior or whether it should be seen as a subfield within the mainstream discipline wherein the general axioms still held but required qualification in terms of specific applications. This debate reflected and perhaps defined similar contestations with respect to other fields as well: tropical medicine, national literatures and arts, agriculture and food security, and so on. Something similar can be observed in architecture between the lineaments of the "modern" vis-à-vis the new "regional" claims that begin to be advanced in the postwar period, with respect to technologies, forms, symbolisms, plan organizations, housing arrangements, and climate responsiveness. Many of the essays in this volume speak to this tension between international and regional attributes, while some direct attention to tensions around the fiscal and formal definition of particular typologies. As they all make clear, these tensions were enunciated not just by nationalist ideologues in developing countries but by the roving circuit of firms and consultants as well, proclaiming a certain expertise specifically applicable to the politically and economically fraught conditions they found in the various development contexts.

By any measure, the challenges faced by the so-called "developing nations" were immense. In Asia and Africa, most of the new nations were defined by geographical boundaries drawn on sand by their departing colonial masters. The waves of factional conflict and war—between, within, and across states—that ensued undermined mass-party formations that were still nascent, opening up paths to autocracy on the one hand and counter-formations in the shape of ethnic or factional strongholds on the other. In these contexts, development policies, such as they were, reflected as much trade-offs in power as the creation of new patronage-clientele networks. The chimera of the state as a uniform space—in which inputs and outputs could be rationally assessed or disbursed through "secular" calculations—remained just that, a daydream of its technocratic elite and a humbug of the subdisciplines that came to be termed development this or that. The epistemological outlines laid out in development textbooks thus present us today not with an account of "what happened" in development but with a historical archive of a powerful mode of speculation whose distortionary effects have still not been fully measured.[23] In terms of the chapters in this volume, some of the principal preoccupations of this archive are worth highlighting, given the effects that these conceptions would have on production in other sectors such as architecture and planning.

In theoretical terms, the primary challenge of developing countries, as outlined in the broad literature, were the obstructions that these societies posed toward their transition to a fully industrialized future: the low productivity endemic to feudal-agrarian societies and the "sectoral imbalances" produced therein between manufacturing and agriculture, mistranslated into imbalances between urban and rural or between regions; skills and knowledge deficits hampering greater technological penetration; the challenge to investments and new technologies in a demand-dampening "surplus labor" environment; and the "selection" of which technologies would be most appropriate to introduce in a given situation. Introducing new ideas, new foods, new machines, new clothes, new music, new architecture, even new freedoms in societies little used to them did not just pose questions of resistance forged by habit but also in terms of choices and priorities. Did the expansion of textile capacity make sense in a society where people were happy to live with two sets of clothing but would prefer to spend conspicuously on watches instead? If new wheat technologies offered the most significant returns to investment in terms of added output, would this fly in a rice-eating region? If cement concrete was the cheapest form of technology that could be applied to solve housing problems, did this make sense in context where a country would lose significant foreign reserves, needed for other purchases, in order to import pozzolanic lime? Choices mattered, and they mattered much more in countries weighed down by scarcity, where options for mistakes and misfiring could prove to be both socially and politically catastrophic, as indeed became the case across the developing world.

Against this landscape of choices and priorities, amongst the identification of needs, techniques, technicians, budgetary constraints, and debt contraction and servicing, it would be hard to argue that for governments in developing countries, architecture mattered more than, say, antibiotics, contraception, hydro-electric dams, fresh water, energy, roads, etc. Yet architecture played a particular role in giving form to many of these investments: large infusions of capital into multiple sectors of culture and economy inevitably implied an upsurge of building activity. In every theater of development, new structures were required to house interventions in health, education, agriculture, media, the arts, and housing, not to rule out the structures needed to house the expanded functions of governments themselves: the new parliaments, assemblies, courts, police and military installations, and thousands of miles of double-loaded corridors laid out across the planet to organize the deepening role of government in almost every social interaction. In vying for these commissions, architects spoke to the uses and appositeness of architecture to each of these realms, employing rhetoric that they hoped would intersect with whatever sensibility or agenda they attributed to their prospective patrons, whether this spoke to questions of symbolic form or ornament, climatic response, organizational logic, use of materials, budgetary use, phasing, the effects of physical form on behavior, or the metaphysical predicaments of aesthetics and morality. If on the one hand this rhetoric may have been voiced across the gamut of convictions, from what game theorists call "cheap talk" to the most sincerely held moral beliefs or "good intentions," then on the other these pitches were also voiced through myriad policy and academic tracts, in syllabi and curricula, as well as academic podiums and even software programs written to express dynamics of control and freedom.

Why is architecture *there*, at all? Why was it necessary, in these postwar decades, to devise architectures that appeared to emblematize the discourses of development? In a more disciplinary framework, can we say that there was an architecture *of* development, in the manner that we say "socialist monument" or "modern housing" (categories that in any case are not absent in developmental contexts)? Or can we only talk of architecture *in* development, in the service of or as an accompaniment to this or that feature of the history of development?

The essays in this book intuitively veer toward this last, "weak" interpretation, which is to say that they place architecture as an important feature among a range of development artefacts and the "artefactual politics" of development.[24] As this collection of essays demonstrates, there is no one mode or articulation of architecture that defines its specific utility for developmental tasks. This becomes particularly salient in these chapters, which read development as an inherently *multilateral* and discordant discourse. Following Abrams's insight mentioned earlier, the chapters see these architectural interventions as gambits or even gambles, moves in a fundamentally uncertain field of discrepant ideologies, mercurial budgetary horizons, difficulties of patronage, abrupt electoral and policy reversals, coups within governments, and bureaucracies, not least within the international development agencies themselves. This overarching sensibility leads many of these writers to foreground new types of artefacts or typologies seldom attended to in mainstream architectural discourse: cattle sheds, grain silos, farms, villages, aboriginal settlement patterns, and so on. These artefacts are all intersectional, to borrow from feminist discourse, in the sense that they are created in the overlaps between the informal exigencies of biopolitics and the formal predicaments of government. Additionally, these types inherently highlight the intersections of the "unmodern" within the modern, intersections that ring true in developed contexts as well but which appear all the more pressing in the context of developing countries.

This book cannot be considered exhaustive, nor as a "field guide" in the traditional sense to the topic of architecture in development. Instead, it offers theoretical reflections "from the field," based on extensive archival research, to a growing field of research. This emerging field marks a turn to postwar globality as distinguished from colonial and postcolonial modernity. Diverging from the tendencies of architectural historiography to particularly privilege modernist aesthetics in national formation, the essays here represent a growing body of research that instead highlights the political and economic aspects that dominated discourses of development, dimensions that have been previously ignored in scholarship. The inception of this book dates back to a panel titled *Systems and the South* organized at the 2012 Society of Architectural Historians Annual Conference in Detroit, where some of the editors first gathered to conceptualize a larger research project involving inputs from scholars working on this topic globally. Subsequently, the project came under the aegis of the Aggregate Architectural History Collaborative, under whose auspices the editors sent out an open request for papers. The papers in this volume represent work of scholars working on countries as diverse as Israel, Ghana, Greece, Belgium, France, India, Mexico, the United States, Venezuela, the Philippines, South Korea, Sierra Leone, Singapore, Turkey, Cyprus, Iraq, Zambia, and Canada. The selection reflects the breadth and scope of submissions we received, which conspicuously lacked scholars working on socialist models of development from the Soviet Bloc and the Nonaligned Movement, although strong work is emerging on those regions that look at comparable phenomena.[25] To some extent, therefore, the findings presented in this book must be seen as restricted to the Bretton Woods universe. The relations between the Bretton Woods system and the Soviet world are complex, not just because the roles attributed to money were different in the two systems—the ruble resembled more a scrip than true currency—but also because certain countries such as Yugoslavia were part of both while others were not. Inevitably these differences created divergences in the manner in which projects, including buildings and urban planning, were conceptualized and executed, consideration of which will have to await some future occasion.

This publication represents the culmination of multiple rounds of peer-review workshops and editing. Amongst the essays, certain themes appeared salient. The chapters are consequently organized around these themes as outlined here, although as will become apparent to the reader, many also overlap in their concerns beyond these groupings. The first grouping pertains to *developmental time*. The chapters by Arindam Dutta and Ijlal Muzaffar speak to this synthetic construct, which is inexorably composed of metaphysical claims that find themselves confronting aporias of various kinds. Focusing on the Le Mirail project in Toulouse and the Ford Foundation's Calcutta Plan, Dutta discusses the logic of phased projects and their morphologies as a response to the phase-bound manner in which budgets were allocated. Muzaffar reflects on Abrams's observations about self-help housing in Ghana, where the housing expert encountered the work of a missionary, to unveil the faith underlying financial thinking. Muzaffar proposes that via its operation as metaphysics, systems offered experts a guarantee against failure. For Dutta and Muzaffar "debt" and the "body"—the sites of technique and biopolitics—present the locus of development discourse's metaphysical claims, through whose management it has to instantiate and establish itself. Discussing the constitutive crises of developmental time, their essays argue that it is in these crises, rather than in their reconciliation, that the trajectories of development history are shaped.

The next section looks at the fates and predicaments of *Expertise*, which includes chapters by Ayala Levin, Nikki Moore, Diana Martinez, and a collaborative work by Sebastiaan Loosen, Viviana d'Auria and Hilde Heynen. Levin's chapter might be said to follow up on Dutta's and Muzaffar's chapters by looking at how incompletion was incorporated into the planning process itself, as a modus operandi that precluded failure. Her chapter highlights the dwindling scope of development planning for its touted international exponents by focusing on the agenda of so-called action planning. First touted by the development practitioner Otto Koenigsberger, this concept can be seen as a last-ditch attempt to corral the growing chorus within the planning community itself on the significance of "implementation" as scores of the well-laid master plans of the 1950s and early 1960s beached themselves on the shoals of the economic and political vicissitudes that we highlighted earlier. The shift in the planner's emphasis on process rather than expert foresight, Levin argues, also augured a deflation of expectations from the planning function itself. If the plan as an originating document was essentially to be seen as a *non sequitur*, and if implementation were to be reduced simply to historical vicissitude, then Koenigsberger's recourse inadvertently laid out a recipe for the eventual obliteration of the planner's epistemic authority, becoming more and more the business entrepreneur he wished to engage, as would indeed be the case in the ensuing decades.

Moore and Martinez both look at the architecture of training campuses for perhaps the most significant cultural heroes of development discourse: the agronomists. Moore's analysis of the *Escuela Nacional de Agricultura* (the National School of Agriculture) in Texcoco, Mexico, and Martinez's study of the International Rice Research Institute (IRRI) in the Philippines look at the two research poles in Latin America and Asia created by the Rockefeller Foundation to engineer high-yield varieties of rice, seen as essential to solving the world's catastrophic levels of hunger. Both essays foreground the political aegis of the state in this technocratic drive and the attendant disputes over knowledge and technology, given developing countries' interests in maintaining research and food sovereignty, the public and private control of food systems, and the economic security of farmers in capital-intensive grain production. Moore looks at the attempts by members of the National School to locate their work in the image of the land reform struggles led by agronomists associated with Emiliano Zapata, and the eventual success of the Rockefellers in subsuming that goal in the name of higher productivity and technical superiority. Martinez charts a similar story of failure, albeit in this case, the shift in emphasis in Philippine goals of development, from food security, manifested in rice research, to export-oriented industries centered around another crop, the coconut. Both Moore and Martinez look carefully at building articulation, layout, and orientation to reveal differentiations in micro-dispensations of knowledge and power.

Loosen, d'Auria, and Heynen's chapter turns to the academic ramifications of Habitat: The United Nations Conference on Human Settlements, held in Vancouver, Canada, in 1976. It is important to note that 1971, the year of the "Nixon shock," represented a bellwether year for development discourse. Nixon's removal of the dollar's convertibility to gold was signally directed at the United States' international debtors, signaling that American debt would be priced in international markets rather than by fiat. The cancellation of fixed exchange rates among international currencies put an end to the viability of long-term planning horizons, eventually diminishing the influence of international development agencies such as the UNTAA and auguring the growth of private consulting firms as states perforce began to emphasize privatized inputs into governmental work. New educational centers addressed this growing privatized development market. Loosen, d'Auria, and Heynen discuss how the establishment on the discourse of "settlements" in the UN conference manifested itself in the Post-Graduate Centre on Human Settlements at the Katholieke Universiteit Leuven, Belgium, one outpost in a network of institutions catering to development studies for architects and planners. Other prominent nodes of this circuit included the Otto Koenigsberger-founded Development Planning Unit in London and the Bouwcentrum in Rotterdam, with some of the key actors—such as John F. C. Turner—also circulating through the Massachusetts Institute of Technology and the University of California, Berkeley. The focus on education and training, particularly in Western graduate programs aimed at Third World students, subsisted in a direct or positivist correspondence between studies of social behavior and studies of form. The emphasis on positive categories, such as the "urban poor" or "the city," the authors suggest, can be seen as foregrounding modernism of a kind that, lodged in fieldwork, was inevitably vulnerable to empirical questioning, and eventually the critiques of positivism such as that of Aldo Rossi.

The third group of chapters pertains to questions of *bureaucratic organization*. This group includes essays by Ginger Nolan, Albert José-Antonio López, and Felicity D. Scott. Nolan's chapter on Christopher Alexander speaks to the technocratic constructions of putative agency formalized on behalf of sundry unmodern subjects, for whom the architect or technical expert poses himself as knowledge facilitator, self-proclaimed advocate, and defender against bureaucracy. Analyzing Alexander's attempts to centralize "native"—or nonprofessional—agency in processes of design, Nolan argues that in his responses, architecture becomes the recourse to erase problems that are not architectural in nature. Tradition is here stylized and affirmed in terms of a modernity that operates by deletion. López's chapter on the (brief) importance gained by architectural and planning discourse at the center of Mexican government and administration in the 1940s and 1950s speaks to a similar logic of deletion that appears at the heart of systems thinking, an erasure of contingency that appears at the very moment of a system's claim to accommodate it. López locates the Alemán government's appeal to the concept of *planifación* as a particular faction's attempt to place a universal architectonic of government and bureaucracy that would presumably abolish faction, and by consequence, disagreement in the sense that a claim to systems would also claim to imbibe all disagreements within itself, as "inputs" for the betterment of the system. López traces this claim in the midst of other claims and counterclaims to political and epistemological authority, placing the eventual ruin of the architect Carlos Lazo Barreiro's career as woven within these tensions.

Looking directly at the proceedings of the Habitat conference, Scott's chapter studies its Audio-Visual Program, which could be considered a precursor to the education programs discussed by Heynen, d'Auria, and Loosen. Given the decline of the UN's so-called "technical missions," such as the ones on which Abrams and Koenigsberger had been sent in the 1950s and 1960s, the creation of Habitat, amongst other such topical UN conferences such as the ones on women and the environment, could be seen as a sign of this *weakened* influence. Scott's chapter highlights nonetheless the continuing fracases over coordination, participation, and representation amongst various development actors. The Audio-Visual Program's focus on film and television, as capital-intensive media, inevitably shone a light on its Western originators given the dearth of production, distribution, projection, and broadcasting technologies it necessitated. Eventually the program went in the way that so many bureaucracies had gone before it, as it obsessed more with its own procedures and protocols rather than delivering much on the ground.

Scott's chapter leads us to the next section on *technological transfer*. This group includes chapters by Melany Sun-Min Park, Manuel Shvartzberg Carrió, and Farhan Karim. Park's chapter analyzes the interfaces of technology and labor and the dissonances that appear therein in the attributions and de-attributions of "skills" to various developmental subjects. Park's essay speaks to definitional questions regarding the competence and scope of the architectural profession in South Korea, whose profile, she argues, was tagged onto the country's—American-assisted—objectives to establish heavy industry. This postwar imperative, Park argues, predisposed architects to define the attributes of their profession in managerial and organizational terms that provided them the best language to enter into the scale of investment decisions being negotiated between the state and its clients. Shvartzberg Carrió's essay looks at the US housing industry's prioritization of steel as a "cheap" form of construction as inherently wedged in an international frame of exploitation. These connections are explored through a case study of native American displacement to accommodate new housing development in Palm Springs, California, and new worker settlements in

Ciudad Guayana in Venezuela, an industrial enclave supplying steel to American markets. If Shvartzberg Carrió's and Park's chapters speak to the fractures of modernization, Karim's chapter speaks to the construction of tradition in fostering development, in the shape of so-called earth-based technologies, deemed as ideal for the undercapitalized poor to build their own homes. The essay speaks to the absurdity of foisting this technological choice as a universal panacea, and the evangelism that development critiques sometimes demonstrate in their bids to foster "agency" in the unwitting subjects of development, the poorer the better.

The next section, titled *Designing the Rural*, contains chapters by Olga Touloumi, Petros Phokaides, Fabiola López-Durán, Martin Hershenzon, and Ateya Khorakiwala. That this section has the largest number of contributions is no coincidence: at the turn of the 1950s, the developing world dwelt, by a large margin, outside of cities and urban settlements, engaged in lives far from the spectra of productivity espoused by modern economics. Touloumi's chapter highlights modernist architects'—at least those seeking to impact development contexts—early recognition of this fact, in the shape of propositions for village design. Touloumi's chapter, like Nolan's, looks at two competing and mutually irreconcilable constructs of the village: on the one hand in the sense of the Rousseauian small community invoked by technological mavens such as Marshall McLuhan and reformists such as Mahatma Gandhi and the Indian National Congress, and the smorgasbord of vocations, interests, ethnic allegiances, and landed and other economies that comprised the rural world that architect-planners such as Jaqueline Tyrwhitt sought to enter. Phokaides's chapter takes up another abortive attempt to plan villages, in this case the commission received by the firm of Constantinos Doxiadis to devise a rural settlement scheme for Zambia, to comport with President Kenneth Kaunda's ambitious territorial objective of pushing up productivity in the countryside. As events were to reveal, this was as much an attempt on Kaunda's part—as with other anti-colonial movements such as the Indian National Congress—to forge a captive clientele outside the cities. The evidently farfetched scope of this ambition, a conscious pipe dream that Doxiadis Associates would hardly be loath to disabuse, mattered less than what both patron and client hoped to obtain through this mutual entanglement, for Kaunda to deepen his reach into the countryside and for Doxiadis to simulate some figment of planning activity and data gathering, in the process totting up the firm's resume in order to move on to the next commission. As with Levin's study of Koenigsberger, here we see knowledge capital staring into the terms of its approaching abasement.

Both Hershenzon and Khorakiwala look at building typologies devised to build up capital accumulation in the countryside. Hershenzon's chapter studies cowsheds designed by the Rural Building Research Center in Israel in the context of the newly established Israeli state's dual objectives of fostering rural productivity as a factor of national wealth and social collectives for its new migrant citizens. The essay traces the intersecting goals of collectivist *kibbutzim*'s shared cattle and land-holdings as they transitioned into formalized state initiatives in the farming and dairy sectors, where they were scaled up into regional planning approaches. This scaling-up posed in turn new kinds of problems of racial integration commensurate with the postcolonial predicament of translating the anti-colonial aspirations to community to the formal challenges of citizenship, as the notion of the "collective" slowly devolved into the single family as the basic unit of socialization. Khorakiwala's essay also looks at the grain storage silo in post-independence India as an indexical object in a discourse of national wealth, somewhere downstream from the research carried out at the *Esquelas Nacional* and the IRRI in the battle to combat, certainly food insecurity, but also the significant challenges to governmental legitimacy from the periodic market crises and inflationary pressures created by capricious agricultural output. Khorakiwala's study of the silo thus locates it as a vehicle not so much of space but of time, as housing a "stage" in a process involving inflationary management, domestic subsidization and support for farmers and consumers, and international flows of technology, commodities, and aid, crosshatched by the intersecting challenges of market and state. In a situation where food security appeared as a major arbiter of sovereignty, the grain silo, devised as part of a government effort to retain (and represent) surpluses, can be construed as an intersectional object, necessarily challenged by limitations in other sectors, from availability of land and technology to the paucity of expertise in devising an imported typology.

Moving to South America, López-Durán's chapter traces Nelson E. Rockefeller's three decade-long strategy to position oil-rich Venezuela as a pilot project that instrumentalized food production to expand capitalism in the Global South. Masterminding the use of Venezuelan oil camps as laboratories for agricultural production and consumption on a national level, Rockefeller developed a comprehensive scheme that responded to Venezuela's food crisis and at the same time compensated for US monopsony in the oil sector. López-Durán's story begins in the late-1930s, when concurrent nationalization of oil production by Bolivia (1937) and Mexico (1938) had made the vulnerabilities of single-sector export economies all too real to American commodity markets and firms—leading to the 1947 creation of Rockefeller's International Basic Economy Corporation (IBEC), a private global initiative with a focus on food and housing. López-Durán's chapter locates the entire chain of agricultural production, commodification, and distribution that Rockefeller, in league with the oil companies and Venezuela's shifting governments between 1939 and the early 1970s, attempted to put into effect in order to "diversify" its economy. It reveals a series of new spaces ranging from agricultural colonies and clubs in the oil camps to the architecture of modern supermarkets in the cities that introduced a new cultural model of food consumption and recreation. What Rockefeller did not foresee was that Venezuelans themselves would recognize and act against a program that benefited just the US and the Venezuelan urban middle-upper class. As a result, in the late 1960s, it would be these very supermarkets that would become the target of political bombings, as insurgents identified the face of IBEC's economic imperialism in these displaced linkages of rural and urban economies.

The last section of this volume focuses on an essential element of architecture that architectural discourse has addressed little in the last thirty years, although modernist thought prior to the Second World War might be seen to be replete with its consideration: *land*. The chapters by Burak Erdim, Panayiota Pyla, and Konstantina Kalfa all locate the question of land as impelling different kinds of responses in architectural production. The liminality of dwelling in architecture and the liminality of architecture in dwelling find unique expression in Kalfa's study of the *antiparochì* framework of "unplanned" apartment development in Athens, Greece. Kalfa's study speaks succinctly to the problem of architects' legitimacy, as conditioned by the eddies of investment, landed interests, and the nature of political authority. In the context of Greece, as with the prodigious growth of informal, unplanned housing development flowering in the myriad pathways between rural and urban terrains, *antiparochì* directly reflected the nature of the state as well, which is to say the compulsions that represent the vulnerability at the base of its authority. Kalfa's chapter also touches on tourism, as she identifies in the construction of the Hilton in downtown Athens two stark contradictions: land for the Hilton was apportioned by violating the very bylaws that urban planners were promulgating to check the wave of informal construction, thus rendering the Hilton itself as of a piece, legally speaking, with *antiparochì*. Additionally, if eradicating *antiparochì* was seen as essential to rebuilding Athens as a global tourist destination, eventually *antiparochì* would itself be reconceived as a picturesque urban typology adding to Athens's traditional charms.

Like Kalfa, in the other expanses of the Mediterranean, the chapters by Erdim and Pyla both focus on Hilton hotels, designated as prominent symbols of American influence in the urban downtowns of their client states, in this case Cyprus and Istanbul. Pyla focuses on the construction of tourism as the "lead sector," to use Rostow's terms, for Cyprus's development, seen as more "modern" than agriculture, and highlights within this construction a further set of paradoxes. If tourism came to the fore, this was because for liberal economists it offered, in a "weak" state setting, the best prospects for private, self-sustaining initiatives that lay at the basis of a robust economy. And yet "retrofitting" Cyprus for the tourism sector represented a substantial task, achieved by the state's creation of new financial bodies and large debts contracted from international financial bodies. In what we could see as a premonition of futures elsewhere, nothing manifested this contradiction more than the Hilton, a private establishment that required substantial government expenditure in the form of infrastructural inputs, financial incentives, and regulatory manipulation to bring it into being. In sum, the Cyprus government had put substantial resources into an entity over which it had no control, whose lever of power lay in its ever-present threat of departure if not kept supplied by future cycles of state benefits.

Erdim's account of the Istanbul Hilton tells a comparable story, although this is narrated in the context of the postwar Turkish state's efforts to modernize land tenurial and construction systems. As a recipient of Marshall Plan aid, Turkey's attempts to support the construction market as the receptacle for surplus agrarian migrant labor necessitated interventions in zoning, building codes, and the creation of an insurance industry. It was in this context that Charles Abrams went to Turkey, ostensibly to provide recommendations for regulatory agencies in the building sector, but in the event he was deemed *persona non grata* given the Turkish government's displeasure with the Americans at the withdrawal of Marshall Aid funds at that time. As Erdim's chapter shows, neocolonial dominance was hardly a guarantee for consonance between the mandates of foreign experts and national governments. Abrams's arrival in Turkey immediately after Marshall Plan aid was withdrawn found him at odds with the government, with officials unwilling to brook technical advice without financial purse-strings attached: the creation of the Middle East Technical University (METU) that would ensue offers a runaway story in the alignment of interests from various factions within the government as well as American and UN development agencies.

That the political economy of land became one of the most fraught problems in development discourse was not a coincidence. Land continues to be exceptionally resistant to its transformation into a purely economic element. Like the money form, it embodies a multitude of social relations within it that govern access, tenure, and its use. This resistance is primarily epistemological, similar to how the blurring of rural–urban distinctions in the developing world proved to be an intransigent obstacle in the West's utopic traditions of conceptualizing the city. By attending to how architecture, as a form of expertise and know-how as well as the producer of technical and aesthetic objects, attempted to manage difference by mediating between competing epistemologies, different scales of intervention, temporal as well as spatial, and various sectors of governance, the chapters that follow consider architecture as a field that fleshes out in concrete form the aporias and crises of development discourse.

NOTES

1 Arturo Escobar, *Designs for the Pluriverse: Radical Interdependence, Autonomy, and the Making of Worlds* (Durham, NC: Duke University Press, 2018), 32.
2 q. Jamie Martin, "Were We Bullied?" *London Review of Books* 35, no. 22 (November 21, 2013).
3 Alain Badiou, *Metapolitics*, trans. Jason Barker (London: Verso, 2005).
4 For the concept "theater of development" see Ayala Levin, *Architecture and Development: Israeli Construction in Sub-Saharan Africa and the Settler-Colonial Imagination, 1958–1973* (Durham, NC: Duke University Press, 2022), 15–18.
5 Mahbub ul Haq, *The Strategy of Economic Planning: A Case Study of Planning* (Karachi: Oxford University Press, 1963), 1.
6 Eric Helleiner, "Bretton Woods and the Endorsement of Capital Controls," in *States and the Reemergence of Global Finance: From Bretton Woods to the 1990s* (Cornell, NY: Cornell University Press, 1994), 25–50.
7 Rosenstein-Rodan first presented this argument in a short paper titled "Problems of Industrialization of Eastern and South-Eastern Europe," *Economic Journal* 53 (1943): 202–211. Also see Rosenstein-Rodan, "Notes on the Theory of the 'Big-Push,'" in *Economic Development for Latin America*, eds. Howard S. Ellis and Henry C. Wallich (New York: St. Martin's Press, 1961), 57–81.
8 Nils Gilman, *Mandarins of the Future: Modernization Theory in Cold War America* (Baltimore: Johns Hopkins University Press, 2003); also see Edward B. Shils, *Tradition* (Chicago: University of Chicago Press, 1981).
9 P. P. Streeten, "International Cooperation," in *Handbook of Development Economics*, eds. Hollis Chenery and T. N. Srinivasan, vol. 2 (New York: Elsevier, 1989), 1154.
10 Noam Chomsky, *Cartesian Linguistics: A Chapter in the History of Rationalist Thought* (New York: Harper & Row, 1966); Albert O. Hirschman, *The Passions and the Interests: Political Arguments for Capitalism Before Its Birth* (Princeton, NJ: Princeton University Press, 1977); Alexandre Koyré, *From the Closed World to the Infinite Universe* (Baltimore: Johns Hopkins University Press, 1957).
11 Michel Foucault, *The Order of Things: An Archaeology of the Human Sciences* (New York: Vintage Books, 1966, 1994).
12 See Keith Michael Baker, "The Language of Science," in *Condorcet: From Natural Philosophy to Social Mathematics* (Chicago: The University of Chicago Press, 1975), 85–128.
13 Paul Krugman, *Development, Geography, and Economic Theory* (Cambridge, MA: The MIT Press, 1997), 71.
14 David Webster, "Development Advisors in a Time of Cold War and Decolonization: The United Nations Technical Assistance Administration, 1950–59," *Journal of Global History* (July 2011): 260.
15 Friedrich A. von Hayek, "The Use of Knowledge in Society," *American Economic Review* XXXV, no. 4 (September 1945): 519–530.
16 Charles Abrams, "Aid: Experts and 'Inperts,'" in *Man's Struggle for Shelter in an Urbanizing World* (Cambridge, MA: The MIT Press, 1964), 93.
17 Ibid.
18 Ibid., 94.
19 Ibid., 101.
20 Albert O. Hirschman, "A Dissenter's Confession: 'The Strategy of Economic Development' Revisited," in *Pioneers in Development*, eds. Gerald M. Meier and Dudley Seers (New York: Oxford University Press/The World Bank, 1984); Albert Hirschman, *The Strategy of Economic Development* (New Haven, CT: Yale University Press, 1958).
21 > If the Treasury were to fill old bottles with bank-notes, bury them at suitable depths in disused coal mines which are then filled up to the surface with town rubbish, and leave it to private enterprise on well-tried principles of laissez-faire to dig the notes up again . . . there need be no more unemployment, with the help of the repercussions, the real income of the community, and its capital wealth also, would probably become a good deal greater than it actually is.
> (John Maynard Keynes, *The General Theory of Employment, Interest, and Money* (New York: First Harvest / Harcourt, 1964), 129)

22 Abrams, "Aid: Experts and 'Inperts,'" 104.
23 See for example Hollis Chenery and T. N. Srinivasan, *Handbook of Development Economics*, vols. 1 & 2 (New York: Elsevier, 1989).
24 Langdon Winner, "Do Artifacts Have Politics?" *Daedalus* 109, no. 1, Modern Technology: Problem or Opportunity? (Winter 1980): 121–136.
25 See, for example, Łukasz Stanek, *Architecture in Global Socialism: Eastern Europe, West Africa, and the Middle East in the Cold War* (Princeton, NJ: Princeton University Press, 2020); Cole Roskam, "Non-Aligned Architecture: China's Designs on and in Ghana and Guinea, 1955–92," *Architectural History* 58 (January 2015): 261–229; Vladimir Kulić, "Building the Non-Aligned Babel: Babylon Hotel in Baghdad and Mobile Design in the Global Cold War," *ABE* 6 (2014).

Part I

Developmental time

1

Incompletion

On more than a certain tendency in postwar architecture and planning

Arindam Dutta

This chapter compares two otherwise unrelated planning projects of the early 1960s. Both projects represent "failures" of some kind. The projects are Candilis-Josic-Woods's (CJW's) propositions for a new township, Le Mirail, on the outskirts of Toulouse, France, and the Ford Foundation's Basic Development Plan for the city of Calcutta (now Kolkata), India. I say otherwise unrelated because the two projects do not share any *dramatis personae*, and although initiated in the same year, 1961, they would have no influence on each other. Much separates the two projects in terms of scope, geography, governmental and institutional frameworks, and the nature of capital formation in the two countries, not to rule out of course social composition and culture. Le Mirail was a much smaller project, a mixed-use development conceptualized for 100,000 people, one piece in a broader regional development plan for the Toulouse region. By contrast, the Calcutta plan catered to a population of some 7 million people, projected to double in twenty years. The territory covered by the plan encompassed 200 square miles, and the economies surveyed were linked to a hinterland of 150 million people.[1] This scalar discrepancy also entailed a difference in planning type: unlike the "physical" propositions of the CJW plan, Ford's Calcutta "plan," such as it was, can be described more as an attempt at administrative reform, incorporating massive infrastructural inputs, the economics of rural-urban linkages, market operations, and so on.

What I focus on in these two projects is the emphasis on *time-modeling* as the central feature of their approach: hence the "incompletion" of my title. Narratives of political and economic transition after the Second World War can be succinctly measured by the shift in fortunes of a particular type of global—and globalizing—document that by the mid-1960s appeared to be at a low ebb. This was the master plan, a genre defined by large, brightly colored and color-coded maps and drawings, covering large tracts of territory—cities, regions, or even whole countries—packed thick with symbols—arrows, legends, diagrams, indices—that correlated them with demographic and economic data of various sorts.

Visually, these plans appear to have to do with the placement of objects—population concentrations, logistics, infrastructure, economic zones—in space. In actuality what they mapped were *expectations*, sequences unfolding in time, concatenations of causes and effects, whose totality was encapsulated in the plan's claim to represent the future. The incompletion

DOI: 10.4324/9781003193654-3

I describe in this chapter is therefore of a double kind. It refers in the first instance to the deportment of the master plan document as a *teleological apparatus*. The modernizing crux of these master plans, and planning in general, lay not in professions of ruling out uncertainty and unpredictability in the future but in their claims of bringing uncertainty within a *viable range* of calculability and rationality. Master plans are by definition incomplete.

In the two decades after the Second World War, these plans would embark on what was literally a downward journey: from tops of tables, the cynosure of heads of states and ministers with their bevy of technical consultants, to bottom drawers in dusty plan chests in planning offices. The actual abandonment of these plans comprises, in our study, incompletion in the second instance. If incompletion in the genre of the master plan represented a warranty against failure, this would prove to be no warranty at all. Plans would fail nevertheless, but not on the terms that the master-planners had anticipated. Incompletion in the first instance would provide the stimulus for massive expansion in the modernizing frames and claims of knowledge; in the second, it would entail a cauterization and a forced closure of these claims, opening up a dispiriting void in the place where expertise had once been.

We started by noting differences between the scope of the CJW and the Ford projects. Much also lay in common between them, as observers noted at the time.[2] Both France and India, like many other countries, had adopted so-called "mixed economy" approaches. Both emphasized the necessity of strong state intervention in the realm of public goods—in Albert Hirschman's terms "social overhead capital," contents of which varied from country to country—with the anticipation that eventually the bulk of economic activity would be carried by a vigorous private sector defined by market principles of competition and entrepreneurship.[3] Both countries were signatories to the Bretton Woods Agreement, ostensibly aimed at securing free trade in goods and services but in effect an arrangement that subjected their economies and governments to the writ of the United States Treasury. Both countries balked at this dependence, countering this by adopting the fiscal strategies of what came to be called *dirigisme* or the command economy, where the state retained the prerogative of defining long-term sectoral priorities, shaped by the temporal structure of "five-year plans," inspired by the socialist world.

In both countries, the prerogative of devising the five-year plans went to what were in fact *extra-constitutional* bodies: in France the Commissariat général du plan de modernisation et d'équipement, and in India the Planning Commission.[4] Both bodies lacked executive authority and occupied strictly "advisory" positions. Throughout their careers, the wherewithal of these expert bodies would remain wholly reliant on their charismatic patrons, Charles de Gaulle and Jawaharlal Nehru, who in turn used them to concentrate decision-making powers against political contenders in their own cabinets. The careers of both expert bodies were consequently defined by intrinsically inimical relationships to their finance ministries, tensions that then undergirded every proposition or project launched under their auspices. Ford's leadership in India understood this well and sought to use intragovernmental divisions to their advantage:

> During the decade following India's emergence as a nation in 1947, "father figures" like Prime Minister Nehru, at the national level, and [West Bengal] Chief Minister B. C. Roy, at the state level, dominated political life. Their power stemmed in part from the inherited paternal governmental mantle of their colonial predecessors and in part from their leadership during the struggle for Independence. When these men took up "pet projects"—as Nehru apparently had done with the urban plan for Delhi—those projects were almost certain to be carried out.[5]

Both the Toulouse and Calcutta projects thus also substantially benefitted from powerful regional patrons: Roy in West Bengal and in Toulouse, the socialist mayor Louis Bazerque. Both cities would see a significant influx in civil war refugees, producing what would be perceived as large-scale demographic "imbalances." In the case of Toulouse, some 27,000 *pied-noirs* would move there from Algeria. Calcutta had received a staggering 2 million people during the partition of India, the world's largest human migration to date. An additional million people would arrive in 1971, with the onset of the Bangladesh War. Both cities boasted a sizeable communist/socialist left, which would lend both projects a regional complexity with regard to reigning political dispensations in Paris and New Delhi. Against the background of the Cold War, these ideological and political tensions—between experts over *dirigisme* and in politics between non-communist and communist adversaries—would cast both projects as international *cause célèbres* in their own right. Le Mirail would be broadcast as "the most important urban project in Europe," meriting a visit from Soviet Premier Alexei Kosygin, amongst others.[6] Likewise, Ford consultants, in keeping with the ineluctable self-promotion demanded of their profession, drummed up the immensity of the challenges involved. Calcutta, they declared, was the "toughest planning job in the world in operation" and the "biggest and most important [job] that would ever engage [the] minds" of its participants.[7] The city would become a vital pit stop for a range of luminaries, from World Bank head Robert McNamara, Harvard and MIT presidents Nathan Pusey and Julius Stratton, US Ambassador John Kenneth Galbraith, and MIT political scientist Myron Weiner to the veritable circus of architects and planners eyeing the global development market. Charles Abrams stopped by, as did Catherine W. Bauer and Gordon Cullen (engaged by Ford for both the Calcutta and the New Delhi projects). Each came riding their hobbyhorse into town: Cullen argued for the urban design approaches espoused by the British townscape movement; more ludicrously, Julian H. Whittlesey, an ex-associate of Albert Mayer and part of the Ford team, proposed that Buckminster Fuller-type geodesic domes be mass-manufactured and deployed to address the pressing challenges of Calcutta's slums.

Both projects benefitted from the regional importance accorded to these cities by their federal governments. Toulouse and the midi-Pyrénées would be designated as an essential node in the Fifth Republic's plans for an *économie concertée*, one of eight *métropoles d'équilibres et grandes agglomérations* by the Délégation à l'Aménagement du Territoire et à l'Action Régionale (DATAR). This distributional "physical planning" strategy was given further impetus by the decision to nominate Toulouse as the new hub of the French aircraft (and eventually electronics) industry, with the objective of enticing technical and scientific expertise away from the lopsided primacy that the Paris metropolitan region enjoyed in all matters economic, cultural, scientific, and political. Pursuant to this policy of *l'aménagement*, Paris's propositions to vest a large number of ancillary research labs and institutes in Toulouse conjured up prospects of the imminent migration of technocratic elites to what was still a small medieval city. Toulouse's socialist mayor, Bazerque, deeming his urban charge as unprepared and little equipped with the modern amenities suited to the approaching surge of metropolitan intellects, sought to requisition large federal outlays toward a conurbation plan equipped with large transportation and infrastructural networks. New zoning ordinances were introduced outlining new industrial and residential zones supported by a system of green belts. The exotic, newfangled modernist propositions of Le Mirail, designed by an architectural consultancy (CJW) whose reputation as "experts" was on the upswing—it would win two other comparable public works projects across Europe, Caen Hérouville

(40,000 inhabitants) and Bilbao Val d'Asua (80,000 inhabitants) in the same period—would be the lynchpin of this regional plan. For Bazerque, CJW's drawings and renderings would serve as both visual totem and marketing billboards for his urban ambitions. Le Mirail was designated a *zone à urbaniser par priorité* (or ZUP), representing the keystone in a bid by the Toulouse municipality to attract key national and regional subsidies, not to rule out investments by developers and commercial partners (with the requisite abetments and enticements) in what was in essence—portentous pronouncements on "*le habitat pour le plus grand nombre*" aside—a suburban residential enclave.

Calcutta, once Britain's imperial capital in Asia, would appear on Ford's radar for quite the opposite narratives than the ones of upward mobility being written in Toulouse. In 1960, the city was still one of the largest conurbations in the world. Mid-century shifts in global commodity supply chains—notably the shift of packaging industries from jute to plastic—as well as the loss of its hinterland during partition set what was hitherto India's largest industrial center on a steady path to deindustrialization. Soaring unemployment, the growing pressures of population and large slum areas—housing an excess of half the city's population—made for an explosive political situation that neo-Malthusian American foreign policy was primed to recognize, particularly with Vietnam escalating in the neighborhood. "I HAVE FELT CALCUTTA, I LOVE IT . . . Fantastic slums . . . I have to pinch myself," trilled the aforementioned Whittlesey.[8] The Americans were well familiar with Calcutta. The city had served as the principal Allied base for the Burma front during the Second World War: some 150,000 Americans had been stationed there, some of them on the large airbase in the city's north, in Kalyani, newly built to run air-supplies to Chiang Kai-shek's embattled, landlocked troops across the Himalayas. In the process they had had to significantly modernize and refurbish Britain's patchy, crumbling, and inferior supply infrastructure in its biggest colony, developments that had been looked on with admiration by planning enthusiasts within the Indian National Congress (then mostly in prison) itself.

Ford officials would play up Calcutta's escalating urban problems as building up yet another political precipice in Asia, another domino in a chain of dominantly agrarian societies imminently susceptible to fall into the powerful lures of communism. "If Calcutta falls into the Communist camp, or into suicidal anarchism, all of Asia will take heed and probably follow . . . strengthening Calcutta is a matter of vital concern to the whole free world."[9] This alarmism represented less ideological conviction than an attempt to attract additional sponsors, namely the US Department of State, to invest in the consultancy effort. After a Marxist government was elected to power in West Bengal in 1967, Ford insiders noted that while Ford's leadership

> had been concerned in 1961 that one purpose of the Foundation's entry into Calcutta would be to help avert West Bengal's loss to the Communists, [they] were perfectly willing to work with the Communists in 1969 if they were prepared to support programs for Calcutta's development.[10]

Between 1961 and 1974, Ford's propositions for Calcutta would find themselves confronting not just its spatial challenges but administrative challenges as well. Anglo-Saxon jurisprudence, both at home and in its colonies, as is well known, signally inveighed against the governance of cities as unified jurisdictional entities, a characteristic that would prove a major stumbling block for Robert Moses in New York and the Labour Party's planning strategies in London alike. Calcutta was no different. The city's name was, at best, mere toponym. Little existed by way of an administrative apparatus armed with the jurisdictional and revenue powers that could leverage externalities across multiple sectors (transportation, education, police, healthcare, property rights, land values, utilities, and so on) that was the leitmotif of modernist planning doctrines.

In this sense, perhaps Ford's greatest contribution was the creation under its guidance of a new bureaucracy, the Calcutta Metropolitan Planning Office or CMPO, to precisely effect such leverage, albeit this too would, symptomatically, be granted few jurisdictional powers. Quite like its archetype in New Delhi, the Planning Commission, the CMPO would primarily remain a knowledge-producing enterprise, tasked with gathering data and mobilizing inputs from citizens' bodies as well as administrative and electoral officials in order to best assist urban decision making, whose wherewithal lay outside its purview (see Figure 1.1). In France, *l'aménagement* likewise involved the construction of what was largely

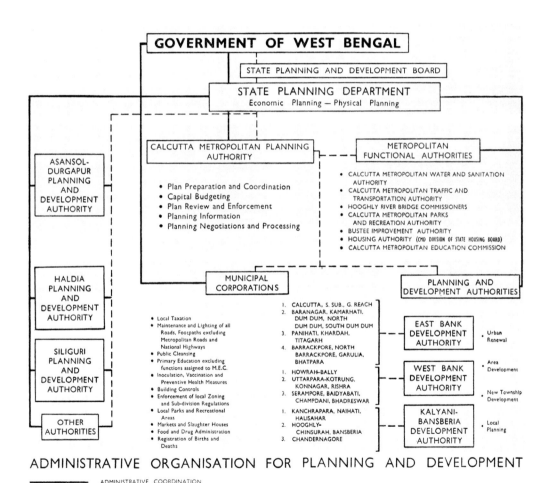

FIGURE 1.1 Diagram showing the decision-making structure pertaining to Calcutta's governance within the West Bengal government and Ford's (i.e. CMPO's) place within it.

Source: Calcutta Metropolitan Planning Organisation, *Basic Development Plan: Calcutta Metropolitan District 1966–1986* (Calcutta: CMPO, 1966).

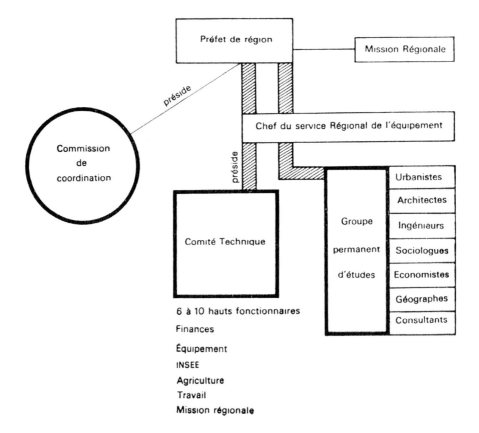

FIGURE 1.2 Diagram depicting DATAR expert inputs in relation to prefectures.

Source: Ministère de l'équipment, Délégation à l'aménagement du territoire et à l'action régionale, *Documents relatifs à l'organisation des études d'aménagement des aires métropolitaines* (Paris: DATAR, October 1966).

a new apparatus of knowledge gathering and inputs, a framework that inevitably placed its "experts" at odds with existing regional power structures (see Figure 1.2). In Calcutta, such tensions between expertise and politics, Ford correctly anticipated, would also take on the inevitable accusations of "foreign intervention," a scenario that Ford Foundation officials sought to counter by carefully positioning Indian personnel in the foreground, in the end to little effect.

In terms of physical planning, the broad recipes followed in Toulouse and Calcutta were remarkably alike, and in keeping with urban planning doxa anywhere on the globe at this time. Both plans advocated ring roads to stave off congestion in the city center, proposing to redirect population density instead toward the urban periphery, dotted by new, township-size residential and office enclaves. Le Mirail would acquire a companion piece in Calcutta with the creation of Salt Lake City to the city's east, designed by the Yugoslavian para-statal infrastructure firm Ivan Milutinovic-PIM. Technical expertise for the Ford transportation plan for Calcutta was sub-contracted to the Connecticut offices of the American infrastructure firm Wilbur Smith and Associates, whose capabilities, like Ivan Milutinovic-PIM, were built on a "deep state" portfolio of public transportation and military contracts.

PLANNED INFLATION IN THE BRETTON WOODS SYSTEM

In either case—as with all master-plans of the time—the scale of proposals far exceeded the budgetary, not to rule out juridical, powers of their promoters. This thus begs the crucial question, responding to which in some fashion establishes the basis for the arguments underlined in this essay: how did planners propose to pay for these projects?

Here we encounter the specter of incompletion in its first sense, which concerns the *phase-bound* approach taken in these large-scale planning exercises. Indeed, phasing—as with five-year plans—represented a critical point of departure for postwar governments, comprising a novel fiscal-technocratic device that would have been unthinkable in the *laissez faire* outlook of prewar governments, one that owed its existence precisely to the Bretton Woods exchange mechanism. As is well-known, the exchange mechanism was not one but many, comprising a veritable alphabet soup of institutions dedicated to different tasks, from infusing liquidity into credit-starved nation-states, to settling international payments, to providing targeted low-interest sovereign loans for modernization projects, to providing technical expertise, and to finding instruments to even out international asymmetries of education, skills, income, rights, food security, and so on. Acting in concert, or so it was argued, these interlinked institutional apparatuses would be critical to stave off nation-states from falling into the crippling financial crises that had led the world into the Great Depression and two catastrophic wars. With the International Monetary Fund always on hand to inject liquidity—and the US dollar acting as global default currency—governments could use the counter-plays of inflation and interest rates as a strategic tool to better define, prioritize, and rationally sequence their fiscal needs and outlays. Fiscal decisions would not be subject to periodic volatilities of national and international markets, but in accordance with long-term objectives of productivity and distribution. "It came to be increasingly accepted . . . that the secular growth rate of the economy was a parameter manipulable by public policy and an appropriate dimension for a social welfare function even in capitalist states."[11]

This approach has been mistakenly described as Keynesian. In fact Keynesian economics, *deliberately* aimed at the "short-run," not only had little to offer in this respect but was also doggedly opposed to long-term state intervention. In Keynes's own view, *laissez faire* principles and the "animal spirits" of the market—where private firms were given wherewithal to determine their own efficiencies of input and output, or fail in the process—offered far superior informational tools to ensure enduring robustness in the economy. Only under certain, presumably exceptional, conditions was the state to intervene, a case in point being the Great Depression. There, deterioration in wage levels—demand—had combined with oversupply and overcapacity in production systems such that the "natural balance" (as per Say's law) between demand and supply could not be reestablished on its own accord. Only in such conditions, and such conditions only, would the state have a role to play, by providing an exogenous but calibrated stimulus in the form of an inflationary money supply until such a point that disequilibria between investment patterns, production, and demand could be restored within a viable range.[12]

As opposed to this "classic" Keynesian doctrine, far more significant within global development circuits was a certain theology of "growth" as it shaped itself in the 1950s and 1960s, fostered by a complex intellectual exchange between post-Keynesians such as Roy Harrod, Evsey Domar, Robert Solow, Hollis Chenery, and an émigré cadre of Central European economic thinkers of quasi-Marxist, "structuralist" persuasions such as Michal Kalecki.[13] For these thinkers, it was precisely their interest in the long run that became the departure point for a new economics. Proponents of growth theory argued that Keynesian short-term fixes or distortions did more harm than good in that monetary infusions created pent-up inefficiencies which otherwise in any case more drastic fluctuations in naturally occurring business cycles would eliminate. More crucially, short-term monetary management offered little by which the economy could graduate from the structural discrepancies of low productivity, high labor surpluses broadly defining the developing world, to the near-full employment, highly industrialized conditions that Keynes's *General Theory* assumed as a *sine qua non* for its propositions. Consequently, Keynesianism, these thinkers argued, was pointedly ineffectual when it came to choosing defining strategic investment decisions in any given sector—not least because Keynes himself had stringently warned against such statist foibles—or for that matter, in laying out a roadmap for how nonindustrialized or semi-industrialized economies would effect the transition to full-fledged capitalism.

The success of growth theories in postwar governmental and planning circles thus owed significantly to their proponents' proclivity toward defining national and international economies in terms of input-output equations of various sorts, models that easily translated into tractable policy strategies for economic planners. The Harrod-Domar model, for instance, offered a simplified and elegant way of understanding GDP as a simple function of investment, wherein planners "choice of projects" could be theoretically measured in advance in terms of their respective capital-output ratios.[14] By transubstantiating complex relationships between money, wages, technology, society, etc. into so many determinable "inputs" along a measurable chain, ersatz concepts such as the "production function" were claimed as effective gauges to measure allocative efficiency. In the process the economists handily rewrote the "economy" as a field formalism, where physical inputs and outputs within a given production process could begin to be visualized almost in the manner that an engineer might worry about how much coal or water to carry to move a train carrying x numbers of people from London to Manchester.[15]

Two implications follow from this, relevant to the idea of phasing that we have highlighted earlier. The first is that given the presumption of relatively steady monetary inflows, growth could be structured as a kind of sequence. A country could, for instance, prioritize, in its first Five-Year Plan, heavy industry and the power sector so as to trigger downstream growth of manufacturing, in the second, agriculture and food security, allowing for greater control over inflation and prices, in the third, small industries to take up large slacks in employment, and so on. Large multi-sectoral projects or priorities within sectors could likewise be broken up and realized in stages. The second implication is equally important. If inflationary fluctuation could be modeled as predictable, then both public and private actors could simply *discount* these effects as part and parcel of their investment decisions. In other words, it was as if time itself, or the discounting of risk that investors typically feared in market unpredictability, could be canceled out as a factor in production decisions. This is one attribute of incompletion that is critical to keep in mind: strategies of incompletion—phasing or staging—were specifically premised on *predictability* in inflationary patterns. *Dirigisme* and incompletion, in other words, represented two faces of the same coin. Planning would be nothing else but the planning of incompletion, the fashioning of unpredictability as a function of predictability, where all social and economic volatility would be subsumed as so many (manageable) errata within a "secular" gradient of change.

ON THE PRIMACY OF TIME

It is within this epistemological strand of translating the economy into a field formalism and its use for various rhetorical claims toward action and decision making made by postwar academic and governing elites that we see the emergence of "space"—in the manner astutely highlighted by Henri Lefebvre at this time—delineated as a new governmental domain.[16] Since risks appearing over time could be discounted via the state's continued interventions in debt and inflationary management, growth could be defined as a distributional question of *where* particular investments or interventions should be concentrated. (In Lefebvre's own writing, firmly grounded in Marx, the primacy of time over space remains unquestioned—Marx addresses this in his treatment of the play between what he called "formal" and "real" subsumption—an essential crux of his arguments that appears entirely lost or misunderstood in characterizations of "spatial-Keynesianism" espoused by recent Lefebvreian enthusiasts.)[17]

A veritable army of geographers, sociologists, statisticians, and planners set to work modeling national space in the image of the mathematical field formalisms propounded by the economists. Where to put that large chemical factory? From where to where should a highway go? Should housing be seen as a private or public investment? Should education be addressed as "social overhead capital" or a commodity like any other? If the former, to what levels (primary, secondary, tertiary)? Research? Should the state install industries producing high-value goods involving large-scale infusions of capital goods and high productivity in a region composed largely of low-income, subsistence agriculture (advisable in political terms but inadvisable in economic terms given costs from higher inefficiencies)?[18] Space, in other words, was another name for geographical unevenness, the inevitable "imbalances" and conflicts emerging from historical divergences of capital formation, technological absorption, cultural habit, political resistance, and so on, between localities and regions.

Both the Le Mirail and Calcutta projects can be read as indices of a double incompletion: a spatial one, which divided the project timeline of Le Mirail, for example, into multiple stages; this in turn hinged on a *prior* temporal apprehension of incompletion, which involved the monetary-fiscal inputs on which they were reliant on to secure their success. CJW's Caen Hérouville and Bilbao Val d'Asua projects would also adopt similar phasing strategies. Ford's phasing strategy in Calcutta likewise expressly split up its sectoral and intra-sectoral priorities along priorities projected for India's fourth, fifth, sixth and seventh Five-Year Plans, with the first two phases sketched out in the greatest detail (see Figure 1.3).

At the time, Shadrach Woods made clear CJW's dawning realization of the hollow premise of uniform space espoused by the old CIAM, their "talk of *cet espace* or of that *mouvement*, absolutely wallowing in the jargon of composition."[19] The CJW propositions consequently specifically address the city as a transformed cognitive object, placed at the interface of economic planning, allocational and locational dynamics, property speculation, and investment patterns. It is no longer a unified container, a bounded entity with a finite set of contents. Rather its boundaries, such as they are, represent arbitrary spatial delimitations

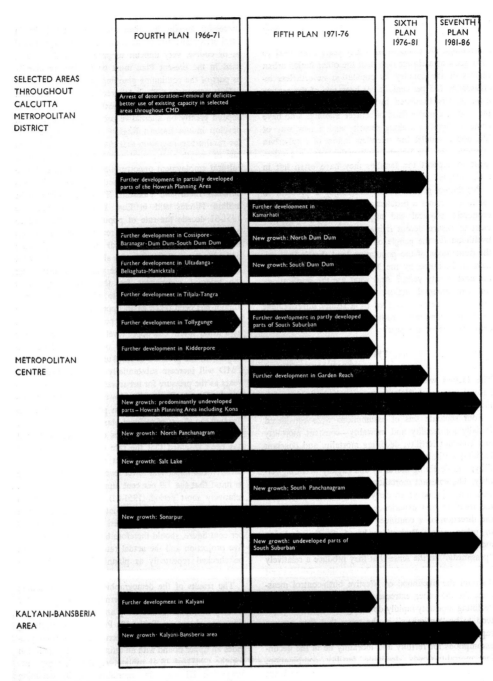

FIGURE 1.3 Ford/CMPO diagram distributing geographically divided growth into Five-Year Plan fiscal phases.

Source: Calcutta Metropolitan Planning Organisation, Basic Development Plan: Calcutta Metropolitan District 1966–1986 (Calcutta: CMPO, 1966).

over multiple, overlapping circuits whose origins and ends lie far from this delimited space, interrelationships among which, moreover, are constantly in a process of flux or uncertainty. To talk of the city is therefore not to talk of a space but of an entity in time; like the capitalist market, it is prone to volatility, mutability, fickleness, and risk. Thus, phasing strategies in planning and architectural discourses of this time do not refer to different parts of self-same entities. Planning would no longer be the simple matter, as the prewar modernists had envisaged, of laying out subdivisions or zones, in the purely spatial sense. Phasing sketches out the calendar of a future that cannot be fully known. Each event, each realized bit of the project in this calendar comprises a fragment or an assembly of fragments, each of which respond in turn new, emergent concatenations of factors, contingencies developing from the volatile mix of all the inputs that go into planned development: executive actions, jurisdictional tensions, legal adjudications, political patronage and opposition, the vicissitudes of consumption patterns, investments, supply, prices, market movements, elections, and allocational preferences, if not the nature of the social contract itself. For Woods, each phase of the Le Mirail would represent

> a fragment of a continuous social reality. . . . As a consequence of being staged, the plan had to allow for modification as conditions changed over the relatively long span of development . . . we had two basic conditions, growth and change, as imperatives of the plan.[20]

Stage 2 would follow Stage 1, but these phases would not resemble each other. The latter stage would rather be as if an "operation . . . held in reserve," open to wholly new considerations, modifications, resolutions for which the previous stage would serve as a test. "It will . . . adapt to new conditions as it is carried into effect. It will react to the conditions which it creates and, in a continuous feed-back process it will, ideally, change constantly."[21] The project is incomplete through and through in its very conception (see Figure 1.4). Failure in the parts would be key to success in the overall.

M. Christine Boyer has described how the *Team 10 Primer* would be constructed in precisely this way, as an assembly of fragments, piecemeal revelations, and jotted-down realizations essaying forth into what appears as an unbounded, limitless conversation. The book is compiled quite like how its authors comprehend the city.[22] Indeed, in the mid-1960s, a sensibility of incompletion can be said to pervade the entirety of architectural thought, all of which begins to revolve around the examination of fragments. Denise Scott Brown explicitly stated as much:

> The development of architectural thought since World War II [has] gone in essentially two directions. One is towards methodical rigor: toward the evolving of concepts and theories of method—planning method or design method—and the use of systems analysis, mathematics and the computer, to make complexity manageable. The other direction is toward the partial and incomplete: towards philosophies of the circumstantial and incremental, and notions of how to live with complexity and contradiction.[23]

A similar tendency can be seen in the Design Methods movement. "We may therefore picture the process of form-making as the action of a series of subsystems, all interlinked, yet sufficiently free of one another to adjust independently in a feasible amount of time."[24] In Japan, all of Kenzo Tange's projects—the Yamanashi and Shizuoka Press and Broadcasting Centers (both 1966) and the Osaka Expo '70 pavilion—realize the *fragments* of the *same*

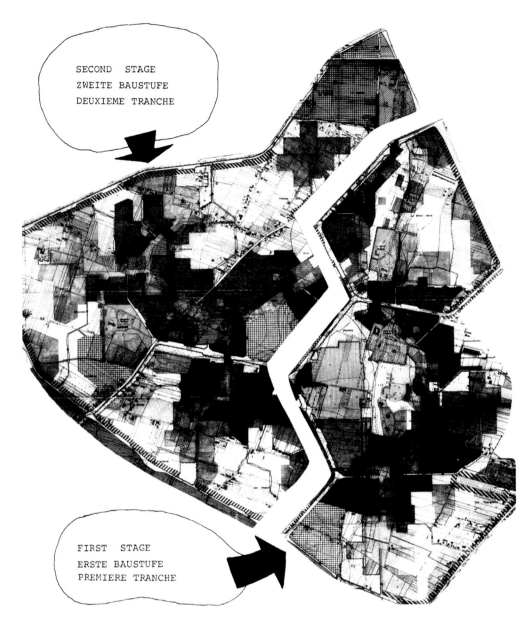

FIGURE 1.4 Plan of CJW's Toulouse-Le Mirail showing its two phases. Only one-third of the first phase would be completed, fully funded by the state.

Source: George Candilis, Alexis Josic, and Shadrach Woods, *Toulouse Le Mirail: Birth of a New Town* (Stuttgart: Karl Krämer Verlag, 1975): 22.

city, first developed *in abstracto* in the Boston Harbor project at MIT (1959) and the Tokyo Bay Plan (1960).

What does an architecture of incompletion look like? What would be its form? At Le Mirail, CJW utilized the organicistic concept of a "stem" to sequester essential infrastructural functions such as circulation and other amenities from more flexible, that is, market-responsive elements such as housing, commercial establishments, entertainment venues and so on. Woods would later rue the relegation of *form* in terms of the ebbing powers of the architect herself: "What we accomplished . . . was the revelation that building could easily be organized without architecture."[25] Within the Ford organization in Calcutta, the dispute over formal specificity went further with a full-fledged war erupting between the planners and the architects. To address the city's burgeoning slum problems, Whittlesey's response was to utilize mass-produced geodesic domes in conjunction with a symbolic ziggurat, the former to combine work and life activities and the latter as a modern totem encapsulating religious and charismatic power of the type that he thought Indians continued to repose in figures like Nehru. Such technological symbolism, he argued, was necessary "to secure publicity and overcome the conservative Bengali mind. . . . Technology must and can win over politics. Nehru knows this. [Deliberative, consultative] politics is a dull weapon."[26] On his part, Ford's mission head Arthur T. Row decried Whittlesey's "picturesque stunts," complaining that they "proposed an architectural solution to a non-architectural problem."[27] At Le Mirail, Woods would take this conflict of architecture and non-architecture more personally, noting that for their clients (Bazerque) the symbolic, mediatic attractions of architecture were precisely what reigned supreme, seen as necessary to attract investors:

> So we, the architects, are called in at a rather late date, as usual, when some of the decisions affecting design have already been taken, although the persons making those decisions probably are ignorant of their effect on the physical environment which is to be created.[28]

As a consequence, he noted elsewhere, "We have to resort to gimmicks, to prestidigitation."[29]

In formal terms, incompletion is thus defined by these countering imperatives of *anti-*architecture (Calcutta) and *part*-architecture (the "stem" in Le Mirail). These countering imperatives toward incompletion will in themselves launch an array of projects, in practice and through a new institutional emphasis on "research"—an activity little evinced institutionally in architectural schools up to this point—into new grammars of form-finding, of a new aesthetics of putting together parts and wholes. Reacting against presumptions of space as a homogeneous, uniformly divisible, entity, totemized in the Corbusierian tower or the Miesian box, this Second Modernism will instead turn toward the intersections of spatial relations and manner in which these relations *unfold in time*.[30] Architectural output will begin to dwell not on outputs but on the processes of output. Thus, to speak of the forms, the morphology—a term that acquires some currency at this time—of incompletion, of what an architecture of incompletion *looks* like, would be strictly speaking a redundancy in that what these approaches specifically discount is the significance of the look or of appearances, of the importance of the finished form.

On the other hand, it would be equally a mistake to take this emphasis on contingency and informality at its word, as lacking in form or concrete formal attitudes. The anti-aesthetic will have an identifiable aesthetic. The embrace of contingency will in fact result in a finite, identifiable, array of shapes, materials, textures, even its own discourse on ornament, that today appear as signature traits of that era. Grammar will not remain mere grammar: rather this grammatology will foster some well-defined modes of expressivity, full-fledged formal patois or poetic dogmas that will foster a recognizable genre of objects (see Figure 1.5). In many cases—for example, Christopher Alexander, as per Ginger Nolan's chapter (Chapter 7) in this volume—the very premium given to flexibility and change will in fact result in far more dogmatic, neurotic approaches than the geometric fixations of the older modernists that they would criticize.

FIGURE 1.5 Single-story (UCOPAN) housing system of prefabricated parts devised for the CMPO.

Source: Calcutta Metropolitan Planning Organisation, Basic Development Plan: Calcutta Metropolitan District 1966–1986 (Calcutta: CMPO, 1966).

In the taxonomy sketched out provisionally that follows, I attempt to identify some key formal characteristics of architectural production of the 1960s, all of which privilege process and incompletion as the overarching rationale behind their approach. The taxonomy provided applies as much to the American pseudo-debate between the Greys and the Whites, the diverse output of Team 10, Third World modernists, the proponents of megastructure and metabolist thought, and more avant-garde practitioners such as Yona Friedman and the Situationists alike. In all these projects, the formal investigations specifically reflect a crisis in the architects' growing sense of their professional marginalization in the face of what Parsonian political scientists would come to call "collective agency problems" in the processes of urbanization.[31] The formal attributes of incompletion here explicitly express a certain contradiction in the temporal imaginary, presenting on the one hand a (utopian) scaling up of architectural scope to reflect these presumptions of *deferred* collective agency, and on the other, a (realist) recognition of the intrinsic fractures in that premise. Incompletion represents as much a claim to epistemological authority as it is haunted by the absence of this authority:

1 *Conflating Plans and Diagrams:* The literal amalgamation of diagrams and plans represented a key device through which architects and planners conflated physical spaces and geography with the thermodynamic field formalisms developed by the economists. Arrows, symbols, legends begin to thicken architectural renderings, loading them with informational ballast that refer not to space or geography but to data, stochastic probabilities, and projections into time.

2 *Bigness/Phalansterization:* The push against "composition," as argued by Woods earlier, expressly read space as a multi-jurisdictional entity. Quite as the economists sought to characterize planning as multi-factoral analyses encompassing multiple jurisdictional terrains, architects play to this technocratic characterization by aggregating, within their projects, multiple types of programmatic usage, such that buildings lose programmatic definition and appear more as relational composites. City and building become one and the same. Larger and larger buildings interiorize all social space, such that public and private behaviors alike come to be "architecturalized" within a planned totality. Postwar architecture resurrects the phalanstery: there is no outside of architecture. Rather, projects emphasize internalized heterogeneity, juxtaposition, interiorized flows.

3 *Organicism:* If formal rigidity is deemphasized, there is on the other hand an overelaboration of linkages, connections, articulations. Parts acquire autonomy in relation to wholes; "composition" is dis-privileged in favor of expressing a grammar of relations. Nineteenth-century, Romantic, paradigms of organic and vegetational images rear their head again, most notably in the repurposing of the concept-metaphor "growth." Among architects, the preoccupation with growth and processes leads to the preponderance of two key "logics" of spatial assembly: the "tree-shaped" logic of stems and branches and the "rhizomatic" logic of the so-called "mat building" or, in Woods's terms, the "groundscaper."

4 *Sachlichkeit/Brutalism/Primitivism:* As with their interwar precursors, postwar architects and planners internalized the premises of economics as a "science" based on the scarcity of resources. There is an embrace of austerity: architects espouse a bias against ornament and symbolism in favor of built expressions that pare form down to its barest, elementary, essentials, reverting to something like a *sachlich* character. The avowed

opposition to ornament will in fact involve recourse to a very specific kind of ornament: the designedly unfinished roughness of "New Brutalism." Both *sachlichkeit* and Brutalism reflect a shared sensibility of temporal deferral or anteriority: these buildings *await* culture (decoration, symbols, fetishes, commodities, meaning). These coarse, "primeval" surfaces anticipate societal time, a future supplementation when occupants come to fill out these built receptacles with the everyday rituals of lived existence. Formal desistance thus has as its counterpart the architects' obsessive preoccupation with ethnography and the study of human behavior.

THE FAILURE OF PROCESS/THE PROCESS OF FAILURE

To say that incompletion "emerged" in the mid-1960s, of course, would only mean to say that it emerged *in a certain way*. If by incompletion we mean simply a certain alertness toward contingency, then this would not be something new: any theory of practice necessarily locates contingency as its central feature, which the practitioner must learn to negotiate. The term design, which owes its origin to theology, also refers to a similar negotiation of contingency. God sculpts the universe from chaos, and it is in this image of creation, a perennially unfinished act whose outcome can never be known, that the *arti del disegno* will seek to craft itself. In Kant's critical philosophy, incompletion acquires a new synonym—*teleology*—a term that redefines divine eschatology and brings it within the open prerogatives of finite, subjective, judgment. In post-Kantian thought, incompletion consequently takes up its modern avatar in being posited specifically as a mode and model of practice, which is to say it begins to produce real objects and actual effects driven by what we may call the romantic logic of the fragment.[32] Research, poetry, the university, museums, bureaucracies, indeed the state itself—all of these will claim to realize what we may call a homeostasis of incompletion, in that their epistemological and censoring powers will be explicitly premised on their commitment toward the continual revisitation, emendation, erasure, rewriting of their actions.[33] In the mid-twentieth century, the management of contingency will define a further set of institutional and epistemological careers, instigating the construction of new machines—computers—as well as a panoply of ersatz knowledge fields, systems science and cybernetics, structural anthropology and linguistics, glimmerings of which shine through the characteristics outlined in the aforementioned taxonomy.

Architects in the mid-1960s inevitably drew on these older, more archaic, strands and contexts. However, I argue that the emphasis on incompletion in this period also manifests a very specific dispensation of state and fiscal prerogatives in this period, a dispensation that can be measured in terms of its effects on the complex downstream interactions of budgetary outlays, procurement of services, and contractual doctrines. If one looks carefully at the contractual documents and correspondence of projects such as Le Mirail or Ford's Calcutta, a far more prosaic picture emerges as to why incompletion acquires such salience in this period, which has to do with the consultants'—CJW for instance—acute responsivity to *the phase-bound manner in which budgets were allocated*. To read architectural output in this manner does not mean reducing these outputs to economistic criteria. Rather, what I am attempting to highlight here is the tenor of state patronage and the implicitly transactional, unsettled and clientelist character by which various domains of knowledge—the economists, hygienists, statisticians, engineers, accountants, and so on—sought to establish control over these budgetary domains, and with which the architects found themselves in competition.

Certainly the architects knew well which side their state-funded bread was buttered on. Here one only has to read Shadrach Woods's own article on Le Mirail published in the *Washington University Law Review*, much of which was devoted to budgetary breakdowns rather than architectural argument, providing the reader with extensive details as to how subsidies from different governmental bodies were essential for the project.[34] In the event, the only portion of the project that would be realized was a "demonstration area," fully paid for by government funds. When further investments failed to appear, the Le Mirail would die on the vine.

Something similar might be said to be occurring with the macroeconomic premises of the Bretton Woods system itself by the end of the 1960s. If Le Mirail and Calcutta projects were "failures," they must therefore be read not as isolated instances but in fact as indices of a larger crisis in an entire global system, an entire way of conceiving and doing projects. Indeed the conceptualization and trajectory of these projects manifest as much the challenges that planning bodies increasingly found themselves confronting by the mid-1960s. As countries piled up foreign exchange deficits from large capital expenditures whose conceptualization remained outside Washington's control, the US Treasury was nonetheless forced to absorb the brunt of these globally accumulating currency deficits. In efforts to reestablish control, outgoing debts to countries began to be weighted with more and more "conditionalities." In 1967, both the United Kingdom and India were subjected to the International Monetary Funds' earliest "Strategic Adjustment Programs," which mandated a massive currency devaluation, producing a deflationary shock that to all intents and purposes put paid to the inflation-based temporal horizon projected by the planners. If in Britain this announced the end of Harold Wilson's "white heat" socialism, both France and India were forced to undertake a so-called "Plan Holiday" and suspend their respective Third Plans (France from 1960–61 and India from 1966–68). The deflationary prescriptions explicitly privileged monetary stability over growth, bringing an end to the high-growth levels of the immediate post-war, sending developed countries into a path of long-term economic stagflation. In France, counter-inflationary policies had already been set underway in November 1964 when the finance ministry began to curtail the powers of the *Commissariat Général du Plan* by inveighing against government "interference" and "guidelines" affecting the private sector. "By opting for balance of payments equilibrium and monetary stability over physical plan targets, the government in effect repudiated its commitment to genuine economic planning."[35] As Valéry Giscard d'Estaing, then France's Minister of Finance and Economic Affairs (1962–1966), put it: "*Le plan, c'est l'inflation.*"[36] In the end the Bretton Woods arrangement would be dismantled by the same country that had created it, with Nixon taking the dollar off the fixed-rate mechanism and allowing it to float on global financial markets.

In developing countries, the first tranches of large capital and capital-goods infusions in the 1950s had proved ripe for capture by dominant "interest groups"—ethnic factions, business lobbies, large and medium landowners—whose hold over political parties created new concentrations of power for which the distributional ethos underlying planning, both economic and physical, itself consisted of a threat. The career of the West Indian development economist W. Arthur Lewis over the 1960s offers us a case in point. Lewis's *The Theory of Economic Growth* (1955) had established some of the principal foundations of development economics and modernization theory, its chapters notable for the way in which it introduced non-economic factors—cultural predispositions, the uptake of knowledge paradigms and ideas, governmental frameworks—as crucial considerations for the proposed new economics.[37] Following the book's publication, Lewis would directly involve himself with development programs in Ghana and the Caribbean, a phase of his career that his own biographer would use as a case study of "why visiting economists fail," a theme that would gain increasing prominence in development literature from the late-1960s onward.[38] By comparison with the earlier book, Lewis's *Development Planning* (1966), published a decade later, reads as much as an inquest into failure, focusing far more on the manner in which planners, divested of the privileges accorded "neutral" expertise, must learn to negotiate with influential power bases—within and without government—that hold critical sway over economic decision-making.[39]

In India, following the deflationary shock administered by the 1967 Structural Adjustment Program, the national planners' ability to "choose" and define projects would be likewise curtailed by a powerful combination of *domestic* interests, notably personified in Giscard d'Estaing's counterpart, the fiscally conservative finance minister Morarji Desai, whose powerbase lay in the business lobbies of western India. One ironic outcome of this drastic curtailment of the planners' power would be the derailing of the Ford planning effort in Calcutta itself. After all, Ford's founding objectives in India had broadly comported with American goals of supporting private capital. The crippling recession set in force by the IMF's deflationary shock in 1967 would provide a major impetus for the prevailing of the communist parties in provincial elections held in West Bengal that year, following which Ford's planners would be caught between two counteracting biases: the right's bias against planning *and* the communists' bias against Americans.

Also ironically, one of the strongest obstacles that would emerge for Ford's ambitions in regional planning, as with planning globally, would be the very rights of private property which the Americans were so positively disposed toward, the thicket of rentier-based tenurial relations in both city and rural hinterland. In the end, it was this factor that most got in the way of the planners' ambitions of remaking space and time. Whittlesey, having enthused about Calcutta's slums, would bitterly express his frustrations in his letters home, concerned about its implications for his future career:

> The venal bastards. . . . These Indians are a damn sight smarter than the Americans who put us here. . . . At present this is a nightmare way beyond the technical and living difficulties. . . . I cannot rid my mind of this, and I want to get away. And I chastise myself for wanting to get away, but I must. The consequences will not be easy to face in New York either.[40]

As for itself, it would never quite recover from the prolonged deindustrialization on which it had embarked in mid-century.

Something similar can also be said, *mutatis mutandis*, about CJW and *dirigisme* in Toulouse, although unlike Calcutta here the story has to do with rising, not declining, regional wealth. Mayor Bazerque's gambit had depended on a regional vision that tied together state-disbursed *l'aménagement* with urban infrastructural improvements. Rosemary Wakeman has narrated in some detail as to how surrounding towns and *mairies* around Toulouse, driven by similar expectations, mobilized private commercial interests and real estate investors to heavily speculate in land, driving up land values and consequently the costs of Bazerque's grandiose ambitions, which included Le Mirail. Correspondingly, the central government cut down subsidies on state land purchases in a drive to privilege privatized initiatives. Consequently, the projected transport linkages to central Toulouse never materialized. Rather than serve as the centerpiece of a new conurbation, Le Mirail would come to resemble a beached liner, its isolated residents disconnected from the thriving region around them. The prospects of a grocery store within the demonstration area would undercut by a massive *Carrefour* located on the well-traveled highway nearby. By 1975 Le Mirail would leave the city of Toulouse with a debt of 531 million francs.[41]

Architects such as Shadrach Woods would deeply internalize these cascading failures of modernist planning around the world, including CJW's, as signaling the marginalization of the architectural profession as such. Upon his return to the United States, Woods would run from pillar to post to obtain a planning commission in New York. "We did not engineer the catastrophe single-handed. We were only representing a stage in the development of the creeping bureaucratic miasma which would have engulfed us."[42] The architects were not alone in what appeared to be the growing devaluation and dereliction of their epistemic authority. Practically that same year, Wood's thoughts were echoed as if verbatim by the development economist Albert O. Hirschman, "But should [the economist] not have a more important role than one of acting as usher and high-level messenger boy for the people who make the real decisions?"[43]

In Calcutta, where Ford had strenuously worked to establish an administrative apparatus aimed precisely at sifting through and coordinating interests and approaches, this dereliction would leave a cadre signally befuddled about its own knowledge paradigms. Even as they were stepping off the tarmac, Ford's planners could imagine little as to what they had done wrong or could have done otherwise. Arthur T. Row's *post-hoc*, disconsolate reflections provide us with an epitaph for Ford's Calcutta venture that serve just as well for the pumped-up aspirations of incompletion in general:

> How could one disagree? What was wrong with employing a traffic engineer to devise the means for sorting out the traffic; a highway engineer to improve the roads; an urban planner to choose a location for a new bridge; a bridge engineer to design it; sanitary engineers to work out improvements to the water supply, the sewerage and drainage systems; an architect to design housing related to people's ability to pay; a public-housing expert to establish a management system for government housing; an anthropologist to see that the housing reflected the social milieu and the culture of the people for whom it was designed; an architect/engineer to plan a development that mixes residence with work on an accessible site; a demographer to estimate the future population for which these several programs would be planned; an economist who would estimate the future economy and quantify space needs; a fiscal scientist to work out how all these improvements could be paid for; and all this under the direction and coordination of an experienced and able urban planner?[44]

NOTES

1 Calcutta Metropolitan Planning Organisation, *Basic Development Plan: Calcutta Metropolitan District 1966–1986* (Calcutta: CMPO, 1966).

2 Ashok Rudra, "French Planning for India?" *Economic and Political Weekly* 2, nos. 33/35 (August 1967): 1533, 1535–1536.

3 Albert Hirschman, *The Strategy of Economic Development* (New Haven, CT: Yale University Press, 1958).

4 For a comparative study of the two planning systems, see essays by Charles Kindleberger and Richard S. Eckhaus in Max F. Millikan, ed., *National Economic Planning: A Conference of the Universities-National Bureau Committee for Economic Research* (New York: NBEA/Columbia University Press, 1967); for the dynamics of French planning bodies, see June Burnham, *Politicians, Bureaucrats and Leadership in Organizations: Lessons from Regional Planning*

in France (New York: Palgrave Macmillan, 2009); for details pertaining to Toulouse post-politics and the Le Mirail project, see Rosemary Wakeman, *Modernizing the Provincial City: Toulouse, 1945–1975* (Cambridge, MA: Harvard University Press, 1997). For a thoroughgoing study of the travails of planning in India, see Francine J. Frankel, *India's Political Economy, 1947–2004* (New Delhi: Oxford University Press, 2005).

5 David Willcox, "Preface," in Arthur T. Row and Kalyan Biswas, *Calcutta: The Great Experiment*, Unpublished manuscript, Reports 013484, Ford Foundation Archives, 3–4.
6 q. Wakeman, *Modernizing the Provincial City*, 127.
7 Arthur T. Row, *An Evaluation of the Calcutta Planning and Development Project, 1961–1974* (New Delhi: The Ford Foundation, 1974), 79, 89.
8 Julian H. Whittlesey, Ford Foundation architect, letter to his wife Eunice Whittlesey July 20, 1961. *Stepping Stones: Letters to Eunice 1932–1974 on Paths of Architecture and Planning and Archaeology, Article, #4439*. Division of Rare and Manuscript Collections, Cornell University Library. Henceforth "Whittlesey Papers."
9 Bernard E. Loshbough to Chester Bowles, "A Proposal for a US-AID for Calcutta," May 22, 1964, "Training and Research Activities of the Calcutta Metropolitan Planning Organization," 1961–1970, Grant Notification Letters, Reel No. 2640, Ford Foundation Archives.
10 Row, *An Evaluation of the Calcutta Planning and Development Project*, 24.
11 Millikan, *National Economic Planning*, 5.
12 See Prabhat Patnaik, *The Value of Money* (New York: Columbia University Press, 2009).
13 See H. W. Arndt, *Economic Development: The History of an Idea* (Chicago: University of Chicago Press, 1987); Joseph L. Love, *Crafting the Third World: Theorizing Underdevelopment in Rumania and Brazil* (Stanford, CA: Stanford University Press, 1996).
14 See George Rosen, *Western Economists and Eastern Societies: Agents of Change in South Asia, 1950–1970* (Delhi: Oxford University Press, 1985), 22.
15 Philip Mirowski, *More Heat than Light: Economics as Social Physics, Physics as Nature's Economics* (Cambridge, MA: Cambridge University Press, 1989).
16 See for example Jean Labasse, *L'Organisation de l'espace: éléments de géographie volontaire* (Paris: Hermann, 1966); also Henri Lefebvre, *The Production of Space*, trans. Donald Nicholson-Smith (Cambridge: Blackwell, 1974, 1991).
17 Neil Brenner, *New State Spaces: Urban Governance and the Rescaling of Statehood* (New York: Oxford University Press, 2004).
18 See Thomas Vietorisz, "Locational Choices in Planning?" in Millikan, *National Economic Planning*, 39–130.
19 Shadrach Woods, "Dwellings, Ways and Places," lecture at Harvard GSD, 1963, manuscript, 16, Box 28, Shadrach Woods Architectural Records and Papers, 1923–2008, the Department of Drawings and Archives, Avery Architectural and Fine Arts Library, Columbia University. Henceforth "Woods Papers."
20 Shadrach Woods, "Discovery of Architecture," lecture given at Yale Fall 1963, drafted in St. Louis September 12, 1963, manuscript, 12–13, Box 27, Woods Papers.
21 Shadrach Woods, "Le Mirail, A New Quarter for the City of Toulouse," *Washington Law Review* 1 (1965): 13.
22 See Christine M. Boyer, *Not Quite Architecture: Writing Around Alison and Peter Smithson* (Cambridge, MA: The MIT Press, 2017).
23 Denise Scott Brown, "Team10, Perspecta 10, and the Present State in Architectural Theory," *Journal of the American Planning Association* 33, no. 1 (1967): 43.
24 Christopher Alexander, *Notes on the Synthesis of Form* (Cambridge, MA: Harvard University Press, 1964), 43.
25 Shadrach Woods, lecture given at Cornell, April 4, 1972, manuscript, 5, Box 27, Woods Papers.
26 Julian H. Whittlesey, "Ford Foundation Architect," letter to his wife Eunice Whittlesey July 29, 1961, Whittlesey Papers.
27 Row and Biswas, *Calcutta*, 71.
28 Shadrach Woods, lecture at American Institute of Planners (after 1978, American Planning Association), October 10, 1963, manuscript, 4, Box 27, Woods Papers.
29 Woods, "Discovery of Architecture," Woods Papers.
30 See Arindam Dutta, ed., *A Second Modernism: MIT, Architecture, and the 'Techno-Social' Moment* (Cambridge, MA: The MIT Press, 2013).
31 See Robert Dahl's classic study of New Haven, *Who Governs? Democracy and Power in an American City* (New Haven: Yale University Press, 1961, 2005).
32 See Jean-Luc Nancy and Philippe Lacoue-Labarthe, *The Literary Absolute: The Theory of Literature in German Romanticism*, trans. Philip Barnard and Cheryl Lester (Buffalo, NY: The SUNY Press, 1988).
33 See Theodore Ziolkowski, *German Romanticism and Its Institutions* (Princeton, NJ: Princeton University Press, 1990).
34 Woods, "Le Mirail, A New Quarter for the City of Toulouse."
35 Richard B. Du Boff, "The Decline of Economic Planning in France," *The Western Political Quarterly* 21, no. 1 (March 1968): 105.

36 Ibid., 106.
37 W. Arthur Lewis, *The Theory of Economic Growth* (London: George Allen & Unwin, 1955).
38 Barbara Ingham and Paul Mosley, *Sir Arthur Lewis: A Biography* (New York: Palgrave Macmillan, 2013).
39 W. Arthur Lewis, *Development Planning: The Essentials of Economic Policy* (London: George Allend & Unwin, 1966).
40 Julian H. Whittlesey, letter to Eunice Whittlesey, "Stepping Stones: Letters to Eunice, 1932–1974," Kroch Asia rare materials archives, Cornell University Library, # 4439, Box 1.
41 Wakeman, *Modernizing the Provincial City*, 133.
42 Shadrach Woods, lecture given at Cornell, April 4, 1972, manuscript, 5, Box 27, Woods Papers.
43 Albert O. Hirschman, *A Bias for Hope* (New Haven: Yale University Press, 1971), 53.
44 Row and Biswas, *Calcutta*, 84.

2

God's gamble

Self-help architecture and the housing of risk

Ijlal Muzaffar

So you are my witness, declares the Lord. And I am God [Isaiah 43.12]. That is, if you are my witness, I am God, and if you are not my witness, I am, as it were, not God.
—Sifre Deuteronomy 346, Finkelstein edition

A group of women walk in a line carrying pans full of cement on their heads (see Figure 2.1). The four in the back seem to be sharing a laugh. The one in the middle appears lost in her thoughts. The woman in the front returns the camera's stare with a clenched twig, or a cigarette, between her teeth. In the background, we see other laborers, all seemingly men, gathered under the roof of one of the unfinished structures, perhaps taking a break. The gendered division of labor notwithstanding, the scene appears routine and ordinary. And it is meant to be. Shown by Charles Abrams, the American housing expert and UN advisor, the image was supposed to attest to the widespread low-cost "core" housing schemes being undertaken in the newly independent Ghana. This particular one was in New Ajena, one of many new towns being constructed in northern Ghana as part of Kwame Nkrumah's ambitious Volta River Valley development project that Abrams viewed positively.[1]

But there is something extraordinary in the photograph as well: the women's dresses. They are all strangely similar, if not alike. Abrams, who included this photograph in his book, *Man's Struggle for Shelter in an Urbanizing World*, as an example of a successful UN mission carried out with this long-term collaborator, Otto Koenigsberger, doesn't comment on this uniformity. For Abrams, the ordinariness of the photograph was a sign of its extraordinariness. It was proof of a "system" at work, an arrangement that, when set up properly, not only crossed spatial boundaries but, more importantly, aligned different temporal processes as well. Koenigsberger had highlighted these qualities of a system in urban context in a report cowritten for the Ford Foundation titled *Infrastructure Problems of the Cities of Developing Countries*:

> There is a need to design urban *systems* which respond both to the resources available in various countries and to the different *time scales* of potential change in these resources. That is: Urban infrastructure systems needs to be designed to fit the income levels of different countries, taking account of the ways in which incomes are likely to *change over time* [emphasis added].[2]

DOI: 10.4324/9781003193654-4

FIGURE 2.1 Women workers transporting concrete for the core-house settlement in Ajena Ghana.
Source: From Charles Abrams, *Man's Struggle for Shelter in an Urbanizing* World (Cambridge, MA: MIT Press, 1964), 181.

But does everyone have to wear the same clothes in a system? Isn't variation a virtue of systemic relations? What does the uniformity of workers' dress represent, and how does it reflect the working of a system when it spills over from the urban to the rural, crossing not only distinct spatial conditions but temporal rhythms as well?

A clue to our puzzle is given in a footnote in Abrams's book praising one Lloyd Shirer, a missionary of the Pentecostal Evangelical Church, who was already working in the Volta River Project Area when Abrams arrived on the UN mission. Discussing precursors to his proposed "core" housing and its other variations, like the "roof loan scheme," in Ghana, Abrams mentions "how the [UN] mission was impressed with the pioneering work of Lloyd Shirer, who [had] worked with the natives and taught them how to use rammed-earth techniques in housing, building dams, and other essential work."[3]

Since there was no uniform for construction work given by the government, could the dresses have been handed out to the women by Shirer's mission? If they were, they would visualize a point that Abrams's praise for Shirer makes apparent nevertheless. The religious dimension plays a particular role in resolving a conundrum Abrams's argument inevitably tangles itself into. If the core house is part of a "system," who gets to speak for this system? How does one know what the system wants?

The conflation of religious and the systemic in one footnote in Abrams's book is not incidental. Both draw their legitimacy from establishing a certain idea of scale and somehow knowing that scale. And this scale, more than spatial, is temporal, as Koenigsberger's statement stressed. To know the system is to know not only what it connects in space, but also in time. It is to know not only what has been but what is to come. Locating this commonality between architecture and religion, however, is not a matter of identifying Abrams's religious beliefs or Shirer's architectural interests. Rather, it is to locate an epistemological overlap between architecture and religion in the development theater. Here we will see that without shaping such an epistemology of systems, which allows religion to operate like architecture and architecture to operate like religion, there can be no claim to the possibility of development.

It is also not a coincidence that Shirer chose to spread the Lord's name by teaching how to build houses and Abrams found in this activity a noteworthy precedent for his own enterprise. Systemic predictions are made, as we will see, by reading a text purportedly hidden in the material world itself. Both Shirer's and Abrams's projects lay out schemas of organizing material in time that allows the expert and the preacher to establish the distinction between individual thinking and systemic thinking, whether it is theological or architectural. As these distinctions are put in place, the religious and the developmental experts gain the right to speak for a larger dimension. This authoritative voice, speaking for God, for system, for God's system and system's god, was sometimes male and sometimes female, but the material world it purportedly organized remained resolutely female. The women walking down the line do not just wear dresses given by the missionaries and shown by the UN experts. They are seen to embody them, the dress and the skin on which it rests being part of a singular world that is being rearranged according to a higher logic.

THE SCALE OF TIME

An argument for a system is an argument for scale. A system is a system inasmuch as it can situate its parts in relation to a larger arrangement, one always managed in the purview of the other. This characteristic was essential to the definition employed by Norbert Weiner, the MIT communication scientist, when he first framed the new field of cybernetics in 1948 as a science of "closed systems," with the observer always outside an enclosing boundary.[4] This was also true when the undefined status of the observer in Weiner's systems came under criticism and was transformed during the Joshua Macy Foundation conferences that brought together prominent scientist and philosophers, including Weiner, during the 1960s. The system soon came be thought of as an open, infinitely extending realm that engulfed the observer as well.[5] Abrams and the Volta River Project show that what became a crisis for cybernetics as a science, its inability to validate the observation as well as its objectivity, however, became an opportunity to outline a particular position, that of a vulnerable expert, who, in striving against fallibility, earns not only the right to an objective observation but to a transcendental outlook as well.

Concurrent with developments in systems theory, Abrams and Koenigsberger use the term "system" in a sense that is somewhere between the two concepts of system, open and closed. The observer steps in and out of what he observes. This impossible position is carved out not by wrestling with the space of the system, who is in and who is out, or how big or small the system is, but by shifting the question of scale from space to time. The expert knows best not because he is objective but because he can predict the long term even if he is wrong in the short term. The gathering of intentions, capturing a multitude of concerns under a single criterion, establishing continuities across disjunctures, occurs under the shadow of a certain temporal scale, a specific dimension of time, a time out of time. This dimension would in fact figure to be more critical for the functioning of the system than its spatial expanse. For it is through establishing a certain temporal scale that the expert is able to locate his intentions outside the vagaries of history and, with it, politics.

This temporal scale appears slowly, surreptitiously, in Abrams's writing: in evaluating the possibilities of generating savings for housing finance in underdeveloped areas, Abrams defends an unusual option: lottery. "The lottery is," Abrams asserts,

> a more respectable device than is generally believed. The distribution of the Promised Land amongst the Twelve Tribes of Israel involved a decision by drawn lot. As a source of national revenue, the lottery was introduced in England as far back as 1569 and continued in use until the 1920s. A lottery helped pay for Virginia Company's colonial expedition, and lotteries were partly responsible for financing the establishment of Harvard, Columbia, Dartmouth, and Williams colleges in the United States.[6]

What connects this arc across religion, monarchy, nationalism, colonialism, and institutions of higher education? What thread knits together the vagaries of patriarchy, divine right, mercantilism, and private and intellectual property? Oddly, it is "respect." But how is respect made to cover the edifice of lottery to make it both financially and morally feasible? What turns the lottery purchaser from a gambler to an investor and the seller from a cheater to an impartial judge? For Abrams, the difference lay in the kind of lottery that was being proposed. Here, Abrams is not asking the inhabitant to buy a ticket and wish for a prize. That indeed would be gambling. Abrams is proposing the lottery to be offered by a bank for only those who save:

> Inducing people to save will entail more than hanging out a bank shingle. In addition to paying interest, the [housing] association must search for other devices that will challenge the established habits and stubborn folkways. A proved device is lottery, which is used to raise general revenues, funds for hospitals, etc. If with every deposit the depositor receives a chance to win a home, this might supply the incentive needed.[7]

But isn't "inducing" a kind of cheating itself? Sure, you don't lose your money if you don't win a house, but you were never saving to buy a house either, you were saving to win one. The bank, here the lottery seller, makes you save under a false pretense, because you are assumed to not understand the true one. Inducing, incentivizing, are all euphemisms for a lie that must be told and sold in the face of "stubborn folkways."[8]

Yet this is not just a moral question, where one side assumes to know more than the other. Instead, herein lies a specific quality of economic, particularly financial, thinking that makes it trump social and political thinking, a quality that makes its logic supersede other logics. This is the quality of the temporal scale we identified earlier. Financial thinking establishes itself as the logic behind, above, around, individual thinking. It is larger, deeper, more complex in time than personal decisions. The individual thinking might ponder to save or not to save, to be thrifty or wasteful, but financial thinking decides where the line between the two lies. It sets the premise for evaluating the former. The bank knows best.

But how can this claim be sustained? Aren't financial plans laid out on shorter horizons than "traditional" ones? What is the nature of this scale that makes economics trump history? Usually the question is answered in terms of the opposition between dynamic and static modes of thought, between change and stability, speed and slowness, as Walter Rostow, the MIT economist and advisor to presidents Kennedy and Johnson, had done in his famous *Stages of Growth*.[9] Abrams too had defined the problem of development in this way. Ghana's problems, Abrams asserted, stemmed from the speed of change that the West had only experienced slowly.[10] The logic that prevailed in the industrialized world, the historical processes of rise and fall, of fortunes, politics, and capital, could not be allowed to follow its waxing and waning in the development arena. We wasted too much time and money the first time around. There was no need to repeat what was now visible in hindsight.

But that argument alone does not give financial thinking its omnipresence over historical thinking. Financial thinking's triumph resides in its claim to a time larger than historical time. Despite the fact that it must be bound to five-year plans, national boundaries, geographical locations, its logic precedes and determines all outcomes. Saving is a success no matter what the result:

> While objections to lottery exist (e.g., they may induce people to rely on luck more than labor), the argument against use of the lottery to draw savings is without much force. The benefits of savings are retained, and thrift rather than speculation is encouraged when the gamble is the inducement to thrift. In this context, it is less a lottery than the accepted and respected prize for participation.[11]

For Abrams, this statement held its force even if one financial world view was replaced by another, even if saving was done away by expenditure, or "investment," as John Maynard Keynes proposed and Abrams attested, with Koenigsberger and Vladimir Bodiansky, in his report for the Gold Coast.[12] In each case, what is replaced is an approach, not the logic of finance. God might change his mind, but he is never dead.

It is not a coincidence that Abrams locates the original moment of the draw at the division of the Promised Land. The logic of savings and draw has a theological dimension. It is an economic theology. Here we are reminded of Max Weber's claim that all social and natural sciences must have this theological dimension as their premise, a transcendental assumption that must precede their findings and give them legitimacy and meaning.[13] In Abrams's case, this theological dimension is *literally* theological. The draw for the division of the Promised Land was holy and impartial, respectable and just, not because it was based on chance but because it was a supplication of one intent by another, a supplication of personal intent by divine intent, of intent by Intent. No matter what the results of the draw, the outcomes were just and were part of God's plans. There were no losers in the draw for the Promised Land. The draw was only the facilitator of bringing intent in accordance with Intent. Here, again, we are not pointing to Abrams's religious belief (the example of the Promised Land is, after all, deployed as an example). Rather, we are uncovering an epistemological structure of development thinking that excludes all political and historical dimensions from it.

For Abrams, lottery acquired a bad reputation only when this transcendental support was missing: "The abolition of lotteries in England and the United States was later inspired by corruption and counterfeiting of tickets."[14] Here the confrontation between history and religion, between politics and economics becomes apparent. What is called corruption and counterfeiting are traces of interest, historical and political, of contingency, that couldn't be part of God's plan, nor of financial planning. The lottery only worked as a legitimate enterprise when all its outcomes could still be explained as part of a larger logic, be it theological or financial.

FROM GOD'S SHADOW TO THE EXPERT'S TOUCH

The God Abrams invokes as the impartial mediator of the draw is the God of the Old Testament, one that frequently expressed anger and carried out destruction, a God who did not stay out of the business of the world. He is a god who is inside the world with the rest, in need of the world as much as the world needs him, a god who suffers not just *for* creation but *with* it.[15] This duality is critical for the mode of authority and expertise Abrams is outlining.

It does not have to be this way. In contrast, Myra Rivera has located this otherliness in sameness as a source of emancipation and interpretation in the figure of the ghost, or the "Spirit," in James' gospel.[16] The Spirit inhabits the gospel as an unknown and unknowable trace of another time and space. The Holy Ghost, the Spirit, descends on Jesus after his death, resurrecting him. Yet it is not the same as Jesus. The Jesus walking about after his death is neither one with the Spirit nor apart from it. This Jesus eludes his followers. They feel his presence more with the lightest movement of the air rather than with the solidity of vision or touch. He passes through closed doors, gets mistakenly identified by Mary Magdalen as a gardener, and is only slowly recognized by others.[17]

Rivera's stresses the strange relationship between the appearance of the ghost and the vulnerability of the witnesses.[18] Mary's tears, though, might not have brought Jesus back, Rivera asserts, "but they at least seem to have brought about a transformed vision."[19] The Holy Ghost too is made vulnerable as a result. After being resurrected, Jesus moves through walls. Yet

> the surprisingly fluid materiality of a body that is undeterred by closed doors is nonetheless indelibly marked by history—and so are the readers haunted by his story. In this scene [when Jesus meets his disciples], it is only after revealing the wounds in his admittedly strange body that his disciples are able to recognize him.[20]

Jesus's wounds, like Mary's tears, open a space of vulnerability shared by the apparition and those who witness it.

For Rivera, this combination of ontological ambiguity and experiential vulnerability amounts to what is nothing short of a "haunting," where the haunted pray to be haunted, to participate in an encounter that "spill[s] over the limits of canonical memory—necessarily and unpredictably."[21] There are great rewards to be reaped from this mutual reliance and fallibility.

> In this theology, the Holy Ghost names the divine in relationship with the past, with ancestors and with their ever multiplying inheritances.... We may indeed call this the Spirit of the truth that blows from the past, appearing occasionally as/in spectral bodies to incite memory and enliven hope.[22]

For Rivera, the ambiguity, vulnerability, and multiplicity open the door to continuously wrench the past, present, and future from the closing confines of a singular meaning and "solid knowledge that replaces spectral memory." In leaning on each other, the Holy Ghost and its witnesses occupy a scale that defies measure, is beyond measure, in space and time: "Animating ghosts to dance in the faults of history, or of ontology, the Holy Ghost incites those still alive to become witnesses. Without such witnesses, there is no dance—and, as it were, no God."[23] A vulnerable God, then, one who is both one and separate from his incarnation as a human, one who is seen by his disciples only when they too become vulnerable, when they forgo their need for proof and replace it with faith.

This interpretive dance doesn't occur at the global margins of development. There, the dance has a guest list of one, one witness who can move to the tune of the Spirit, or the system, only one witness who can see the ghost and touch its presence. Do we take the expert's touch, the missionary's embrace, to be a stand-in for the divine presence? Does this witnessing still amount to an interpretative dance, or is it a choreography predetermined from the beginning?

The missionary at the margin promises the freedom of the first option but delivers only the second, a singular interpretation, always offering one to shore up the other. Rivera is all too well aware of this move. As she notes, "the mysterious quality of a ghostly body is too often replaced by a straight argument for hyperpresence on both Jesus and the knowledge gained through the agency of the Holy Ghost—solid knowledge that replaces spectral memory."[24]

The missionary and the expert in Ghana try to have it both ways, to lay a claim to a larger realm outside of time and space, outside of scale, and then have it only accessible to their interpretation. Both Shirer and Abrams, the missionary and the expert, were able to appeal to ambiguity when needed and uphold precision when convenient, demand faith yet withhold interpretation, appear vulnerable yet turn that vulnerability into a new mode of claiming authority.

This economy of uncertainty and assertiveness is sustained, however, by displacing responsibility onto another register, one which is partially theological, partially worldly, a space and time in-between that, in the case of John's Gospel, was neither owned by God the father, nor Jesus the son, but by the Ghost which was neither and both. In the case of the expert, this Ghost is the system.

TIME OF INTENT

We can see this operation at work in a particular term in Abrams's discussion on generating savings: "induce." Lottery "induces," Abrams asserts, the participant to be thrifty. What kind of decision making-process is inducement, and many of its synonyms like encouragement and incentive? What is the nature of agency that needs inducement for action? It is in this regard that the particular footnote on Shirer in Abrams' book stands out. Abrams informs us that Shirer

> had come to the Northern Territories [the site of the Volta River Project] as a missionary and was later employed by the government. He was made a chief by one of the larger tribes for the valuable services he rendered, but later he left Ghana with his wife because, following independence, he was not *encouraged* to stay [emphasis added].[25]

Between Shirer encouraging natives to build with rammed earth, his appointment as a government officer, his consecration as an honorary chief, and the government's lack of "encouragement" that forced him to depart, lies a spectrum of ways in which intent is inscribed, imagined, and recognized, from the position that can induce to the position that requires inducement. It is this spectrum that we are delineating in the overlap between Shirer's and Abrams's claims.

Shirer lost favor from both the government and the Pentecostal Evangelical Church for actions that are described obliquely and only in passing by the Assembly of God minister, Rosemarie Daher Kowalski, as "moral failure."[26] Yet whatever the actions that result in that inscription, their association with morality (even if with only its "failure") ascribes them to a subject in possession of, with access to the play and privilege of, belief and vulnerability. Failure in this realm, like of Shirer's, is a validation, a consolidation, rather than a nullification, of an expansive subjecthood.

This fallibility is different from the one experienced encountering the ghost of history. This fallibility is a mark of infinite omni-comprehension, of access to not only particular subject positions but to the premise of all subject positions, to the realm of intra-subjectivity. This difference is evident in the asymmetry between who can and cannot have moral failures. The natives who were "taught to build with rammed-earth techniques" couldn't lay claim to such shortcomings. As the wards rather than guardians of development, they were "foreclosed" from such moral failures.[27] This foreclosure results not just from the opposition between Shirer, the teacher, and the natives, the taught, or Shirer the singular subject and the natives the plural group. The ascription of intent stems from the very manner in which intent is defined. Intent here is coupled not only with who can hold belief but who can also be vulnerable enough to falter from that belief. This is not a question of possessing a thought that is either true or false but a thought the veracity of which remains intact even when it contradicts itself.

THE BODY OF VULNERABILITY

God's voice can only be heard at the margin. The missionary and the expert can only establish direct communication with the Spirit, or the system, in a place seen to be marked by risk. The intersection between God and system occurs only in the context where the boundary between thought, body, and the world appears blurred. Only in the face of this uncertainty can the missionary suffer, and in that suffering read God's signs. Only in this context can the expert be uncertain and purpose uncertain plans. Risk, thus, is not external to godly systems but forms their very condition.

In this sense, architecture is not something added to the context. Rather, it is the context imagined as a forever-changing script in which bodies, landscape, and materials need to be continuously intermingled as one pursues reading God's, or system's, signs. Architecture as context turns suffering, failure, and risk into a form of production and expertise. As such, it is the mode and medium of both missionary salvation and development.

This contextualization becomes particularly evident in the journey of Margaret Shirer, Lloyd Shirer's wife and a Pentecostal minister herself, to the perceived margin. Margaret's first revelation came through her own mouth when she started speaking "in tongues," we are told, in a Pentecostal church in Philadelphia.[28] The occurrence was seen as sign, and she was immediately ordained as a faith missionary to be sent, not surprisingly, in search for an appropriate context in Africa. More signs followed. Margaret suffered fever, delusion, and delay traveling upriver on the Volta.[29] Reading these hardships as an invitation to blur the boundaries between body and the world, Margaret didn't hesitate to "tackle traditionally male work like construction, which would have been condemned as 'unfeminine' at home."[30] Her labors didn't go unnoticed. She was ordained a pastor on a furlough back to the United States. On her return she met Lloyd on a mission and developed an ever-expanding preaching routine. "Often Lloyd would drop her off on his motorcycle to preach in one village, drive on to speak in the next, and pick her up on the way home."[31]

A particular economy of distance and insight emerges in this account. God's voice becomes immediate at distance. God reveals himself in the hinterland to the missionary. His singular voice acquires meaning as the missionary becomes vulnerable to disease, loneliness, and personal safety. The two processes, traveling and clarity, enduring bodily hardships and reading God's signs, are coupled. Only the missionary in wilderness, the wild missionary, hears the voice of God. Wilderness becomes the analogue of a place before and between worlds.

There is also an economy of materiality, an architectural economy, imbedded in this account. Seeing the self and the world in architectural terms, as composed of movable, organizable parts, imbues them with an associative quality. It is not a coincident that on their daily escapades, the Shirers insisted on teaching the natives rammed-earth building techniques along with preaching. The act of building connected one form of embodiment with the next, one surface to the another, bringing one fluid, one solid, in continuity with the other, food with the mouth, sweat with air, skin with tools.

This architectural outlook makes the reading of God's script synonymous with writing one's own. It forms a miraculous, instantaneous, connection between otherwise irreducible mediums. The boat floating up the Volta, the motorcycle puttering through the jungle, the sweat emerging on the skin, the fever passing through the body, the exhaustion imbedding itself in the limbs, the calluses erupting on hands ramming earth into bricks, all yield themselves as parts of a divine script that is simultaneously reading and writing, a conjoining of God's will with self-realization. In building her hut, the preaching station, the rammed earth dwelling for the natives, the missionary not just builds a structure but structures her body, allowing it to be organized, inscribed into the world, according to the will of the Spirit. A body like the native's, already seen to be too stable, too inscribed into the world, and settled in its associations, cannot be readily reorganized. That body cannot be the slate on which the divine script makes its letters appear. It is the vulnerable body of the missionary, out in the perceived wilderness, that is open to this re-inscription, this malleability, this re-arrangement.

To be vulnerable, then, is to possess a body and a consciousness that can be rearranged according to a larger will and be able to discern the logic of that arrangement. This vulnerability allows one to occupy a unique position in a hierarchy of arrangements. To see one's self at the edge of the material world, immersed in it only as a test of one's resolve, to be part of it yet not be lost in it, is to possess the power both to claim access to this material world yet also be able to pass judgement on it. And with the ability to straddle the material and the conceptual worlds comes the privilege of occupying a time that is both of this world and without it, to be in history and outside it. With this closure, the fault line of history located in the wilderness is closed. The gate onto the past, rather than summoning ghosts that dance in this undetermined space and insist on new interpretations, as Rivera would hope, is closed shut.

To be sure, there are gradations of this authorship; some are nearer to the material world than others. Margaret could not claim the distance from this bodily and material economy at will, as Lloyd could. Margaret was able to parse the divine script through the fog of association not because she thought it through but because she felt it. This wasn't the work of mind and reason. It was her body that traversed established boundaries of skin and country and endured the continuity of associations across distance and disease. Lloyd too suffered through his body, but he was able to claim a distance from it as well. Tellingly, Lloyd's failure in the end was of "judgment." Margaret's steadfastness forever remained tied to the vulnerability of her body.

Yet the native women in our opening photograph do not even enter this duality. They can never read the script they are written into, whether through their body or mind. The same outlook that makes the colony appear as wilderness, the rural as hinterland, also makes the native appear too close to the wilderness to understand it. They never have access to the fiction of singular thought, of a singular word, of singular system. Their time is of the moment, while the missionary's time, after being of the moment, can fold back on itself, to validate intent with Intent. It is this folding that binds (Pentecostal) missionary with (UN) mission, the Shirers with Abrams, religion with development.

THE WEIGHT OF HISTORY

The hierarchical claims to hear God's voice, to see system's signs, in the hinterland is marked not just by gender but also by race. These distinctions become apparent by another character in this story. During their stay in Volta, the Shirers received a skeptical visitor, the African American writer Richard Wright, who had taken the trip to Ghana to test the calculus of distance and insight. Does traveling far bring closeness in time? For Wright this question was cast in racial terms. Did the color of his skin intimately tie him to another cultural milieu despite the gulf of space and history?

Hoping to find a sense of belonging, Wright, however, found himself alone in the crowd. Landing in Accra, Wright was hosted by none other than Prime Minister Kwame Nkrumah. Initially, Wright was exhilarated by how the crowd hailed the freedom leader at the height of his popularity with shouts of "Kwame! Free-dooom!"[32] As Lynn Weiss notes,

> He was "riveted by the exuberant dance of the women." But then suddenly he realized, "I'd seen the same snakelike, veering dances before. . . . Where? Oh, God, yes: in America, in store front churches, in Holy Roller Tabernacles . . . on the plantation of the Deep South."[33]

With that connection, jubilation gave way to doubt. Wright's sense of distance and separation was exaggerated. How could centuries of separation, of having traveled on different paths of history, be overcome by momentary realizations?

Troubled, Wright wanted to travel to the North, out of the clamor of the city, in search for a purer source. Nkrumah put him in touch with none other than Lloyd Shirer, who held an appointment at the Department of Welfare at the time and had made a name for himself building houses as a missionary that Nkrumah saw as an extension of this development programs. Traveling with his new host across the northern territories, Wright interviewed various native religious figures, asking them how they perceived his relationship with ancestral spirits after a gulf of centuries. The men couldn't give Wright a satisfactory answer. "It's hard to tell sar, [one of them declared,] . . . I'm afraid, sar, that your ancestors do not know you now."[34] Wright found it difficult to comprehend how the missionaries who hosted him found immediacy and clarity in this context, how they felt they belonged and he did not.

One day, Wright and Shirer wandered into a funeral of a chief. Initially, the two foreign set of eyes saw a very different scene. Where Shirer had found the voice of God, Wright only found the clamor of alterity. As Lynn Weiss recounts, "[t]he scene was organized chaos, replete with "half-nude women" in raffia skirts, whose faces were streaked with white paint. Men fired guns into the air and beat drums, as the coffin jerked erratically from one direction to another: "I had understood nothing, nothing [Wright thought,] . . . I looked closer and saw that the faces of the women and children were marked with a reddish paint on the left cheek. . . . My mind reeled at the newness and strangeness of it. Had my ancestors acted like that? and why?"[35]

This question, however, was finally settled by finding an uncanny affinity across space and time with gyrating hips. It is women's bodies once again that give meaning to Wright's dreamlike experience. While men fire weapons that shatter the present, it is women's "half-naked" bodies whose arrangement and rearrangement offered the opportunity for reclaiming another timeless time. In this regard, it does not matter if Wright didn't get an answer to his question. It was already moot. The concluding question above, "Had my ancestors acted like that? and why?" turns the present into a scene from the past, colored bodies and faces into ghosts.

It is important to note that these realizations congeal once Wright is out of the confines of the city. It is only in the presumed hinterland that the impossibility of aligning history and agency is turned into an opportunity of meaningful narratives. After the initial frustrations, for Wright, too, the out-of-joint present becomes the ever-present. On the one hand, for Wright, all marks, all writing, appeared historical and multiple. It yielded dual meaning. But on the other, women and environment, women as environment, allowed for a conflation of space and time that enabled Wright to dismiss the weight of that history.

This sublimation reached its apex when one evening Wright asked Lloyd Shirer how he understood this displacement himself. Shirer, to Wright's dismay, saw it only a problem for the natives. "[T]o leave a spot where [their] ancestors are buried creates terror in some African tribes. . . . They feel they are leaving their very souls behind them."[36] No stranger to the brunt of racism in the United States, Wright knew well that the question of belonging couldn't be sliced so neatly between American "us" and African "them." Unconvinced, Wright asked to talk to Shirer's African cook. We do not know what the cook said. He remains nameless in Wright's accounts of his visit. But his words, paraphrased into a series of questions by Wright, point to the economy of time and space that seem to be a privilege of men, regardless of race. African beliefs were, Wright concluded, "but dreams, dreams dreamed with eyes wide open! Was it the jungle, so rich, so fertile, was it that life, so warm, so filled with ready food, so effortless, [that] prompted *men* to dream dreams like this?"[37] Wright's conclusion is not far from Shirer's. Africa provides him insight into a universality of men, not the particularity of history. "It may be that such beliefs fit the soul of man better than railroads, mass production, wars. . . . And the African is not alone in holding that these dreams are true. All men, in some form or another, love dreams."[38]

In Wright's wondering, too, women seem to vanish, merge, and be replaced by the jungle and nature, by the availability of effortless food, that lead to men dreaming with men. Despite his dissatisfaction with Shirer's response, Wright follows Shirer on the path the latter charts a few steps ahead of him on account of his proclaimed racial superiority. The short-circuiting of women out of the economy of dreams revealed a three-tiered system. White men confronting God, white women confronting their bodies, black men attempting to confront white men by communing with black men. The black women only confront erasure.

SOLID NAMES, HOLLOW EFFECTS

Lynn Weiss has argued that for Wright and other American writers, such as Gertrude Stein, who tried to analyze the relationship between names and body, labels and identity, subject and origin, the bridge between these terms always seemed fractured, simultaneously connecting and distancing, making revolutionary slogans and racial insults out of the same names. "I dislike it," Stein asserted, "when instead of saying Jew they say Hebrew or Israelite or Semite, I do not like it and why should a Negro want to be called colored."[39] For Stein, a noun was indeed a "stupid thing," but those like "Negro," "Jew," were "nice strong solid names and so let us keep them."[40]

We have two different modes of naming: one, the inscription of God that reveals clarity, the other political strategies that are bound up with incoherency and multiplicity. One's strength comes from the lack of human agency in it, the other's precisely, as Weiss argued, because of the "offensive strategy that argues for a reappropriation of a name that in a hostile mouth is a curse."[41]

But in making this differentiation, we must take caution. The difference between the two forms of signs is not dependent on just the presence or absence of "agency." We must ask, what is agency, and how is it afforded? The equation of agency has two sides, both haunted by irreducible remainders, effects which are more than the sum of identifiable causes. These remainders always challenge the necessity of equating. The equals sign in this respect can be imagined as a hinge or a fold that must hide or suppress the surplus to facilitate comprehension of an event or action.

On one side of this equation is intention, what the subject desires. On the other side is perception, what is recognized or read as action. The subject can do whatever she wants, but those actions can produce very different results depending upon how they are perceived by other subjects in other social and cultural contexts, institutional and political settings. Agency then is the tangential effect, the torque, that is thrown off by the colliding vectors of intention and perception.

And it is indeed a collision, for it produces debris that muddles meaning. We are always seeing events with squinted eyes through dust clouds of non-sense that escape history. We must dust off the debris, cough away what we cannot breathe into sense. Understanding and event, intention and effect, are thus never equal. They are always separated, affected, contaminated by dust blowing from the conflict of other systems, other intentions and perceptions.

Yet this irreducibility, this excess, doesn't turn the world into senselessness. Sense is produced, actions are recognized, behavior is curbed, sources are allocated, substance is moved—all of which are dimensions of exercise of systemic power. A system is an arrangement of turning dust into writing. The irreducible remainder, the incalculable difference between intention and perception, desire and result, revolution and governance, protest and democracy, is a challenge that is managed through different kinds of systemic power. This remainder continuously makes any system unstable, displacing it toward new ends.

All this is important to keep in mind as we ourselves try to understand the different modes of agency being articulated by Shirer, Abrams, and Wright for themselves and for the natives. The missionary and the expert desire clear vision, eyes that can see through the dust of context. They want to clear the remainder of history, see intention equal perception, desire equal result. The missionary clears the dust by emphasizing the singularity of the word of God behind its worldly multiplicity. The expert does so by insisting on the systematic equivalence of disparate acts and materials. Their agency is claimed, sustained, by the ability to not recognize the possibility of other meanings in natives' actions.

It is not as if the natives do not have agency. From the chief to the cattle herder to the women tending the cocoa crops, hawking wares in the market, or carrying pans full of cement on their heads, they all have agency that produces effects in other equations of intentions and perceptions, in other systems of power. The agency of the missionary and the expert, however, has the power to subsume these agencies under its own system. It has the power to recognize them according to criteria that preserves its own role, manages its own exercise. All agency is not equal; neither are all possibilities of power. The missionary and expert's agency culls away the possibility of power from natives' agency. It is willing to evaluate natives' actions in terms that preserve only its own role. Since it is these roles that guard the path to governance, other agencies—collisions of other intentions and perceptions in whose dust lurk other possibilities of power—appear as corruption, backwardness, ignorance, tradition.

The expert-missionary agency depends upon securing continuity of singular meaning across material boundaries. And this systemic continuity, whether be it theological or developmental, can only be secured by suppressing the multiplicity of meaning from action. But how is this continuity preserved? How can a letter remain a sign to a singular concept? What allows one meaning to win over others? What allows the missionary to say this is the sign of God, and the expert to declare this method of housing will generate this much economic growth, generate this much savings?

This singularity is secured by summoning substance, materiality, as alibi. It is not the signified that asserts its power over the sign, nor just the symbolic dimension of the sign that claims a singular association with a signified. Rather it is the link between the two, the substantive dimension of the sign, the ink on the page, the rammed-earth block on the foundation, in whose material and mute depths the sign must disappear before it can claim an association with the signified that is mobilized to make the singular association.

While a host of phenomenological evaluations of vernacular as well as modern architecture would ascribe an inherent meaning to this material depth, we don't need to assume such a meaning to see the singular association of sign and signified in action.[42] It is the very muteness, distance, irreducibility of substance to concept that allows for an association to be made. This is the gap where the premise of an argument can be hidden. This gap makes the association vulnerable to challenge but also allows it to be established without being explained in the first place. How can a straight wall produce an economic value of 2 cents, or a fever of 102 the verification of God's will? It is precisely the ambiguous material gap, the weight of the wall, the heat of the body, that allows for a sign to take refuge in it and emerge as a referent of a particular concept.

Yet this gap, this material muteness is not neutral. It adds a texture to meaning that is beyond description, which is always in excess of description. An aluminum roof can claim impermanence, become a sign of continuous change, even though in reality it might never be taken off. It is precisely this specific yet irreducible dimension of materiality that is summoned to secure a connection to a signified. The texture it adds to meaning is held up as evidence of that singular relationship. That texture can be held up as evidence precisely because it cannot be explained, precisely because it is a support that is in excess of the explanation but can undergird that explanation.

This might appear contradictory, since projects such as core housing in New Ajena were based on providing choice to the inhabitants, to build their own house over time under the roof provided to them on loan. But that choice is based on a rigid matrix of singular associations not only across mediums—material and conceptual—but also across conceptual realms that are irreducible to each other but are made to appear so through the mute materiality of architecture. How much concrete, how much time, how thick the posts, how wide the sheet metal, not only map out a calculus of risk and capital flows but also how solid the resulting community would be, how stable the reputation of the lendee would be, how broad the social impact of a well-built house would be.

And as the web of these singular associations expand, we see the metalepsis of cause and effect in operation. The individual subject and the world of capitalist relations surrounding him (again, we must not forget the gender specificity of the desired effect) are presented as a source of developmental change. But as we have seen, the individual subject and his capitalist foundations are only an illusion, continuously produced by employing the very social structures of "tradition" and patriarchy it is meant to replace. Now, at the end of this essay, we see how this illusion is sustained on the women's bodies that remain invisible even when they are in the center of the frame. This illusion betrays how rationality is indeed a dream. Computers are idols to a singular God. For thought is never singular, nor is computation. The multiplicity of thought results in "moral failure" in the subject and "errors" in the computer. Not only does the software resist singular meanings, but the hardware also defies singular states of on and off, of 0s and 1s. Transistors heat up, linger in infinite states between their binary identities, crashing computers, bringing down systems that demand continuities based on singularities. Throughout the history of Western enlightenment, as George Canguilhem would remind us, we have only attempted to exorcise these delirious machines of these irreducible dimensions, to bring them into the fold of rational thought, so much so that our bodies too have long appeared as machines to us.[43] But there is always a ghost in the machine, in all machines, from systems to computers, to architecture, that forever murmurs the violence perpetuated through them.

NOTES

1 Abrams's caption to the photo calls the town Ajena, even though that was the name of the old town that was flooded by the waters of the Volta river reservoir. The settlement under construction shown in the photo was thus called New Ajena after its now submerged namesake. See Iain Jaackson, Ola Uduku, Irene Apeaning Addo, Rexford Assisie Opong, "The Volta River Project: Planning, Housing and Resettlement in Ghana, 1950–1965," *Journal of Architecture* 24, no. 4 (2019): 512–548.

2 Otto Koenigsberger and Beverly Bernstein, ed. *Infrastructure Problems of the Cities of Developing Countries: An International Urbanization Survey Report to the Ford Foundation* (New York: Ford Foundation, 1971), 265.

3 Abrams, *Struggle for Shelter, Man's Struggle for Shelter in an Urbanizing* World (Cambridge, MA: MIT Press, 1964), 187.

4 Norbert Weiner, *Cybernetics: Or Control and Communication in the Animal and the Machine* (Paris: Hermann & Cie, & Cambridge, MA: MIT Press, 1948). I borrow this interpretation of Weiner's idea of cybernetics as a closed system from Catherine Hayles as described in her *How We Became Posthuman: Virtual Bodies in Cybernetics, Literature, and Informatics* (Chicago: The University of Chicago Press, 1999), 9–14.

5 For a historical account of systems thinking in cybernetics, see Catherine Hayles, "Toward Embodied Virtuality," in *How We Became Posthuman: Virtual Bodies in Cybernetics, Literature, and Informatics* (Chicago: University of Chicago Press, 1999), chap. 1, 1–24.

6 Abrams, *Struggle for Shelter*, 156.

7 Ibid.

8 Escobar has shown how the definition of modernization as a dynamic process facing off with rigid traditional practices was prevalent in the founding documents of the UN. See Arturo Escobar, *Encountering Development: The Making and Unmaking of the Third Word* (Princeton, NJ: Princeton University Press, 1985), particularly chapter 1, "Introduction: Development and the Anthropology of Modernity," 3–20.
9 Walter Rostow, *The Stages of Economic Growth: A Non-Communist Manifesto* (Cambridge: Cambridge University Press, 1960).
10 Abrams, *Struggle for Shelter*, 156.
11 Ibid., 157.
12 That "savings" might be individually beneficial but collectively detrimental was a central argument of Keynes's *General Theory of Employment, Interest and Money* (London: Palgrave Macmillan, 1936). See Charles Abrams, Vladimir Bodiansky, and Otto Koenigsberger, *Report on Housing in the Gold Coast* (New York: United Nations Technical Assistance Administration, 1956).
13 See Weber, "Part 1: Science as a Vocation, and Politics as a Vocation," in *Max Weber: Essays in Sociology* (New York: Routledge, 1991, 1948), 77–148, 149–158.
14 Abrams, *Struggle for Shelter*, 157.
15 See, for instance, Terence E. Fretheim and Walter Brueggeman, *The Suffering of God: An Old Testament Perspective* (Philadelphia: Fortress Press, 1984); Johann Baptist Metz and J. Matthew Ashley, "Suffering Unto God," *Critical Inquiry* 20, no. 4, Symposium on "God" (Summer 1994): 611–622.
16 See Myra Rivera, "Ghostly Encounters: Spirit, Memory, and the Holy Ghost," in *Planetary Loves: Spivak, Postcoloniality, and Theology*, eds. Stephen D. Moore and Mayra Rivera (New York: Fordham University Press, 2010), 118–135.
17 Ibid., 129.
18 See Carolyn Bynum's description of the distinction between the God of the Old and the New Testaments and how this vulnerability in corporeality forms the site of female piety in her "The Body of Christ in the Later Middle Ages: A Reply to Leo Steinberg," in *Fragmentation and Redemption: Essays on Gender and the Human Body in Medieval Religion* (Cambridge, MA: MIT Press, 1990).
19 See Rivera, "Ghostly Encounters," 128.
20 Ibid.
21 Ibid., 129.
22 Ibid., 133–134.
23 Ibid., 134.
24 Ibid., 129.
25 See Abrams, *Struggle for Shelter*, 187.
26 See Rosemarie Daher Kowalski, "What Made Them Think They Could? Assemblies of God Female Missionaries," *Assemblies of God Heritage* 34 (2014): 45–78. For an account of the origins of Pentecostal Church in Missouri in 1920s, see Rosemarie Daher Kowalski, "The Missions Theology of Early Pentecost: Call, Challenge, and Opportunity," *Journal of Pentecostal Theology* 19, no. 2 (2010): 265–291.
27 While the term "foreclosure" was introduced into psychoanalysis by Jacque Lacan in the late 1930s, I am here employing it in the sense it in used by Gayatri Spivak to describe how Kant's entire edifice of moral philosophy and judgment is premised on conjuring a figure of the native informant, the New Hollander and the inhabitant of Tierra del Fuego, who stand before the tribulations of full subjecthood to establish the European as "the human norm." See Gayatri Chakravorty Spivak, "Philosophy," in *A Critique of Postcolonial Reason* (Cambridge, MA: Harvard University Press, 1999), vol. 6, 1–111.
28 Ibid., 57.
29 Rosemarie Daher Kowalski, "What Made Them Think They Could?" *op cit.*, 61.
30 Ibid., 68.
31 Ibid.
32 Richard Wright, *Black Power: A Record of Reactions in a Land of Pathos* (New York: Harpers, 1954), 56. Quote in Lynn Weiss, *Gertrude Stein and Richard Wright: The Poetics and Politics of Modernism* (Jackson: University Press of Mississippi, 1998), 68.
33 Wright, *Black Power*, 56.
34 Ibid., 195.
35 Lynn Weiss, *Gertrude Stein and Richard Wright*, 130. Wright quote from *Black Power*, 68.
36 Quoted in Yoshinobu Hakutani, *Cross-Cultural Visions in African American Literature: West Meets East* (New York: Palgrave Macmillan, 2011), 57.
37 Wright, *Black Power*, 217. Quoted in Hakutani, *Cross-Cultural Visions*, 58. Emphasis added.
38 Ibid., 217. Quoted in Hakutani, *Cross-Cultural Visions*, 58.
39 Gertrude Stein, *Everybody's Autobiography* (New York: Random House, 1937), 200. Quoted in Weiss, *Gertrude Stein and Richard Wright*, 66.
40 Ibid.

41 Weiss, *Gertrude Stein and Richard Wright*, 66.
42 Such phenomenological associations can be seen at work in Karsten Harries, *The Ethical Function of Architecture* (Cambridge, MA: The MIT Press, 1996), which, following Heidegger, locates in materiality the essence of being and a particular authentic way of relating to the environment. For a critique of such claims of authentic belonging and the racialized and anti-Semitic theories they supported, see Mark Jarzombek, "Husserl and the Problem of Worldliness," *Log* (Winter/Spring 2018): 67–79.
43 George Cangiulhem, "Machine and Organism," in *Incorporations*, eds. Jonathan Crary and Sanford Kwinter, trans. Mark Cohen and Randall Cherry (New York: Zone Books, 1992), 44–69.

Part II

Expertise

3

Planning for an uncertain present

Action planning in Singapore, India, Israel, and Sierra Leone

Ayala Levin

In 1963, a UN team comprising architect-planner Otto Koenigsberger, traffic economist Susumu Kobe, and Charles Abrams, a legal advisor on land issues, arrived in Singapore at the request of the country's government. Frustrated by the British colonial administration's lengthy planning procedures in the preceding decade, the Singaporean client wanted the team to provide a broad urban renewal plan quickly. To satisfy the government's desire for immediate results while also pursuing a more comprehensive vision for the island, Koenigsberger presented the idea of "action planning"—an open-ended process broken down into short-term action programs—which he devised as a planning method appropriate specifically for developing countries.[1]

In critical accounts of development, there is perhaps no easier target than planning. Whether economic, social, or physical, planning has been considered a top-down apparatus doomed to fail by critics such as James Scott and Arturo Escobar.[2] What these critics have not acknowledged, however, is how planners understood and responded to this predicament. Action planning departed from the long-range blueprint approach with its conception of a fixed future that constitutes the high modernist paradigm described by Scott (which could be said to have characterized planning up to the 1950s) to a more flexible, user-responsive approach in the 1960s (see also the chapters by Arindam Dutta, Petros Phokaides, and Martin Hershenzon in this volume).[3] The new action-oriented planning was the result of Koenigsberger's extensive experience working for the government of Mysore in British India in the 1940s and as a UN consultant for Nigeria and Singapore in the 1950s and 1960s. As this chapter shows, action planning was also informed by Albert Mayer's experiments in India and by Israeli practices that planner Aryeh Doudai translated to Sierra Leone before he also joined a UN Singapore mission in the late 1960s. These planning endeavors addressed the growing need for governments operating with a high deficit and expecting rapid modernization to rely less on prolonged, careful planning and more on shorter-term implementations or "action." Since meticulous plans based on extensive surveys were unable to respond to changing circumstances in real time, they quickly became outdated and were seen as a waste of resources. In other words, plans were increasingly considered failures not because they were unable to predict a distant future but because they could not respond to

DOI: 10.4324/9781003193654-6

processes taking place in the present. At stake in rebranding planning as "action planning" was nothing short of revising the concept of the master plan and redefining the role of planners, whose professional authority and legitimacy were undermined by the master plan's diminishing status.

Developing countries tested planning paradigms and forced planners to rethink their methods. In addition to high deficits, planners in developing countries faced challenges in gathering information and translating it into usable data and in identifying the local actors on whom governments depended to implement plans. Action planning addressed both problems: as attempts at implementation became part of the planning mechanism itself, this new method eliminated risk and the very possibility of failure. No longer aiming to produce a fixed blueprint for the future, planning became a machine for learning the present—a black-box for processing ever-accumulating data, heralding the incorporation of computer analysis. As such, action planning diverged completely from Scott's characterization of high modernist planning, with its emphasis on the future, its approach to territory as a clean slate, and its structure as a series of preconceived goals. While Scott's generalized formulation may not be historically accurate, as most development plans even in the 1950s did not consider territories a tabula rasa, I use it as a foil to highlight action planning's stark differences: it emphasized the present, understood countries or regions as constituted by social and economic interactions, and consisted of actions rather than set goals.

ACTION PLANNING: SINGAPORE

As early as 1950, following his experience of planning in India, Koenigsberger expressed misgivings about the applicability of the master plan in Third World countries. Master plans and reports are not enough, he argued. Echoing the decentralizing measures some developing countries undertook in order to foster participation, Koenigsberger suggested that it would be best "to create a live organisation preferably anchored in the structure of the local government . . . which constantly deals with planning problems and keeps the basic conceptions of the plan alive."[4] It was not, however, until 1963, when he, Charles Abrams, and Susumu Kobe were commissioned by the UN Center for Housing, Building and Planning to report on "Growth and Urban Renewal in Singapore," that Koenigsberger named this approach "action planning."[5]

The main objective of the Singapore commission was to propose an alternative to the 1955 master plan attributed to prominent British planner George Pepler, who acted as Town Planning Advisor to the Colony from 1950 to 1954. The piles of information Pepler's team produced at the time—which consisted of numerous reports and three sets of maps—had become obsolete in just a few years.[6] Initiated in 1951 under the British colonial administration, the plan delineated a medium-size town to be served by a system of radial and ring roads and surrounded by a green belt.[7] Koenigsberger's team defined their British predecessors' failure in terms of the rapid changes that Singapore had undergone since the inception of the plan, especially population growth and urban migration. According to the UN team's critique, it was

> a plan for a medium size town with rural hinterland, not a plan for a metropolis. Its road pattern is unsuited to the motor age. Above all, it is conceived more as an instrument of control for private investment than a programme of public action.[8]

It was that last point that Koenigsberger wished to overturn via his "action planning" proposal. As Koenigsberger emphasized, the 1955 plan was flawed not because of its level of execution—the planners had followed then-current planning techniques to the letter—but because the profession's underlying assumptions and methodologies regarding the regulation of real estate development were not conducive to planning in developing countries.[9] According to him, the key assumptions on which the master plan was based emerged from the European experience of the Great Depression and the world wars and were "fundamentally conservative in outlook and practically unanimous in considering the preservation of the achievements and institutions of the past as a main objective of all planning."[10] Though he put it only in terms of planning in Europe and the United Kingdom, his critique resonated with the professional hangover from colonial development, where planning was used as an instrument of control, especially in countering rapid urban migration during late colonial rule. This approach perdured in the ranks of UN planners, many of whom were former imperial officers who found an outlet for their colonial expertise in the United Nations.[11] Parallel to economists' turn from gradual growth to the "Big Push" theory, Koenigsberger called on planners to reconsider their procedures and devise models appropriate for the postcolonial era and for independent governments' desire to accelerate modernization.

At stake in planning for Singapore was more than its unpredictable population growth: the aim of accelerating housing and industry modernization was to serve the urgent political agenda of repressing the strong left wing that had given rise to the self-rule government in 1959. In February 1963, just a few months before the UN consultants arrived, the one-party government had repressed all communist organizations and arrested radical-left politicians. This political purge was the culmination of years of conflict between British-educated professionals and Chinese-educated left-wing unionists within the party's leadership—conflict that escalated over the terms of a merger with Malaya the same year.[12] This short-term merger further ignited already existing racial tensions, which reached their climax in the 1964 riots. The following year, Singapore's expulsion from the federation of Malaysia exacerbated unemployment. Singling out housing as both the problem and the solution to these social and economic tensions, the government sought to preempt and diffuse conflicts by constructing satellite towns and multiethnic public housing starting in 1960.[13] This emphasis on mass housing as a means of development would set the pattern for Singapore's growing economy in the coming decades—public housing programs were vehicles of political legitimacy and control, as the government would deny housing to those who objected to its rule. Furthermore, the Singaporean state took decisive steps to industrialize the country, finance a home-owning middle class, and transform the dense historical neighborhoods of Singapore's Central Area into a global hub.[14]

The Singaporean government's request for the UN consultants should be considered in light of its aims to repress the radical left, assuage racial conflicts, and undertake a determined program of rapid industrialization and public housing. According to the UN planners, their role was to address the unexpected rate of population growth, the rapid expansion of the built-up area, traffic congestion, and "Central Area decay."[15] While that last concern betrays the influence of US urban renewal discourse, the planners opposed its sweeping connotations. Warning about "bulldozer addicts," Koenigsberger, Kobe, and Abrams advised against wholesale demolition.[16] In fact, as H. Koon Wee has recently suggested, it was the Singaporean government that promoted the language of urban renewal, seeking UN expertise to legitimize its mass resettlement and clearing of the Central Area.[17] Perhaps the government did not realize that Abrams, the New York housing expert on the team, was a fierce critic of the rhetoric and reality of "slum clearance."[18]

The *Growth and Urban Renewal* report—published after Howe Yoon Chong, the permanent secretary of the Ministry of National Development, expressed his disappointment in the planners' reluctance to support his agenda—can be read as the planners' attempt to appease their unhappy clients around this very issue of renewal. Proposing a mode of action that would satisfy the government's expectation of fast results, they also did not cede their expert authority.[19] Urban renewal and its attendant "slum clearance" were not enough, they argued, as the city-state needed "more *new* housing than *re*-housing, more new development than redevelopment."[20] The right strategy would therefore undertake urban renewal as part of a comprehensive plan for the entire island.

Urban renewal programs not only rendered the built environment obsolete but also threatened the planning profession itself, reducing it to a servant of real estate development. This pressure was expressed in the Singaporean government's demand for "a more flexible plan" and "a more positive approach"—euphemistic language for encouraging capitalist development rather than impeding it by strictly regulating land use.[21] This clash of expectations continued well into the early 1970s, when another UN planning consultant complained that Singapore's government was "action- [i.e. profit-] oriented" and had no respect for planners.[22] Given the Singaporean government's overarching desire for rapid modernization, "action planning," among its other objectives, aimed to restore the status of planners and win back their hitherto unchallenged authority: at stake was reasserting the necessity of planners in the face of such pressures for actionable plans and immediate results.

As a response to the Singaporean government's pressure to hasten construction and increase real estate revenue, and perhaps in an attempt to link the plan with Singapore's ruling party, the People's Action Party, Koenigsberger rebranded planning as *action*. Distancing his method from the textbook approach of his British predecessors who authored the 1955 plan, Koenigsberger proposed a conceptual shift from the fixed master plan to planning as a process. Rather than serving as a tool for the control and regulation of private interests, as he perceived the planning profession in Europe to do, he argued that planning should be conceived as a tool for public action. In Singapore,

> practically all of the development of land, roads and utilities, four-fifths of all housing and more than half of the industrial development on Singapore Island is due to the initiative of public agencies. Singapore's first need is therefore for a *plan of action* to guide, accelerate and coordinate public development. The control of private investment is less important.[23]

Witnessing the germination of Singapore's unique model of highly incentivized ownership of government-provided mass housing, Koenigsberger considered public and private development mutually dependent in the process of modernization. In the context of Third World challenges in funding and implementing development projects, he further considered "public action" the shared domain of governmental initiatives and private entrepreneurship—a distinction that the government of Singapore has blurred considerably with its form of state capitalism. Proposing a series of "action programmes" instead of a master plan, Koenigsberger offered the government a flexible tool that, in the hands of both the planner and the policymaker, would encourage and coordinate private and public investments. Produced piecemeal in a mosaic pattern, this series of plans was to gradually supersede the 1955 master plan in various designated areas until it supplanted it altogether via the Dutch-inspired concept of the ring city (Figure 3.1).[24]

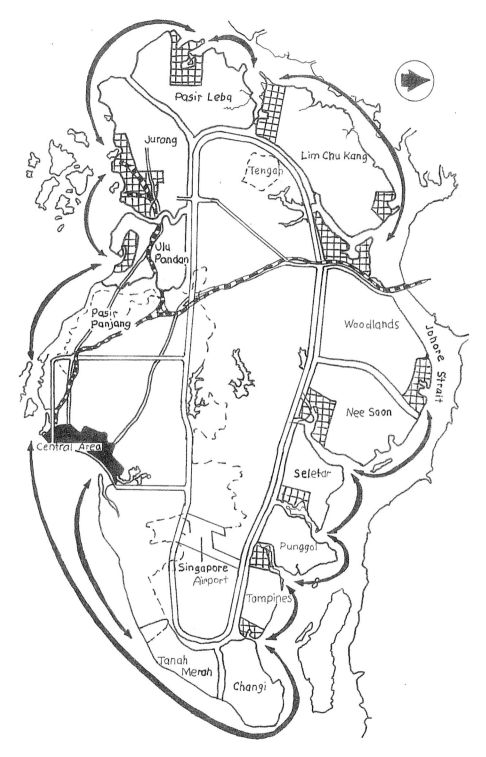

FIGURE 3.1 "Ring City" concept applied in Singapore.

Source: Redrawn from Charles Abrams, Susumu Kobe and Otto Koenigsberger, "Growth and Urban Renewal in Singapore," *Habitat INTL* 5, nos. 1/2 (1980): 105.

MANAGING PARTICIPATION: INDIA AND SINGAPORE

Koenigsberger strengthened broader claims for action planning by denying sole authorship of this new method and instead arguing that it was an emergent planning condition, writing that "this process of re-thinking has been in progress since about 1957," the year he took over the directorship of the Department of Tropical Studies at the Architectural Association (AA) in London. In addition to the AA and the UN, he mentioned MIT, Berkeley, Delhi, Vancouver, and the Institute of Social Studies in the Hague as some of the places and institutions where this rethinking was underway.[25] As Koenigsberger himself had applied some of his findings in Lagos a year earlier to Singapore, experts at the institutions he cited tended to gain their expertise by learning on the ground and transporting their knowledge from one country to another. Recent scholarship has shown how, in the case of colonial expertise, professional knowledge-production occurred via travel and translation *in* the colonies. Yet when it comes to the postcolonial era, there continues to be a perceived binary whereby theory is produced in the north and tested out in the south. While "action planning" could not have attained esteem as a theory without Koenigsberger's institutional ties to the authority of the AA and the UN, its conception also challenges this assumption by demonstrating that, much like colonial expertise, postcolonial knowledge was produced *in* the Global South by a network of itinerant characters, like Koenigsberger, who traversed both the developed and developing worlds. Postcolonial knowledge production differs sharply, however, from the colonial variety in that its centers of knowledge production also included locales *in* and experts *from* the Global South—a fact that is often neglected in the historiography of development. Attentive to the rise of this cadre of local experts, and most probably as a result of governmental stipulation, Koenigsberger and his team engaged Singaporean professionals and intellectuals who were better positioned to perform research for the plan.[26]

Koenigsberger's marriage of applied research with planning recalls American architect and planner Albert Mayer's experimentation in rural reconstruction in Uttar Pradesh, India. In fact, Koenigsberger may have discovered the language and methodology for action planning in Mayer's Research and Action Institute in Lucknow, the capital of Uttar Pradesh. Mayer established the institute in 1952, the year the Indian government launched its national "community development" program of nationwide rural reconstruction. Known for his involvement in New Deal planning, Mayer was invited by India's Prime Minister Pandit Jawaharlal Nehru to plan various cities, including Chandigarh, following his experience as an army engineer in India during World War II. Mayer set up the institute in Lucknow to coordinate his ambitious reorganization of one of India's most agriculturally productive states. While its focus on the rural sector cannot seem further removed from the planning of the island of Singapore as a global metropolis, Mayer's experimentation paved the way for Koenigsberger's transformation of the master plan from a fixed object to a tool of action and his attendant conversion of the planner from a detached technocrat to an involved participant and a mediator between the government and local stakeholders.

The idea for Mayer's Research and Action Institute germinated as early as 1946, the same year that social psychologist Kurt Lewin, known for developing the field of group dynamics, published his article "Action Research and Minority Problems" based on a study of interracial and interreligious relations in Connecticut.[27] Emphasizing applied research that was geared toward problem-solving and conflict resolution, action research postulated the guiding involvement of the researcher in the group's decision-making process. Developed in the Center for Group Dynamics at MIT, Lewin's group dynamics approach had broader implications for human relations, a subfield of scientific management. In addition to corporate management, action research's threefold feedback circle of "planning, action, and fact-finding about the result of the action" reached audiences in fields such as education, mental health, and anthropology, the last of which introduced Mayer to the concept, who implemented the method in his attempts at restructuring Indian rural life via the participatory structure of the village council.

One valid critique of Mayer's experiment with the reorganization and mobilization of rural labor is that it applied ideas of scientific management via "action research" to a romantic image of the village as a natural unit of communitarian life.[28] While Mayer failed to acknowledge the complex and rigidly hierarchical system of the panchayats (village councils), this romanticization should not be understood as simply naivete on the part of the foreign planner: misconstruing the effects of the caste system on peasants' lives was important to the very efficacy of the project. With its emphasis on identifying and cultivating "local leaders," action research reinforced rather than dismantled rural power structures, including a complex caste system, deep-seated patriarchy, and a landholding class that forced peasants to work as landless laborers or sharecroppers.[29] Despite its claims for democratization through participation, the Nehruvian panchayati raj system was unable to resolve these contradictions. Facing this irresolvable conflict, Mayer's preservation of the village as a traditional institution was meant to play a dual role in the process of rural modernization. First, common heritage would create an emotional basis for generating enthusiasm for new practices.[30] Second, the village played a political role, as it allowed modernization to bypass structural hindrances. By securing the cooperation of the rural elite, Mayer circumvented the entrenched land tenure system—a thorny issue for many postcolonial governments—and ensured the enlistment of "voluntary" workers in the cause.

Koenigsberger would have known about Mayer's experiment, if not through personal communication, then by reading about it in the Second Development Plan published by the Indian government in 1956, which recommended expanding the Uttar Pradesh model to other parts of the country.[31] Koenigsberger's action planning followed certain key principles in Mayer's action research approach. First, Koenigsberger paid attention to Mayer's emphasis on group psychology—the "human factor." Mayer relegated physical planning to a secondary place in the reorganization of villages and, for this reason, rejected the creation of a "model village" as a fixed visual and spatial entity to guide future planning.[32] Similarly, although Koenigsberger maintained a visual concept—"the ring plan"—that gave general guidelines for the planning process, his image was very flexible and mainly served a psychological function in communication between the planner and the public (which, in reality, consisted of select participants in the planning–implementation–planning process). The ring image, Koenigsberger surmised, was "more easily understandable than maps and density figures."[33] Second, in Mayer's action research approach, the planner's role was no longer that of producing blueprints for the future but of mediating between the government and local stakeholders. Likewise Koenigsberger, as a planner in the Global South, saw his main function as collaborating with local developers and expanding their field of operation. This strategy was an attempt to win over key members of the public and ensure their participation in the implementation of the plans. When the word "development" exerts "a certain mystique, and is rarely used without strong emotional overtones," Koenigsberger complained, the private developer acquires symbolic capital, "thinking of himself not as a speculator but rather as a national hero." Together with landowners, private developers formed "the most vocal part of the community" and constituted the greatest hindrance to the planner.[34] In both Mayer's and Koenigsberger's projects, it was not a matter of engaging people whose voices were usually unheard—as "participation" is typically heroicized in planning discourse—but rather of ensuring the collaboration of those who had the power to thwart the plan.

While this redefinition of the planners' role presumably enhanced their ability to implement plans, it also diminished their authority as experts, as the hierarchy dividing expert from layman dissolved. Ironically then, to make themselves more relevant, planners had to play down their expertise—only to reassert it again in another guise. For Koenigsberger, the planner needed to become adept at "corporate thinking" and be capable of inducing "public authorities to plan their operations similar to those of large financial and commercial undertakings."[35] The planner was to act like a savvy entrepreneur, setting in motion a sequence of carefully timed procedures:

> Timing was to be such that the planner would always be one jump ahead of the official dealing with land acquisition, who in turn would be expected to be always one jump ahead of those who were to plan and build roads and public utilities. These, in their turn, would always have to be one jump ahead of the public and private investors.[36]

Since it cannot be planned in advance or fully orchestrated by the planner, the planning-implementation sequence is imagined as a series of responses that occur concurrently, with each feeding back into the others, so that the temporal gaps between them are eliminated. With quick responses as the key to this "four dimensional plan," the time lag between planning and implementation was reduced to an almost complete overlap. If, in Uttar Pradesh, the physical plan was sidestepped in favor of social organization at the scale of the village, then in the Singapore action plan, the physical plan was, by design, perpetually postponed, as it comprised multiple moving pieces.

THE PLAN AS BLACK-BOX: ISRAEL, INDIA, AND SINGAPORE

The elimination of the temporal gap between planning and implementation was meant to relieve one of the most pressing concerns planners faced in developing countries, namely the rapid changes that rendered protracted planning attempts futile. Preparation of the survey and master plan for Singapore's 1955 plan took four years, from January 1952 to the end of December 1955. By the time Singapore achieved self-rule in 1959, the data on which the plan had been based was no longer valid. This was not an isolated event: Michel Ecochard's plan for Dakar, commissioned in 1963, was outdated by the time of its completion.[37] Other examples include the plan for Abidjan, produced in 1961 by the French engineering office SETAP under the authority of the French cooperation program Fonds d'Aide et de Coopération, and the plan for Kinshasa that became obsolete the moment the Mission Française d'Urbanisme published it in 1967.[38] For this reason, in 1972 Plan Organization, the planning authority of Tehran—like the government of Singapore a decade earlier—commissioned Constantinos Doxiadis to produce an action plan in just three months. The urgency forced Doxiadis to abandon the elaborate analytical procedures of the ekistics approach in which he took pride.[39]

As these examples demonstrate, it was not only the institutional disconnect between planning and execution that hampered the successful implementation of plans. The root of the problem was located a step earlier, in the temporal gap between the survey and the conceptualization of the plan. The survey was the information bank on which planning was based, but it was inevitably outdated by the time the plan was conceived. Reacting to this structural deficiency, action planning not only rendered the masterplan obsolete but more importantly eradicated the survey as a stand-alone entity that had served as the plan's epistemological basis.

A case in point is the planning of the Lakhish region in Israel in the mid-1950s as a rural experiment in settling North African Jews in cooperative villages. Due to the arrival of masses of immigrants before the plans were even halfway complete, people were housed in the new villages while planning and construction took place and while basic infrastructure was lacking.[40] According to the agricultural economist Ra'anan Weitz, one of the key authors of the project, their phased approach, which combined implementation with planning so that they at times overlapped, was not a by-product of external conditions but essential to the project's modus operandi. When he told his team to enlarge "a basic map which the British had done" and use it, they objected:

> The team said that in order to plan houses, roads, and villages, you need to do topography. I said, "Yes, you do need to do topography. If we mobilize all the certified surveyors in Israel, how many topographies could we produce in a year? The one we need is with levels of ½ meter, 10 centimeters, with details 1 to 1,000."
>
> They said, "Well, maybe between 10 and 15."
>
> I said, "Since this year we are establishing 120 villages, we would have to wait for the topographies. Some of us would have to wait ten years. In the meantime, what will people do? Who will build their houses?"
>
> So, I said, "the mistakes you'll make by waiting to do it without mistakes will be a hundred times bigger than the mistakes you will make by using the maps we have."[41]

Here, full data is represented as not just an impossibility but also unnecessary or even undesirable.[42] Writing in 1986, Weitz retroactively used Koenigsberger's logic of action planning to rationalize his contingent planning as a methodology.[43] Yet the influence might actually have been mutual. By 1962, Lakhish had become a site of pilgrimage for development experts and Israel's flagship project for export to other developing countries. Koenigsberger had visited the site in the spring of 1962 and reported on "the value of Israeli experiences for other countries," recommending that his report should be distributed not only to academic and UN readership but also to administrators and politicians.[44] We can speculate that contingent planning in Lakhish inspired Koenigsberger's "action-planning" approach in Singapore the following year.

Another prominent UN consultant, American anthropologist Margaret Mead, visited the Lakhish region in the summer of 1956. Confronted with such a project, another country, she noted with a hint of irony, would have approached the UN, which would have appointed sociologists, anthropologists, historians, and other experts to study the subject. These experts would then have formed committees that, in turn, would have sat for three years and issued a detailed report in the fourth, explaining ultimately why it would be impossible to build settlements in the area. Amused, she said, "you skipped all these phases and just went on to build the settlements."[45]

The process of extensive research and deliberation that Mead described is reminiscent of the "root approach" that American economist Charles E. Lindblom criticized in his influential 1959 article, "The Science of 'Muddling Through.'" Driven by the same objective as action research—to remedy the divorce between academic knowledge and real-life decision making—Lindblom argued that policymaking should do away with the "comprehensive rational approach" of academic experts. The "branch approach" he proposed instead, akin to the "decision tree" that proliferated in systems theory, precluded the use of blueprints or models, since policymakers could no longer assume the fixed trajectory these entailed. For Lindblom, the problem lay in the fact that the "root approach" was "greedy for facts." In the context of limited time and resources—as he argued was the case in developing countries—it was "even more absurd as an approach to policy."[46]

Alongside the difficulty of accumulating and processing information, developing countries presented the added challenge of identifying new information and converting it into usable data. In the early 1950s, the UN had singled out information gathering as an urgent problem that led to "defective knowledge and [the] consequent inability to make rational plans was a major constraint."[47] The aim was not just to make accurate future predictions but to comprehend present conditions—especially the societal patterns of countries in transition—and effectively render them into analyzable data. Given these epistemological stakes, the task of the planner changed dramatically from accumulating and processing readily available data to identifying relevant new information from the field, including localized forms of knowledge, that could be converted into familiar forms of analysis in northern institutions.

Again, action planning, linked to action research, was just what the doctor ordered. In action research, as anthropologist Laura Thompson, whom Mayer consulted in Uttar Pradesh, put it, "*The event precedes the understanding of it.* Activity leads to discovery and not vice versa."[48] According to Mayer, his experiment assumed that "the ideas thus discovered will be constantly filtered into the system," turning the project itself into a mechanism for processing information.[49] By folding information gathering into a continuous planning–implementation–planning process, Mayer laid the foundations for incorporating feedback into the physical planning process, which effectively turned the process into a black-box mechanism that prefigured the incorporation of computers into planning. The grassroots democratic process to which Mayer aspired had the potential to become an all-encompassing machine for gathering and processing data. Similarly, as Koenigsberger suggested, action programs in Singapore were to "be combined with market research, annual reviews of population forecasts and housing targets with annual surveys of social and economic changes and the *feed back* of survey results into new programmes"—a vision that anticipated the introduction of computers into Singapore's planning in the late 1960s.[50]

In effect, the plan was no longer a final product built on data that had been gathered and processed but rather a means for generating data. Paradoxically, despite the waning authority of the plan as prescription and planners as experts, their rhetorical, if not operative, power *increased*. Although fragmented into "a series of *action programmes*," wrote Koenigsberger, plans would not lose their comprehensive scope "as they should deal with all aspects of urban life." These aspects included employment, shelter, communications, traffic, education, welfare, capital formation, stimulation of savings, community development, and public relations.[51] For Koenigsberger, action planning's pragmatic methodology did not come at the expense of the masterplan's comprehensive scope—indeed, it only multiplied planning's reach exponentially, as more and more information was fed into the plan's moving parts. Action planning actually concentrated even more power in planners' hands.

IMAGING CHANGE: SIERRA LEONE

If underestimating how much Singapore's population would increase was the 1955 masterplan's fundamental failure, another, according to Koenigsberger, was its very stipulation that city and country constituted two separate entities.[52] Conceiving the plan in terms of a town–country binary, Pepler transported the precepts he had advocated as a member of the council for the preservation of the English countryside to the island of Singapore. Yet the rural and the urban were inherently linked in the developing world—where typically 90 percent of the population was agrarian—a fact that refuted the planning profession's traditional presumptions. Rural migration to urban centers presented a data challenge, for example, not just because mechanisms of counting and surveying were insufficient but also because it disrupted any assumptions about the rural and urban as fixed and distinct categories. In Africa in particular, urban–rural migrations were not unidirectional processes, and urban residents had continuing ties with rural communities. These urban–rural linkages—a subject of copious analysis in development literature at the time—not only pertained to technocratic issues of resource management but also entailed the problems of governance, as support for governmental action was mediated by rural leadership.

In a 1965 attempt to remedy this professional predicament, Israeli planner Aryeh Doudai redirected urbanization in Sierra Leone from the coastal capital, Freetown, to its hinterland and turned the problem of rural migration data into the driving mechanism of his Sierra Leone national urbanization plan. Then head of the Institute for Planning and Development (IPD), which was established in 1962 by the Israeli Ministry of Foreign Affairs' Division for International Cooperation (Mashav), Doudai consulted the Sierra Leone government as part of Israel's attempt to foster diplomatic relations with decolonizing African countries in order to win their support at the UN.[53] Doudai convinced the government to invest in the production of a survey, on the assumption that this investment would yield a UN Special Fund grant to support further planning.[54] For Sierra Leone's government, the timing was especially ripe: in 1965, it was about to draft a Five Year Plan of Economic and Social Development to elaborate on the Ten Year Plan published in 1962, a year after Sierra Leone gained independence.[55]

In Doudai's hands, the survey, aimed at soliciting UN funds quickly, turned into a "broad-sketch plan" of an urban network for the entire country. Due to the rapidly changing conditions of Third World urbanization, Doudai maintained, there was no point in conducting elaborate surveys, as these would become outdated by the time the planning process was completed. For this reason,

> The planning process should be multi-dimensional. . . . In terms of time it should be designed not for a predetermined sequence of activities, but on the basis of an ever-deepening process in which the first broad intuitive decisions feed back as information and experience on which to set off another series of processes, in a continuous, on-going, succession. . . . To some degree survey, research, planning, programming, decision making and implementation overlap in all situations, and in Africa one single and continuous process is particularly suitable.[56]

Doudai's emphasis on feedback as a core principle in planning is indicative of how systems theory was broadly employed as a way out of the relatively narrow definitions of planners' expertise, and planning's dependence on particular operations and sets of data. Since Doudai did not use the term "action-planning," he may have conceptualized this planning methodology independently of Koenigsberger based on lessons in Israel, specifically the aforementioned Lakhish region. The pragmatic approach taken in Lakhish informed Doudai's consultancy projects in other developing countries where the challenge, as he explained in 1963, was to draft a comprehensive national plan despite a lack of data.[57]

Doudai turned the absence of exact and up-to-date data into the driving force of Sierra Leone's urbanization plan. The survey-cum-plan was presented in the form of a large booklet containing a series of unified templates of the country's scaled-down territory, each isolating variables such as soil, agriculture, population movement, and services, based mostly on information obtained by the former British colonial administration. This simplified visualization of data was consistent throughout the book, even as the narrative turned from accumulating data to processing it by using tracing paper to juxtapose and superimpose information. The visual analysis concluded with a series of flow maps that shift from depicting existing conditions to representing a desired outcome that can ostensibly be deduced from the preceding maps (see Figures 3.2–3.5). In this conflation of map and diagram, the arrows

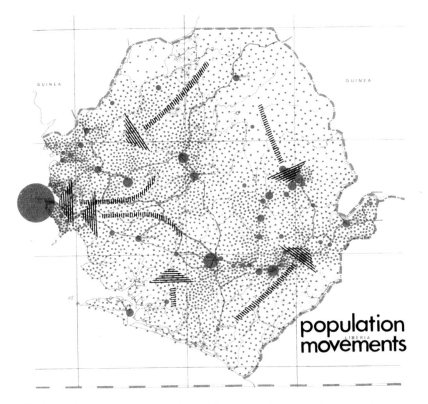

FIGURES 3.2–3.5. Sierra Leone Population Movements; Regional Patterns; Emerging Regions; and Urban Frameworks.

Source: Aryeh Doudai and Ursula Oelsner, *Sierra Leone National Urbanisation Plan* (Tel Aviv: Institute for Planning and Development, 1965).

PLANNING FOR AN UNCERTAIN PRESENT

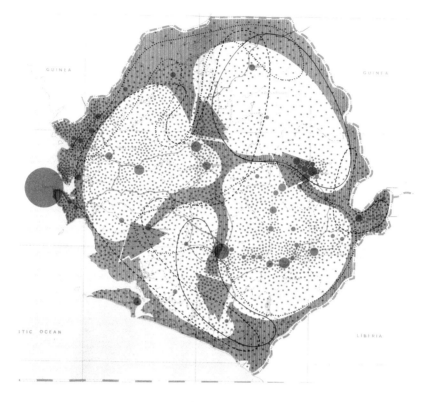

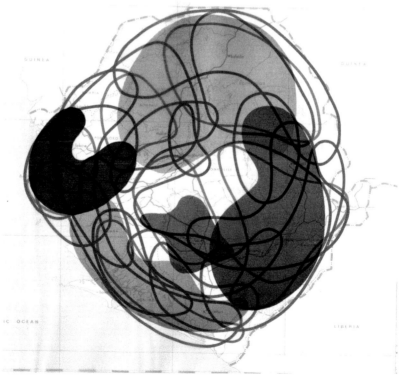

FIGURES 3.3–3.4. (CONTINUED)

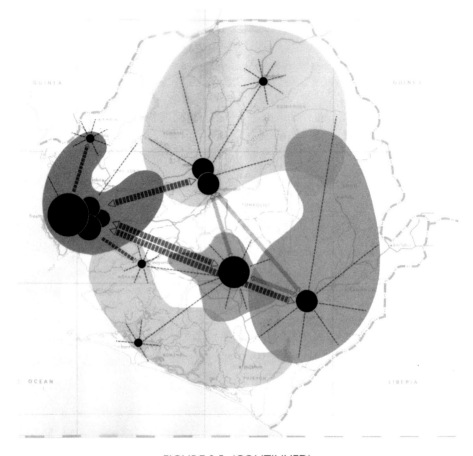

FIGURE 3.5 (CONTINUED)

represent not only the movement of population and resources but also their future consolidation into regions of economic differentiation.

Such maps heralded the burgeoning use of computer graphics as instruments for information processing and corresponded with what semiotician Jacques Bertin defined in 1967 as graphic representation's two basic functions: storage and research. Bertin argued that juxtaposition and permutation could change "dead images" into "living" ones, transforming them from representation to a "point of departure" for the processing of information.[58] Advocating "put(ting) cartography back into action," Bertin proposed that "(t)he best graphic operations are those carried out by the decision-maker himself."[59] And indeed, with its schematic diagram maps, the Sierra Leone national urbanization plan offered a useful and flexible tool for the layman policymaker in his dealings with the country's various stakeholders. Reminiscent of what Koenigsberger termed a "concept plan," with its advantages of flexibility and communicability, Doudai conceived his "broad-sketch plan" as an open-ended tool for policymaking and negotiation, whose inconclusiveness was fundamental to its very functioning.[60] As a flexible template for the policymaker, the more schematic and general the plan was, the more effective it would be.

In Sierra Leone's hinterland, the unequivocal stakeholders were the country's chiefs—they had inherited their role as the dominant power-brokers from the British colonial system of indirect rule. In 1946, as part of the Colonial Welfare and Development Act, twelve Paramount Chiefs were installed to administer funds and carry out public works. In addition to these twelve—who, with self-rule and independence, came to hold seats in parliament alongside elected members—the government depended on local chiefs for both electoral support and implementation of its plans, for which they provided unpaid labor and access to land.

To secure the chiefs' support, one of the urbanization plan's objectives was, ironically, "to encourage the population to remain in rural villages."[61] By including this objective, the planner appealed to a major concern of the chiefs, who were losing their youth, an important source of rural labor, to the lures and paying jobs of the city. It can also be assumed that this objective of keeping people in villages meant directing more funds to chiefs to carry out the plan, in continuity with the public works role they had assumed under British rule. To curtail rural migration to Freetown, Doudai identified existing urban nuclei that could become regional centers for agricultural processing and distribution, following the model of the Lakhish region. Unlike the distant coastal capital, Freetown, these medium-sized towns would ostensibly satisfy the urban ambitions of young men while still binding them to the chiefdoms' farms, to which they could migrate seasonally.[62] Located in feasible proximity to the villages, these urban centers would strengthen village agricultural production by providing the facilities necessary for survival in a modernizing economy, albeit without introducing radical changes to social or economic structures. In this process, Doudai promised, "chiefdom units"—and, by implication, the authority of the chiefs—will "be disturbed as little as possible."[63]

In its conclusion, four bean-shaped figures emerge in a seemingly organic fashion out of the booklet's visual analysis. Standing for unnamed regions that were to supplant and override colonial administrative boundaries, they were the ultimate development objects of the plan. Presented as abstract organic shapes superimposed over the country's territory, their forms had neither clear territorial boundaries nor any indication of how such regions would correspond to physical or social divisions. The emphasis on flows and connections over composition and the blurring of scalar distinctions served to turn the region into a concept rather than a definite territorial unit (reminiscent of the organicist aesthetic analyzed in Chapter 1). Presented as the result of both physical variables and cultural data, such as ethnicity and language, the plan constructed Sierra Leone's regions as economic units of specialized activities yet to come. Apparently guided by the invisible hand of liberal economy rather than the state, the regions were expected to transform over time by increasing their economic differentiation.[64] In this "broad-sketch plan," inconclusive data and contingent future projections translated visually into intentional "fuzziness."[65] This visual ambiguity allowed room for ongoing negotiation between the policymaker and the chiefs—and among the chiefs themselves, who represented ethnically and socially differentiated communities with often-conflicting interests that would be harnessed for economic competition and thus would harmonize with the state's goals.

Conceived as a tool of policymaking and negotiation, the plan was more significant at the rhetorical level than as a binding document. It was flexible enough to address and include the input of customary leaders across the country as well as other "populations of interest" in international and national institutions, such as the UN and Sierra Leone's government.[66] Its inherent open-endedness not only allowed policymakers to change its objectives over time, as Lindblom suggested, but also absolved them of responsibility for its full and complete implementation.[67] As Weitz explained in relation to Lakhish: "if you expect that after 25 years Lachish [sic] will look exactly as we described it in the beginning, then we failed."[68] This flexibility was especially useful in the hands of so-called weak governments in Africa, whose lack of administrative infrastructure far from capital cities presented a challenge for governance and that therefore depended mainly on the cooperation of chiefs.

This intentional "fuzziness" radically contradicts the aesthetics of legibility James Scott attributed to high modernist planning. Furthermore, this planning approach also conflicts with Scott's argument that high modernist planners resorted to miniaturizing their schemes into contained model units after failing to implement them in large-scale territories.[69] Understanding the creation of a model unit as limiting, the territorial impulse exemplified in the Sierra Leone national urbanization plan—where the dynamic temporal-spatial figure of the region supplanted hard administrative boundaries—also runs through the work of Mayer, who conceived of his village experiment as part of a regional network, and in the work of Koenigsberger, who saw no purpose in planning the city of Singapore without considering the entire island.[70]

The territorial impulse, encapsulated in the figure of the region, considers political and administrative divisions as inhibiting factors. As exemplified in the cases of Lakhish in Israel, Ciudad Guayana in Venezuela, the Tennessee Valley Authority in the United States, the Jordan Valley project in the Middle East, and the Mekong River Delta project in Asia, the flexible figure of the region allowed planning to cut across governmental and ministerial jurisdictions and even traverse national boundaries.[71] For this reason, regional development projects often entailed the establishment of new administrative apparatuses that bypassed existing structures and their attendant obstacles, and as such, they presented opportunities for radical social and economic transformation.

POSTSCRIPT: SINGAPORE

Ironically, it was at the pleading of Singapore's notoriously centralized government that planning's open-endedness and responsiveness to a variety of users was formalized. Ironic, but not entirely contradictory: as demonstrated earlier, this open-ended approach did, in the end, concentrate ever more power in the hands of planners and policymakers.

Open-ended planning's source of power, however, is very different from that of the authoritarian, top-down approach that Scott described, whether or not that conception actually existed in practice. Moreover, the new planning model was not grounded in statutory power—in fact, the Singapore planners resisted legal formalization.[72] Rather, the plan's power lay in its indeterminacy and its ability to move among different actors, whether rural elites or middle-class entrepreneurs. As a non-binding document, it opened up space for negotiation, which at its best fed back into the plan. From the centralized government of Singapore to the weak government of Sierra Leone, action planning served as a machine capable of constantly updating. As such, the plan was not an end in itself; instead, it was a proto-computer black-box for the production and processing of data. Paradoxically then, the survey, now eliminated as a precondition for planning, became the plan's very raison d'être. As planner E.E. Peacock—of an Australian firm involved in the UN project in Singapore—put it, the plan "isn't perfect . . . it will always need careful updating, refining and management in order to keep it alive."[73] In need of constant nurturing, the plan was an insatiable beast, always hungry for more data, or at least the appearance thereof, to justify its own existence and that of the planners.

The mechanisms put in place by Koenigsberger's team laid the groundwork for feeding the beast. In 1967, a Plan of Operation was signed to implement the Urban Renewal and Development Project, which was to be carried out by the State and City Planning organization set up specifically for the project in Singapore's Ministry of National Development. By mid-1968, it had completed a land use survey, an accommodation survey, a series of transport surveys, and a home interview survey covering 5 percent of all households in the urban portion of the island. Two hundred and sixty temporary workers were trained from scratch to conduct these surveys, and another team of eleven punch operators had to be recruited to handle the resulting 750,000 punched cards. This team of "girls" labored in evening shifts in a punching room especially leased from the Port of Singapore Authority.[74] By 1970, confronting an ever-growing volume of data, the planning coordinator insisted on setting up efficient mechanisms for storage, retrieval, and regular updating. To this end, he recommended that the Project's Survey Research Unit serve as the nucleus for a Statistical Unit linked to all the departments in the ministry, thus laying the foundation for Singapore's Smart Nation initiative, which was established in 2014.[75]

The manager of the UN Singapore Project was none other than Doudai, who took up this position in 1968.[76] If, in Sierra Leone, Doudai rushed to sidestep the survey in favor of planning, in Singapore he foregrounded the collection of data as the planning objective. Like Koenigsberger, he understood planning as a process: "its completion is only a first step, the beginning, the laying of foundations for the long, continuous planning process that lies ahead."[77] Departing from the proposal of Koenigsberger's team, however, Doudai insisted on the need for a long-term plan. Adding an intermediary category of "ideas"—plans that served as a testing ground before concept plans could be formalized—he further deferred the plan as a moving target.[78] In 1971, he boasted that "an enormous amount of data and information was accumulated, analysed, and evaluated by the Project. A data bank and an adequate survey and research machinery [for updating the data bank regularly] were established."[79]

If, for Koenigsberger, even consumer surveys could feed into the plan, then data produced for the plan could in turn be used for other purposes, such as monitoring public opinion and political dissent.[80] Thus, the UN planning project for Singapore's urban growth has helped the Singaporean government use democratic practices of "political participation and public policy feedback" to reverse conflict and "absorb and contain" dissent.[81] This seeming contradiction is explained by the People's Action Party's social democratic origins and its disavowal of liberalism.[82] More broadly, however, and in line with Singapore's contemporary "smart" status, by heralding the conversion of population and territory into quantifiable data, the UN plan anticipated smart cities, whose fantasy of self-governing urban machinery necessarily overrides the liberal underpinnings of human action and decision making. As action planning's unplanned progeny, smart cities mark both its logical conclusion and its limits.[83]

NOTES

1 Otto Koenigsberger, "Action Planning," *Architectural Association Journal* 882 (May 1964), 306–312. An early version of this paper was presented at the European Association for Urban History Biannual Conference in Rome in 2018, in a panel convened by Susanne Schindler and Gaia Caramellino.

2 James C. Scott, *Seeing Like a State: How Certain Schemes to Improve the Human Conditions Have Failed* (New Haven, CT: Yale University Press, 1998); Arturo Escobar, "Planning," in *The Development Dictionary: A Guide to Knowledge as Power*, ed. Wolfgang Sachs (London: Zed Books, 2010), 145–160.

3 Chapters 1, 14, and 16. This shift is documented in Eric Mumford, "From Master-Planning to Self-Build: The MIT-Harvard Joint Center for Urban Studies" and M. Ijlal Muzaffar, "Fuzzy Images: The Problem of Third World Development and the New Ethics of Open-Ended Planning at the MIT-Harvard Joint Center for Urban Studies," in *A Second Modernism: MIT, Architecture, and the 'Techno-Social' Moment*, ed. Arindam Dutta (Cambridge, MA: SA+P Press, MIT Press, 2013), 288–309, 310–341.
4 Rachel Lee, "Self-Help-City," in *Otto Koenigsberger: Architecture and Urban Visions in India*, eds. Tile von Damm, Ann-Katrin Fenk, and Rachel Lee (Liverpool: TAG Press, 2015), 81.
5 Charles Abrams, Susumu Kobe, and Otto Koenigsberger, *Growth and Urban Renewal in Singapore: Report Prepared for the Government of Singapore*, UN Department of Economic and Social Affairs (under the UN Technical Assistance Programme), November 1963, Otto Koenigsberger's Papers. I am grateful to Jiat-Hwee Chang for sharing documents from Renata Koenigsberger's estate with me, as well as for his assistance in navigating Singapore's planning history.
6 Teo Siew Eng, "Planning Principles in Pre- and Post-Independence Singapore," *TPR* 63, no. 2 (1992): 168.
7 Beng-Huat Chua, *Political Legitimacy and Housing: Stake Holding in Singapore* (London: Routledge, 1997), 32.
8 Charles Abrams, Susumu Kobe, and Otto Koenigsberger, "Growth and Urban Renewal in Singapore," *Habitat INTL* 5, nos. 1/2 (1980): 89.
9 Ibid.
10 Ibid., 98.
11 Richard Harris and Susan Parnell, "The Turning Point in Urban Policy for British Colonial Africa, 1939–1945," in *Colonial Architecture and Urbanism in Africa*, ed. Fassil Demissie (Burlington, VT: Ashgate, 2012), 127–151.
12 The disagreement over the merger with Malaya reflected a broader disagreement over the terms of independence, including demands to abolish the Internal Security Council, dismantle British military bases, grant citizenship to those who helped fight colonialism, and allow freedom of the press and of speech. See Cheng Lian Pang, "The People's Action Party, 1954–1963," *Journal of Southeast Asian History* 10, no. 1 (March 1969): 150.
13 Michael Hill and Loan Kwen Fee, *The Politics of Nation Building and Citizenship in Singapore* (London: Routledge, 1995), 113–120.
14 H. Koon Wee, "The Emergence of the Global and Social City: Golden Mile and the Politics of Urban Renewal," *Planning Perspectives* 35, no. 4 (2020): 689–718.
15 Abrams, Kobe, and Koenigsberger, "Growth and Urban Renewal in Singapore," 87.
16 Ibid., 104.
17 Wee, "The Emergence of the Global and Social City," 695. American urban renewal was not adopted wholesale in Singapore but was subject to criticism and adaptation. Nancy H. Kwak, *A World of Homeowners* (Chicago: University of Chicago Press, 2015), 123.
18 Paul Walker, "Charles Abrams vs. Robert Moses: Contested Rhetoric of Urban Housing," *Rhetoric Review* 31, no. 3 (July 2012): 289–308.
19 Wee, "The Emergence of the Global and Social City," 695.
20 Abrams, Kobe, and Koenigsberger, *Growth and Urban Renewal in Singapore: Report Prepared for the Government of Singapore*, 9–10.
21 Abrams, Kobe, and Koenigsberger, "Growth and Urban Renewal in Singapore," 94.
22 Agency for International Development, *Bureau for Technical Assistance Urban Development Staff*, Report on a Visit to Singapore, January 1972, 8.
23 Abrams, Kobe, and Koenigsberger, *Growth and Urban Renewal in Singapore: Report Prepared for the Government of Singapore*, 11.
24 Abrams, Kobe, and Koenigsberger, "Growth and Urban Renewal in Singapore," 90, 104.
25 Koenigsberger, "Action Planning," 307.
26 Wee, "The Emergence of the Global and Social City," 691.
27 Nicole Sackley, "Village Models: Etawah, India, and the Making and Remaking of Development in the Early Cold War," *Diplomatic History* 37, no. 4 (2013): 758.
28 Daniel Immerwahr, *Thinking Small: The United States and the Lure of Community Development* (Cambridge, MA: Harvard University Press, 2015), 86–87.
29 Ibid.
30 Sackley, "Village Models," 760.
31 Albert Mayer, *Pilot Project, India: The Story of Rural Development at Etawah, Uttar Pradesh* (Berkeley: University of California Press, 1958), 289.
32 Sackley, "Village Models," 757.
33 Abrams, Kobe, and Koenigsberger, *Growth and Urban Renewal in Singapore: Report Prepared for the Government of Singapore*, 3.44.
34 Koenigsberger, "Action Planning," 307.
35 Ibid., 307, 310.

36 Ibid., 309–310.
37 Tom Avermaete, "Framing the Afropolis: Michel Ecochard and the African City for the Greatest Number," *OASE* 82 (2010): 97.
38 Yetunde Olaiya, "Systemic Shifts: The Case of Abidjan's Urban Planning, 1945–60," *Journal of Architectural Education* 68, no. 2 (2014): 190; Luce Beeckmans, "French Planning in a Former Belgian Colony: A Critical Analysis of the French Urban Planning Missions in Post-Independence Kinshasa," *OASE* 82 (2010): 63, 69.
39 Ali Madanipour, "The Limits of Scientific Planning: Doxiadis and the Tehran Action Plan," *Planning Perspectives* 25, no. 4 (2010): 493.
40 Smadar Sharon, "Not Settlers But Settled: Immigration, Planning and Settlement Patterns in the Lakhish Region in the 1950s," (Ph.D. diss., Tel Aviv University, 2012), 113–114, 127, 141 (In Hebrew).
41 John Forester, Raphael Fischler, and Deborah Shmueli, eds. *Israeli Planners and Designers: Profiles of Community Builders* (Albany, NY: State University New York Press, 2001), 325.
42 This kind of reasoning was used in India in 1948 to set up the National Sample Survey Organization (NSSO), where quick "sampling" rather than decadal census-taking became the modus operandi starting with the First Plan. I thank Arindam Dutta for this important parallel.
43 Ra'anan Weitz, "Interview with Shimeon Amir," *Kidma* 33, 9, no. 1 (1986): 25 (In Hebrew).
44 Otto Koenigsberger to Aharon Remez, July 6, 1962, ISA, MFA 1908/18.
45 "Sikhot Maariv," *Maariv*, June 14, 1965, 4 (In Hebrew).
46 Charles E. Lindblom, "The Science of 'Muddling Through,'" *Public Administration Review* 19 (1959): 80–81.
47 Doug J. Porter, "Scenes from Childhood: The Homesickness of Development Discourse," *The Power of Development*, ed. Jonathan Crush (London and New York: Routledge, 1995), 72.
48 Laura Thompson, "The Clinical Situation in Psychotherapy, Dependency Government, and Applied Anthropology," *Human Organization* 18, no. 3 (Fall 1959): 132.
49 Mayer, *Pilot Project, India*, 291.
50 In 1968, the Singapore Service Bureau used IBM System 360, model 30. See Republic of Singapore, State and City Planning, Notes on the United Nations Assistance in Urban Renewal and Development Project, Singapore, January 1969, Koenigsberger's papers.
51 Abrams, Kobe, and Koenigsberger, "Growth and Urban Renewal in Singapore," 89.
52 Ibid., 89, 103.
53 On the role of Israeli architectural aid in fostering these relations, see Haim Yacobi, *Israel and Africa: A Genealogy of Moral Geography* (London: Routledge, 2016), 19–55; and Ayala Levin, *Architecture and Development: Israeli Construction in Sub-Saharan Africa and the Settler-Colonial Imagination, 1958–73* (Durham, NC: Duke University Press, 2022).
54 IPD Board Meeting No. 15, October 26, 1964, Israel State Archives, MFA 469/7 (130).
55 Sierra Leone Government, *Draft, Five Year Plan of Economic and Social Development, July 1, 1966–June 30, 1971* (Freetown: Sierra Leone Government, 1965).
56 Aryeh Doudai and Ursula Oelsner, *Sierra Leone National Urbanisation Plan* (Tel Aviv: Institute for Planning and Development, 1965), 4–5.
57 Meeting at the Tel Aviv Engineering Club, December 27, 1963, Israel State Archive, MFA 1898/16.
58 Jacques Bertin, "General Theory, from *Semiology of Graphics*," in *The Map Reader: Theories of Mapping Practice and Cartographic Representations*, eds. Martin Dodge, Rob Kitchin, and Chris Perkins (Chichester and Hoboken, NJ: Wiley-Blackwell, 2011), 9–10.
59 Cited in Denis Wood, Review of *Graphics and Graphic Information Processing* by Jacques Bertin, *Association of Canadian Map Librarians* 54 (March 1985): 118.
60 Doudai and Oelsner, *Sierra Leone National Urbanisation Plan*, 5.
61 Ibid., 88.
62 Ibid., 32.
63 Ibid., 90.
64 Ibid., 80.
65 Muzaffar, "Fuzzy Images," 341.
66 Akin Mabogunje and Adetoye Faniran, eds., *Regional Planning and National Development in Tropical Africa* (Ibadan: Ibadan University Press, 1977), XI.
67 Lindblom, "The Science of 'Muddling Through,'" 86.
68 Forester, Fischler, and Shmueli, *Israeli Planners and Designers*, 323.
69 Scott, *Seeing Like a State*, 257–261.
70 Koenigsberger, "Action Planning," 306.
71 On the case of Ciudad Guayana see Muzaffar, "Fuzzy Images," 314.
72 Aryeh Doudai, "Singapore's United Nations-Assisted State and City Planning Project," *Singapore Institute of Planners Journal* (1971): 7. This was common in many countries, such as Israel and India, where planning units existed only as

advisory chambers to the prime minister's office or other ministries. In Israel, the first national physical plan (1951) did not gain statutory power until 1965.

73 "Rewarding City and the Master Plan," *The Straits Times*, April 30, 1971, 7.
74 Notes on the United Nations Assistance (op cited note 53).
75 "Planning Co-ordinator's Briefing," February 27, 1970, Koenigsberger's Papers. The report cites "The Ministry of Law and National Development" as the home of the project but these were, in fact, two different ministries.
76 By then, Doudai was no longer employed by IPD. Still, the strong military ties that Israel and Singapore initiated in December 1965 might have contributed to his appointment.
77 Doudai, "Singapore's United Nations-Assisted State and City Planning Project," 4.
78 Notes on the United Nations Assistance (op cited note 53).
79 Doudai, "Singapore's United Nations-Assisted State and City Planning Project," 5.
80 Koenigsberger, "Action Planning," 309.
81 Garry Rodan, *Participation without Democracy: Containing Conflict in Southeast Asia* (Ithaca, NY: Cornell University Press, 2018), 4.
82 Beng Huat Chua, *Liberalism Disavowed: Communitarianism and State Capitalism in Singapore* (Ithaca, NY: Cornell University Press, 2017), 5.
83 Orit Halpern, Jesse LeCavalier, Nerea Calvillo, and Wolfgang Pietsch, "Test-Bed Urbanism," *Public Culture* 25, no. 2 (2013): 294–295. See also Manfredo Tafuri, *Architecture and Utopia: Design and Capitalist Development* (Cambridge, MA: MIT Press), 173–175.

4

To which revolution? The National School of Agriculture and the Center for the Improvement of Corn and Wheat in Texcoco and El Batán, Mexico, 1924–1968

Nikki Moore

In 1968, three models of agricultural development, coupled with student protests against the growing authoritarianism and brutality of President Gustavo Díaz-Ordaz's regime, fractured the unfinished university campus of the National School of Agriculture in Texcoco, Mexico. One might say that the design of the campus, undertaken in March 1963 by the architect William C. Brubaker of the Chicago firm Perkins + Will in partnership with Augusto H. Álvarez and Enrique Carral Icaza of Mexico City, was commissioned by Mexico's secretary of agriculture and the Rockefeller Foundation to prevent precisely this type of fallout. The campus was, in fact, an attempt to salvage nearly two decades of collaborative advances in soil and seed improvement fostered by Mexico's national and international agronomists and expertise provided by the Rockefeller Foundation. Mexico's agronomists saw their role as supporting the use of modern agricultural methods to further the land restitution and subsistence aims of the Mexican Revolution. A smaller subset of this group saw those goals best achieved through alignment with the International Communist Party. And both groups contrasted with Rockefeller Foundation-supported researchers who saw agricultural modernization and surplus as the means to strengthen Mexico's position within the emerging global market. Looking to a unified campus to manage what bureaucracy and shared funding could not, Plan Chapingo—the campus expansion named for the school's original and historic plantation, Hacienda Chapingo—was designed to unite each of these factions and approaches.

This chapter traces Brubaker's steps in the development of Plan Chapingo and argues that while embedded in complex political and economic negotiations between North American and Mexican institutions, the architect attempted to leverage bio-sensitive planning to resolve heated opposition between proponents of divergent national and international models of agricultural development. In his application of what we could call the aesthetics of scientific neutrality, Brubaker's Plan Chapingo campus illustrates precisely how the built environment, utilizing a seemingly apolitical, scientific method of problem solving, stakes a highly political claim for the shape of post-Bretton Woods development in central Mexico. Though ultimately Brubaker's solution would not hold and Plan Chapingo failed in its attempt to unify growing opposition among its faculty, the bifurcated model for agronomic modernization that

DOI: 10.4324/9781003193654-7

emerged in Mexico set the stage for the Rockefeller Foundation's approach to agricultural development in South America, North Africa, and South Asia throughout the 1960s and 1970s.[1] While the national agronomists who remained at Chapingo after the split focused on developing agricultural solutions to aid Mexico's arid-climate farmers, many of the globally focused researchers would leave to develop a new International Maize and Wheat Improvement Center, or CIMMYT, seeing this Mexican episode as a formative step in nothing less than the technoscientific transformation of global agriculture now known as the Green Revolution.

THE NATIONAL SCHOOL OF AGRICULTURE, MEXICO'S REVOLUTIONARY CAMPUS

Before the 1967 division of the campus, Chapingo was both a living monument to the agricultural aims of the Mexican Revolution (1910–1920) and an emerging international initiative for agricultural research.[2] The school's revolutionary history was rooted in both the selection of its site and the crucial role of its early alumni in formulating postrevolutionary national policy. In 1924, the Chapingo Hacienda, one of the Mexican Revolution's prized land reclamations, was dedicated to the Mexican people by the revolutionary president Álvaro Obregón as the new site of the National School of Agriculture (see Figure 4.1).[3]

FIGURE 4.1 The National School of Agriculture Administration Building and heart of former Hacienda Chapingo. The original Jesuit convent and chapel (right) were renovated between 1886 and 1887 by architect Antonio Rivas Mercado during the tenure of former Mexican President Manuel Gonzalez (1880–1884) to reflect the nation's European aspirations. The Chapingo Chapel later became the site of Diego Rivera's homage to Mexico's agricultural future when the school was dedicated to the people of Mexico in 1924.

Source: Rockefeller Archive Center, Rockefeller Foundation Photographs, Record Group 323 + 323D, Box 96, Folder 1905.

Built from the acreage, barns, distillery, and the grand Spanish colonial, neoclassical, and baroque country home of former president Manuel González (1880–1884)—the puppet for the 35-year dictatorship of Porfirio Díaz (1877–1911)—the new National School of Agriculture within the old hacienda served as a landmark and showcase of the postrevolutionary government's redistributive program for the nation's oldest plantation-style estates and its promise of land tenure to those who had been pushed off both their own private acreage and communal village holdings.[4]

The dedication of the new site of the National School of Agricultural was but one step in the longer history of the institution. As early as 1853, the Ministry of Development was created to address rural problems and oversee agricultural advancement, opening the first National College of Agriculture in the northern sector of Mexico City. During Porfirio Díaz's tenure, leaning on French, German, and Italian models and purveyors of agricultural expertise designed for the benefit of the landholding elite, the ministry oversaw the importation of supplies ranging from tractors and irrigation equipment to seeds and fertilizers to augment the commercial viability of Mexico's agro-industries. By 1908 the National College of Agriculture, which included both an agricultural and a veterinary school, would be renamed the National School of Agriculture. Following suit, similar satellites for the transfer of technical knowledge in agriculture, horticulture, zootechnics, veterinary science, rural industry, and farm engineering were established in Juarez, Oaxaca, Rio Verde, and Tabasco.

By 1917, under the revolutionary government of Venustiano Carranza, further agricultural stations were established in Tabasco, Yucatán, Morelos, Guanajuato, Querétaro, Guerrero, and Michoacán, with plans for additional stations in Nuevo León, Chihuahua, Zacatecas, Chiapas, and Quintana Roo. By 1928, the government of Plutarco Elías Calles commissioned agronomists and educators at Ciudad Juarez's Private School of Agriculture (1906) to study agronomic schools and development in Europe, Asia, and North Africa in order to integrate their findings for the modernization of Mexican agriculture.[5]

THE AGRICULTURAL FREE SCHOOLS: FIRST NATIONS AND THE COMINTERN

Under the postrevolutionary government of Obregón, international agronomist Pandurang Khankhoje—a political refugee, the founder of India's revolutionary Ghadar Party, and a professor at the National School of Agriculture—was conducting Mexico's first genetic experiments in hybrid corn and other cereal developments.[6] In 1926, Khankhoje fostered friendships with the photographer Tina Modotti, the muralists Xavier Guerrero and Diego Rivera, and Úrsulo Galván Reyes, the founder of the Xalapa Mexican Communist Party and the National League of Agrarian Communities.[7] The group's alignment with the Communist International, or Comintern, would lead not only to a visual archive of photographs and murals of the Chapingo school but, by framing the communal farming practices of Mexico's First Nations through the ideological lenses of class struggle, this same group of agronomists, farmers, activists, and artists simultaneously drafted a working model for Mexico's own national political and agrarian development in the Agricultural Free Schools. Guided by a board of directors that included Diego Rivera, Marte Gómez, Ramón P. de Negrí, Moisés Sanz, Manuel Meza, and Manuel Ávila, the Agricultural Free Schools filled a gap in postrevolutionary education, offering practical and communal agricultural and farm management training to rural, Indigenous, and often elderly subsistence farmers.[8] By 1932, more than 33 Agricultural Free Schools were in operation across rural Mexico.[9]

THE ROCKEFELLER FOUNDATION: THE AESTHETICS OF SCIENTIFIC NEUTRALITY

In 1941, former Chapingo director Marte R. Gómez, then Secretary of Haciendas under the administration of Manuel Ávila Camacho, invited an eager Rockefeller Foundation to Mexico to conduct experiments in agricultural improvement within the Office of Special Studies (OSS) in Mexico City. Foundation-inflected histories have built an imperial hero-story out of insertion of Rockefeller scientists into Mexico's national and international research consortium. Yet when Rockefeller-sponsored agronomists joined the faculty at the National School of Agriculture between 1942 and 1943, they entered preexisting teams of scientifically minded peers who had been working since the late nineteenth century to diversify Mexico's crops while improving agricultural yields and soil conditions.[10]

Given the long genealogy of Mexico's advances in agronomy, what distinguished the Rockefeller Foundation's agricultural work at Chapingo from that of its Mexican counterparts was less the application of new scientific solutions to agricultural projects than a way of seeing the world through the lens of what I am calling the aesthetics of scientific neutrality. Which is to say, if architectural modernism is defined as an architectural response to—and participation within—the twentieth-century inclination to propose scientific and technological solutions to what were often also cultural and political problems, the aesthetics of scientific neutrality, in line with the tenets of positivism, reveals a way of looking at objects—including humans, plants, and reinforced concrete—as "resources" or "value-neutral factors"—the components of a uniform economic space, best handled and optimized through a combination of technocratic and scientific approaches. The aesthetics of scientific neutrality present what Foucault would call a dispositive or apparatus, establishing the conditions for the modernist solutions and production that follow.[11]

Concretely, the aesthetics of scientific neutrality pinpoints a way of seeing shaped directly by the post–World War II Bretton Woods reorganization of global power, marked by the creation of the International Monetary Fund and the World Bank, which reframed previous colonial arrangements in terms of the new, purportedly more neutral market-driven forces of industrial production, expertise, and technocracy.[12] Taking up the mantle of this scientifically neutral reorganization of the First, Second, and Third Worlds, the United Nations, the World Bank, and the Point Four Program, as well as the Rand, Ford, and Rockefeller conglomerates, created expanding networks focused on the rationalization of domains ranging from welfare and farming to tourism, urban planning, and economic growth. Yet as Louis Marin has argued, neutrality is never neutral. Speaking directly to the purported neutrality of the liberal university, per se, Marin describes neutrality as something more akin to dissimulation. It is, he states,

> not simply an inert screening-off of a deeper reality. It is, rather, a means to an end, a means possessed by an end for its own self-realization. It is the mark of a force aiming at a goal, a mask of the violence of this force or, in different terms, its "reactivity."[13]

The disintegration of the Chapingo campus begins and ends with the Rockefeller Foundation's dissembling of scientific neutrality in the face of more entrenched ideological debates and interests. Agricultural experiments conducted by the Rockefeller Foundation's OSS and the Mexican government's Office of Experiment Stations in the early 1940s did, initially, align in their efforts to disseminate improved seed corn to small farmers. The earliest differences were driven by little-studied political considerations that played out in methodological differences. On the one hand, Rockefeller scientists focused on improving open-pollinated corn varieties—open pollination is a quick method to gain moderate yield improvement that allows farmers to save and reuse their seed year after year. Mexico's agronomists, on the other hand, including Khankhoje, dedicated their efforts to hybrid corn development and its potential for dramatically increased yields, which was achieved by purifying and then breeding for specific genetic traits. This method, following the model of the North American Midwest, often required annual seed purchase to eliminate contamination, which carried the threat of low yields. While the OSS's choice would initially be most appealing to farmers working within tight budgets, the Rockefeller decision to pursue open-pollinated varieties had more to do with the program's need to produce quick results to fortify allegiances during World War II than with saving small farmers the cost of annual seed purchases. When the OSS methodologies produced unpredictable yields, the Rockefeller and Mexican agronomists continued to diverge and, moving into the 1950s, were unwilling to collaborate.[14] Faced with lackluster results in corn development for small farmers, Rockefeller scientists drew upon Khankhoje's early genetic hybrid research as they shifted their focus to wheat, where high-yield experiments achieved through partnerships with large landholding exporters were showing dramatic results.[15]

Hoping to force a truce between competing objectives and methods, in 1960, Mexico's Secretary of Agriculture, Julián Rodríguez Adame, brought both research groups under the umbrella of the Secretariat by forming the National Institute for Agricultural Investigations (INIA) at the National School of Agriculture at Chapingo. When this bureaucratic shift failed to bridge agronomic and ideological divides, Adame and the foundations began to look for an architectural solution. Thus, in March of 1963, William C. Brubaker of Perkins + Will made his first visit to Chapingo. A consultant in school design for the Ford Foundation Educational Facilities Laboratory, founded in 1958, Brubaker was brought in by the Ford and Rockefeller foundations as the school design expert of choice, touting his experience in cost-saving, component-based architecture, design strategies to support innovative curricula, and record of successfully integrating new media into unconventional learning spaces.[16]

In order to assist with navigating the day-to-day challenges of campus planning and construction at Chapingo, architects Augusto H. Álvarez and Enrique Carral Icaza, of Álvarez and Carral, were hired as Brubaker's Mexican counterparts. In an interview some three decades later, Brubaker described this and other partnerships between firms as part of the functional necessities of the planning and execution of large projects, reflecting colonial-era practices of multinational firms and their local agencies.[17] In Álvarez and Carral's employment by Perkins + Will, we thus see a refashioning of the "native informant" within the development-era hiring structure, which posed new hierarchies and boundaries in the realms of technology and knowledge transfer in the form of this putative "collaboration" between global architectural expert and the local architectural assistant.[18]

REORDERING THE CAMPUS

Brubaker's notes from this first meeting of the Plan Chapingo stakeholders clarify the end goal of all proposed construction—209,000 square feet in total—with one "Ultimate Objective—a coordinated program, a unified institution for education, research, and extension."[19] Brubaker's unifying challenge plays itself out in the architect's proposals for a complete campus plan, including a new library, departmental buildings, student center, and additional student housing. Brubaker recorded his initial designs in a sketchbook that he presented in Chicago on April 23, 1963. In attendance for the preliminary design presentation was John Nagel, the Ford Foundation's representative for Mexico and Central America; Dr. Ralph Richardson, the Rockefeller Foundation's associate director for agriculture; and F. Lee Cochran, Robert Palmer, and a person listed only as Tinney, from Perkins + Will. No one from Chapingo was recorded as attending the presentation.

While in the early pages of the architect's sketchbook the Chapingo hacienda anchors each scheme and composition, just as it anchored the revolutionary history of the school's founding, the newly proposed buildings would shift the balance of both the built and political environments on campus. Pages from Brubaker's sketchbook, dated April 23, record that in Scheme 1, the campus's southern border wall would be opened to accommodate training facilities for the Ford Foundation's most prized component of Plan Chapingo, the INIA extension program. This proposal takes up valuable irrigated field space, though Brubaker notes that this schematic offers a "good housing plan," which would be accomplished by positioning new dormitories in close proximity to the student center. In this same scheme, the hacienda maintains its centrality, with newly proposed buildings radiating out around it. Yet simultaneously, "the old hacienda," once the heart of the school's educational program, is relabeled as the proposed site for the alumni center.[20] While accompanying notes indicate that the iconic building might have kept its current classrooms and administrative offices, this potential reassignment was the first indication of a symbolic relegation of what was previously the revolutionary heart of the campus from being an active presence in the educational direction of the school to a sidelined archive, a marginalization by memorialization, as it were.

Scheme 2, presented on the same day, offered a "less desirable plan for student housing," and ultimately it was Scheme 3 that would be realized. In the final schematic for Plan Chapingo, the INIA extension facilities are positioned in the northeast corner of the campus, in an area of dense trees beyond the perimeter. Accordingly, the student center joins the centralized library at the heart of the campus plan, while the original hacienda becomes something of a monument at the periphery.

The implications surrounding the decision to move forward with Scheme 3 and its centralized library echo the aims of the foundation representatives present at the meeting in the following ways. First, and namely, it heralded the decentralization of the Mexican post-revolutionary agronomists and founders of the Agricultural Free Schools, whose combined mission statement was frescoed like a sonnet in the entry, stairwell, and chapel murals by Diego Rivera inside "the old hacienda."[21] Next, this schematic moved existing dairy barns and laboratories for animal husbandry to irrigated land much further south of the main campus, thereby shifting previously powerful faculty interests off of the primary campus and out of the spotlight.[22] Finally, focusing the campus around a new library funded by the International Development Bank would place the Ford and Rockefeller foundation's objectives for Plan Chapingo—namely, access to international communities of science—at the heart of the school's physical configuration.

CONFIGURING THE DEPARTMENTAL BUILDINGS

With the campus configuration in place, Brubaker was drawn back to the project of integrating the campus's divergent faculty into departmental buildings. As noted in the Ford Foundation's records for the project, the faculty preferred a plan wherein national and internationally focused teams of agronomists would each obtain their own set of facilities.[23] The foundations disagreed, noting that this duplication of laboratories and offices would not only further silo each group but would also involve the replication of resources. They suggested instead a campus organized by subject matter, regardless of ideological orientations within.[24]

If anything, the foundations' shared departmental buildings proposal exacerbated the tensions that Plan Chapingo was tasked to overcome. In response, in a November 6, 1963, meeting with only Perkins + Will, Ford Foundation, and USAID representatives, Brubaker attempted to reconfigure the political terrain with a purportedly apolitical solution. To do so, he drew from early sketches by Robert Palmer to propose an organization that emphasized the site's solar orientation, thus literally taking matters out of terrestrial entanglements and redescribing the plan as a strictly rational—and purportedly apolitical—order in its configurations of laboratory, office, and departmental space.[25] Palmer's sketch shows the classrooms oriented to ideal solar conditions, with offices, labs, and workrooms facing east and all corridors between classes facing west to create shaded breezeways outside each room. Each breezeway was lined with an elongated, checkerboard-patterned, cinder block brise-soleil to allow light into the outdoor hallways while blocking the region's intense sun. Air conditioning would be available only to the library and administration center. Thus, in the departmental buildings' final configuration, Brubaker formulated a cross-sectional diagram where sun, shade, and breezes began to dictate the architectural forms for the labs and classrooms. Borrowing from a previous project in Florida, Brubaker sought to shade the offices to the east and south sides of each building. To do so, he installed a series of extended, shade-giving window casings made from bush-hammered, precast concrete, which preserved the look of a window wall from the front.

Extending a solar rationale to the central library, Brubaker glazed each exterior wall, yet shaded the interior from the sun through the use of another form of brise-soleil, which appeared to hang or float from the building's farthest edges. Patterned like a woven wicker basket or a porous membrane, in functional terms the trellis-like form created an effective breezeway around the building's perimeter, shading the library workspace at all times of the day. In symbolic terms, we could say that this basket pattern reiterated this new building's centrality to both the school's changing curriculum and its new global orientation. It was from this breadbasket that the school's most important products—the accumulation and dissemination of agricultural knowledge and scholarship to international academic communities elsewhere—would be harvested.[26]

In structuring the school's architecture around Copernican logic, Brubaker produced a rationale for the department buildings' configurations that both displaced and deflected the conflicts that it was intended to supplant. It was as if, in this aesthetics of scientific neutrality, Brubaker reshaped the terrain of the social discussion: no longer would it be a question of which revolution—Mexican, Red, or Green—to which the school would be beholden. Rather, his designs resolutely announced a fourth revolution, the documentation of scientific knowledge as sure as the movements of the earth around the sun, which would eventually forestall conflict and bring the campus to order. Architectural heliotropy would provide, in Brubaker and Álvarez y Carral's final plans for Chapingo, the symbolic legitimacy that Rockefeller espoused in its efforts to solve social and political challenges around the world.

THE NATIONAL SCHOOL OF AGRICULTURE AND THE GREEN REVOLUTION

In the experimental fields of the National School, these aesthetics would give birth to the methods of the Green Revolution itself. The Green Revolution is perhaps best known for improving yields in wheat by upwards of 400 percent and winning the American scientist and Chapingo professor Norman Borlaug the Nobel Peace Prize in 1970.[27] By moving seeds that grew in Chapingo's central Mexican altiplano in the traditional wheat growing season to the northern coastal lowlands of Sonora for a second season each year, Borlaug was able to escalate the speed of naturally occurring hybrid crossings.[28] Initially, Borlaug drew from ancient seed strains collected from sites across Mexico and transplanted them at sites with contrasting growing conditions in a process now called shuttle breeding. His objective was to speed up the growing capacity of native strains and improve their disease resistance and yields, particularly selecting for flexible seeds that were able to adjust to the differences in sunlight exposure (photoperiods), climatic conditions, and environmental factors experienced in each location.[29] His signature triumph was thus almost inadvertent: the creation of seeds that could thrive when dislodged from their native conditions.

The process was not without its failures. After testing native seeds and bringing them to their productive limit, Borlaug found that most of them, adapted over centuries to Mexico's dry soil conditions, would grow such tall stalks when fertilized that the plants would bend and break under their own weight. After testing more than 20,000 varieties of wheat, the path to success emerged by crossing Japanese dwarf varieties of wheat (namely Norin 10) with some of Mexico's top-performing seed.

While the science behind this discovery is sufficiently championed, what is essential to pinpointing the resonance between Borlaug's shuttle breeding process and the architecture of Plan Chapingo is this: taking something constitutive, both local and transcultural in its origin, and cultivated from the soil, history, and cultures of Mexico, both Borlaug and Brubaker worked through iteration after iteration of that specificity until they could arrive at something purportedly universal, adapted to a variety of applications, and depoliticized in its implications. This becomes patent if we notice a salient characteristic of Brubaker's final design, which, as noted, sidelined the erstwhile centrality of the hacienda.

Paradoxically, Brubaker would replicate the essential compositional scheme of the Chapingo Hacienda—its two-story elevation and rectilinear plan wrapped around an open courtyard—as if it were a piece of DNA (see Figure 4.2). While the dimensions of the buildings vary, whether one looks at the departmental buildings, which took the hacienda plan and replicated it into a molecular arrangement of interlocking rectilinear rings, or the plan for the faculty center, dining hall, or the central library, it is clear that Brubaker repeated the hacienda plan again and again across the new modern campus. In doing so, he not only unwittingly reasserted that plan's colonial, subjugational logic, but in its ongoing repetition he also watered down the very symbol of the school's revolutionary identity, making the original hacienda just one of many in the campus's new Plan Chapingo.

The explicit decentering of specificity, born of replication and displacement, represented the heart of the Green Revolution's signature experiments. The same could be said for the corporate International Style of architecture championed in Plan Chapingo. Emphasizing each building's functional, technical rationale while stripping away signs of locality, nationality, and specificity, the Green Revolution did for seeds what the International Style did for architecture. This shared aesthetic—the aesthetics of scientific neutrality—are not coincidental.

FIGURE 4.2 Neil MacLellan, "Campus Development Plan, Chapingo, Mexico, 1964 (Byron McClellan)." A model of the original Chapingo Hacienda, with its open central courtyard, is visible to the right of the densely wooded area near the campus's center. Below right, the hacienda footprint is replicated in a trio of departmental buildings and the unbuilt faculty center in the lower right, which was instead reconfigured to serve as the campus dining hall.

Source: Rockefeller Archive Center, FA003 100–1000 Photographs, box 96, Folder 1888.

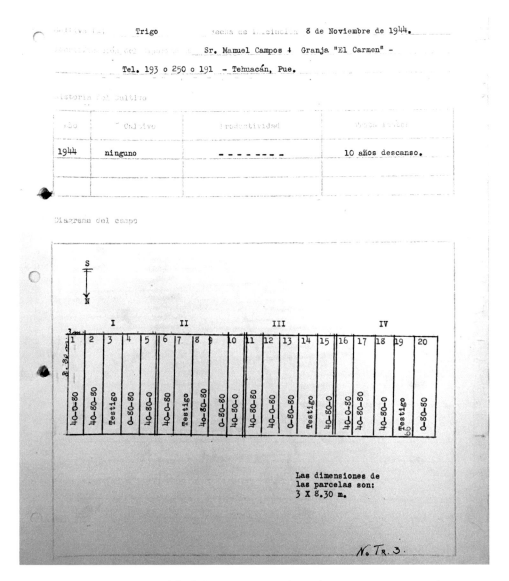

FIGURE 4.3 "Trigo/Wheat" (1944). Sample planting charts for testing application of nitrogen, phosphorus, and other chemicals on maize, wheat, and barley. Their form was repeated in the horizontal windows of Alvarez's Chapingo Campus.

Source: "Report of the Oficina de Estudios Especiales S.A.F. February 1, 1943–June 1, 1945." Rockefeller Archive Center, Rockefeller Foundation Projects, 1.1 Projects, Series 323 Mexico, Box 6, Folder 38.

In fact, the precise form of the Green Revolution's earliest field tests is reflected in Brubaker's final design language for the architecture of Chapingo (see Figures 4.3 and 4.4). A strong proponent of bringing outdoor light into the classroom—a practice inspired by Mies van der Rohe, Le Corbusier, and other exemplars of the International Style—the architect created a series of window walls along the south and east facades of each set of laboratories, offices, and classrooms. However, Brubaker and Álvarez deviate from Le Corbusier's injunction to horizontal casements by replicating the very form of the Green Revolution's early

FIGURE 4.4 Neil MacLellan, "Chapingo Project," (1967). Brubaker's window walls, as completed for the departmental, laboratory, and extension buildings, replicating the grid of the Green Revolution's early planting charts (left).

Source (right): Rockefeller Archive Center, Rockefeller Foundation Photographs, Record Group 323, Box 96, Folder 1888.

field experiments in the narrow punctuated vertical windows that define the campus expansion.[30] While Le Corbusier's ribbon windows serve to create an even distribution of light across his interior spaces, their narrowed frame truncates both the sky above and the land below from a viewer situated deep within a room's interior. At Chapingo, however, Brubaker would introduce floor-to-ceiling casements throughout the classrooms, offices, and facilities, such that when students and researchers looked out of their laboratories onto the world, the casement mullions would seem to replicate the same longitudinal divisions amongst the field rows that had propelled the research arm of the National School of Agriculture to its success. Dividing everything from the proximate to the horizon into a palimpsest of near and far furrows, Brubaker's design moved the planar vivisection of the nonhuman field of research into a kind of embodied phenomenological experience of the upright viewer, conflating the methodologies of science into a striated visual field, tying together living and nonliving objects within a continuous pattern.

Brubaker's "neutral" assimilation of local predicaments played out in other facets as well, most notably in his perhaps inadvertent step into Alvarez's complicated relationship with the distinct history of Mexican modernism. Between 1950 and 1952, the architects Mario Pani and Enrique del Moral led more than 150 architects, landscape architects, and engineers in the design and construction of one of Mexican modernism's most iconic projects, the Autonomous University of Mexico (UNAM).[31] Built around the ruins of Cuicuilco, a settlement that arose in approximately 600 BCE and was abandoned after a volcanic eruption sometime before 200 BCE, the campus brought together both the art and architecture of the region's First Peoples and the glass, steel, and volumetric tenets of modernism to craft an image of both the present and future of the postrevolutionary nation.[32]

Álvarez matriculated at the department of architecture at UNAM in 1933 and, along with Carral, became part of the faculty in the late 1930s. His personal history, as the grandson of a wealthy plantation owner in the Yucatan dispossessed of the family's land during the Revolution, put the architect at political odds with the aims of the postrevolutionary avant-garde who had designed the school and curriculum that formed his professional outlook.[33] As a practitioner, Álvarez welcomed the import substitution industrialization models fostered by the Mexican state during World War II, as well as the opening of the country to foreign corporations and global trade as a means to stimulate economic growth and new, private commissions.[34] His projects, the best known of which are the corporate campuses for IBM (1970–72) and El Centro Operativo Bancomer (1974–76), clearly distinguished him from the early Mexican modernists. His body of work is made up of rationalist and brutalist buildings, echoing the aspirations of multinationals whose expansionist aims are visible in their "neutral," modern, concrete, and glass facades.

While there is no record of Brubaker making a trip to UNAM, Plan Chapingo's signature incorporation of local stone stacked in pyramidal cross sections in both the departmental buildings and the auditorium may, ironically, have come from the Chicago-based architect rather than Álvarez or Carral. A sketch in Brubaker's notes from a trip to the Conjunto Habitacional Unidad Independencia, or "Unidad Independencia," a public housing project created to house factory workers in Mexico City, specifically takes note of very similar pyramidal forms incorporated by the architects Alejandro Prieto and José María Gutiérrez in 1960.[35] Prieto and Gutiérrez's inspiration would have come obliquely from the pyramids of Teotihuacan and Cuicuilco and more precisely through Albert T. Aria's homage to the Calderas mountains in UNAM's lauded handball courts in 1952. The appearance of these same elements in the design of the end walls of Chapingo's departmental buildings are first visible in the proposals of the Perkins + Will team in what now appears as an attempt to contextualize this new university plan by placing it in conversation with the very model Álvarez and Carral had been working to escape.

If Brubaker and Álvarez differed in their approach to the campus's precedents, they came together to respond directly to the unresolved problem of Chapingo's opposing faculty groups. Within the departmental buildings, as each faction hoped to maintain divisions by capturing opposing sides of the rectilinear plans, Brubaker leveraged his experience with the Ford Foundation's Educational Facilities Laboratories to build flexibility into the structure of each building. Thus, none of the walls between laboratories, offices, and workspaces were load bearing. If faculty configurations changed, spaces could be opened and rooms recombined to accommodate the possibility of institutional unity. In Alvarez's own plans for the courtyard landscape, he created intersecting walkways, spanning from corner to corner and meeting in a tree-shaded space in the middle. The design worked as if to say that for now faculty and students could best head toward greater camaraderie when stepping outside of the breezeways and offices that still divided them and into the handcrafted biological space that connected and interested them all. Despite these careful technocratic propositions, however, these landscape solutions and flexible spaces were not enough to save the original plan for the campus.

PROTESTS

By the mid-1960s, an active student movement joined with national and regional labor unions to rise up against the country's authoritarian government. As benefits from Mexico's import substitution industrialization methods, including the Green Revolution's agricultural exports, failed to materialize, protests erupted from the city to the countryside and on the Chapingo campus. These tensions would reach their peak in 1968 with the slaughter of 300–400 university students in Tlatelolco Square.[36] The massacre marked but one spectacular instance of President Díaz-Ordaz's growing tendency toward authoritarianism and state violence, involving the kidnapping, torture, disappearance, and death of students, union workers, and leftist guerrillas at the hands of the US-backed and monopolist PRI, the Institutional Revolutionary Party, in what is now known as Mexico's Dirty War.

National conditions hit home for Chapingo students in 1967, in the midst of Plan Chapingo's construction.[37] Standing together under the newfound banners of the National Federation of Students in Agricultural and Forest Sciences and the National Strike Council, agricultural students across the country launched their own campus strikes.[38] While the protests were most directly aimed at domestic governance, fomented by North American support for Díaz-Ordaz, many students had grown to see Rockefeller Foundation researchers and faculty as one more avatar of the same appropriative foreign agenda whose agro-industrialization project was draining the resources of the Mexican people.

Occupying buildings across campus, the student body brought the school's built environment into political contention. The students' first point of grievance was the Ford Foundation's decision to remove students from the committee for school governance.[39] Students also voiced opposition to the 1924 militarization of Chapingo, which required students to wear military uniforms and participate in regimented military activities. Brubaker's architecture fared no better, as students bemoaned the loss of their former campus plan, heavily criticizing the new administration building that hovered above the school's beloved main road. They demanded new dorms, pledged by the Mexican Government in 1963 and never built. Additionally, students petitioned for a department of languages, as well as proper audiovisual equipment—identifying a blind spot in the Ford and Rockefeller foundations' vision—to aid in translating the newly acquired books and articles in the library that they were now required to consult when writing their theses.

President Díaz-Ordaz and other political leaders, including the school's former director Marte Gómez, condemned Chapingo's campus protests as the result of outside communist agitators. The students decried this political ploy aimed to draw North American support for some of the regime's most heinous crackdowns against its own people. Using language and references from the Mexican Revolution of 1910, most student protestors described themselves as more directly inspired by the aims of Emiliano Zapata than by Karl Marx, even if the Agricultural Free Schools, fostered by Chapingo faculty, had conflated the two.[40]

DISPERSAL

The breakdown of Plan Chapingo left at least three models of agricultural education in its wake. Furthering the path of scientific neutrality, in 1966 President Díaz-Ordaz and Mexico's Secretary of Agriculture and Ranching, Gil Preciado, signed an agreement giving legal status to the Rockefeller Foundation's CIMMYT, or International Center for the Improvement of Maize and Wheat. While the project was first housed and inaugurated within the walls of Plan Chapingo, by 1967, after months of intractable conditions at the National School of Agriculture, the Rockefeller Foundation accepted the President's gift of land from the prerevolutionary Rancho El Batán, located less than 20 miles from Chapingo.[41] The first designs for the campus, executed once again by Brubaker of Perkins + Will, combined modernist glazing with elaborately landscaped brutalist architecture. While these emergent plans would go unbuilt, the formal qualities of the facility's proposed architectural identity emerged directly from the Chicago-based architect's vision for the site's second water tower, which featured a geometric pair of semicircles, joined in a boat-like configuration, balanced atop an open rectilinear stair-filled column.

The focus on water and irrigation brought the history of this parcel of land into high relief. As early as 1440, drawing from the Texcoco River, the land chosen for the CIMMYT was watered by some of the nation's earliest irrigation systems. Utilizing a series of manmade canals designed during the reign of Netzahualcoyotl, the region's first water wheel (and the ranch's namesake) was later established on this very site. Combining natural resources with human ingenuity, El Batán became a prized agricultural site for the Nahua and Mexica as well as colonial Spain and modern Mexico, famed for the nation's earliest wheat harvests as well as a large supply of *pulque*, or agave wine, made from maguey.

Poised like a chalice at the campus's entrance, Brubaker's proposed water tower was to mark the next phase of human history, where, through the agricultural technoscience developed by the CIMMYT, water and irrigation would bring dry land to an as yet unseen fecundity. Inverting and replicating this same semicircular geometry across the campus in the form of windows, stairwell lofts, and vaulted ceilings, each building carries the water tower's form in elevation. A 1967 rendering of the facility's administration building, signed by an unknown Radke, reveals Brubaker's intent. Upending the same semicircular form of the water tower in the facility's uppermost windows, the tower's now inverted semicircles seem to pour their contents back out onto the land below. At the same time, the shape of the building's multi-story colonnade draws the eye from the landscape up along the buildings columns to the same windows that open into laboratories and classrooms, creating a metaphorically reciprocal irrigation system in which agricultural innovation, scientifically improved landscape, and modern resources are coproduced. Planted within shallow pools from which the entire campus seems to rise, each building emerges from the essential albeit controversial nature of one of the Green Revolution's primary tools for success: heavy irrigation.

Upon seeing the first maquettes, CIMMYT's director, Edwin Wellhausen, reported being extremely pleased with the proposal, stating that this new campus, defined by modular, cellular units and filled with lush landscapes, would be something truly new, appropriate to the research to be conducted therein.[42] Despite the director's enthusiasm, funding for the project hinged on whether or not the Ford Foundation was interested in fully partnering with the Rockefeller Foundation on this second Mexican campus. While Ford did sign on, the project's plans were reduced to a cipher as the foundations' ambitions vis-à-vis the Green Revolution had already begun to reach beyond the CIMMYT. Subsequent Rockefeller projects, drawing upon the fundamentals of Borlaug's research, were already under negotiation in Colombia, the Philippines, Nigeria, and India.[43]

In the wake of these shifts, CIMMYT's architecture became a product of the global expansion of the Green Revolution project and the wide distribution of a now-shared facilities budget. In Álvarez and Carral's description of the final functional CIMMYT campus, as well as a booklet published by the Rockefeller Foundation in 1967, the project is discussed as a second collaboration with the Perkins + Will team.[44] In appearance and function, and perhaps as a consequence of the foundations' dispersed budget, however, it draws directly from Álvarez's oeuvre. The gridded fenestration, broken by heavy concrete beams and columns that will become Álvarez's signature corporate calling card, create the CIMMYT's two-and-a-half-story façade. The building itself is visually anchored to the ground by two raised concrete staircases that form bridges between the raised first floor at the building's front and rear. To the left of the entrance, a horizontal brutalist building, paid for by the Japanese government in honor of Borlaug's success in crossing Japanese and Mexican seeds in the Green Revolution's signature experiments, sits heavy on the landscape like an outsized bunker. The brise-soleils of Chapingo, designed to negotiate the region's climate, have been replaced by thick walls that enclose fully air-conditioned spaces. Here the universal, international culture Alvarez sought to champion takes the form of ubiquity, utility, and corporate office parks.

The completed architecture of the CIMMYT points to a new stage in the life of the Green Revolution. Drawing upon their experience creating expansive private development networks around the globe, the Ford Foundation leveraged the Rockefeller Foundation's scientific expertise to form a coalition of economic support. The result was a collaborative source of funding not just for the CIMMYT but also for a worldwide network of commodity-driven facilities, known as the Consultative Group for International Agriculture Research (CGIAR). National governments from Sweden to Japan signed on, along with further entities ranging from the United Nations to private agribusinesses. To ensure impartiality and protect the intellectual as well as genetic property rights of CGIAR discoveries, the Ford and Rockefeller foundations would negotiate special legal recognition for the CIMMYT and each institute to follow, including embassy-like protections and privileges—ranging from tax exemptions to intellectual property rights—for the knowledge workers and discoveries involved therein.

The Agricultural Free Schools fared no better. Scripted in the 1923–1927 murals of Diego Rivera within the once-Jesuit chapel at the heart of the old Chapingo administration building, where the germination, cultivation, and rich agricultural harvest of postrevolutionary Mexico were fed and fertilized by the blood of martyrs like Emiliano Zapata and defended by Mexico's Marxist rural laborer, the Agricultural Free Schools melded Khankhoje's wealth of both agricultural and activist training. A student of military revolutions and one of the founders of India's nationalist Ghadar Party, Khankhoje also held advanced degrees in agriculture, specifically dry farming, from Washington State Agriculture College in Pullman.[45] An anecdote illustrates the degree to which the two were, for him, entwined. Focused on ways to utilize his agricultural acumen for the benefit of his homeland, in a series of papers published by *Chitrramaja Jagat*, Khankhoje managed to disseminate both his research and the status of revolutionary actions he was undertaking from abroad by encoding his scientific papers.[46] Embedding the transnational within the national and particular, Rivera, too, encoded his work with Khankhoje's projects. The scientist–revolutionary appears at the head of the table in *Our Daily Bread* (1928), a mural for the Secretary of Public Education building, and his experimental fields and biological innovations are featured in *Man at the Crossroads* (1933) created for 30 Rockefeller Plaza and recreated on canvas for the Palace of Fine Arts in Mexico City (1934) after the New York project was destroyed for its depiction of Lenin.[47]

Shaped by the agrarian aims of the Mexican Revolution, the Agricultural Free Schools and the CIMMYT represent but two transnational development strategies that attempted to grapple, by divergent means, with the nation's confluence of politics and agriculture. Between them sits the National School of Agriculture at Chapingo. There, histories of the built environment, from Antonio Rivas Mercado's reconfiguration of the Chapingo Hacienda to Plan Chapingo, record the national processes of political, agricultural, and educational trial and error. As the politically committed Free Schools, along with Khankhoje's research in hybrid cereal grains were first sidelined and then subsumed, Brubaker, Alvarez, and Carral attempted to design scientifically neutral answers to intrinsically political questions by orienting Plan Chapingo toward neither the Mexican Revolution nor the Green Revolution but rather toward another less-contested revolution: that of the earth around the sun. When this approach failed to unite Chapingo's agricultural factions, less than 20 miles away the CIMMYT set the stage for Rockefeller and Ford foundations' agricultural schools and institutes throughout the Global South, as the divided campuses of the first site of the Green Revolution were replicated in facilities around the globe. They became, in fact, the model. In Colombia, the National School of Agriculture in Palmira would soon find itself next door to an international research facility, the International Center for Tropical Agriculture in Cali. In Peru, the same division would support both the National Agrarian University in Lima and the International Potato Center, now in a nearby suburb. In Nigeria, the Philippines, India, Japan, and, formerly, Syria, the bifurcated model for agricultural modernization built from the failure of the aesthetics of scientific neutrality continue to hold even if—or primarily because—the original Plan Chapingo campus could not.

NOTES

1 Building on the Mexican agricultural development experience, between the 1960s and 1970s the Rockefeller and Ford foundations formed the Consultative Group for International Agriculture Research (CGIAR) to found research institutions in the Vavilov Centers for Biodiversity throughout the Global South, including the International Rice Research Institute (IRRI) in Los Baños, Philippines (1960); the CIMMYT in El Batán, Mexico (1967); the International Institute for Tropical Agriculture (IITA) in Ibadan, Nigeria (1967); and the International Center for Tropical Agricultura (CIAT) in Cali, Colombia (1972).

2 The Mexican Revolution, which ended the dictatorship of Porfirio Díaz, was fought primarily between 1910 and 1920, though rebellions and uprisings continued until 1930. Forces leading to the revolution were varied, from the personal power-seeking aspirations of the privileged to the discontent fomented by the encroaching hacienda system. For more on the Mexican Revolution, see Alan Knight, *The Mexican Revolution*, 2 vols. (Lincoln: University of Nebraska Press, 1990).

3 Álvaro Obregón Salido, a general in the Mexican Revolution, was the president of Mexico from 1920 to 1924. For the early history of the Escuela Nacional de Agricultura, see Ministerio de Fomento, Colonización, Industria y Comercio de México, *Ley y Reglamento Interior de la Escuela Nacional de Agricultura* (Mexico City: Ignacio Cumplido, 1856). See also Ramón Fernandez y Fernandez, *Chapingo: Hace 50 Años* (Chapingo, Mexico: Colegio de Postgraduados, Escuela Nacional de Agrícola, 1976), 35.

4 José de la Cruz Porfirio Díaz Mori was first elected in 1877 and ruled Mexico until 1911, a regime interrupted only by the election of his ally and puppet President Manuel Gonzalez from 1880 to 1884 and truncated by the Mexican Revolution that opposed him. Díaz ruled under the banner of "Order and Progress," relying on both an inner circle

of privileged *científicos* (scientists) to support his national development aims and brutal enforcers who roamed city and countryside to bend the nation to Díaz's will. Mexico's 1910 census counted 8,245 haciendas (or plantations) in the country. Of these, "300 contained at least 10,000 hectares; 116 around 25,000 hectares; 51 had approximately 30,000 hectares; while 11 are believed to have measured not less than 100,000 hectares." G. M. McBride, *The Land Systems of Mexico* (New York: American Geographical Society of New York, 1923), 155–156.

5 Adolfo Olea-Franco, "One Century of Higher Agricultural Education and Research in Mexico (1850s–1960s), with a Preliminary Survey on the Same Subjects in the United States" (Ph.D. diss., Harvard University, 2002), 310.

6 Juan Manuel Cervantes Sánchez and Juan José Saldaña, "Las estaciones agrícolas experimentales en Mexico (1908–1921) y su contribución a la ciencia agropecuaria mexicana," in *La Casa de Salomón en Mexico: Estudios sobre la institucionalización de la docencia y la investigación científicas*, ed. Juan José Saldaña (Mexico City: Facultad de Filosofía y Letras, Universidad Nacional Autónoma de México, 2005), 306–338; Olea-Franco, "One Century of Higher Agricultural Education and Research in Mexico," chap. 7.

7 Nikki Moore, "Nations of Maize: Mexico's Agricultural Free Schools, 1926–1940" (paper presented at the Society of Architectural Historians Annual International Conference, April 16, 2021); Gabriela Soto Laveaga, "Largo Dislocare: Connecting Microhistories to Remap and Recenter Histories of Science," *History and Technology* 34, no. 1 (2018): 24–25.

8 Artemio Cruz León and Marcelino Ramírez Castro, "Escuelas libres de agricultura de Mexico: Proyecto de la Liga de Comunidades Agrarias y antecedents de las escuelas campesinas," *Revista de Geografía Agrícola* 57 (2017): 143.

9 Listed in order of proximity to Chapingo, a selection of the schools are as follows: Emiliano Zapata, Chiconcuac; Emiliano Zapata, Ocopulco; Tocuila; Netzahualcóyotl, Cuautlalpan; Netzahualcóyotl, San Salvador Athenaeum; Tlalnepantla. León and Castro, "Escuelas libres de agricultura de Mexico," 143.

10 Marte R. Gómez, *Galería de Ministros* (Chapingo, Mexico: Colegio de Postgraduados, 1976), 16.

11 "The apparatus is precisely this: a set of strategies of the relations of forces supporting, and supported by, certain types of knowledge." Michel Foucault, "The Confession of the Flesh," in *Power/Knowledge: Selected Interviews and Other Writings, 1972–1977*, ed. C. Gordon (New York: Pantheon Books, 1980), 194–196.

12 For the impact of the Bretton Woods Conference for development thinking and architectural production, see the Introduction to this volume.

13 Louis Marin, "'Le Neutre' and Philosophical Discourse," in *Neutrality and Impartiality: The University and Political Commitment*, ed. Alan Montefiore (Cambridge: Cambridge University Press, 1975), 86–127.

14 Jesus Uribe Ruiz, *Problemas y Soluciones*, Adolfo López Mateos Files, 506.1/15, National Archives of Mexico, Mexico City. Uribe Ruiz's objections are also mentioned in "U.N. Group Warns on Push to Cities," *New York Times*, 21 July 1964.

15 Karin Matchett, "At Odds Over Inbreeding: An Abandoned Attempt at Mexico/United States Collaboration to 'Improve' Mexican Corn, 1940–1950," *Journal of the History of Biology* 39, no. 2 (Summer 2006): 345–372.

16 William Brubaker, *Planning and Designing Schools* (London: McGraw-Hill, 1998), 6; C. William Brubaker, oral history interview by Betty J. Blum, 1999, transcript, Chicago Architects Oral History Project, Ernest R. Graham Study Center for Architectural Drawings, Art Institute of Chicago, 109–11; Elizabeth B. Kassler, *Built in USA, 1932–1944* (New York: Museum of Modern Art, 1944), 74–75. The Educational Facilities Laboratories (1958–1986) received over $26 million in grants from the Ford Foundation in order to explore connections between school architecture, classroom design, and learning outcomes. Judy Marks, *A History of Educational Facilities Laboratories (EFL)*, rev. ed. (Washington, DC: National Clearinghouse for Educational Facilities, 2009), 2–3.

17 Brubaker Oral History, *Perkins + Will Corporate Archives, Ryerson and Burnham Library* (Chicago: University of Chicago, 1998).

18 Ayala Levin, "Beyond Global vs. Local: Tipping the Scales of Architectural Historiography," *ABE Journal* 8 (2015): 6, https://doi.org/10.4000/abe.2751.

19 C. William Brubaker, *National School of Agricultural Education, Chapingo Mexico Meeting Notes Sketches, 1962–1963*, 19–20, C. William Brubaker Papers, Ryerson and Burnham Archives, Ryerson and Burnham Libraries, Art Institute of Chicago (hereafter Chapingo Sketchbook).

20 Brubaker, Chapingo Sketchbook, 23.

21 Diego Rivera was one of the leaders of the Mexican Mural Movement, one of the founders of the Revolutionary Union of Technical Works, Painters, and Sculptors (1922), and a member of the Mexican Communist Party until he was kicked out in 1929. Rivera married Frida Kahlo in 1929. The two hosted the exiled Soviet revolutionary and Marxist theorist Leon Trotsky in Frida's childhood home in Mexico City from 1937 to 1939. Leonard Folgarait, *Mural Painting and Social Revolution in Mexico, 1920—1940: Art of the New Order* (Cambridge: Cambridge University Press, 1998). See also Alan Knight, "The Mexican Revolution," *History Today* 30, no. 5 (May 1980): 28–34.

22 Ford Foundation, Report #000303, *Catalogued Reports*, Ford Foundation Archives, Rockefeller Archives Center, Sleepy Hollow, New York.

23 Ford Foundation, Report #000303.

24 Ibid.

25 Brubaker, Chapingo Sketchbook, 25.
26 The modern library moved the stacks out from behind secured walls and doors, giving students direct access to materials at will. A bindery was included to encourage publication of the school's research findings. Dorothy I. Parker, the librarian for the Rockefeller Foundation, managed the organization and operations of the new library. Biographical information on Parker is found in the finding aid to the Dorothy I. Parker Papers, Rockefeller Archive Center, Sleepy Hollow, New York.
27 Leon Hesser, *The Man Who Fed the World: Nobel Peace Prize Laureate Norman Borlaug and His Battle to End Hunger: An Authorized Biography* (New York: East End House, 2010).
28 Thomas Payne, director of the CIMMYT Global Seed Vault, interview by author, El Batán, Mexico, May 24, 2016.
29 Hesser, *The Man Who Fed the World*, 48–49.
30 Le Corbusier, *Towards a New Architecture* (New York: Dover Publications, 1985).
31 Celia Ester Arrendondo Sambrano, "Modernity in Mexico: The Case of the Ciudad Universitaria," in *Modernity and the Architecture of Mexico*, ed. Edward R. Burian (Austin: University of Texas Press, 1997), 95–106.
32 J. Artigas, *Centro Cultural Universitario: Visita guiada en torno de su arquitectura* (Mexico City: Universidad Nacional Autónoma de México, 1994); Mario Pani and Enrique del Moral, *La construcción de la Ciudad Universitaria del Pedregal: Concepto, programa y planeacion arquitectonica* (Mexico City: Universidad Nacional Autónoma de México, 1979); Burian, *Modernity and the Architecture of Mexico*. See also Albert José-Antonio López's chapter (Chapter 8) in this volume.
33 Alvarez and his family escaped to Cuba during the Revolution and took refuge there until 1921. Lourdes Cruz González Franco, *Augusto H. Alvarez: Vida y obra* (Mexico City: Facultad de Arquitectura, 2004, Universidad Nacional Autònoma de Mexico), 11.
34 González Franco, *Augusto H. Alvarez*, 7.
35 C. William Brubaker, Chapingo Notebook 2, C. William Brubaker Papers, Ryerson and Burnham Archives, Art Institute of Chicago, 24. A brief note on page 24 also says that the design for the Unidad Independencia, or Independence City, was "based on Athens Charter."
36 In 1968, a group of students met in Tlatelolco square, northwest of the National Palace and the Zocalo, to demand the release of the 1958–59 railroad strike prisoners, the firing of Mexico's chief of police and his deputy, autonomy for university and college campuses from both political and military oversight, and the revamp of Articles 141 and 145 of the Constitution, which authorized imprisonment of all political enemies, both foreign and domestic. As police opened fire on the crowd, triggered by gunshots issued from the Díaz-Ordaz Olympic Protection Unit, hundreds of students were trapped in the open plaza. While official state reports published in the next morning's papers counted 25–28 dead, recently opened state archives on the Tlatelolco Massacre, which include the accounts of eyewitnesses, have placed the number at 300–400 students. Antonio Gómez Nashiki, "1968: Cronología del movimiento estudiantil mexicano," *Nexos* (January 1988); Elena Poniatowska, *La noche de Tlatelolco: Testimonios de historia oral*, 2nd ed. (Mexico City: Era, 1998); Procuraduría de la República, *Informe Histórico a la Sociedad Mexicana* (Mexico City: Procuraduría de la República, 2006).
37 Participants in student and faculty strikes at Chapingo referenced the violent crackdowns against railroad strikes, which were organized and executed throughout 1958–59 and functioned as early signs that the PRI was no longer operating as a democratic force in Mexico. During this period, railroad strikers as well as petroleum workers, members of the democratic opposition, and communists were jailed for their dissent and opposition. Núñez, Hiram, Jorge Gustavo, Ocampo Ledesma, and Rosaura Reyes Canchola, eds., *Chapingo y el movimiento del 68* (Mexico City: Universidad Nacional Autónoma de México, Centro Cultural Universitario Tlatelolco, 2018).
38 *Chapingo y el movimiento estudiantil popular del 68*, eds. Gutierrez, Ledesma and Canchola (Mexico City: Universidad Nacional Autónoma de México, 2018); Susana Draper, *1968 Mexico: Constellations of Freedom and Democracy* (Durham, NC: Duke University Press, 2018).
39 Ford Foundation, Report #000303.
40 As O'Neill Blacker demonstrates in his case study of Guerrero, most of the protests arising in the late 1950s and 1960s were driven by local grievances, the leaders of which looked to the Mexican Revolution for ideological inspiration. O'Neill Blacker, "Cold War in the Countryside: Conflict in Guerrero, Mexico," *The Americas* 66, no. 2 (October 2009): 181–210, https://doi.org/10.1017/s0003161500006076.
41 International Maize and Wheat Improvement Center, *CIMMYT Charter and Civil Partnership Agreement*, 1966, CGIAR Legal Records, CGSpace, https://cgspace.cgiar.org/handle/10947/372.
42 Edwin J. Wellhausen, Diary, Officers' Diaries, 1967–1968, RG-12, FA 394, Box 514, Rockefeller Foundation Records, Rockefeller Archives Center, Sleepy Hollow, New York.
43 For the history of the Rockefeller Foundation agricultural facilities in the Philippines, see the chapter by Diana Martinez, Chapter 5, in this publication.
44 González Franco, *Augusto H. Alvarez*; "CIMMyT: The International Maize and Wheat Improvement Center, a Project of the Rockefeller Foundation," *Rockefeller Foundation* (April 1967), Augusto H. Alvarez, AHA Doc-3, Folder 1: Conjunto de Edificios para el Centro Internacional para el Mejoramiento del Maiz y Trigo CIMMYT, Archive of Mexican Architects, National Autonomous University of Mexico, Mexico City.

45 The secular Ghadar Party arose in India and abroad during World War I. The party's aim was to restore national sovereignty through the overthrow of the British Raj. While the Ghadar Party's actions took place in Punjab, many of the party's members, including Khankhoje, lived and operated from within Canada and the United States. Maia Ramnath, *Haj to Utopia: How the Ghadar Movement Charted Global Radicalism and Attempted to Overthrow the British Empire* (Berkeley: University of California Press, 2011).

46 Abhidha Dhumatkar, "From Nationalism to Internationalism: Pandurang Sadashiv Khankhoje: Apostle of Indo-Mexican Friendship," *Proceedings of the Indian History Congress* 72, no. 2 (2011): 1124.

47 For more on the appearance of Khankhoje's portrait and research in Rivera's murals, see Soto Laveaga, "Largo Dislocare," 24–25. For more on the decommissioned mural, see "Diego Rivera: Fiery Crusade of the Paint Brush," *New York Times*, April 2, 1933; "Rockefellers Ban Lenin in the RCA Mural and Dismiss Rivera," *New York Times*, May 10, 1933; Catha Paquette, *At the Crossroads: Diego Rivera and his Patrons at MoMA, Rockefeller Center, and the Palace of Fine Arts* (Austin: University of Texas Press, 2017).

5

From rice research to coconut capital

Diana Martinez

The International Rice Research Institute or the IRRI (see Figure 5.1) and the *Tahanang Pilipino* [Filipino Home], colloquially known as the "Coconut Palace" (see Figure 5.2), appear in every way to be opposites. The high modernist style of the former marks its position on the far reaches of postwar internationalism's endless frontier; the latter meanwhile, designed in a modernized regional idiom, roots the building firmly to a bounded national place. Merely stylistically opposed, the histories behind their design and construction represent distinct though inseparable moments in the complex story of the country's development politics.

While visibly international, the IRRI is not without "context." Approaching the complex, one's view is partially obscured by a screen of coconut palms. While a familiar sight, their precise arrangement in a point grid echoes the exactitude of the building itself. Beyond their swaying trunks the IRRI sits upon a 5 foot-high flat plinth, the battered retaining walls of which are faced in rough volcanic rock—a texture that like the coconut palms grounds the building within a specific environment—a "nature" permitted to appear only if tightly controlled.

FIGURE 5.1 The Headquarters of the International Rice Research Institute.

Source: Rockefeller Archive Center.

FIGURE 5.2 *Tahanang Pilipino* (Filipino Home), colloquially known as the Coconut Palace.

Source: Wikimedia Commons.

DOI: 10.4324/9781003193654-8

Wedged in a fertile flat between Mount Makiling, a dormant volcano, and Laguna de Bay, the Philippines' largest lake, the IRRI is strategically located in the town of Los Baños, at the center of what had long been the source of Manila's fresh water, aquacultural, and agricultural produce. It lies about a two-hour drive south of the capital, the location of the Coconut Palace, a building that unlike the IRRI relentlessly expresses every aspect of its "locality." While its architect, Francisco "Bobby" Mañosa, made elaborate claims about the building's organic relationship to place, the site was far from "natural." Set in the heart of Metro Manila, the palace occupies the corner of a large piece of reclaimed land—a surface set atop a tight grid of concrete piles driven hundreds of feet into Manila's heavily silted bay. Planters bursting with naturalistically grouped copses of coconut trees foreground a building conspicuously built, and purportedly entirely, out of coconut parts. While its architectural language is harder to specify than the IRRI's, one hardly has to read the architect's paeans to the genius of native form to place it within the category of "Critical Regionalism"—Kenneth Frampton's call to adopt modernism's universal progressive qualities without losing sight of geographical and cultural context.[1]

The IRRI's rhythms, low lying forms, and general attitude toward its surrounding landscape directly descend from Eero Saarinen's General Motors Technical Center in Warren, Michigan. Described in *Life Magazine* as GM's "Industrial Versailles," the Technical Center established the standard language of corporate modernism.[2] The style had become synonymous with a certain kind of work, not the industrial labor of the Ford factory but that of "technical research," intellectual labor that centered around administration, design, and engineering.[3] While GM's increasingly remote factories carried on the blue-collar work of industrial production, the Technical Center signaled new global divisions of labor characteristic of the postwar emergence of the multinational corporation.[4] Indeed, the imperative of "research" and its associated formal characteristics tie the GM Center and the IRRI campus together as two iterations of an organizational homology. Driven primarily by lower labor costs, greater capacities for production, and material/resource proximity, GM's corporate model of centralized decision making and decentralized operations was repackaged at the IRRI as an international model of cooperation, though one headquartered in the "developing world" that distributed "shared" knowledge across the globe.

Drawing inspiration from Frank Lloyd Wright's concept of "organic architecture," the Coconut Palace marked a clear departure from IRRIs modernism. While the specifics of Wright's organicism changed over time, in general, his ideas adhered to some basic tenets: emphasis of the site's "natural" features and more broadly the regional landscape; making visible the "innate" nature of materials; and most of all, demonstrating an internal coherence or unity that subsumed everything from window mullions, to furniture, to building systems under a single formal logic. In appealing to the "native genius" of an "*Arkitekturang Filipino*," it was to the authority of Wright's formal systems and organic "philosophy" that Mañosa turned in order to make his claims internationally legible.

Playing specific roles with respect to two different national agricultural development strategies in the two periods described here, the IRRI signifies Philippine leadership's first focus, at the onset of decolonization, on rice—a subsistence crop—before the country made a large-scale shift to coconuts—a cash crop—a changed relationship with the global market represented by the construction of the Coconut Palace. While these two investment strategies reflect distinct development programs, both played a role in shaping what are widely viewed as the dysfunctional turns of Philippine society and its political economy in the postwar period and beyond. Today, the Philippines' high levels of poverty, high crime rates, and lack of economic opportunity are almost solely understood as the lasting effects of Marcos's decadent corruption, his inability to contain radical Communist and Islamic separatist threats, and a general perception of the nation's seemingly endemic technological and cultural "backwardness." However, as this chapter argues, the Philippines' so-called dysfunctional economy is a condition that should be understood in the context of larger internationalist and global humanitarian ideologies and the role these played in the Philippines' position within the global economy. Describing the systemic complexities involved in the Philippines' agricultural development programs and their entanglement with the global circulation of building materials, currency, and agricultural commodities will shed new light on the persistent conditions that characterize the Philippines' "underdevelopment."

THE ORIGINS OF THE INTERNATIONAL RICE RESEARCH INSTITUTE

In 1952, two prominent scientists working for the Rockefeller Foundation—Warren Weaver, a polymath, "science advocate," and then director of the Rockefeller Foundation's Division of Natural Sciences and Agriculture, and J. George Harrar, director of the RF's Mexican Agriculture Program (MAP), visited several countries in Asia to familiarize themselves with the state of rice research—surveying rice farms, visiting scientific and educational institutions, and speaking with government officials (see Nikki Moore's chapter (Chapter 4) in this volume). In October of 1954 the two presented a paper based on their findings to Rockefeller Foundation trustees. Declaring a "real need for an international rice research institute in Asia," Weaver and Harrar suggested a radical departure from the RF's previous country-specific approach, which had structured Harrar's work in Mexico. The weakness of the country-based programs was that sponsoring institutions had been seen as inserting themselves too conspicuously into national politics. By contrast, the new rice research institute, built in the spirit of "international cooperation," would furnish "a basis for international friendships and understanding" and contribute "toward a pattern of global living which is undoubtedly a desirable and necessary part of the future."[5] Other arguments for the international model included concentrating the best experts in a single place, financial savings related to efficiency, sharing of expensive instrumentation, and limiting the production of papers to a single or limited set of languages, which Weaver argued would facilitate the dissemination of scientific knowledge. Most notably, however, the two scientists argued that the basic problems concerning rice were not local but "*universal* problems" in which "(m)any of the . . . fundamental physiological, biochemical, and genetic problems are . . . independent of geography and . . . (thus) independent of political boundaries."[6]

Despite the paper's favorable reception, the Rockefeller Foundation (RF) lacked the funds to meet its ambitions. This changed one day in August of 1958, when Harrar and Robert Chandler, a horticulturalist and eventual founding director of the IRRI, were invited to join a group of Ford Foundation (FF) officers for a luncheon, the purpose of which was to discuss cooperation between the Rockefeller and Ford Foundations on the establishment of an agricultural university in Lyallpur, Pakistan (Faisalabad). As Chandler recalled, the IRRI was an unusual project for the FF to fund. Unlike the RF, which viewed its work in the broadest terms, that is, the application of *science* to the universal category of *humanity*, the Ford Foundation focused on limited units of intervention, that is, villages, farms, schools, public administration, etc. Such was the case with the FF's early efforts in Lyallpur, a rural development program that placed too much emphasis, in Chandler's opinion, on the inherent benefits of a moralizing "self-help" strategy, the failure of which, Chandler argued, lay in its dependence upon the labor and knowledge of "uneducated and unexperienced village workers" instead of relying upon "hard science" to increase crop yields.

Whatever the case, by the end of the lunch, Forrest "Frosty" Hill, one of the attending FF officers, was fully convinced of the proposal's worthiness and concluded the meeting with a soft agreement to fund the rice research institute. Realizing what was once a pipe dream for the RF scientists, this agreement inaugurated a new era of collaboration between the Rockefeller and the Ford Foundations as a supranational combine. In Hill's words, "we've got money, we've got similar purposes . . . you've got the experience, you've been abroad in these places, you know how to run it, let's get together and see what we can do."[7]

Matters moved quickly following that first meeting. In search of a site, Weaver and Harrar determined that India lacked the infrastructure to support such an institute. Meanwhile, Japan and Taiwan, as relatively advanced producers, were not in need of the direct benefits such an institute could offer. The Philippines offered several advantages. First, it was in need. For many years it had been importing rice at unsustainable levels. The Philippines also enjoyed good relations with all of the potential beneficiary nations. Additionally, English was more widely spoken in the Philippines (per capita) than any other nation in Asia—the result of an intensive English education program instituted during the American colonial period. Weaver and Harrar were also impressed by research already being conducted at the University of the Philippines (UP) College of Agriculture in Los Baños; an institution established fifty years prior, in the early years of the American colonial period, and modeled directly after American land-grant universities. The university had also already received significant funding for various projects from both the Rockefeller and the Ford Foundations. However, not only was it already an international center for agricultural research, much of its faculty were American trained, which facilitated interactions between RF scientists and the UP faculty. It was, in sum, largely on account of various legacies of American colonialism that made the Philippines, and Los Baños in particular, an obvious site for the IRRI.

THE "LOCAL" ARCHITECT AND THE AMERICAN CONSULTANT

Moving to the Philippines in September of 1960, Chandler's first task was to find a local architect. Beginning with a tour of Manila, the first buildings to catch his eye were those of the new World Health Organization (WHO), designed by Alfredo J. Luz. A recent graduate of the University of California–Berkeley, Luz was well versed in contemporary trends of American architectural design. Heavily influenced by the work of Eero Saarinen, the WHO's auditorium was a barely modified version of MIT's Kresge auditorium, while other elements were variations on the modernist idiom first standardized at the GM Technical Center. Luz's adaptations included the introduction of a deep façade of vertical louvers, which protected the building's users from the direct rays of the tropical sun. These details made little difference to Chandler, who was mostly interested in the fact that the WHO had been constructed of mostly imported materials, meaning Luz had experience with purchasing from foreign suppliers.

While Luz was largely responsible for the design, and while Chandler (both believing in Luz's abilities and for reasons of efficiency) resented the idea that an additional architect was needed, the Ford Foundation wanted to involve a prominent US architect. They selected Ralph Walker, founding partner at Voorhees, Walker, Foley, and Smith (VWFS). The firm had not only worked with the Foundation before but also wrote the authoritative book on the design of the modern laboratory.[8] Simply titled *Laboratories*, the book outlined many of the principles first explored in VFWS's campus designs for General Electric and Bell Labs, where VWFS first proposed individual lab modules, each with benches that looked out upon the bucolic landscape of Murray Hill, New Jersey. These modules, arranged around open areas called "Idea Factories" included redundant and/or stretched circulation spaces that encouraged a traffic of free interchange between specialists from different fields as they traversed the single interconnected campus.[9]

At the time of the Philippines commission, VWFS's Bell Labs approach, which introduced the concepts of modularity and knowledge sharing by seeding chance encounters was a model "universally agreed upon"—codified in the architectural press, research-management trade journals, special laboratory design handbooks, and scores of built projects.[10] Still, Luz's design owes more to Saarinen's influence on Luz than it does to Walker's oversight, though Saarinen's work was itself, as Reinhold Martin describes in *Organization Complex*, a topological transformation of the VWFS approach. This adaptation can be seen in Saarinen's then recently completed Bell Laboratories in Holmdel, New Jersey, a building that Martin argues inverts the VWFS model by "replacing workers sitting at tables looking out windows" with an organized community of *introverts* inhabiting the "deep space" of air-conditioned office buildings illuminated by fluorescent light. The same inversion happens at IRRI, though here, introverts turn away from their lush surrounds in order to focus on the vast realm of genetic information bound up within tiny grains of rice.

The "deep space" of the design was designed to accommodate the "universal problems" associated with rice research—problems not related to the Philippine context but reducible to biochemistry, genetics, and physiology—aspects of "hard science" that required isolation from the external environment. Programs that demanded a greater degree of isolation, such as the spectroscopy and isotope-counting laboratories, were placed deep within the building's interior, while offices and trainees' benches were placed closer to the exterior. As was the case with the WHO, Luz's contribution lay in adapting Saarinen's system to the tropical climate. His most notable modification to this end was a walkway that surrounded both buildings, sheltered by slender aluminum columns, which, like the deep louvers of the WHO, shaded the interior windows and the buildings' inhabitants from the radiant heat of tropical light. This walkway, a sort of late modernist *stoa*, pushed the "idea factory" to the exterior of the building. Casual encounters, where new ideas might cross fertilize, happened under the sheltered colonnade that mediated between the inwardly focused laboratory and a gridded green vista of experimental rice paddies, which were, as I will discuss shortly, themselves extensions of the laboratory. This relationship to the working landscape, reconfigured the VWFS-Saarinen laboratory topology by orienting the gaze of introverts once again toward the exterior—rendering the *world as laboratory*.

By the time Luz designed the IRRI, the "idea factory," and associated innovations, first introduced at Bell Labs, were ubiquitous and internalized by American trained practitioners like Luz. Indeed, while Luz welcomed Walker's input, in the end, the American was hardly needed. Effectively, Walker's main role was to endow the design with a stamp of American authority. While his role at the IRRI was minimal, Walker characterized foreign expertise in the tropics (he executed dozens of projects in the Caribbean) as "a new type of imperialism [based on] specialized knowledge generously given to backwards peoples."[11] Despite his imperious derogations of tropical natives, when Walker first visited the Philippines in October of 1960, he was deeply impressed by Luz, and he commented to Chandler after seeing Luz's design, "these boys are good. I wish I had them in my shop in New York!"[12] Accordingly, Walker made only minor changes to the design; he included the use of volcanic rock to line the retaining walls and planted coconut palms near the buildings as a means of returning context to the site—a coconut grove before it was acquired by the IRRI.[13]

Though a seemingly minor detail, the reference to coconuts drew from Walker's lifelong approach to design. A pioneer of Art Deco, Walker took modern ornament seriously. Rejecting what his decorator and frequent collaborator Hildreth Meière described as the "asceticism of Left-wing Modernists," Walker emphasized architectural finishes and applied art—upholstery, carpets, murals, and mosaics—and not industrially produced steel or glass as the standard bearers of modernist meaning.[14] Exemplifying this approach were the opulent surfaces of Walker's Irving Trust Building. There, three decades before his association with the IRRI, Walker specified a thin, luminous layer of Philippine capiz shell to gild the elaborate faceted ceiling of the tower's top floor "Grand Lounge." The walls meanwhile were covered in a gold and red fabric based on Native American feathered headdresses. Combining the symbology of an almost annihilated native culture with materials yielded from a recently acquired colony served up every Old-World Orientalist trope and tragedy for a New Imperial American Age. For Walker, however, this use of expressive décor mitigated the inhuman scale and anonymous logics of industrial architecture and culture. Despite the fact that the IRRI's organization derived from VWFS's "modular" innovations, it was the communicative function of the coconut palms and the volcanic rock cladding that were Walker's most significant contribution.

Under Walker's influence, Luz became concerned by his design's lack of cultural references. Shortly after Walker's second visit, in a move uncharacteristic for an otherwise committed modernist, Luz proposed replacing his colonnade of aluminum mullions with a series of precast concrete arches. Luz promised that while this less "ascetic" treatment expressed something of the Philippines' colonial architectural heritage, it would not affect the project's interior arrangement, ostensibly Chandler's primary concern. When Luz presented the idea to Chandler, however, the geneticist commented that it gave the buildings a "more cloistered look than was strictly in keeping with a scientific institution."[15] When the scheme was presented to the other scientists and officers of the Rockefeller and Ford Foundations, they voted to retain the original, modern, more "scientific" design.[16]

INTERNATIONAL SOIL

IRRI's internationalism was articulated not only through the building's introverted topology, universal imperative, and ambiguous relation to its surroundings but also by physical alterations to the site itself, quite literally, to its *soil*. Foregrounding Luz's modernist complex was an 80 hectare experimental rice paddy engineered as an international patchwork of ersatz tropical environments. Each plot was filled with imported soils from, for example, Java, the Mekong Delta, and the Plain of Jars. Underneath the soil, an intricate network of underground pipes allowed individual plots to replicate the rainfall and drainage patterns of any part of the tropical zone. Thus, the vista that the scientists looked out toward was not the Philippines as such but rather a pixelated grid of a miniaturized and rationalized Asia. The point of this international palette, however, was not to breed rice strains that catered to particular climatic conditions. Rather, it was to test the hardiness of a truly international breed—a strain of rice that could flourish in a variety of environments. This breed would allow the IRRI to avoid what Chandler considered the "failure" of the FF approach, which in his opinion lay in its dependence upon untrained village workers "unequal to the task of helping farmers." The IRRI's goal, in other words, was to create a grain of rice that withstood what Chandler saw as myriad disadvantages facing the "developing" world, not the least of which were varied soil conditions and the assumed ignorance of its village populations.

Erasing local contingencies was a strategy also used to attract a multinational coterie of top-notch scientists to the Philippines. Looking to establish an attractive standard of living, Chandler directed Luz toward his early days in Manila, where Chandler and his wife spent time socializing at the exclusive Manila Polo Club. Speaking at length with Luz about the club's swimming pool, the couple asked Luz to replicate its crystal blue hue for their own pool at the IRRI. Attention to such detail was appended to specifications that brought the IRRI living quarters in sync with the living conditions of the "developed world." Officers' quarters included washers, dryers, and individual generators, amenities that allowed the grantees to live isolated from the area's poorly maintained infrastructural grid. Astonished by the IRRI's luxurious accommodations, a visiting grantee from a Ford Foundation village development project commented that "What this seems to say . . . is that IRRI residents should never be without electricity and water . . . none of us (here) are in that enviable situation."[17] Chandler replied that the homes were not only for Americans, but for Asian grantees: "From their air-conditioned offices and living rooms, trainees from Karachi to Saigon would view the problem of underdevelopment from the vantage point of modernity."[18]

The IRRI's autonomous infrastructure was matched by the careful crafting of the institution's international status. Even before Chandler set foot on the Philippines, President Carlos Garcia issued an executive order that made the IRRI the first tax-exempt research foundation in the Philippines. IRRI's status as a "nonprofit, nonstock, philanthropic organization" insulated the institution from a variety of statist responsibilities. To bring the costs of building the IRRI to an absolute minimum, Harrar also proposed a "philanthropic exchange rate" for the conversion of US dollars to Philippine pesos. Thus, perhaps counterintuitively, savings in construction materials (which came into the country tariff free) were another strong motivation for specifying American materials.[19] Arrangements such as these perpetuated certain advantages for international "aid" organizations. Filipino enterprises—both large corporations and small domestic farms and firms—received no such benefits. Relatedly, traditional farming methods became untenably expensive, exerting a devastating effect on small farmers. In sum, the IRRI not only created an island of physical, economic, and infrastructural stability, at large it contributed to increasing levels of economic instability.

"PROGRESS IS A GRAIN OF RICE"

In 1966, only four years after the official dedication of the IRRI, Allied leaders with forces in South Vietnam led by a beleaguered President Johnson and the recently inaugurated Ferdinand Marcos descended upon two sites with high symbolic value to the United States—Corregidor Island and Los Baños—to attend the Manila Summit, the purpose of which was an attempt to negotiate a peace deal between Allied and North Vietnamese forces. The two sites were selected to demonstrate two different kinds of war. Corregidor, an island located at the entrance to Manila Bay, was the site of one of the most consequential battles of World War II. Los Baños was the site of a new kind of war, which in Johnson's words was "the only important war that really counts . . . [one] against poverty, against disease, and against ignorance . . . illiteracy, and against hungry stomachs."[20] With his stirring speech—delivered amidst the IRRI's experimental rice paddies—Johnson, Marcos, and the IRRI scientists officially introduced IR8, more popularly known as "The Miracle Rice," to the world (see Figure 5.3).

FIGURE 5.3 IRRI Director Robert Chandler explaining the importance of semi-dwarfness in IR8 to US President Lyndon Johnson and Philippine President Ferdinand Marcos. Also in the photo are Peter Jennings (standing) and Hank Beachell, the IRRI breeders responsible for IR8's development.

Source: Rockefeller Archive Center.

First bred in 1962 and yielded from the very first round of hybridization, IR8 was the eighth of thirty-eight crossbred varieties. The result, scientists effused, had the potential to end world hunger.[21] IR8 matched all eight characteristics belonging to an "ideal plant type" predefined by the IRRI: including a short stature to avoid wasting materials on stalk; a dark green color to absorb sunlight better; rigidity, to allow for machine harvesting; regional interchangeability; and of course higher yield. A perfectly timed debut, IR8's arrival in 1965 coincided with an El Niño year—a shift in weather patterns that promised famine conditions across Asia. That same year, US ground forces first arrived in Vietnam. Both conditions renewed the urgency of IRRI's mission, now charged with proving the American claim that free men ate better. It was also an election year in the Philippines in 1965, and rice was at the center of both leading presidential candidates' campaigns. The incumbent, Diosdado Macapagal, campaigned on the strength of his relationship with the United States, touting a successful trip to the United States in October of 1964. Anticipating catastrophic shortages, he secured a pledge of 25,000 tons of free rice and an additional 100,000 tons to be purchased under the so-called "Food for Peace Act."[22] Ferdinand Marcos, meanwhile, promoted a potential future of permanent food security, aligning himself with the IRRI's global "Green Revolution" by campaigning on the slogan "Progress is a Grain of Rice." Marcos, aided by the tailwind of a corruption scandal, won in a landslide.

Under the auspices of the Green Revolution, biology became the province, if not the property, of a transcendent meta-state, the domain not of nations but of Knowledge. Rice research today provides 75% of rice varieties grown, varieties that have increased potential yields from 4 to more than 10 tons per hectare per crop.[23] Lodging internationalism into the grain itself, the IRRI produced not only biopolitical subjects but actual new forms of biological life. Translating Enlightenment ideals into genetic code, Green Revolution projects supplanted old universal humanist values with new global "humanitarian" benchmarks. Its successes, expressed in the quantifiable terms of minimum calorie counts and factors of increased yield, rendered the "developing" world as a place where survival supplanted living.

Following the election, Marcos sharply aligned his image and political program with the aims of this global humanitarianism. Accordingly, he filled his cabinet with Harvard-trained technocrats, many of whom served on IRRI's board. Shortly after his inauguration, Marcos consummated the relationship between foreign aid institutions and his national development policy by inaugurating SPREAD, a USAID initiative approved by Chandler, which introduced a large-scale multiplication of IR8 field trials. USAID also began to distribute IR8 (dependent upon both fertilizers and pesticides) in a package with Atlas and Esso farm chemicals, while another leading manufacturer of farm chemicals, Caltex, built a nationwide distribution network.[24] That corporations benefitted from IRRI's work is no coincidence: while IRRI officers claimed that "hard science" operated above the political fray, they understood the dependence of "modern" breeds on industrial chemical inputs. That is to say, while the stated ideological commitments of internationalist scientists were to the universal human subject, those professed benefits were tightly bound to the success of multinational corporations.

DEBT AND DICTATORSHIP: CHARACTERISTICS OF INTERNATIONALISM

Soon after his inauguration, Marcos and his technocrats began to focus on ambitious infrastructural projects—irrigation, roads, schools, and communications infrastructures, a development strategy patterned after the Philippine relationship with the Ford and

Rockefeller Foundations. Marcos's infrastructural projects would, however, mostly be funded through external borrowing from US-based foreign aid and internationalist intergovernmental organizations like the World Bank. Most of the loans were high interest and short term. This pattern of funding construction projects while accumulating massive foreign debt continued unabated until 1970, when Marcos's advisors informed him that for the fiscal year ending in June of 1970, the high interest on the loans would require that the Philippines dedicate more than half of its export earnings to pay for interest.

For a solution, Marcos again looked outwards. In January of 1970, Marcos allowed the Philippines' major official creditors, led by the World Bank and the IMF, to form a "Consultative Group,"[25] which restructured the Philippines' external debt in exchange for Philippine compliance with an IMF stabilization program. That program required that the peso either be sharply devalued or allowed to float. The Philippine government accepted the latter condition, and by years end the peso fell from 3.9 to 6.4 per dollar. The devaluation, "austerity measures," and a forced reorientation of the economy toward the production of export commodities faced bitter political opposition from both the Filipino industrial elite (a capitalist class almost fully represented in the Philippine Congress)[26] who fell victim to the abolition of protectionist laws ordered removed by the World Bank, and the urban working class, whose cheap labor was the main incentive for foreign multinationals to open operations in the Philippines.[27] To circumvent opposition, Marcos declared martial law in 1972, citing a communist threat in the North and a Muslim separatist threat in the South. This move, validated by US and US-based supranational institutions, legitimized Marcos's turn to dictatorial rule in the eyes of an "international community." As Marcos made brutal shows of punishing Communist militias, he busily cleared the path for a host of IMF and World Bank development objectives.

Under the leadership of Robert McNamara, and during martial law, the World Bank drastically stepped up its lending program to the Philippines at the instigation of the US government, whose own aid program was handicapped by democratic pressures to reduce bilateral aid to human rights violators. Not only was the bank unhindered by Marcos' human rights record, martial law made the Philippines more attractive as a "favorite testing ground" in which to push development projects "free from the endless legislative debates of a democracy."[28] In real terms this meant that while overall World Bank lending rose by a factor of three from the early 1970s to fiscal year 1979, loans to the Philippines rose by a factor of eleven, making it the World Bank's eighth-largest recipient of loans. The main significance, however, of the World Bank's post-1972 relationship to the Philippines did not lie in the actual value of its loans but rather in how it commanded Marcos's attention, thus occupying a central position in national policy making.

THE SHIFT TO COCONUTS

Though the IRRI continued to be a much-celebrated example of the powers of international cooperation to serve a putative humanity, IR8 did little for the Philippine economy. The "miracle rice" was not a particularly valuable market commodity. While useful for preventing famine, many considered it unpalatable—both chalky and hardened after cooking. Rice farmers were reluctant to put it on their tables, and more importantly, relative to World Bank and IMF objectives, it did nothing to service the rapidly inflating Philippine debt. Coconuts, not rice, were by this measure the most important crop in the Philippines. The year martial law was declared, coconuts generated between 15% and 20% of Philippine export revenues and accounted for ~20% of total agricultural crop production. In addition to this, according to the United States Agency for International Development (USAID), about a third of all Philippine households derived some income from coconut and related by-products. It was believed that a massive reorganization of the industry would further strengthen an already top-performing cash crop. To facilitate World Bank interventions, Marcos centralized the coconut industry, placing all existing coconut research and development organizations under the authority of the Philippine Coconut Authority.

Attempting to duplicate the science that produced IR8, the World Bank sponsored a plan to introduce a new "precocious and high yielding seed nut"—a hybrid between the West African tall and Malaysian dwarf varieties—a new "target" for the Philippine nation. Almost as quickly as Filipinos were introduced to the image of their modern selves through their modernized diet, they were asked to refocus their attention toward marketing an exoticized version of self by identifying with a new agricultural product cum national symbol— the coconut. On an economic level, the focus on coconuts signaled a shift away from import substitution toward an export-oriented economy. In ideological terms, a coconut economy represented a turn away from food security initiatives, the aim of which was to produce subjects loyal to a capitalist system, toward the world economy as such, the global health of which was assumed to produce salient benefits for nations that assented to the authority of its systems of governance. An investment in coconuts thus oriented Philippine development policy toward the return of "external balance" to its economy by imposing a focus on the payment of its debts.

That the coconut was the Philippines' largest export industry had little to do with a global "taste" for the tropical. In fact, food uses accounted for a fraction of the coconut market. Rather, the coconut's uniquely high saturated fat content made it a universally valuable commodity. This value steeply escalated during World War II, when coconut oil was used as a key ingredient in an improved fuel for flamethrowers, replacing gasoline, whose rapid evaporation limited its ability to burn its targets. In 1943, Dr. Louis Fieser, a Harvard organic chemist, combined naphthenic acid derived from crude oil and palmitic acid derived from coconut oil to produce a gel-like fuel he named napalm (a portmanteau of "na" from naphthenic and "palm" from palmitic). Napalm could be "thrown" greater distances than gasoline, decreasing the danger of blowback in flamethrowers, while clinging to whatever it touched. In creating a sizeable blaze around its target, it also decreased the need for accuracy when dropping bombs. One of its first uses was in the Philippines itself, where it was deployed in the American "liberation" of Japanese-occupied Manila. It is no small irony that what was branded in the Philippines as the "Tree of Life" was used in the manufacture of the fuel that destroyed much of Manila while decimating its population. Notably, the coconut husk also served as an important source of activated carbon, most destined for use in American gas masks. It was the United States' wartime demand for weapons-related coconut products that established the foundation for the Philippines' coconut export economy. In peacetime, coconut glycerin was heavily used in the skin care and cosmetics industries, and before World War I, in its refined and "deodorized" form, coconut oil served as a cheaper substitute for lard and butter.[29] In other words, unlike rice, which merely fed people, the coconut possessed a perpetually diversifying variety of uses in times of both war and peace. Shifting the agricultural economy toward the production of coconuts was thus motivated by the coconut's convertibility, fungibility, and ability to substitute for other things. In short, it was valued for its similarity to currency (see Ateya Khorakiwala, Chapter 17 in this volume).

THE COCONUT PALACE

Completed in 1978, in the fifth year of Marcos' martial law regime, the Coconut Palace was commissioned by first lady Imelda Marcos to serve as an official government guest house. She tapped Mañosa, champion of a modernized Filipino vernacular, for the job. Presenting the coconut as an important marker of cultural identity, the palace was also designed as a showcase for the versatility and export power of the coconut. To illustrate this versatility, Mañosa exhausted the use of coconut as a building material, specifying coco-parquet floors, lacquered coco-laminates, and carpets and wallpaper of both fine and coarse coconut fibers. His centerpiece—a massive coconut and crystal chandelier that dangled above a dining table inlaid with an intricate mosaic of over 40,000 coconut shell fragments (many ceremoniously placed by a long and patient queue of elementary school students)—formed a sublime coconut assemblage that served as an enlivening conversational backdrop for state dinners.

Even the plan, heavily reminiscent of Frank Lloyd Wright's late career use of the hexagonal grid, was, according to Mañosa, derived from coconut—in this case, from its processing logics. "When sewn for planks," Mañosa wrote, "a coconut tree trunk is first shaped into a six-sided column. A fresh coconut is also opened by trimming the husk along six sides." The hexagon was thus used in the inlay pattern on the marble floors, echoed in the shape of the swimming pool, mirrored in the lobby's twin staircases, and repeated throughout the interior's many subtle details. Collectively, the architect continued, "the recurrent hexagonal shapes within and without [lent] a sense of organic unity to the *Tahanang Pilipino*." Extending the coincident logic of abstraction and traditional forms, Mañosa described the building's six-sided domed double roofs—covered in coconut wood shingles—as suggestive of the shape of a "salakot," or farmer's gourd hat.[30]

Unlike the IRRI, which spoke the language of universality, the Coconut Palace communicated in a modernized national idiom. Intended to highlight the Philippines' competitiveness within the global economy, the representational burden of the Coconut Palace was twofold. First, it was to create a strong identity for the coconut, mostly a surreptitious ingredient in its final processed forms. Second, that image had to be bound to a national identity. The challenge placed in front of Mañosa was to fabricate a unifying native symbol for the Philippines, an internally diverse archipelago whose identity was forged through colonization and colonial resistance. It is often forgotten that the Philippines was named after its colonizer, King Philip II. In fact, it was not until Spanish was introduced as a lingua franca that *illustrados* from various corners of the polyglot archipelago could take up the united banner of *rebolusyon*. The representation of a nation bound together by its Hispanization, however, ran counter to the goal of the Coconut Palace, which was to produce a unique, and thus necessarily *native*, national identity.

To do this, Mañosa dug deep into the history of precolonial cultures, which he incorporated in the Coconut Palace as distinct "themes" for each guest room; the Zamboanga, Pampanga, Marawi, Bicol, Mountain Provinces, Iloilo, and Pangasinan. Each culture was placed within their own hexagonal cell and was furnished in artifacts produced in each respective province. The Pamapanga room, for example, showcased crafts carved out of lahar (a slurry of pyroclastic material) from Mt. Pinatubo. The Maranao bedroom, meanwhile, displayed that group's traditional weaving and metalwork.[31] As important as it was to claim the Philippines' precolonial heritage was to Mañosa, this "interest" was shaped by a motivation to make an economic contribution to the nation. In very direct ways, Mañosa advanced this cause by transforming once worthless by-products of coconut oil production into "materials suitable for a luxurious mansion."[32] These coconut finishes were not only saleable products but also served as effective advertisements for the Philippines, carrying with them a meaningful residue difficult to delink from their geographic origins. Viewing "traditional" cultural artifacts against the backdrop of Mañosa's dizzying palette of value-added coco-materials meant that the visitor could view together the skill of traditional artisans with an idea of how that labor might be exploited toward the production of marketable commodities.

The value added to the coconut by cheap labor was, however, eclipsed by the scientific contributions that were the legacy of the IRRI, best demonstrated in the Coconut Palace's most spectacular detail, which by design appeared to be the most "natural." At once emblematic and structural, Mañosa's coconut column was nothing more than an inverted and undressed coconut trunk that met the ground with a simple stainless-steel cap (to prevent end rot). When inverted, the root bulb, the characteristic bulge at the bottom of the tree, served as a ready-made capital—one that in its emergence from the column shaft biologically reified the metaphor of "organicism." The specification of the coconut column was more complex than Mañosa's drawing suggested—its design was not drawn but was rather genetically engineered. Drawing upon the strength of the country's cross-breeding program, Mañosa collaborated with Philippine scientists to develop a cultivar of structural lumber. Dedicating this not yet existing cultivar to the building's notoriously narcissistic patron, he named it *Imelda Madera*. In the end, the quest for Imelda Madera failed. In order to meet his deadline, Mañosa settled for a thin steel piloti sheathed in fiberglass—carefully modeled after the crinkled segments of a coconut tree. In short, this was internationalist architecture in national drag. These distinctions mattered little in that the *Tahanang Pilipino* "succeeded" in its goal of making a robust overture to a doubly defined diversity by conflating the commodity that it pushed with the identity that it forged.

ROBERT MCNAMARA AND UNCTAD V

By speaking in a language of a monumentalized vernacular, the palace seemed to make its primary appeal to a national audience. Yet its most important gesture was in fact outwards. It was, after all, a guesthouse—a symbol, in the architect's words, of "Philippine hospitality." Located directly on Manila Bay, the building captured not only a panorama of its famous sunset but also a clear view of several recently constructed export processing zones—gateways to a global market. The Coconut Palace then was only the most symbolic gesture of the Philippines' willingness and ability to support an agenda oriented toward the development of a trade economy. Fittingly, the building's inauguration was precisely timed to coincide with the fifth United Nations Conference on Trade and Development (UNCTAD), which took place in May of 1979.[33]

While coconut development would at least theoretically enable the return of external balance to the Philippine economy, the coconut's liquidity—its convertibility to capital, the very property that assured World Bank consultants of their sound investment in coconuts—is also the property that made the giant seed a particularly "corruptible" commodity. Coconut capital coursed through many of Marcos's corruption schemes, including the notorious "Coco Levy Fund" scandal. The fund, financed through a tax, the "coco levy," was set up in order to underwrite the development of the coconut industry, with promises that most of the money would be channeled toward scientific research conducted by the Philippine Coconut Authority (PCA). In contrast to the IRRI, the laboratories associated with the PCA were geared not toward the production of a single superior seed but rather toward the production of marketable exports—most of them "value-added" goods—which made use of otherwise disposed of by-products of the already lucrative coconut and palm oil industry.[34] Also, unlike the IRRI, the laboratory architecture of the PCA was prosaic and unremarkable, and the costs negligible compared to that of Marcos's extravagant coconut duck.[35]

Ultimately the Coco Levy fund provided an all-too-convenient vehicle for siphoning money off of the wages and profits of coconut farmers, and much of it would disappear in a cloud of the Marcos's conspicuous consumption.[36] The Coconut Palace was, however, considered a "legitimate" use of the fund in that its intended role was to create market exposure for the coconut. Still, at an estimated cost of US$10 million, it was widely viewed both then and now as the symbol *par excellence* of Marcos Era opulence and corruption. In fact, it was a manifestation and representation of an internationalist development strategy pushed not only by Marcos's infamous cronies and technocrats but by an elite cadre of global players headed by the World Bank.[37] It was at the UNCTAD V conference, just around the corner from the Coconut Palace, that Robert McNamara announced that the World Bank would consider making "structural adjustment loans" to assist developing countries to undertake "needed structural adjustments for export promotion."[38] With this announcement, McNamara disclosed that the World Bank, an institution that long operated in a conservative fashion, would be moving into IMF territory in order to more quickly mobilize funds for projects aimed at reorienting developing economies toward the production of profitable exports. The Philippines was among the first, along with Bolivia, Kenya, Senegal, and Turkey, to receive structural adjustment loans. Placing the history of UNCTAD V and the Coconut Palace together reveals the two central aims of its construction; to shore up the confidence of foreign capital in the coconut industry and to communicate, through the opulence of its hand-made finishes, the skill and commitment of Philippine labor. In sum, it served as an impressive symbol that demonstrated to a global community of statesmen, foreign investors, and creditors the Philippines' dedication to a particular niche within an interdependent global capitalism.

CONCLUSION

While most interpretations of Marcos's building program flatten his architectural ambitions as outcomes of what has been called the dictator's pathological "Edifice Complex," a close examination of both the headquarters for the IRRI and the Coconut Palace tells a more complex story and illuminates how transnational capitalism both works and transforms.[39] In insulating itself from the economic instability of its host countries, the IRRI presented its results as being achievable anywhere. The perceived success of the IRRI hinged precisely on the its locational ambiguity—a necessary precondition for an institution that claimed to benefit humanity at large. Yet the IRRI was not merely a trumpet for internationalism and its stated humanitarian goals. It was a place where internationalism was realized in genetic code. While defenders of the Green Revolution claim that it saved the world from famine, in the process, it impoverished small farmers, introduced a large-scale dependency on chemical inputs, and enriched large multinational corporations.[40]

Drafting off the IRRI's "successes," Marcos initiated countless and expensive infrastructural projects, but unlike the IRRI, these projects were not funded by private foundations but with loans lent by subsidiaries of the UN—most notably the IMF and the World Bank—which, in their push to develop economies and with their ability to distribute loans, transformed the world into a map of creditor and debtor states. The governments of debtor states were impelled to reorient their economies toward satisfying the dictates of their creditors. In this milieu, Marcos found conditions favorable to personal enrichment and the accumulation of power—a power backed by the military force of creditor nations whose desire to implement their policy suggestions trumped any desire to uphold democratic ideals.

In the short time between the construction of the IRRI and the Coconut Palace, there at least appears to be a turn, from an attempt to erase difference through an imperative to modernize—the putative aim of which was to provide for the basic needs for a universal human subject—to an adoption of diversity as a value. Diversity here is of two kinds. The first diversity is strictly economic and tied to a conception of the globe as a collection of varied resources. The second kind of diversity is invoked as a value tied to the integrity of cultural and/or national difference. The adoption of the latter kind of diversity is commonly presented as a corrective to the "oppressive" force of high modernism and colonialism alike. This is taken up as a moral position when framed as an ostensibly more sensitive and critically informed regionalism. If we look past the register of representation, beyond the smokescreens of ideological posturing, we can more clearly see each building's position within subsequent stages in the evolution of the increasingly complex machinery of transnational capitalism. The Coconut Palace, in fact, is both motivated by and demonstrative of an acceleration of the forces set into motion by the IRRI. The vicissitudes of style are revealed here not only as symptomatic, but also as strategically deployed tools of the internationalist institutions that choreographed the emergence of a global economy.

NOTES

1. In *Modern Architecture: A Critical History*, Frampton characterizes Critical Regionalism not as a movement but as a "critical category oriented towards certain common features." Thus, many of the examples that Frampton uses are built before Tzonis and Lefaivre's articulation of the category.
2. "Architecture for the Future: GM Constructs a Versailles for Industry," *Life* (May 21, 1956): 102–107.
3. That "technical" work was considered distinct from industrial work is highlighted by the fact that the closest GM factory—a transmissions factory—was located on a close by but physically separate site in Warren.
4. Not coincidentally, the opening of the Warren Technical Center coincided with the opening of GM's first factory outside of North America, in Bogotá, Colombia.
5. Robert Chandler, *An Adventure in Applied Science: A History of the International Rice Research Institute* (Manila: The International Rice Research Institute, 1992), 2.
6. Ibid.
7. The Ford Foundation endowment was and is approximately three times the size of Rockefeller's.
8. Voorhees, Walker, Smith, and Haines, *Laboratories* (New York: Voorhees, Walker, Foley, Smith, & Haines, 1961).
9. Jon Gertner, *The Idea Factory, Bell Labs and the Great Age of American Innovation* (New York: Penguin Books, 2012), 77.
10. Roland J. Wank, Introduction to *Laboratory Design*, ed. H. S. Coleman (New York: Reinhold Publishing, 1951), 3; quoted in William Rankin, "The Epistemology of the Suburbs," *Critical Inquiry* 36, no. 4 (Summer 2010): 776.
11. Ralph T. Walker, *Ralph T. Walker, Architect of Voorhees, Gmelin, and Walker* (New York: VWFSH, 1957), 225.
12. Ralph T. Walker quoted in Chandler, *An Adventure in Applied Science*, 28.
13. My description of Walker runs contrary to Nick Cullather's in *Hungry World,* where Cullather characterizes Walker as a "modernist." In fact, Walker spent much of his life railing *against* modernism, and in particular against Corbusier's modernist designs for the tropics. Walker preferred adapted "native" solutions to what he viewed as Corbusier's oversimplified cure-all, the brise soleil. More problematically, Cullather makes no mention of Luz or Carlos Arguelles (responsible for IRRI's housing), despite their frequent appearance in the archival material (and the

relative infrequent appearance of Walker in those same archives). Cullather's focus on Walker, and his omission of the Filipino architects advances a narrative consistent with his story of white, Western experts bringing a disastrous modernism to the "Third World."

14. Meière quoted in "The Question of Decoration," *Architectural Forum*, July of 1932. Most information on the Irving Trust Building is from Kate Holliday's "Walls as Curtains: Architecture and Humanism in Ralph Walker's Skyscrapers of the 1920s," *Studies in the Decorative Arts* 16, no. 2 (Spring–Summer 2009): 39–65.
15. Chandler, *An Adventure in Applied Science*, 28–29.
16. Ibid., 29–30.
17. Harry L. Case to George F. Gant, "International Rice Research Institute Budget," October 12, 1966, FF grant files, PA06500055. Quoted in Nick Cullather, "Miracles of Modernization: The Green Revolution and the Apotheosis of Technology," *Diplomatic History* 28, no. 2 (April 2004): 227–254.
18. Chandler, *An Adventure in Applied Science*, 94.
19. Ibid., 10.
20. Lyndon Johnson quoted in *Rice Today: Special Supplement Focusing on IR8* (Los Baños: IRRI, 1996), 25, http://books.irri.org/RT_Supplement-IR8.pdf.
21. IR8 was a cross between a high yield rice variety from Indonesia (PETA) and a dwarf variety from China.
22. US Public Law 480 was signed into law in 1954 under Dwight D. Eisenhower. See also Chapter 17 by Ateya Khorakiwala in this volume.
23. J. L. Maclean, D. C. Dawe, B. Hard, and G. P. Hettel, eds., *Rice Almanac: Source Book for the Most Important Economic Activity on Earth*, 3rd ed. (Wallingford: CAB International, 2002).
24. Wesley C. Haraldson, "The World Food Situation and Philippine Rice Production," *Journal of the American Chamber of Commerce* (February 1966): 59.
25. The "Consultative Group" was modeled after the "Inter-Governmental Group for Indonesia" (IGGI), which directly managed the finance policies of the pro-Western Suharto military clique that overthrew the nationalist Sukarno government in the mid-1960s, Walden Bello et al., *Development Debacle: The World Bank in the Philippines* (San Francisco: Institute for Food Development Policy), 22.
26. Most of whom were or would become Marcos's top political rivals.
27. Bello et al., *Development Debacle*, 27. Marcos provided the World Bank almost absolute power in the field of foreign investment toward "economic development."
28. Armado Castro, quoted in Robin Broad, *Unequal Alliance: The World Bank, the International Monetary Fund, and the Philippines* (Berkeley: University of California Press, 1990), 63.
29. In the 1930s, US dairy farmers threatened by coconut oil's versatility successfully lobbied for an excise tax. Though the tax was placed on all coconut oils, the United States granted the Philippines a preference of 2 cents/pound over "foreign" sources. In the Philippines, tax proceeds were returned to the Commonwealth government, where it made up a significant portion of its annual budget. Because demand for coconut oil did not decrease (in soap making there were few affordable substitutes), the Philippine coconut industry did not suffer. This arrangement demonstrates how the Philippine Commonwealth government leveraged its colonial status toward its benefit. An independent Philippines lost both preferential status and tax revenue. Lloyd P. Rice, "Philippine Copra and Coconut Oil in the American Market," *Far Eastern Survey* (October 9, 1935): 156–161.
30. Eric S. Caruncho, *Designing Filipino: The Architecture of Francisco Mañosa* (Manila: Tukod Foundation, 2003), 22.
31. Ibid., 41.
32. Ibid., 20.
33. According to an often repeated story, Pope John Paul II refused to be the first guest at the Coconut Palace, citing indulgence in the face of overwhelming poverty. In fact, the Coconut Palace was rushed to completion not for the Pope's visit (in 1981) but for the UNCTAD V conference in 1979. Following the Pope's refusal, Imelda invited Brooke Shields and George Hamilton to be the Palace's first guests. This story paints a picture of Imelda and Ferdinand as corrupt and ostentatious spendthrifts. While correct, this characterization problematically deemphasizes the far larger role that both the United States and US-led international organizations played in impoverishing the Philippines.
34. While a multi-billion dollar industry today, coconut water was mostly disposed of in the 1960s. The technology did not exist to ship it in shelf-stable form. In 1949, a Filipina chemist named Teódula Kalaw África invented "nata de coco," which transformed coconut water into chewy cubes by introducing *Komagataeibacter xylinus* to produce a gel of microbial cellulose. A huge variety of shelf-stable coconut products became popular additions to Filipino cuisine starting in the 1950s.
35. "Ducks," a term coined by Denise Scott Brown and Robert Venturi, explicitly represent their function through their shape. This typology is defined in opposition to "decorated sheds," generic structures with appended signs that denote their purpose. Both types accept the central function of architecture as communicative, considered a central feature of postmodern architecture.
36. Money siphoned from the Coco Levy Fund was used to start the United Coconut Planters Bank and to buy a majority stake in the San Miguel Corporation, then controlled by one of Marcos's political rivals. These were vehicles through which Marcos and his cronies amassed huge amounts of cash.

37 Before 1974, reconstruction and development loans provided by the World Bank (WB) were small. The size and number of loans greatly increased following Johnson's appointment of Robert McNamara as WB President. McNamara implored WB treasurer Eugene Rotberg to seek new sources of capital outside of the northern banks that were the primary sources of revenue to increase the capital available to the bank. One consequence of "poverty alleviation lending" was the rapid rise of Third World debt. From 1976 to 1980, developing world debt rose at an average annual rate of 20 percent.
38 Robert McNamara, quoted in Patrick Allan Sharma, *Robert McNamara's Other War, the World Bank and International Development* (Philadelphia: University of Pennsylvania Press, 2017), 138.
39 Gerard Lico, *Edifice Complex* (Quezon City: Ateneo de Manila University Press, 2003).
40 Recent scholarship argues that the Green Revolution led not to faster agricultural growth or more food per capita but only to a higher percentage of wheat in the diet. See Glenn Davis Stone, "New Histories of the Indian Green Revolution," *The Geographical Journal* (February 1, 2019), https://rgs-ibg.onlinelibrary.wiley.com/doi/full/10.1111/geoj.12297.

6

"The city as a housing project"

Training for human settlements at the Leuven PGCHS in the 1970s–1980s

Sebastiaan Loosen, Viviana d'Auria, and Hilde Heynen

INTRODUCTION

The "science" of human settlements was given official recognition on the occasion of Habitat, the United Nations Conference on Human Settlements, held in Vancouver in 1976. There, the problem of "shelter" was given official patronage on an international basis as part of a new global governance apparatus.[1] The event endorsed human settlements as a nebulous but powerful terrain of action for experts in socioeconomic planning and urban management without dismissing the involvement of the design disciplines as key contributors to technical assistance and humanitarian aid.[2] The use of both "habitat" and "human" as epithets is telling: both terms, strongly linked with the impact of decolonization, had been cultivated within post-war architectural debates and were now mobilized to accompany the rhetoric of "planetary housekeeping".[3] While "habitat" underlined the idea of crafting an all-encompassing home for mankind on earth, the recurrence of "human" promoted a balancing act when it came to those global transformations occurring under the aegis of "development."

The presence of "Man" and "Earth" as simultaneously operating objects of management and protection enlarged the spectrum of disciplines that, together with urban design and planning, could support the so-called Third World in its path toward "development." Environmental and social sciences, for instance, were increasingly called upon to corroborate approaches to housing and broader urban transformations,[4] gradually becoming part of urban planning and design curricula in Europe, which emulated, with a certain delay, the example of the MIT Center for Urban and Regional Studies initiated in 1957.[5]

Once it was firmly placed on the international agenda, the concept of human settlements followed two trajectories that were not perfectly aligned. On the one hand, it became part of an increasingly professionalized discourse within intergovernmental organizations such as the UN and the World Bank. On the other hand, the concept found a home in many academic schools, where it was central to research and educational programs, often in collaboration with national development agencies, but where it was also elaborated with a certain degree of autonomy vis-à-vis the intergovernmental approach to the issue. By critically contextualizing and reviewing the establishment of the Post Graduate Centre Human Settlements (PGCHS) at the KU Leuven, Belgium, this contribution tackles the professional legitimacy of architects

DOI: 10.4324/9781003193654-9

and urban designers as manifested throughout various training programs established to tackle development issues. Thus, it contributes to understanding how the field of human settlements was consolidated not only by profiling a particular kind of expertise within professional practice but also through its iterations with academic research and pedagogies.

This chapter engages with the PGCHS's theoretical framing of the human settlements endeavor throughout its maturation phase, where it sought to establish international connections, developed a UN-mandated short-term training program, and set up an institutional framework that assembled its many dispersed activities into a holistic approach toward the built environment. In focusing on the center's self-conceived role within the rising development impetus, and in particular on the personal experiences that informed two of its key protagonists, Han Verschure and André Loeckx, this chapter investigates how the center engaged with the accumulation of experiences with so-called Third World participants and projects. In zooming in on the rather unusual way of mobilizing contemporaneous theoretical concepts in making sense out of these experiences, it also scrutinizes the leeway left for individuals to negotiate certain tendencies inherent to the development apparatus (see Arindam Dutta, Chapter 1 in this volume).

THE POSTWAR LANDSCAPE OF TRAINING

During its first decades of existence, the United Nations' policies toward "developing countries" increasingly identified training as a key component in the response to those countries' "need for assistance." In 1963, the UN established an autonomous training and research institute called UNITAR (United Nations Institute for Training and Research) mandated to increase UN effectiveness and increase national action impact. In its official account, it is described as follows:

> The UNITAR's creation occurred at the most opportune time in the history of the UN, coinciding with the addition of 36 States since 1960, including 28 African States. That unprecedented wave of decolonization created a critical need for assistance, as many of the newly-independent States lacked the capacity to train their young diplomats.[6]

While the UNITAR targeted public policy officials and young diplomats, other branches of the UN had attended to training in architecture and urban planning. Early UNTAA (United Nations Technical Assistance Administration) missions in the 1950s had already emphasized the importance of long-term university-based planning education in the "developing" world. An early key-figure was the Yugoslav Ernest Weissmann (1903–1985), Assistant Director of the Town and Country Planning Section of the UN Division of Social Affairs, who envisioned a global system of research and training institutes.[7] Weissmann's vision notwithstanding, the establishment of such institutes was kindled more by particular individuals and contingencies than by a firmly decisive policy. The establishment of the School of Architecture and Community Planning at the Middle East Technical University (METU) in Ankara, for instance, was a consequence of Charles Abrams's (1901–1970) changing the scope and content of his 1954 UNTA mission.[8] Informed by the particular conditions in Turkey, in stressing how education in housing and planning would be an essential component of sound policy development, Abrams countered the UN's general unwillingness to engage directly in establishing schools—a reluctance that was based on the debated role of foreign experts. Comparably, also in 1954, Jaqueline Tyrwhitt's (1905–1983) engagement with Indonesia would begin, leading to the foundation of the School of Regional and City Planning at the Bandung Institute of Technology (BIT) in 1959.[9]

In this context, Weissmann was regularly receiving requests for UNTA fellowships and overall UN patronage from a variety of schools and training staff. While no real consensus and direction seemed to emerge in the choice of schools supported, this can largely be seen as a consequence of the fact that, as Weissmann himself reminded a large majority of his interlocutors, technical assistance resources were allocated by governments themselves, and it was they "alone [who] must decide whether or not these funds should be used for fellowships, [as well as on the] field of training and place where such training is desired."[10] Nonetheless, various communications from 1957 onwards testify to the growing agreement about the idea that physical planning was a distinct field requiring an interdisciplinary training that could support national and regional development. At the time, this mainly meant supporting regional planning—including river basin development schemes—mostly building on the UN Seminar on Regional Planning held in Tokyo in 1958.[11] Thus, besides the METU and the BIT, by 1961, the list of planning schools that had received UN assistance included departments in Peru, Colombia, Venezuela, and India.[12] Other countries, such as Ghana, had been the object of advisory missions to evaluate the establishment of regional training centers.[13]

As attested by Charles Abrams, there was a strong need for "South-oriented" training programs: by the early 1960s, there was still "not a single comprehensive university course in the problems of international urbanization, housing, or international urban land economics," which in turn was needed in order "to develop a pool not only of visiting experts but of 'inperts,' i.e., qualified nationals within the countries themselves."[14]

Thus, universities in Europe and North America also contacted Weissmann to inform him about their new physical planning training programs, catering to this need by offering trainings that most mid-career professionals would not find in their home countries—often at the instigation of staff with a track record as UN advisors. In this regard, the Canadian UN consultant and Head of the Department of Community and Regional Planning at the University of British Columbia (UBC), Peter Oberlander (1922–2008), would state vis-à-vis the physical planning course launched at UBC in 1958 that it was a unique technical assistance program because it departed from the approach conducted until then, whereby future planners would either be trained in foreign institutions in existing programs or in regional training centers which might be established in the "developing countries" themselves. Rather, the UBC program could combine the best advantages of both forms by offering "a training geared to the needs and conditions of the developing countries, access to a wide range of views, library materials, course possibilities and personal experience in a university setting."[15] Likewise, now little known initiatives such as the full-time course in town and country planning led by the Tropical Study Group in Birmingham and the four-month course in comprehensive planning at the Institute for Social Studies in The Hague similarly requested UN action for the promotion of a new educational offer.[16]

Some of these were developed alongside new institutional actors established to cater to an emerging market opened up by the myriad aid programs' need for expertise. In Greece, for instance, after launching the Graduate School of Ekistics (GSE) in October 1959 to prepare students for international practice with the aim of transcending conventional planning education, Constantinos Doxiadis (1913–1975) founded the Athens Center for Ekistics (ACE) in 1963 as a place to link research, documentation, international cooperation, and education with the support of the Ford Foundation.[17]

Other training experiences in Europe found their footing in institutes with a historical pedigree, in some cases tied to earlier colonial involvements, such as those at the Development Planning Unit (DPU) in London and of the Institute for Housing Studies (IHS) in Rotterdam (both recently turned 60). The DPU started life in 1954 as the Department of Tropical Architecture at the Architectural Association.[18] As Hannah le Roux and Jiat-Hwee Chang have shown, it grew out of colonial knowledge networks dealing with "tropical building"—a term sufficiently neutral to allow depoliticized utilization in a postcolonial context.[19] Initially inspired and animated by committed architects such as Otto Koenigsberger (1908–1999), Maxwell Fry (1899–1987), and Jane Drew (1911–1996), the program in tropical architecture waxed and waned depending on the amount of incoming students and the success rate in obtaining financial support from various sources. Framed by Koenigsberger as a program whose job it was "to do itself out of a job" (since it was training trainers who would at a certain point be able to take over the job themselves), the DPU reinvented itself several times, identifying new challenges and approaches to legitimize its continued existence.[20] Whereas it was originally understood to be a special program aiming at development cooperation, it gradually became fully integrated in the academic structure of the Bartlett School, part of the University College London (UCL). In its current reincarnation, the DPU combines academic research and postgraduate teaching, drawing resources from research grants and tuition fees rather than solely from development aid programs.[21]

A similar evolution characterizes the Rotterdam based IHS (currently the Institute for Housing and Urban Development Studies). Its history goes back to the Bouwcentrum ("Center for Building"), a facility created immediately after the war in response to the Dutch housing shortage. Its objective was to investigate and propagate building technologies and methodologies that would foster fast production of affordable housing. A decade later, in response to an increasing, international demand for its expertise, the Bouwcentrum established an "International Course on Building" in 1958, which evolved in the early 1970s into an independent, international training institute, the Bouwcentrum International Education (BIE), which would transform into the IHS in 1982. After several decades of standing on its own, it became integrated into the Erasmus University Rotterdam in 2004.[22]

The "Second World" (the Communist bloc) was also quite active in development cooperation programs related to the fields of architecture and planning, as the research of Łukasz Stanek and others is unfolding.[23] And there, too, training programs for architects and planners were organized, such as the "International Postgraduate Course of Urban and Regional Planning for Developing Countries" at the Technical University of Szczecin, Poland, which lasted from 1966 to 1992.[24]

For other schools, it was the 1976 Habitat Conference that provided the impulse to start working in the field of human settlements or gave new research impetus and legitimacy to existing programs, as in the case of UBC, which founded a Centre for Human Settlements (CHS) in the wake of the conference.[25] The Vancouver conference not only put human settlements high on the urban design and planning agendas, it also bolstered an increase in training efforts. One of the "Guidelines for Action" formulated at the Vancouver conference stated that "international and national institutions should promote and institute education programs and courses in the subject of 'human settlements.'"[26] Thus, among the conference's follow-up activities was the coming together, in August 1978 in Enschede, the Netherlands, of experts solicited by the UN Centre for Housing, Building and Planning (UNCHBP)—shortly before it was absorbed in the new UN Centre for Human Settlements

(UNCHS, a.k.a. UN-Habitat) that same year. The goal of the experts' meeting was to examine the training programs that would be "necessary to improve the slums and squatter areas in urban and rural communities throughout the Third World," making it the time to significantly review training courses.[27] In this vein, higher education institutions and other training centers rearticulated their offer to encompass the human settlements agenda.

Among the 41 participants to the Enschede meeting in 1978 was Han Verschure (born 1942), founder and driving force of the Post Graduate Centre Human Settlements (PGCHS) in Leuven, which—in tune with the course of events highlighted here—was gradually taking shape in those years and was establishing a UN-mandated training program on human settlements.

A CASE IN POINT: THE LEUVEN PGCHS

In contrast to the DPU and the IHS, the founding of the center in Leuven was not immediately tied to a colonial prehistory. Although the University of Leuven had close ties with Lovanium University in Kinshasa, founded in 1954 in the former Belgian Congo, these connections did not stretch to the architecture department. The urge to initiate a human settlements center rather came from the ambition to strengthen the international profile of the university, as well as from a more general post-1968 desire of reconnecting architecture to a social agenda that had somehow been lost in the preceding decades. In 1968, the initially bilingual university had split into Dutch- and French-speaking counterparts, resulting in a brain drain for both parties, especially for the Flemish side. Hence, under the impulse of its first rector, Pieter De Somer, the Katholieke Universiteit Leuven (KUL) sought to strengthen its international ties, appeal, and know-how.[28] The PGCHS grew out of an internationally oriented program that started to be developed when rector De Somer attracted Verschure to the architecture department for his considerable experience abroad.[29]

After graduating in Architecture in Brussels in 1966, Verschure had further specialized in urbanism and planning at the Norwegian Institute of Technology in Trondheim with Arne Korsmo (1900–1968) and at the University of Washington, Seattle. In the late 1960s he briefly joined the University of Colorado, Boulder and the Center for Environmental Structure at the University of California, Berkeley, where Christopher Alexander (born 1936) was in the midst of his work on the PREVI competition in Lima, basing his design method on patterns developed from existing settlements.[30] Following a call by systems theorist Kenneth Boulding (1910–1993)—considered a progressive voice amongst the economists at the time for taking "environmental costs" into account—Verschure briefly joined a group of 12 young professionals, tackling issues of environmental planning and policy from an interdisciplinary perspective.[31] Impressed by Charles Abrams's work for the UN, Verschure applied for commissions for the UNCHBP and subsequently worked in Indonesia and various countries in the Middle East.

After being appointed part-time at the KUL in the early 1970s, Verschure combined missions abroad with teaching and research. At the university, he found himself in a fledgling academic environment, where a first generation was exploring the scope of "research in architecture" and where the first PhD in architecture was awarded in 1969, to Jan Delrue (born 1939), a specialist in hospital building and rationalized construction methods.[32] At the same time, at the engineering faculty a general graduate research program saw the light, attracting international students to conduct specialized research.[33] The PGCHS organically grew out of this international research experience. With no proper graduate program in place, the need for one rose with the prospect of a batch of Indonesian students coming to Leuven when an exchange agreement was signed between the KUL and Parahyangan Catholic University in Bandung (UNPAR), an outcome of the two universities' long-lasting ties based upon their shared Catholic background (see Figure 6.1). In the absence of a clear framework for academic research, and with the requirement of obtaining a doctoral degree in order to get full tenure, Verschure's doctoral research was devoted to establishing a base course for such a graduate program. In the subsequent years, his dissertation on "Housing and Development" would develop into the backbone of the human settlements program in Leuven. Its main hypothesis was simple yet challenging and entirely in the spirit of the 1976 Vancouver conference: a proper housing policy cannot solely rely on "formal" housing programs but requires looking at the city as a whole, both its formal and its informal areas.[34]

Meanwhile, the enthusiasm evoked by the Habitat conference had also resulted in crucial funding opportunities for the PGCHS. Verschure managed to convince the Minister of Development Cooperation to have Belgium be among the first contributors to UN-Habitat, contributing 10 million Belgian Francs (the equivalent of 250.000 Euro) on a yearly basis (which lasted for over 20 years) (see Figure 6.2).[35] This contribution ensured that UN-Habitat would favorably look at Belgian proposals for training courses. Hence, from 1979 to 1993 the short-term UN Training Program "Housing in Development", targeting mid-career professionals from Africa and Asia, was one of the center's main preoccupations, aiming to develop a comprehensive understanding of the housing process. Since the Training Program

FIGURE 6.1 Discussion on a project for a school building in Bandung, c. 1974. From left to right: Jan Delrue (PGCHS), Tam Hway Tak (China), Adjie Harsadi (Indonesia), Han Verschure (PGCHS), Mark Van Naelten (PGCHS), Sandi Siregar (Indonesia), Simion Salaam Abdulahad (Iraq), Miguel Caluza (Philippines), and Jeffrey Kijono Utomo (Indonesia).

Source: KU Leuven, Department of Architecture, archives PGCHS.

FIGURE 6.2 Executive Secretary of UN-Habitat Arcot Ramachandran, Belgian Ambassador to Kenya and the Kenyan-based UN organizations Cristina Funes-Noppen, and Han Verschure at the Headquarters of UN-Habitat, Nairobi, while negotiating the program "Housing in Development," 1979.

Source: KU Leuven, Department of Architecture, archives PGCHS.

was funded directly by Belgium as a multilateral contribution to UNCHS, it had something of a special status, and as a consequence, the PGCHS arguably had more leeway to steer an independent course vis-à-vis UN-Habitat.[36]

From the mid-1980s onwards, another structural feature was crucial to the center's functioning: a continuous stream of Belgian graduates, who became acquainted with the center through optional courses in the regular architecture program, kept working at the center as "conscientious objectors," converting their nine-month military conscription into an eighteen-month service in the socio-cultural sector, constituting a relatively cheap labor force.

By the late 1970s, the PGCHS had grown into a full-fledged center focused on the problems of the built environment in the developing world. It encompassed a patchwork of activities that well exceeded the university's core business. Besides the gradual development of its postgraduate program in human settlements and the UN-Habitat-sponsored short-term training program, the PGCHS had multiple applied research projects running, which were informed by a logic of development cooperation rather than by an urge to produce academic research. These projects were commissioned by a panoply of NGOs and ranged from a self-help housing project in Kigali and a study of pozzolan as an alternative for cement to the development of new housing typologies in Algeria.[37] Thus diffused in a heterogeneous amalgam of projects, the PGCHS's functioning arguably was drawn by the post-Bretton Woods-era landscape of development programs. Operating as a node in a broader conglomerate of governmental, intergovernmental, and nongovernmental organizations, the center responded to the political transformations that had led to state policy-based interventions giving way to more small-scale project-driven endeavors involving a more diverse pool of stakeholders.

FORM, INSTITUTIONS, RESOURCES

In developing its overall approach, the PGCHS relied both on in-house expertise at the KUL and on that of regular visiting experts such as John F. C. Turner (born 1927) of the DPU, Cor Dijkgraaf of the IHS, and Geoffrey Payne (born 1942) of Oxford Polytechnics. John Turner, in particular, played a crucial role in the further development of the PGCHS' intellectual identity. By the time of his involvement, he had gained an international reputation as the main advocate of people's autonomy in designing their dwellings, based on his experiences with squatter settlements in Peru; his ideas had left a substantial mark on the 1976 Vancouver conference's self-help agenda (albeit stripped of its relationship with the autonomy of decision-making); and he had directed courses at renowned institutes such as the MIT, the AA Graduate School and the DPU.[38]

As international expert at PGCHS, Turner suggested a way of working that would long characterize the center's distribution of labor among its staff members. In his 1979 discussion paper, "What to Do About Housing: Its Part in Another Development," Turner outlined three fields of action that would structure the PGCHS approach.[39] Insisting on seeing housing as an activity rather than as a material demand, in a reformist fashion he reframed the challenge of providing adequate housing into identifying the fields of action that could transform the existing housing system for the better. Without claiming any comprehensiveness, Turner identified nine potential "pressure points" to take action and to transform the housing system as whole, grouped in three sets: *Forms*, the forms the housing goods and services take as *ends*; *Resources*, or the *means* by which they are developed; and *Institutions*, or the *ways* in which access to resources and forms is governed (see Figure 6.3).[40]

For Turner, "Forms, Resources, and Institutions" grouped the possible actions in descending order of ease with which changes can be effected and ascending order of impact they have

Fields of Action	PROGRAMMES Establishment	Improvement	Development	Priorities
INSTITUTIONS				
O - organisation	x	x	x	I
R - rules (law, norms)	x	x	x	I
E - exchange (finance)		x	x	II
RESOURCES				
L - land	x	x	x	I
W - work		x	x	II
T - technics		x	x	II
FORMS				
B - boundaries			x	III
N - networks			x	III
S - spaces			x	III

FIGURE 6.3 Scheme of John Turner's fields of action to intervene in a housing system, with stated priorities.

Source: John F. C. Turner, "What to Do About Housing—Its Part in Another Development," in *UN Follow-up Workshop on Housing, Nairobi, 11–29 January 1982: Background Papers* (Leuven: PGCHS, 1982), 8.

on the housing systems. Forms, in other words, was the easiest field of action to intervene in but also the least influential.[41] For a center such as the PGCHS, Turner's well-reasoned identification of different fields of action provided an attractive framework to conceptualize the field of housing as a whole. It combined a comprehensive view on housing with the possibility of being active on different fronts, as any of the discrete fields of action could be a starting-point for change.[42] Even if it served mainly as a pragmatic, organizational framework for the PGCHS to align the dispersed efforts of its staff members, it did manage to build in some guarantees that in each project and design each of these aspects received sufficient attention.

While the themes covered by "Resources" and "Institutions" were quite common in the development context, that of "Forms" was more ambivalent. The IHS and DPU, for instance, embraced Turner's suggestion that housing first of all needed to be addressed from an institutional point of view, for example, through urban management strategies leading to "site and services" or self-help solutions via "incremental development." Also, the more technical themes covered by "Resources," such as climatic design, rationalization of the construction industry, or appropriate technology, were household terms in the field. But under the rubric of "Form," the tripartite structure of collaboration suggested by Turner's framework also carved out a role for some kind of architecture specific knowledge that exceeded the purely technical aspects related to architectural and urban form.

At the PGCHS, this opening took a course of its own. Remarkably, architectural theory, as elaborated in very different contexts by Aldo Rossi in Italy or by Philippe Panerai and Jean Castex in France, was turned to as offering important clues for a better understanding of building and dwelling practices in relation to culture, tradition, and history. There were several factors that led theory to gain currency in this context. What certainly paved the way was that the PGCHS developed its curriculum at a moment when the international community already had a couple of decades of familiarity in training for human settlements. Facing up to the truth that after considerable years of experience there were no signs that these programs were "doing themselves out of a job," as Koenigsberger had put it, this lasting concern motivated substantial changes in the nature of the training on offer, gradually making room for the less tangible sociocultural aspects of the built environment, to which architectural theory sought to contribute.

DPU's history might be taken as somewhat emblematic of ongoing curricular changes in the field, showing an evolution from technical concerns of climatic design in the 1950s (the "Tropical Architecture" paradigm), toward more general planning issues in the 1960s.[43] Inspired by the turbulent years of the late 1960s, more social and political themes would be treated to foster a kind of critical awareness of imperialism and the logic of development itself. Thus, in the 1970s, inspired by work such as Paulo Freire's radically dialogical pedagogy, training programs were further reoriented toward the aim of educating independent intellectuals rather than transmitting partial expert knowledge—which, in the more critical of voices, was considered to reinforce the existing relations of dependency. American-Indian architect and planner Christopher C. Benninger (born 1942)—who had helped founding the Ahmedabad School of Planning with the Ford Foundation in 1971—captured this spirit vividly:

> Training must go beyond the mere imparting of technical and administrative skills; it must better equip practitioners to conceptualise reality in terms of the contexts within which they work. Training has a sensitising role to play. It must create [an] understanding of the human condition as well as knowledge about how to change it. Training becomes a development

process when the traditional role between student and teacher is broken and a new relationship evolves wherein, using real environments as laboratories, they learn from each other and from studies in contexts which reveal patterns and options for effective action.[44]

"Conceptualising reality" and "understanding the human condition" were among the new pedagogic objectives that helped pave the way for theory in the context of development, as found at the PGCHS. But also the nascent academic climate at the KUL played its role: in trying to get a grip on the novel phenomenon of "research in architecture," the first generation of scholars tried to position their investigations within a wider, systematic, and holistic understanding of the world. This drive toward an encompassing theoretical frame effectuated a productive interaction between the human settlements paradigm and architectural theory. That interaction was in large part due to the appointment of André Loeckx (born 1949) on the chair of architectural theory in 1982, who simultaneously was involved in the activities of the PGCHS, taking the lead in its inquiries into "Form."

"THE CITY AS A HOUSING PROJECT"

Staff member in Leuven since the late 1970s, Loeckx had earlier fulfilled his own civil service as a "conscientious objector" in socialist Algeria, constructing several schools during Boumédiène's push to modernize the country. Exposed to building in that environment, and with the prospect of starting a PhD in Leuven, he sought to complement his architectural experience with courses in anthropology, studied the latest works in semiotics, and attended several modules at the DPU in London.

Bringing these multiple backgrounds together, his PhD dissertation offered a post-structuralist informed analysis of building and dwelling practices in Kabylia, a Berber region in Algeria impacted by drastic modernization. Partly overlapping with the PGCHS's agenda, the fieldwork in Kabylia doubled as a research project in collaboration with the Algerian *Institut National d'Études et de Recherches du Bâtiment* (INERBA, National Institute of Studies and Research on Building), an institute founded in 1978 to orient the future work of the then newly established Algerian Ministry of Housing. The main ambition of Loeckx's PhD, titled "Model and Metaphor. Contributions to a Semantic-Praxiological Approach towards Building and Dwelling,"[45] was to understand the built environment through a textual metaphor, thus seeking to benefit from the linguistic turn in the humanities, confronting authors as diverse as J. L. Austin, John Searle, Jacques Lacan, Julia Kristeva, and the *Tel Quel* scene to more architectural specific theories such as N. John Habraken and SAR 73's "tissue analysis" and the French school of typo-morphology, as propagated by Panerai and Castex in Versailles. In emphasizing building and dwelling as a cultural practice—as practices that have cultural "meaning" and that can be analyzed as "text"—Loeckx sought to inscribe this theoretical work in the then current debates in cultural anthropology, where post-structuralism was gaining a footing. He sought to theorize an inherently open "reading grid" that allowed the interpretation of the Kabyles' changing dwelling practices on their own terms, without relying on a universal framework nor reverting to an idealized set of supposed "traditional" Kabyle values.

In sum, the ultimate aim of these theoretical endeavors was to reap the benefits of post-structuralism by transposing it from the linguistic to the built realm. Rooted in ongoing dwelling practices and based on inherently contextual signifying practices, it offered a solid point of critique to those methodologies that skip the moment of interpretation and allude to a supposedly objective description of the built environment—and this critique would strongly mark the PGCHS's own framework when aiming to train mid-career professionals from Africa and Asia.

Throughout the years, the engagement with architectural theory to address the issue of "form" became more explicit—not in order to draw any prescriptions from theory, but as a more basic search for the right vocabulary to address the changes in the built environment as they manifested themselves in reality. Thus, well-known paradigms such as Habraken's "support and infill" approach and Alexander's pattern language were mobilized in the UN training course as tools for participants to help in analyzing the built environment.[46] To the aims of the short-term course, these approaches had the benefits of being practice oriented, of emphasizing the need for fieldwork, of allowing readings of the built environment on different scale levels, and most of all of being able to be inscribed into a design program.[47] It offered a systematic way to analyze the whole of the built environment up to its smallest socio-spatial patterns, and despite its limitations, it offered a manageable format of understanding the built environment that allowed an informed guess as to how adequately certain spatial solutions would respond to the challenges at hand.

As the numerous fieldwork experiences started to accumulate, however, the analytic reach offered by such hands-on concepts was gradually dwarfed by the tremendous richness of built reality as found, turning urban analysis more to an end in itself, eschewing a direct link with design solutions or construction. Compared to the toolkit presented by MIT's Horacio Caminos and Reinhard Goethert in their 1978 *Urbanization Primer*, the PGCHS methods complemented the *Primer*'s detailed site analyses with a more sociocultural interpretation focusing on acts of inhabitation.[48] Their turn toward the Italo-French school of typo-morphology offered two major shifts, mainly inspired by an Aldo Rossian frame of mind.[49] The first was the assertion of architecture's autonomy: through its material permanence, architecture contains a spatial logic that cannot be reduced to a social logic, or, for that matter, to a logic of "development." The second shift was the emphasis on the fundamental link between architecture and the city. As a consequence of this link, any proper analysis will have to operate at different scale levels, acknowledging that even the level of the individual house is connected to the entire city.

The strongest insight they found in Rossi's work that resonated with their experiences in the developing world was the analogical relation that Rossi drew between analysis and design. Rossi's work provided arguments that questioned the possibility of providing a priori, schematic spatial solutions, and even of establishing a set of design criteria to assess a project independently from an analysis of the existing built environment. With a nod to Alexander, without *analysis* of form, *synthesis* of form was thought to be out of the question. Thus, following a Rossian logic, where the labor of the project coincides with the analysis of the built environment, it is hard to favor in advance a specific spatial logic as the best way toward "development." Hence a critical intervention in a housing system requires in the first place a thorough understanding of the existing architectural and urban forms and the sociocultural logic they embody—much like the post-structuralist informed challenge of Loeckx's work on modernizing Kabylia.

The PGCHS's baseline was thus that a proper housing policy requires looking at the city as a whole, in both its formal and informal expressions. As the argument grew that the capacity of low-income housing cannot be limited to some particular segments of the built environment—those being planned by development organizations—but is potentially part of every settlement type available in the city, the 1980s UN workshops expanded the notion of housing

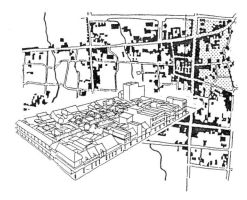

FIGURE 6.4 Cover of 1986 UN course handouts, with an allegory of "The City as a Housing Project."

Source: André Loeckx and Sandi Siregar, "Bandung, the City as a Housing Project" (Leuven: PGCHS, 1986).

to include the city as a whole. In this sense, the idea of "the city as a housing project" became the main theoretical line underlying the PGCHS's activities in the 1980s (see Figure 6.4).[50]

In the context of the annual UN workshops, alternately organized in Africa and Asia, those cities were Nairobi and Bangkok, where the PGCHS partnered up with various local partners such as the Housing Research and Development Unit (HRDU) of the University of Nairobi or the Asian Institute of Technology (AIT) in Bangkok. As a locale of intensive field work—for participants once during their training, for the PGCHS staff on an annual basis—Nairobi and Bangkok served as platforms on which the issues pertaining to the housing process could be projected. Thus, serving as a locus of reflection, the real heroes of theory for the PGCHS, one can argue, were not Rossi and company but Nairobi and Bangkok.

An important element in that was the strategic choice of sites with which participants would be confronted for their five to ten days of fieldwork. In the Bangkok course, three very different sites were carefully selected.[51] The first two suited the dominant housing paradigms: Rangsit, a not very successful 1973 site and services project, and Tung Song Hong and Lad Krabang, which dealt with issues of appropriate technology and participation. Klong Toey, the third site, was more unusual, as participants were required to study the "morphological efficiency" of the existing slum and slum reconstruction project, which, in terms of space use, was deemed exemplary for other housing projects (see Figure 6.5). Similarly, three

"THE CITY AS A HOUSING PROJECT"

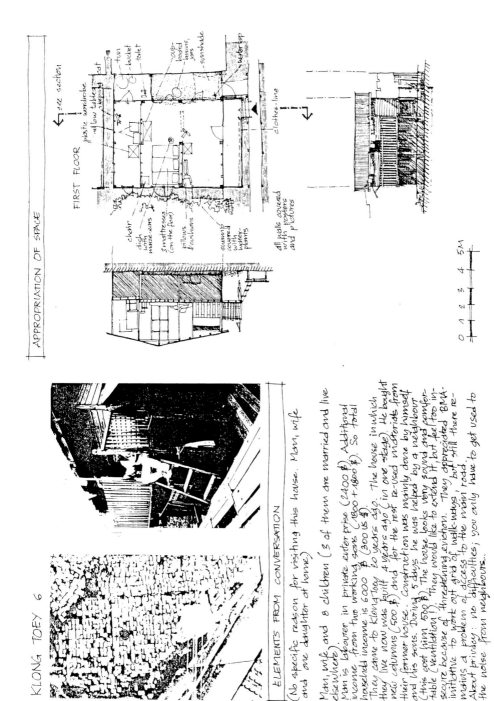

FIGURE 6.5 Excerpts of typo-morphological tissue analyses of Klong Toey, Bangkok, 1986.

Source: André Loeckx, Noël Naert and Bart Wouters, "'Typo-Morphological' Tissue Analysis, Case Study: Klong Toey" (Leuven: PGCHS, 1986).

sites were selected in Nairobi, including Kariobangi, a 1964 (and again not entirely successful) site and services scheme, developed in isolation from the city, and Kibera, a slum where no considerable upgrading attempts were being undertaken. The third site, Eastleigh, would hardly register on the radar of the UN's approach to human settlements: a private low- and middle-income residential area, established in the 1920s for extended Asian families. When Africans gradually took the place of Asians after independence, the traditional Asian courtyard-type houses were being remodeled into single room tenements for small families and bachelors working in the nearby industrial area. Which housing paradigm could engage with the complexities of such socio-spatial reality?

By turning to the city's history, the PGCHS staff tried to apprehend urban dynamics and to identify the various characteristic settlement types, their own specific histories and underlying logics, and their potential for low-income housing.[52] Through their turbulent histories, most cities in development literally display a live exhibition of housing solutions, allowing the recognition of low-income dwelling capacity in areas that are not commonly considered as being low-income, such as in Eastleigh. The PGCHS thus tried to twist the UN approach to housing into one that would take its clues from what existed already in each specific context rather than offering "technical" solutions supposedly applicable everywhere.

CONCLUSION

The nebulous notion of human settlements took root in two contexts: that of a globally oriented professional practice professed by intergovernmental organizations and that of architecture and planning schools, often in a university context, where it gradually converged with an academic research agenda. More than in the decades before or after, in the 1970s and 1980s these two contexts strongly overlapped in the various training programs for "Third World" professionals, such as the PGCHS's UN Training Program "Housing in Development."

In his anthropologically inspired critique of Caminos and Goethert's *Urbanization Primer*, Amos Rapoport—one of the giants in Man-Environment Studies—aptly captured the double bind in which a pedagogical program such as the PGCHS found itself.[53] Rapoport argued that generalizing categories such as the "urban poor"—the subject of Caminos and Goethert's considerations—were inadequate to assess the spatial quality of a project, for such categories lack sociocultural specificity. "Not only is poverty alone insufficient for such definition; if one considers cultural variables as central, and design as culture-specific, then 'Third World' is much too broad a term."[54]

Rapoport's insistence on having cultural variables play a role as form determinants and evaluative criteria is challenging, for it essentially refutes the idea of a universally valid spatial knowledge. The theoretical and urban historical endeavors at the PGCHS can be seen as the efforts of a European architectural school caught in the double bind of the university and the development context. In emphasizing the limitations of technical solutions, in stressing the need for fieldwork (for many mid-career professionals a novel experience), and in encouraging participants to rely on their own background and knowledge, the center evidenced a certain willingness to take up Rapoport's critique and to confront European knowledge frameworks with cultural realities elsewhere. Yet they operated in the context of, in collaboration with, and with a mandate by an intergovernmental body with a global agenda, posing an ultimate constraint to the level of symmetry in the exchange between experts and mid-career professionals. In a very pragmatic sense, this constraint was felt by many schools of that epoch with a comparable double mandate in having to balance the efficiency of easily transferable design schemes and criteria with a far thornier plea for sociocultural sensitivity.

In terms of what could register in reports and proposals as a solid housing *strategy* toward development, the needle was more likely to tilt toward the former. More specifically: an optimized set of universal criteria to develop a site and services scheme able to adapt to local circumstances—the most common approach during the 1970s and 1980s—was for many of the UN decision makers a more trustworthy component of an architectural training program than a narrative that argued that the best solution can only be found by looking at the whole of the built environment and might equally consist of, for instance, rehabilitating a modernist neighborhood designed under colonialism.

Though the PGCHS's spatial and architectural bias was initially supported by UN middlemen such as MIT-trained Tomasz Sudra, Chief of UNCHS's Training Unit, by the early 1990s the UNCHS mindset started to shift and the program was less suited to UNCHS's aim to "promote a global and systematic approach to human settlements training."[55] In the years to come, the PGCHS would thus refocus its activities elsewhere. It would still be involved with the UNCHS program *Localising Agenda 21*, which resulted in a publication that documented and legitimized their approach of spatial planning and strategic projects,[56] but intensive courses under the patronage of UNCHS gave way to a "normal" international master and doctoral program, which were fully inscribed in the logic of the university (although still fueled by scholarships from the Belgian Ministry of Development Cooperation).

In short, like DPU and IHS, the PGCHS found its financial basis in the late 1970s and 1980s largely through development aid programs. Like them, it became more fully academic in the 1990s, shifting toward more research-oriented funding programs. While financial support from development aid programs diminished—coinciding with the growing exclusion of the discipline of architecture from the field of housing (see Arindam Dutta's contribution, Chapter 1, this volume)—there was a pressure from the side of the university to more strongly compete for research funding. In its mutation into a full-fledged academic research center, "development" was no longer the driving concept, and the directives of the UNCHS became somewhat sidelined. The legacy of the concerns of "housing in development" are, however, still there, even today, for the field of human settlements, as currently taught and researched in Leuven, is infused with ecological approaches, landscape urbanism, and postcolonial urban studies—disciplines that, for better or for worse, took up the baton where the system thinkers and developmentalists dropped it.

In recounting the PGCHS's adoption of the Turnerian triad "Forms," "Institutions," and "Resources" and the center's attempt to consider architectural and urban form as a meaningful entry point for intervening in a housing system, we discussed how the UN's "developing" efforts resulted in theoretical ideas that were inextricably entwined with a Western university context (such as anthropology and semiotics), finding their way into many African and Asian professionals' intellectual baggage—but also, on the other hand, how the KUL protagonists' investment in theory was greatly impacted by an accumulation of experiences in the South, being involved in the program on an annual basis.[57] At the PGCHS, theory was challenged by reality, up to a point that only the reality of the urban whole could form the keystone to the center's approach.

This approach, informed by post-structuralist tendencies in anthropology and attempting to recognize the unstructured aspects of everyday life, gave leeway to a form of uncertainty that was ultimately at odds with the imperatives of global governance. It installed a sense of indeterminacy with regard to development, because specific paradigms, schemes, or perspectives were always presented as provisional and approximate rather than final. Perhaps in this light we could consider the PGCHS's 1980s training program as an emblematic battlefield between a post-structuralist form of thinking, accepting an illogical part in reality that escapes any form of rationality, on the one hand, and the structuring tendencies of a global order aiming to set an empirically divergent group of societies on the same path of development on the other.

NOTES

1. Felicity D. Scott, *Outlaw Territories: Environments of Insecurity/Architectures of Counterinsurgency* (New York: Zone Books, 2016).
2. For a general account, see Viviana d'Auria, "Retracing the Emergence of a Human Settlements Approach: Designing in, from and with Contexts of Development," in *The Routledge Companion to Architecture and Social Engagement*, ed. Farhan Karim (New York: Routledge, 2018), 49–63.
3. Barbara Ward, "The Home of Man: What Nations and the International Must Do," *Habitat International* 1, no. 2 (September 1976): 125.
4. While social sciences such as anthropology were already entangled with early colonial planning, interdisciplinary work between social sciences and urban planning and design was not consistently and overtly endorsed. During late colonial times, for example, the marriage of architecture with anthropology was not a given, nor considered necessary to advance housing solutions by key professionals. On this last point see, for example: Viviana d'Auria, "In the Laboratory and in the Field: Hybrid Housing Design for the African City in Late-Colonial and Decolonising Ghana (1945–57)," *The Journal of Architecture* 19, no. 3 (2014): 329–356.
5. Eric Mumford, "From Master-Planning to Self-Build: The MIT-Harvard Joint Center for Urban Studies, 1959–71," in *A Second Modernism: MIT, Architecture, and the 'Techno-Social' Moment*, ed. Arindam Dutta (Cambridge, MA: SA+P Press/The MIT Press, 2013), 288–309.
6. "The Institute's History," UNITAR, October 13, 2008, www.unitar.org/institutes-history.
7. Ellen Shoshkes, "Jaqueline Tyrwhitt and the Internationalization of Planning Education," in *Urban Planning Education: Beginnings, Global Movement and Future Prospects*, eds. Andrea I. Frank and Christopher Silver (Cham: Springer, 2018), 65–80.
8. Burak Erdim, *Landed Internationals: Planning Cultures, the Academy, and the Making of the Modern Middle East* (Austin: University of Texas Press, 2020). See also Erdim, Chapter 18, this volume.
9. Ellen Shoshkes, *Jaqueline Tyrwhitt: A Transnational Life in Urban Planning and Design* (Farnham: Ashgate, 2013). See also Olga Touloumi, Chapter 13, this volume.
10. Letter by Ernest Weissmann to Pedro Paolo Morillo, December 29, 1960, UN Archives.
11. United Nations Department of Economic and Social Affairs, *United Nations Seminar on Regional Planning: Tokyo, 28 July to 8 August 1958* (New York: United Nations, 1959).
12. Letter by Ellen Schoendorff to Ruth D. Spaeth, September 19, 1961, UN Archives. These institutes were: the Centro de Planificación Urbana y Regional, Universidad Nacional de Ingeniería (Lima, Peru); Estudios de Graduados en Planeamiento Municipal, Facultad de Arquitectura, Universidad del Valle (Cali, Colombia); Centro de Estudios de Planificación del Desarrollo, Universidad Central de Venezuela (Caracas, Venezuela); and the Department of Town and Country Planning and Housing, School of Planning and Architecture (New Delhi, India).
13. For instance, the Canadian Peter Oberlander was involved in supervising the Institute for Community Planning at the Kwame Nkrumah University of Science and Technology at Kumasi.
14. Charles Abrams, *Man's Struggle for Shelter in an Urbanizing World* (Cambridge, MA: The MIT Press, 1964), 103–104.
15. Letter by Peter Oberlander to Ernest Weissmann, May 17, 1961, UN Archives. The UBC course notwithstanding, in 1962 Oberlander had sent out a timely warning with regard to the relevance of planning curricula in North American schools for overseas students, and stressed the importance of setting up training programs in the newly

independent countries themselves. H. Peter Oberlander, "Planning Education for Newly Independent Countries," *Journal of the American Institute of Planners* 28, no. 2 (1962): 116–123.

16   The Birmingham course was advised by Otto Koenigsberger (1908–1999) and the course in The Hague led by the Dutchman Jacobus P. Thijsse (1896–1981). Both had earlier already worked for the UN as housing and planning advisors.

17   For more on the history of the GSE and the ACE, see Lefteris Theodosis, "Victory Over Chaos? Constantinos A. Doxiadis and Ekistics 1945–75" (Ph.D. thesis, Universitat Politècnica de Catalunya, Barcelona, 2015).

18   Patrick Wakely and Caren Levy, *Sixty Years of Urban Development: A Short History of the Development Planning Unit* (London: DPU, 2014).

19   Hannah le Roux, "The Networks of Tropical Architecture," *The Journal of Architecture* 8, no. 3 (Autumn 2003): 337–354; Jiat-Hwee Chang, *A Genealogy of Tropical Architecture: Colonial Networks, Nature and Technoscience* (London: Routledge, 2016).

20   Patrick Wakely, "The Development of a School," *Habitat International* 7, no. 5/6 (1983): 337–346.

21   Wakely and Levy, *Sixty Years of Urban Development*.

22   "Our History: 60 Years of Making Cities Work," *IHS*, 2018, www.ihs.nl/en/about/ihs-history. This website does not mention any connections to colonial knowledge networks.

23   Łukasz Stanek, *Architecture in Global Socialism: Eastern Europe, West Africa, and the Middle East in the Cold War* (Princeton, NJ: Princeton University Press, 2020); Stanek, ed., *The Journal of Architecture* 17, no. 3: Cold War Transfer: Architecture and Planning from Socialist Countries in the 'Third World' (2012).

24   Alicja Gzowska and Piotr Bujas, "Development Aid from Socialist Poland: Knowledge Transfer and Education on Tropical Architecture and Planning for Developing Countries," *Journal of Architectural Education* 74, no. 2 (2020): 209–221. Over the course of its two and a half decades of existence, the Szczecin course accommodated some 500 students. Its head, Piotr Zaremba (1910–1993), clearly was a global expert, traveling extensively all over the globe to offer assistance for spatial planning in China, North Korea, Iraq, Vietnam, India, Guinea, and Mexico.

25   Centre for Human Settlements, "Our Mission," (University of British Columbia, 2018), www.chs.ubc.ca/index.html. Today the CHS is a unit within the School of Community and Regional Planning (SCARP), involving faculty and student associates from various departments at UBC in multidisciplinary research and capacity-building programs related to regional, urban, and community development.

26   "The Vancouver Declaration on Human Settlements" (Vancouver: United Nations, 1976), Guidelines for Action, par. 12.

27   Morris Juppenlatz, "A Comprehensive Approach to Training for Human Settlements," *Third World Planning Review* 1, no. 1 (Spring 1979): 86. The twelve experts present were Christopher C. Benninger, Thomas L. Blair, Olga Bronstein, Jacques Bugnicourt, Abhijit Datta, Cor Dijkgraaf, Albert Kartahardja, Otto Koenigsberger, Jacob O. Maos, Tom J. Segaar, Fredj Stambouli, and K. C. Sivaramakrishnan, "List of Experts and Participants in the Ad Hoc Meeting of Experts on a Training Programme for the Improvement of Slums and Squatter Areas in Urban and Rural Communities," *Habitat International* 4, no. 1/2 (1979): 227–229.

28   Jo Tollebeek and Liesbet Nys, *The City on the Hill: A History of Leuven University, 1968–2005* (Leuven: Leuven University Press, 2006).

29   For this section we mainly relied on extensive interviews with Han Verschure and André Loeckx (November 16, 2017 and January 23–24, 2018, Leuven) as well as Verschure's earlier brief account of the center's history: Han Verschure, "PGC Human Settlements: Evolution of a School," *MaHS MaUSP Newsletter*, Special Edition Emeritus Celebration of Professor Han Verschure (2009): 4–5. For more on information on the PGCHS and particularly on its UN Training Course "Housing in Development," see Sebastiaan Loosen, "Shaping Social Commitment. Architecture and Intellectuality in the 1970s and '80s" (Ph.D. thesis, KU Leuven, 2019), chap. 3.

30   Christopher Alexander et al., *Houses Generated by Patterns* (Berkeley, CA: Center for Environmental Structure, 1969); Fernando García-Huidobro, Diego Torres Torriti, and Nicolás Tugas, eds., *Time Builds! The Experimental Housing Project (PREVI), Lima: Genesis and Outcome* (Barcelona: Gustavo Gili, 2008).

31   Cf. Kenneth E. Boulding, "The Economics of the Spaceship Earth," in *Environmental Quality in a Growing Economy: Essays from the Sixth RFF Forum*, ed. Henry Jarrett (Baltimore: Johns Hopkins University Press, 1966), 3–14.

32   Jan Delrue, "Architecturale grondslagen voor een rationalisatie in de bouwnijverheid. Modulaire maatcoordinatie als ontwerpmethodiek" [Architectural Groundwork for a Rationalization in the Building Industry. Modular Measure Coordination as Design Methodology] (Ph.D. thesis, Katholieke Universiteit Leuven, 1969).

33   "Postgraduate Studies, Faculty of Engineering, University of Leuven," information booklet, [1969–1970].

34   Han Verschure, "Housing and Development: An Evaluation of Concepts and Ideas with Case Studies Focussing on Housing Policies and Spontaneous Settlements in Third World Cities" (Ph.D. thesis, Katholieke Universiteit Leuven, 1979). For its attunement to the Habitat spirit in this regard, see f.i. D. A. Turin, "Exploring Change: What Should Have Happened at Habitat," *Habitat International* 3, no. 1/2 (1978): 190.

35   Raf Tuts et al., "Housing in Development Programme: Experience, Achievements, Lessons, and Impact" (Leuven: PGCHS, May 1995), 3.

36   On this special status, see "UNCHS Launches Comprehensive Training Programme," *UNCHS Habitat News* 1, no. 3 (1979): 20–21. After outlining three main categories of training programs launched under the UNCHS umbrella, the

ongoing Leuven program is mentioned as a category of its own. Five years later, a UNCHS report reviewing the landscape of training for human settlements paints a rather disappointing picture of the importance of training within then-current bilateral approaches. Along with four other initiatives, the PGCHS is credited for being exception to the rule. "Training for Human Settlements (HS/C/7/3)," *UNCHS Habitat News* 6, no. 1 (April 1984): 4.

37. Several of the PGCHS projects were included in Bertha Turner, ed., *Building Community: A Third World Case Book* (London: Building Community Books, 1988).

38. Richard Harris, "A Double Irony: The Originality and Influence of John F.C. Turner," and Ray Bromley, "Peru 1957–1977: How Time and Place Influenced John Turner's Ideas on Housing Policy," *Habitat International* 27, no. 2 (June 2003): 245–269, 271–292.

39. This internally circulated paper dates June 1979 and would subsequently be published in a reworked and abridged form in *IFDA Dossier*, no. 15 (February 1980): 63–73, by the International Foundation for Development Alternatives (Nyon, Switzerland). It was reprinted in *Habitat International* 5, no. 1/2 (1980): 203–211. When possible, we refer to the 1980 version in *Habitat International*, and to the 1979 version as included in one of the PGCHS's course readers: *UN Follow-up Workshop on Housing, Nairobi, 11–29 January 1982: Background Papers* (Leuven: PGCHS, 1982), 1–23.

40. John F. C. Turner, "What to Do About Housing—Its Part in Another Development," in *UN Follow-up Workshop on Housing, Nairobi, 11–29 January 1982: Background Papers* (Leuven: PGCHS, 1982 [1979]), 5–6; Turner, "What to Do About Housing—Its Part in Another Development," *Habitat International* 5, no. 1/2 (1980): 207.

41. Ibid., 10/204.

42. Ibid., 6/207.

43. Wakely, "Development of a School". Further insightful sources on the changing nature of such curricula: Martin Evans, "Education for Responsive Climatic Design," and Michael Lloyd, "Design Education in the Third World," *Habitat International* 7, no. 5/6 (1983): 347–355, 367–375; Geoffrey Payne, ed., *Open House International* 21, no. 4: British Academic Institutions: Their Contribution to the Improvement and Development of the Built Environment in Developing Countries (1996).

44. Christopher Benninger, "Training for the Improvement of Human Settlements," *Habitat International* 11, no. 1 (1987): 154.

45. André Loeckx, "Model en metafoor. Bijdragen tot een semantisch-praxiologische benadering van bouwen en wonen" (Ph.D. thesis, Katholieke Universiteit Leuven, 1982).

46. N. J. Habraken, *Supports: An Alternative to Mass Housing* (London: The Architectural Press, 1972); Christopher Alexander, Sara Ishikawa, and Murray Silverstein, *A Pattern Language: Towns, Buildings, Construction* (New York: Oxford University Press, 1977).

47. André Loeckx, "Appropriate Design Patterns. The Issue of Form: Concepts and Practices," in *UN Follow-up Workshop on Housing, Bangkok 4–21 August 1981: Background Papers* (Leuven: PGCHS, 1981).

48. Horacio Caminos and Reinhard Goethert, *Urbanization Primer: Project Assessment, Site Analysis, Design Criteria for Site and Services or Similar Dwelling Environments in Developing Areas, with a Documentary Collection of Photographs on Urbanization* (Cambridge, MA: MIT Press, 1978).

49. The PGCHS staff outlined their indebtedness to authors such as Aldo Rossi, Vittorio Gregotti, Giorgio Grassi, Salvatore Muratori, Carlo Aymonino, Philippe Panerai, Jean Castex, Christian Devillers, and Bernard Huet in a theoretical piece that sought to reflect on their accumulated experiences of fieldwork: André Loeckx and Paul Vermeulen, "Note on the Methodology of Urban Analysis" (Leuven: PGCHS, September 1986).

50. André Loeckx, "The City as a Housing Project: Statements and Methods Concerning the Architecture of a City in Development" (Leuven: PGCHS, 1985).

51. *UN Workshop on Housing, Bangkok, 7–18 December 1982: Report and Proceedings* (Leuven: PGCHS, 1983); Loeckx, "The City as a Housing Project".

52. André Loeckx, "The Architecture of Housing in Development: Learning from Nairobi," in *Report and Proceedings: Workshop on Housing, Nairobi, January 18th-31st 1987* (Leuven: PGCHS, 1987), 57–82.

53. Amos Rapoport, review of *Urbanization Primer*, *Journal of the Society of Architectural Historians* 38, no. 4 (December 1979): 402–403.

54. Ibid., 402.

55. "Overview of UNCHS (Habitat) Training Activities," *UNCHS Habitat News* 11, no. 1 (April 1989): 43.

56. André Loeckx et al., eds., *Urban Trialogues: Visions, Projects, Co-Productions: Localising Agenda 21* (Nairobi: UN-HABITAT, 2004).

57. This impact can for instance be recognized in the theoretical focus on topics such as displacement and migration, using the empirical evidence of fieldwork studies of human settlements. Cf. Hilde Heynen and André Loeckx, "Scenes of Ambivalence: Concluding Remarks on Architectural Patterns of Displacement," *Journal of Architectural Education* 52, no. 2: Patterns of Displacement (November 1998): 100–108.

Part III

Bureaucratic organization

7

Folders, patterns, and villages

Pastoral technics and the Center for Environmental Structure

Ginger Nolan

BUREAUCRACY

The Indian government buildings for the State of Gujarat are (or were) two and three story buildings ... with great white cows walking through the corridors, uninterrupted by anyone, because of their sacred nature. Inside the offices themselves each civil servant sat behind a desk, piled high with legal size manila folders, brown in color—and from each folder there stuck out a tab, a marker, colored red, blue, green, white ... to indicate the degree of urgency of the project in the folder. These tabs were marked URGENT, IMMEDIATE, AT ONCE, and so on ... and they, and the folders, sat idly on the desks, in huge dusty piles, for weeks, months, years. A project, or problem, passes through the government by means of a series of steps which consist, concretely, of an act whereby the folder representing that project moves from one persons [sic] desk to another, accumulating signatures as it goes. The concrete physical moving of a folder is therefore the essence of the matter.

To expedite my request for funds, I went into the office where the folder for my request lay buried, had tea with the official there, and then sat down. He, thinking that our interview was over, asked if he could do anything further. I said, politely, that I would be glad to take the folder with me to its next destination—and made it clear that I would not leave the office until the folder did. I sat there. In the end I was able to get half the money for the school, in a few days, by walking the folder from desk to desk like this.[1]

In 1961 a young European architect, overseeing his first building project—a small schoolhouse for the rural village of Bavra in Gujarat—found himself confronting the methods of state bureaucracy. Having arrived in Bavra a half-year earlier to conduct research as part of his PhD at Harvard University's architecture department, Christopher Alexander was wrapping up his fieldwork by overseeing the design and construction of a small schoolhouse, a project suggested to him by the residents of Bavra (see Figure 7.1). He later credited his research in Bavra for inspiring his renowned architectural "pattern language." The pattern language was a comprehensive rubric of rules governing good architectural and urban form, based on a sampling of global precedents and ranging in scale from domestic ornamentation to urban and regional planning and dictating, among other things, the organization and scalar relationships for cities, town centers, suburbs, etc. It might be said that the pattern

DOI: 10.4324/9781003193654-11

FIGURE 7.1 Construction of Bavra schoolhouse, India, n.d.
Source: The Christopher Alexander Archive.

language served as a proxy for the more intimate forms of collaboration and construction involved in the design and construction of the Bavra schoolhouse.

The funding required for the schoolhouse was 5,000 rupees, a modest sum Alexander sought to collect from the state government, then sited in Ahmedabad. The system of state bureaucracy he encountered in Ahmedabad struck him as at once transparent and inscrutable: on the one hand, a simple "concrete" matter of folders being transferred from one desk to another, gathering signatures as they moved (or failing to gather signatures as they lay supposedly dormant); on the other hand, a system defying rational logic, as attested by the seeming superfluity of the designations "URGENT, IMMEDIATE, AT ONCE," to say nothing of meandering cows and chatty tea-breaks whose rhythms were at contretemps with the efficiency required of administrative process. Thus, Alexander took it upon himself to perform the task of moving his folder from one desk to another, strolling complacently, like one of the great white cows, among offices, desks, and civil servants. The incident appears in Alexander's and Janet Johnson's account as a clever circumvention of the senseless stoppages in the system, a strategy devised by dint of a simple insight (concerning a manila folder's torpid tendencies) and by dint of an equally simple solution (*move the folder*).[2] By extending this reasoning to its logical conclusion, it might be inferred that, had rural residents only thought of this innovation themselves—of personally moving a manila folder from one desk to another—their villages may have already been equipped with schoolhouses. A corollary implication that might be inferred from such reasoning is that the same magical worldview that authorized cows to enter willy-nilly into administrative buildings might be held accountable for enshrouding that administration's byzantine processes in a veil of impenetrable authority. Alexander, in this recounting, simply tore asunder the veil.

Let me offer, however, a different interpretation of the event, one that casts the practices Alexander regarded as deferrals and superfluities as integral to the workings of the administrative system. Alexander's freedom, as a foreign figure, to meander through the offices was not so dissimilar after all from the bovine prerogative to wander; not dissimilar, that is, from the cows' sacred exceptionality: an exceptionality that did not disrupt the system but belonged properly to it. The bureaucratic process worked to effectively winnow out non-exceptional from exceptional applications, channeling both into appropriate piles, all the while submitting each application to *more or less* the same uniform process. The bureaucratic system was characterizable *not* merely by "an act whereby the folder . . . moves from one person's desk to another" but by various impinging interests and power relations, determining the urgency of a particular project relative to another.

At the interstices between parliamentary democracy, industrial capitalism, and the remnants of colonial feudalism, bureaucratic administration would have constituted a potentially flexible mechanism, helping to negotiate and prioritize diverse and often conflicting agendas. Bureaucracy, then, far from being rigid (as clichés would have it), in fact mediated the fundamental contradiction of capitalist democracy—the inequality between putative equals—bending protocols this way or that according to the sway of money, politics, and social relations. The presumed tendency of folders to stagnate corresponded to state interests to impede the flow of money from state coffers to small rural outposts. As Alexander had divined, there were ways to make the folders move. Yet these movements surely had at least as much to do with social-economic statuses and exchange as they had with what Alexander described as the "concrete" laws of physical inertia. It would be unlikely that an indigent rural denizen presuming the right to move her own folder from one desk to another would have been suffered to see her task through to completion. And few such residents would have been in the economic position to offer, as an alternative, a petty favor or bribe to hasten the passage of a folder through the circuit of office desks. The difference between a bribe and Alexander's action is nothing more than the difference between money and cultural capital.

In the encounter described by Alexander, the role played by social relationships surfaced through a small ritual: what appears in the report as a detail of no consequence—the act of sitting down to a cup of tea with a civil servant as a prelude to the shuffling of folders—was probably no mere diversion from the administrative process at hand but rather helped determine the rate at which a given folder might move through the system. While sipping tea, applicants' social status, affiliations, and connections could be assessed, their agenda clarified, and perhaps reciprocal favors hinted at. Tea, by offering the ruse of a *break* from administrative work, in fact enabled certain factors that were legally excluded from consideration to be converted into *de facto* criteria within the administrative alembic that sifted folders into either dammed-up piles or flowing channels. That is, tea-breaks helped negotiate the discrepancies between two competing economic-political frameworks: on the one hand, the socioeconomic hierarchies that, in combination with the state's industrial developmental priorities, helped naturalize the dearth of public amenities like schoolhouses for the rural poor; on the other hand, a political ideal of modern democracy that supported a notion of universal rights (e.g., to formal education *cum* schoolhouses), such that any human could presume to apply for government funds for village improvements, whether or not such a request was likely to be granted.

Tea-breaks carved out a caesura within the homogeneous anonymity of administrative protocol, allowing a more nuanced presentation of social factors and thereby setting in motion the gears for distributing (or withholding) government funds. For example, information exchanged during this particular instance of drinking of tea likely included Alexander's impressive credentials as a PhD student in Harvard's architecture department and perhaps his prior studies at Cambridge University in mathematics, architecture, and computation, as well as his seven months of anthropological fieldwork in Bavra sponsored by the Harvard Society of Fellows. Such details could have easily supported Alexander's presumed right to intervene in civil servants' protocols. The exchange of information enabled by tea-drinking was, moreover, reciprocal, allowing Alexander to take stock of the situation, establish a degree of amicability, and thereby feel sufficiently at ease to venture the impertinence of transporting his own folder.

In other words, the ritual of tea-drinking can be placed at the chiasmus between the putative macroscopic homogeneity of administrative procedure and the more microscopic relationships determining a particular folder's ability to draw money—or not—to a proposed project and to thereby alter—or not—the forms of life available to citizens as they were either granted or denied the basic infrastructural lineaments of civil society. The sacred cows, chatty tea breaks, and lethargic folders, which may have appeared to European eyes as so many quaint symptoms of the obdurate backwardness of Third World bureaucracy, were in fact not incidental but integral to the ways state government managed popular claims to a more equitable distribution of resources. By comparison, the pattern-language, though also establishing homogenous standards and protocols, involves a shift of scale from the municipal politics of bureaucracy to global systems of architectural production and economic development.

The Bavra schoolhouse had emerged from a rather unlikely comingling of interests—between the aspirations of a small rural group and those of a well-pedigreed European architect whose career was informed by his interests in anthropology, cognitive science, and computation.[3] In the decades to follow, however, Alexander's projects would usually conform to more typical forms of architectural patronage. Whereas the Bavra schoolhouse had been proposed by the village residents, then designed by Alexander with respect to local ceramic techniques, subsequent housing projects typically responded to a moneyed client's behest. Following a client's prompt, Alexander often did, however, propose procedural mechanisms for involving residents in design or construction processes. In India, the passage of his manila folder through the government offices—an event occupying a surprisingly significant portion of his brief report on the Bavra fieldwork—appears indeed to have been instructive for the subsequent trajectories of his newly founded Center for Environmental Structure (CES) in Berkeley, California, in 1963. The CES's housing work and Alexander's scholarship would largely revolve around the problem of how occupants' personal preferences and cultural differences could be processed within a system that operated according to uniform standards and protocols. The CES was far from alone in attempting to allow a degree of individuation within the rubrics of modern architectural production. However, relative to most vanguardist architects of the 1960s, the CES—with its nostalgia for pre-industrial times—more staunchly rejected modernist stylistics. Moreover, while some of the CES's housing projects could be classed as self-help architecture, the center's approach was quite distinct from the stripped-down core self-help model promulgated widely in the 1950s.[4]

It is in regard to Alexander's struggle to negotiate between the architect's large-scale organizational prerogatives and the occupant's prerogative to develop and change a house over time that I turn to Michel Foucault's notion of pastoral power. The CES's low-cost housing schemes essentially conceived of the architect's (or really, for Alexander, the "master builder's") relationship to housing occupants in terms homologous to the relationship between a pastor and his lay flock, a trans-individuating relationship through which personal responsibility could be partly transferred from the laity to a leader deemed more capable of handling that responsibility.[5] Such leadership cannot readily be attributed to mere technical expertise, given that Alexander cast doubt on the efficacy of architectural expertise, which, he claimed, had produced far more monstrosities than had nonexpert forms of architectural production.[6] The right to govern in a pastoral sense derived from a special ability to apply nature's macroscopic principles to the specifics of particular social and cultural conditions, an ability that required a more intimate knowledge of individual building occupants than what was typical in the design of low-cost mass-housing. In keeping with decades of anthropological efforts to *indigenize* developmental programs, the pattern language offered a means of transposing existing local practices and methods of modernization.[7]

Pastoral power has to do with the way personal responsibility is redistributed among humans and nonhumans, this redistribution not, however, assuming a straightforward partitioning. Rather, the density of refractory relationships between actors blurs the partitions between various channels of responsibility and in this sense might be contrasted to bureaucracy, which at least *attempts* to clarify channels of responsibility (even while it may often appear to have the opposite result).[8] While pastoral power—at least in its magico-religious origins—is seen to represent a form of interpersonal intimacy (e.g., between pastor and laity), bureaucracy is often thought to displace human relationships, being understood by Max Weber in terms homologous to Marxian alienation, insofar as immediate social relations are supposedly converted into the scope of intermediating procedures. That is, bureaucracy reifies "traditional" social relationships as a set of depersonalized protocols and processes.[9] Alexander, in his account of Gujarati bureaucracy, supposedly *re*-converted documentary relationships into human ones by personally transporting his folder between desks. This claim to restore human social agency rested on the assumption that bureaucracy didn't already allow personal negotiation of the rules, whereas in fact bureaucracy could be seen as an interface between the abstractness of state-scaled legal procedures and the nuanced minutiae of local, personal claims. Thus, it might constitute an expedient mechanism (however flawed) *between* what Weber classed as "traditional" and "rational" modes of authority, so that the rational (for Weber, instantiated by bureaucracy) could be seen as more a liminal than actual condition. The *ideal* of bureaucracy would be to instate a seamless, unvarying process of arranging humans and nonhumans within the organizational rubrics of the state. The reality was messier, allowing for negotiation between the governed and apparatuses of governmentality.

Pastoral power, however, tends toward dissolving the distinction between governance and the self-determination of the governed, short-circuiting the domain of social negotiation.

Beginning with the bureaucratic encounter in Ahmedabad, Alexander's career would largely consist in efforts to reform bureaucratic procedures, to alter the vectors of responsibility between architectural actors and thereby repartition responsibility in such a way that pastoral intimacy could be effected *through* bureaucracy, albeit a new form of bureaucracy that had been re-scripted with the goal of allowing *nature* to assert a guiding role in architectural development. Bureaucracy (for Alexander, an alienating device) was to be transformed into a pastoral model of power with the aid of new architectural procedures, mechanisms, and guidelines. Architectural typologies, in the form of Alexander's "pattern language," were to form the basic semiosis undergirding the CES's proposed bureaucratic systems of architectural production. The pattern language would allow a degree of personal responsibility within the scope of self-help architectural projects, albeit by dint of its regulating tenets. The pattern language's precepts of "good" architectural form were the distinguishing characteristics of what Alexander called "natural cities," defined as "cities which have arisen more or less spontaneously over many, many years".[10] As a procedural interface between architects, builders, clients, and building occupants, the pattern language was to allow the conversion of occupants' personal architectural needs into a schema derived from nature's strict aesthetic and spatial prescriptions. There would be thus no need for any discrepancy between universal principles and personal needs (including the particularities of culture).

Alexander's whole notion of pattern language served as an architectural analog for the trans-individuating convergence between the missionary-professional and local laities. (The rudiments of the pattern language were worked out as early as 1964, with a subsequent manual appearing in 1968, although it was not until 1977 that Alexander and his CES collaborators published a comprehensive compendium, followed decades later by the series *The Nature of Order*.)[11] The pattern language constituted a sacred scripture among its devotees, received less as an authored-work than as a work of revelation that interpreted the true nature of good architecture and urbanism. The book's intended readership seems to have been primarily architects and urbanists, although the CES's architectural work was also oriented toward forms of quasi-autoconstruction regulated by professional expertise. To the extent that autoconstructed housing might be understood as a form of self-care (in a Foucauldian sense), a self-help architecture guided by the architect's command of the pattern language represented a transfer of care from the architectural occupant to the aesthetic pattern language meant to safeguard the occupant from him- or herself—that is, from the poor choices that might lead to the degradation of the built environment.[12] Although the CES's housing settlements were intended to evolve slowly over time, following the unforeseeable developments of its occupants' lives and fortunes, they would do so only under scrupulous architectural guidance that assumed an almost bureaucratic form.

Alexander's implicit critique of bureaucracy could be contrasted to recent social-scientific observations on autoconstructed settlements, most notably Partha Chatterjee's formulation of the "politics of the governed" as well as work that engages similar themes, including *inter alia* Teresa Caldeira's notion of "transversal logics."[13] This, along with a related body of social-scientific literature, traces a concatenation of relationships through which residents of autoconstructed settlements negotiate claims to rights and services, often involving their engagement—direct or indirect—with bureaucratic processes. Actors—such as settlement leaders, landlords, patrons, schoolteachers, developers, utilities workers, party representatives, bureaucratic procedures, building regulations, NGOs, roads, and hydraulic pipes—form a web of intermediating nodes through which different interests, actors, and scales of institutional power are brought into negotiation with each other.[14] Chatterjee, for example, describes a local schoolteacher who served the residents of an autoconstructed settlement as a mediator of sorts—an organic intellectual capable of moving between empowered actors, bureaucracy, and the residents of the settlement.

However, an emphasis on the efficacy of popular politics risks neglecting a decades-long drift toward forms of local voluntary (or semi-voluntary) participation in large-scale developmental programs that often obfuscate the distinction between top-down and bottom-up. The CES's proposals for a form of self-help housing that allowed homes to be personally tailored to individuals sought to render housing occupants into personalizing agents of development. What are we to make of the impulse on the part of some international experts, including many architects and international NGOs, to enter into a role resembling, *mutatis mutandis*, the schoolteacher of Chatterjee's account?[15] Clearly, the latter is distinguishable from the former insofar as s/he is largely internal to the community. Nonetheless, there exist many forms of international expertise and mediation, ranging from, on the one hand, social workers and activists seeking to attain an intimate knowledge of local needs and conditions and to thereby serve as conduits of those needs, to—on the other end of the spectrum—digital and non-digital means of data collection used in large projects of urban planning and redevelopment. More recently—and this is the phenomenon that I will read backward into Alexander's oeuvre and through a theory of what I will call *pastoral technics*—we witness the increasing blurring of these two poles, as tasks of data-production, data collection, and interpretation are delegated along a chain of command stretching from native informants up to large funding and policy institutions.

This is the case, for example, in recent movements of urban redevelopment according to which communities self-enumerate, self-map, and formalize their property holdings under the aegis of bodies like UN-Habitat.[16] In such cases, top-down programs of property surveying, census-taking, and land privatization are reformulated as bottom-up activities. In the computational forays of Alexander and his contemporaries such as Yona Friedman and Nicholas Negroponte, the purportedly bottom-up processes of housing design are transacted through prescribed formula and frameworks, displacing the intervention of professional architectural design with a series of depersonalized architectural protocols, enabling local practices to be translated into modernizing programs while still retaining some significant vestige of local practices.[17] In a strictly geographic sense, the CES's work spanned Northern–Southern divides. However, a great portion of the office's work was focused on low-cost housing, including a homeless shelter in northern California, workers' housing in Mexico, miners' housing in Venezuela, and several research reports on the issue of low-cost housing in places ranging from the United States to India. Even if the ambitions of the pattern language extended well beyond the Global South or a global indigent, the redistribution of responsibility between the self and the architectural programs of modernity landed in the Global South in conjunction with the apparatus of development.

DOCTOR OF THE ENVIRONMENT

Scholarship has characterized modernity according to the administrative penchant for imposing macroscopic, reductive, and rationalistic schema in disregard of the world's cultural, ecological, and economic diversity. While there is certainly some accuracy to such characterizations, a myopic preoccupation with "how states see" (to use James C. Scott's formulation) has missed how microscopic gradations of difference come to be *differently* processed within seemingly macroscopic systems of governmentality.[18] Alexander's career is useful as a device through which to examine the tensions between the macro- and microscopic proclivities of development, as his dealings negotiated between large agglomerations of techno-economic power and the finely grained textures of rural villages and urban or peri-urban domiciles. Attempting to mediate between these two scales, we find not only the pattern language for which Alexander would soon become famous but also proposals for drastically reforming modes of architectural production, including a proposal for village design based on his work in Bavra.

Although impatient with the lassitude of bureaucracy—as we saw with the vignette in Ahmedabad—Alexander also chafed at the accelerated pace of modernist architectural production, to which he attributed the profession's dismal failures to create a humane environment.[19] In nonindustrialized villages, centuries of gradual "unselfconscious" architectural transformation had led to perfected models of habitation, Alexander argued in his 1964 book *Notes on the Synthesis of Form*. In this book Alexander described the slow pace of "unselfconscious" architectural evolution found in rural villages. For example, the perfection (or what Alexander called the "nonarbitrariness") of the Mousgoums' architectures in Cameroon was the result, he said, of an unselfconscious, centuries-long process of natural selection. Occupants' small random mutations to architectural form ("aimless changes") would be integrated into standard architectural practices and perpetuated over generations *if* those transformations turned out—by chance—to be beneficial. Conversely, nonbeneficial mutations would most likely not be replicated.[20] "Ritual and taboo," he wrote, "discourage innovation and self-criticism."[21]

Effectively, what distinguished this slow-creeping form of natural selection from the sluggish process of selection Alexander encountered at government offices in Ahmedabad—that is, the sifting of folders into either stagnant or trickling piles—was that in the government offices, consciously conceived processes and a profane agenda interfered with nature's own processes of selective adaptation. Ideally, design and construction protocols would be retooled so that bureaucracy could be supplanted by an invisible hand guiding natural self-regulating processes of architectural adaptation and evolution. Folders—or rather, *projects* of architectural transformation—*should* be dammed up in stagnant piles, condemned to fruitlessness, so as to allow only a few select projects to "move" forward and bear fruit. But the mechanism of selection had to be altered so that what was filtered out was market-driven stylistic novelty for novelty's sake. This process required new procedures for guiding homeowners to appropriately plan and transform their homes.

In their 1973 report, "The Grassroots Housing Process," Alexander and his colleagues proposed to counter "the monotonous and alienating sameness" of modern housing tracts by a new model of producing housing clusters financed by a "sponsor." This model, eschewing real estate marketing and bank mortgages, aimed to restore housing from its role as a "commodity" to its erstwhile role as an "activity."[22] The authors argued that a "builder" (a term they preferred to "architect") might guide small "clusters" of a dozen families in their incremental development of family domiciles and communal spaces, allowing for gradual changes over time, as families' needs and means evolved. The report's appeal to voluntary forms of patronage (i.e., the "sponsorship" of a housing cluster) bore a curious resemblance to models of autoconstructed settlement in many cities of the Global South where an individual landlord, a private corporation owning unoccupied urban land, or a group of persons holding unofficial claim to a plot of land might rent out a tract to groups of newcomers, allowing them to build houses.

Unlike autoconstructed settlements, however, the CES required centralized aesthetic management over residents' architectural decisions. A local "builder" would therefore function as a kind of village witch-doctor; "his" healing techniques consisting not in charms, herbs, and poultices but rather in a combination of pastoral intimacy with the building occupants (the laity) and a hermeneutic application of pattern language: that is, the expert interpretation and application of that language—much as a priest interprets and applies sacred texts and incantations—according to the specific needs of specific homeowners yet in harmony with the architectural needs of the larger group. The CES described this in terms more medical than theological, suggestive of the transfer of self-care over to expert diagnostics and treatment. Referring to the continual, lifelong architectural "diagnoses" proffered by the builder, the report suggested that the builder be thought of "as a kind of family doctor of the environment."[23] The pattern language would help ensure fidelity to nature's presumed tendency to self-correct and self-perfect, as the pattern language itself was derived from a comparative sampling of "unselfconsciously" developed world architectures.

Yet the builder's role was not only architectural. "He" was also to act in a broader governing capacity:

> Since the twelve families in a cluster will, together, make many decisions about their common land, they are acting like a local government in microcosm. This function is perfectly natural. . . . *However, the group processes which are needed, both for reaching consensus and for encouraging distinctions, are unfamiliar ones at this particular moment in history*. The builder will help these processes to become fruitful; and to this extent will function as a manager, whose task it is to ensure smooth and cooperative decision making by the group of families.[24]

The cluster was conceived not only as an architectural community but a small-scale polity engaged in democratic processes that were "natural" but at the same time oddly "unfamiliar . . . at this particular moment," suggesting that, just as conventional architectural knowledge and related skills had been lost to modernity, so too had "natural" abilities to self-govern. Indeed, the proposal could be read—in part—as an effort to reinstate feudalist forms of social interdependency found in villages like Bavra. Based on Alexander's lifelong critiques of the dehumanizing effects of industrialization on the built environment, and based on his penchant for architectures produced under feudal regimes, he and his coauthors may have been implying that modern architectural and artistic deskilling had been accompanied by political deskilling—the withering away of humans' "natural" social capacities to self-govern. While certainly the modern nation-form has eroded various local conventions of direct political negotiation, it is not clear that this would necessarily entail a concomitant erosion of people's natural *faculties* of political negotiation. It was furthermore unclear what qualified the builder to act as a steersman of democratic process and whether this didn't risk undermining the democratic process envisioned.[25] More importantly, though, the proposal begged the question of whether it really made sense to treat a suburban cluster of families as a unit of political community, that is, whether it made sense to see the private domestic sphere as a democracy in microcosm. Did it make sense for capitalist society to be structured on the foundations of feudalist-inspired villages?

ARCHITECTURE: "THE CONTINUING PRESENCE"

Alexander's fieldwork in Bavra informed his first published book, *Notes on the Synthesis of Form*, a work that brought his training in computer science to bear upon his anthropological and architectural interests.[26] The book expounded the need for a form of architectural notation capable of transcribing complex programmatic requirements into spatial diagrams. In the appendix, Alexander showed how the many social and economic needs of an Indian village could be worked into a system of visual notation—a spatial hieroglyphic that could be then fine-tuned according to site and context (see Figure 7.2).[27] However, the village occupied an ambivalent status in Alexander's analysis, being treated ostensibly as a static, unchanging object but also as a pliable one. In long lists detailing villagers' needs, Alexander's anthropological posture suggested that he was simply noting existing social practices and preferences. However, he interpolated into these lists various state-dictated goals for village modernization. Hence, extant rural customs and implicit critiques of those same customs were merged into a single, deceptively cohesive program. For example, in the long tabulation of village requirements, we find the criterion "eradication of untouchability" a few lines below these preceding criteria: "Harijans regarded as ritually impure, untouchable, etc."; "Members of castes maintain their caste profession as far as possible"; and "Members of one caste like to be together and separate from others, and will not eat or drink together."[28]

FIGURE 7.2 Diagram of a "Worked Example."

Source: The Christopher Alexander Archive.

FOLDERS, PATTERNS, AND VILLAGES 153

The dilemma posed by caste politics recalls the debates over the role of the panchayats (village councils) in the years leading up to Indian independence. The panchayats had been described by British administrators as indigenous microcosms of republican self-governance, adduced as evidence of an organic kinship between British liberal values and Indian customs.[29] Subsequently, Mohandas K. Gandhi proposed that local panchayats constitute India's base unit of national sovereignty, a suggestion allied to his notion of rural villages as the preserves of authentic national culture. Gandhi's preference for a highly decentralized federal government was hotly contested by the Dalit economist and statesman B.R. Ambedkar, who argued that the village was in fact India's basic unit of social oppression, insofar as village practices supported caste-based hierarchies.[30] His arguments highlighted the error of presuming localized forms of governmentality to be necessarily anti-hegemonic and anticipated how populist ideology (such as Gandhi's romantic evocations of village culture), along with majoritarian electoral politics, risked exacerbating economic and ethnic privilege.

Alexander's village analysis, however, circumvents any political confrontation between local practices and modernizing reforms—egalitarian or otherwise—through an array of architectural *dispositifs* that attempt to *spatially* reconcile contradictory agendas. His proposal for the organization of domestic space effectively replicated existing caste-based segregations with clusters of five to ten families living inside discrete compounds, walled-off to protect both caste-purity and feminine purity (see Figure 7.3). However, Alexander maintained (counterintuitively) that this enforced seclusion might in fact embolden females, converting them gradually to conform with the state agenda for female education.[31] Social-engineering is thus camouflaged within traditional architectural configurations, attempting to subtly transform village practices without engaging residents in direct negotiation around contentious issues like gender politics.

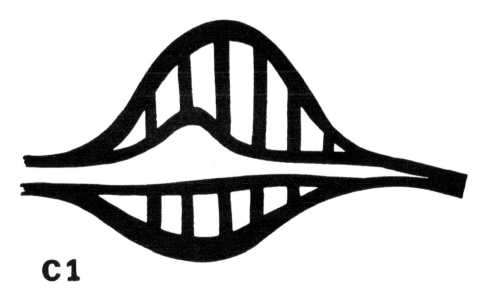

FIGURE 7.3 Diagram of group compounds from a "Worked Example."
Source: The Christopher Alexander Archive.

FIGURE 7.4 Diagram of communal space from a "Worked Example."
Source: The Christopher Alexander Archive.

Public space was to be arranged by a more novel contrivance, one that skirted the issue of caste politics. Alexander noted the importance of "a community center which somehow manages to pull all the communal functions together" but perceived that any such central meeting space ran the risk of being "associated with one party, or certain families" and thus might "not contribute to social life at all."[32] To resolve this dilemma, he proposed, instead of a central square, "a *linear* center, containing some buildings facing in, some out, zigzagging between the different compounds"[33] (see Figure 7.4). In other words, to prevent one group's domination of public space, a miniature public niche, nestled between the walls surrounding the compound, would be accorded to each caste-based enclave. The separate niches were connected by a serpentine path, but its narrow winding form did not readily suggest a space where people could gather *en masse*; nor was it clear what might induce members of different castes to promiscuously comingle here, since caste-appropriate spaces had been provided. Alexander was correct to observe that a central public space ran the risk of domination by one group, but at least the centrality of that space—its hypothetical availability to all—renders such domination a visible matter of public concern and thus opens up the possibility of challenging that domination. Indeed, "public" amenities such as shared wells and religious edifices have long constituted the contested objects of caste-based activism in India. The representational function of a public space, serving to index relationships of power, also provides the ground upon which those relationships can be tested and transgressed.

Alexander suggested that the walls lining this path between the "public" niches would serve a didactic purpose. The walls would be inscribed "with the alphabet and messages written in such a way that their continuing presence forces people to absorb them."[34] Literacy constituted one among numerous priorities of Indian rural developmental schemes. However, the inscription of an alphabetic primer on village walls suggests quite a different form of pedagogy than that of a village schoolhouse.[35] Short-circuiting the contentious politics of *who*—which castes and genders—might benefit from formal schooling, this proposal suggested that habitual, semi-conscious exposure to information might be an effective substitute for student–teacher relationships.

The presumed efficacy of habitual exposure was also evident in Alexander's approach to agricultural modernization. Agricultural demonstrations and model farms—programs begun under colonialism and continued under national rural development schemes—required, Alexander noted, not a "physical plan" so much as "a change of attitude in the villagers":

> This change of attitude cannot be brought about by sporadic visits from the agricultural extension officer and village-level worker, but only by *the continuing presence* of demonstration methods, on site; there should be a demonstration farm, government or panchayat-owned, perhaps run by the village-level worker. . . . [T]he farm [should] be placed in such a way that every farmer passes it daily, on his way to and from the fields [emphasis added].[36]

Alexander makes the state's infrastructure of education—both schools and agricultural demonstrations—dissolve into the architecture of the village, so that the continuing presence of the thing (be it the alphabet or state-sponsored agricultural reform) could eschew two extremes: state coercion or state ineffectualness. Unaddressed in Alexander's spatial proposal was the villagers' demand—noted in his list of requirements—to dismantle the inegalitarian zamindari system of land ownership.[37] Certainly, reforming land policies may have exceeded the purview of architecture, but architectural planning could have helped imagine and visualize the possibility of land redistribution. Yet rather than supporting farmers' popular resistance against agrarian feudalism, the project of village modernization assumed a rearguard position. Alexander had good reason to camouflage this regressive version of modernization, rendering it into a discrete "continuing presence." The bureaucracy of state programs could cease to be bureaucracy (and thus avoid the pitfalls of bureaucratic ineptitude or bureaucratic intrusiveness) if bureaucracy metamorphosed into architecture. This transformation offered a strategy for reforming rural "backwardness" without an obvious incursion of state officers, effectively dissolving the distinction between village insiders and outsiders.

Architecture as a pastoral technology displaced the human agent of governmentality with nonhuman actors (e.g., alphabetic walls and model farms), intended to reform unconscious habits and attitudes without discussion. It was not a new strategy. Planners of colonial and national programs often presumed an epistemic impasse between rural residents and state actors that they sought to overcome by mimicking native media.[38] The political theorist and historian Subir Sinha describes the role played by such efforts in various late-colonial-era precursors to India's early national programs of rural village development:

> [The colonial governor of Punjab] set up stalls in village fairs, using the magic lantern and the gramophone, and distributed illustrated booklets of moral stories. Gandhian activists were involved in "mass contact" programs, and in setting examples through their own behavior. Gandhi urged them to enter into "every detail of village life." . . . [A] YMCA activist and [missionary's] wife, experimented with local dance and theatre forms to popularize the programs . . . [emphasis added].[39]

Sinha's description highlights how local media helped serve as an interface between village and state—"the cusp of community and the outside world"—an interface that, for Alexander, could become architectural, such that what was formerly outside could be brought within, thereby "nativizing" state-sponsored reforms, similar to the use of "local dance and theater forms" by US missionaries. The reforms could be rendered seemingly indigenous insofar as the architecture was largely derived from Alexander's fieldwork observations. Elements likely to provoke conflict—whether in the form of caste politics, state agricultural programs, or female schooling—were provided for architecturally and rendered minimally visible. Villagers' interests and the state's interests were subtly woven into a single fabric. Pastoral intimacy was to be effected through habit-forming devices supplementing human-to-human efforts of persuasion and thus displacing processes of negotiation and contestation.

PATTERN LANGUAGE

In 1961, immediately following Alexander's work in Bavra, he was invited by the industrialist Gautam Sarabhai to apply his fieldwork findings to the design of a new village for one of the rural communities displaced by Gujarat's various dam construction projects.[40] Sarabhai, one of the heirs to a textile empire, was involved at the time, along with his sister Gita, in a number of modernist design initiatives, including the National Institute of Design (NID), which had officially opened in Ahmedabad that same year. The NID was a joint initiative between the federal government, the Ford Foundation, and the Sarabhais, having emerged from programs to create village-based export industries, with Pupul Jayakar and Ray and Charles Eames serving as cultural advisors.[41] The Eameses, in suggesting that the NID's primary challenge would be the move from "unconscious" craft technique to conscious design methods, anticipated Alexander's framing of the putatively unconscious evolutions of various world architectures.[42] Indeed, when Alexander declined this commission, he attributed his decision to a perceived dearth of consciousness on the part of rural Indians:

> I gave this [commission] a great deal of thought, and realised that no village which I built, could ever be a living place, and that, in fact, the village would only come to life in a significant way *if the people of the village would understand these diagrams*, and would then build a village, in their own way, *under the impetus of these patterns* (diagrams). This realisation, was the birth of the thought which is now contained . . . in the theory of pattern languages.[43]

There is a striking inversion here between the respective roles of the "native informant" and the anthropological observer. It is the village residents who are seen to lack any knowledge of their village's form and spatial requirements because they lack an understanding of these *diagrams* (diagrams that represented a mix of federal developmental agenda and the extant conditions of another Gujarati village). Thus, the residents would need to be made conscious of their own village by being taught to understand the anthropologist's diagrammatic abstractions of another (presumably similar) village, albeit in a quasi-modernized form. Although only these residents could make the resulting village "come to life," they could offer nothing more than this vitality; for they lacked the requisite structuralist understanding of their own spatial practices.

Alexander confessed furthermore that his "own ignorance of India was far too great, and the diagrams were too naïve, and . . . the project would never succeed, without years and years of further effort, and closer knowledge of India."[44] Alexander's uncharacteristic humility here is somewhat belied by his immediately prior suggestion that, although *he* might possess insufficient knowledge of India, the pattern language—a sacred scripture of which he and his co-authors were merely the prophetic scribes—could compensate for this deficiency, providing a way to bypass the disjunction between the local and the universal through the device of structuralist comparison and abstraction. According to the paradigm of scriptural hermeneutics, the pattern language bears universal relevance but must be selectively interpreted, thickened, and applied to particular contexts under the careful professional guidance of the "missionary" expert. As such, a macroscopic understanding of architecture (of the *nature* of architecture in general) can be applied to the fine-grained variations of different world contexts. However, whereas a pastor (to abide with the Christian metaphor) must intimately know the flock so as to translate the sacred tongue into the vulgar, the pattern language defers the work of translation. On the one hand, Alexander avowed that seven months of village fieldwork cannot yield sufficient intimacy with local context; on the other hand, the pattern language, like a magical Rosetta stone, can obviate the need for translation as such; can obviate, that is, the need to know the "vernacular."

The pattern language had presumably digested a sufficient number of world architectures as to be appropriate to any local context, albeit still requiring the active effort of anthropological interpretation, of knowing what typologies to apply, where, and how. The work of interpretation was something for which architectural professionals were deemed qualified (assuming they were convertees to the pattern language sect). Of the residents to be displaced by the dam project, Alexander writes "*if* [they] *would* understand these diagrams," suggesting a glimmer of potential comprehension but also the unlikeliness of such an attainment. It seems that the rural residents would need to be first *modernized* so that they might be able to interpret the very diagrams that were to protect them against the depredations of modernity.

Concerning the CES's ambivalence toward modernization, it should be pointed out that Alexander declined Sarabhai's invitation *not* out of discomfort with the project's premise, that is, not because of the displacement of the residents under programs of industrial development. Indeed, the pretext of displacement is wholly endemic to his diagrammatic analysis of Bavra, insofar as the construction of a village *ex nihilo* presumes that villagers have been relocated. Structuralism, as a form of cultural comparison, lent itself to displacement: the identification of the shared essence or structure of the thing in question allowed for the transposition and conservation of that constant amidst relocation and modernization. Particularities could change so long as some (anthropologically divulged) essentiality was conserved. According to longstanding colonial discourses, though, this knowledge of the essential or structural was precisely what a rural subaltern lacked. According to such a diagnosis, a village resident could be thoroughly acquainted with her particular village layout but still utterly unable to adapt that layout to a new geographic context, allegedly not discerning between the necessary and the contingent. As such, fluency in the pattern language presupposed a form of epistemic subjectivity that was allegedly foreign to the rural resident. The village resident was thus placed in a double-bind in relation to the pattern language: to make use of the pattern language, s/he must be converted to a modern subject-position; but, once converted, s/he was no longer the properly rustic subject of village culture.

In Foucault's linking of pastoral power to Christian origins, the flock's religious affiliation appears as a given. However, pastoral power would seem to be especially expedient in contexts of conversion—not only religious conversion but also programs of modernization. The intimate knowledge of the native is what secures the authority of the missionary who must, to some degree, "go native." Because conversion must mediate between the local/

pagan and the Christian/universal, the missionary's local expertise has to exceed the local expertise of the actual locals. It must penetrate to the deep inner core of local practices and beliefs, dissect them, and thence establish kinships—fungibilities—between those beliefs and practices and the new body of beliefs and practices. The question is whether the convertee—in this case, let's say the subject of development—is ever deemed capable of negotiating her or his own relationship to the programs of modernization.

Scholarship on autoconstructed settlements shows residents capable of translating their needs and politics into the professional idioms and bureaucratic protocols of various social programs.[45] In these processes, they activate their relationships to documents, eking out documentary paths toward political ends. Yet, lest any romanticization of the "politics of the governed" beget political complacency at the cost of others' exploitation, it must be considered how different kinds of social practices once organized around (and by) different kinds of documentary relationships (under paradigms of modern bureaucracy) are increasingly being reorganized in the present day around assemblages of data collection and data interpretation whose primary claim rests on the promise, like Alexander's village proposals, of bypassing political and bureaucratic negotiation.

Regarding this question, the pattern language serves as a harbinger of two tendencies gaining ground in present-day contexts of transnational developmentalist schema: on the one hand, the establishment of procedures for local data collection that often leverage direct user-input (i.e., involving minimal intervention of human bureaucrats at the ground level, beyond initiating the user's participation); on the other hand, the (often secular) missionary-style rural and peri-urban architectural projects in which the foreign "missionary" displaces the need for any interaction between local residents and bureaucratic or political institutions because s/he carries full responsibility for managing the financial, political, and legal aspects of a given project. As such, a growing danger to the viability of popular politics is posed not by the alienating effects of bureaucracy so much as the severing of the populace from that bureaucracy by dint of pastoral technics. The pattern language, by purporting to suture the division between the macroscopic domain of universal nature and the microscopic domain of local particularity, simultaneously threatened to suture that space of indeterminacy and conflict that might otherwise be mediated through politics. As an array of organizational *dispositifs* intended to enfold local practices into the rubrics of governmentality, pastoral technics also enfolded the presumed agency of the former within the prerogatives of the latter.

NOTES

1 Christopher Alexander and Janet Johnson, "Center for Environmental Structure, Project 1, 1962: Elementary School, Bavra, India," n.p.

2 It is unclear what Janet Johnson's role was vis-à-vis Alexander's Bavra fieldwork, as the fieldwork report was coauthored by them but nonetheless uses the first-person pronoun in describing Alexander's activities. The two were romantically involved, and there are photographs and personal letters indicating that Johnson visited Alexander in Bavra but with no indication of whether she was there in an academic or purely personal capacity. Her collaboration with Alexander ended after the coauthored report. The subsequent development of this work into *Notes on the Synthesis of Form* appears under his sole authorship.

3 Alexander was involved in Harvard's new Center for Cognitive Studies, cofounded by the psychologists Jerome Bruner and George Miller. See Jon Kracauer, "Christopher Alexander," unpublished manuscript, 1985 (Christopher Alexander papers). On Alexander's influence on the field of interface design, see Molly Wright Steenson, *Architectural Intelligence: How Designers and Architects Created the Digital Landscape* (Cambridge, MA: MIT Press, 2017), chap. 2.

4 On self-help housing see Nancy H. Kwak, *A World of Homeowners: American Power and the Politics of Housing Aid* (Chicago: University of Chicago Press, 2015). See also Ijlal Muzaffar, "The Periphery Within: Modern Architecture and the Making of the Third World" (Ph.D. diss., Massachusetts Institute of Technology, 2007).

5 On pastoral power, see Michel Foucault, *Security, Territory, Population: Lectures at the Collège de France, 1977–78*, ed. Michel Senellart, trans. Graham Burchell (Basingstoke: Palgrave Macmillan/République Française, 2007), 203, 209. See also Michel Foucault, "*Omnes et Singulatim*: Towards a Criticism of Political Reason," in *The Tanner Lectures on Human Values*, ed. Sterling McMurrin (Salt Lake City: University of Utah Press, 1981), vol. 2, 225–254.

6 The ills of modernist architecture form a common theme of Alexander's writings. See, for example, Christopher Alexander, *The Timeless Way of Building* (New York: Oxford University Press, 1979), chap. 13.

7 On efforts to render developmental programs more locally persuasive by adapting certain local conventions, see Nicole Sackley, "The Village as Cold War Site: Experts, Development, and the History of Rural Reconstruction," *Journal of Global History* 6, no. 3 (2011): 481–504. See also Subir Sinha, "Lineages of the Developmentalist State: Transnationality and Village India, 1900–1965," *Comparative Studies in Society and History* 50, no. 1 (January 2008): 68–69.

8 On bureaucracy as a "diffusion of responsibility," see Matthew S. Hull, *Government of Paper: The Materiality of Bureaucracy in Urban Pakistan* (Berkeley: University of California Press, 2012), 115.

9 Max Weber, *Economy and Society*, trans. Keith Tribe (Cambridge, MA: Harvard University Press, 2019), chap. 3.

10 Alexander, "A City Is Not Like a Tree," *Architectural Forum* 122, no. 1 (April 1965): 58.

11 See Christopher Alexander, Sara Ishikawa, and Murray Silverstein, *A Pattern Language Which Generates Multi-Service Centers* (Berkeley: Center for Environmental Structure, 1968). See also Alexander et al., *A Pattern Language* (New York: Oxford University Press, 1977); and Alexander, *The Timeless Way of Building*.

12 Michel Foucault, *The Hermeneutics of the Subject* Lectures at The Collège de France, 1981–82, ed. Frederic Gros, trans. Graham Burchell (New York: Palgrave Macmillan, 2005).

13 Partha Chatterjee, *Politics of the Governed* (New York: Columbia University Press, 2004); Teresa Caldeira, "Peripheral urbanization: Autoconstruction, Transversal Logics, and Politics in Cities of the Global South," *Environmental Planning D* 35, no. 1: 3–20.

14 Some examples of work in a similar vein, tracing concatenations of actors implicated in the agency of autoconstructed or other quasi-legal polities, includes Nikhil Anand, *Hydraulic City: Water and the Infrastructures of Citizenship in Mumbai* (Durham, NC: Duke University Press, 2017); James Holston, *Insurgent Citizenship: Disjunctions of Democracy and Modernity in Brazil* (Princeton, NJ: Princeton University Press, 2008).

15 Chatterjee, *Politics of the Governed*, 55–56.

16 See for example UN-Habitat, *A Practical Guide to Designing, Planning, and Executing Citywide Slum Upgrading Programmes* (Nairobi: United Nations Human Settlements Programme, 2014), 32–33.

17 See, for example, Nicholas Negroponte, *The Architecture Machine* (Cambridge, MA: MIT Press, 1970).

18 James C. Scott, *Seeing Like a State: How Certain Schemes to Improve the Human Condition Have Failed* (New Haven: Yale University Press, 1998). As a welcome counterpoint to Scott's representation of the state's rationalizing and macroscopic tendencies, see Daniel Immerwahr, *Thinking Small: The United States and the Lure of Community Development* (Cambridge, MA: Harvard University Press, 2015).

19 Christopher Alexander, *Notes on the Synthesis of Form* (Cambridge, MA: Harvard University Press, 1964).

20 Ibid., 52–53.

21 Ibid., 34.

22 Christopher Alexander, Mike Cox, Halim Abdel-Halim, et al., "The Grass Roots Housing Process," unpublished manuscript, Center for Environmental Structure, June 1973, 11–12.

23 Ibid., 24–25 [emphasis added].

24 Ibid., 37–38 [emphasis added].

25 Alexander, Cox, Abdel-Halim, et al., "The Grass Roots Housing Process," 39.

26 On the intersection of architecture and computation at Cambridge University, see Scott Keller, "Fenland Tech: Architectural Science in Postwar Cambridge," *Grey Room*, no. 23 (Spring 2006): 40–65.

27 Alexander, *Notes on the Synthesis of Form*: "Appendix I: A Worked Example."

28 Ibid., 137.

29 James A. Jaffe, "Layering Law upon Custom: The British in Colonial West India," *FIU Law Review* 10, no. 1 (2014): 85–110.

30 BR Ambedkar, "On Village Panchayats Bill," in *Dr. Babasaheb Ambedkar Writings and Speeches*, eds. Vasant Moon and Hari Narke, 2nd ed. (New Delhi: Dr. Ambedkar Foundation, 2014), vol. 2, 101–121.

31 Alexander justified the perpetuation of walled compounds by claiming they might eventually encourage women to emerge from purdah because of the mediating protection of this domain of semi-seclusion. However, as he claims to derive the organizational device of the compound from Bavra's existing arrangement, the claim to liberation seems far-fetched. Alexander, *Notes on the Synthesis of Form*, 171.

32 Alexander, *Notes on the Synthesis of Form*, 170–171.

33 Ibid., 167–168 [emphasis added].

34 Ibid., 168.

35 Decades later, the architect Yona Friedman proposed to UNESCO the use of "*journaux murals.*" See Ginger Nolan, *Savage Mind to Savage Machine: Racial Science and Twentieth-Century Design* (Minneapolis: University of Minnesota Press, 2021), chap. 4.
36 Alexander, *Notes on the Synthesis of Form*, 160.
37 Ibid., 137, 162. On debates and policies around postcolonial land redistribution, see Benjamin Siegal, *Hungry Nation: Food, Famine, and the Making of Modern India* (Cambridge: Cambridge University Press, 2018).
38 On the British colonial use of "native" media, see Ginger Nolan, *The Neocolonialism of the Global Village* (Minneapolis: University of Minnesota Press, 2018).
39 Sinha, "Lineages of the Developmentalist State," 68–69. On the use of folk arts and media in colonial and postcolonial development programs, see also F. L. Brayne, *The Remaking of Village India* (London: Oxford University Press, 1929); Albert Mayer, *Pilot Project India* (Berkeley: University of California Press, 1958); Sackley, "The Village as Cold War Site."
40 On the role of dam construction in Indian nation-building, see Ateya Khorikiwala, "The Well-Fed Subject: Modern Architecture in the Quantitative State, India (1943–1984)" (Ph.D. diss., Harvard University, 2017), chap. 2.
41 On the founding of the National Institute of Design, see Eugene S. Staples, *Forty Years: A Learning Curve, The Ford Foundation Programs in India, 1952–1992* (New Delhi: Ford Foundation, 1992), 51.
42 The Eameses wrote of craft practices in India:

> The decisions that are made in a tradition-oriented society are apt to be unconscious decisions—in that each situation or action *automatically* calls for a specified reaction. *Behaviour patterns are pre-programmed, pre-set.* . . . The nature of a communication-oriented society is different by kind—not by degree. All decisions must be conscious decisions evaluating changing factors."
> Charles and Ray Eames, "The India Report" (Ahmedabad: National Institute of Design, 1958), 3 [emphasis added]

43 Christopher Alexander and Janet Johnson, "Elementary School, Bavra, India" [emphasis added], n.p.
44 Ibid.
45 See Chatterjee, *Politics of the Governed*, 56–64. See also Anand, *Hydraulic City*, chap. 2.

8

The technical state

Programs, positioning, and the integration of architects in political society in Mexico, 1945–1955

Albert José-Antonio López

A POLITICAL SOCIETY IN TRANSITION

From the late-1930s through the mid-1950s, Mexico's political society, state administrative bodies, and various civil and professional organizations underwent a series of transformations heralding what some have called a "transition" between "revolutionary" and "postrevolutionary" chapters in modern Mexican history. Key amongst these changes was the creeping empowerment of the executive branch in claiming new jurisdictions and resolving—sometimes forcefully—structural issues within the national political economy. This trend was initiated toward the end of the term of President Lázaro Cárdenas (1934–40). With the troubled and violent elections of 1940, Manuel Ávila Camacho (1940–46) established a consolidatory politic of so-called "National Unity," in practice a contested rhetorical strategy deployed on numerous fronts that lingered in the Mexican political lexicon well into the administration of Miguel Alemán Valdés (1946–1952). "Unity" variously could be used to describe a pragmatic ideological centrism, an imagined popular-frontism, a balancing of various regional dynamics of power and economic development, as well as a forceful co-option or neutralization of both far-right and left-wing political challenges.[1] The postrevolutionary transition was notably marked by a redistribution of power as well as a generation change. With the reorganization of the country's dominant political party, renamed in 1946 as the *Partido Revolucionario Institutional* (PRI), and the election of Alemán, the Mexican state was increasingly led by a younger, largely civilian and professional leadership rather than by former revolutionary military commanders; the military lost a portion of political authority despite producing the occasional electoral challenger and being a lingering influence on political culture well through the 1950s. This complex period of political and social transition contributed to the complicated mid-twentieth century Mexican state's characterization as an "inclusionary" as well as "bureaucratic" authoritarian apparatus.[2]

Within this sociopolitical environment, a small handful of Mexican architects became critical agents within key bureaucratic institutions, most notably with the appointment of Carlos Lazo Barreiro (1914–1955) as head of the *Secretaría de Comunicaciones y Obras Públicas* (SCOP) during the administration of Adolfo Ruiz Cortines (1952–1958). The elevated position of power attained by architects within the nascent postrevolutionary state was out

DOI: 10.4324/9781003193654-12

of keeping with the discipline's traditional social stature among other professional experts—some of which were colloquially referred to as *técnicos* according to their perceived "scientific" qualifications.[3] Membership to this techno-professional class was typically extended to persons in the various fields of engineering, the sciences, and increasingly the relatively new profession of economists.[4] This essay thus attempts to offer a response to the question: how did a small group of architects—members of a profession of privilege, respectability, and mass public appeal in Mexican society but not traditional recruits for the highest levels of public office—manage to achieve such prominence in the construction of Mexico's postrevolutionary *political* society and developmentalist political economy?

While architectural historians have correctly focused on the role of differing modes of historicism, architectural functionalism, monumentality, and spectacle as formal expressions of redefined national identity, revolutionary ideology, or state expressions of power, and political theorists have often attended to more hegemonic narratives of unidirectional professional co-option, I emphasize a more politically complex, contested, and dynamic narrative of modern architecture's indispensability to the state. I acknowledge the critical import of the built legacies of this moment but emphasize the equal importance of architecture's *claims* within political, professional, and economic *discourses*, their insertion and rhetorical use in broader forums of the national political imaginary, and their reception by political society.

Drawing on the work of sociologist Andrew Abbott, I interpret the notion of architecture as both a jurisdictional profession and one that is shaped by connected external fields.[5] For Abbott, professional jurisdiction relies on the ability of members of a profession to claim a certain area of expertise within a competitive interprofessional environment via sanctioned formal knowledge and therefore authority over specific tasks. Changes to the dynamic of the system of professions derive from the interplay of competing professional claims, external regulatory, legal, and organizational factors, or technology. I add that some of the most important causes of these shifts—at least in this period of Mexican history—came from a complex yet relatively small political arena marked by interpersonal relations, loyalties, and competition between areas of political and ideological exclusion. The system of professions in which modern Mexican architecture operated was closely tied to shifts of power within Mexican political society due in part to a complicated process of postrevolutionary political reorganization that gradually led to what is referred to as the professionalization of politics.

As noted by historian Aaron Navarro, during this moment of political transition, political communication relied less on physical acts of violence like those that characterized the county's earlier transitions of power. Instead, a more "modern" form of political speech was adapted by Mexico's dominant political party that relied on new forums and technologies of political engagement, political restructuring, ideological improvisation, and rhetorical strategies to co-opt and neutralize the threat of opposition.[6] It is critical that we add to this assertion, however, by noting that as the Mexican state became increasingly dominated by university-educated civilians, these newest members of political society became the greatest articulators of the country's modern political speech. In the case that I describe, concerted efforts were made by a small group of architects to inject their professional terminology into political discourse with hopes that it would be accepted by the more established leadership not only for nationalistic purposes of ideological coercion but also for maximum professional integration.

As more established members within this amorphous and dynamic political environment sought both signs and new actors to contribute to the briefly integrationalist postrevolutionary project of social, political, and economic renovation, the new class of educated professionals—architects aggressively at the vanguard—saw an inroad into the expanding bureaucratic organizations that administered the growing powers of the Mexican executive branch of government. Activist architects' claims to ever-higher positions of technical authority and expertise momentarily translated into meaningful political appointments that gave a means by which to make their modernist and politically provocative visions of social, political, and economic development manifest. Complementary to this, architects, especially those involved in urbanism and planning, lent special credential and legitimacy to the political leadership, particularly during the term of Miguel Alemán, Mexico's first civilian president. This was done not only by interventions in the built environment but also in their occasional contribution of politically useful concepts to the ideologically unstable brew of inchoate developmentalism as well as their addition of further nuance to the defining but semantically transitory political rhetoric of the period. For a brief period, architects and politicians established an exceptionally intimate but also very complicated relationship of mutual political dependency that stretched the definitions of what an architect or *técnico* was in Mexican political society.

PLANNING, PROPAGANDA, AND THE GOVERNMENT PROGRAM

Let us turn to the architect and planner Carlos Lazo Barreiro (1914–1955) in order to explore in concrete detail some of these architectural/political developments in the 1940s and 1950s. Lazo was an influential and critical voice during this period. In 1943, following his publicized travels in the United States to research regional planning and industrial architecture under the AIA's Delano-Aldrich Fellowship, he authored numerous articles in *Construcción*—a smaller but noteworthy technical journal directed by Basque journalist, intellectual, and Spanish Republican exile Almiro P. Moratinos.[7] Lazo's writing furthered advocacy for the Mexican state's more effective adoption of national planning—a campaign launched by Carlos Contreras Elizondo (1892–1970) two decades prior.[8] Lazo's contribution to the language of Mexican planning discourse was notable in that he advocated an "organic" and most importantly "*integral*" planning of all social and economic projects regardless of particular institutional jurisdiction.[9] In 1945, Lazo was recruited into the *Comisión de Programa*, or Program Commission, for Alemán's presidential campaign.[10] By June 1946, we see the melding of his roles as a contributor to *Construcción* and member of the Alemán campaign in his article "*La Planificación y La Política: Programa de Gobierno.*" While this work represented one of his earliest attempts to fully articulate all of the planning and administrative components of his theory of *planificación integral*, it more importantly served as a vehicle in criticizing the aging political cohort that had steered the Mexican state since the conclusion of the Revolution. These general criticisms of incompetent and corrupt military leadership were not-so-indirect jabs at the outgoing President Ávila Camacho's appointment of his famously capricious, violent, and self-indulgent brother, Maximino, to the helm of the SCOP.[11] In the PRI's ostensibly renovatory exercise in relegitimization during the 1945–1946 campaign period, an internal voice critical toward the erstwhile regime and party shortcomings was apparently seen by some political leaders as a valuable asset for an incoming civilian administration intended to further the reorganized dominant party's hegemony. What made Lazo's criticism stand out, however, was his skill in balancing the ritualistic deposition found in anti-corruption rhetoric with the anticipatory tone central to a messianic modernism that painted the image of an inevitable technical leadership guided by reason, education, expertise, and more importantly a sense of political vocation and national duty. He contrasted the nepotism and cronyism of the decadent *"caudillaje"* with the age of the *técnico*, "the generation that is 'sufficiently' restorative."[12]

The moralizing and pro-technical professional theories of governance contained within Lazo's *Programa* appear to have contributed to the development of Alemán's political promises of modernization, reform, and clean government in the later stages of his campaign.[13] Lazo's growing value to Alemán was confirmed when, in 1947, the newly elected president appointed the architect as an *Oficial Mayor*, or senior official, of the newly created *Secretaría de Bienes Nacionales e Inspección Administrativa* (Secretariat of National Resources and Administrative Inspection).[14] The architect was put in charge of the Secretaría's *Comisión Técnica de Arquitectos* (Technical Commission of Architects) and *Comisión Federal de Planificación* (Federal Commission of Planning), positions which he used to further develop the planning study that he continued to call a *Programa de Gobierno* (see Figure 8.1). By late 1948, however, members of the Alemán administration were proving to be no less corrupt than their predecessors. With the efficacy of the new secretariat in doubt, its director—the renowned anthropologist and archeologist Alfonso Caso (1896–1970)—decided to resign. After receiving clear political pressure, Lazo resigned soon after.[15] Despite this, the architect managed to remain close to Alemán, becoming a *Consejero de la Presidencia de la República Mexicana*—a close presidential advisor.[16]

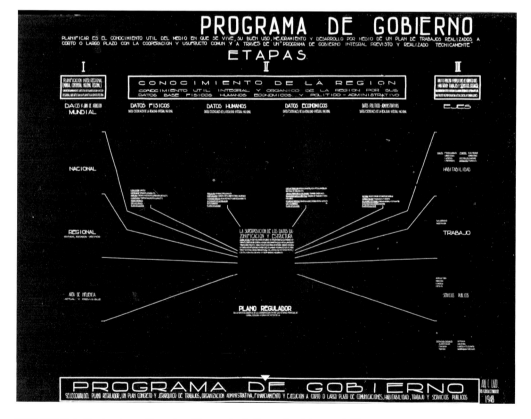

FIGURE 8.1 Carlos Lazo Barreiro (drawn by J. Gonzales Naranjo), "Programa de Gobierno" (1948).

Source: Published in Lazo, *México: Programa de Gobierno* (Mexico City: Editorial Espacios, 1952).

In maneuvering through the expanding political mire and bureaucratic shuffles, Lazo took the tremendous amount of work that he and his staff had compiled during his tenure at *Bienes Nacionales* and put it toward the construction of a renewed public campaign in favor of coordinated planning and major government reform. By early 1950, his writings were being featured in *Excélsior*, the second largest newspaper circulated in Mexico City at that time and known for being generally pro-development, with an assortment of authors highlighting economic matters, planning, and architecture. In the twenty full-page Sunday articles that he published over the course of several months, Lazo returned to the topic of a well-planned *Programa de Gobierno*.[17] These installments offered the newspaper's readers a broader understanding of *planificación integral* as a policy of regional reorganization and national economic development, centralized planning administration, political-administrative consolidation, and greater executive powers of oversight and execution. Out of the many proposals in the "Programa," Lazo offered three critical ideas to these ends: the formation of *Unidades Regionales* or new delineations of regional administration, *Zonas Vitales* of natural resource extraction and manufacturing, and the creation of a new *Secretaría Técnica de Planificación de la Presidencia* enabling an administrative consolidation more firmly under the charge of the president and his key technical advisors—institutions that echoed contemporary administrative reforms being made by the corporatist regime of Juán Perón in Argentina (see Figure 8.2).[18]

FIGURE 8.2 Proposed location of a *Secretaria Técnica de Planificación* in the Mexican Executive Branch of government.

Source: Carlos Lazo Barreiro, "México: Programa de Gobierno, V. Proposición para México, C. Organización del Ejecutivo," *Excelsior*, September 3, 1950. Archivo General de la Nación, Archivo Carlos Lazo.

Within Lazo's hybrid regionalist, economic-nationalist, technocratic, and presidentialist framework, the multivalent rhetoric of "national unity" was given further structural nuance. To be sure, Lazo's delineation of new "regional unities" and their larger "vital zones" was a strategy for localized regional investment and development.[19] These new "unities" clearly pointed to recent regional planning activity and inter-secretarial coordination such as the *Comisión del Papaloapan*, a vast hydrologic, sanitary, industrial, and agricultural project administered by the *Secretaría de Recursos Hidráulicos* and encompassing a total of 17,800 square miles, including portions of the states of Oaxaca, Veracruz, and Puebla.[20] However, the redrawing of Mexico's regional territorial map also argued the obsolescence of its current political-administrative map, in short posing a potentially significant challenge to the established structures and systems of regional authority.

In describing how this new Mexican politico-administrative reality could be brought about, Lazo stated the current relationship between Mexican politics, civil society, and the general public was equally at a point of supersession. With disdain for the current electoral system, he echoed Renan by advocating for a "daily plebiscite" as the only viable means for a Mexican National regeneration defined by what he saw as a new, insurgent, and rational "planning" attitude as well as a more emotional unifying sentiment that he summarized as an almost mystical "passion for Mexico."[21] He supplied a new corporatistic functional schematic for public order, urged a unified polity for its rational and ordered manifestation, and prophesied that with its manifestation, Mexico's chief source of political power—the executive—would finally have a suitable "foundational structure" by which to execute "*una política*"—a single unified policy amongst all levels of government, administration, public, and private interests.[22] And yet, with his disdain for liberal capitalism and emphasis of a unified national policy, Lazo—in an effort to defend against accusations of being a fascist or a communist—was sure to vocally denounce totalitarianism as incompatible with his idealized polity. Ideologically, he positioned his *planificación* and *programa* in the vein of various late nineteenth- and early twentieth-century Catholic integralist movements in the hispano, franco, and lusophone worlds as well as into the category of "third-way" economic activist political systems common to the larger developing countries caught up in a growing "Cold War."[23]

The *Secretaría Técnica de Planificación* was intended to be the cornerstone of the new "foundational structure" that both articulated and supported presidential political action and, perhaps most importantly, asserted the power of the presidency. It was as much an instrument of coordination as it was of ostensible anti-corruption oriented moralization—which in this context connoted both a critique of the failures of the *Secretaría de Bienes Nacionales* and a renewed crackdown on graft and unsanctioned networks of patronage. Loosely echoing Fayolist administrative thought, Lazo's proposed new secretariat was to be functionally compartmentalized into three organizational branches whose responsibilities were to plan, coordinate, and monitor. Taken together, I argue that Lazo's *Programa de Gobierno*, along with its defining policy of *planificación integral*, was a serious, if conceptually radical, contribution to the contemporary discourse of *Mexicanidad*—a term used to describe the revolutionary-era project of national identity formation but later appropriated by *Alemanistas* as a byword for the administration's efforts toward statist industrialization and integrative national development.[24]

Excélsior had a wide readership. Lazo's articles—saturated with striking graphics and integralist, developmentalist rhetoric—were tests in the efficacy of his technicist planning language in persuading a broad public. More important to the political traction of this rhetoric, however, was the reception of these same ideas in political society. The architect-planner sent copies of the articles in *Excélsior* to a number of fellow technocrats and established politicians, including former presidents such as Ávila Camacho.[25] At the same time, he maintained an active correspondence with Lázaro Cárdenas, often seeking the former president's input in regard to planning policy.[26] Taken together, we may consider Lazo's efforts as a multi-objective project of jurisdictional expansion and collective professional mobility but also a grand maneuver at attaining personal political gain. The *Programa de Gobierno* is an example of Mexican political *futurismo*.[27] It aided in demonstrating to the established political class that *técnicos*, and especially *arquitectos planificadores* (planner-architects) such as himself, were capable of producing convincing and viable theories for rationalizing the systems of political administration.[28]

THE ARCHITECT-POLITICIAN

For an architect-planner, the ability to both project grand images into the national imaginary and wield a broad technical language meaningful to the discourse of socioeconomic development was key to their political participation. However, in the construction-frenzied late 1940s and 1950s, prestigious building projects were central, especially for the newly emergent architect-planner, as a means of furthering a powerful public image. Up until this point Lazo's planning theories were more abstract than physical, but he was soon given the opportunity to transform these abstract proposals of planning and management into something more concrete in what would become Mexico's most iconic architectural assemblage to emerge from this polity.

Toward the last two years of his presidency, President Alemán was concerned with the fact that construction of the new *Ciudad Universitaria* (CU) of the Universidad Nacional Autónoma de México (UNAM)—a project designed and led by the architects Mario Pani (1911–1993) and Enrique del Moral (1905–1987)—had stalled. The president decided to push the CU to completion, a decision no doubt reflective of a desire for an additional legacy project that would soften criticisms of his socioeconomic policies as well as deflect any accusations that corruption under his rule had impeded the material progress of the nation. He named Carlos Novoa, the director-general of the Bank of Mexico, as president of the governing body in charge of the university's construction. In April of 1950—while Lazo was in the process of mailing copies of his *Programa de Gobierno* to high-ranking members of the PRI—Novoa officially hired the architect-planner to be the *Gerente General*, or general manager, of the design and building of the new campus.[29]

The CU was to be completed in two years, and to achieve this deadline, Lazo applied an administrative structure similar to the one outlined in the *Programa de Gobierno* to its construction program. Echoing Lazo's position on the role that a decadent political society played in delaying socioeconomic development, it was determined that many of the challenges in completing the UNAM resided within the inner politics of the Mexican architectural profession. Not long after his appointment as general manager of the CU, Lazo's initiatives—and resistance to them—became a lightning rod for a major professional dispute that in many ways epitomized the generational and ideological conflicts that existed for some years amongst competing factions of elites within the new dispensation. The rift came to a head in late 1950 with the formation of the *Movimiento de Unidad y*

Renovación (Movement for Unity and Renovation) by members of the *Sociedad de Arquitectos Mexicanos*, or SAM. The movement's leadership consisted of the architects Carlos Lazo Barreiro, Raúl Cacho, Augusto H. Alvarez, Juan O'Gorman, Augusto Pérez Palacios, Santiago Greenham, Pedro Ramírez Vázquez, and Jorge L. Medellín.[30] The group issued a manifesto which promised the membership of the SAM that under a new leadership, the professional society would be able to orchestrate a "practical plan of action" imbued with "national sentiment" and "professional consciousness" that would enable the profession to achieve a number of collective goals including "the inclusion of [their] concrete proposals into future constructive Government Programs that were to be realized within the country."[31] In addition, it also promised that a reformed professional society would from then on ensure that future nationalist projects of great symbolic import, such as the *Ciudad Universitaria*, would be the task of a unified profession rather than of one exclusive and well-connected faction. This was a clear if indirect reference to Mario Pani's relation to former Secretary of Finance Alberto J. Pani, his oversized influence in Mexican architecture, and his leadership along with Federico Mariscal in the *Colegio de Arquitectos Mexicanos* (CAM)—a rival professional society to the SAM that had been established in 1945. In this light the manifesto's call for "unity and renovation" was nothing short of a project of coalition between ideologically disparate groups of architects in order to disrupt entrenched professional cliques, their protected relationship with the state, and their monopolization of architectural work.

With questionable campaign tactics and a rushed election, the CAM was merged with the SAM under Lazo's leadership.[32] Given Lazo's good rapport with the Alemán administration, the president's private secretary, Rogerio de la Selva, offered to settle any resistance.[33] Lazo refused this initial offer of direct presidential intervention, noting that such partisanship would cost him his legitimacy in the eyes of many of his fellow architects. Still, in the days that followed, the movement was met with fierce opposition and included a classic Cold War era attack with red-baiting that made front page news in *Últimas Noticias*, the afternoon edition of *Excélsior*.[34] Lazo actions were condemned, as he was denounced as the leader of a communist cell, a somewhat curious choice of attack against a man known for openly espousing his beliefs in Catholic–humanist social justice and injecting the rhetoric of a corporatistic, *integralist* nationalism into the discourse of Mexican economic development—the latter being a talking point more in line with various far-right "action" groups. Nevertheless, it was a weighty denouncement, fueled no doubt by his close friendships with various Marxist intellectuals, his apparent closeness to Cárdenas, his employment at the historically left-wing *Instituto Politécnico Nacional*, or IPN, and his general critique of liberal governance in the *Programa de Gobierno*. Responding to the personal political smear, Lazo promptly issued a statement to the press defending his reputation and the integrity and nationalist credentials of the *Movimiento*.[35] To further legitimize his position, Lazo agreed to a more monitored election—which he also won. At a large banquet held in the newly purchased headquarters of the unified CAM/SAM, he also managed a public display of accord with the architect Federico Mariscal, who in less than two months went from denouncing Lazo as a subversive communist to praising his work, declaring loyalty to him and urging the whole profession to work under him.[36] As president of the unified CAM/SAM, Lazo was now the official spokesman and mediator between the state, current presidential administration, and the architectural profession. He now commanded the necessary professional and political power to test his administrative project upon the *Ciudad Universitaria* and bring the campus to completion, therefore satisfying both his and the president's political objectives.

As the *Ciudad Universitaria* rose out of the rocky Pedregal in the southern reaches of Mexico City, Lazo furthered his efforts at turning the construction zone into a test site of administrative coordination. The success of the new administrative model rapidly hastened its completion and turned the campus into a set where mass construction was its greatest drama. This spectacle served to the political benefit of the Alemán administration. Lazo similarly benefited from the spectacle of construction to visually convey the efficacy of his managerial strategies and the promise of his political vision. With the campus rapidly becoming a usable backdrop for public assembly, Lazo utilized his positions as head of the CAM/SAM, general manager of the CU, and representative of the Alemán administration to activate its spaces in ways that further bolstered his image not only as a professional leader and political spokesman but as a public intellectual and visionary. In 1952, the campus was used by the CAM/SAM to host the VIII *Congreso Panamericano de Arquitectos* (Pan-American Congress of Architects). Lazo included within its many exhibitions a sizeable display of his *Programa de Gobierno*, conveying his ideas on regional and national planning and the future *integral* developmentalist ethos that he desired for Mexico to an international audience of fellow architectural professionals (see Figure 8.3).[37]

FIGURE 8.3 Carlos Lazo Barreiro, Exhibition of *México: Programa de Gobierno* (1952).

Source: Archivo General de la Nación, Archivo Carlos Lazo.

Lazo built off of his reputation as one of the primary public figures behind the completion of the CU to disseminate more of his political thought via printed media. In the same year, he had key speeches that he delivered during the construction of the CU and other works of his political thought published and distributed. One of these was *Pensamiento y Destino de la Ciudad Universitaria de México*, a medium-sized book containing the decidedly nationalist, humanist, and cosmic language of Lazo's vision of the new campus, proposals for a new *Instituto de Planificación* that would be capable of giving the UNAM's highest terminal degree, and a very concrete but never implemented 100-page draft for a new Organic Law for the UNAM.[38] Another book that came that year—notably in time for Mexico's presidential elections—was a lavish professional portfolio-like compilation of materials from his *Programa de Gobierno* published by *Editorial Espacios*—an architectural press headed by the architect Guillermo Rossell de la Lama (1925–2010). It was produced in very small numbers and distributed to a select few, with some evidence that this publication was designed to be circulated amongst Mexico's more established leadership. Lazo's visionary capabilities, managerial capacity, service to the PRI and the outgoing administration, growing public popularity, and his successful recruitment of a team of skilled professionals made him exceptionally viable for higher political recruitment. Adolfo Ruiz Cortines, former head of the *Secretaría de Gobernación* under Alemán, was elected in 1952. His administration promptly named Lazo as the head of the SCOP—the first architect to hold this post traditionally reserved for either engineers or generals. The significance of this achievement for the architectural profession was such that differences were partially cast aside, with Lazo receiving a telegram of begrudging congratulations from Mario Pani.[39]

PUBLIC WORKS AND THE "HEROIC" *TÉCNICO*

Lazo transferred much of the cadre of administrators that he brought together for the construction of the CU into the SCOP. They had to reckon with numerous discrepancies inherited from the Alemán administration. Lazo's predecessor at the SCOP, Agustín García López, was notoriously corrupt.[40] Under his tenure, the Alemán administration had accrued 80 million pesos of debt, and several highways had been paid for yet only existed in name.[41] President Adolfo Ruiz Cortines, a former accountant, campaigned on public financial accountability, personal political austerity, and restoring the image of the hard-working, patriotic, honest, and intelligent civil servant.[42] To combat these problems and political expectations, Lazo initiated an overhaul of the SCOP that was rationalistic as much as it was symbolic, pragmatic as much as it was political. His tenure was marked by administrative reform initiatives inspired by his *Programa de Gobierno*. Many of its boldest plans did not come to pass—such as the lofty desire to create an entirely new executive dependency with the powerful authority of supervening the divisions of the federal bureaucracy; an effort to arrange for a presidential decree that would have made the SCOP's *Dirección de Planificación* a similarly powerful apparatus of inter-secretarial coordination was stillborn.[43] Still, the tripartite administrative functions of "planning," "coordinating," and "monitoring" (later rephrased as "controlling") were retained within the schema of the SCOP's internal administrative layout. The SCOP's administration, organized according to the praxis of *planificación integral*, was now directed at the SCOP's given and expanding jurisdictions over the construction and operation of telecommunications, transportation, and public works. Meanwhile, the dream of authoritative inter-secretarial coordination was reduced to a noteworthy apparatus of coercion. The SCOP's *Gerencia de Promoción*, was created to "[seek] the cooperation of all national sectors so as to express a true government plan."[44] It was headed by Guillermo Rossell de la Lama, whose team—largely culled from *Editorial Espacios*—expended great effort in printing and distributing informative pamphlets amongst the SCOP employees, massive and lavishly illustrated *Memorias* detailing both the completed, ongoing, and proposed work of the dependency among high-profile government officials, and propagandistic exhibitions directed to the more general public.

This politico-administrative reorganization took monumental architectural form in the rehabilitation of a structurally deficient, massive, unfinished hospital belonging to the *Instituto Mexicano del Seguro Social*, or Mexican Social Security Institute (IMSS), located in the Mexico City neighborhood of Narvarte.[45] The hospital had been designed by Raúl Cacho—a close supporter of Lazo's in the *Movimiento de Unidad y Renovación*. The adaptive reuse of the structure enabled a rapid architectural centralization of the SCOP's many scattered offices, thus making possible the fullest working implementation of the new administrative program within a year of coming to office. For the project, Lazo formed a team that included himself, the building's original architect, and Augusto Pérez Palacios (also a key supporter from the *Movimiento*) to strengthen the building's framework, reprogram the function of its spaces of circulation, and make it representative of the new mission of the expanding planning bureaucracy. This last task was given to a team of artists including the architect-painter Juan O'Gorman, José Chavez Morado, Jorge Best, Arturo Estrada, Rodrigo Arenas Betancourt, and Francisco Zúñiga. All were commissioned to integrate their plastic arts—including 6,000 square meters of mosaic murals—over the building's principal facades.

The Centro SCOP has often been cited as one of the paragons of the movement of *integración plástica*. While *integración plástica* was often regarded as a didactic interface pregnant with content reflecting the manifold and often contradictory facets of Mexican nationalism and the particular political and ideological perspectives of its artists, it also came to represent—especially by the mid-twentieth century—a more coercive turn in the relationship between the Mexican state, architecture, and the plastic arts. It had evolved more or less into an "official" mode of artistic production.[46] While the hallowed characterization of the historical and revolutionary figures critical to the mythos of the revolutionary Mexican nation-state persisted and continued to be embodied by the figural representation of *jefes*, *caudillos*, *campesinos*, and *obreros*, this pantheon expanded over time so as to extol an emergent hero of the postrevolutionary period: *técnicos*.

Material from the process of the building's early stages of rehabilitation portrayed both the shifting perceptions of the *técnico* in the capacity of planner, constructor, and manager in Mexico as well as the claims to authority made by this new class in the ostensibly inclusionary, bureaucratic-authoritarian state. The concept of the rational, authoritative, and heroic vision of the *técnico* is fully present in a preliminary treatment sketched by Augusto Pérez Palacios for the Centro SCOP's facades (see Figure 8.4). On an elevation sketch showing the northern facing facades dating from February 1953, Pérez Palacios envisioned a nearly nine-story figure covering the terminating face of the building's central north-south block.[47] (This is the same façade over the Calle Xola entrance upon where Juan O'Gorman's mosaic mural, *Canto a la Patria*, was actually placed.) Before the male figure in Pérez Palacios's sketch and under his outstretched muscular right arm are the tools and product of

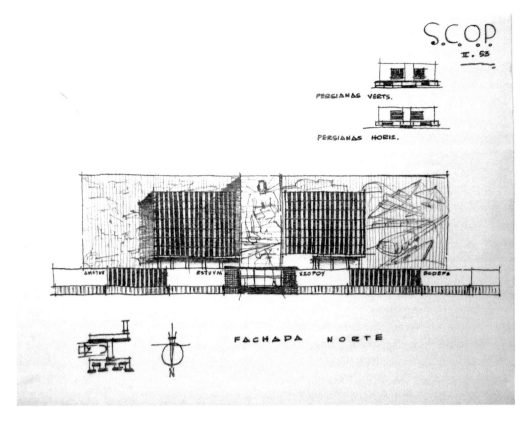

FIGURE 8.4 Augusto Perez Palacios, sketch for north facade of the Secretariat of Communications and Public Works (February 1953).

Source: UNAM Facultad de Arquitectura, Archivo de Arquitectos Mexicanos, Fondo Augusto Pérez Palacios.

his work: a drafting triangle and multiple construction plans. His head, cast over his right shoulder, is backlit by rays of light. The proposed mural appears to be praising individual might and arguably embodied Mexican conceptualizations of *personajismo* (a not-so-easily translated practice that resembles hero-worship, personality or celebrity cult formation, and the assignment of impossible capabilities and responsibilities upon a single, typically male figure), and *liderismo* (an appropriated term from English that connotes strong, authoritative leadership). In the foreground, a curious spherical—either atomic or planetary object—sits upon a table. This was a frequently reappearing sign in the global and atomic age, and one that reoccurs in Lazo's different iterations of the *Programa de Gobierno*. It would have referred both to Lazo's notion of "*el sentido actual*"—which in short was a postwar, socioeconomic integrationist, world consciousness—as well as the "*summa cósmica*"—which for him was a Catholic–humanist–evolutionist vision of physical and moral telefinality for the rationally planned society (see Figure 8.5).

Compelling though this imagery may be, especially in that it conveyed continuity with a cosmic, scientific, and constructive theme in Mexican muralism that had existed since the early 1930s, it nevertheless possessed a visual language that reflected the changing dynamics of authority of the architect-planner within the political discourse of technicism. The representation hailed this new professional figure's supposed elevation within Mexican political

FIGURE 8.5 Carlos Lazo at his office with a drawing of the "Summa Cósmica" or "Evolution of Evolutions," ca. 1952.

Source: Fondo Saúl Molina Barbosa/Carlos Lazo Barreiro, IISUE/AHUNAM.

society to greatness and best captures the highest extent to which Pérez Palacios and similarly inclined technical architects sought to make themselves seen in the eyes of the public: as a techno-messianic leadership with empowered executive authority to will telecommunication and transportation infrastructures—explicitly described as the new tools of "social justice" in contemporary SCOP literature—into existence.[48]

A POLITICAL LIFE CUT SHORT

Given his brief political life and tenure at the SCOP, it is difficult to assess the long-term effects of Lazo's policy of *planificación integral* and moralizing technocratic administrative reform. It is worthy to note, however, that his late political career as a member of the

Ruiz Cortines administration demonstrated a failing in his previous ability to craft a unitary rhetoric of coalition and consensus. While at the SCOP, Lazo's political status among the political establishment grew; there were even rumors of his possible candidacy for *el dedazo*—selection as the PRI's presidential candidate.[49] However, he managed to alienate many of his leftist friends in the process: when Juan O'Gorman described his working collaboration with Lazo on the new secretariat building between 1953 and 1954, he revealed the tension:

> I had a conflict with Lazo because on the principal wall of the building, facing Xola Street, I planned a sign that read "Anti-imperialist Democratic National Unity." This apparently didn't suit Lazo because he was secretly doing politics in order to make it to the Presidency of the Republic, for which reason he ordered the taking down of the lettering on the sign previously mentioned. That attitude demonstrated his bad faith and political stupidity. Luckily for Mexico, he never realized his golden dreams. He died in an accident in the mud of the ex-lake of Texcoco.[50]

While a very worked-out and nearly finalized preparatory drawing of the facade by O'Gorman from 1953 shows that a more neutral placard stating simply "National Unity" had also been proposed, the lettering on the facade, as built, demonstrated the greater political breakdowns and transformations in postrevolutionary Mexico. The spot intended for the placard remained unfilled for a brief period of time until it was simply covered up with blank mosaic panels.[51] The multivalent, incorporative rhetoric of "National Unity" that in many ways shaped the transitory and fragile strategies of coalition, détente, and co-option that made the formation of the PRI possible had finally been exhausted.[52]

Lazo's sudden death in a plane crash brought shock and highly symbolic acts of political and professional mourning. Most profound amongst these was President Ruiz Cortines's order that the architect be named a *General de División*—the next to highest level of rank in the Mexican army—and granted a military burial.[53] In his message of technicist political regeneration and authoritative planning, he had been a critic of military generals being in command of Public Works; with a mixture of irony and symbolic appropriateness he returned to the earth as one. Professional tributes were no less bold: Pedro Ramírez Vázquez (1919–2013), the new president of the CAM/SAM, proposed—quite polemically—the erection of a monument to Lazo at the CU, which he claimed was the architect's "masterpiece." The monument in question, the work of Augusto Pérez Palacios, would have taken the form of a nearly 7 meter-tall concrete bust of the deceased architect emerging out of an outcrop of volcanic stone near the *Estadio Universitario*. The proposed monument immediately came under attack, however. Many architects took offense to Ramírez Vázquez's gesture of bestowing creative authorship to an individual that they regarded as a state-appointed managerial figure; some went so far as to insinuate that the new president of the CAM/SAM had ulterior motives in giving unjust credit to Lazo so as to further ensure the persistence of his memory.[54]

Taken together, the polemic in Lazo's memorialization and O'Gorman's bitter criticism points to a certain professional schadenfreude that appears to have come with Lazo's sudden death. The sense of relief within some sectors of Mexico's political society may have been even greater. Noting both the rumors of his eligibility for the presidency and the sudden silence in the press in the weeks following the architect-politician's death, the journalist Rubén Salazar Mallén mused that Lazo's popularity, charisma, and bold plans might someday have posed a threat to the PRI's political system if they didn't in fact chose him as the presidential candidate.[55] Clarifying that Lazo—a PRI politician—was also an internal representative of Catholic interests and the opposition *Partido Acción Nacional* (PAN), Salazar Mallén went so far as suggesting the potential for a situation similar to when Juan Andreú Almazán—a previous head of the SCOP—received enough popular support via a coalition of business leaders, conservative social groups, and some factions of the military, to prompt his challenge of the dominant party's candidate, Ávila Camacho, in the 1940 election.[56] With such weighty commentary, there has appeared from time to time speculation about the possibly intentional nature of Lazo's death.[57] Proof of any wrongdoing has never come to light, but rumor carries special weight in the formation of political consciousness.[58] The existence of these suspicions represented a lingering breach of trust between the general public and political society. The sentiment that "political speech" in Mexico no longer relied on physical violence was held in suspicion almost as soon as it arrived.

The relative autonomy in socioeconomic planning by *técnicos*, especially in the form of an architect-planner in control of a major state entity with exceptionally wide jurisdiction such as the SCOP, was a fleeting phenomenon in Mexican political economic practice. The breadth of authority that the SCOP once possessed diminished after 1955 with a turn from costly transportation oriented public works to telecommunication infrastructure. At the beginning of the presidency of Adolfo López Mateos (1958–1964)—a figure considered by some as an ideological equilibrialist as well as another great orator of his generation—a new *Ley de Secretarías y Departamentos de Estado* was passed. With this, the SCOP was broken up into two separate ministries: the *Secretaría de Comunicaciones y Transportes*, or SCT, and the *Secretaría de Obras Públicas*. National planning was no longer conceived as an institutional appendage of Public Works; not unlike Lazo's propositions at the onset of the 1950s, the authority to plan and coordinate the economy was maintained as a key executive power function but within the purview of a newly created *Secretaría de la Presidencia*.[59] For much of the existence of this *Secretaría* and the broad Mexican consensus on statist economic policies, this institution would be home to more left-leaning economic "structuralists," "Keynesians," and "quasi-populists."[60] Architects remained critical actors in the Mexican federal government, but in different capacities.[61] Broadly speaking, as Mexico transitioned into a later and less inclusionary phase of its techno-bureaucratic authoritarianism, architects lost their claim to being *técnicos*—a term which in its maximum sense connoted both high-level managers of socioeconomic administration as well as powerful visionaries and spokesmen of the Mexican nation-state. While the idea of broad socioeconomic and government planning and coordination was ostensibly maintained in successive administrations as a useful tool of political power, its methodologies and key actors shifted with a diminished focus on the skills of grand administrative, architectural, and infrastructural projection in favor of more technical economic modeling and forecasting. With that shift, the title of *técnico* would be claimed more successfully by another professional, as pointed out by Raymond Vernon in his classic book *The Dilemma of Mexico's Development:* the economist.[62]

NOTES

1 My understanding of "national unity" is derived in part from the following works: for a study on state control, regionalism, and economic development, see Susan M. Gauss, *Made in Mexico: Regions, Nation, and the State in the Rise of Mexican Industrialism, 1920s-1940s* (University Park, PA: Pennsylvania State University Press, 2010); for a history of electoral strategy and political consolidation via the use of intelligence, see Aaron W. Navarro, *Political*

Intelligence and the Creation of Modern Mexico, 1938–1954 (University Park, PA: Pennsylvania State University Press, 2010); finally, for an understanding of how Mexican Marxists interpreted and utilized the rhetoric of "unity," see Barry Carr, "The Frenesí of Developmentalism," in *Marxism & Communism in Twentieth-Century Mexico* (Lincoln, NE and London: University of Nebraska Press, 1992), 142–186.

2 For more on the "inclusionary" and "bureaucratic" authoritarian qualities of the Mexican state, see Alan Knight, "The Modern Mexican State: Theory and Practice," in *The Other Mirror: Grand Theory through the Lens of Latin America*, eds. Miguel Angel Centeno and Fernando López Alves (Princeton, NJ: Princeton University Press, 2001).

3 For a study on twentieth-century Mexican elite social structures, political qualification, and recruitment, see Peter H. Smith, *Labyrinths of Power: Political Recruitment in Twentieth Century Mexico* (Princeton, NJ: Princeton University Press, 1979).

4 For the rise of the professional economist in Mexico, see Sarah Babb, *Managing Mexico: Economists from Nationalism to Neoliberalism* (Princeton, NJ: Princeton University Press, 2001).

5 Andrew Delano Abbott, *The System of Professions: An Essay on the Division of Labor* (Chicago: University of Chicago Press, 1988), 86–113.

6 Aaron W. Navarro, *Political Intelligence and the Creation of Modern Mexico, 1938–1954* (University Park, PA: Pennsylvania State University Press, 2010), 259–268.

7 For details on Lazo winning the Delano-Aldrich fellowship, see "Jovenes que Triunfan" *Construccíon* 20 (September 1942): 15. A more widely read account of Lazo's trip can be found in the "Urbanismo y Arquitectura" column of the newspaper *Excélsior*. See Lorenzo Favela, "Un Raro Caso Ejemplar: la beca Delano Aldrich, su Usufructuario, el Arquitecto Carlos Lazo Jr. y una Conferencia," *Excelsior*, May 30, 1943.

8 For more on Carlos Contreras, see Alejandrina Escudero, *Una Ciudad Noble y Lógica: Las propuestas de Carlos Contreras Elizondo para la Ciudad de México* (Mexico City: Universidad Nacional Autónoma de México, 2018).

9 Carlos Lazo, "Planificación," *Construcción* (January 1944): 23; Carlos Lazo, "La Planificación y la Política," *Construcción* (July 1946): 37.

10 The program commission was charged with creating the candidate's political platform. It was situated within the Comité Nacional Alemanista. Letter from Comité Nacional Alemanista and Ramon Beteta to Carlos Lazo. October 1, 1945. AGN, Archivo Carlos Lazo, Caja 2, Exp 61.

11 For more on the excesses of Maximino, see Stephen R. Niblo, *Mexico in the 1940s: Modernity, Politics, and Corruption* (Wilmington, DE: Scholarly Resources, 1999), 281–291.

12 Carlos Lazo, "La Planificación y la Política" . . .; for more on the act of "ritualistic deposition" in anti-corruption rhetoric, see Bruce E. Gronbeck, "The Rhetoric of Political Corruption," in *Political Corruption: A Handbook*, eds. Arnold J. Heidenheimer, Michael Johnston, and Victor T. LeVine (New Brunswick, NJ: Transaction Publishers, 1989), 175–180.

13 For Alemán's campaign promises, see "Síntesis del Programa de Gobierno que sustenta el Candidato a la Presidencia de la República, Señor Lic. Miguel Alemán y que expone ante la Opinión Pública del País," *El Economista* (October 1945): 33–57. For documents suggesting Lazo's edits to the original program's contents, see "Programa de Gobierno del Sr. Lic. Miguel Alemán: INDICE" (n.d.). AGN, Archivo Carlos Lazo, Caja 67, Exp 161.

14 Official letter to Carlos Lazo naming him Oficial Mayor, July 1, 1947. AGN, Archivo Miguel Alemán Valdes. Caja 0733, Exp 702.11/2.

15 Initial letter of resignation of Carlos Lazo to President Aleman, December 8, 1948. AGN, Archivo Carlos Lazo, Caja 5 Exp 141; Final Letter of resignation of Carlos Lazo to President Aleman, February 1, 1949. AGN, Archivo Miguel Alemán Valdes. Caja 0806, Exp 703.6/37—. Note: further details of the problems within the *Secretaría de Bienes Nacionales* can be found in Jesús Silva Herzog, *Una Vida en la Vida de México: y mis últimas andanzas, 1947–1992* (Mexico City: El Colegio de México; Siglo XXI, 1993), 294.

16 Lazo was named a presidential advisor sometime in 1949; see Carlos Lazo, *Pensamiento y Destino de la Ciudad Universitaria de México* (Mexico: Porrúa, 1983), 223.

17 Proofs and copies of these are in: AGN, Archivo Carlos Lazo, Caja 7, Exp 79 and Caja 8, Exp 81–82. A list of these articles can be found in Lazo, *Pensamiento y Destino de la Ciudad de México*, 222.

18 Carlos Lazo, "Programa de Gobierno: V. Proposiciones para México, C. Organización del Ejecutivo," *Excelsior*, September 3, 1950. AGN, Archivo Carlos Lazo, Caja 8, Exp 81. Note: A similarly phrased *Secretaría Tecnica de la Presidencia* was created by Perón in 1946, later becoming the *Ministerio de Asuntos Técnicos* in 1949, itself regarded as a "*unidad de comando*" for the Peronist regime. See Maria Mercedes Prol, "Arreglos institucionales en el regimen politico del primer peronismo, 1946–1955," *Nuevo Mundo Mundos Nuevos*, December 9, 2007, http://journals.openedition.org/nuevomundo/12592.

19 Lazo contributed to a broader dialogue on region-oriented strategies of development. Arguments for regional development were offered by the technocrats of Mexico's *Oficina de Investigaciones Industriales* (OII) as well as Carlos Novoa, the Director-General of the Bank of Mexico, later president of the governing body that managed the construction of the Ciudad Universitaria. Lazo also maintained some level of dialogue with the Hungarian-Jewish émigré, Dr. Laszlo Radványi, Chair of the *Escuela Nacional de Economía* at the UNAM, another proponent of regional development. For more on contemporary regional planning in Mexico, see "Rival Visions of Mexico's Industrial Geography: Region Versus Center," in Gauss, *Made in Mexico*, 123–126.

20 Note: This regional project was initiated in the early 1940s by the formation of a *Comisión Intersecretarial de Agricultura, Comunicaciones y Marina* and was later transformed by Alemán's presidential decree of February 1947 into Mexico's equivalent to the TVA. Thomas T. Poleman, *The Papaloapan Project: Agricultural Development in the Mexican Tropics* (Stanford, CA: Stanford University Press, 1964).

21 Lazo cites Ernest Renan's "Qu'est-ce qu'une nation?" (1882) in "Programa de Gobierno, V. Proposición para México, A. Esquema Funcional de la Organización Pública." AGN, Archivo Carlos Lazo, Caja 8, Exp 82; he mentions a "Pasión por México," in "Mexico: Programa de Gobierno, I. Objetivo y Criterio, 1. Objetivo. AGN, Archivo Carlos Lazo, Caja 7, Exp 79.

22 "Programa de Gobierno, V. Proposición para México, A. Esquema Funcional de la Organización Pública" in AGN, Archivo Carlos Lazo, Caja 8, Exp 82.

23 Programa de Gobierno, IV. Proposiciónes Mundiales, B. La Planificación Como Medio" in AGN, Archivo Carlos Lazo, Caja 8, Exp 82.

24 For more on the notion of Aleman's *Mexicanidad,* see Gauss, *Made in Mexico*, 3–4; 17–18. For the role that this nationalism played in the construction of the Ciudad Universitaria, see Alfonso Pérez-Méndez, "Conceptualization of the Settlement of El Pedregal: The Staging of the Public Space in the Master Plan of the Ciudad Universitaria," in *Living CU 60 Years*, eds. Salvador Lizárraga Sánchez and Cristina López Uribe (Mexico City: Universidad Nacional Autónoma de México, 2014), 59–81.

25 Letter from Lazo to Alfredo Becerril Colin, April 27, 1950; Letter from Lazo to Alfredo del Mazo, April 27, 1950; Letter from Lazo to Ing. Carlos Ramirez Ulloa, April 28, 1950; Letter from Lazo to Manuel Avila Camacho, April 28, 1950. AGN, Archivo Carlos Lazo, Caja 3, Exp 74.

26 Letter from Lazo to Lázaro Cardenas June 8, 1950. AGN, Archivo Carlos Lazo, Caja 3, Exp 74.

27 *Futurismo* is a Mexican political term used to describe the informal practice of hopeful political candidates publicly gauging their political strength among unions, factions of the PRM/PRI, and Mexico's many publics while angling for nomination. While the term is often used in connection with presidential candidates and the general elections, the practice extended to nearly all levels of political office, especially elected but also appointed. In addition, while it especially describes individual political viability, it can also be used to describe the collective viability of *camarillas* or political cliques, since candidacies and campaigns were organized by committees and were driven by the efforts of cliques, class and profession-based organizations, and other networks of socio-political power. Navarro, *Political Intelligence*, 11; 198–200.

28 On claim making and professional jurisdictions, see Abbot, 86–113. On the collective mobility project, see Magali Sarfatti Larson, *The Rise of Professionalism: A Sociological Analysis* (Berkeley: University of California Press, 1977), 66–79.

29 For the full narrative of Lazo's role in the CU, see Pérez-Méndez, "Conceptualization of the Settlement of El Pedregal," 37–83.

30 "A Los Miembros de La Sociedad de Arquitectos Mexicanos: Movimiento de Unidad y Renovación, Noviembre de 1950," AGN, Archivo Carlos Lazo, Caja 5, Exp 141.

31 Ibid.

32 "Carlos Lazo: Candidato a Presidente," *Excelsior*, November 26, 1950; "Legalidad y Unidad al Elegir la Planilla del Movimiento Unitario," *Excelsior* or *Últimas Noticias* (?), December 17, 1950, AGN, Archivo Carlos Lazo, Caja 5, Exp 145, Note: Newspaper references in my research come from clippings that Lazo collected. Here, the newspaper name was missing. Similarities in type-face, writing style, and bias led me to infer that it was published by one of these two sources.

33 Letter from Carlos Lazo to Rogerio De la Selva, November 30, 1950. AGN, Archivo Miguel Alemán Valdes. Caja 1040, Exp 630/12306.

34 "El Comunismo Amenaza con Agrietar a los Arquitectos," *Últimas Noticias*, December 14, 1950. Note: Raúl Cacho noted Federico Mariscal and Carlos Contreras were leaders in the movement against the *Movimiento*. See Letter from Raúl Cacho to Sr. Cantú, December 11, 1950. AGN, Archivo Carlos Lazo, Caja 5, Exp 145.

35 "Los Arquitectos Repudian a los Rojos y se Agrupen," *Últimas Noticias* (?), (n.d). AGN, Archivo Carlos Lazo, Caja 5, Exp 145.

36 "Arquitectos e Ingenieros Dieron fin al Pleito que Durante Muchos Años los Tuvo Separados" Excelsior, January 26, 1951. AGN, Archivo Carlos Lazo, Caja 5, Exp 145.

37 Cristobal Jácome-Moreno, "Construcción y persuasion: El VIII Congreso Panamericano de Arquitectos en México como plataforma política," *Latin American and Latinx Visual Culture* 2, no. 1 (January 2020): 101–114.

38 Carlos Lazo, *Pensamiento y Destino de la Ciudad Universitaria de México* (México D.F.: Universidad Nacional Autónoma de México, 1952); This book was later re-edited and reprinted and can be found as Carlos Lazo, *Pensamiento y Destino de la Ciudad Universitaria de México* (Mexico: Porrúa, 1983).

39 Telegram from Mario Pani to Carlos Lazo, December 1, 1952. AGN, Archivo Carlos Lazo, Caja 2, Exp 40.

40 For mention of García Lopez's corruption and subsequent political castigation, see: Peter H. Smith, "Mexico since 1946: Dynamics of an Authoritarian Regime," in *Mexico Since Independence*, ed. Leslie Bethell (Cambridge: Cambridge University Press, 1991), 347; also see Smith, *Labyrinths of Power*, 273–274.

41 Jesús Silva Herzog, "Capítulo Séptimo: Jesús Silva Herzog, Economista e Historiador," in *México visto en el Siglo XX*, eds. James W. Wilkie and Edna Monzon de Wilkie (Mexico City: Instituto Mexicano de Investigaciones Económicas, 1969), 685; Enrique Krauze, *Mexico: A Biography of Power: A History of Modern Mexico, 1810–1996* (New York: Harper Collins, 1997), 604.
42 Smith, "Mexico since 1946," 347; Frank Brandenburg, *The Making of Modern Mexico* (Englewood Cliffs, NJ: Prentice-Hall, 1964), 108.
43 The draft of the proposed decree, likely dating from late 1953, can be found as "Decreto que Crea la Dirección de Planificación del Programa de la Secretaría de Comunicaciones y Obras Públicas." AGN, Archivo Carlos Lazo Barreiro, Caja 59, Exp 193.
44 See: "Tesis.—Gerencía de Promoción de Comunicaciones y Transportes," in *SCOP Memorias 1953–54* (Mexico City: Secretaría de Comunicaciones y Obras Públicas, 1954).
45 A lengthy narrative of the design and construction of the secretariat was featured in a specially devoted edition of *Espacios: Revista Integral de Planificación, Arquitectura y Artes Plásticas* 21–22 (October–December 1954).
46 Mary K. Coffey, *How a Revolutionary Art Became Official Culture: Murals, Museums, and the Mexican State* (Durham, NC and London: Duke University Press, 2012), 1–24; Robin Adèle Greeley, "Muralism and the State in Post-Revolutionary Mexico," in *Mexican Muralism: A Critical History*, eds. Alejandro Anreus, Leonard Folgarait, and Robin Adèle Greeley (Berkeley and Los Angeles: University of California Press, 2012), 13–36.
47 SCOP. II.53, Fachada Norte. UNAM Facultad de Arquitectura, Archivo de Arquitectos Mexicanos, Fondo Augusto Pérez Palacios, (S.C.O.P Croquis) Caja 14, Exp. 42.7.
48 "Las Comunicaciones—Instrumento de Justicia Social: Discurso pronunciado en representación del señor Presidente de la República, por el señor arquitecto Carlos Lazo, Secretario de Comunicaciones y Obras Públicas, en la asamblea anual de la Asociación Mexicana de Caminos, en el Hotel del Prado, el día 20 de abril de 1953." AGN, Archivo Carlos Lazo, Caja 87, Exp 88. Note: Augusto Pérez Palacios was the head of the SCOP's Department of Social Service.
49 Spoken rumors of Lazo's eye on the nomination may have started as early as 1954, if not earlier, if we are to take O'Gorman's following anecdote at face value. A published rumor of a future presidential run appears in "¿Carlos Lazo candidato a la Presidencia?" *Atisbos*, September 29, 1955, 3.
50 Juan O'Gorman, *Autobiografía* (Mexico City: Universidad Nacional Autónoma de México, 2007), 166.
51 The facade drawing that was consulted is a photographed reproduction within a large binder assembled for a retrospective on O'Gorman in the 1980s. *Papeles O'Gorman, Fondos Especiales*, Biblioteca de las Artes, Centro Nacional de las Artes (CENART). The phrase "Unidad Nacional" was placed onto panels on this façade only after the building's reconstruction following the earthquake of 1985.
52 For a better understanding of the break-up and various reinterpretations of "National Unity" in the late 1940s, see Carr, 142–186.
53 On Lazo's military appointment and funeral, see: "Verdadero Impacto Constituyó el Deceso del Titular de SCOP," *La Prensa*, November 7, 1955; Carmen Baez, "La Trágica Muerte del Srio. de Comunicaciones Produjo Duelo Nacional," *El Nacional*, November 7, 1955. AGN, Archivo Carlos Lazo, Caja 5, Exp 44–45.
54 Note: A letter of protest was signed by Enrique de la Mora, Fernando Fineda, Enrique del Moral, Mario Pani, Salvador Ortega F., José Hanhousen, Enrique Landa, José Villagrán García, Juán O'Gorman, Gustavo Saavedra, Enrique Yañez, Enrique Guerrero, Fernando Barbara, Antonio Pastrana, Hilario Galguerra III, Luis Martínez Negrete, José Luís Certucha, Enrique Carral, and Augusto Álvarez. The letter was reprinted in a major newspaper, possibly *Excélsior*, and a clipping exists—sans any information of the publisher—in a file in Lazo's archive. See Letter to Pedro Ramírez Vázquez, November 25, 1955. AGN, Archivo Carlos Lazo, Caja 5, Exp 43. Note: A more insinuative protest was published by the architects Enrique Yañez, Enrique Guerrero, and Salvador Ortega in the same newspaper column as the letter, under the title "Los Proyectos de la Ciudad Universitaria."
55 Rubén Salazar Mallén, "La Muerte de Carlos Lazo," *Quién Es?* (November 1955).
56 Navarro, *Political Intelligence*, 30–78.
57 Guillermo Rossell de la Lama, *Caminos Andados del Político Arquitecto* (México City: Porrúa, 1996), 106.
58 Claudio Lomnitz, "Ritual, Rumor, and Corruption in the Formation of Mexican Politics," in *Deep Mexico, Silent Mexico* (Minneapolis, MN: University of Minnesota Press, 2001), 145–164.
59 Gauss, *Made in Mexico*, 16.
60 Babb, *Managing Mexico*, 118.
61 Pedro Ramírez Vázquez (1919–2013) is one of the most famous Mexican architect/state-functionaries of the 1960–80s. He served as the President of the Organizing Committee of the 1968 Olympic Games in Mexico City and as the Secretary of Human Settlements and Public Works under the administration of José López Portillo (1976–1982). See: Luis Castañeda, "Pre-Columbian Skins, Developmentalist Souls: The Architect as Politician," in *Latin American Modern Architectures: Ambiguous Territories*, ed. Patricio del Real and Helen Gyger (New York: Routledge, 2013), 93–114; also, *Spectacular Mexico: Design, Propaganda, and the 1968 Olympics* (Minneapolis, MN: University of Minnesota Press, 2014. Guillermo Rossell de la Lama, another Lazo protégé, was the Secretary of Tourism from 1976–1980 and the Governor of Hidalgo from 1981–1987.
62 Raymond Vernon, *The Dilemma of Mexico's Development* (Cambridge, MA: Harvard University Press, 1965), 136–137.

9

"Foreigners in filmmaking"

Felicity D. Scott

In "Biggest Communication Experience Ever," *Film News* enthusiastically reported on media-technical innovations recently introduced at Habitat: The United Nations Conference on Human Settlements, which took place in Vancouver, Canada, in June 1976. As editor Rohama Lee explained, Habitat "was the first UN conference to use audio-visual (films, slides, videotapes) as an intrinsic tool" for international diplomacy. To this end, she recalled, 236 films were made specifically for the conference, ranging in length from 10 to 27 minutes, each of which was condensed into a 3-minute capsule to be "used as part of official statements" in plenary sessions and committee rooms such that, as she put it, "Whatever was talked about was shown in a visual statement of reality."[1] Repeatedly drawing upon the often-idiosyncratic lexicon of Habitat's Audio-Visual Program, Lee detailed aspects of the modus operandi and logistics of the elaborate program of film and video production and the expansive (and expensive) mechanisms instituted for those films to be delivered to delegates and press gathered in Vancouver, to be broadcast to "the world's eyes and ears." She also stressed the UN's stated imperative that "the films be made by the countries themselves" in order to "produce more authenticated documentation" and went on to briefly detail a series of aid initiatives launched to mitigate against "uneven representation" among countries on account of their differing economic and technical capacities. In addition to financial support, technical assistance involved: staging regional pedagogical workshops; distributing cameras and other equipment to countries demonstrating need; sending a team of circulating filmmakers and producers to help make films; use of temporary postproduction facilities in Nairobi; and providing raw-stock from the United States, footage from which typically "was sent back for processing in U.S. laboratories."[2]

"It was startling," Lee noted in a patronizing tone of the program's pedagogical achievement and epistemological ambitions, "how quickly the delegates, even from non-technological countries, learned to use the [audiovisual] materials, and how they responded to the learning process as well as to the material itself, giving reality to the spoken word and expediting decision making."[3] Concluding, she underscored the global imaginary at play in this new diplomatic media as well as its instrumental character when put to work at its primary destination—the UN conference:

> Above all, [the films'] content emphasizes the one-ness of the world and the generality of its problems. Unique in cinematic history, the use of film and slide presentations prepared all over

the world will surely convince national policy makers that solutions are available, the while they underline the necessity for international commitment and cooperation.[4]

Lee thus pointed to two distinct if both strategic sectors of the UN's body politic to which the audiovisual program was addressed: people from the "non-technological countries" that were the overt target of development aid and often the subject matter of the films and national delegates and international media, the latter two groups driving the supposedly global decision-making process to establish international policies for so-called human settlements. Moreover, she integrated what might initially seem to be contradictory mandates. In the first instance, the films were to somehow perform authenticity, allowing developing countries to speak for themselves about their experience of modernizing processes, while functioning as pedagogical aids for local communities being integrated therein. Additionally, in the second instance, the films simultaneously had to speak to an international audience about the shared, supposedly planetary issues facing human settlements throughout the world, thus encouraging national delegates to approve a global policy agenda, regardless of where their country fell on UN development indexes. And, indeed, at stake for the UN was to produce an audiovisual technique and distribution system that would absorb such distinctions into a single narrative of the global telos of development, one that foregrounded a certain liberalism while simultaneously managing the disposition of economic and political trajectories and how different economies were located within them.

Lee made little mention of the "human settlements" and housing technologies depicted in the Habitat films, let alone the populations inhabiting them. Yet she was evidently moved by the heroic roles for film demonstrated by the initiative, including the possibility of worldwide film production and reception achieved through development aid, film's "utilization for training and educational purposes" of people from "non-technological" countries, its capacity to effect change through facilitating policy making in an international context, and more. Hence she concluded that the "fantastic thing" that happened in Vancouver had not yet "received the publicity and acclaim that it deserves."[5] It was not, however, that Habitat's Audio-Visual Program was not visible at the UN conference: indeed, many reviewers commented on the ubiquity of screens and seemingly endless films and broadcasts they encountered in the "wired city," some enthusiastically, others noting their uniformity and tendency to distract. Together the barrage of films and the proliferation of screens, their infiltration into almost every space at the UN conference, led to its reception as a "poverty spectacular."[6] Many reviews also pointed to the humanitarian ambitions of using "movies to move," putting films to work to mobilize sympathy for development aims that might propel governments to act.[7] But only a handful of articles discussed the AV program in any detail, those that did typically coming from film contexts and hence addressed to film audiences, and the program was largely deemed an unsuccessful if costly experiment. That the budget for the film initiative amounted to US$12 million ($50 million in today's terms), rivaling the cost of the conference itself, suggests that it was a calculated experiment.

I take Lee's remarks as an entry point for revisiting Habitat's Audio-Visual Program not just for her concise identification of multiple systems that converge in this apparatus—media-technical, semantic, institutional, economic, scientific, bureaucratic, and architectural— Nor simply as a reminder of the cynical (if to many appealing) imaginary encapsulated in her reference to the "one-ness of the world" and humanitarian aid—both effective weapons for motivating Western audiences—or even for her symptomatic obfuscation of structural paradoxes between that global imaginary and the conference's more specific target, managing environments throughout the Global South, although all are relevant here. Additionally, "Biggest Communication Experience Ever" stands as one of the few reports of Habitat to foreground the expanded, variegated, and dispersed mechanisms and range of agents through which the UN's development agendas and idioms migrated into and assimilated multiple fields of expertise related to the environment. For at Habitat, architectural technologies and the infrastructural and planning systems that were the stated focus of the conference find themselves entangled not only with economic and techno-scientific discourses familiar from the UN's Development Decades but with expertise related to time-based media, as films came to supplement speech and printed reports as platforms for disseminating expert knowledge and diplomatic forms of exchange. Indeed, in a move that uncoupled the built environment from its conventional material domain, we find attention to human settlements shifting quite literally from a focus on modernization or planning schemes and techniques for their implementation in cities, towns, and villages to encompass the mediatic circulation of such expertise and its role in international diplomacy.

More specifically, Lee alluded to the role of an otherwise anonymous agent, Andreas Fuglesang, whom she called an "international expert on communications and the use of audio-visual in developing countries."[8] Fuglesang provided material for her report, effectively channeling the claim that as "visual statements of reality," films were more effective tools through which to *educate* and to *convince* than texts, diagrams, reports, tables, charts, and other print media or, we might add, even architecture. I will come back to Fuglesang in some detail, for upon closer inspection he turns out to be a significant vector for systems logics as they informed the lexicon of aid, visualization, participation, function, and cognition, all of which helped to cast the films as "visual statements of reality," thus helping to fulfil the "authenticity" mandate while not leaving filmmaking untouched. Fuglesang worked behind the scenes in advance of the conference, archival evidence suggesting that developing new audiovisual techniques and managing the films' production as well as their interface with the apparatus for display in Vancouver was no small feat. This difficulty was not merely technical, although the practicalities of supplying equipment, film stock, financing, training, and ensuring the circulation of bodies and materials throughout the Global South at this historical moment remain an important part of the story.

In addition, Fuglesang contributed in particular ways to an idiosyncratic but distinctly epistemological agenda for film. His weapon was a new audiovisual genre, one designed to educate and to convince, and to do so in two distinct if historically entangled forums: theaters of "poverty," illiteracy, and development throughout Africa, Asia, and Latin America, and the UN's world conference in Vancouver. This was the moment, to recall, shortly after the World Bank, another key player in this story, had come to more fully recognize the strategic role of housing in development agendas, having previously focused on agriculture, industry, utilities, and infrastructure as key means by which to economically integrate countries from the Global South into the International Economic Order emerging in the wake of World War II and of decolonization struggles. This focus on housing and the built environment did not, of course, seek to render those countries in the image of the North but rather ensure their capacity to act as functioning labor pools for productive and extractive industries. Hence Habitat's expanded focus on squatter settlements, self-help initiatives, and sites and services projects, among other less costly "solutions" to the rapid urbanization of developing countries and the threatened depopulation of the countryside. With Habitat's audiovisual project, to underscore, the centrality of architectural and planning expertise gives way, or is refunctioned and put to work differently. While focusing on films of development projects might seem to be a lateral move, it is a wager of what follows that this shift in attention from built systems to media-technical ones, with their distinct semantic logics and forms of distribution, is not incidental to the historical trajectory and shifting ambitions of the UN and its affiliated agencies for governing populations and environments through new forms of "know-how."

Habitat's Audio-Visual Program, replete with the ambition to produce "visual statements" about human settlements, its claims to fostering a politically neutral technology (film), one that could educate and convince, and its claim of offering an "intrinsic tool" or mechanism to reach the "world's" eyes and ears at an intergovernmental conference, serves as a platform to interrogate these new forms of instrumentality directed toward the built environment and toward instituting policies for steering emerging systems of development. There are other dimension to this story that I address elsewhere, including the audiovisual program's claims to creating a "world picture" circa 1975 and the aporias and cracks embedded within that "global snapshot"; the evidentiary and epistemological status assumed in the notion that the films were documents of reality and the politics of such observations; the media-technical infrastructure installed in Vancouver, and the modes of classification, storage, retrieval, dissemination, and display to which it gave rise; and individual films that operated either in alignment with the Audio-Visual Program, as intentionally out of sync with it, or even that managed to creatively appropriate the larger apparatus and make it function otherwise.

HABITAT EXPO-76

Habitat was the fifth of the UN's so-called "World Conferences," a series launched in 1972 with the Conference on the Human Environment in Stockholm, which led to the founding of the UN's Environment Program (UNEP), and out of which the idea for a separate event focusing on housing and the built environment emerged. In the interim, the UN hosted conferences on World Population in Bucharest (1974), World Food in Rome (1974), and Women in Mexico City (1975), each event staging a calculated and carefully scripted relationship between an "urgent" "global" or planetary crisis that warranted an international gathering dedicated to advancing global mechanisms of governance in the developing world. Fueled by growing neo-Malthusian anxiety about population growth, as well as food and resource scarcity in developing countries and concerns that changing gender roles could interrupt norms of social reproduction so key to producing a manageable work force to serve capitalist enterprises, these conferences, as I have argued, sought to institute distinctly biopolitical paradigms of governance that would touch down unevenly in different parts of the world. Trafficking in a similar rhetoric of crisis, scarcity, and security, Habitat was intended to be the most synthetic conference in the series, to mark a point at which all vectors impacting forms of life converged. Recognizing the degree to which the built environment "conditioned human life," as secretary general of the conference, Enrique Peñalosa, put it, Habitat was geared toward nothing less than the redesign of "social organization." This redesign would take place through instituting national and international policies for planning and land use, infrastructure and services, and housing (or in Habitat parlance, "shelter"), as well as by designing institutional systems through which to manage territories, built environments, and populations.⁹ The question is why or how audiovisual media came to be seen as more effective weapons to engage the built environment than speech and print, and how it came to take on such an idiosyncratic logic.

Habitat built upon the world conference formula first instituted in Stockholm—with its pre-scripted Declaration of Principles and recommendations for national action and international cooperation, its tightly regulated nongovernmental forums, and its vast media presence. Yet from the earliest planning phase, the organizers sought to stage a departure through updating forms of visual demonstration, rhetoric from which would linger in the lexicon of the film program.[10] The initial proposal was for a world "exposition" on human settlements to supplement the conference with a multimedia installation dedicated to technology transfer and national demonstration projects, the latter being the initial destination of development aid affiliated with the conference. A 1973 report indicated that the "conference-exposition" would "feature simple and down-to-earth solutions for developing countries in an ongoing demonstration of low-cost construction techniques and selected aspects of community ecological systems."[11] The aim was to display solutions for the rationalization of low-tech building methods, recycling, waste disposal, and other intermediate or alternative technologies as well as examples of self-help and mutual aid strategies being tested in situ. UNEP initially encouraged governments to identify or launch demonstration projects to be considered by UN committees for financial aid and in turn for inclusion in the Vancouver exhibition, and they hired the design firm Chermayeff-Geisman to design the "global exhibit."[12] If the technical solutions were to be low-tech and low-cost, as deemed appropriate to their target populations, the presentation methods were, from the start, conceived differently. As Maurice Strong, secretary general of the Stockholm Conference and first executive director of UNEP, reported to his Governing Council in April 1973, "As a result of international co-operative efforts, such as Expo 67 and Expo 70, techniques of presentation have advanced constantly. Emphasis will be placed on audio-visual techniques; and other modern communication media can be used to great advantage."[13] To the UN General Assembly, he posited, "the Exposition will make this event unique in that there will be graphic, audio-visual, and model presentations of the various solutions. This will be a highly significant innovation in methods of international communication of knowledge and experience."[14]

In February 1974, Kurt Waldheim announced the appointment of Colombian-born economist Enrique Peñalosa to the position of secretary general for the Habitat conference. Peñalosa was perfect for the job: then administrative manager of the Inter-American Development Bank, he trained under the long arm of the US Central Intelligence Agency and World Bank as they steered inter-American agencies and development initiatives in Latin America. As noted in the UN press release, in 1954 "he participated in a one-year training course on economic development, given in Washington by the International Bank for Reconstruction and Development," going on to work with Lauchlin Currie in World Bank missions, to serve on the Permanent Advisory Panel on Agriculture and Rural Development at World Bank, and to found the Colombian Institute of Agrarian Reform (INCORA).[15] He was also a fellow at the University of Chicago-based, Ford Foundation funded Adlai Stevenson Institute of International Affairs, all alliances and appointments suggesting a perfect alignment with the UN development apparatus as it sought to steer the global economic order.

Peñalosa's appointment began in April 1974. "The first thing I did," he claimed in an interview, "was to eliminate anything dealing with tri-dimensional exhibitions," clarifying that by this he meant maquettes, models, and other material displays.[16] He argued that the decision was taken in response to two objections: developing countries believed their contributions would be "overwhelmed" by their industrialized counterparts, while "socialized countries" objected that it would turn the conference into a trade fair in the interest of Europe and North America. "Politically speaking," he noted of the prospect of producing such a divide, "that would have been more than a disaster. And so I decided to change the allocation of assistance," redirecting UNEP and other aid programs from providing technical and financial assistance for demonstration projects to sponsoring films about them. This, he posited, would help "to develop a sense of participation among the countries involved."[17] "Then," he concluded, "I decided to hire the experts," appointing Andreas Fuglesang to senior information officer and head of the AV program for the UN's Habitat Secretariat in September 1974. According to Peñalosa, Canada, Sweden, and the United States had simply not thought about whether developing countries could contribute audiovisual material instead of built demonstration projects that could then be translated into exhibition materials in Vancouver. This official story was repeated in UN press releases and by spokespeople in Canada's Habitat Secretariat (CHS), the body responsible for the host country's administration of the conference, albeit without acknowledging that the introduction of film was hardly an equitable substitute. As announced by CHS in "Use of Audio-Visuals an Unqualified Success," "The idea of illustrating human settlements solutions through traditional three-dimensional displays [was] discarded as requiring too much space and as highlighting the differences in capabilities between rich and developing countries to mount elaborate expositions. Film was a natural alternative."[18]

Like architecture and planning projects, expositions and large-scale exhibitions are, indeed, time-, money-, personnel-, and space-intensive endeavors. And distinctly material. Peñalosa later acknowledged that it was not just financing, technologies, and expertise in the realm of housing and planning that were unevenly distributed among UN member states but also filmmaking expertise. Film, we might say, was anything but a "natural alternative," and it remains ambiguous as to whether this was simply a massive oversight or, rather, if the organizers recognized an opportunity to test a more thoroughgoing shift from material presentations to new media formats. That the UN, CHS, and in turn the Canadian International Development Agency (CIDA, which stepped in to help fund the initiative in 1975) all dedicated enormous resources to Habitat's Audio-Visual Program suggests that something of another order was being put to the test, and in retrospect the shift in aid from buildings and infrastructure to film is perhaps better read as part of a history of forging techniques within an emergent form of power-knowledge, a form of global governmentality to be mediated by time-based substrates. For such an agenda, Canada was a perfect collaborator. With a prominent film industry centered in the National Film Board (NFB) and with its media credentials much celebrated in the wake of Expo 67 and a burgeoning worldwide McLuhanism, Canada, and particularly CIDA, had a stake in this shift to supplement diplomatic talk with film. Here we find an updated version of Canadian aid, for the country had been a "leader" in agricultural reform in Latin America, instituting aid programs that opened enormous new markets for its industrial farming equipment. A new market for film and media technology was potentially big business for Canada, an opportunity to be a leading player in the instrumentalization of audiovisual techniques and systems of display that might have larger applications, even replacing a US-dominated technology like television as a dominant form. This story line would not, of course, come to pass: indeed, celluloid and soon after magnetic tape would soon read as archaisms within a media-technical world increasingly connected via a computerized information network and operating in even more dispersed and perhaps even less evident ways as mechanisms of control. But in the technical infrastructure implemented in Vancouver to distribute the films on demand, we find a moment of that future imaginary, an image of endless bodies neatly coupled with small screens that integrated audiovisual material into a communication environment.

"A GLOBAL LEARNING EXPERIENCE"

In early April 1975, Peñalosa invited filmmakers, producers, and other representatives of UN member states from the developing sector to attend regional audiovisual production workshops, announcing the goal of "making Habitat a global learning experience."[19] Designed to "assist text-oriented information officers to work in the visual medium,"[20] the workshops had three stated objectives: "To give the participants a general introduction to the technical specifications and the methodology of the audio-visual presentation; to assist in the completion of a manuscript and production plan . . . [and] to assess the need for assistance."[21] The reference to methodology and script-writing assistance did not mean that participants would learn conventional filmmaking techniques. Rather, such instruction was necessary on account of the idiosyncratic nature of the genre, the "audiovisual statement." The UN was not just soliciting short documentary films of urban and rural demonstration projects to screen in Vancouver. As Penalosa announced in "Habitat Introduces New Technique: The Audio-Visual Statement," his team had conceived a new medium with "its own particular standards."[22] The six-day workshops took place throughout April and early May. Headed by Fuglesang, they convened in regional Offices of the Economic Commission; that for Latin America in Mexico City, Mexico, for Africa in Addis Ababa, Ethiopia, and for Asia and the Pacific in Bangkok, Thailand. Penalosa also wrote to European countries, the United States, Australia, and Japan requesting financial assistance for the workshops and inviting them to attend (unfunded) in an observer capacity. Given the idiosyncratic nature of the audiovisual materials requested, he later convened a two-day workshop in Geneva for filmmakers from the developed world to explain the format.

Peñalosa's invitation was accompanied by documents detailing the workshop's multiple agendas, along with technical guidelines for the narrative content and unified formats recently codified by Fuglesang, and a survey questionnaire on "local film technology resources" to be filled in by national delegates to establish requirements for financial and technical assistance. Additionally, the package included scripting templates and their visual counterparts, storyboards. Claiming that a "common format" would better facilitate comparison across national contexts, the films had to address, in sequence, "nature of the problem," "aim of the solution," "action taken," "honest evaluation," and "specific recommendations." If seemingly technical in orientation, these documents offer a symptomatic lens onto the epistemological ambitions at work. "The demonstration projects have a purpose which goes beyond that of representing the National Government," the guidelines reminded their users, adding, "The projects are supposed to be LEARNING EXPERIENCES for all the other national delegations. . . . The solutions must also show ADAPTABILITY—if other countries are going to learn from a national experience." Underscoring the imperative of a common format for informational value, instructions for the story board suggest that "the presentation should be conceived like a TEACHING AID. The more the demonstration project is presented in a VISUALIZED way, the greater the value is for all the viewers from other countries and cultures."[23] If technical guidelines and storyboards are conventional tools of the trade for filmmakers, here we find a distinct genealogy at work. In setting out guidelines for Habitat's audiovisual program, Fuglesang again stressed that "the film and slide presentations were not intended to be entertainment or propaganda but teaching aids," a medium he had developed over the last decade.[24]

When Fuglesang suggested to a journalist in Vancouver that "film is largely a 'new' medium as far as governments are concerned," he did not mean that governments had not encountered film or television in their own countries.[25] Indeed, even countries without a commercial filmmaking industry had cinemas and even television stations, the latter often under government control even if remaining dependent upon "foreign" content for programming. Rather, Fuglesang was speaking to the potential to use film for governing populations, quite literally to change or modernize their habits, norms, and practices. This too was hardly new. Beyond a longer history of colonial film units,[26] UNESCO had been experimenting with the use of "new media"—radio, television, and film—in educational and other initiatives throughout the Global South and Eastern Bloc countries for over a decade. Now an expert in using communications media for development within a burgeoning field, Fuglesang had earlier forged a lucrative career in marketing and advertising before turning to development work in the field of childhood nutrition, a role that had taken him to Zambia from 1967 to 1971, then to Ethiopia, where he worked at the Ethiopian Nutrition Institute until his appointment to Habitat. *Film News* simply noted that "He is also known as a freelance journalist, photographer, graphic artist, and producer of educational films," overlooking this transposition from the commercial sector to humanitarian causes, the entanglement of which would continue to haunt the project.[27]

At the regional workshops, Fuglesang presented a slideshow demonstrating how audiovisual material could be conceived as a format and method for applied communication in development work. In October 1974, right after his appointment to head Habitat's Audio-Visual program, he presented his communications–development philosophy under the title "The function of film as a communication medium—the film language," at a seminar at the Dag Hammarsjöld Foundation, Sweden, that served as a testing ground for the UN project. Titled "The Function of Film as an Educational Medium in Development Work" and directed by Fuglesang, the seminar brought together "participants" from English-speaking countries within Africa and South Asia alongside "resource persons" from Sweden and North America, the latter including filmmakers and other experts, such as those working in "film *audience* research in Africa" and "*visualization* in the film language." "Participants" were, however, the intended test subjects: invited from Ethiopia, Ghana, India, Kenya, Nigeria, Senegal, Sri Lanka, Tanzania, and Zambia, they included film and television producers working in "the information units of relevant ministries or in the general broadcasting/information services." At stake, participants were told, was developing guidelines to address "economic and cultural" implications of the use of film in adult education in the developing world. On the economic front, Fuglesang explained, was the question of the impact of foreign filmmakers operating in the Third World. Commercial film producers from industrialized countries, those "engaged in the production of promotion and advertising films," he wrote in a semi-autobiographical tone, "are increasingly turning to the developing countries in order to find new markets for their know-how," including "offering their expertise to international and voluntary organizations, working in the developing countries, and also to the national governments." This, the document proposed, could be counteracted through training local professionals, transferring that know-how into other hands and hence instituting its mechanisms more thoroughly.

But it was the "cultural" question that Fuglesang focused upon most, which concerned as he put it both "cultural values and functional technique." "Can film function optimally as a communication medium in development work, when the film-maker and his target group have different cultural backgrounds?" he queried. Pointing at once to a neocolonial refunctioning of cultural techniques and of visual literacy, he continued,

> Does this not lead to a superimposition of cultural values and filmatic techniques. . . . Is the modern, highly sophisticated filmatic language, which has been developed in the westernized societies, suitable as a means of communicating with a rural population, which to some 70 or 80 percent may be illiterate and often has only scant experience of how to perceive and interpret pictorial and filmatic messages?[28]

The seminar, he concluded, leaning upon the common claim that technocratic approaches were somehow beyond politics, would thus focus on film production, questioning how to optimize "filmatic technology as related to defined target groups." Technology, he clarified, going on to detail the conjunction of techniques and knowledges that might couple effectively for such a biopolitical agenda,

> should here be taken in the widest sense including both technical equipment and procedures and psychological approach. In educational terminology, this is the micro-teaching situation . . . the encounter between the film-maker, represented by the pictures on the screen, and the individual mind in the audience and the effects of this encounter.[29]

Finally, Fuglesang stressed that because

> communication is a two-way process . . . the seminar will not discuss the *educational film* only but also the *documentary film* in so far as it can provide an opportunity for the rural people to express themselves in films illustrating their social and political situation.

According to Hammarsjöld Foundation Executive Director Sven Hamrell, Fuglesang had convinced the foundation that film and television "have a greater potential for involvement of the people than perhaps any other media."[30] In recognition of the expanding role of communication media within UN agencies and the development sector more broadly, he funded the "Applied Communication" book series in 1973, the first volume addressing Fuglesang's 1972 workshop "Communication—An Essential Component in Development Work," the second translating his pedagogical slideshow from that event into a manual. This detailed techniques for shifting, as he put it, "from perception to creativity," for translating observations of subjects targeted for development into "creative" tools of visualization geared toward techniques of visual literacy and in turn to provide media for "motivation and change."[31]

The Uppsala seminar was initiated prior to Fuglesang's formal appointment at the UN and formed the third installment of "Applied Communication." It was published as *Film-Making in Developing Countries 1: The Uppsala Workshop*, and rushed to press for delivery in time for the regional Habitat workshops in Addis Ababa, Mexico City, and Bangkok.

Fuglesang introduced the book by proposing a model of filmmaking explicitly driven by behavioral psychology and applied social-scientific knowledge, as if these functioned more neutrally, less commercially, than other forms of disciplinary expertise, and as if they operated without rhetoric. He also alluded to the urgency to develop new techniques and new understandings of media given the "growing presence of the electronic picture." Reminding the reader that the book was not the treatise of a film scholar, he also identified its target audience:

> the communicators, the practitioners in the field, the researcher, the script-writer, the director, the cameraman—those who toil with the practical problems of visualizing the educational message and shaping the film image to a meaningful tool of development in their own social environment.[32]

By 1974, however, Hamrell felt the need to distinguish "participatory" techniques from the "manipulative outlook" that was increasingly evident within development communications strategies. Pointing to the use of opinion polls, "measurement of knowledge levels and attitudes to change," he suggested that the potential for coercive use of film and video was "revealed by the enormous demand for investment in the hardware of development communication: the offset press, the radio transmitter or the TV studio." To him there remained a solution to this dependency model: in place of hardware-oriented approaches, such as providing printing presses, radios, etc., he suggested paying attention to the social function and the psychology of communication, as though social-scientific knowledges could be put to work less coercively than other machines. "The so-called 'moulding of minds' expresses a bad way of looking at human relationships," he posited of a previous regime, going on to connect the need for a new epistemological framework to participatory potentials inhering within the feedback-based logics of new information technologies. Invoking the period's techno-utopianism, he argued, "In this age of computerized information and satellite systems, we must work for the growth of what might be called a 'communicatarian' democracy, giving everybody access to the technical resources of the mass media."[33] Hamrell thus reiterated Fuglesang's thesis that villagers might be more functionally integrated into a system of communication and hence educated in the ways of development through the added dimension of cognitive and other social-scientific data about them and giving them the opportunity to express themselves on film. He did not see this as coercive.

FUNCTIONAL LANGUAGE OF FILM

Fuglesang's seminar presentation, "The function of film as a communication medium—the film language," was published as "Sorry, I don't speak Swahili" in *Film-Making in Developing Countries I*, alluding to a language dominant in countries throughout eastern and southeastern Africa.[34] Heavily illustrated with cartoonish "visualizations" of communication theory, as well as of intersubjective and cross-cultural encounters—between filmmakers (foreign and native), their subjects, and viewers—the slideshow explained how all communication functioned through shared systems of signification, that is, within a common framework agreed upon by social convention. These systems ranged from spoken and written language to pictorial and what he termed "film language," the latter conceived as a "flow of visual information" with "its own set of symbols and rules for their use, for syntax and grammar."[35] Fuglesang qualified that at stake was not reproducing the "one-way manipulative persuasion pipeline" manner of mass media but of reconceiving film as a shared platform of communication such that a filmmaker from or working in the development sector might communicate with illiterate rural villagers.[36] To operate within film's semantic system, he posited, subject matter had to be reconceived as "pictorial information bits," pictures, and sequences, together forming celluloid components that could function as the "visual documents of reality" sought by Habitat's audiovisual program. As demonstrated in Venn diagrams, producing shared platforms of understanding did not mean that people "speak exactly the same language," for "two can never be one," but rather aimed "to have as much as possible in common."[37] If, he posited, people from a world conceptualized only in circles could not communicate with people who had only experienced squares, once the circle people reconceptualized their world in triangles, there would be productive overlap (two triangles created a square). Film language, he posited, was an ideal vehicle for such a cross-cultural system of communication. Once sharing techniques of camerawork, lighting, sound, editing, and other aspects of a modern film apparatus, he declared, people could "talk" through film; "it is international!"[38]

Fuglesang went on to explain that such an international film language had epistemological and cultural limitations, that it could only function as a "sublanguage," and this is where "culture" came in. Villagers, he noted, had not been to film school; they came from a distinct cultural domain with its own "meta-language." Foreign filmmakers, he argued, were not equipped to identify relevant "pictorial information bits" to feed into an educational or documentary film, for they could not access a culture's "cognitive system"; hence, the technical apparatus itself was not sufficient to allow film to mediate speech with those "illiterate rural audiences" that were their ostensible target of film as an "educational medium." At stake then, in hosting the workshop, was answering the question "How can we make our film language more FUNCTIONAL?" How could it be retooled to speak to, about, and from the world of those villagers?[39] Fuglesang's answer was twofold: in the first instance he insisted on the need to involve a "local" filmmaker with expertise not just in film but, on account of his cultural background, in local symbolic codes, hence serving as a type of cultural translator between film language and the "cognitive systems" and viewing habits of his subjects. Blind to the role of social and economic distinctions, it was assumed, that is, that a filmmaker born in an African state but educated in a modern institution, most likely in the Global North, shared a local cognitive system with the peasant.

In the second instance, and returning us to the nexus of educational and documentary films, Fuglesang offered instructions on how to "change the roles of the film-maker and the viewer" by putting the camera into the hands of the villager. The techniques' operative potential trafficked in the belief that embedded in gestures made with a camera was evidence of a culturally specific "cognitive system" and with it a conception of reality that might be rendered visible or legible through the formal and semantic aspects of a film—what they chose to shoot, how they used the camera, editing decisions, etc. Here was an opportunity, he posited, to "learn from a film produced by a rural villager," to "study how he would express himself with it," to use the film as a vehicle for knowledge about the other, even as a technique through which to claim access to a cultural truth and with it authenticity.[40] Here, too, was an intelligence gathering technique wherein, once coupled with a movie camera, a Third World subject revealed clues that could be read by the communications development expert, like a filmmaker who could not otherwise "speak" their language. Through such a switch in position, that is, participation facilitated data collection.[41]

This gesture of putting cameras in the hands of "others" was not new but derived from anthropological filmmaking and programs such as the Canadian National Film Board's Challenge for Change, both of which were represented by speakers and films in the Uppsala seminar. A key reference was Sol Worth's Navajo Film-Maker Study of 1966, a social research experiment seeking to demonstrate that, having put the cameras in Navajo hands, the films produced somehow reflected Navajo culture and patterns of cognition.[42] Professor at University of Pennsylvania's Annenberg School of Communications, Worth was invited to the Uppsala workshop but could not attend and in his place asked team member Annette Jere to report on the study. Noting that she was not a filmmaker but a social anthropologist, Jere outlined the use of film as a research technique focused on the Navajo and their findings, also screening two films from the study—*Navajo Weaver* by Susue Benally and *Intrepid Shadow* by Al Clah. Reflecting on the value of Worth's study for the Habitat initiative, Fuglesang claimed it gave people "the opportunity of expressing themselves, their lives, and their views on the filmstrip," adding that "extremely interesting, culturally conditioned phenomena revealed themselves in the pictorial language used."[43] Mike Mitchell, representing Challenge for Change and the North American Indian Traveling College, offered an insightful critique of the idea that cognitive and cultural elements were somehow transmitted in the use of a film camera:

> Experts were poking in it when we were learning to make films. They were telling us why we were doing this, that or the other. . . . They did not understand that we were hesitant to express ourselves until we knew how to use the technology. When they asked me: "Why, did you do that?", I could only say: "Because I was trying to learn to use the camera."[44]

With the presentation of the Navajo film study in Uppsala, things did not go as Fuglesang planned. Under the subheading "A Point of Confusion," he added an editorial comment expressing concern that "Some African participants appeared rather to identify with the Navajos than with the professionals who undertook the study."[45] As with those invited as foreign filmmakers working in African countries, the African filmmakers had been invited as already "part of modern film technology," as sharing a common education in a Western film or television school. Their role, as he had outlined in his presentation, was as cultural go-between or translator. Joseph Mahiga, education officer and director of the Audio-Visual Institute in Dar es Salaam, Tanzania, noted that films "made in Tanzania" are invariably made by foreigners, with African members of the crew reduced to porters, guides, and interpreters, and pointed to mechanisms by which the status quo was likely to be perpetuated under the rubric of development aid, even if cameras were put in the hands of local filmmakers.[46] Moreover, challenging Fuglesang's reading of local filmmakers being able to access cultural codes of illiterate villagers, he recalled that "Even a local film-maker who has been trained exclusively abroad using alien resources and techniques and whatever, when this local man comes down to the people, if he has assumed the tastes and the values of Europeans, he is not the same."[47] Responding to "Challenge for Change," he noted the risk of such participation: "What we think the white man is doing is always considered as progress, and this is where we go wrong. Technological development may be termed progress, but I fear this might be progress towards self-extermination."[48] Segun Olusola,

Controller of TV Programs for NBC Television in Lagos, Nigeria, questioned the motivation for such immense funding, asking why the Canadian government would undertake such an expensive enterprise if it were not to *its* benefit. Seth Adagala from the Kenyan Ministry of Information and Broadcasting in Nairobi queried in turn whether the promise of control by "participants" was genuine or "just a tactic to get your work going." Working to clarify, Low desublimated the surveillant character of this enterprise, and implicitly its role within a larger biopolitical apparatus: "This process has to do with government and government enters into it. Government wants information from the people" in order to pursue what he nevertheless believed were lofty development goals.[49]

CONCLUSION: CAPTURING "REALITIES"

In "Sorry, I don't speak Swahili," Fuglesang insisted that film was not just "mediating" but somehow actually capturing "reality," that "A film is an extract of reality," even that a film was made up from "pieces of reality."[50] Reality, he argued, "is literally passing through the film-maker and his team mates before it comes out in the release copy. They are making the film with pieces of reality and of course some other pieces go into it."[51] He did not elaborate on what those "other pieces" might be, but in addition to the film apparatus—cinematography, editing, narrative, text, sound, celluloid, camera, screen, projector, etc.—we can interpret them to encompass the techno-scientific knowledge framework he believed indispensable, an epistemological dimension inseparable from the historical, institutional, economic, political and geopolitical factors informing the films' deployment in the development sector in the first place. All such factors, and through them the political disposition fostered, would be harbored in any "reality" captured in films affiliated with Habitat. On account of the carefully scripted format and narrative structure design in Uppsala and put to work in the audiovisual program's technical guidelines, such forces would in some sense pass through the filmmakers and their teams before manifesting at 24 frames per second, and in turn being transferred to videotape for delivery in Vancouver.

Unlike the Navajo of Worth's study, or the Indigenous people, "illiterate villagers," or other actors affiliated with this story, and to whom cameras had been or might be given, Western filmmakers and those seeking to deploy them in the interest of global governance were considered unmarked. But as I have tried to show, we might refract such a claim to accessing the meaning of decisions and of gestures, not through individual filmmakers, who like any other test subject could adopt heterogeneous relationships to any such system, nor even through individual films, similarly marked by complex historical traces that implicitly refute claims to global adaptability upon which the film program relied (both are addressed in other aspects of my research), but through the multi-faceted apparatus of the UN's audiovisual program itself as an object of study. We might, that is, attempt to read the history of its technical and narrative guidelines and through them certain institutional, economic, and political frameworks, including gestures that sought to elide or manage specific histories, geographies, and cultures that would raise the specter of politics. The language of equity across nations was not the bearer of an ethos of social or economic justice, just as aid programs have long served the aid-giver both in an immediate sense and in the long-term patterns of dependency they hoped to institute. The very idea that "human settlement" technologies and practices from one context might be applicable to a point elsewhere within a global network of built environments is of course a mark of systems thinking at work. The mandate of conforming to a "common format" in films is in turn evidence of a drive to systematize and to integrate and control in the name of adaptability to a global system.

In addition to guidelines and format requirements, the Uppsala seminar gave rise to other, less evident legacies and contradictory or ambiguous tendencies manifest at the Habitat conference. The anxiety about authenticity, about how films could access cultural truths (as if they might remain unmarked by the institutional framework), led to the mandate that films be made by "local filmmakers" or that cameras be put into the hands of the "people," creating a complex topology of switching positions between viewer and viewed, of filmmaker and subject, as well as of self-surveillance and self-presentation that was not lost on seminar "participants." Coupled with the dual mandate that the films educate and convince, that they functioned as teaching aids and documentary films, we find equally complex tensions or irresolution between local and global destinations, for which the elaborate techniques to standardize narratives and formats and to mobilize the rhetoric of participation or self-representation seem symptomatic, or compensatory at best.

When, in "Sorry, I don't Speak Swahili," Fuglesang suggested that people from the circular world could be reframed or reframe themselves as a triangular world—more like but not the same as the square world—he cast this not as akin to epistemological dimensions of colonial violence but in the more palatable language of "understanding" and cross-cultural communication. When countries were invited to speak through film about their social and political realities from the perspective of a "common format" and according to a narrative telos of development, they were not called upon to voice disagreement or to enter into a sphere of political exchange. Indeed, the diagrams serve as a reminder that, like the Habitat films, development aid was designed to bring poor countries *partly* into alignment with the industrialized world and its economic matrix, but only just enough for them to be rendered compatible to the system, put to work and therefore less likely to foment revolution. But the allegorical gesture, like the Development Decades more generally and the proliferating field of experts it deployed, remained haunted by structural inequities and hence by the potential of insurrection. We might interpret this mandatory common format, the requested shift from circle to triangle, as a strategic or cynical refunctioning of the parable of the Roman Plebeians who, according to Jacques Rancière, constructed the scene of argumentation in order to make their claims legible to the patricians on Aventine Hill, and who did so by mimicry, "in such a manner that the patricians might recognize it as a world in common."[52] For Fuglesang the question was how Western filmmakers might come to know the "other," how to enable the other to speak via film, ambiguously situated between "expression," evidence, and surveillance. The task was determining how, at the Habitat conference, Western governments might come to know the developing sector. This understanding was not positioned as an ethical or political issue but, to underscore, as a "functional" one, something that could be achieved through common format, through narrative, and with recourse to social scientific techniques. But such a system remained unstable and did not only function unidirectionally (in which filmmakers from industrialized countries instructed less developed counterparts, although it certainly also functioned that way). In staging such an opportunity for encounter, having invited others to speak about themselves, potentials for revalencing emerge, returning us to the question of who was being educated and who was being convinced, answers to which become increasingly less self-evident than they at first appeared.

NOTES

1. Rohama Lee, "Biggest Communication Experience Ever," *Film News* 33, no. 4 (September–October 1976): 20–25.
2. Ibid., 24. As evident in the archives, film footage was also often sent to Europe and the UK for processing.
3. Lee, "Biggest Communication Experience Ever," 25.
4. Ibid.
5. Ibid., 20.
6. "Poverty Spectacular," *Jericho: The Habitat Newspaper*, June 3, 1976, 4.
7. See, for instance, Wolf von Eckardt, "The Habitat Conference, Using Movies to Move," *Washington Post*, June 11, 1976, B14.
8. Lee, "Biggest Communication Experience Ever," 20.
9. Quotes are from Enrique Peñalosa, as recounted in "Proceedings of the Conference," in A/CONF.70/15 Report of Habitat: United Nations Conference on Human Settlements, Vancouver, 31 May–11 June 1976 (New York: United Nations, 1976), 130.
10. See Felicity D. Scott, *Outlaw Territories: Environments of Insecurity/Architectures of Counter-Insurgency* (New York: Zone Books, 2016).
11. United Nations Environment Programme, "United Nations Conference-Exposition on Human Settlements, Note by the Secretary-General," 28th Session, Agenda item 50, A/9238, October 30, 1973, 16–17.
12. Letter from Enrique Peñalosa to Ivan Chermayeff, 05/03/1974, Series S-0445, Social Affairs, Box, 0310 Social Development, Co-operation and Consultation, File 0002, Social Matters, Habitat, United Nations Conference on Human Settlements, Administrative Arrangements and Financial Implications. United Nations Archives and Records Management System.
13. "United Nations Conference-Exposition on Human Settlements: Plan for and Anticipated Costs of the Conference-Exposition, Report of the Secretary General," UNEP/GC/6, April 12, 1973, page 11. For Governing Council, first session, Geneva, 12–22 June 1973.
14. United Nations Environment Programme, "United Nations Conference-Exposition on Human Settlements, Note by the Secretary-General," 3.
15. United Nations Office of Public Information, Press Release SG/A/150, BIO/1091, HE/178, February 25, 1974. The appointment ran from April 15, 1974 to December 31, 1976. On Lauchlin Currie's work in Colombia, and an important reference for many terms at work here, see Arturo Escobar, *Encountering Development: The Making and Unmaking of the Third World* (Princeton, NJ: Princeton University Press, 1995).
16. Brian Johnson, Anthony Smith, and Cathy Echenberg, *Worth a Thousand Words? A Report on the Audio-Visual Component of the Habitat Conference at Vancouver* (London: International Broadcast Institute, 1976), 67.
17. Ibid., 68.
18. "Use of Audio-Visuals an Unqualified Success," *Bulletin* (Ottawa), no. 10 (August 1976): 11.
19. Template for letter from Enrique Peñalosa to UN member states, April 10, 1975. Appendix H of Johnson, Smith, and Echenberg, *Worth a Thousand Words?*, 85.
20. Malcolm Cobley and Gerald Graham, "Audiovisual Programs at the United Nations Conference on Human Settlements," *SMPTE Journal* 87 (April 1978): 219.
21. Johnson, Smith, and Echenberg, *Worth a Thousand Words?*
22. "Habitat Introduces New Technique: The Audio-Visual Statement," *Audio-Visual* 2, no. 1 (March 1976).
23. Storyboard form, reproduced in Johnson, Smith, and Echenberg, *Worth a Thousand Words?* This document also notes a maximum length of 26 minutes, with maximum length of credits as 30 seconds.
24. Johnson, Smith, and Echenberg, *Worth a Thousand Words?* 9. First quote is Johnson and Smith, second is a quote of Fuglesang.
25. "Spools Rush in for Unique Show," *Jericho: The Habitat Newspaper*, May 31, 1976, 6.
26. See, for instance, Brian Larkin, "*Majigi*, Colonial Film, State Publicity, and the Political Form of Cinema," in *Signal and Noise: Media, Infrastructure, and Urban Culture in Nigeria* (Durham: Duke University Press, 2008).
27. Lee, "Biggest Communication Experience Ever," 20. As indicated on the front page, Lee's "exclusive report" was "based on material supplied by Andreas Fuglesang."
28. The 1974 Dag Hammarskjöld Seminar on "The Function of Film as an Educational Medium in Development Work," four-page memo with description and objectives. Page 1.
29. Ibid., 3.
30. Sven Hamrell, "Light-Setting on the Background," in *Film-Making in Developing Countries 1: The Uppsala Workshop, 7–18 October 1974*, ed. Andreas Fuglesang, Applied Communication, vol. 3 (Stockholm: The Dag Hammarskjöld Foundation, 1975), 7.
31. The first two volumes in the series derived from the 1972 workshop: *The Story of a Seminar in Applied Communication* and *Applied Communication in Developing Countries*, both of 1973.
32. Fuglesang, "Preface," to *Film-Making in Developing Countries*, 12.
33. Hamrell, "Light-Setting on the Background," 8, 9.

34 Uppsala, August 27–September 9, 1972. The second volume of Film-making in Developing countries was a film of the workshop.
35 Fuglesang, "Sorry I don't Speak Swahili," in *Film-Making in Developing Countries 1*, 24–25.
36 Ibid., 23.
37 Ibid., 24.
38 Ibid., 26.
39 Ibid., 29.
40 Ibid., 28.
41 Ibid.
42 See Sol Worth and John Adair, "Navajo Filmmakers," *American Anthropologist* 72, no. 1 (1970): 9–34. JSTOR, www.jstor.org/stable/670752. See also www.youtube.com/watch?v=FWMO2UGfaBI.
43 Andreas Fugelsang to Patrick Hailstone, Director ACSOH, 22 November 1974. Association in Canada Serving Organizations for Human Settlements fonds, 1974–1976, Rare Books and Special Collections, University of British Columbia.
44 Mike Mitchell, cited in Fuglesang, "Editor's Comment," *Film-Making in Developing Countries 1*, 108.
45 Fuglesang, "Editor's Comment," in *Film-Making in Developing Countries 1*, 107.
46 Mahiga, "Our Technical and Educational Problems and Needs," in *Film-Making in Developing Countries 1*, 72.
47 Joseph Mahiga, cited in "Foreigners in Film Making," in *Film-Making in Developing Countries 1*, 77.
48 Joseph Mahiga, cited in "The Role in Society," in *Film-Making in Developing Countries 1*, 101.
49 Olusola, Seth Adagala, and Colin Low, cited in "The Role in Society," 100–101. Segun Olusola. "The overall problem," Olusola remarked, "whether we like it or not is that this world is coming to a confrontation between white and black. In my view how to counter this should be the goal of people who make films in our society," 101.
50 Fuglesang, "Sorry I don't Speak Swahili," 29.
51 Ibid., 26.
52 Cited in Thomas Keenan, "Drift: Politics and the Simulation of Real Life," *Grey Room* 21 (Fall 2005): 94–111.

Part IV

Technological transfer

10

The making of architectural design as *Sŏlgye*

Integrating science, industry, and expertise in postwar Korea

Melany Sun-Min Park

In *Kŏnch'uk ch'ŏrhak ŭro sŏŭi ŭijangnon* (A philosophy of architecture), a design compendium from the late 1970s, we find a pithy recommendation from the architect Pak Hak-jae on how to "change the form of the factory into an office building": lift a matchbox upwards.[1] His crisp tone was accompanied by an equally concise image. An ink pen sketch of three identical skyscrapers, windowless volumes that suggested neither an empty nor filled interior but rather a series of nondescript boxes resembling unremarkable corporate offices (see Figure 10.1). Taken together, Pak delivered a message that was less about the capacity of architects to creatively respond to a design problem than to their ability to accommodate shifting corporate interests. In a separate passage, Pak framed the terms of his question regarding the role of the architect in the context of the burgeoning scientific fields:

> If you refer to the specialist in design planning as a designer and the practical planner as an engineer, the person who deals with both of these aspects synthetically will be called an architect. . . . This is even more the case, if we consider that the development of science, at present and in the future, will advance at a rapid rate.[2]

Pak's description of the architect, stuck midway between designer and engineer, anticipated the late 1970s moment when architectural practices began to broaden their work scope beyond the industrial projects that dominated the immediate decades following the Korean War (1950–1953). By the early 1980s, Junglim, South Korea's earliest corporate architecture firm, would increase six times in size to over 100 employees, precisely to match its expert competence with increasing corporate commissions. A set of linked questions arise from locating architectural expertise in its interaction with expanded patronage groups: How did architecture, industry, and science become implicated in the state imperative to develop its postwar economy? How did South Korea's first-generation architects respond to patterns of technical proficiency and scientific knowledge, which dominated the postwar discourse on industrial development? How did architecture's technical associations challenge not only the primacy of "design" as an imported pedagogy but also the related positioning of "design" as a specialist and coherent form of architectural knowledge?

DOI: 10.4324/9781003193654-15

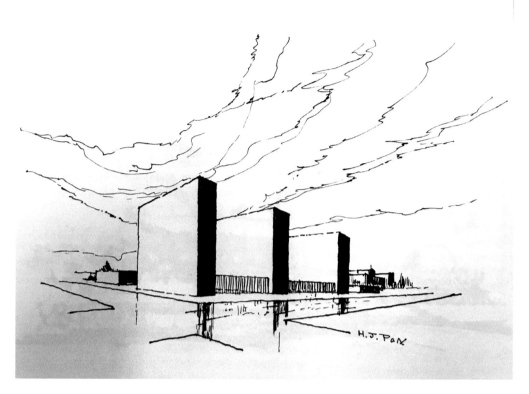

FIGURE 10.1 Pak Hak-jae's sketches of three identical skyscrapers in *Kŏnch'uk ch'ŏrhak ŭro sŏŭi ŭijangnon* (A philosophy of architecture, 1979).

Source: Image courtesy of Seoul Museum of History.

To address these questions, we will begin our story in the immediate post-Korean War years, a time when neither architecture nor the more conventional sciences had concretized their disciplinary codes and standards. For instance, it was not until the mid-1960s that South Korea first issued its licensing exams codifying architecture into a formally recognized profession.[3] Moreover, the fragile economic context of the late 1950s also overlapped with disjointed training paradigms in architecture, comprising remnants of the Japanese education system enforced during colonial rule and American techno-scientific priorities adopted during the early Cold War years. Importantly, architecture was viewed as a crucial part of the resource and manpower development scheme that the United States envisaged for the country. During the time, architectural inputs were largely limited to construction technology, repair, maintenance, and managerial decisions, which almost exclusively defined the architects' role within the limits of a deliberately industrial field.

This initial, marginal role within larger state-led industrialization would provide Korean architects a formative experience necessary to eventually expand into their own large-scale operations. A central example can be found in the career trajectory of Kim Chŏng-sik (1935–), the founder of Junglim, whose earliest employment dates to Ch'ungju Piryo, South Korea's inaugural fertilizer plant. The involvement of Kim and the first cohort of architectural hires at the planned industrial development would illustrate how the professional formation of

Korean architecture was strongly catalyzed by encounters with foreign aid and its accompanying technical transactions and vocational training programs. Moreover, this chapter argues that the imperatives of industrial development would be played out in organizational terms through the corporatization of architectural expertise. In other words, the development of architecture as a fully integrated service can be best understood through an analysis of its industrial beginnings. Indeed, this industrial experience reflected and in some ways preempted architecture's corporate models of practice that could neither prioritize nor do away with "design" in its full scope of rendered services.

MURKY BEGINNINGS

Before we turn to the corporate transition of South Korean architecture, let us examine the economic and political context in which architecture and fertilizer came to dominate the developmental imagination. The fertilizer industry would emerge as the first site of this catalysis, producing a key interface between nascent forms of architectural and scientific expertise that would respond to nationwide development challenges. Seeded with a $23 million investment from the American state agency, the International Cooperation Administration (ICA), the government-owned fertilizer plant Ch'ungju Piryo (subsequently known as "Ch'ungbi") aimed to supply 40 percent of the national demand for synthetic fertilizer. Conceived just prior to South Korea's first Five-Year Plan under Park Chung-hee (1962–1966), Ch'ungbi was a seminal foray into long-term economic planning.

In these early years, when Korea had yet to establish a steady economic planning infrastructure, technical managers were installed in place of economic planners so that many educated individuals were employed in areas secondary to their primary training. The freshly minted architectural graduates at Ch'ungbi were the subject of similarly incongruous placement—they made up the official "*sŏlgye*" or "design" team even though, as we shall see, their university training told an alternative story and their responsibilities at Ch'ungbi rarely touched the scope of design (see Figure 10.2). (The Korean term *sŏlgye*, derived from the Japanese word *sekkei*, loosely translates to "design" in its modern usage and encompasses a range of definitions, including "planning".) Instead, the design of the fertilizer plant was left to McGraw-Hydrocarbon, an American consortium of engineers and chemists with strong experience in the sector.[4] Responsible for the construction of the plant's facilities and oversight of the factory operations, McGraw-Hydrocarbon provided exterior support for the state-centered Korean chemical industry.

In 1955, when the Ch'ungbi contract was officially signed between McGraw-Hydrocarbon and the South Korean government, the country also joined the International Monetary Fund (IMF). This entry set the stage for an export-led economy, a process further abetted by trade liberalization and normalization of relations with Japan in the mid-1960s. The modern export-oriented Korean economy and its fledgling industries relied on the early promises of international aid as the primary instrument of postwar recovery. To be sure, Korea was not alone in this regard. As of January 31, 1959, the United States' ICA provided financial assistance to countries in the Far East, Near East, and South Asia, Africa, Europe, and Latin America. Within this scheme, South Korea received the greatest allotments in the region with technical cooperation, second only to the Indonesian Republic (see Diana Martinez, Chapter 5 in this volume).[5] Additionally, between 1953 and 1960, the United Nations Korean Reconstruction Agency (UNKRA—see Farhan Karim, Chapter 12 in this volume) provided

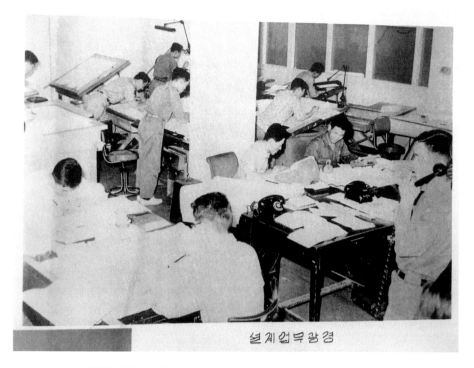

FIGURE 10.2 Ch'ungju Piryo's *sŏlgye* team at work, ca. 1963.

Source: Ch'ungju Fertilizer Plant photo album (1963) from Kim Chŏng-sik's private collection, Mokchon Foundation.

relief through the United Nations Civil Assistance Command in Korea (UNCACK) and the United States' bilateral assistance program. Still, in this time period leading up to 1960, official American aid to South Korea was tenfold that received from UNKRA and totaled $1.7 billion.

Indeed, the prodigious amount of aid from the United States, UNKRA, and other United Nations agencies had created its own problems because they came without coherent allocational criteria regarding spending priorities in various sectors.[6] Overvalued exchange rates and lack of productive output had inflated the South Korean economy, motivating its entry into the IMF. Consequently, it was not a paucity of American aid that had *ipso facto* urged its entry into the Bretton Woods system. Instead, the high infusion of underutilized capital had forced the Korean economy to open to international markets, linking aid, debt, and developmental aspirations in a self-perpetuating cycle.

This self-perpetuating logic is especially evident in the manner in which American agricultural surplus found its way into the $158 million worth of goods delivered under Public Law 480, signed in 1954. The law enacted a bulk infusion of wheat into a rice-consuming country, and this was part of a new calculus involving the interactions of land, farmers, nutritional needs, and technological inputs. This logic was evident in the ICA report on its coordination of the Ch'ungbi program, which stated that "cultivated acreage" in South Korea had reached its "maximum developments," meaning that additional "production" would require intensification of both land and crop.[7] This observation ultimately comprised an Orientalist view of Korea's "traditional" agricultural patterns, presumably rigid and unchanging in its outlines. In this light, land-use intensification could be resolved with the use of commercial fertilizer from Ch'ungbi, while crop intensification could be achieved by developing "improved seed varieties."

Importantly, though, the rationale behind this emphasis on intensification drew on a misrepresentation of land resources as diminishing. Missing from a 1958 ICA evaluation was how the ongoing national rice shortage was fueled, in part, by the infusion of American agricultural surplus, which saturated the domestic grain market and significantly lowered the price of rice—this, in turn, pushed Korean rice farmers into financial strife.[8] In other words, the unmanageable amount of wheat that the Americans supplied to South Korea spurred the *need* to intensify the nation's major domestic crop. "Intensification" thus became yet another criterion for production in the wheel of development where cause and effect were often unclear. In catalyzing a series of problems (inflation, balance of payments, and the disturbed rice economy), American financial and food handouts left South Korea with little choice but to depend on and consequently legitimate this uneven system of exchange.

The mutual link of fertilizer and foreign aid in this discourse of resource intensification resonated in economic policies put in place by then Minister of Commerce and Industry An Tong-hyŏk. Fundamental to Korea's industrialization, An declared, was a "3F" policy of three national assets: force (fuel or power), funds, and fertilizer. Intended as a political catchphrase, the 3F policy made clear that among all domestic products, fertilizer would be cast as a trailblazer of modern industrial development. Fertilizer would comprise the flipside of foreign funds and a crucial ingredient in the Korean state's fiscal mechanisms. At the same time, activity surrounding fertilizer manufacture and its industrial facilities responded to the state's clarion call for "*saengsan*," the catchall term for "production" that connotes measurable and quantifiable growth. Under the developmental qualifier of calculable material abundance, the fertilizer plant faced pressure for expedient delivery. Ch'ungbi both signified and contained the inputs of policy makers—as an economic ploy and a site of knowledge transaction—that would legitimize architectural and scientific expertise as a crucial constituent of resource intensification.

While mobilized as an explicit state resource, Korean architects occupied ambiguous roles on projects of national interest, particularly in collaboration with foreign experts. The unclear and often secondary position of local architects at Ch'ungbi is best represented in a 1956 nationally televised scene that depicts a McGraw-Hydrocarbon engineer with a Korean representative discussing a rudimentary architectural model of the new industrial landscape that would replace an agrarian area of over 660,000 square meters. Ch'ungbi's buildings and machinery were represented by a stockpile of elementary shapes—spheres, cylinders, and rectilinear volumes—that sit on top of the mock "block plan" loosely inscribed with a transportation network (rail) and storage areas for fuel (anthracite coal and petroleum). The uniform ebony coating on these industrial miniatures disguised the functional distinctions between buildings devoted to storage, processing, and operation. What we see in this model is McGraw-Hydrocarbon's provisional attempt to lock buildings and relations in place. As the next section will reveal, despite this seeming diorama of top-down planning scheme devised by American experts, its execution would be realized by a group of local architects whose experiences and training would largely be wide ranging and unconsolidated.

KISUL AND *KISULCHA*, TRAINING TECHNIQUES AND TECHNICIANS

In its initial recruitment, the Ch'ungju Fertilizer Plant hired over 150 graduates from the chemical engineering department at the elite Seoul National University but only a handful of architectural graduates. Despite this imbalance, the Ch'ungbi project's hiring of architects provided employment security amidst an otherwise tenuous professional field. In project records, it appears that at least three members of the sixteen-person *sŏlgye* team had institutional credentials in architecture: Kim Chŏng-sik, a graduate of the Seoul National University's architecture program, Yi Sŏng-ch'ul, from Hanyang University, a postwar Korean institution, and Ŏm Ŭi-sŏn, from Kyŏngsŏng Technical College, a colonial-era establishment.[9]

Located at the plant's main administrative building, the architects assumed multiple roles—at times designated as *kamni* ("technical supervisor") and otherwise as *sŏlgyesa* (loosely equivalent to "designer" or "planner"). Architects were also hired as Ch'ungbi's industrial facilities were nearing completion, meaning that this late timing and uneven patterns of recruitment reflected a process steeped in trial and error, blurring the boundaries of design, management, and technical supervision. As pathbreakers, architectural forays in industrialization verged on a kind of bricolage, shuttled between the nimble and the cursory, the inexperienced and the experimental.

Hired as quasi-technical workers and quasi-conjuring artists, these postwar architects embodied the skill sets of another set of ad hoc inventive precursors, the *haebang moksu* or the "liberation carpenter." The *haebang moksu* were an occupational category that had been informally coined only in the wake of decolonization (1945–), when the Japanese presence in Korea gave way to American military camps with expedient building types such as industrial sheds that required ready architectural details and component assemblies.[10] Coincidentally, South Korea was not equipped with an industrial base capable of producing standardized building components such as I-beams.[11] Instead, as at Ch'ungbi, construction materials were procured, produced, and converted spontaneously; for instance, when closed, rectangular-shaped channels were needed for the fertilizer sheds, C-channels were quickly welded on site. In other words, technical challenges became unplanned opportunities to experiment with novel solutions. New construction techniques, including the use of nails and metal fasteners, were adopted to complement limited access to imported, standardized construction material. Material uncertainty, combined with an emphasis on rapid deployment, would push a large number of unskilled laborers to perform building tasks typically assigned to a trained *moksu* or carpenter. The improvised solutions that resulted were thus central to closing the distance between the image of development and the material reality of industrially manufactured building parts.

This hybrid tendency characterized the practice of Pae Ki-hyŏng, a Korean architect whose position at Ch'ungbi was exceptional. Unlike the other Korean "design" team, his hire came from a competition entry his firm, Kuzosa Architects and Engineers, submitted for the housing quarters (or the "Industrial Village," as noted in the archives) of the Korean and American employees at Ch'ungbi.[12] As Kuzosa's first competition entry, Pae's winning design filled the residential program missing from McGraw-Hydrocarbon's industrial portfolio.[13] These houses were conceived as single-family structures that varied in size (50, 55, or 60 square meters), roofed with assorted sheet metal or tile. This amalgam of building materials and spatial dimensions suggested a proto-modularization with housing as a kit of parts. When examined closely, these residential units posed greater technical challenges than their size and materials might suggest.

THE MAKING OF ARCHITECTURAL DESIGN AS *SŎLGYE*

A case in point is the truss roof system for which Pae designed a timber frame strengthened with metal fasteners. Pae, who had studied at Kyushu University and later trained at steel factories in Japan during the 1940s, would no doubt have been familiar with the Japanese architects' preoccupation with truss construction and the kinds of structural calculations that were considered integral to the education of a modern architect. In fact, Pae's years in Japan coincided with the development of "Western carpentry," consisting of supplementing timber framing with metal stiffeners. This technique, combining American and British methods of construction with the Japanese finesse for working with wood, formed a crucial piece of aseismic knowledge that *daiku* (traditional Japanese carpenters) as well as architects were expected to master.[14] In drawing from this hybrid know-how of early twentieth-century Japanese architects, Pae's training and approach anticipated the challenges that postwar Korean architects would encounter.

Conflicting and overlapping measurement units further reveal this hybrid context. On Pae's 1958 section drawing for the workers' housing at Ch'ungbi, Korean and imperial units appear combined, written in English and unelaborated beyond the simple statement: "All sizes are shown in Korean *cheok* unit. But lumber sizes in 'inch' unit" (see Figure 10.3). The architect's notation for the nonuniform units thus separated out traditional Korean forms

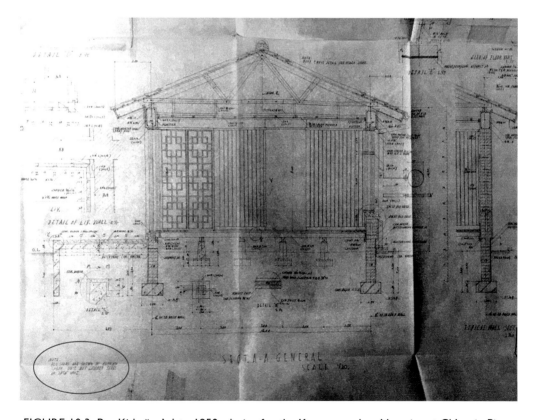

FIGURE 10.3 Pae Ki-hyŏng's late 1950s design for the Korean workers' housing at Ch'ungju Piryo. Notation on the bottom left reads "All sizes are shown in Korean cheok unit. But lumber sizes in 'inch' unit."

Source: Image courtesy of Mokchon Foundation.

of mensuration from the specifications received from the American timber suppliers. While this detail hinted at local challenges of realization, less clear are the implications for those handling the different building elements tasked with understanding their accompanying units. Would the McGraw-Hydrocarbon contractors be expected to work with the Korean units? Conversely, how efficiently could the American terms be converted for Korean technicians and workers? This compound notation registered the complexities that emerged when different constructional knowledge systems were overlaid. This idiosyncratic mode of melding instructions made visible the double bind inherent in import substitution. On the one hand, this approach aimed to universalize technologies, materials, objects, and people through quantitative attributes. On the other hand, import substitution intended to build up "local" capacities and abilities to realize these universal goals. In architectural practice, this was literally expressed in terms of the technical limits and conventions of the multiple parties involved, exposing a transaction or translation difficulty that, at least in this period, could not easily be elided by or reduced to abstract economic principles of exchange.

Pae's housing project further diverged from American inputs by experimenting with vernacular dwelling references. His elevations prominently featured a traditional fenestration pattern called *wanja*, motifs derived from the shape of the Buddhist cross or the Chinese character *wan*, meaning "continuity." His sectional drawing reveals a traditional kitchen arrangement of pots and fireboxes connected to an integrated under-floor heating system known as *ondol*, a timeworn tradition of accommodating the Korean domestic way of living with minimal, stationary upright furniture. To these more traditional elements, Pae added shoe storage and clothes cabinets for each household and introduced Lauan plywood, a Southeast Asian mahogany, for the interior surfaces. Overall, Pae's meticulous attention to detail could not be further from South Korea's otherwise substandard state of postwar housing, which the ICA reported in 1957 as the most problematic "rehabilitation" item left on its laundry list.[15]

By 1959, Kuzosa was a full-service architecture firm of around fifty employees, complete with *kamni* (supervisors) and technical experts in services like lighting, electricity, power, hygiene, and plumbing. In light of the firm's extensive experience with industrial commissions, Kuzosa could have easily filled the role of McGraw-Hydrocarbon.[16] But why, then, was Pae's firm exclusively engaged in building Ch'ungbi's residential quarters, the most aesthetically inclined and carefully planned aspect of the plant? One partial answer is that Kuzosa's vernacular references—however slight—departed from the ICA's set of priorities around this time. Regarding installation of more institutionalized versions of knowledge exchange, the American agency was far removed from engaging questions that had to do with vernacular forms or traditional practices.

To that effect, the ICA's procurement of McGraw-Hydrocarbon was linked to the signing of an education reform program called the Minnesota Plan (1954–1962). One of approximately forty "university contracts" the ICA coordinated internationally, this educational investment became the most significant channel through which knowledge exchanges took place between the United States and South Korea. It supported faculty members from Seoul National University's architecture, medical, forestry and agricultural programs, among others, to receive at least one year of graduate education at the University of Minnesota in the absence of autochthonous graduate-level training.[17] Meanwhile, Minnesota faculty and administrators helped conceptualize Seoul National University's curricula, grading, and pedagogical methods as well as evaluated the condition of the research facilities.

The Minnesota Plan, which aimed at a direct pedagogical reform within the ivory tower, fell into one of two forms of knowledge transaction that took place in postwar South Korea.[18] Vocational training in the late 1950s occurred via either local or overseas training schemes—institutional pathways that would be formalized through new national licensure requirements. Architectural vocational training consisted of either (1) local on-site technical apprenticeships (as was the case for the Ch'ungbi employees) or (2) international postings for educated elites whose lengthy appointments were oftentimes contrived as part of official governmental strategies (as was the case in the Minnesota Plan).[19]

The Minnesota Plan's emphasis on vocational disciplines—including architecture—demonstrated education and knowledge transfer as entrenched in, if not merged with, developmental agendas, reiterating the ICA's commitment to linking technical knowledge with *saengsan*, "industrial productivity." In this respect, any form of knowledge would become a vocation, a "*chigŏp*" (job), an expedient means of gaining employment so long as the new positions measured up to these overlapping constraints in industrial production: lack of funds in a certain sector, material unavailability, and absence of knowledge in a given technology. These challenges, in turn, led to the convergence of epistemological, disciplinary, and professional domains propelled by the impetus of economic development.

The 1962 Five-Year Plan first addressed these parallel concerns surrounding technical expertise, knowledge production, and economic aid. From the mid-1960s, the promotional language for national development was fully couched in expressions like *kwahak ipkuk* ("nation building through science") or *kisul charip* ("technological self-reliance"). With the 1967 Science-Technology Promotion Act, the Korean government combined the two words *kwahak* (science) and *kisul* (technology) into a single idiom, *kwahak kisul* or "science-technology," officiating science and technology as a single developmental achievement.[20] Public and official discourse soon began to use the acronym "S&T" to refer to the newly minted term, *kwahak kisul*. The same acronym appears in the 1959 Ministry of Commerce and Industry meeting notes on the "S&T contract" signed between McGraw-Hydrocarbon, the ICA, and the Korean government. In the latter, however, the "S&T" stood for a "service and technical training contract" or a "technical training and operation service contract."[21] The architectural services of American technocrats thus fell under the double definition of "S&T"—as both a service (as per the contract) and as a quasi-scientific discipline (as per its English acronym).

Meanwhile, Korea's Illyŏk Kaebal Yŏn'guso (Manpower Research Institute) maintained this line into the early 1970s, designating architecture as a form of "scientific and technical manpower." Among the country's official technical occupations or *chigŏp—kwahakcha* (scientist), *kisulcha* (engineer), *kisulgong* (technician), *kinŭnggong* (technician), listed here in descending order of expertise and social rank—architects were assigned to the second-tier category of a *kisulcha* (engineer).[22] According to the Institute, a "*kisulcha*" was "a person who performs the functions of a department that utilizes the knowledge of the natural sciences and who is responsible for planning, executing and supervising one's given task."[23] Following this definition, architects fell under the job title "*kŏnch'uk kisulcha*" (architectural engineers) and were viewed as a subset of the engineering profession, obliquely incorporated into and professionally tangential to the world of the natural sciences.[24]

The inclusion of science—and indeed architecture—within the *kwahak kisul* sphere must be understood within the mid-1950s context, when research positions and facilities in Korea were barely funded, leading to a perception of research as a somewhat lavish, self-indulgent exercise.[25] There was a dearth of experimental facilities, even for the chemists at Seoul National University leading its most distinguished scientific department. Similarly, the closest training in scientific research one could receive outside of the university setting was a 10-month-long program at the Central Industrial Research Institute (Chungang Kongŏp Yŏn'guso), another recipient of ICA's funding.[26] The Institute produced its first cohort in 1957, precisely in response to the rising fertilizer, cement, and tungsten industries. The hiring of chemists at Ch'ungbi during the late-1950s thus signaled the incipient scientific status of the aforementioned national institutions.[27]

The Minnesota Plan, which paralleled institutionalizing efforts, included architecture in its programming and was symptomatic of the state's effort to square architecture with science's disciplinary development as *kwahak kisul*. From this perspective, one would expect that the almost exclusively technical focus of Korea's architectural programs would be applauded. Yet the technically oriented pedagogy of the Department of Architectural Engineering at Seoul National University was at the heart of the Minnesota advisor Carl Graffunder's critique. In December 1955, Graffunder observed that lecture-focused teaching methods in structures and construction dominated the architecture curriculum:

> The most worthwhile objective of this Department would be to provide an atmosphere in which both students and faculty could apply themselves to the study of creative architectural design. At present the limitations of equipment, curriculum, faculty and space all conspire against this objective. The study of architecture consists principally of lectures about architecture and provides very little laboratory work in the design and planning of buildings....
>
> Although the lecture courses are generally of high quality and are well attended, they do not take the place of concentrated daily work in the drafting room. Consequently, although the students and graduates are well versed in the technical aspects of building construction, they have very little experience in creative architectural planning and design.[28]

Graffunder demanded that the architecture department shift its priority to increase the number and quality of "laboratory courses in planning and design." From the second to fourth years, he advised that the lecture courses be "compressed" so that the afternoons would be dedicated to "laboratory work in architectural design."[29] To refer to design work as "laboratory" work resonated with the techno-scientific training in support of an industrial economy that defined the ethos of the Minnesota Plan. Further, "laboratory work in architectural design" was a convenient summation of the two ends of design heuristics: creative artistic experimentation ("architectural design") and scientific formulations of problems ("laboratory work"). Above all else, the synthesis of "design" and the "laboratory" presented design as the process of coming up with an "individual solution" to a problem, a process that supposedly shared the nature and goals of any scientific research involved in a laboratory setting.[30]

The architecture student was trained to operate as a solitary inventor whose instructions would be collectively monitored in a classroom setting, reminiscent of a studio model of design pedagogy. Yet how would one teach the principles of design, if its guiding definition—a problem-solving process—was not at all familiar to the faculty, most of whom had graduated from Kyŏngsŏng Technical College? As Yi Sang-hŏn has shown, the closest thing to "design" in the Japanese training curriculum was "*ŭijang*," which had to do with skimming "simplistic theories of design" and "mastering drawings about western architecture and decorative motifs."³¹ Furthermore, this colonial architectural education was based on resolving the technical issues and approaching the task of building design through a piecemeal approach. In this way, design, which, as of the late 1940s, was taught to third- and fourth-year Seoul National University architecture students, must be understood through this limited colonial legacy.

To remedy the situation, Seoul National University faculty would pay special attention to the methods of teaching in architectural design during their visit to the University of Minnesota the following year.³² To this effect, architecture was sorely underrepresented and, in some ways, misrepresented within the Minnesota Plan itself. Architectural participation was limited to a year—from 1956 to 1957—and restricted to three architects: Kim Hŭich'un (1915–1993) from Shin Kŏnch'uk Culture Research Institute, Yun Chŏng-sŏp, and Kim Chŏng-su (1919–1985), who upon their return would become the leading figures of modern Korean architecture.³³ The tangible skill sets acquired by the Korean architects are somewhat difficult to ascertain, with the exception of Kim Hŭi-ch'un, who had learned Western architectural history—perhaps undermining the program's technical focus—and later strove to make history a fundamental part of Seoul National University's architecture program.³⁴ The effects of this training on the architecture faculty remained dubious to the advisory, who wrote in a 1957 progress report that "after having three men trained under this project no specific improvements in either designing or curriculum in this department has been noticeable."³⁵ This negative review stood in opposition to the optimism aired by the university's president and deans, who commented that, on the whole, the institution witnessed the "modernization and up-grading of course content" and "stimulation of research activities."³⁶

The final shortfall in pedagogical reform can be ascribed, in part, to the ways Graffunder's recommendations *symbolized* design as a coherent architectural pedagogy despite his broad connections to design education. As the head draftsmen of Antonin Raymond's office (1946–1947) and a graduate of Harvard Graduate School of Design, where the Bauhaus lineage of modernism and its studio culture had fully taken hold by the late 1940s when he was a student, Graffunder was familiar with the principles of design heuristics. At Minnesota's School of Architecture, the modernist architect Ralph Rapson (1914–2008) had become dean in the same year the Minnesota Plan was signed. Known equally as an experimentalist and a pragmatist, Rapson was fully entrenched in the modernist circles.³⁷ By the time of his Minnesota appointment, Rapson had taught design with Laszlo Moholy-Nagy at the Chicago Institute of Design (previously called the New Bauhaus) and alongside Serge Chermayeff and Carl Koch at MIT.³⁸ The various institutional lineages of design that were relayed exclusively through Graffunder thus exposed the Korean educators to the motley yet highly filtered definitions of design pedagogy.

While inchoate, the broader strokes of modern design discourse familiar to Rapson and Graffunder could not have contrasted more pointedly with Seoul National University's technical curriculum, which had little to do with heuristics underscoring the practice of design: "learning by experience." The technical focus of the Korean architecture department was a polar opposite of the Bauhaus studio culture, especially its emphasis on the "psychological aspects of design" and the instructions in "form and affect,"³⁹ which left an enduring legacy in many American architectural schools. Meanwhile, the design education Graffunder invoked had little in common with the comparatively esoteric undercurrent of the Bauhaus principles. Instead, the American advisor's recommendations recalled mechanical and process-driven ideas about design as a mode with which to "analyze" and "solve" a problem.[40] Moreover, Graffunder's guidelines suggested that creativity was an inherent source and inevitable by-product of architectural education, so long as the curriculum's focal point could be redirected to design exercises. Taken together, "design" remained a sweeping if vague panacea for reforming Korean architectural education.

As far as the American advisors could tell, though, the gap between Seoul National University's program and their expectations of what an architecture school should look like, what it should teach, and how it should function institutionally had everything to do with the lack of "proper space and equipment."[41] In response, Graffunder recommended more "books, periodicals, and slides" as well as "drafting room equipment," and, lastly, "shop equipment for concrete testing and experimental student construction work."[42] However, between Graffunder's 1955 recommendation, Kim Chŏng-sik's undergraduate graduation in 1958, and his master's graduation in 1966, the physical conditions for hands-on architectural research remained largely stagnant at the nation's most prestigious institution.

During his graduate years, Kim experienced the subpar research environment Graffunder had observed nearly a decade prior. For his 1965 master's thesis, completed during his employment at Ch'ungbi, he experimented with glass fiber as a form of concrete reinforcement. Yet the lack of adequate research facilities hindered proper experimentation necessary to generate a new architectural material. In the end, his research went from a hands-on trial to a synthetic overview of secondary scholarly literature that was eventually published as a two-part article in the journal *Kŏnch'uk* (1968). In place of Korean-language sources regarding concrete reinforcement, Kim relied on technical details and research findings from Japanese journal articles and American trade catalogs, including the Concrete Reinforcing Steel Institute's Design Handbook and Owens-Corning's *Textile Fiber Materials for Industry*, both published in 1962.[43] In this way, he experienced firsthand the difficulties of bringing an experiment to fruition when research facilities were scarce and poorly resourced.

Ch'ungbi's own laboratory building most vividly captured the lagging circumstances around scientific experimentation. As early as 1961, Kim Chŏng-sik had conceptualized the laboratory facility alongside a hospital for Ch'ungbi's workers and their families. Kim envisioned the two structures as a visual and physical antidote to unsavory manufacturing outputs such as noise, gas, and air pollution.[44] While a potential remedy, the laboratory building was largely an afterthought to the primary production facilities. In essence, scientific research did not precede industrial production. This contrasted with the official picture, which advertised state-of-the-art laboratories as a prerequisite for every South Korean fertilizer factory. The necessity of accelerated production effectively put research on hold, reflecting diverging conditions and temporal demands in the two spheres. The never-built research laboratory at Ch'ungbi would, in a sense, exemplify the dissonance between production and experimentation, even as official narratives presented them as simultaneous feats of national accomplishment. With few exceptions, the opportunity to "design"—the very thing the Minnesota Plan sought to establish pedagogically—would also lag behind in the name of industrial productivity. In short, "design," as a paradigm of practice and pedagogy, was absent from the Korean architects' experience, especially for those at the center of resource development.

CORPORATIZING PRACTICE

The primary lessons learnt from the institutions and industries of *kwahak kisul* would not be the kind of "design" practice espoused by the Minnesota advisors nor the accompanying research strategies. The most significant takeaway involved the ways in which technical expertise was integrated into the managerial structure of the emerging industries. In the concluding section, we will explore how technical expertise, which American advisors initially deemed a hindrance to architectural design, became foundational to defining the corporate operation of architecture.

Through his employment at Ch'ungbi, Kim Chŏng-sik gained organizational exposure that he carried forward into Korea's first corporate architecture firm, Junglim Architecture Research Institute, which he co-founded in 1967 with his older brother Kim Chŏng-ch'ŏl (1932–2010). From 1959, the senior Kim was employed at the Bank of Korea in the *yŏngsŏn'gwa*, a division akin to facilities management but whose responsibilities extended beyond upkeep and maintenance.[45] This group was tasked with designing bank branches, with architects participating in comprehensive roles as in-house designers and facilities managers. For the Kim siblings, a combination of professional networks established throughout the financial sector and pragmatic construction experience provided the impetus to open their own firm.[46] Moreover, since the Korean state controlled the circulation of capital and national industries via the Bank of Korea, itself overseen by the Ministry of Finance, these aspiring architects successfully found leverage within the tight bond between financial control and industrial management. Together, their enterprise drew on dual experiences rooted in the transaction of capital across the different registers of money and fertilizer.

From the time of its founding in the 1960s to its corporate heyday in the late 1970s, Junglim's growth was commensurate with its ever-proliferating scale and diversity of commissions. The firm's corporate projects, most notably the mid-1970s winning competition entry for the Korea Exchange Bank, prompted internal expansion by creating new roles within the company. In particular, the bank commission became a test bed for managing a new advisory role known as *komun*, consultants responsible for communicating with outside contractors in technical areas: electricity, heating, and fixtures. Pushed to meet industry standards—and in some ways put into place—by Junglim, increasingly competent contractors soon graduated from their subcontractor status to active bidders on projects. This transition would eventually make the *komun* role redundant and undermine the advisory system altogether. Thus, the management system Junglim adopted in response to an internal organizational challenge would unwittingly help expand and produce new forms of competence, firm structure, and specialization within the building industry.

To be sure, Kim Chŏng-ch'ŏl was no stranger to the slippery nature of consultancy. While employed full-time at the Korea Exchange Bank (his second bank appointment after the National Bank), Kim was hired at Junglim Architectural Research Institute as a *komun* in the mid-1960s. In this capacity, Kim observed his own architectural practice as a consultant, while likely benefiting from the bank's higher remuneration. Interestingly, it was only a few years earlier that the Ch'ungbi plant, where his younger brother was hired, had also seen the need to utilize the services of a *komun*. In May 1961, with the expiry of the 33-month-long S&T contract signed with McGraw-Hydrocarbon, a *kisul komun* or "technical advisor" role was set up to replace the more direct technical training mandated in the previous American contract. In this way, technical expertise was integrated into the industry itself, which in turn promoted the need for these abstract roles that represented rather than performed such expert skill sets.

The fertilizer industry's integrated structure also anticipated the Kim brothers' experience around shifting company hierarchies, new job assignments, and divisions of expertise which became crucial for corporatizing their firm into a *chonghap sŏlgye samuso* (literally "comprehensive design office").[47] In particular, the large scale of the 1972 bank commission precipitated not only the need for greater manpower but also the internalization and diversification of expertise that were central to the firm's founding ethos.[48] "By organizationally carrying out comprehensive creative activities, we will execute technological innovations and perfect total design practices" read its early mission statement.[49] The comprehensive organization of the corporation was thus equated to a comprehensive—and "total"—design practice, connoting the firm's structure and its service outputs as being aspirationally symbiotic.

Indeed, by 1983, Junglim expanded in size and systematized its organizational structure. The 115 employees were all divided and assigned into the specialist areas of construction—planning, design, international business relations, structure, finance, machine, electricity, *kamni*, and administration—to replace the previous twenty-nine-person company lacking any divisional structure.[50] This by no means suggests that Junglim was the first architectural firm to offer an integrated service; almost three decades prior, Chonghap Kŏnch'uk and Kuzosa had offered an amalgam of services.[51] Yet what distinguished Junglim from these two—or indeed other firms of a comparable scale including Konggan and Ŏmi Kŏnch'uk—was that it had proactively modeled itself after and into an architectural corporation.[52]

Junglim's corporate model was Welton Becket and Associates, one of America's largest architectural offices of its time, which would later become one of Samsung Corporation's most favored hires (they were commissioned for its subsidiary company office buildings, including for Samsung Life Insurance (1984) and the newspaper *JoongAng Ilbo* (1985)). The American firm's principle of "total design," along with its organizational charts published in *Total Design: Architecture of Welton Becket and Associates* (1972), became the single most important reference for Junglim's service integration (see Figure 10.4).[53]

According to the architect William Dudley Hunt, Jr. who authored the monograph, "total design" had emerged out of the firm's desire to both defend and diminish the status of "design."

> Here design is function; it is aesthetics; it is problem solving; it is process. In this firm, the talk centers around the facts of design, insofar as that is possible, not around the abstractions of design. Even among themselves, the designers and other key people here avoid, by choice, the rather esoteric jargon that many architects employ, by choice, when discussing design.[54]

According to the American firm's definition, design was an all-encompassing term for the organization and production of architecture. By turning architecture into a "total design," design was no longer the charge of architects, reflecting a tension that is central to the twentieth-century history of the architectural profession. Design—and by extension architecture—could now encompass a complete range of experts including "detailers, cost estimators, draftsmen, inspectors, and workmen."[55] From this perspective, the lone figure of the genius would be replaced by an assemblage of experts who would help shed the esoteric undertone that had burdened the status of architects and designers.

THE MAKING OF ARCHITECTURAL DESIGN AS *SŎLGYE* 211

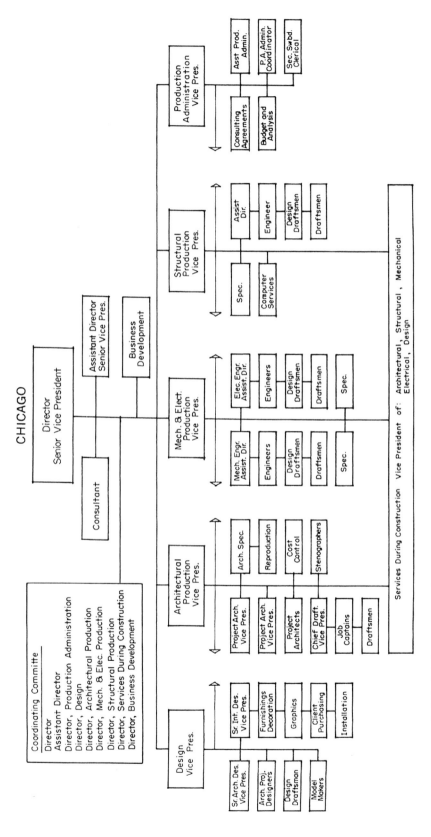

FIGURE 10.4 An example of an organizational chart from Total Design: Architecture of Welton Becket and Associates (1972).

Source: Total Design: Architecture of Welton Becket and Associates (1972), 41.

While Junglim and Welton Becket might have shared the idea that "total design" was fundamentally about architecture's democratization, there were at least two points of divergence. As Pak Chŏng-hyŏn has suggested, Junglim's provision of specialized experts helped to expedite the Korean government's repair and maintenance programs—for example, the colonial-era Seoul City Hall—which needed immediate technical attention in the early 1980s.[56] In this shift, architecture's "totalization" was less about disciplinary questions (the focus of the American firm, even as it discussed "design" in its broader applications) but instead responded directly to the state's urgency to handle architectural assignments. In this way, the Korean architectural profession was brought back full circle to the state imperative of expediency that had been fundamental to its industrial engagement. If the corporate commission had instigated Junglim's expansion into a corporation of its own, the state agenda came to sustain its corporate model to a certain degree.

The second point of departure is that, as of 1949, when Welton Becket and Associates was incorporated, no individual from the firm was publicly credited with an architectural commission.[57] This contrasted radically with the Korean corporate model in two distinct ways. First, the lead partner or executive was attributed—often wrongly—to a project for which one had little involvement in the *sŏlgye* process.[58] As a result, the said individual became a "designer" in name only, confirming architecture's complicity in corporate bureaucracy. Second, in Korea's immediate postwar context of heavily state-led development, there was hardly any room for the model of the architect as a charismatic, top-down designer who could advocate for social—let alone architectural—values of his or her own.[59] The institutional circumstances generated by the state and by the whole-hearted embrace of developmentalist policy forged a certain "style" of architectural practice that either diminished the general persona of the architect or misattributed the design decisions.

In concluding, let us cross-reference Junglim's corporate development with a diagram that was drafted around the same time by Pak Hak-jae, whose insight into architecture's response to corporate needs opened this chapter. According to this diagram of professional knowledge (see Figure 10.5), "architecture's total planning" was newly divided into "design planning" (*ŭijang kyehoek*) and "practical planning" (*shiryong kyehoek*), each encompassing aesthetic modes of production (architecture, garden, and allied arts) and engineering categories (structure, facilities, and construction). At the same time, Pak's diagram hinted at *sŏlgye* in terms of its definition as a "design" practice: a cognitive process that lay midway between concept and production. Furthermore, Pak represented architectural planning as a specialist category of its own. Taken together, "design" was an aspirational intellectual rubric that could also be taken as a standalone "expertise." This was precisely the opposite of the condition we saw at Ch'ungbi, wherein design, along with facilities management and site planning, had figured as a disparate and internally evolving patchwork of services. Consequently, architectural expertise known as *sŏlgye* at Ch'ungbi had demonstrated an early if unresolved version of "total design" knowledge that architectural firms sought to incorporate under one roof.

Between Welton Becket's corporate model and Pak's diagram, the "total planning" of architecture correlated with Junglim's new sectors of architectural expertise that could cut across the different scales, stages, and forms of practice. This correlation signified not only the production of architectural knowledge and the production of a professional services firm as coincidental; it also reconfigured the epistemological stakes of "design" by leveling it as a fixed and definable service, just like the technical specialties. As Yi Sang-hŏn has

THE MAKING OF ARCHITECTURAL DESIGN AS *SŎLGYE*

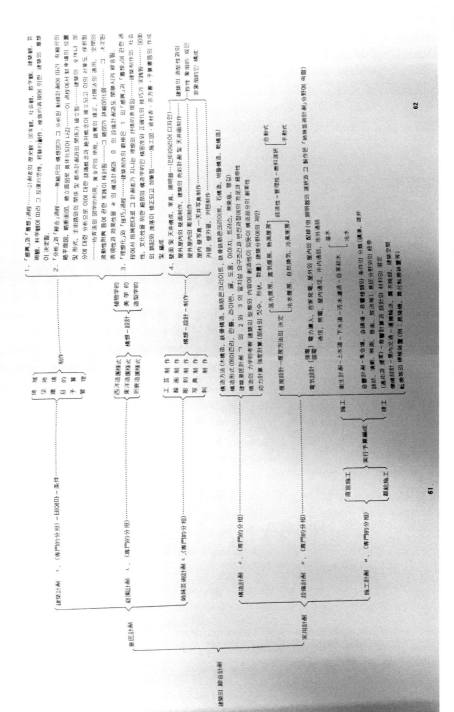

FIGURE 10.5 Pak Hak-jae's chart of architectural knowledge in *Kŏnch'uk ch'ŏrhak ŭro sŏŭi ŭijangnon* (A philosophy of architecture, 1979).

Source: Seoul Museum of History.

observed, the financial terms attached to architectural services continue to demonstrate such a technical association; the fee structure of *konchuk sŏlgye* or "architectural design," in practice and for any given project, always follows that of *enjiniŏring sŏlgye* or "engineering design."[60] Unlike engineering, however, where the problem—and, likewise, the financial remuneration—is likely prefixed, the problem that comes with architectural *sŏlgye*—the labor of design and creative production—is certainly far more abstract and thus difficult to quantify.[61] In this light, when companies like Junglim were transformed into a comprehensive "design" practice, *sŏlgye* most likely bypassed a specialist service or expertise per se (as Pak had idealized in his diagram) and instead became a conceptual framework for organizing architecture's corporate structure. Henceforth, the Korean practice of architecture, either at Ch'ungbi or in its mature corporate version at Junglim, exemplifies how the labor of architectural design will never be fully grasped by engineering's fiscal and technical parameters, even as it continues to be defined by them.

NOTES

1 Pak Hak-jae, *Kŏnch'uk chŏrhak ŭro sŏŭi ŭijangnon* [A philosophy of architecture] (Seoul: Industrial Book Publishing Corporation, 1979).

2 Ibid.

3 The first "Kŏnch'uksa pŏp" or legal statute for architects was established in December 1963, and in the same year a two-tier system distinguishing between "1-kŭp" and "2-kŭp" (first- and second-tier) architects was installed. In April 1965, the first professional licensing exam took place together with the creation of the Korea Institute of Registered Architects (Taehan Kŏnch'uksa Hyŏp'oe).

4 Sun Jae-Won, "Building of Human Resources and the Introduction of Technology," *Review of Korean Studies* 10, no. 4 (December 2007): 61.

5 Office of Statistics and Reports, *ICA Management Report* (January 31, 1959), 14.

6 Charles R. Frank Jr., Kwang Suk Kim, and Larry E. Westphal, "Development of the Trading and Exchange Rate System: Phase I, 1945 to 1953, and Phase II, 1953 to 1960," vol. 7 of *Foreign Trade Regimes and Economic Development: South Korea* (New York: National Bureau of Economic Research; distributed by Columbia University Press, 1975), 25–41.

7 International Cooperation Administration: Office of the Assistant to the Director of Evaluation, *Evaluation of Korea Program*, by Vance Rogers, Evan M. Wilson, and Thomas Stern (Washington, DC, April 15, 1958), 45.

8 Between 1955 and 1958, national wheat production dropped from 70 percent to 25 percent with America PL480 sources filling in the remaining demand. See Kim Tae-ho, "T'ongilbyŏ ŭi kiŏk kwa 'imgŭmnim ssal' ŭi yŏksa mandŭlgi" [Memories of Unification Rice and the Making of the History of 'King's Rice'], *Sarim* 57 (July 2016): 40.

9 Information obtained from an interview with Kim Chŏng-sik on July 3, 2017.

10 An Ch'ang-mo, *Han'guk hyŏndae kŏnch'uk 50-yŏn* [50 Years of Contemporary Korean Architecture] (Seoul: Chaewŏn, 1996), 17.

11 Structurally sound and architecturally functional I-beams were first produced in Korea with the establishment of P'ohang Chaech'ŏl in 1970. Previously, steel produced by Inch'ŏn Chaech'ŏl, Korea's earliest and main manufacturer of the industrial material, was made mostly from recycled iron and inadequate in strength for construction applications. See Lee Yun-suk and Jung In-ha, "1950–60nyŏndae han'guk kŏnch'uk ŭi kisul chŏk tamnon e kwanhan yŏn'gu—chonghap kŏnch'uk kwa shin kŏnch'uk munhwa yŏn'guso rŭl chungshim ŭro" [A Study on the Technical Discourse of 1950–1960s Korean Architecture Centered on Chonghap Kŏnch'uk and Shin Kŏnch'uk Munhwa Yŏn'guso], *Taehan kŏnch'uk hak'oe haksul pal p'yodaehoe nonmun chip—kyehoek kye* 23, no. 2 (2003): 660.

12 Newly established in 1956 with architectural and engineering graduates from Korean and Japanese universities, Kuzosa revived the recently disbanded architecture collaborative, Shin Kŏnch'uk Munhwa Yŏn'guso (New Architecture Cultural Research Institute), that Pae had helped establish in June 1954. Between 1958 and 1959, Kuzosa brought over the architects Sin Ŭn-su, O Ung-sŏk, Yi Ch'ae-yŏng, Mun Yŏng-chae, and the engineer Ch'oe Yŏng-kyu from Chonghap Kŏnch'uk, South Korea's architecture collaboration established a year prior to Shin Kŏnch'uk. Kuzosa thus partially consolidated two of South Korea's pioneering architectural groups under one roof.

13 The competition entry for Ch'ungbi was initiated by Ŏm Tŏk-mun, its architectural drawings drafted by Wŏn Chŏng-su, and perspective drawings drafted by Lee yun-hyŏng. See Wŏn Chŏng-su, "Han'guk ŭi kŏnch'ukka(10)—Pae Ki-hyŏng(2)" [Korean architect(10)—Pae Ki-hyŏng(2)], *Kŏnch'uksa* (November 1997): 45.

14 For an exhaustive account of the *daiku* and their exposure to foreign construction methods in late nineteenth- and early twentieth-century Japan, refer to Gregory Clancey, *Earthquake Nation: The Cultural Politics of Japanese Seismicity, 1868–1930* (Berkeley: University of California Press, 2006).

15 International Cooperation Administration, *Evaluation of Korea Program*, 87.
16 Prior to Ch'ungbi, Kuzosa had designed factories for Taehan Heavy Industry (1953); Cheil Mojik (1954), Samsung Corporation's textile business; and Tongyang Yŏmjik (1957), Korea's leading silk manufacturer.
17 In 1956, ninety-two out of the 102 Korean faculty were studying at University of Minnesota, three at MIT, two at Lowell Technological Institute, and one each at Ohio State, Yale, and the Pasteur Institute in Paris. "Fourth Semi-Annual Progress Report to Foreign Operations Administration and Seoul National University of Korea in [sic] behalf of Regents of the University of Minnesota covering the period April 19, 1956–October 19,1956," published on October 19, 1956, 10.
18 The Minnesota delegation occasionally commented on the national construction standards through its civil engineering advisor, Paul Andersen, who recommended a Korean building code and the replacement of the Japanese regulations. See "Fifth Semi-Annual Progress Report to Foreign Operations Administration and Seoul National University of Korea in [sic] behalf of Regents of the University of Minnesota covering the period October 19, 1956–April 19, 1957," published on April 19, 1957, 36.
19 Sun, "Building of Human Resources," 43–69.
20 Sang-Hyun Kim, "Science, Technology, and the Imaginaries of Development in South Korea," *Journal of Asian Sociology* 46, no. 2 (September 2017): 352–358; see especially 355. The formulation and usage of the term *kwahak kisul* was certainly not new to the 1960s. Kim attributes the earliest colonial usages of *kwahak kisul* in Korean and *kagaku gijutsu* in Japanese to 1941, the year when the Faculty of Science and Engineering was created at Kyŏngsŏng Technical College and the "New Order for Science-Technology," tying science and technology to Japan's national defense strategies, was installed. Ibid., 348–349.
21 "Chŏngbusŏ tongŭi haltŭt" [Government appears to consent], *Tonga ilbo*, March 19, 1960.
22 Illyŏk Kaebal Yŏn'guso, *Kwahak kisulgye illyŏk chawŏn chosa* [A Survey on Scientific and Technical Manpower] (Seoul: Kwahak Kisulch'ŏ, 1973), 18–19.
23 Ibid., 18.
24 The term "*kŏnch'uk kisulcha*" appears under the 1969 *Han'guk chigŏp sajŏn* (Dictionary of Korean Occupations) published by the Illyŏk Kaebal Yŏn'guso.
25 Han'guk Wŏnjaryŏk Yŏn'guso, *Han'guk wŏnjaryŏk isimnyŏn sa* [20 Years of Korean Nuclear Power] (Seoul: Han'guk Wŏnjaryŏk Yŏn'guso, 1979).
26 Kukka Kisul P'yojunwŏn, *Kukka Kisul P'yojunwŏn 130-yŏnsa* [130 Years of Korean Agency for Technology and Standards], 2 vols. (Kwach'ŏn-si: Kukka Kisul P'yojunwŏn, 2013), 96–97.
27 Scientific research conducted for engineering applications was only institutionalized formally at a national scale with the establishment of the Korea Institute of Science and Technology (KIST) in 1966, paralleled by a ninefold increase in state investment between 1963 and 1970 (from 1.2 billion Korean Won to 10.5 billion Korean Won). See Song Wi-jin, Yi Ŭn-gyŏng, Song Sŏng-su, and Kim Pyŏng-yun, *Han'guk kwahak kisulcha sahoe ŭi t'ŭksŏng punsŏk* [A Study on the Characteristics of the Korean Science and Technology Community] (Seoul: Kwahak Kisul Chŏngch'aek Yŏn'guwŏn, 2003), 42.
28 Carl Graffunder, "Report and Recommendations Pertaining to the Department of Architectural Engineering Seoul National University," December 1, 1955, 1–2.
29 Ibid., 2.
30 Ibid. For the comparisons and distinctions made between the scientific laboratory and artistic workshops, both regarding the Bauhaus and more generally as it appeared in modernist discourses, see Zeynep Çelik Alexander, *Kinaesthetic Knowing: Aesthetics, Epistemology, Modern Design* (Chicago and London: University of Chicago Press, 2017), 168–171.
31 Yi Sang-hŏn, *Taehan Min'guk e kŏnch'uk ŭn ŏpta: Han'guk kŏnch'uk ŭi saeroun ch'aip'olloji ch'atki* [There Is No Architecture in Korea: Finding a New Typology in Korean Architecture] (P'aju: Hyohyŏng Ch'ulp'an, 2013), 151. Similarly, Tonga konggwa hagwŏn, the precursor to Hanyang University, had a "design" curriculum in the early 1940s, but this also likely focused on drawing techniques.
32 Graffunder, "Report and Recommendations," 4.
33 Out of the three, Yun Chŏng-sŏp alone studied city planning at University of Minnesota. See Lee and Jung, "1950–60nyŏndae han'guk kŏnch'uk ŭi kisul chŏk tamnon e kwanhan yŏn'gu," 659.
34 Cho Ch'ang-han, "Kim Hŭi-ch'un ch'udo t'ŭkchip," *Kŏnch'ukka* (September 1993): 24, quoted in Kim Ye-jin, "A Study on Artistical Growth Background of Korean Modern Architects" (Master's thesis, Sŏnggyun'gwan University, 2005), 26.
35 "Sixth Semi-Annual Progress Report to Foreign Operations Administration and Seoul National University of Korea on behalf of Regents of the University of Minnesota covering the period April 19, 1957–October 19, 1957," published on October 19, 1957, 45.
36 "Fifth Semi-Annual Progress Report to Foreign Operations Administration and Seoul National University of Korea," 26.
37 See chap. 7 of Daniel Barber, *A House in the Sun: Modern Architecture and Solar Energy in the Cold War* (New York: Oxford University Press, 2016).

38 For Rapson's MIT connection, see chaps. 3 and 4, ibid. Rapson's teaching philosophy stands out in the two articles: "The Goals of Professional Training," *Journal of Architectural Education* 11, no. 2 (June 1956): 11–12; and "Objectives of Architectural Education," *Journal of Architectural Education* 14, no. 2 (September 1959): 21–23.
39 Alexander, *Kinaesthetic Knowing*, 175.
40 Graffunder, "Report and Recommendations," 2.
41 Ibid., 5.
42 Ibid., 3.
43 The single Korean literature he referenced was the Korean Standards Association's *Korean Industrial Standards* (1964). Other consulted publications included the third edition of *The Theory and Practice of Reinforced Concrete* by Clarence W. Dunham (1953) and the *Manual of Steel Construction* by the American Institute of Steel Construction, AISC (1963).
44 "Ch'ungju piryo kongŏp chushik hoesa chonghap pyŏngwŏn" [Ch'ungju Fertilizer Industry Co., Ltd. General Hospital], *Kŏnch'uk* 8, no. 2 (1964): 45.
45 Pak Chŏng-hyŏn, *Kimjŏngch'ŏl kwa chŏngnim kŏnch'uk 1967–1987* [Kim Chŏng-ch'ŏl and Junglim Architecture] (Seoul: P'ŭrop'aganda, 2017), 84.
46 Ibid., 85.
47 At the time, only a firm with a minimum of three licensed architects could be legally established as a "*chonghap samuso*," meaning that the licensure became the most salient factor for architecture's corporatization.
48 Pak, *Kimjŏngch'ŏl kwa chŏngnim kŏnch'uk 1967–1987*, 101.
49 Ibid., 92.
50 In 1972, the firm size numbered twenty-nine. By 1997, with 293 staff, Junglim employed over a tenfold amount from its early beginnings. Kwŏn To-un, *Kŏnch'uk sŏlgye 45-yŏn: pyŏnhwa wa sŏngjang, namgigo sipŭn charyo tŭl* [45 Years of Architectural Design: Changes and Development, Documents I Wish to Leave Behind] (Seoul: Kimundang, 2014), 96–97.
51 Pak, *Kimjŏngch'ŏl kwa chŏngnim kŏnch'uk 1967–1987*, 100.
52 Ibid., 112.
53 Kwŏn, *Kŏnch'uk sŏlgye 45-yŏn*, 94.
54 William Dudley Hunt, *Total Design: Architecture of Welton Becket and Associates* (New York: McGraw-Hill, 1972), 46.
55 Ibid., 45.
56 Pak, *Kimjŏngch'ŏl kwa chŏngnim kŏnch'uk 1967–1987*, 101.
57 Hunt, *Total Design*, 16.
58 Yi, *Taehan Min'guk e kŏnch'uk ŭn ŏpta*, 229.
59 Exceptions to this model include Kim Jung-up (1922–1988), who returned to Korea after having worked with Le Corbusier in the early 1950s, and Kim Swoo-geun (1931–1986), who ran a smaller atelier model. By the late 1960s, however, Kim Swoo-geun's practice was implicated in the state-led Korea Engineering Consultant Corporation. See Melany Sun-Min Park, "The Paradox of Excess: Kim Swoo-geun's Môt and His Economical Architecture," *The Journal of Architecture* 22, no. 6 (August 2017): 1027.
60 Yi, *Taehan Min'guk e kŏnch'uk ŭn ŏpta*, 92.
61 Ibid., 93.

11

Infrastructures of dependency

US Steel's architectural assemblages on Indigenous lands

Manuel Shvartzberg Carrió

Indigenous infrastructures foreground interdependence among humans and nonhumans—a radical relationality that is inherently disrupted by settler colonialism.[1] Infrastructures like railroads, working in concert with juridical constructs like the doctrine of discovery, have been key to the colonial disruption of systems of interdependence by systems of "dependence."[2] But what role have architecture and urbanism played in this historical process? This chapter examines this question through a critical reading of two projects spearheaded by US Steel Corporation in the early post-World War II period: a series of prefabricated steel houses in Palm Springs, California, and the iron-ore mining settlement that would become Ciudad Guayana, Venezuela. The projects illustrate how architectural expertise structured US Steel's operations—from resource extraction and production to distribution and consumption—as a fungible infrastructural system critical to the United States' bid for hegemony in the Cold War and to the maintenance of settler-colonial capitalism. Located on Indigenous lands, the projects' designers organized displacements of Native sovereignty and racialized segregation, naturalizing these processes through an architectural discourse of modernist regionalism. Through the use of specific architectural devices—the grid and the patio—they sought to enact a "transition" for Indigenous populations and racialized workers: from rural to urban life and from noncapitalist societies to capitalist modernity.

At the micro-scale, US Steel's sponsorship of the homes in Palm Springs—built on the Agua Caliente Band of Cahuilla Indians' land—demonstrates how architects mobilized the basic "intellectual technologies" theorized by liberal technocrats to explain and produce techno-economic integration. Via automation and standardization, the whole housing construction process could be optimized, leading to ever-higher efficiencies and profits. Imagined at an industrial scale, architectural techniques of labor mobilization, specialization, and decentralization suggested that a rationalized prefabricated housing system could embody the secular mechanics of national growth. Yet instead of shared growth and social integration, this resulted in dynamics of racial dispossession and what Agua Caliente Tribal Chairwoman Vyola Olinger called "fragmented jurisdiction."[3]

The western United States grew dramatically in the early postwar period, with US Steel supplying over a quarter of all its steel needs. To cope with this demand, US Steel sought

Venezuela's substantial mineral resources.[4] Thus, at the macro-scale, techniques of architectural mobilization were put to work in the conceptualization and design of Ciudad Guayana: a city explicitly designed as a "resource frontier" for US Steel and as a "growth pole" for southern Venezuela.[5] This project, originally planned for US Steel by José Luis Sert and Paul Lester Wiener in the early 1950s, was later expanded in the 1960s by MIT and Harvard's Joint Center for Urban Studies, working with the governmental Corporación Venezolana de Guayana (CVG). US Steel's original settlement began extracting iron ore in 1953, making it the first large-scale industrial project of today's expansive Orinoco Mining Arc, a region still populated by dozens of Indigenous nations, such as the Kali'na, the Warao, and the Pemón.[6] Sert and Wiener's urban plan was designed to assimilate these Indigenous and other migrating rural populations into modern and industrial patterns of life. The Joint Center's subsequent project consolidated the orchestration of mineral resource extraction as a motor of Venezuelan national growth while also guaranteeing the flow of iron ore to the United States, strengthening the symbiotic relation between US hegemony and pro-capitalist Venezuelan political parties. Between 1959 and 1969, US Steel shipped almost 40 percent of all imported iron ore into the United States from this one site.[7]

Both architectural projects displaced Indigenous systems of interdependence through "infrastructures of dependency"—reconstituting migrant labor and Indigenous land as "factors of production" and relegating them as a "periphery" of US Steel's central productive "core."[8] Architectural expertise was instrumental in designing these infrastructures as vehicles of neocolonial interpellation: first construing Indigenous and rural populations as "primitive" or "prehistorical," then assimilating them through specific biopolitical enclosures to assist in their urban "transition." Indigenous life and land were treated as residual excesses to be relocated and reformed. These modern architectures, working as interconnected parts of US Steel's extraterritorial infrastructure, mediated this double operation of displacement and assimilation.

AN "AMERICAN INDIAN POINT IV PROGRAM"

After World War II, the most influential models and case studies for comparative analysis on Native American development were found in Latin America.[9] Native activists and liberal reformers argued for two kinds of models. On the liberal side, spearheaded by Indian Commissioner John Collier in the late 1930s, was the idea that Indigenous peoples in both North and South America would greatly benefit from being incorporated into world markets, as producers and consumers of a US-led sphere of democratic capitalism. By connecting North–South Native programs to the United States' own needs for markets and resources, Collier sought to appeal to US policymakers who viewed Latin America as a new exploitable frontier.[10]

The other model, developed in the 1960s and 1970s, attempted a structural analysis along Marxist lines, positing Indigenous populations akin to the rural "subsistence" peasants and farmers of the transition from feudalism to capitalism.[11] Indigenous activists and scholars used this approach to establish an interpretive frame of "internal colonialism" applicable to the "intranational" condition of Latin American tribes and the US Indian reservations system, as well as other nations undergoing processes of decolonization in Africa and Asia.[12] They adopted the center-periphery paradigm central to these discourses, attempting to understand the spatialization of cultural and economic power relations over Indigenous nations. In the United States, critics argued that the reservation was structurally *under*developed, with its resources—both primary materials and unskilled labor—exploited for the benefit of the metropolis and orchestrated by a system of "corporate colonialism."[13] This suggested a framework wherein "assimilated" Native elites (akin to "comprador" bourgeoisies in Latin America) remained dependent on the "aid" institutions established by the Bureau of Indian Affairs (BIA).

Dependency theory thus appeared to offer a universal structure—a narrative and a methodology—that could potentially unite diverse struggles. However, McCarthyism marginalized political actors with any association to potentially "subversive" nations and organizations.[14] Mainstream postwar Native American activism was thus consigned to being a nonpartisan and exclusively US-based effort, but construed in direct analogy to postcolonial nations seeking self-determination and development as rewards for allegiance to US hegemony. In this context, the National Congress of American Indians attempted to build a coalition in favor of an "American Indian Point IV Program"—a dedicated development plan to mirror Truman's Point IV program of international aid but specifically tailored for Indian reservations in the United States.

This mode of activism, combined with the radical American Indian Movement of the 1960s and 1970s, eventually brought about an era of relative autonomy based on the federal "recognition" of Native Tribes, ushering what is now called the era of tribal "self-determination." But with this concession, the question of whether or not the critical model of dependency theory also applied to Indigenous nations was effectively displaced by the assimilative forces and dynamics of liberal recognition.[15] More ambitious arrangements for a decolonial sovereignty and global political economy were thus muted.[16]

Yet the mechanics of liberal recognition were not merely rhetorical. Rather, "recognition" was articulated *architecturally* as a means to incorporate vast numbers of Indigenous and racialized workers into American—and US Steel's—jurisdictions.[17] In both Palm Springs and Ciudad Guayana, architecture offered an instrument to mobilize Indigenous land and labor, continuing the long project of structuring settler-colonial dependency.

THE INTELLECTUAL TECHNOLOGIES OF DEVELOPMENT

In the aftermath of World War II, the US began to vigorously impose policies of tribal "termination," implemented through two main approaches: assimilation and relocation.[18] "Assimilation" involved undoing the cultural bonds and legal institutions that tied Native Americans to their tribes, turning them into individuals enmeshed in the market relations of the "free-enterprise system" by allotting previously communal land to individual tribal members.[19] "Relocation" was a policy encouraging Native Americans to leave their reservations for cities, where BIA agents would encourage their integration into the US labor market and culture. While the vast majority of tribes were opposed to termination, allotment was a divisive issue among Native communities, often forcing a brutal choice on tribal members.[20]

This was the situation of the Agua Caliente Band of Cahuilla Indians in the late 1940s and 1950s, whose reservation was located within and preexisted Palm Springs, California.[21] The small and exclusive tourist resort attracted much media attention as celebrities, corporate executives, and politicians vacationed and built second homes there.[22] After World War II, Palm Springs began to grow exponentially, with the majority of the influx constituted by a working-class that serviced the resort—including Latin Americans, African Americans,

FIGURE 11.1 Wexler & Harrison, Development House for Rheem Manufacturing Company with United States Steel Corporation. Promotion rendering, ca. 1962.

Source: Donald Wexler Collection, College of Environmental Design, Archives-Special Collections, California State Polytechnic University, Pomona.

and Asian Americans, plus the Agua Caliente Tribal members still residing on their reservation. Among the local architects shaping this growth were Donald Wexler and Richard Harrison, who would come to build a number of homes in Palm Springs, in close association with US Steel. The homes were designed and marketed as exemplary case studies in efficient steel design and construction, published all over the world in architectural, steel-trade, lifestyle, and other publications.[23]

Glamorized in their Palm Springs location (see Figure 11.1), Wexler and Harrison's housing prototypes seemed to provide evidence that techno-organizational innovations could generate a life of abundance for America's new "consumers' republic."[24] According to sociologist Daniel Bell, the year 1956 marked a shift in the US labor market from a predominantly industrial to a services economy. Postwar technocrats from the state, corporations, and the professional classes had conquered both the "game against nature" and the "games between men," heralding "the coming of post-industrial society."[25] In practical terms, Bell argued, this was made possible by a new set of "intellectual technologies" deployed by experts to ensure continuous economic growth for society as a whole—a surplus that would then have to be apportioned as more personal income, more social investment, or more leisure time.[26]

Palm Springs appeared to offer a tangible vision for such a society of leisure. Yet the city itself had been founded within the Agua Caliente reservation—a "slum" according to local newspapers—and the US Steel houses were built directly on Native land. Though the tribe had struggled against land dispossessions since the end of the nineteenth century, in the postwar period the city of Palm Springs carried out a series of landmark legal and urban maneuvers for tribal termination, seeking to gain jurisdiction over the Agua Caliente's land and the population living on it.[27]

Although most tribal members now owned highly valued real estate in the center of Palm Springs, under federal trusteeship laws they were not allowed to sell or lease it for more than five-year periods, so the land remained undeveloped. In addition, the city refused to supply utilities like water, gas, and electricity to the reservation, effectively producing the unsanitary conditions used as an excuse for emergency "slum-clearance." This opened the door to an act of Congress which, for the first time in US history, transferred civil and criminal jurisdiction from a reservation to a state, thus empowering the city over the tribe's security, health and safety, building codes, sanitation, policing, and fire.[28]

Throughout the 1950s, the city, the tribal council, and the Bureau of Indian Affairs were locked in complex negotiations while trying to develop a plan that would "allot" the land held in common by the tribe into equally valued plots of property for each tribal member. Multiple plans were put forward over time by the different parties—including the tribe's own proposal, produced by Victor Gruen Associates.[29] The final Indian Equalization Act, passed by Congress in 1959, privatized Native American lots and extended leases from five to ninety-nine years, while also ensuring that tribal lands (and development over such lands) would be managed and overseen by state-sanctioned "guarantors" assigned to the Agua Caliente.[30] Yet the act also made possible a new subdivision of tribal land that had been unoccupied until then. The subdivision was bought in 1959 by Palm Springs' most prominent developers of tract housing, the Alexander Construction Company, who had recently expanded from the crowded Los Angeles real estate market to Palm Springs in search of more lucrative profit margins. They promptly hired local architects Donald Wexler and Richard Harrison to design—in collaboration with US Steel—thirty-five prefabricated steel homes as prototypes for the middle-income housing market.[31]

AUTOMATION AND DECENTRALIZATION

The US Steel homes in Palm Springs offered private middle-class housing by pioneering modes of automation in design and construction that would make local construction workers, most of whom lived on the reservation, unemployed. The logic of capitalist growth—rearticulating decades of land dispossession into a technology of labor displacement—thus had parallel but asymmetric effects upon the Indigenous and racialized working class living in Palm Springs.

"Internal migrations" resulting from technological unemployment were seen as a sign of national-economic vitality,[32] so even though social reformers attempted to ameliorate "urban blight," the fundamental logic of racialized displacement was left intact. In this context, automated prefabricated housing exacerbated the dynamic of mobility while also promising to resolve its contradictions—from the relation between private developers and government funding to the problem of achieving a market-based solution to housing affordability.[33]

Rather than addressing affordable housing, US Steel would leverage Palm Springs' status as a national symbol of postwar leisure and glamorized modernist architecture to market its own products for steel housing to builders and developers.[34] The project offered prototypical solutions to broad issues facing US Steel at large, including corporate overproduction and how to finance a massive and ever-growing distribution infrastructure. The most direct way to deal with these issues was to cheapen or automate labor; to enter new markets (such as establishing the US Steel Homes division in 1953);[35] and to capitalize (sell or rent) their supply and distribution chains.[36] Sited in a place where labor was radically and structurally oppressed, Palm Springs was a safe testing ground for automation processes in construction. Furthermore, by spectacularizing a standardized fabrication and assembly process, the project also advertised US Steel's growing network of "Service Center" warehouses—steel "supermarkets" stocked with standard parts—to thousands of smaller steel producers who might then fulfill their own steel inventories without having to pay the heavy costs of storage and distribution themselves.[37]

US Steel's infrastructure—comprising mines, steel mills, logistics, research and marketing centers—had grown substantially since World War II, and the company struggled to maintain it while also turning a profit. Though US Steel's close relations with government allowed it to maintain a high level of demand through defense contracts, regular steelworker strikes were a real threat to the corporation. In this context, Wexler's and Harrison's housing prototypes were explicitly designed as experiments in automation and efficient logistical operations—a comprehensive kit of prefabricated steel parts enabling a construction and assembly process that required less than half the skilled labor of a regular home.[38]

Structural and finished steel sections would be procured from US Steel's Geneva plant in Utah, shipped to the engineering factory in Huntington Park, California, for prefabrication and preassembly, and then delivered to the building site for installation. This systematic approach—a vertically integrated chain for housing—infused the whole project, from the formal design to construction processes like casting the foundation slab with the aid of pre-engineered steel templates. So standardized, the entire house could be packed and transported on a single truck to the site, where a single crane and a team of three workers would hoist and fix each element in place, completing the house in just three days. By reducing site machinery and labor, the project radically reduced the costs of construction.

But despite its slick steel and techno-managerial allure, this system was never a real solution to the housing problem at mass-scale. It wasn't just that its cost was only accessible to middle-class families. In fact, the dream of a *private solution* to the housing crisis through the technological innovations of automation was both a utopian ideological product of the Cold War and a structural contradiction within a free-market capitalist economy.[39] Rather than stabilizing housing, automation would set it in perpetual motion, as the temporary efficiencies gained through automation generated surpluses of both capital goods and labor that could not be easily recycled through market processes alone. Without sufficient labor-intensive investments, as labor was increasingly automated, housing supply would soar, but demand would wane. In such instances, as in Palm Springs, the surplus labor released by automation could both generate and exacerbate the housing problem—potentially worsening the unemployment and poor living conditions of the construction workers living on the reservation.

Indeed, in the wake of tribal termination policies, similar dynamics of racialized proletarianization led tens of thousands of Native Americans to take up the various programs of the Relocation Act of 1956, moving to large cities like Los Angeles and Chicago, where they were often housed in inner-city "slums" as they tried their luck at the "free-enterprise system of development."[40] During the massive internal migrations of World War II—7 million workers moved to defense production locations[41]—economists like Alvin H.

INFRASTRUCTURES OF DEPENDENCY 223

Hansen and Guy Greer argued that prefabricated housing would be a crucial component to structure this mobilization. They also stressed, however, that government could not interfere with local real estate markets. The problem of "blighted areas and slums," Greer claimed, were of "peculiar difficulty," for they represented a racialized *"excess"*—urban areas had unduly high valuations, meaning that the market would only start investing if the land was cheap enough or if racial demographics were inverted. This racist, "free market" rationalization sought to prevent government support for urban redevelopment and public housing.[42]

In other words, race and ethnicity effectively pierced the net of jurisdictional protections, whether in terms of access to "adjustment" policies or other state-sanctioned modes of political-economic enfranchisement, like unionization, adequately funded public housing, or federally insured mortgages. Following the intellectual technologies of economic optimization, Wexler and Harrison's prefabricated housing project effectively extruded this rationale into an imaginary three-dimensional space, interlacing the site in Palm Springs with US Steel's national production and distribution infrastructures in order to architecturally eliminate the racialized worker (Figure 11.2).

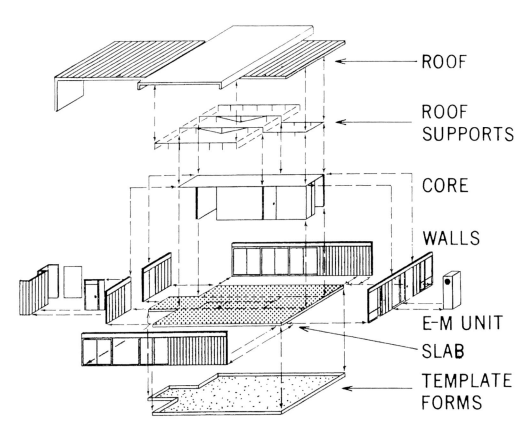

FIGURE 11.2 Wexler & Harrison, Development House for Rheem Manufacturing Company with United States Steel Corporation. Construction sequence diagram, ca. 1962.

Source: Donald Wexler Collection, College of Environmental Design, Archives-Special Collections, California State Polytechnic University, Pomona.

RECENTRALIZATION AND TRANSITION

The problem of how to "redevelop" inner cities would constitute the major focus of large liberal philanthropic institutions like the Ford and Rockefeller Foundations in the 1950s and 1960s. In collaboration with economists and planners, they sought to find ways of assimilating racialized urban migration. Responding to the same issues, architects would start defining ways to revitalize "urban cores," moving away from purely suburban models and trying to shape city centers afflicted by the seemingly unstoppable phenomena of market-driven decentralization. The accumulating expertise on this issue—combining urban policy and design—was key to the formation of the MIT-Harvard Joint Center of Urban Studies in 1959, which would instrumentalize research on urban blight and labor mobilization for an international discourse of "development."[43]

The United States' dominant suburban growth model constituted a complex and conflictive grid of techno-jurisdictional intersections, including for US Steel. One problem was growing miner strikes.[44] But another was the supply of raw materials. Already during World War II, US Steel's calculations of available iron ore reserves in the Mesabi Range indicated that reserves would dwindle in about 25 years.[45] As the American frontier was being depleted, US Steel funded dozens of expeditions across the world in search of plentiful, reliable, and accessible sources of iron ore. Finally, in 1947, working together with Venezuelan officials and the US Army, US Steel found the largest deposit of high-grade iron ore in the world—estimated at 500 billion tons—near the Orinoco river in southern Venezuela.[46] The deposit, "Cerro Bolívar," was dubbed the "Ten Billion-Dollar Mountain."[47] Reports suggested that US Steel would be able to extract 5 million tons of ore in the first year and up to 10 million per year thereafter.[48] By 1969, after a $300 million investment, US Steel was shipping 15.7 million gross tons of iron ore per year from the development—nearly 40 percent of all the iron ore being imported into the United States.[49]

In 1948, US Steel began construction on the mine, as well as a miners' town next to Cerro Bolivar called Ciudad Piar and a riverside settlement 90 miles east, Puerto Ordaz, in which an ore-crushing plant, docks, utilities, and managers' housing would be built. Across Puerto Ordaz, on the Caroní's eastern side, was an existing small fishing village called San Félix. Ships would leave Puerto Ordaz daily, transporting about 6,000 tons of iron ore each, to US Steel's largest production plant, over an eleven-day trip (Figure 11.3).[50] The massive East coast Fairless Works, opened in 1952 to supply the whole country (shipping steel products to the West Coast via the Panama Canal),[51] was precisely planned in the late 1940s to take advantage of the cheap iron ore that would soon flow from Venezuela.[52]

By 1953, US Steel's local subsidiary, the Orinoco Mining Company, was ready to begin exporting ore. All the investment capital was US Steel's; the Venezuelan government granted fifty years of mining rights with no immediate financial obligations, after which profits would be shared equally between the foreign corporation and the host state. A number of US corporations built the infrastructural elements of the settlement, with architecture firm SOM originally designing the plan for the mining town at Cerro Bolivar.[53] However, in 1950, after political pressures against the design of another "company town," US Steel hired Venezuelan architects, who then subcontracted Paul Lester Wiener and José Luis Sert as the main urban planning consultants for both Ciudad Piar and Puerto Ordaz.[54]

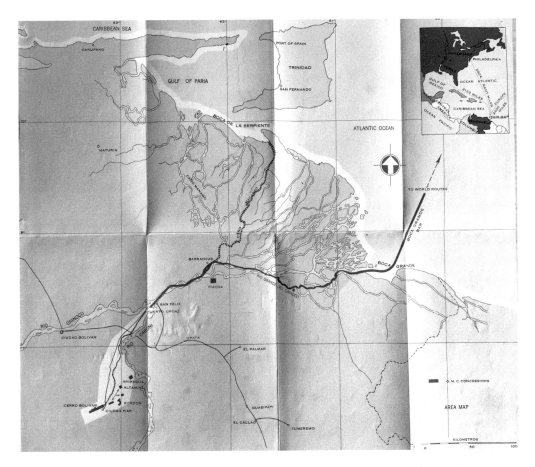

FIGURE 11.3 Diagram of shipping routes from Cerro Bolivar to US Steel mills.
Source: Orinoco Mining Company: A Résumé. US Steel, 1959.

Although they never claimed credit for what was actually built there, Wiener and Sert's work with US Steel extended until late 1953 (just before the first shipment of iron ore in early 1954), and US Steel's urban designs for both the miners' and the managers' towns appear to be substantially based on their plans (Figure 11.4).[55] Indeed, Sert and Wiener widely published the designs for Puerto Ordaz's "Civic Center" (Figure 11.5).[56]

Since the mid-1940s, Wiener and Sert had been producing plans for new industrial towns across South America, including those of Motor City, Brazil (1945), Chimbote, Peru (1948), and Medellin (1949) and Bogota (1951–1953), Colombia. Their plans for Ciudad Piar and Puerto Ordaz bear significant similarities with these other South American projects: they were all organized around civic centers formed by municipal and cultural buildings and surrounded by low-rise housing. US Steel's promotional literature described the urban character of Puerto Ordaz as based on an "open city" principle, built around "the traditional Venezuelan plaza, bordered by a church, its parish house, a recreational center, a supermarket, a cafeteria, the post-office, barbershop, beauty-parlor, shops, etc., all accessible to the general public."[57] Many of the buildings on the central plaza contained their own internal courtyards.

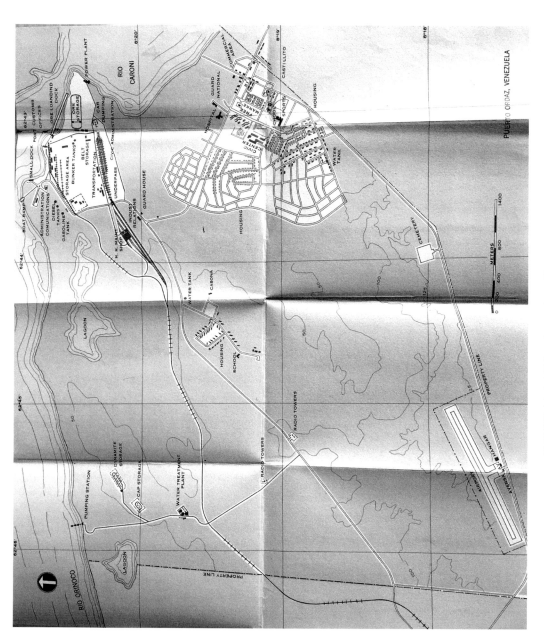

FIGURE 11.4 US Steel site plan of Puerto Ordaz.

Source: *Orinoco Mining Company: A Résumé*. US Steel, 1959.

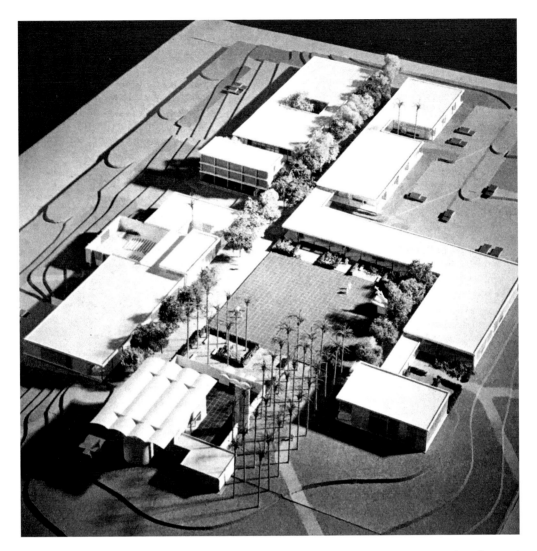

FIGURE 11.5 Model of proposed "civic center" for US Steel at Puerto Ordaz, by José Luis Sert and Paul Lester Wiener, 1953.

The formal architectural device that tied all these plans together was the "patio." Sert claimed this was a typological instrument that could help re-humanize cities after the perils of suburban decentralization and urban congestion. At the scale of the home, patios offered inward-looking calm to possible "unpredictable changes occurring in the neighborhood."[58] At an urban scale, patios could be as big as plazas, a basic "module" across different kinds of spaces and scales. By using patios, Sert hoped to create "outdoor rooms" more amenable to human connection, thus stopping the "centrifugal habits" of the modern metropolis. The patio-form was thus pitched as a universally scalable and typical unit for producing "a *coherent* city—as opposed to an informal town at one end of the scale, or a monotonous collection of identical units at the other."[59]

Sert's development of the patio as a humanistic typology was at the center of CIAM's preoccupations in the early 1950s, where it played a prominent role in the discussions at CIAM 8 about "the heart of the city."[60] Yet the patio was initially explored by Sert and Wiener as an instrument to accommodate the displaced populations of rural to urban migration. In 1946, they were commissioned by the Peruvian government to design the monumental project for a new city and port that would process mining resources. The main issue, as they saw it, was how to assimilate the new masses of farmers and peasants coming from the countryside to work in industry for the first time. Patio-houses were a central dimension of how to achieve this:

> The great majority of these people cannot live in apartment houses. They will have to continue living near the ground, close to their animals, making use of the patios or courtyards as their roofless living rooms. Their houses have to be *transitional forms* between past and future; their customs and habits cannot be changed suddenly. The North American or European ways of living are not applicable here even were they economically feasible—which they will not be for many years to come.[61]

In other words, the patio's flexibility was not only spatial but temporal. It functioned as a zone of transition between rural and urban, traditional and modern, but also *within* the structure of permanent change constituted by the metropolis—"between past and future." The patio's universality was argued historically—"fully developed in Mesopotamia in Ur around 2000 BC"[62]—as well as culturally—present in the Mediterranean countries and "India, Japan, China, Latin America, and the South and Southwestern United States."[63] Moreover, it represented dynamics of transition in land use: under the pressures of urban migration, it offered rural space in the heart of the city.

The patio was thus ideal for developing nations because it offered a techno-economic enclosure that could, through its very form, aid in the assimilation to urban and modern life. Its structure was a kind of half-way house for informal settlers to adopt more "coherent" ways of life—a moral and normative ideal which was also central to Venezuelan dictator General Marcos Pérez Jiménez's urban reforms for civilizing rural migrants.[64] The "civic center" at Puerto Ordaz was conspicuously flanked by a large church (the largest building in the central square), as well as schools, hospitals, and municipal buildings. The towers of the National Guard, located at the edge of each civic center, kept a watchful eye at both Puerto Ordaz and Ciudad Piar.

Yet the civic center's open patio-structure did not prevent socio-spatial segregation—it naturalized it. While American corporate managers and high-level technicians were housed in US-designed suburban-style modern homes at Puerto Ordaz, the bulk of the mine's workers had to make do in shacks across the river or at the mining town of Ciudad Piar. Even at Puerto Ordaz, the corporate hierarchy was diagrammatically reproduced in three housing sectors—Camp A, Camp B, and Camp C—arranged in ascending order of rank, size, and amenities.[65]

Most workers lived primarily in the informal settlement across the Caroní river, in the town of San Félix, which accommodated a large influx of migrants in search of work at the mine and the other steel facilities. This population had migrated mostly from the surrounding provinces and from multiple Caribbean countries, constituting San Félix's new service labor force.[66] Despite US Steel's "open city" declarations, the corporation enforced a strict policy of allowing only company workers to occupy the areas around the civic center, thus accentuating the divide between San Félix and Puerto Ordaz. In 1958, as the area grew and informal settlements began to encroach upon the managers' town, the Venezuelan government began removing squatters at the behest of US Steel. This informal settlement was continuously targeted for elimination, including by the "diversion of its through-traffic and purposeful neglect of its infrastructure."[67]

Furthermore, while a variety of commercial and social offerings housed in glass-clad modernist buildings were available in Puerto Ordaz, this theatrical openness jarred with the daily flow of workers from San Félix that had to cross the river and pass through the managers' civic center to get to the steelworks west of Puerto Ordaz. This meant crossing the river by boat, as there was no bridge, and traveling the rest by bus—a distance of about 24 kilometers. The commuting never flowed in the opposite direction, thus accentuating the spatial, social, and racial division between the two towns.[68]

A "GROWTH POLE" FOR VENEZUELA—AND US HEGEMONY

Venezuela had welcomed US Steel's investment, marketed by General Pérez Jiménez as a national security asset as well as a motor for national modernization. When in 1959 the General was deposed and succeeded by a development-friendly democratic president, Rómulo Betancourt, the activities of US Steel in the Orinoco river were supported ever more strongly by the Venezuelan state. With national power highly concentrated in the north of the country, the new government proposed to "sow the oil" revenues in the Orinoco, expanding Sert and Wiener's relatively small project into a massive city to jump-start a broader regional economy in the south of Venezuela.[69] The plan sought to connect Puerto Ordaz and San Félix, which had continued to drift apart despite the development's constant growth over the 1950s. The new city, Ciudad Guayana, promised to be a "city of the future"—upgrading the original "open enclave" into a "laboratory of Third World development."[70] This would be accomplished through heavy national economic investment on top of US Steel's existing infrastructure, to be expertly deployed in the shape of a detailed urbanization plan designed by Harvard and MIT's Joint Center for Urban Studies. Thus, the Joint Center's expertise assimilating racialized migrants in the United States would now become the foundation for a much larger project to systematize "development" as an international urban policy field. By consolidating and growing US Steel's original settlement, the Joint Center would help Venezuela rebalance its economy geographically while also strengthening ties with its main trading partner, the United States.

The Joint Center's involvement in the project—a contract worth nearly $2 million over five years for a total construction budget of nearly $4 billion over ten years (10 percent of Venezuela's national budget)—was a triumph of US-led development predicated on the export of technical assistance. The Joint Center accepted the commission with the proviso that they would be able not only to design the masterplan for the city but also to survey their design iterations and publish public reports on them, thus turning the project into a live test-site at the scale of a whole region.[71] Indeed, if the business of development was codified *in* and *as* design research, scientific publications were its main currency.[72]

The planning team consisted of thirteen planners and technocrats from MIT and Harvard, twelve of whom were based in Caracas throughout the duration of the project.[73] When the project began in 1962, it encompassed the working-class town of San Félix, with 45,000 people, and the managerial enclave of Puerto Ordaz, with 4,000.[74] While US Steel wasn't officially involved in the Joint Center's design, the whole undertaking was premised on the idea that explosive national growth could and should go hand in hand with foreign investment in heavy industry—it only required a deep modernization effort achievable through the urbanization plan. But while ostensibly designing a "new" city that would subsume the old layout, the Joint Center's planning efforts were heavily focused on the Puerto Ordaz area and barely attempted to incorporate the "informal" encampments of San Félix.[75]

The focus upon the managerial classes was not accidental, it was a central aspect of the research conducted by John Friedmann, a planner on the MIT-Harvard team, who used the Ciudad Guayana project to explore his ideas of core-periphery regional development. Friedmann made use of French economist François Perroux's "growth pole" theory, importing this paradigm to rationalize the uneven growth happening at Ciudad Guayana as a net benefit for Venezuela as a whole.[76] The new city was conceived as a "flexible structure" to accommodate the large influx of unskilled workers migrating to the area in search of work.[77] Friedmann posited that the right type of urbanization could not only adequately absorb this migrant labor, but also accelerate the efficiency and productivity of the industrial processes that sustained the whole development, in turn rebalancing the national economy by making Southern Venezuela into a strong national "growth pole."[78] The paradigm, therefore, was one of scalar articulation rather than qualitative reorientation: the micro-scale of the city's design—beginning from Sert and Wiener's patio-based civic center and housing design—could spur the nation's macro-development. To achieve this, the planners accepted the spatial, social, and racial segregation that US Steel's "open city" had put in place, merely enlarging and extending the configuration.

In Friedmann's account, these inequalities were a necessary condition for explosive growth. Furthermore, not only was this inherent in the concept of "center-periphery," but the model operated universally, in all places and at all scales: "World, continent, nation, and city—the center-periphery hypothesis appears on all the relevant scales of explanation simultaneously as cause and effect of economic transformation."[79] Thus, while temporary inequalities were regrettable, it was a necessary price for economic growth. Echoing Sert's necessary "transitional forms," growth based on large "metropolitan regions" required broad transitional policies to manage shifts in social power. As Friedmann admitted, "the center-periphery relationship may be described as essentially a 'colonial' one."[80] Social upheavals were to be expected, but following the liberal development expert's principles of distribution, these might be guided in the right direction.

Accordingly, the Joint Center's main proposal was to institutionalize the existing distribution and flow of workers, creating a central "spine" around which everything else would be organized, providing what Friedmann called the plan's main objective: "urban hierarchy." Avenida Guayana, as the spine was called, "connected the steel mill on the western edge of the city with the old town of San Félix on the eastern edge, linking industry, the airport, the commercial center, the cultural center, the river, and the medical center as nodes along the way."[81] Yet while these urban amenities were distributed evenly along the length of the "spine," the distribution of housing neighborhoods, "unidades vecinales," remained in place according to the previous social divisions—with "elite" housing in the west and worker housing in the east.

San Félix's workers protested that their requirements—such as the urgent need for a bridge across the Caroní river—were being disregarded.[82] As one of the planners noted, the managers' housing was conceived—following US Steel's development pattern—as a tool for social differentiation and moralization: "a demonstration of the CVG's intention to provide high quality environments for the elite and a demonstration to the residents of Ciudad Guayana of a better way of life."[83]

In contrast, workers' housing was planned in the manner of John Turner's "self-build" paradigm, with residents of San Félix receiving "manual-like drawings that visualized easy steps for progressive upgrades to each individual home." Eventually, while billions were poured into governmental and social infrastructures for the managerial class, the workers' housing "project was pared down to a parceling exercise."[84] In a cruel irony of the core-periphery theory's principles at work, the CVG's own headquarters in Ciudad Guayana, one of Venezuela's largest steel-framed buildings designed by noted architect Jesus Tenreiro-Degwitz, had to use steel imported from the US for its construction.[85]

SYNTHESIS OR DECOLONIZATION

If Marxist critics had identified the core-periphery dialectic as something to be *abolished*, for liberal technocrats the dialectic's inherent inequalities were something to be *managed*, for the sake of explosive growth. Driven by this imaginary synthesis, they accepted capital's prerogatives, limiting the potentials for more egalitarian, sustainable, and decolonial kinds of development. Although US Steel had transformed the productive economy of the Orinoco region, its local economic impact was quite limited. This was partly because the mining process itself was being automated, so that by 1961 US Steel's jobs in the region were already in decline. As one critical reviewer of the project observed, while this modernization effort was organized around "the belief in mixed economies, economic take-off and expectations of trickle-down effects to benefit and integrate the population," the ultimate result "was a restructuring of relationships between multi-national companies and an increasingly rich and powerful patrimonial State which had turned to State capitalism."[86]

However, the attempt to "integrate the population" was not new; it was grounded in a longer process with a beginning in the colonial administration of Imperial Spain and the "logical positivism" that inspired the Venezuelan War of Independence in the nineteenth century.[87] Focusing on the "traditional Venezuelan plaza," US Steel redeployed a planning device from the Laws of the Indies, which pioneered the city square as the center of a territorial grid for the appropriation of land by settlers, subsuming Indigenous cities, infrastructures, and sovereignties.[88]

The grid and the patio were thus construed as "transitional forms" through which subjects became interpellated into neocolonial laws and history. As Giedion claimed in 1954 with reference to Sert and Wiener's patio housing for Cuban workers, this "New Regional Approach" was a synthesis of modern architecture's internationalism of the 1920s—an architecture of invisible grids which "hovers in mid-air, with no roots anywhere"—and the environmental and cultural specificities of "primitive" and "Eastern" cultures, thus encompassing "both cosmic and terrestrial considerations."[89] Via this hurried synthesis, regional modernism would foster development while becoming "humanized" through the "authentic" ways of life of Indigenous peoples and traditions.

This primitivist fiction, however, was directly undermined by the historical realities of the Indigenous peoples affected by US Steel's developmentalism. Rather than merely synthesizing an embodied humanity with a disembedded modernity, the project at Ciudad Guayana had differential effects on each particular Orinoco nation it intersected with. Thus, for the

Karinya Mamo tribe—which was located a few miles upstream from the development—the opportunities for urban employment were broadly beneficial, allowing for ties to and between the community to be strengthened, including the establishment of a robust critical discourse about the development itself.[90] Conversely, downstream from Ciudad Guayana, the Warao had to face the effects of pollution, which severely disrupted their fishing and economic practices.[91]

Similarly, in Palm Springs, the mobilization of architectural parts spectacularized by US Steel's housing prototypes was beneficial to those Agua Caliente tribal members who were able to profit from the land's allotment, while those who were excluded from the state's property adjudications were at risk of becoming proletarianized by the architects' drive toward total labor automation.

Regionalist modernism, then, enacted two kinds of "settlement fantasies"[92] constituted by a continuous process of mobilization between the two. Growth at the so-called "core" was managed by techno-economic modes of expertise—particularly the twin dynamics of labor automation and spatial decentralization. This expertise was imagined as the infinite interoperability of different axes of jurisdiction, suggesting the total disentanglement of architecture from territory—and thus ignoring jurisdictional incommensurabilites while profiting from them. Wexler and Harrison's diagrams represented this desire for a total architecture which sought to completely systematize the process of economic growth; an imagined synthesis that invisibilized the core's own internal peripheries.[93] The use of steel was an attempt to reduce the complexities inherent in any prefabrication project seeking to harmonize distinct jurisdictional regimes. One material—steel—amounted to one sovereign jurisdiction, so to speak, in the form of a monopolistic corporation with a diverse and coherent body of technological and sales expertise; a techno-political bridge over the Agua Caliente's "fragmented jurisdiction."

Yet compound growth both required and produced endless relocations of labor, capital, and materials.[94] Thus, at the so-called "periphery," regional development sought to "humanize" the upheaval of labor migration and industrial integration by which iron ore could continue being exported, strengthening the US and Venezuela's geopolitical arrangement at the expense of the Orinoco's Indigenous nations. At both ends, the mechanics of the core-periphery model produced growth, but also differentially reproduced certain "infrastructures of dependency." This dependency was not merely economic but, more fundamentally, it was *epistemic*: the imaginary gulf between the primitive vis-à-vis the modern, which required symbolic "transitional forms" like patio-houses to enter settler history and law. In spatial terms, regionalist modernity required a bounded and contained jurisdiction which was nonetheless porous in certain ways; enabling performances of systematicity and the ritual regimentations of industrial life, while continuously expelling racialized labor and iron ore. The same porosity, however, was also a sign of settler colonialism's paradigmatic un-systematicity—a system constantly overwhelmed by that which it could not fully contain, as demonstrated by both the Agua Caliente's and the Warao's continued existence as Indigenous peoples.

NOTES

1 Winona LaDuke and Deborah Cowen, "Beyond Wiindigo Infrastructure," *South Atlantic Quarterly* 119, no. 2 (April 1, 2020): 243–268.

2 Native polities in the United States are still considered "domestic dependent nations." See: Joanne Barker, "The Corporation and the Tribe," *American Indian Quarterly* 39, no. 3 (Summer 2015): 243–270. On settler-colonial railroads,

see: Manu Karuka, *Empire's Tracks: Indigenous Nations, Chinese Workers, and the Transcontinental Railroad* (Oakland, CA: University of California Press, 2019).

3 Vyola J. Ortner and Diana C. du Pont, *You Can't Eat Dirt: Leading America's First All-Women Tribal Council and How We Changed Palm Springs* (Santa Barbara, CA: Fan Palm Research Project, 2011), 57, fn. 142.

4 Kenneth Warren, *Big Steel: The First Century of the United States Steel Corporation, 1901–2001* (Pittsburgh, PA: University of Pittsburgh Press, 2001), 203, 205.

5 John Friedmann, *Regional Development Policy: A Case Study of Venezuela* (Cambridge, MA: MIT Press, 1966).

6 Uzcategui and Marianna Belalba Barreto, "Arco Minero del Orinoco: la crisis de la que pocos hablan en Venezuela," *El País*, September 11, 2018.

7 Warren, *Big Steel*, 210; William T. Hogan, *Economic History of the Iron and Steel Industry in the United States*, vols. 4 and 5 (Lexington: Heath, 1971), vol. 4, 1491, 1659.

8 The concept "infrastructure of dependency" was coined by Susan Bodenheimer, in "Dependency and Imperialism: The Roots of Latin American Underdevelopment," in *Readings in US Imperialism*, eds. K. T. Fann and Donald C. Hodges (Boston: Porter Sargent, 1971). For the classic Marxist historical narrative on core-periphery dynamics, see: Immanuel Wallerstein, *The Modern World-System* (New York: Academic Press, 1974).

9 *Beyond Red Power: American Indian Politics and Activism Since 1900*, eds. Daniel M. Cobb and Loretta Fowler (Santa Fe: School for Advanced Research, 2007), 162.

10 Paul C. Rosier, *Serving Their Country: American Indian Politics and Patriotism in the Twentieth Century* (Cambridge, MA: Harvard University Press, 2009), 80–84.

11 José Carlos Mariátegui, *Seven Interpretive Essays on Peruvian Reality* (Austin: University of Texas Press, 1971 [1928]); Raúl Prebisch, *The Economic Development of Latin America and Its Principal Problems* (New York: United Nations, 1950); Andre Gunder Frank, *Capitalism and Underdevelopment in Latin America* (New York: Monthly Review Press, 1967); Aníbal Quijano, "Dependencia, Cambio Social y Urbanización en Latinoamérica," *Revista Mexicana de Sociología* 30, no. 3 (July–September 1968): 525–570; Celso Furtado, *Economic Development of Latin America*, 2nd ed. (New York: Cambridge University Press, 1976).

12 Robert K. Thomas, "Colonialism: Classic and Internal," *New University Thought* 4 (1966): 37–43; "Powerless Politics," *New University Thought* 5 (1967): np; Pablo Gonzalez Casanova, "Internal Colonialism and National Development," *Studies in Comparative International Development* 1 (April 1965). See also: David E. Wilkins, "Modernization, Colonialism, Dependency: How Appropriate Are These Models for Providing an Explanation of North American Indian 'Underdevelopment'?" *Ethnic and Racial Studies* 16, no. 3 (July 1993): 390–419.

13 Cardell K. Jacobson, "Internal Colonialism and Native Americans: Indian Labor in The United States from 1871 to World War II," *Social Science Quarterly* 65, no. 1 (March 1984): 158–171; Gary C. Anders, "Theories of Underdevelopment and the American Indian," *Journal of Economic Issues* 14, no. 3 (September 1980): 681–701; "The Internal Colonization of Cherokee Native Americans," *Development and Change* 12 (January 1978): 41–56.

14 Paul C. Rosier, "'They Are Ancestral Homelands': Race, Place, and Politics in Cold War Native America, 1945–1961," *The Journal of American History* 92, no. 4 (March 2006): 1300–1326; 1318.

15 Glen Sean Coulthard, *Red Skins, White Masks: Rejecting the Colonial Politics of Recognition* (Minneapolis: University of Minnesota Press, 2014).

16 For exceptions, see George Manuel and Michael Posluns, *The Fourth World* (New York: Free Press, 1974); *Economic Development in American Indian Reservations*, ed. Roxanne Dunbar Ortiz (Albuquerque: University of New Mexico, 1979).

17 On this "steel fundamentalism," see Judith Stein, *Running Steel, Running America: Race, Economic Policy, and the Decline of Liberalism* (Chapel Hill: University of North Carolina, 1998).

18 Vine DeLoria Jr., "Chapter 3: The Disastrous Policy of Termination," in *Custer Died for Your Sins: An Indian Manifesto* (Norman: University of Oklahoma Press, 1988).

19 Donald Fixico, *Termination and Relocation: Federal Indian Policy, 1945–1960* (Albuquerque: University of New Mexico, 1986), 147.

20 Heather Ponchetti Daly, "Fractured Relations at Home: The 1953 Termination Act's Effect on Tribal Relations throughout Southern California Indian Country," *American Indian Quarterly* 33, no. 4 (2009): 427–439.

21 Ryan M. Kray, "Second Class Citizenship at a First Class Resort: Race and Public Policy in Palm Springs" (Doctoral diss., University of California, Irvine, 2009).

22 Lawrence Culver, *The Frontier of Leisure: Southern California and the Shaping of Modern America* (Oxford and New York: Oxford University Press, 2010).

23 Helmuth Odenhausen, "Future Scope for Steel Building with Special Reference to Housing," *Acier-Stahl-Steel: International Review for the Development of the Uses of Steel* (Bruxelles: Centre belgo-luxembourgeois d'information de l'acier) 29th Year, no. 10 (October 1964): 421–433; Frank M. McKeller, "New All-Steel Home System," *Home Builders Journal* (August 1962); "New Steel Components Let You Bolt Together a $9/sq. ft. House," *House and Home* (April 1962): 127–129.

24 Lizabeth Cohen, *A Consumers' Republic: The Politics of Mass Consumption in Postwar America* (New York: Vintage Books, 2004).

25 Daniel Bell, *The Coming of Post-Industrial Society: A Venture in Social Forecasting* (New York: Basic Books, 1973).

26 For Marxist versions of this argument, see Paul M. Sweezy and Paul A. Baran, *Monopoly Capital: An Essay on the American Economic and Social Order* (New York: Monthly Review Press, 1966); Paul A. Baran, *The Political Economy of Growth* (New York: Monthly Review Press, 1957).

27 Manuel Shvartzberg Carrió, "Designing 'Post-Industrial Society': Settler Colonialism and Modern Architecture in Palm Springs, California, 1876–1977" (Doctoral diss., Columbia University, 2019).

28 Public Law 322, *An Act to Confer Jurisdiction on the State of California Over the Lands and Residents of the Agua Caliente Indian Reservation*. 1949. Between 1951 and 1967, the city maneuvered to condemn Section 14—the area where most workers lived—on the grounds of "insalubrity." By the end, almost two-thirds of Palm Springs's entire adult population was forcefully dispossessed and ejected from the city. See Manuel Shvartzberg Carrió, "Palm Springs and the *Nomos* of Modernity: Prefabricated Steel Houses, Automation, and Settler Colonialism in Postwar America, 1943–1968," in *Productive Universals—Specific Situations: Critical Engagements in Art, Architecture and Urbanism*, eds. Anne Kockelkorn and Nina Zschocke (Berlin: Sternberg Press, 2019).

29 Victor Gruen and Associates, *Indian Lands Palm Springs* 14 (1957), Agua Caliente Cultural Museum Archives.

30 The act's provisions were abused by the guarantors, leading to charges of fraud in the 1970s. George Ringwald, *The Agua Caliente Indians and Their Guardians* (Riverside: Press-Enterprise, 1967, 1968).

31 Lauren W. Bricker and Sidney Williams, *Steel and Shade: The Architecture of Donald Wexler* (Heidelberg: Kehrer Verlag, 2011), 21; Bernard Perlin, "Background of the Rheem-Calcor Construction System," *Rheem Home Program: Business and Technical Data for the Federal Housing Administration*, December 1961; Rheem Manufacturing Company, "Metal Home Program," *Press Release*, February 24, 1962, Donald Wexler Collection, ENV Archives-Special Collections, Cal Poly Pomona.

32 See, for example, Simon Kuznets and Dorothy S. Thomas, "Internal Migration and Economic Growth," in *Selected Studies of Migration Since World War II* (New York: Milbank Memorial Fund, 1958), 198–200.

33 Avigail Sachs, "The Pedagogy of Prefabrication: Building Research at MIT in the Postwar," in *A Second Modernism: MIT, Architecture, and the 'Techno-Social' Moment*, ed. Arindam Dutta (Cambridge, MA: SA+Press, Department of Architecture, MIT, 2013); Douglas Knerr, *Suburban Steel: The Magnificent Failure of the Lustron Corporation, 1945–1951* (Columbus: Ohio State University Press, 2004).

34 Alice T. Friedman, *American Glamour and the Evolution of Modern Architecture* (New Haven: Yale University Press, 2010).

35 Knerr, *Suburban Steel*, 184.

36 Stein, *Running Steel, Running America*.

37 Donald Wexler, "Innovations in Steel," presentation at the "Study in Steel, 1962—Design Program" conference, May 7, 1962, in San Francisco, sponsored by US Steel. Donald Wexler Collection, ENV Archives-Special Collections, Cal Poly Pomona.

38 Knerr, *Suburban Steel*, 199, fn. 4.

39 Prefabricated homes constituted the last "bulwark against socialized housing." Burnham Kelly, *The Prefabrication of Houses: A Study by the Albert Farwell Bemis Foundation of the Prefabrication Industry in the United States* (New York: The Technology Press of MIT and John Wiley and Sons, Inc., 1951), 96.

40 Fixico, *Termination and Relocation*, 147. Many tribes denounced the 1956 Act as a strategy to capture their lands. On technological adjustment, see William Metzler, "Relocation of the Displaced Worker," *Human Organization* 22 (Summer 1963): 142–145.

41 Eric Mumford, "Defense Migration and the Transformations of American Urbanism, 1940–1942," *Journal of Architectural Education* 61, no. 3 (February 2008): 25–34, 27.

42 Eric Mumford, *Defining Urban Design: CIAM Architects and the Formation of a Discipline, 1937–69* (New Haven: Yale University Press, 2009), 34–35.

43 Eric Mumford, "From Master-Planning to Self-Build: The MIT-Harvard Joint Center for Urban Studies, 1959–71," in *A Second Modernism: MIT, Architecture, and the 'Techno-Social' Moment*, ed. Arindam Dutta (Cambridge, MA: SA+Press, Department of Architecture, MIT, 2013), 292–296.

44 *First Disclosure of Iron Ore in Venezuela: US Steel's Policies on Costs, Prices, Plants, Productivity*. Testimony by Officials of United States Steel Before the Joint Committee on the Economic Report (Washington, DC, January 24, 1950), 34.

45 Hogan, *Economic History of the Iron and Steel*, 2089.

46 John Stuart MacDonald, *Planning Implementation and Social Policy: An Evaluation of Ciudad Guayana, 1965 and 1975* (Oxford and New York: Pergamon Press, 1979), 9.

47 Leigh White, "Ten Billion-Dollar Mountain," *Saturday Evening Post*, September 30, 1950, 17.

48 Thomas E. Mullaney, "Cerro Bolivar Ore Is Due in January: Venezuelan Mountain Is Rich Source of Iron Ore," *The New York Times*, October 25, 1953.

49 Warren, *Big Steel*, 210; Hogan, *Economic History of the Iron and Steel*, 1485; 1491; 1659.

50 Megan Morrissey, *The Architecture of Inequality: Foreign Influence and Urban Planning in Ciudad Guayana, Venezuela* (MA thesis, Georgetown University, 2008), 22.

51 Stein, *Running Steel, Running America*, 214.

52 Hogan, *Economic History of the Iron and Steel*, 1657–1658.
53 Mullaney, "Cerro Bolivar Ore Is Due in January."
54 Viviana d'Auria, "Caracas's Cultural (Be)Longings," in *Latin American Modern Architectures: Ambiguous Territories*, eds. Patricio del Real and Helen Gyger (New York: Routledge, 2013), 132, fn. 17. See also: Carlos Brillembourg, "Sowing the Oil: Brutalist Urbanism—Ciudad Guayana, Venezuela, 1951–2012," X Seminário Docomomo Brasil, *Arquitetura Moderna e Internacional: Conexões Brutalistas, 1955–75*. Curitiba, October 15–18, 2013, 4–5.
55 Mumford, "From Master-Planning to Self-Build," 298–300, fn. 32.
56 "Can Patios Make Cities?" *Architectural Forum* 99 (August 1953): 124–130; *José Luis Sert: Architecture, City Planning, Urban Design*, ed. Knud Bastlund (New York: Praeger, 1967), 78–83.
57 *Orinoco Mining Company: A Résumé* (US Steel, 1956).
58 *José Luis Sert*, ed. Bastlund, 135.
59 "Can Patios Make Cities?" 128–129.
60 Mumford, *Defining Urban Design*, 95–96; 103–111. See also the CIAM 8 catalogue, *The Heart of the City: Towards the Humanisation of Urban Life*, eds. J. Tyrwhitt, J. L. Sert, and E. N. Rogers (New York: Pellegrini and Cudahy, 1952).
61 *José Luis Sert*, ed. Bastlund, 54 [emphasis added].
62 Sigfried Giedion, "Introduction," in *José Luis Sert*, ed. Bastlund, 7.
63 *José Luis Sert*, ed. Bastlund, 134.
64 Viviana d'Auria, "Caracas's Cultural (Be)Longings," 132, fn. 17.
65 Morrissey, *The Architecture of Inequality*, 28.
66 Ibid., 32; MacDonald, *Planning Implementation and Social Policy*.
67 MacDonald, *Planning Implementation and Social Policy*, 23–24.
68 Morrissey, *The Architecture of Inequality*, 39.
69 Fernando Coronil, *The Magical State: Nature, Money, and Modernity in Venezuela* (Chicago: University of Chicago Press, 1997).
70 Morrissey, *The Architecture of Inequality*, 51.
71 Ibid., 55–59.
72 See, for example, Friedmann, *Regional Development Policy*; MacDonald, *Planning Implementation and Social Policy*; Lloyd Rodwin, ed., *Planning Urban Growth and Regional Development: The Experience of the Guayana Program of Venezuela* (Cambridge, MA: MIT Press, 1969); Lisa Peattie, *The View from the Barrio* (Ann Arbor, MI: University of Michigan Press, 1968); and *Planning: Rethinking Ciudad Guayana* (Ann Arbor, MI: University of Michigan Press, 1987); Donald Appleyard, *Planning a Pluralist City: Conflicting Realities in Ciudad Guayana* (Cambridge, MA: MIT Press, 1976).
73 The exception was anthropologist Lisa Peattie, who lived in San Félix and became a fierce critic of the planning process produced by the Joint Center.
74 MacDonald, *Planning Implementation and Social Policy*, 17; Morrissey, *The Architecture of Inequality*, 64.
75 The Joint Center's project for Ciudad Guayana seems to have completely excluded Ciudad Piar, the miners' town, as part of its "growth pole" modernization.
76 François Perroux, "Note on the Concept of 'Growth Poles,'" in *Regional Economics: Theory and Practice*, eds. David L. McKee, Robert D. Dean, and William H. Leahy (New York: Free Press, 1970); François Perroux, "Economic Space: Theory and Applications," *Quarterly Journal of Economics* 64, no. 1 (1950): 89–104.
77 Felipe Correa, *Beyond the City: Resource Extraction Urbanism in South America* (Austin: University of Texas Press, 2016), 96.
78 Friedmann, *Regional Development Policy*, 62. Friedmann based this assessment on Kuznets and Thomas, "Internal Migration and Economic Growth," 198–200; Amy Bellone Hite, "Natural Resource Growth Poles and Frontier Urbanization in Latin America," *Studies in Comparative International Development* 39, no. 3 (Fall 2004), 50–75.
79 Friedmann, *Regional Development Policy*, 12.
80 Ibid., 13.
81 Correa, *Beyond the City*, 98.
82 Morrissey, *The Architecture of Inequality*, 68. The Joint Center did perform "bottom-up" planning surveys, but these did not seem to disrupt the material flows of iron ore and power being deployed through the "mobility infrastructure." Ijlal Muzaffar, "Fuzzy Images: The Problem of Third World Development and the New Ethics of Open-Ended Planning at the MIT-Harvard Joint Center for Urban Studies," in *A Second Modernism: MIT, Architecture, and the 'Techno-Social' Moment*, ed. Arindam Dutta (Cambridge, MA: SA+Press, Department of Architecture, MIT, 2013).
83 Correa, *Beyond the City*, 108.
84 Ibid.
85 Barry Bergdoll, "Learning From Latin America: Public Space, Housing, and Landscape," in *Latin America in Construction: Architecture 1955–1980*, ed. Barry Bergdoll (New York: Museum of Modern Art, 2015), 29–30. See also in the same publication: Jorge Francisco Liernur, "Architectures for Progress: Latin America, 1955–1980," 73.
86 MacDonald, *Planning Implementation and Social Policy*, 11–12.
87 Ibid., 12.

88 Setha M. Low, "Indigenous Architecture and the Spanish American Plaza in Mesoamerica and the Caribbean," in *Gridded Worlds: An Urban Anthology*, ed. Reuben Rose-Redwood and Liora Bigon (Springer International Publishing, 2018); Bernhard Siegert, "(Not) In Place: The Grid, or, Cultural Techniques of Ruling Spaces," in *Cultural Techniques: Grids, Filters, Doors, and Other Articulations of the Real* (New York: Fordham University Press, 2015).

89 Sigfried Giedion, "The New Regional Approach," *Architectural Record*, January 1954, 137.

90 Karl H. Schwerin, *Oil and Steel: Processes of Karinya Culture in Response to Industrial Development* (Los Angeles: Latin American Center, University of California, 1966), 145, 139–148, 197.

91 Manuel Joel Díaz Capdevilla, "Environmental Penal Control in Venezuela: Amazonia and the Orinoco Mining Arc," in *The 21st Century Fight for the Amazon: Environmental Enforcement in the World's Biggest Rainforest*, ed. Mark Ungar (New York: Palgrave Macmillan, 2017).

92 Siegert, "(Not) In Place," 107.

93 For another example, see Konrad Wachsmann, *The Turning Point of Building: Structure and Design* (New York: Reinhold Pub. Corp., 1961).

94 Paul Burkett, "Total Factor Productivity: An Ecological-Economic Critique," *Organization & Environment* 19, no. 2 (June 2006): 171–190.

12

Reinventing earth architecture in the age of development

Farhan Karim

INTRODUCTION

During the 1950s and 1960s, earth architecture became an important component of global development discourse. Architects and researchers in the field of building technology invested in discovering new construction techniques and developing the structural behavior of earth and its environmental performance. The cumulative research efforts of various intergovernmental and national entities transformed earth from a vernacular cultural category to a subject of techno-scientific investigation—a distinct epistemological category of the human condition. Even as extensive scientific studies of earth aimed at bridging development and technology through this material, for some it also became a harbinger of an ecologically and socially conscious building industry. For many developmentalist architects, earth architecture was the last resort to the housing problems of the developing countries. For advocates of earth architecture, the significance of earth was three-pronged. First, it was considered a freely available material. Experts in earth architecture argued that developing societies could easily procure *earth* without incurring any significant cost. Second, the advocates believed that earth architecture was preindustrial and thus free from the conditions of industrialization and large capital accumulation that an industrialized society would require. Third, the experts contended that, through collective involvement in hands-on construction of earth architecture, the poor would experience the transformation of a perceived nothingness into *homes*. This experience, the advocates of earth architecture argued, would give the poor hope for transfiguring their impoverished present into a prosperous future. To borrow the words of the eighteenth-century French architect and first modern advocate of earth architecture, Francois Cointeraux, earth contains the "magic" that turns nothingness into habitation.[1] Earth architecture thus provided evidence that even a blatant emptiness could be invested with promise: the premise of development with zero cost.

This chapter shows that the advocates of earth architecture capitalized on the emerging desire for postcolonial technological change and presented earth as a quintessential vernacular agency for social transformation. The idea of building from nothingness gained impetus, especially in the postcolonial moment, when the spirit of reconstruction and sentiments of nation-building were at their height. The experts concerned, however, did not consider earth architecture as the permanent solution to low-cost housing. Earth architecture was rather considered as a temporary response and a makeshift strategy against a specific moment of crisis, that of economic scarcity, a specter that it sought to manipulate and capitalize on. In a crisis, earth architecture would thus offer a way to escape the laws of material exchange (import-export) within a defunct and unpredictable market. Such "magic," of course, would not work as well in regular times. At the same time, in the imaginary of the development consultant, crisis is never far away. There is no space or time outside crisis—crisis is ongoing. If things appear normal, this is because the crisis has been only temporarily suppressed or is not immediately experienceable. The subject of development, as development thinkers perceive it, is perennially trapped in a continuum of crisis whose degree may vary but is nonetheless an a priori constant. Perhaps one reason for this contrapuntal logic of crisis, presumed precariousness, as we will see in this chapter, was that earth architecture tended not to be economically profitable, or even convenient, in times of so-called "normalcy." Neither builders, realtors, nor communities in times of noncrisis were particularly attracted to the "magic" of earth architecture: the assertion of "hope" thus directly covered over the agency of its supposed beneficiaries.

RAMMED EARTH AS AN EPISTEMOLOGICAL CATEGORY

During the Korean War (June 1950–July 1953), nearly a half million people either lost their homes or became refugees of war, making this one of the first major humanitarian crises after the establishment of the United Nations (UN). Toward the end of the war, the South Korean government roughly estimated that the country would need 1 million housing units, a challenge far beyond the capacity of the government to manage.[2] To address this crisis, a civil agency within the UN entitled the United Nations Korea Reconstruction Agency (UNKRA, 1951–60) was formed in the UN General Assembly in December of 1950.[3] Within a decade, UNKRA had spent $122 million in construction projects on 4,944 sites. Among these new construction projects, 5,500 housing units were built of rammed earth.[4] UNKRA also worked with the Korean Civil Assistance Command (KCAC) and produced an additional 32,000 houses, of which a significant portion were made of rammed earth (see Figure 12.1).[5]

UNKRA's turn to rammed-earth architecture was a response to the wartime condition of the building industry. UNKRA officials' first preference was to import prefabricated housing elements either from both the Hodgson Company and the Airform Corporation of the United States or from West Germany, Sweden, and Italy. The agency ultimately abandoned this plan owing to its financial and logistical unfeasibility.[6] After a year of indecision about the appropriate strategy, material, and technology appropriate for the challenge in hand, Barton P. Jenks, director of UNKRA's Program Analysis Division, decided to recommend the use of rammed earth and earth block structures in combination with lightweight, locally made roofing material.[7] Given the cheapness of this option, the US Housing and Home Finance Agency also backed this choice.[8] In 1953, after almost a year of surveying different possibilities, UNKRA settled on procuring the popular South African Landcrete machine as best suited for the situation.[9] A group of experts from South Africa arrived in South Korea along with the first batch of 100 machines, staying for about three months to teach the North Korean refugees how to operate them.[10] The first batch was South Korea's last requisition from Landcrete. Korean government engineers developed a local prototype based on the South African technology, whose marketing UNKRA approved for the South Korean market.[11] By 1954, therefore, rammed-earth architecture had been accepted as a quick but temporary solution to the housing problem of war-torn Korea, so much so that, besides the

FIGURE 12.1 Workers laying the first row of rammed-earth blocks at UNKRA housing in South Korea.
Source: United Nations Photo Archives, S-0526–0350–7.

prototypes developed by the government engineers, local private manufacturers also began to produce competing versions of the Landcrete machines (see Figure 12.2).[12]

The first four rammed-earth block houses were constructed in 1953 as a demonstration project, followed by 5,500 housing units using rammed-earth blocks. The demonstration housing units cost US$1,945 and were built in about two weeks.[13] The units were sold either for Korean hwan at 256,000 per unit ($1,420 per unit in 1953 US dollars) or with a down payment of 20 percent of the total cost and an eight-year credit plan.[14] By June 30, 1957, the construction of 8,316 permanent-type housing units in Seoul, Pusan, and thirty other cities were built. Almost $4.6 million in building materials and equipment had been provided by UNKRA for the housing program to construct permanent housing for approximately 50,000 individuals.[15] The South Korean wartime government took UNKRA's intervention as an opportunity to open a broader discussion on a national postwar housing program. With this view, the Ministry of Social Affairs arranged a National Housing Authority to work with UNKRA. In this broader discussion of a national housing program, rammed-earth architecture was never considered as a permanent solution; it remained a technological necessity tied mainly with the temporary citizenship status of the refugees from North Korea.

FIGURE 12.2 Korean prototype machine to produce rammed earth block at the UNKRA refugee housing.

Source: United Nations Archives, photograph by author.

Parallel to UNKRA's massive rammed-earth block housing projects in South Korea, a different group of development experts were also experimenting with how to make a cheap, lightweight, and portable hand press for creating rammed-earth blocks. In 1956, Raul Ramirez, the chief of engineering studies for the Center Interamericano de Vivienda y Planeamiento (CINVA) research program on stabilized earth, developed a low-cost version of the then available but expensive manual, rammed-earth block press. CINVA was one of the US government's Cold War organizations that oversaw US-aided development projects in the Caribbean islands and thus, so went the belief, deterred communism. Ramirez's low-cost machine came to be popularly known among the global development experts as the CINVA-RAM. The machine was less sophisticated than the South African Landcrete or its South Korean variations, but it was also far less expensive and relatively easy to operate compared to the other models available from private manufacturers. In the next two years, the CINVA-RAM was promoted in the reports of various government-housing agencies across the developing world. In CINVA's view, the low cost and simple operational method of this machine would make it popular among the governments of the poor, developing countries.

UNKRA's rammed-earth refugee housing project was distinctive not for its material and technological innovation but because its experts believed that the self-operated CINVA-RAM would nurture positivity and cultivate communal feeling in refugee communities and developing societies in general. The machine was evidence that even a developing country in its most vulnerable state would be able to create its own unique path to progress. The experts of rammed earth were acutely aware that earth housing was only a partial and temporary answer to the perceived overall crisis of underdevelopment. Yet for them, the value of rammed earth lay not just as a form of technological solution but also as a social catalyst, in its touted power to foster sentiments of camaraderie and to galvanize attitudes toward labor in an otherwise underemployed population.

This bid to build self-reliance was palpable in one of the South Korean refugee housing projects where, instead of providing ready-made rammed-earth housing, a group of refugees were given land and a CINVA-RAM to build their own houses. The UN, with the help of the South Korean government, had acquired land previously owned by the Japanese, called vested properties, which were distributed among groups of refugees, each headed by a leader.[16] Each group with a leader and land was called a "project." The UNKRA officials expected that over time each project would grow into a "community,"[17] a somewhat mystical social unit widely used by development experts everywhere.[18] (For a discussion on community, see Martin Hershenzon, Chapter 16, this volume.) Ownership of land would have prompted the refugees, UNKRA officials assumed, to recreate new communities on the basis of old communal ties, common political beliefs, or religion. Each "project" was grouped into a smaller Community Development Group (CDG) and was given a CINVA-RAM as an "external stimulation" to build houses and "community." The experts treated earth architecture as a way to involve the users in a hands-on, sensory and immersive experience of participation that would be essential to building a spirit of community.

Like the CINVA experts, the UNKRA experts thus saw the machine as not just an assemblage of techniques but an aspirational symbol that could forge community out of nowhere and even confer a new identity of citizenship on uprooted refugees. A memorandum prepared by UNKRA experts emoted a "happy" picture of the reconstruction work, and stabilized rammed-earth structures were the centerpiece of that happiness.[19] Quoting from the memo,

> The supervisors taught the project leader and the people to use the CINVA-RAM Block Press. They let the people 'play' with the press making mud bricks. Playing with [the] CINVA-RAM, the people became enthusiastic and eager to make blocks for their own houses.[20]

By turning work into play, and by this reasoning, the CINVA-RAM into a toy, rammed earth became a technique to sustain unwaged labor and to preempt the demands of the refugees.

TECHNOLOGY TRANSFERS

In the emerging subfield of development economies in this era, the problem of underdevelopment was studied as a combination of economic and technical concern. W. Arthur Lewis's seminal 1954 paper *Economic Development with Unlimited Supplies of Labor* argued for an alternative technology and updated the existing development toolkit of the Harrod-Domar model, which focused mainly on the steady-state properties of the developed economy and the saving-pushed growth competing with population growth.[21] Amartya Sen's 1960 publication *Choice of Techniques: An Aspect of the Theory of Planned Economic Development* expanded a similar thesis. In broad terms, Lewis's and Sen's arguments focused on maximizing investible capitals by adopting techniques that relied on partially unemployed, surplus labor. Their arguments had great influence on how development architects reconceived the relationship between the production of architecture and the technique of its production.

The choice of labor-intensive and crude techniques offered a platform to redefine the relationship between the large, surplus labor force in developing countries and theories of development. The first Agent-General of UNKRA was J. Donald Kingsley, a former executive secretary of President Truman's Scientific Research Council and former chief of the International Refugee Organization (IRO). As an administrator of the New Deal program, Kingsley could be considered the heir of the American political culture of the New Deal, rooted in harnessing community spirit by repurposing scant economic resources. Kingsley had also served as director of the UN International Refugee Organization, established following World War II, a resume that bolstered an impression of him as the seasoned administrator deft in striking a balance between wartime humanitarian crisis and reconstruction. The primacy of American experts in the upper echelons of UNKRA was not coincidental. Historian Or Rosenboim has discussed how the United States mobilized the UN's global platform to inject its techno-social Cold War ideology into the Third World.[22] Among the thirty-six countries contributing to UNKRA, the United States was not only the largest financial contributor but also provided the majority of the staff and leaders.[23] Therefore, although UNKRA is theoretically an intergovernmental organization and was supposed to act autonomously, its stakes were condemned to respond to Cold War contests of influence.

UN experts were drawn to earth architecture because they saw an enormous potential in the "simple" technology's power to fight communism by providing housing to the Third World poor at the lowest possible cost and effort. What could be more elementary, the rationale went, than providing housing made from earth to the homeless of the Third World? Aside from these ideological hues, experts at CINVA seriously considered the stabilized rammed-earth technique as the only realistic way to instantly provide low-cost housing in the Caribbean—the most vulnerable region to communist intervention in American eyes.[24]

In a feature, *Time* magazine described the machine as *the* solution to the Latin American housing problem.[25] A machine with a promise to turn earth into economic prosperity: such would be the panacea for Latin American housing and low-cost housing challenges everywhere. Eric Carlson, director of CINVA, and Ernest Weissmann, Chief of the Housing and Town and Country Planning Section of the UN, argued in terms of this technology's potential to battle economic downturn and combat political unrest, seen as a natural breeding ground for communism. Earth was, after all, an unused and abandoned resource in any poverty-stricken tropical country.[26] Weissmann's and Carlson's rationale thus went beyond the mere technicalities of its usage to the larger mechanics of global deployment. Their objectives could be summarized in three main themes: first, to create a "low-cost" version of the technique that would be lucrative to Third World societies; second, to explore the political implication of this technique in varied Third World contexts; and finally, to develop a transnational bureaucratic network to disseminate information about the technique.

The operational techniques of CINVA-RAM was simple, but it was its effect on human emotion and behavior patterns that would present the greater challenge and complexity, or so believed its creator, Raul Ramirez. A 1959 manual for the CINVA-RAM for use in Jamaica explained that in order to fully understand the social and economic effect of this machine, one would need to understand the role of mass psychology (see Figure 12.3). Meant for the use of housing officers, village workers, and community development and agricultural advisers of the Jamaica Social Welfare Commission and the Jamaica Agricultural Society, the manual was written in nontechnical language. Despite the use of the low-cost, simple machine and the abundant supply of earth, the manual argued, a project

REINVENTING EARTH ARCHITECTURE

Close up shot prototype "CINVA-RAM" soil-cement block making machine.   Photos Bright - CINVA

4. The lever is depressed till horizontal to apply pressure to the soil and form the block.

5. The top is opened, and the lever returned to the opposite side to eject the block.

6. The block is removed. After 20 days curing, protected from sun and rain it will be ready for use.

FIGURE 12.3 Step-by-step instruction on how to operate a CINVA-RAM.

Source: CINVA, Manual for Supervising Self-Help Home Construction with Stabilized Earth Blocks made with the CINVA-RAM Portable Block Press, January 1959, United Nations Archives; photograph by author.

could fail because of mental fatigue among its users and beneficiaries, followed by eventual loss of interest in the development process itself. To avoid such an outcome, the manual suggested applying two strategies so that the local community would not lose heart with this endeavor of building with earth. The first strategy was disciplinary: teaching people how to follow instructions word for word. Any local improvisation, the manual warned, might have a negative impact on collective psychology. This was based on the presumption that, since Indigenous people did not have any scientific knowledge of soil and its mechanical and chemical properties, revising technical procedures would very likely lead to accidents or failure. Machine-users were thus better off following instructions without question. The second strategy involved cultural mobilization. A development officer would need to continuously encourage local people, cultivating a spirit of sustained optimism and hope, about the benefits of the machine, new housing, and long-term development outcomes. Only by providing this psychological support could one make the development endeavor a success.[27]

Earth architecture thus would help in constructing a rosy picture of a better and yet undetermined future—a "hope" that would alleviate other sentiments regarding the political reality of poor, and feeding on their meager palette of options.

The UN's efforts to market the CINVA-RAM on a global scale earned the machine and rammed-earth architecture significant popularity.[28] In a letter, Carlson spoke enthusiastically of the press and a wave of queries emerging from different parts of the globe.[29] As a consequence, the UN partially funded the research program at CINVA and also backed the agency's supply of sample machines to be provided to housing centers sponsored by the United Nations Technical Assistance Administration (UNTAA) across the world.[30] One year after the "invention" of the CINVA-RAM, more than twenty-five countries had purchased the machine and used it in their rural construction projects.

NETWORK OF EXPERTS: CONFLICTS AND COLLABORATIONS

The UN's promotional materials and report created an optimistic view of rammed earth and its possible future in the Third World. However, stabilized earth construction was not without challenges, as local experts found. C. B. Patel, Chief of Housing and Building Materials and Techniques Section of the UN's Economic Commission for Asia and the Far East (ECAFE), was one of the main critics of CINVA technology.[31] In Patel's view, earth architecture would prove to be an economic, social, and scientific failure. In a memo sent to the UN on behalf of the UN Regional Housing Centres for both India and Indonesia, he expressed concern that, despite the UN's good intention in providing low-cost houses of stabilized rammed earth, the scheme might not work in "Asian countries."[32] Patel argued that in designing the prototypes of stabilized earth structure the foreign experts did not consider the character of local soil or of social aspirations. This proved prescient. UN experts were theoretically well aware of regional differences in soil composition and the challenges they posed for this technology but had carefully elided such concerns in their enthusiasm for a global panacea. For instance, A. E. S. Alcock, UN Housing and Physical Planning Expert, warned Weissmann about the danger of using cement paint in a West African climatic context. He argued that the success of the cement paint in Israel was due to the dry and hot climate of the region, while in a West African context, it would be a total failure, which indeed it was.[33]

Patel's other reservation pertained to the method of using cement to stabilize earth structures. UN scientists took soil as a generic building material and depended solely on cement as the stabilizing agent. As Patel pointed out, echoing concerns emanating from experts in various UN Regional Centres, "in most Asian countries [cement] is still a foreign and imported product, which limits its use."[34] Officials in Regional Centres called for more thorough research on specific regional contexts and local soil contents, such as soil with rich lime content or volcanic soil with high pozzolanic content. Patel's concern shows that, although the UN and CINVA promoted rammed earth as an ingenious technological solution based on a seemingly basic and natural element that could be acquired almost without any cost, there were disagreements, based on sound empirical findings, on this very "basic" attribute of soil. In other words, the UN's touted local technology was not "local" enough. In support of his argument, Patel also forwarded several reports to the UN produced by a regional Public Works Department (PWD) in India. These reports documented various experiments conducted by PWD engineers regarding construction of low-cost housing with unbaked brick or adobe structure that was stabilized by local biological ingredients such as tamarind seed or bitumen emulation.[35]

The third criticism from Patel was directed at the UN's naivety about the social aspirations of local communities and the inner dynamics of local construction industries. In a letter to Vittal Gornov, Director of Housing, Building and Planning Branch, Bureau of Social Affairs, Patel pointed out that the UN experts did not consider the economic implications of the new stabilized earth technique. Quoting Patel, "I find from the outline that the technical details of soil stabilization are dealt with in a comprehensive manner, but the economic aspect of the technique in relation to the traditional materials in the building industry are not discussed at all."[36] Patel contended that the cost of brick was fairly low in India in comparison to cement-stabilized earth. In addition, owing to the heavy monsoons, in many parts of India the maintenance of rammed earth, even when it was stabilized, was a serious inconvenience. In general, Indians, the poor included, preferred brick to adobe structures, Patel suggested, and whenever possible would revert to brick rather than adobe. This preference also expressed their sense of social aspiration, as mud houses were a symbol of poverty while brick represented affluence. So much for the optimism that UN officials wanted to foster in its beneficiaries. Patel continued: Indian government research organizations had already experimented with cement-soil structures, but only in unique situations where India had experienced a great shortage of coal dust for burning bricks. The idea of stabilized earth had never worked in India, and he concluded that the UN's earth housing project in India was destined to fail. Instead, he suggested alternatives that could follow the examples offered by Indian government research organizations such as the Regional Housing Centre in Delhi that had been trying to develop efficient, non-stabilized mud wall techniques, which the Centre believed was economically and socially appropriate for rural housing.

Here, government research institutes such as the Central Building Research Institute (CBRI) in Roorkee played the role of regional powerhouse; we cannot rule out a certain contest over technical dominion in this respect. For its part, the CBRI had developed their own version of a compressed earth block machine based on the Landcrete machine but at an even lower price than that of the CINVA-RAM. A sample was sent to the Building Material Research Institute in Burma.[37] We might say that in this refusal to brook the UN's universal recommendations, Patel instead wanted to see himself and India in a position to advise the UN. He urged UN officials to consult the Indian government's report on non-stabilized earth structures entitled *Report on the Comparative Tests on Waterproof Renderings for Mud Walls* (1958). Patel's arguments went toward a further contextualization: however local and indigenous the rammed-earth blocks might look, they would still have to respond to the complex social and economic condition in any given country.[38]

In a sense, Patel might be seen as upturning the UN's understanding of "traditional" and "modern" building techniques. For Patel, earth architecture was a modern, imported technique that would disrupt existing social and economic fabrics, while brick represented a traditional technique that works in harmony in a given society. UN officials felt differently about the question of modernization. For their part, they firmly believed that they were reviving and revamping an "ancient" technique of building technology that had been corroded with the advancement of modernity. For instance, Weissmann, in the *Manual for Supervising Self-Help Home Construction with Stabilized Earth Blocks*, suggested that the engineers of CINVA include a comparative analysis between CINVA earth blocks and traditional Jamaican construction methods in terms of material use and its economic effects.[39] Through these analyses comparing traditional ways of making mud houses and the new technique, the UN wanted to convince developing societies that stabilized earth was not undoing local economic and social fabrics but enhancing it, expanding and upgrading existing social practices of technology.

Responding to Patel's criticism of the CINVA-RAM, CINVA appointed E.W. Eller, Director of Ellson Equipment of the US, to do an external review of the CINVA-RAM. Before the CINVA-RAM, a lightweight version of the original Ellson machine, nicknamed the Brickmaster, had been the CINVA engineers' most favorite.[40] However, this appointment proved a conflict of interest. Eller's review was negative, but the negative review may have partly arisen from the fear that full operation of the new machine might cause Ellson Equipment to lose its market to CINVA. It is no wonder, then, why Ellson would have been unhappy with this new product; in the process, Ellson sent a memo to CINVA citing Eller's report, in addition to every other housing agency and every potential buyer around the globe.[41] The machine was "terribly crude," wrote Eller in his report. The CINVA-RAM uses "a great deal of physical effort and a great deal of movement," and was consequently not at all a "good machine."[42] In his criticisms, Eller wrote, "the most important practical criticism that I have is . . . 'Points for Circular Criticism' . . . that maximum load to be applied on an operating handle at or below the operator's knees. Labor fatigue must be serious." The next paragraph recounts the unfortunate implications that would have in terms of labor fatigue: "there is every likelihood that the tired worker will not produce blocks of the density necessary for soil stabilization."[43] Finally, the report accused CINVA of being intentionally exploitive: "[the machine] . . . would constitute positive exploitation of the buyer's ignorance."[44]

CINVA's vision, predictably, differed. Some crudity and some imperfection was not only acceptable but desirable since, per the economic surplus theory mentioned earlier, the more one could engage the surplus or idle labor force in mechanical production, no matter the lower levels of efficiency, the more the developing countries would head toward development. Therefore, in a way, the "crudity" was a desired precondition for the developing countries' own good and their future prosperity. A 1957 CINVA publication suggested to the potential users of the machine, "naturally, to take full advantage of the cost reduction, you must work the machine yourself or with your family. It is a 'do it yourself' operation, and if you pay operators the blocks may well be costlier than brick or concrete blocks."[45] More labor, preferably a collective or group labor from one family and less currency expenditure, was thus offered as CINVA's mantra. By virtue of their menial labor, the thought went, the Third World poor would not only be able to construct their homes but would also, in the process of the construction, solidify their family and community ties.

For Eller, CINVA argued, a machine was no more than a mechanical artefact. CINVA argued the crudity of the machine could be compromised for the sake of keeping the price low. "This machine, like every human effort, is not perfect," contended Ramirez. He continued, "and in consequence, we find ourselves dedicated to the task of reducing even further its weight, its cost, and in the improvement of its design."[46] In the following memo, CINVA further explained the complex nature of their organization and the machine, correlating a number of socio-political and technical issues.

But underneath the highly technical details of the notes and memos made by the CINVA engineers, what was posed most of value was not the technique per se but a new kind of social organization, in terms of a self-help family or community. CINVA and Ellson's conflict exposed that the main point of the debate was not the efficiency and accuracy of the machines' construction and mechanisms but rather the socio-political understanding of technique in a specific historic moment. Mechanical effectiveness does not carry any meaning unless it fails to relate questions of labor and technology in relation to broader socioeconomic predicaments.

A RESPONSE TO CRISIS

The postwar reincarnation of rammed-earth architecture has evolved in different directions through different governmental and intergovernmental organizations. Nonetheless, two beliefs bind all these disparate and contested views about earth architecture in its putative essence. First, earth is a primitive substance and therefore represents authenticity. Second, building with earth would ensure political emancipation of economically marginal populations. Is this "modern" meaning of earth a unique postwar and postcolonial formation? Or can this meaning be understood as a cultural construct produced in the course of changing notions within Western political institutions? The first major attempt in modern times to institutionalize and standardize earth architecture and elevate earth from a meaningless material to an ethical substance occurred during the French Revolution. François Cointeraux (1740–1830), an architect from Lyon, France, whose career spans revolutionary and post-revolutionary France, dedicated his entire career to establishing rammed-earth, or pisé, architecture as the symbol of the Revolution and as an instrument of social justice, and political freedom.[47] In 1789, just a few months before the Revolution broke out, Cointeraux established the École d'Architecture Rurale in Paris, a school for rammed-earth architecture. Three years earlier, he had established another school in Grenoble that lasted for only one year. The Comité de Salut Public, a provisional government during the Reign of Terror of the French Revolution, appreciated Cointeraux's focus on rural architecture and pisé and picked up earth as a symbol of poverty-stricken rural France as opposed to the tyranny of its urban elites. Cointeraux's school and writings can be considered as a daring riposte to the Neoclassicism that dominated architectural discourse in France at this time. An argument similar to the mid-twentieth-century one on the oscillation between modernity and tradition appears to have developed at this time. Cointeraux animatedly pointed to the technique's classical roots in Europe, highlighting in his writings that pisé was introduced to France by the Romans. At the same time, his argument for pisé in revolutionary France lay in its symbolic celebration of the vernacular aesthetic and political emancipation of the rural poor.

Thus, while pisé was not entirely unknown to prerevolutionary France, Cointeraux's advocacy of this material gave it new meaning.[48] In the face of dire shortage of lumber, Cointeraux argued that pisé was a more appropriate alternative material for building given that the shortage of wood not only threatened the building industry but also affected the bakery industry, causing a perpetual short supply of bread, a key concern of the state and one of the principal triggers of the Revolution. In other words, the use of pisé would help to retain and balance the economic and social fabric of France in its wider understanding, as well as help landless classes resist exploitation. Cointeraux thus expanded the meaning of pisé and associated it with the overall social revolution of rural peasant life.[49] The emphasis on earth architecture at the UN, UNKRA, and CINVA might thus be seen as a continuation of the Enlightenment ideas that emerged in the course of the French Revolution.

Cointeraux's idea of fostering political justice was based on four assumptions.[50] The first was that the construction of rammed-earth architecture would give destitute peasants a sense of dignity. The second assumption was that pisé architecture ought to be conceived as part of the larger economical system of agricultural production and its resultant social relationships. By combining architecture and agriculture, he coined the term *agritecture*, and in his school, he not only taught the students hands-on pisé building construction but also trained them to become well-rounded people in agricultural enterprise. Pisé, in this view, was an opportunity to redefine the human relationship with land and earth in economic terms. *Agritecture* would teach people how to transform earth into both food and shelter.[51] The third assumption was the idea of "interdiscipline," combining theory with practice, which was at odds with the epistemological framework of his time. The epistemological questions of Enlightenment France tended toward empirical challenges, involving problems of specialization, differentiation, classification, categorization, and organization of knowledge as exemplified in Diderot's Encyclopedia. Cointeraux instead argued for breaking down disciplinary boundaries and conflating different modes of knowledge and their applications. The last assumption was the construction of an autonomous world for the peasantry. Using pisé was a way to reimagine the social and economic relationships of the peasants as citizens of a new republic who would minimize dependency on other economic guilds such as masons and other skilled tradesmen. Predictably, this isolationist position was repudiated not by the land-owning class but by skilled workers in the building industry, as they feared pisé would make their profession obsolete. For instance, the master masons and master carpenters in Amiens filed a complaint against Cointeraux with the police, and no skilled construction workers were legally allowed to work with him.[52]

Cointeraux's technique was almost identical to the method for producing rammed earth blocks which were at the heart of UNKRA and CINVA's. Cointeraux's technique used demountable wooden scaffolding, which he called *nouveau pisé*, subsequent to which he also developed a hand press similar to the CINVA-RAM (see Figure 12.4). In 1807 Cointeraux finished designing a portable hand-press machine more amenable to use by the rural population, which he called *crécize* and received a patent for in the same year. Between 1807 and his death in 1815, Cointeraux widely publicized the *crécize*, publishing a total of sixteen lectures explaining the diverse use of the machine—from producing small details to creating an entire complex.[53] In one of these lectures, he presented a plan for a total agricultural complex consisting of residential units, agricultural fields, barns, and storage.

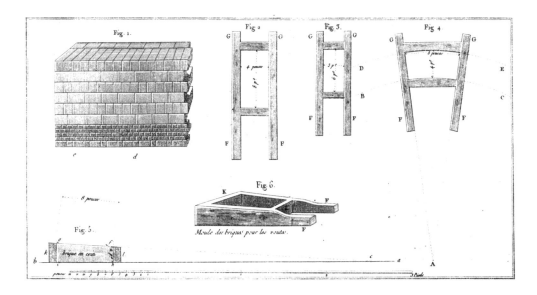

FIGURE 12.4 "Moules de briques" (molds for pisé bricks).

Source: François Cointeraux, *Architecture periodique, ou, Notice des travaux et approvisionemens que chacun peut faire . . . par François Cointeraux, professeur d'architecture rurale* (Paris: Au bureau de l'école d'architecture rurale, 1792), plate 1.

Cointeraux's works were published as four volumes between 1790–91 entitled *École d'Architecture Rurale*. These publications helped the prospects of rammed earth to quickly spread across Europe, in Germany, Holland, Finland, England, and Russia, and then to the United States and Australia.[54] In 1793, the German architect David Gilly established his *Bauschule* in Berlin, where experiments with rammed-earth architecture were carried out. Modeled after Cointeraux's school, the *Bauschule*'s—later renamed *Bauakademie*—championing of rural architecture and pisé acquired considerable influence in ensuing years. Within a decade, in Russia, under the support of Tsar Paul I, the neo-Palladian architect Nicolay L'vov established two schools focused on earth architecture: one in Torzhok and the other one in Tiukhill near Moscow.[55] Farmers from different regions of Russia were summoned for a period of eighteen months to learn about earth architecture, a large state undertaking that came to an end in 1803, two years after the assassination of Paul I. Pisé was never adopted widely; rather, it remained experimental and popular with small groups of idealists who envisioned it as an instrument for social change in rural areas.

In the United States, it would be Thomas Jefferson (1743–1826) who brought Cointeraux's method of pisé architecture to the country. Jefferson had met Cointeraux during his tenure in France as minister to the Court of Louis XVI from 1784 to 1789 and was aware of the latter's work and arguments for pisé as an appropriate and just economic and cultural instrument for the peasantry. At the same time, Jefferson remained unconvinced by these claims; for him, the language of Neoclassicism was closer to the spirit of the American Revolution and the new republic. In contrast to French conceptions of peasantry, Jefferson had a very different vison of "gentlemen farmers" for the new America. Cointeraux asked Jefferson several times to help him and his family to migrate to America. Jefferson, though he admired Cointeraux's work, never positively replied to his plea. Nor did he actively promote pisé building, though he may have inspired others to take on pisé projects. In the United States, other figures took on the promise of rammed earth as the symbol of hope and liberty for the rural poor, particularly in the context of enslaved African Americans. Three people would become its main advocates: General John Hartwell Cocke (1780–1866), St. George Tucker (1752–1827), member of the Virginia Legislature and prominent law professor, and Bushrod Washington (1762–1829), an activist in the American Colonization Society, an organization created to aid freed slaves to migrate to new settlements on the West African coast. This group of men perceived rammed-earth architecture as better suited and culturally appropriate for the betterment of slaves and built a number of pisé buildings in New England.[56] Other than these piecemeal experiments, rammed earth would have a minimal influence in the United States until the mid-twentieth century.

At the end of World War I, rammed-earth architecture again attracted interest, given the great scarcity of building materials in Europe. The English architect and writer Williams-Ellis, in his 1919 book *Cottage Building in Cob, Pisé, Chalk & Clay: A Renaissance*, advocated using rammed earth for postwar housing reconstruction. However, the Building Research Board for the Privy Council for Scientific and Industrial Research rebuffed these claims as naïve and ill-informed. Williams-Ellis did not lose heart. The next year, in 1920, he published a revised and updated version of his book to reflect some of the criticisms posed against the technology. In its second iteration the book attracted some fruitful interests not from the United Kingdom but from the United States, where the *Literary Digest* began to reprint Williams-Ellis's essays in the late 1920's. Public discussion and opinion on earth architecture grew significantly in the United States in the context of the great economic depression, and the US Department of Agriculture (USDA) was drawn to the ideas of rammed earth and its applicability in rural America. One of its key advocates was T. A. H. Miller, an officer of the Division of Agricultural Engineering at the USDA who had read the essays in *Literary Digest* and warmed to the potential of the technology.[57] Miller's interest overlapped with the publication of Karl J. Ellington and Inez Ellington's popular book *Modern Pisé-Building* (1924), which argued that rammed earth could be the appropriate solution for housing for the poor at a time of economic crisis. Miller had a chance to apply his new-found knowledge when he was commissioned to repair the rammed-earth Church of the Holy Cross at the Hillcrest Plantation in North Carolina. Miller later published *Farmers' Bulletin No. 1500: Rammed Earth Walls for Buildings* and became the principal advocate for rammed-earth architecture during the Depression era.

The economic crisis of the Depression era provided a background for renewing the US federal government's interest in pisé, and especially in creating a body of scientific knowledge for this lesser-known construction technique. The federal government was interested in learning whether pisé was a financially and logistically feasible option for the rural poor. A comprehensive database of technical information about pisé in reference to America's geographical and economic context ensued. Under the New Deal, various Agricultural Experiment Stations (AES)—government research centers at the state land-grant universities—created a system of exchanging, producing, and disseminating knowledge about earth architecture. USDA gained the impression that rammed-earth architecture could provide a quick and cheap solution to the housing problems of the migrant, landless farmers of Dust Bowl areas. The South Dakota Station of the AES, under the direction of Ralph L. Patty, subsequently became the lead research center where most of the research publications on rammed-earth architecture were produced.[58]

In the next decade, the US Resettlement Administration, the Works Progress Administration, and the National Youth Administration (NYA) conducted a series of experiments using the technology. Rammed earth continued to be associated with self-help community development projects such as the North Casper Clubhouse in Wyoming (1938–39), built by the North Casper Improvement Association, supported by the NYA's appeal to voluntary labor donations to aid in the project. The experiments of the AES were to provide a reliable, public knowledge database for the research community, builders, and investors. At the same time, the AES had a limited mandate: it was not interested in exploring the possibilities of creating an industry or providing government-built public housing. For its part, the federal government also had no intention of mass-producing pisé public housing. Rather, based on the information generated by the AES, the federal government wanted to limit its remit by creating a handful of model housing projects that could set an example of low-cost housing for the poor. In that context, the two most important rammed-earth housing projects of the New Deal program sponsored by the federal government were the Gardendale Resettlement Project near Birmingham, Alabama (1933–1937) and the Cameron Valley housing development near Alexandria, Virginia, by the Federal Works Agency (see Figure 12.5).[59] Both were designed by the architect and engineer Thomas Hibben. In the Virginia project,

FIGURE 12.5 Rammed earth house in Gardendale, Jefferson County, Alabama. Photograph by Arthur Rothstein. Source, Arthur Rothstein, Photographer. Rammed earth house at Gardendale, Alabama. Alabama Gardendale Jefferson County United States, 1937.

Source: Library of Congress, 2017775756.

Hibben tried to systematize and standardize a method for mass production by introducing new techniques such as reusable and standardized metal scaffolding and compressed air mechanical dampers. Both techniques, however, proved to be inappropriate for rammed-earth structures, and these efforts were discontinued.

Hibben's efforts to mechanize the process, however, was somewhat at odds with the USDA and AES interest. The AES's central assumption about rammed earth was that it ought to be a labor-intensive project and therefore should explore different ways to incorporate the unemployed or surplus of human resources in the construction. The numerous scientific research projects regarding structural stability and material properties of pisé architecture that we see in the AES reports were all conditioned by this socio-political assumption regarding the active participation of underemployed, low-income populations. Using rammed earth, these agencies believed, would capitalize on these populations' availability of their "free" or unemployed time as a voluntary input into building assets. In other words, the premise behind the data-gathering revolved around a certain assertion regarding human psychology: that unemployed people would be willing to sacrifice their labor if mobilized by the promise for a greater good. It was thus in the context of the Great Depression that rammed earth emerged into its developmentalist avatar as an instrument of hope, fostering enthusiasm amongst the underemployed and the marginalized in a time of crisis. Historians have identified this time as a transformative moment within American society, wherein American society in general, at least temporarily, embraced the idea of a strong and centralized government and supported federal intervention to give jobs to the unemployed.[60] The political culture of the Great Depression crafted a narration of salvation that is not eternal but temporal, and rammed earth seemed to embody all of these characteristics.

CONCLUSION

In the 1960s, the discussion on rammed earth took a different course, where the value of earth construction was recoded in terms of its environmentally friendly virtues. As described earlier, the UN's postwar discourse of stabilized earth structure was geared toward a novel social technique that would provide minimal living conditions for the poor while sustaining a collective hope for future prosperity against the threat of communist insurgency. The architectural historian Felicity D. Scott has suggested that the venture of self-help housing and the UN and global aid did not intend to produce an active middle class or working-class population, but it worked to keep the poor docile and agreeable by providing the bare minimum.[61] In the 1970s counterculture movement in the United States and France, rammed-earth architecture often was considered as a symbol of empowerment through self-help. In this context, the original UN-initiated idea of self-help as a tactic to use regional resources to fight poverty and political totalitarianism eventually gained a new meaning regarding individual empowerment and autonomy as opposed to the overarching structures of capitalist exploitation and super-exploitation. For instance, French cultural theorist and philosopher Paul Virilio argued for self-building as an emblem of freedom over one's territory and active participation in the production of space. Earth architecture and adobe constructions thus began to symbolize radicalized notions of land ownership and the right to build.[62]

In the 1960s and 1970s counterculture movement, the semiology of earth architecture evolved significantly, given new environmental conceptions of the planet itself as a compendium of *dirt*. Take, for instance, the cover page of the last issue of the seminal *Whole Earth* catalogue, where we see the familiar shape and image of a deconstructed globe. Portrayed against a striking pink, the image was advanced as an alternative, post-nationalist view of earth. No longer should the Earth be seen as a collection of nation states but as ONE system of *earth* filled with wriggling earthworms and dark compost. In development discourse, dirt and earth architecture thus was reworked as a cultural sign representing the underdeveloped, traditional, and peripheral societies of the Global South, in contrast to societies availing themselves of industrially driven international modernism. Patronized by technocratic development experts on the one hand and appropriated by Euro-American counterculture movements on the other, earth architecture thus acquired a complex image. On the one hand, low-tech earth architecture stands for an inevitable preliminary stage of development toward industrial society, but on the other hand, earth architecture persuades us to imagine an alternative future, a basis to which industrial societies would *return*.

NOTES

1 François Cointereaux, *Nouvelle architecture pratique* ([Paris]: n.p., n.d. [1813]), 18.
2 "Housing," 1, August 20, 1953, in file Housing, in series United Nations Korean Reconstruction Agency, S-0526-0118-08, UN Archives.
3 American regional Office, "UNKRA History," February 5, 1960, in file History Outlines, in series United Nations Korean Reconstruction Agency (hereafter UNKRA), S-0526-0168-07, UN Archives.
4 *United Nations Korean Reconstruction Agency Historical Narratives*, 52, n.d., in series United Nations Korean reconstruction Agency, S0526-0025-07.
5 Report on UNKRA Earth Block Housing Program," 1 (December 15, 1954), in file Earth Block Equipment, in series UNKRA S-0526-0088-04.
6 Letter from Paul J. Sullivan, Hudgson Co. to Frank Ray, UNKRA, July 23, 1951, in file Relief Programme, Provision of Shelter: Housing Survey, in Series UNKRA, S-0526-0026-01. Letter from Earle C. Marshall to Frederick C. Spryer, UNKRA, December 30 23, 1952, in file Relief Programme, Provision of Shelter: Housing Survey, in Series UNKRA, S-0526–0025-07. ACME, "On Built Specifications," October 1952, in file Relief Programme, Provision of Shelter: Housing Survey, in Series UNKRA, S-0526-0025-07.
7 Barton P. Jenks, "Korean Housing Survey," August 26, 1952, in file Korean Housing Survey, in series UNKRA, S-0526-0025-07, UN Archives.
8 Housing and Home Finance Agency, "Preliminary Outline of Investigation for UNKRA of Building Methods and Materials for Korea," November 21, 1952, in file Relief Programme, Provision of Shelter: Housing General, in series UNKRA, S-0526-0025-07.
9 The hand-pressed machines used to produce compressed earth blocks were not new but were not in wide use. During the 1950s, several commercial models were available from American, European, and South African manufacturers. UNKRA preferred Landcrete because of its good reputation and relatively light weight. Letter from Russel S. McClure to Frank Ray, Chief of UNKRA Geneva Office, September 3, 1952, UNKRA S-0526-0026-01.
10 Letter from John E. Goodison to J. R. Jordaan, January 21, 1953, UNKRA S-0526-0025-07.
11 Letter from George S. Hall, *Assistant Agent General to Ernest Weissmann, Chief Housing, and Town and Country Planning Section, United Nations*, February 11, 1955; The UN Archives.
12 Dongmin Park, "Free World, Cheap Buildings: U.S. Hegemony and the Origins of Modern Architecture in South Korea, 1953–1960," (Ph.D. diss., University of California Berkeley, 2016).
13 "U.N. Makes House for South Korea Out of Earth Blocks," *The New York Times*, December 14, 1953.
14 Park, "Free World, Cheap Buildings."
15 Report of the Agent General of the United Nations Korean Reconstruction Agency for the Period July 1, 1956, to June 30, 1957, General Assembly Official Records: Twelfth Session Supplement No. 17 (A/3651), New York 1957. URL: http://community.eldis.org/.59ec460c. However, we must contextualize the UN's involvement in Korea's housing problem as part of the broader social movement toward achieving technological autonomy. See Sang-Hyun Kim, "Social Movements and Contested Sociotechnical Imaginaries in South Korea," in *Dreamscapes of Modernity, Sociotechnical Imaginaries and the Fabrication of Power*, eds. Sheila Jasanoff and Sang-Hyun Kim (Chicago and London: University of Chicago Press, 2015).
16 Memorandum, A CINVA-RAM Case history (Case Study Earth Construction use in Housing Korea, March 31, 1961. Folder Low Cost Housing Earth Construction SO 144 August 3–1, 1968; The UN Archives.

17 Daniel Immerwahr, *Thinking Small: The United States and the Lure of Community Development* (Cambridge, MA: Harvard University Press, 2018).
18 For a discussion on community, see Martin Hershenzon, Chapter 16, this volume.
19 Memorandum, A CINVA-RAM Case history (Case Study Earth Construction use in Housing Korea, March 31, 1961. Folder Low Cost Housing Earth Construction SO 144, August 1968; The UN Archives, 2.
20 Ibid.
21 Roy F. Harrod, "An Essay in Dynamic Theory," *Economic Journal* 49, no. 193 (1939): 14–33; Evsey Domar, "Capital Expansion, Rate of Growth, and Employment," *Econometrica* 14, no. 2 (1946): 137–147.
22 Or Rosenboim, *The Emergence of Globalism: Visions of World Order in Britain and the United States, 1939–1950* (Princeton, NJ: Princeton University Press, 2017).
23 As of September 1953, 161 staffs out of 417 were American. See The United Nations Korean Reconstruction Agency, *UNKRA in Action* (New York: United Nations, 1956).
24 For a detail discussion of America's housing aid to Latin America, see Andrea Renner, "Housing Diplomacy: U.S. Housing Aid to Latin America, 1949–1973" (Ph.D. diss., Columbia University, 2011).
25 "For Dirt-Cheap Houses," *Time*, July 8, 1957.
26 *Interamerican Housing Center Bulletin* 1, "CINVA-RAM, Soil-Cement Block Making Machine," June 26, 1957 (emphasis in original).
27 CINVA, Manual for Supervising Self-Help Home Construction with Stabilized Earth Blocks made with the CINVA-RAM Portable Block Press, January 1959; The UN Archives.
28 Letter from Eric Carlson to Ernest Weissmann, February 18, 1958, the UN Archives.
29 Letter from Eric Carlson to Ernest Weissmann, August 6, 1957; the UN Archives.
30 Interoffice Memorandum. From Ernest Weissmann, Assistant Director Bureau of Social Affairs, in charge of the Housing, Building and Planning Branch, to Mr. Myer Cohen, Director Programme Division, Technical Assistance Administration. Subject: Soil block-making machine, September 5, 1957. File No: SO 144(3–1). The memo suggested sending two machines to the Housing Centres in Afghanistan, Bolivia, Burma, Ceylon (Sri Lanka), Ecuador, Haiti, India, Indonesia, Israel, Jamaica, Jordan, Lebanon, Libya, Pakistan, the Philippines and the Fundamental Education Centres in Egypt and Mexico; The UN Archives.
31 Patel worked with members from other UN organizations. See Alfred E. S. Alcock, K. N. Misra, J. L. McGairl, and C. B. Patel, "Self-Help Housing Methods and Practices in South-East Asia," *Ekistics* 16, no. 93 (1963): 81–87; also see The United Nation's *Report of the Mission to Survey and Evaluate Self-Help Housing Methods and Practices in South-East Asia*, New Delhi, January 1962.
32 Letter from C. B. Patel, Chief, Housing and Building Material Section Industry and Trading Division to Vitali Gornov, Officer-in-charge, Housing, Building and Planning Branch, United Nations, September 1, 1959; The UN Archives.
33 Letter from Alfred E. S. Alcock, Consultor en Planeamiento Nationes Unidas, Republic of Panama to Ernest Weissmann, June 8, 1957; The UN Archives.
34 Letter from C. B. Patel, Chief, Housing and Building Material Section Industry and Trading Division to Vitali Gornov, Officer-in-charge, Housing, Building and Planning Branch, United Nations, September 1, 1959; The UN Archives.
35 S. V. P. Ambekar, Use of Forest Products, Forest Product Derivative and Bitumen Emulsion as Soil Stabilizers, in Government of Mysore, Public Works Department, Mysore Engineering Research Station Krishnarajsagar, Undated; the UN Archives.
36 Letter from Patel to Gornov, January 15, 1959, IN/11/6013; the United Nations Archives.
37 Letter from the Resident Representative. U.N.T.A.B Programme Court Rangoon, Burma to S. Habib Ahmed, Chief Office for Asia and the Far East Programme Division, May 13, 1957; The UN Archives.
38 Letter from C. B. Patel to Vaisali Gornov, January 15, 1959; The UN Archives.
39 Letter from Weissmann to P. Campbell, United Nations Housing Expert, Ministry of Housing and Social Welfare, May 5, 1959; The UN Archives.
40 Letter from D. H. Mo Neal, Building Research Consultant to Eric Carlson, Subject—CINVA-RAM Block-Making Press, November 30, 1957; the UN Archives.
41 Letter from Eric Carlson to Ernest Weissman, CINVA/C/DIR/53, date unknown, the UN Archives.
42 Letter from Raul Ramirez to Eric Carlson, Subject, Report of Mr E.W. Eller, Director, Ellson Equipment (P.T.Y.), Report on the CINVA-RAM Machine, December 1957; the UN Archives.
43 Comment on Reply of Engineer Ramirez, Report by E. W. Eller on the "CINVA-RAM" Machine, February 4, 1958; the UN Archives. Letter from Eric Carlson to Ernest Weissmann, February 18, 1958, the UN Archives.
44 CINVA Memo./4, I/13/58/120, 7, February 4, 1958; The UN Archives.
45 The Cinva-ram prototype low cost soil cement block making machine, March 1957; the UN Archives.
46 CINVA Memo,/3, I/10/58/550, 2, February 4, 1958; The UN Archives.
47 Louis Cellauro and Gilbert Richaud, "Thomas Jefferson and François Cointereaux, Professor of Rural Architecture in Revolutionary Paris," *Architectural History* 48 (2005): 173–206.

48 Francois Rozier, *Cours complet d' agriculture theorique, pratique, economique, et de medecine rurale et veterinaire, vii* ([Paris]: n.p., n.d. [1781–96]), 719–720; Jacques-Francois Blondel, *Cours d'architecture, ou Traite de la decoration, distribution et construction des bâtiment* (Montana: Kessinger Publishing, LLC, 2010, original publication 1773).

49 Jean-Philippe Garric, "François Cointereaux (1740–1830) L'Avant-garde de Art de Ba^tir aux champs," *In Situ* 21 (2013): 1–14.

50 For a review of Cointereaux's work, see: Laurent Baridon, Jean-Philippe Garric, and Gilbert Richaud, *Les leçons de la terre: François Cointeraux (1740–1830) professeur d'architecture rurale* (Paris: Cendres, 2016).

51 Paula Lee, "François Coiantereaux and the School of 'Agritecture' in Eighteenth-Century France," *Journal of Architectural Education* 60, no. 4 (2007): 39–46.

52 François Coiantereaux, *E´cole dárchitecture rurale, transporteé de paris a´ Lyon en 1796* (Lyon: dans l'E´cole dárchitecture rurale, au Faubourg de Vaise, 1796), 12.

53 François Cointereaux, *Confere´nces tenues par le sr. Cointereaux . . . 'a la suite dúne récente découverte qu´il vient faire d´une manir`ere de bâtir, 6`eme conference* (Paris, 1880).

54 Louis Cellauro and Gilbert Richaud, "François Cointereaux's École d'Architecture Rurale (1790–91) and Its Influence in Europe and the Colonies," *Architectural History* 49 (2006): 129–148.

55 Alexei Makhrov, "Earth Construction in Russia: A Scottish Connexion," *Architectural History* 40 (1997): 171–183.

56 Jessica Golebiowski, "Rammed Earth Architecture's Journey to the High Hills of Santee," (Master's thesis, Master of Science Historic Preservation, Clemson University and the College of Charleston), 108–112.

57 Anthony Merril, *The Rammed Earth House* (New York: Harper and Brothers, 1947).

58 National Register of Historic Places Continuation Sheet, United States Department of the Interior National Park Service. Between 1930 and his death in 1941, Patty built three buildings, two garden walls, and twenty-nine smaller wall sections at South Dakota State College.

59 The Federal Works Agency, FWA (1939–49) was one of the three agencies of the federal government that was created through President Roosevelt's Reorganization Act of 1939. FWA administered construction and management of a number of important public works.

60 Kenneth J. Bindas, *Modernity and the Great Depression: The Transformation of American Society, 1930–1941* (Lawrence: University of Kansas Press, 2017).

61 Felicity D. Scott, *Outlaw Territories/Architectures of Counterinsurgency* (New York: Zone Books, 2016).

62 Caroline Maniaque-Benton, *French Encounters with the American Counterculture 1960–1980* (Franham, Surrey: Ashgate, 2011), 141–143. Also see, Paul Virilio, "Létat d'urgance ou l'autogestion de l'espacé (1968)," in *Histoire (s) de l'anarchisme, des anarchists et de leurs foutues idées au fil de 150 ans du Libertaire et du Monde Libertaire*, vol. 9 1968/1975 (Paris, Bruxelles, 2001), 38–39.

Part V

Designing the rural

13

Globalizing the village

Development media, Jaqueline Tyrwhitt, and the United Nations in India

Olga Touloumi

INTRODUCTION

In the early 1960s, Marshall McLuhan told us that the movable type was worldmaking, allowing for books to travel along colonial paths of trade and conquest. In his erudite prose, he named this new world the "global village." In numerous presentations and interviews in the years to follow, McLuhan stretched the meaning of the term "global village" to describe everything from Cold War diplomacy to the effects of radio and television. The term subsequently acquired its own history. McLuhan dressed up his "global village" with the literary aura of James Joyce's *Finnegans Wake* and Wyndham Lewis's *America and Cosmic Man* while employing anthropological constructions of tribalism for the foundation of his media theory, as Ginger Nolan argued recently.[1] What would it mean, though, if this decidedly marquee term was brought in dialogue with its most immediate historical context: the era of decolonization and global development institutions such as the United Nations and the Bretton Woods organizations? Even as McLuhan was developing his media ideology, new international systems of bureaucracy were replacing older imperial orders, and the "village" was slowly emerging as a new way to fold in decolonizing nation states. Development was deployed as a world-making engine that slowly and steadily produced new economic and social divisions in the world, as M. Ijlal Muzaffar notes.[2] What can we learn about development and the role that media played in this new world order if we revisit the emergence of the "global village" from the perspective of UN developmentalism?

Offering an alternative genealogy to McLuhan's "global village," I will focus on the 1954 UN Seminar on Housing and Community Improvement and the Village Centre exhibition, where Jaqueline Tyrwhitt along with the Indian Government and the UN Technical Assistance Administration (TAA) construed the village as a medium for development (Figure 13.1). Villages, as Ayala Levin and Neta Feniger have shown, entered the practice and discursive formation of modern architecture and planning on a scale that is still to be reckoned with.[3] Behind this exploration lies the hypothesis that Tyrwhitt, planner, McLuhan's colleague at the University of Toronto, an avowed disciple of Patrick Geddes, and key actor within the Congrès international d'architecture moderne (CIAM), brought the "village" as a globalizing medium into McLuhan's horizon at a moment when an interdisciplinary cohort at the

FIGURE 13.1 Jaqueline Tyrwhitt with delegates in front of the UN Seminar Hall, New Delhi, 1954; © The Ernest Weissmann Archive.

Source: Courtesy of the Frances Loeb Library, Harvard University Graduate School of Design.

University of Toronto sought to chart the relationship between media and empires, technology and culture. By bringing forward UN conversations on development and the form of the "village," I hope to cast a new set of actors and political imperatives into the historical picture surrounding theorizations of globalization in media studies and to recover the role of media in the post-World War II development ideology of international institutions.

THE UN SEMINAR

In 1952, Ernest Weissmann, chief of the Housing and Town and Country Planning Section (HTCP) of the UN Department of Social Affairs, mobilized TAA resources for an International Exhibition on Low-Cost Housing and a United Nations Regional Seminar on Housing and Community Improvement in New Delhi.[4] The Indian government had been petitioning TAA for support to acquire construction material and equipment for a "trade fair" on low-cost housing to market its developing building sector, and so it accepted the UN's proposal to compliment the exhibition with a regional component that would network India with other South and Southeast Asian countries and an international seminar.[5] The seminar and exhibition, which were three years in the making, aspired to introduce and reinscribe South Asia within TAA's conduits of knowledge transfer. In fact, TAA postponed all other projects to focus its resources on the seminar and exhibition, hoping to embed the UN in the "housing field" in Asia.[6]

At that time, Jaqueline Tyrwhitt was looking for ways into the UN's housing and planning work. Born in South Africa, raised in England, educated in Germany, with experience at major professional organizations for architecture and planning, she was the perfect candidate. She was immersed in modernist debates, concerned with the education of planners (she had led a wartime correspondence course in the United Kingdom and taught in a number of Canadian and US institutions), well traveled, and cosmopolitan and had the capacity to not only traverse informational networks but also expand them, all of which were important qualities for a UN technical adviser on a mission to connect developing peripheries with world organizational centers.[7] Her edited book *Patrick Geddes in India*, containing a selection of the reports of the Scottish planner and sociologist for British governors and administrators in India, had brought her international attention and a new set of professional connections, including Charles Abrams, Albert Mayer, and Constantinos Doxiadis.

By the time she set foot in India, Tyrwhitt already had a rough sketch for the entire event. The seminar would be organized around three themes, headed by technical advisers and discussion leaders: Jacob Crane with Rafael Picó and Constantinos Doxiades for Housing and Community Improvement, Charles Abrams with Frederick Adams and Arieh Sharon (who replaced the Tennessee Valley Authority's David Lilienthal) for Physical Planning, and Robert Fitzmaurice with Jacob Thijsse and Anthony Atkinson for Building Materials and Techniques.[8] She also proposed an "educational exhibition" to illuminate the topics addressed in the seminar for a nonspecialist audience. The exhibition was slated to display representative projects from the broader region, modernist plans for model cities, the CIAM grids (which never arrived), and periodicals dedicated to planning, including Weissmann's UN HTCP Bulletin.[9] In addition, she suggested the creation of a "community centre" around which low-cost housing prototypes would showcase model alternatives "live."[10]

When Tyrwhitt returned to New Delhi after her short break to attend CIAM, she complained to McLuhan:

> This Indian experience is intensely interesting. . . . I have no idea if I really am achieving anything in connection with the Government Exhibition on Low-Cost Housing. Its [sic] rather like my first year at Toronto: one goes on, hopefully, but can't see how anything is working out. And the extreme politeness of the Indian manners is as difficult to guage [sic] as the first contact with Toronto 'never-give-yourself-away'ness. Usually when I come home in the evening, I feel just nothing whatever has been achieved during the day: one seems to be standing still, or to be digging a hole on the seashore which next day has completely disappeared—though it looked like a real hole when you left it.[11]

Tyrwhitt was equally perplexed and frustrated by the lack of transparency and progress, despite endless meetings and work, an experience that most UN consultants and advisers shared to a greater or lesser degree. She canvassed South and Southeast Asia in a forensic trip to locate collaborators and assemble the pieces of her life-size exhibition to cast the potential of the rural as the pragmatic and future agent of development.[12] In villages around Punjab but also outside New Delhi, she captured scenes from village life, turning the "village" into a kit of parts. "A Village Well," a "Village Carpenter," a "Village Cart," read the captions of photographs that she mailed to Giedion late in October (Figure 13.2).[13] Her

FIGURE 13.2 Tyrwhitt's photograph of village in Punjab, India, 1953.

Source: © gta Archives/ETH Zurich, Sigfried Giedion.

tour, culminating in the seminar and exhibition, served well the Economic and Security Council and its nascent regional division of the world, articulating the Economic and Social Commission for Asia and the Far East (ECAFE) group of countries as a coherent cultural, economic, and political region.

THE WORKS OF THE VILLAGE

Tyrwhitt arrived in India with an idea for a "community centre" in New Delhi, bringing UN-based technical assistance to CIAM's conversation on urban cores.[14] The idea for an exhibition was aired first in an ECAFE meeting in Thailand in May 1952, shortly after the TAA and the Indian Government had signed a contractual agreement to co-organize the seminar.[15] In communications with Shri N. P. Dube, the deputy secretary of the Ministry of Works, Housing and Supply, TAA suggested to the ministry that Tyrwhitt's "Model Community Centre" become the central stage for "services . . . available to the Indian village communities."[16] Although she agreed with Krishna Shridhar Joglekar, the chief architect of the Central Public Works Department (CPWD), that they should think of the exhibition as a "village nucleus" instead, she kept alternating the two, revealing the conceptual conflation.[17] In a letter to friends and family, she claimed the CIAM "core" as the originary point of her "Village Centre," an otherwise "open space enclosed by community buildings."[18] Resisting "rural materials" and "rural work," the Public Works Department (PWD) got around Tyrwhitt's request to hire S. P. Raju, a prominent government engineer whose work on smokeless chulas placed him closer to the "rural" she was getting acquainted with, and assembled instead a small crew of architects and engineers (names included D. V. Rao, Din Dayal, Joginder Bahadur, Gulshan Rai, and others).[19] Weissmann welcomed Tyrwhitt's center for adding a "tone of reality" and visibly marking the difference between "developing" and "more developed countries,"[20] while demonstrating "the social aspects of community development . . . in a practical manner."[21] By producing a model for development, the UN would also claim its form—even while professing sole concern for content—and as a result actively articulate an "ascetic modernity" for the Global South's future, as Farhan Karim notes.[22]

For the Indian Government's Planning Commission, however, villages held symbolic and political importance. They constituted primary sites of Nehruvian agrarian reform, where the prime minister sought to divest past political structures of their power. Nehru hoped that the first two five-year plans, with their administrative and economical strategies, would undermine the older imperial class of landlords and intermediaries who held disproportionate power and access to land. The goal was to make the state the "ultimate owner" of land. Another area of concern for the progressive elite was the caste system, seen as an obstruction to freedom and economic growth. Nehruvian cohorts proposed a transfer of power to the *panchayati raj* system, a decentralized but networked form of village self-government that directly connected villages to the central government, circumventing any form of local governance—*zamindars* and landlords—particularly the ones blocking the Nehruvian top-down technocratic project of capitalist development.[23]

The Indian government was also running a growing program of community development projects that targeted villages as both physical and administrative entities, at the time under the auspices of the Community Project Administration (CPA) and the National Extension Services. The first set of those experiments was administered by Albert Mayer, an American planner who reached India with the US Army during World War II and stayed to see his pilot project grow beyond the Etawah region of Uttar Pradesh.[24] Mayer described to Nehru "model" villages that would lead a self-help "revolution" in rural India. He proposed a slow grassroots process to identify "needs" and laid out a plan to meet them with some external guidance and "commonsense engineering." In 1948, he chose sixty-four villages in the Etawah region, set up the "pilot project," and returned to the United States, from where he maintained distant and somewhat perfunctory supervision while angling for new projects, among them the plan for Chandigarh.[25] Building Tyrwhitt's village center, therefore, would serve as a live advertisement of the nascent community development program and an invitation to solidify connections among the various state departments involved (PWD, CPA, and so on).

The Gandhian village quickly emerged as a concept and a technology that various sides wished to put to work. For the colonial government, villages had signified an older premodern order of kinship, social hierarchies, shared property, and collective identity against and, at times, through which rulers aimed to govern and assess their sovereignty. Henry Maine, the British jurist and legal historian who spent the early part of his career in colonial India, claimed that "village communities" and their "mode of holding and cultivating land" were the originary point of proprietary and private law, as well as the sites for colonial "indirect rule."[26] In the postindependence imagination, certainly in the Gandhian narrative, villages held the significance of an "authentic" pre-imperial social and spatial order that supervened other internal boundaries such as caste and religion. Gandhi, who had been planning a nation from his Ashrams, resuscitated the image of a precolonial Indian village in the construction of some essential Indian identity, offering a visual vocabulary for Indian independence to be accompanied with the figure of the artisan and *khadi*—the handspun cloth of the *swadeshi* movement. "[I]f the village perishes, India will perish too," he wrote, declaring the national significance of its political value.[27] For him, rural India held the key to independence, while urbanity represented the very forces of modernity—capitalism and industrialization—that had depleted the country of its resources. He invigorated the image of the village to criticize Western materialism, transforming villages into the primary sites of *hind swaraj* (home rule) and resistance to the economic and cultural colonization of the Englishman.[28] He developed a full program for village *swaraj* (village self-rule) aimed at economic independence, education, and a new relationship to the world. His ideal India would be a "world of cottage crafts and intensive, small-scale farming co-operatives" where "everybody is responsible for his immediate environment and all are responsible for society," advocating for the disciplining potential of labor and the virtue of asceticism.[29] But even more interestingly, Gandhi hoped villages would become schools to educate the new Indian. Unlike international fairs and their global stage for imperial exploitation, Gandhi believed village exhibitions to be countercultures of consumption, as staging grounds for an emancipatory economics.[30]

Tyrwhitt, on the other hand, had been articulating her ideas on the fringes of CIAM debates on "urban cores." She insinuated that claims of universality—not so much those of cultural specificity or regionalism—drove her proposal for a village center.[31] At the time of her appointment, Tyrwhitt had just finished editing *The Heart of the City*, which concluded the CIAM 8 efforts to address the question of "cores" during post-World War II reconstruction. For those modernist architects, "cores" constituted an essential part of the grammar that organized communities across scales, from villages and neighborhoods to metropolitan areas.[32] During a discussion that mostly revolved around Giedion's earlier call for a new monumentality,[33] planners and scholars alike divorced these centers from the economic infrastructures that supported them—the home, the colonies, the church—producing cores as iconic forms devoid of social context. Tyrwhitt, however, disagreed: "The Core is not the seat of civic dignity: the Core is the gathering place of the people," she claimed.[34] Tyrwhitt identified "cores" (either physical or social) as congregative sites for the formation of publics.[35] At the New Delhi Seminar, she brought CIAM thematology, recruiting CIAM members for presentations and even soliciting the CIAM 9 grids to furnish discussions with models (although in the end only photographs of a smaller selection of panels were dispatched to India).[36]

She also programmed screenings for visiting technical advisers and experts. J. Arthur Rank's film, "Homes for All," Pyrene Manufacturing Company's "A New Development in Building," "Good Neighbours," "How to Look at a Village," and "The Road to Kelshi," all produced by the Rational Planning Corporation, Tyrwhitt thought, would effectively illustrate various forms of planning and development in India and abroad for the visiting experts, willfully forgetting that most of those films were aimed at a nonexpert local audience. She set up a small theater for the films, clearing the evening agenda for screenings, an initiative that most planners and architects found unnecessary and a waste of their time. They did not need to be convinced of the value of expertise and planning. They were already experts.[37]

PERFORMING THE VILLAGE

At the Village Centre, Tyrwhitt's "core" made room for international institutions to organize the very space of idealized informality and communal living (Figure 13.3). A health center, an industrial center for craftsmanship, and an educational center served as footholds for the World Health Organization, the Food and Agriculture Organization, the International Labor Organization, and UNESCO. Tyrwhitt's village center was designed to hook the rural into other networks of the distribution of modernity.[38] In fact, to convince UN representatives, Tyrwhitt argued that a community center would be "a valuable field demonstration centre for the Agencies involved."[39] Designed to replace the cultural and political centers of the past, this new type of rural community center would act as an extension of the state machinery into the countryside, creating a platform for the introduction of national policies, but also would act as an avenue for international organizations to educate local villagers according to standards and procedures developed at a distance. Tyrwhitt, who claimed that the organization and structure of the village center held more gravity than its outward appearance betrayed, placed the school and the *panchayat* assembly under the same roof, thus architecturally articulating a connection between "learning and responsibility" at the very center of the village.[40] In other words, what Tyrwhitt hoped to be "the basis of village life"—the place where decisions would be made and the place that guaranteed the autonomy of the village's existence—would already be perceived by villagers as an administrative extension of a center located elsewhere. Tyrwhitt's plan located the village center separately in space yet connected with the "experimental village houses."[41] The education center, health clinic, grain storage, and craftsmen's sheds were all built from sun-dried bricks and rammed earth and defined an open platform, constructing a "microcosm of village culture," illustrating, to the view of the UN, "certain fundamental principles of community living."[42] The exhibition posited an environmental infrastructure that was "integrated with the village life and displayed

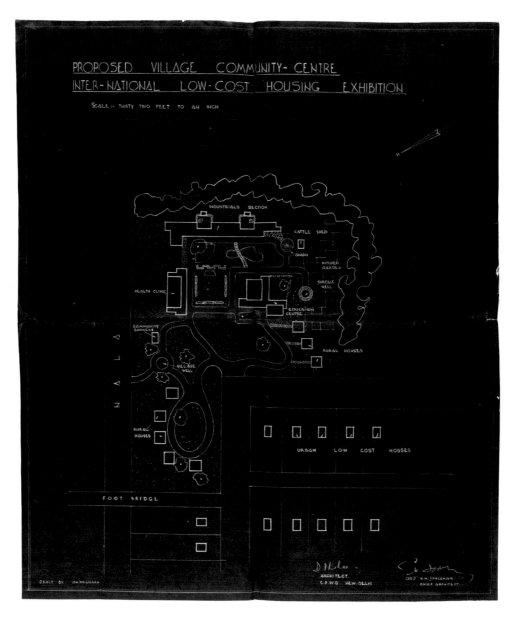

FIGURE 13.3 Plan of exhibition grounds and village center, 1954.
Source: © Tyrwhitt Papers, RIBA.

for all to see" as a model for a modern rural life.[43] In a way, the village center constituted a spatial metaphor for the relationship that the UN wished to have with its periphery in terms of a centrifugal expertise that was implemented locally as indigenous, erasing issues of difference and hierarchy and presenting the two as inseparable. In designing a structural system that incorporated social unevenness and inequality within itself, Tyrwhitt saw local variance as ornamental excess that would eventually wither away and thus intrinsic neither to the universal structure nor to village life itself. "I am a town-planner who is convinced that town-planning starts with the re-development of the core of the Community rather than by concentrating all efforts upon its outer fringes," she announced during a BBC broadcast to England in anticipation of the opening.[44]

Strikingly, although the exhibition posited tradition as the path toward postcolonial India, the model village itself lacked any religious center. To reckon with religious pluralism in India, TAA made no space for a shrine, temple, or mosque in the model village. Tyrwhitt, and by extension the UN, hoped that a structural shift in the organization of the village would create a condition wherein the superfluity of caste would disappear. In place of a shrine, Tyrwhitt's team built a replica of Gandhi's hut, proclaiming it a communal site of spiritual commemoration of core values of Indianhood shared by all.[45]

A particularly acerbic reaction to Tyrwhitt's proposal came from the Gandhian faction itself, in the form of Mridula Sarabhai, an heir to the family that had sponsored Gandhi, Le Corbusier, and Louis Kahn, as well as Secretary of the Congress Party S. N. Aggarwal, who insisted that Tyrwhitt should first visit the ashram. In a manner of speaking, they were asserting their control over Gandhi's legacy.[46] Tyrwhitt contested this gatekeeping. She found the Ashram "pretty phoney [sic]" and argued that Gandhi's disciples were transforming a "natural way of life . . . into a formalised religion,"[47] possibly echoing the sentiments of Sarabhai and contemporary Gandhians as well, who mournfully witnessed the gradual withering away of the Gandhian ideal after independence.[48]

For Tyrwhitt, the principal desire was not to enter into the intricacies of rural society and economy but rather to fix the position of the village within a network of expertise and distribution of resources. During the event, the dynamics of funding and financial support that followed laid bare the character of institutional interests involved. The UN backed away from the exhibition project, with the argument that housing constituted predominantly a national problem and that its mandate required the UN to abstain from investing in local building industries. Without the financial support she envisioned,[49] Tyrwhitt importuned the Indian authorities to step in.[50] Eventually it was the Indian CPA and CPWD that built her village center.[51] For labor and resources, the UN (via Tyrwhitt) urged CPA and CPWD to use locals and regionally available building material to "fire" up rural communities visiting the exhibition "with enthusiasm."[52] The exhibition would thus end up modeling the economy that produced it: all the construction and housing was erected with local material and labor. As for the displays, models donated from South and Southeast Asia organizations, as well as in situ constructions—hardly uniform or systematic in tenor—gradually filled up the live exhibition.[53] Eventually the exhibition featured around 70 models of "low-cost" housing, in addition to products sampling outputs from the building industry (Figures 13.4 and 13.5).[54]

Tyrwhitt was dismayed to find that, although the Indian government had embraced the networking opportunity offered by the UN seminar, the reception of her village center left much to be desired. "[A]ll my buildings are hated by the whole organization," she complained to her friends. The Cement and Concrete Organization and the CPWD had little, if any, interest in the "mud and thatch, locally made tiles, sun dried . . . brick" and the Village Centre at large, and for good reason.[55] There was very little of the expertise surrounding the production of the Village Centre that CPWD and CPA did not already know. Tyrwhitt's focus was on the village as a social space; the Indian organizations, on the other hand, were more interested in equipment and low-cost housing.

Tyrwhitt had proposed a return to tradition, in that sense opposing Nehru's technological vision of progress that would provide the superstructure to rationalize and efficiently

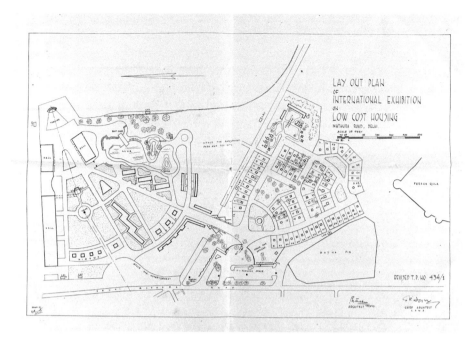

FIGURE 13.4 Plan of the village center, 1954.
Source: © Tyrwhitt Papers, RIBA.

FIGURE 13.5 Slide of the village center with low-cost housing exhibition models, 1954; © The Ernest Weissmann Archive.
Source: Courtesy of the Frances Loeb Library, Harvard University Graduate School of Design.

organize local expertise and technique. Rather than embrace a modernist aesthetic that would disrupt the colonial past, as the Nehruvian faction and the bulk of Indian architects would soon be urging, she wanted the village center to revive precolonial village life, producing the fiction of a long continuity that had briefly been interrupted.[56] Here Tyrwhitt's ideas might be seen as reverting to those of her proclaimed mentor Patrick Geddes, whose writing on India she had studied in detail, excerpted, and published.[57] This fiction would be accompanied through the requisite material signifiers.[58] Bricks, bamboo, and rammed earth, Tyrwhitt argued, constituted the material of an unspoiled and precolonial South Asia. They would perform an authentic rural identity that transcended even nationalism, an Indian identity per se. She encouraged architects, engineers, and builders to render this autochthonous material universe the platform from where modern India would move forward toward development by moving backward and away from the cement concrete that epitomized Western modernity.[59]

In Tyrwhitt's plan, universality would be localized through strategic recourses of material and form—the "core" in her mind. Tyrwhitt's specifications for the exhibition were explicit: the life-size models should use local material; the overall cost of the house should be affordable by the "average villager"; and the building must respond to climatic requirements, with the necessary infrastructural provisions to connect with facilities for education, water, and agricultural services. "Climate" can be read here as a geopolitical category in that it referred specifically to tropical countries from the former British Empire. The manual labor used for the village center reinscribed within development the body of the villager as a catalyst and agent of progress. The process itself became a diorama: visitors were treated to views of a Punjabi potter making cottage tiles and a blacksmith putting on bolts and hooks, while carpenters and weavers went about practicing their trades. The labor on display was not meant to produce any surplus value but to present the life of the village as a kind of homeostasis.[60]

Throughout the exhibit, smokeless chulhas, drainage systems, and wells displayed the UN's technological imperative for development tempered by local knowledge. The model village comprised of a Nehruvian recalibration of the Gandhian idea of a village economy for rural development, where the clandestine reach of the technologic would sneak in and undo the limits posed by tradition. In subsequent publications following the exhibition, Tyrwhitt actively negotiated this fine line, pronouncing her village center as the materialization of Gandhi's vision while underplaying the Nehruvian imperatives behind it.

THE MODEL VILLAGE

To offer her "Village Centre" as a model for development, Tyrwhitt mobilized media. She understood intuitively that models needed systematic abstraction and that the impact of the village center would be measured in terms of its circulation. The UN provided rolls of Kodachrome for Tyrwhitt and other delegates to photographically document both exhibition and seminars and asked her to meticulously record newspaper articles and correspondence, producing the institutional archive that regardless got lost within the chaotic workings of this massive bureaucracy.[61] Tyrwhitt invited G. F. Middleton, the Australian architect who built a rammed earth house for the exhibition with a mold he had perfected in Israel, to bring his camera and film the village center for the UN.[62] In addition, she had the Indian Films Division produce a short documentary on the Village Centre for domestic audiences,[63] a film that included Gandhi's Ashram in Sevagram and CPA villages at Panipat, hence insinuating UN's intervention into national and regional planning efforts.[64]

Where films and photographs could not reach, radio would. At UNESCO, Tyrwhitt was encouraged to connect with All India Radio (AIR), the national broadcasting organization that offered her dedicated airtime for the event.[65] The UN believed radio to be an important medium for reaching rural publics despite literacy barriers, pointing Tyrwhitt to examples of rural radio: the National Farm Radio Forum in Canada; the short-lived NBC program for rural America, "The People Act"; and "radio" schools for villagers deployed across Colombia.[66] Although advertised as a social equalizer, rural radio set hierarchies of expertise along literacy standards, separating village experts and educators from the villagers, creating a two-class citizenship system. Radio infrastructure, as the British had demonstrated before, brought rural areas under colonial control. One thinks here of radio sets installed in village squares for communal listening of educational programs and news, aiming at "village uplift" but inevitably reinforcing the tie with the empire. Radio programming aimed to limit mobility and create a new sense of gratitude to the state, important for urban elites and their idea of citizenship postindependence.[67]

However, Tyrwhitt did not engage the rural radio imperative in its full incarnation. The seminar was organized for experts and professionals, with no intention to invite the general public and farmers into its meeting rooms, even simply as audience. Instead, she prepared two announcements—one for AIR and one for the BBC Empire Service—to address the two worlds of the "global village." To the Indian audience, Tyrwhitt focused on low-cost housing and the self-help techniques presented at the seminar, promising to "see that the meetings come to some conclusions" and to publish a "useful handbook on how to get about the business of providing good and low-cost houses in the very near future." There was not a single word on her village center.[68] To the British audience back in the United Kingdom, she talked about the exhibition, indulging her audience in elaborate descriptions of the prototypes and her village center, with a passing mention of the seminar only at the very end.[69] In short, for her Indian audience she construed expertise as progress without form and for her compatriots back home she confirmed the continuation of British involvement in the production of physical form and planning, albeit in the guise of internationalism and progress.

In the years to follow, Tyrwhitt would refer back to her Village Centre as the "Model Village," situating her UN work within the broader landscape of global development. At Princeton she asked students to design a "model village," and during lectures at Harvard and North Carolina Chapel Hill she reified her conviction that it was a "model" that she had delivered and not just a "centre," further divorcing her creation from its particular context. She repeated her stance in articles published initially for the UN and later for *Ekistics*. To Indian bureaucracies, however, Tyrwhitt presented her exhibition as an inhabitable solution that deserved a life after the UN seminar, urging them to continue using her core after the exhibition was over. Indeed, she approached CPA, PWD, or any part of the Indian government that would lend its ear to discuss the future of her Village Centre as a new pilot next to the older ones.

During her yearlong stay in India, Tyrwhitt also corresponded with McLuhan. Just before leaving Toronto, she had started working with McLuhan and his collaborator, the anthropologist Ted Carpenter, on a Ford Foundation grant for a new project on media and culture. Titled "Changing Patterns of Language and Behavior and the New Media of Communication," the research project catered to the appetites of the Ford Foundation, which had just launched a funding program for interdisciplinary research on behavioral sciences and adult education to benefit its expanding global operations.[70] Tyrwhitt received notice of the winning proposal while abroad,[71] and although the Toronto group convened in her absence, McLuhan relied on her to shape its research agenda. He was anxious about the lack of a common ground and a shared language.[72] In their correspondence, the two would figure out the structure of the seminar and the allocation of funds, outlining an organizational structure and a research plan for the next two years.[73] Following Sigfried Giedion's proposition for "interfaculty study" and in hopes of creating "more knit and interwoven" groups, Tyrwhitt proposed a comparative study of methodological approaches that involved reading representative texts and discussing research papers.[74] Each meeting would be structured around a paper presentation by the members of the seminar and their guests, reframing a gamut of entities—money, language, art, for instance—as media. Tyrwhitt also put on the table a proposal for a "pilot study" at Ryerson University on the perception of the built environment. The project offered McLuhan an opportunity to develop a research platform for future critical collaborations, such as the collaboration with CBC on a mass media and education project that formed the empirical foundation of McLuhan's groundbreaking *Understanding Media* or his later project *City as Classroom*.

The story of the Toronto seminars has been extensively explored.[75] What has drawn less attention is McLuhan's growing interest in Tyrwhitt's UN work in India and international institutions at large. Initially McLuhan had seen in Tyrwhitt a conduit for Sigfried Giedion's thought and architectural culture.[76] However, Tyrwhitt's elaborations on her "Village Centre" and her travels to workshops around South and South East Asia piqued his curiosity. She had spent a fair amount of time discussing with him her ideas around "cores" and the CIAM 8 publication she had coedited with Josep Lluís Sert and Ernesto Rogers, *Heart of the City* (1952), which McLuhan included in the reading list that featured the likes of Sigfried Giedion, Karl Deutsch, and Dorothy D. Lee.[77] In addition, he scheduled her for a presentation on cores and asked her for an essay on the UN seminar and exhibition in India to include in *Explorations* (Carpenter's pet project that McLuhan had deftly appropriated for the seminar's outreach campaign).[78] Tyrwhitt's work offered glimpses into the new world order and its communication systems, and for that reason it was invaluable to McLuhan. At the time, McLuhan had been exploring the theoretical framework of Harold Innis, the Canadian political economist who had been researching transportation systems as communication networks, considering in particular the different perspectives his work brought to media theory. Departing from his earlier work on staples (cod, timber, fur) and their structuring role in colonial peripheries, Innis had launched a new research program around a communications theory centered on imperial formations.[79] "It has seemed to me that the subject of communication offers possibilities in that it occupies a crucial position in the organization and administration of government and in turn of empires and of Western civilization," Innis claimed in his introduction to *Empire and Communications* (1950). Innis believed that the media and communication infrastructures were structural to empires and hence defined their operational characteristics, resulting in "monopolies of knowledge" that only aggravated differentials.[80] Stripping Innis's theory of its political implications—McLuhan notoriously reduced media to "sensory factors" and "art forms"—he also set out to define the media "bias" of an emerging global condition for which the UN appeared to be the principal organ and Tyrwhitt a point of access to the institution's networks and database.

Yet Tyrwhitt's influence on McLuhan's work is hard to trace within this particular archive. In the years that followed her return and eventual departure, McLuhan slowly replaced "tribe" with "village," creating the now overused moniker for globalization of any kind, economic or cultural—the "global village." McLuhan's papers say very little as to the nature of this change, but the questions are worth asking: Why, suddenly, did McLuhan decide that "tribe" was not enough of a descriptor for the global imaginary that mass media were probing? Why did "village" enter his vocabulary and how? In terms of his correspondence with architectural and planning figures, his admiration for Sigfried Giedion and his collaboration with Edmund Carpenter do not substantiate this shift. For that matter, neither Giedion nor Carpenter spent much time thinking about the physical realities of villages. The only person in that group to bring to the table a conversation around cores, perceptions of the environment, and the value of contextual knowledge and experience was Tyrwhitt. In such a context, how is a historian or scholar to do feminist work in an archive that is not feminist by either design or inclination? How is one to unearth influences and appropriations that do not have a record, particularly in a field and context where very few actors could imagine that women held any position in society other than that of assisting and curating the "auteur"? Perhaps a first step would be to destabilize the certainty surrounding archives and the information they deliver, the evidence borne by mere fact, but also the certainty surrounding authorship and the fixation on singular figures.

The world that Tyrwhitt was navigating becomes very palpable if we consider her role as ghost editor and serial amanuensis for a veritable queue of men, first Geddes, then Giedion, and eventually Doxiadis. Giedion, as Ellen Shoshkes has meticulously demonstrated, at times even appropriated her language, acknowledging her input only in the fifth edition of *Space, Time and Architecture*.[81] Can McLuhan's citational silence not be added to this list? Tyrwhitt spent her thirties and forties in unstable, visiting teaching positions around the world, with no job security at a time when most of her male peers had permanent positions in prestigious institutions. When she considered applying for the UN position, Giedion tried to shepherd her toward UNESCO as an institution with a clear agenda toward culture and hence more appropriate for women. He declared the larger UN fabric as too "big" of an organization and "too much involved in the politics of the day" for Tyrwhitt to participate there. Weissmann, the man who offered her the directorship of the UN seminar, confided his doubts to Giedion about the UN wanting to "hire a woman"—presumably for a leading position, since most of the secretarial work and human infrastructure was filled with women. Only Catherine Bauer, urban planner and close friend, supported her ambition to pursue the position that could have the most influence on the fields of planning and housing.[82]

Within a year of the Toronto seminars, Tyrwhitt convinced McLuhan to expand the university library's collection and add a section on development research. New acquisitions included Erwin Anton Gutkind's *Community and Environment: A Discourse on Social Ecology* and UNESCO reports on communications and education.[83] The economists of the group, most significantly William Thomas (Tom) Easterbrook, foregrounded development as one of the most pressing issues that economists were seeking to resolve in terms of "studies of communications."[84] Carpenter and McLuhan, on the other hand, were more interested in seeing "underdeveloped countries" as the sites of media primitivism—Tyrwhitt, not as much. When asked to discuss her work in India, instead of talking about villages, she turned her attention to one of the UN field trips to Fatehpur Sikri, the Mughal emperor Akbar's historic and abortive capital city, foiling the Toronto group's efforts to project onto Indian villages media tribalism.[85] In "The Moving Eye," the article to follow her initial presentation to the group, she argued that the "western gaze," with its "single viewpoint" and "dominating eye," was slowly being replaced with new modalities of viewing, outside the empirical sciences of the West, that she believed structured Fatehpur Sikri in distinct ways.[86] She told McLuhan and the readers of *Explorations* that what she had learned was the presence of another view that was yet out of her field of comprehension. McLuhan later expanded her argument to claim that the "electronification" of communications replaced the single perspective with a field of multiple perspectives. "Today with electronics," he wrote to Tyrwhitt as he was contemplating his *Gutenberg Galaxy*, the first publication to introduce the term "global village," "we have discovered that we live in a global village, and the job is to create a global *city*, as center for the village margins," alluding to Tyrwhitt's cores but furthermore to the international institutions that this core hosted as the managers of education and differential internationalism: mud and bricks in the village, film and paper in the new metropolises.[87]

When McLuhan looked at Tyrwhitt's work, he saw something that perhaps she herself did not particularly attend to: at work in the model village was the construction of a new "center without periphery." That new "center without periphery" reclaimed old colonial channels as its own pathways of communication and tied the entire globe into "a community of continuous learning": learning to earn a living, learning one's role within the community, eventually learning how to inhabit and occupy even the most familiar structures as if they were foreign. Unlike a tribe, it was as if the "village," especially Tyrwhitt's village, materialized in space what he argued was happening with the advent of mass media. Everyone had a place in Tyrwhitt's village—the Indian farmer, the Indonesian builder, the UNESCO delegate, the CIAM planner—and it was their place in the chain of development that determined their relative position to the systems of information circulation that sought to reiterate the structural asymmetries that made their presence necessary. These social and economic differences structured the way local communities experienced their linkage to and place within global networks and the postcolonial world.

CONCLUSIONS

Tyrwhitt's Village Centre is revealing of the differential internationalism that informed the governmental logic of the UN. During the seminar, it was not "Nehru showing India" but rather Tyrwhitt "showing Nehru India" anew, pointing to the ever more prominent role that technical advisers played in the ordering of the world.[88] Tyrwhitt's innovation was to produce something mundane and replicable, as opposed to the spectacular, which traditionally draws crowds. She showed people what they already knew, the Indian village, and told them that they actually did not know it. "This 'Village Centre' incorporates nothing that is not in the existing programme of the Community Projects Administration," Tyrwhitt claimed. "It is simply a visual expression of the idea," she noted.[89] In its effort to impart technique without form to the Indian government, the UN ended up locking both international experts and local communities into their respective positions.

At the same time, developmentalism in the village activated anew the movement of North American and European experts, reconfiguring the network of urban planning actors in the post–World War II period as the CIAM was heading toward its resolution. The seminar introduced Tyrwhitt to Doxiadis at the same time that it introduced Doxiadis—and other UN consultants such as Charles Abrams and Jacob Crane—to the developing world. *Ekistiks*, the journal around which Doxiadis built a community of planners, started in 1954 as an annotated bibliography under the title *Tropical Housing & Planning Monthly Bulletin*, a response to conversations between Doxiadis and Tyrwhitt in Delhi. These conversations, and the journal coming out of them, aimed to actively produce the common ground between development and planning.[90] Tyrwhitt returned to the role of a UN technical consultant three more times, establishing programs on town and regional planning in universities around the world, from Toronto to Bandung and from the UK to Mumbai. Rather than shrinking the consultant's operative territory, the village ended up expanding it.

Bringing McLuhan's conceptual term vis-à-vis this history allows us to demythologize the "global village" and the narratives of "prophecy" with which it has been associated. McLuhan was not interested in predicting the effects of economic and cultural globalization, the causal outcomes that so many development experts professed in hawking their intellectual wares. He limited himself to observing the new communications infrastructures and systems of information circulation that international institutions put forward after 1945. To introduce it in media theory, McLuhan had to divorce the global village from its empirical grounding in the UN's development work and depoliticize it from its governmental mission, recasting it as a metaphor to describe a new form of colonialism. To put it in the words of Gayatri C. Spivak, McLuhan's appropriation of the rural to describe the electrification of communications was "colonialism's newest trick."[91] The "village" as a conceptual tool of globalization would make it possible to imagine rearranging the physical world, redistributing resources, and expanding the operations of capital while disguising itself as a form of self-determination, an ideological sleight of hand necessitated in the post-1945 world order given the decolonizing fervor amongst the UN's newest nation-states. The "global village" was never meant to be singular; rather, it was many parallel systems that may or may not have overlapped and that functioned to separate the circulation of information from that of capital, a process that sustained rather than resolved social and economic difference on a global scale. And within these overlapping systems, development, in its essence, mobilized media—the technical adviser, film, radio, the village—to actually enlarge and stabilize the organization, not the world.

NOTES

1 Nolan addresses poignantly in her work the production of the "primitive" and "savage" as analytical categories in anthropology and media: Ginger Nolan, *The Neocolonialism of the Global Village* (Minneapolis: University of Minnesota Press, 2018); and Ginger Nolan, *Savage Mind to Savage Machine: Racial Science and Twentieth Century Design* (Minneapolis: University of Minnesota Press, 2021).
2 Arturo Escobar, *Encountering Development: The Making and Unmaking of the Third World* (Princeton, NJ: Princeton University Press, 1995); M. Ijlal Muzaffar, "The Periphery Within: Modern Architecture and the Making of the Third World" (Diss., Cambridge, Massachusetts Institute of Technology, 2007).
3 Ayala Levin and Neta Feniger, "Introduction: The Modern Village," *The Journal of Architecture* 23, no. 3 (2018): 361–366; Ayala Levin, "The Village Within: An Alternative Genealogy of the Urban Village," *The Journal of Architecture* 23, no. 3 (April 3, 2018): 392–420.
4 The basic agreement was signed on April 2, 1952. See: Supplementary Agreement No. 7 to the Basic Agreement concerning Technical Assistance between the United Nations and the Government of India, October 30, 1953. TyJ/31/9, RIBA.
5 Jaqueline Tyrwhitt, History of UN Seminar on Housing & Community Improvement, May 3, 1954. TyJ/32/1, RIBA.
6 Letter from Hinder to Steinig, February 24, 1953. TyJ/31/9, RIBA.
7 Shoshkes's thorough biography shows how integral Tyrwhitt was to post-World War II planning culture. See: Shoshkes, *Jaqueline Tyrwhitt*; Shoshkes; Ellen Shoshkes, "Jaqueline Tyrwhitt and the Internationalization of Planning Education," in *Urban Planning Education: Beginnings, Global Movement and Future Prospects*, eds. Andrea I. Frank and Christopher Silver (Berlin: Springer, 2018), 65–80. For more details on the war correspondence course, see: Ines Maria Zalduendo, "Jaqueline Tyrwhitt's Correspondence Courses: Town Planning in the Trenches," 2005, https://dash.harvard.edu/handle/1/13442987.

8 Letter from Hinder to Steinig, May 14, 1953. TyJ/31/9, RIBA.
9 Letter from Tyrwhitt to Hinder, October 11, 1953. TyJ/31/9, RIBA.
10 Letter from Tyrwhitt to Hinder, June 23, 1953. TyJ/31/9, RIBA.
11 Letter from Tyrwhitt to Marshall McLuhan, August 30, 1953. 43–5–6–10–6, Gta archiv/ETH.
12 Letter from Tyrwhitt to Mr. Ebrahim al Kazi, September 4, 1953. TyJ/31/3, RIBA; and Letter from H. L. Keenleyside to Indian Minister of Foreign Affairs, June 16, 1953. TyJ/31/9, RIBA.
13 The set is here: 43–5–6–10–4-F1; 43–5–6–10–4-F3, and 43–5–6–10–4-F4, Gta archiv/ETH.
14 Letter from Hinder to P. S. Lokanathan, June 3, 1953. TyJ/31/9, RIBA. For more on Tyrwhitt's use of the "core" in the exhibition, see: Shoshkes, "Jaqueline Tyrwhitt," 141–164; Farhan Karim, "Negotiating a New Vernacular Subjecthood for India, 1914–54: Patrick Geddes, Jaqueline Tyrwhitt, and the Anti-Utopian Turn," *South Asia Journal for Culture* 5 & 6 (n.d.): 51–72.
15 Memorandum from Jaqueline Tyrwhit to N. P. Dube, June 23, 1953. TyJ/31/9, RIBA.
16 Letter from L. Steinig to Shri N. P. Dube, June 10, 1953. TyJ/31/9, RIBA.
17 Letter from Tyrwhitt to Hinder, June 19, 1953. TyJ/31/9, RIBA. For more information on the architects and place of the UN seminar within Nehru's program, see Peter Scriver and Amit Srivastava, *India* (London: Reaktion Books, 2015), 134–137, 147–151.
18 Letter from Tyrwhitt, February 12, 1954. TyJ/32/1, RIBA.
19 Tyrwhitt, "Preliminary Budget for the UN–TAB Village Centre," July 8, 1953; Letter from Tyrwhitt to Hinder, September 19, 1953; and J. Tyrwhitt, Memorandum on Position of Work, November 14, 1953. TyJ/31/9, RIBA.
20 Ernest Weissman, *Opening Remarks, International Federation for Housing and Town Planning*, Proceedings of the South East Asia Regional Conference, February 1–7, 1954. TyJ/29, RIBA.
21 Untitled document, May 19, 1953. TyJ/31/9, RIBA.
22 For an in-depth discussion of the debates and practices that informed Tyrwhitt's embedded model village, see Farhan Karim, *Modernism of Austerity: Designing an Ideal House for the Poor* (Pittsburgh: Pittsburgh University Press, 2019).
23 Partha Chatterjee, *A Possible India: Essays in Political Criticism* (Delhi and New York: Oxford University Press, 1998), 31–34, 40–50; M. S. Swaminathan, "Jawaharlal Nehru and Agriculture in Independent India," *Current Science* 59, no. 6 (1990): 303–307. For a conversation about Nehru's technocratic policies and the emergence of a "quantitative state," see the important conversation set up by Ateya Khorakiwala: Ateya Khorakiwala, *The Well-Tempered Environment: Modern Architecture in the Quantitative State, India (1943–1984)* (Ph.D. thesis, Harvard University, 2016). Ginger Nolan's chapter in this volume (Chapter 7) highlights further issues pertaining to these initatives.
24 Alice Thorner, "Nehru, Albert Mayer, and Origins of Community Projects," *Economic and Political Weekly* 16, no. 4 (1981): 117–120.
25 For a historical examination of the project, see Nicole Sackley, "Village Models: Etawah, India, and the Making and Remaking of Development in the Early Cold War," *Diplomatic History* 37, no. 4 (September 2013): 749–778; Nick Cullather, *The Hungry World: America's Cold War Battle Against Poverty in Asia* (Cambridge, MA: Harvard University Press, 2013), 80–94.
26 Karuna Mantena, *Alibis of Empire: Henry Maine and the Origins of Indirect Rule* (Princeton, NJ: Princeton University Press, 2009), 2–11, 119–147.
27 Mohandas Gandhi, *Village Swaraj*, ed. H. M. Vyas (Ahmedabad: Navajivan Publishing House, 1962), 30–32.
28 Here I am extending Trivedi's argument that the *khadi* constituted a critique to Western materialism to also include the village. See: Lisa Trivedi, *Clothing Gandhi's Nation: Homespun and Modern India* (Bloomington, IN: Indiana University Press, 2007), 1–37.
29 Gandhi, *Village Swaraj*, 10.
30 Ibid., 170–172. For a discussion of the place of craftsmanship in Gandhian and post-Gandhian thought, see Arindam Dutta, *The Bureaucracy of Beauty: Design in the Age of Its Global Reproducibility* (New York: Routledge, 2007), 235–277.
31 Jaqueline Tyrwhitt, "The Village Centre at the Exhibition on Low Cost Housing, Delhi, 1954," *Ekistics* 52, no. 314/315 (1985): 430.
32 Eric Paul Mumford, *The CIAM Discourse on Urbanism, 1928–1960* (Cambridge, MA: MIT Press, 2000), 201–204.
33 Sigfried Giedion, "The Need for a New Monumentality," in *New Architecture and City Planning: A Symposium*, ed. Paul Zucker (New York: Philosophical Library, 1944).
34 Jaqueline Tyrwhitt, "Cores with the Urban Constellation," in *CIAM 8: The Heart of the City: Towards the Humanisation of Urban Life*, eds. Jaqueline Tyrwhitt, Josep Lluís Sert, and Ernesto N Rogers (London: Lund Humphries, 1952), 103.
35 Tyrwhitt, Sert, and Rogers, *CIAM 8*, 36–40.
36 Letter from Tyrwhitt to Hinder, November 9, 1953; and Letter from Hinder to Tyrwhitt, December 23, 1953. TyJ/31/9, RIBA.
37 Letter from Hinder to Tyrwhitt, December 22, 1953. TyJ/31/9, RIBA.
38 Memorandum from Jaqueline Tyrwhit to N. P. Dube, June 23, 1953. TyJ/31/9, RIBA.
39 Letter from Hinder to P. S. Lokanathan, June 3, 1953. TyJ/31/9, RIBA.

40 Jaqueline Tyrwhitt, "Creation of the Village Centre (Delhi)," *Ekistics* 52, no. 314/315 (1985): 431.
41 Jaqueline Tyrwhitt, "Many Problems in the Evolution of the Ideal Village," *The Statesmans Engineering Feature*, n.d. TyJ/39/2, RIBA.
42 Technical Assistance Programme, United Nations Seminar on Housing and Community Improvement in Asia and the Far East, New Delhi, January 21–February 1954, December 1, 1954. TyJ/28/3, RIBA.
43 United Nations Regional Seminar on Housing and Community Improvement, Final Draft of Conclusions. TyJ/28/3, RIBA.
44 Broadcast Talk to England, Script January 19, 1954. TyJ/32/1, RIBA.
45 Jaqueline Tyrwhitt, "Many Problems in the Evolution of the Ideal Village," *The Statemans Engineering Feature*, n.d. TyJ/39/2, RIBA.
46 Letter from Tyrwhitt to Hinder, December 22, 1953. TyJ/31/9, RIBA.
47 Letter from Tyrwhitt, February 12, 1954. TyJ/32/1, RIBA.
48 Tyrwhitt, "The Village Centre at the Exhibition on Low Cost Housing, Delhi, 1954," 430.
49 Housing and Town and Country Planning Section, Department of Social Affairs, United Nations, United Nations Regional Seminar on Housing and Community Improvement, New Delhi, 20 January–17 February 1954. TyJ/28/3, RIBA.
50 Letter from Tyrwhitt to Hinder, June 19, 1953. TyJ/31/9, RIBA.
51 Letter from Tyrwhitt to Hinder, October 15, 1953. TyJ/31/9, RIBA.
52 Tyrwhitt to Dube, Memorandum, June 23, 1953. TyJ/31/9, RIBA. Farhan Karim's chapter in this volume (Chapter 12) explicates a similar currency of optimism and "hope" in the construction section.
53 Tyrwhitt, Low-Cost Housing, October 1, 1953. TyJ/31/9, RIBA.
54 Tyrwhitt, "The Village Centre at the Exhibition on Low Cost Housing, Delhi, 1954," 430.
55 Jaqueline Tyrwhitt, "My UN Job in Delhi, 1954," *Ekistics* 52, no. 314/315 (1985): 489–489.
56 See: *Seminar on Architecture, March 1959* (New Delhi: Lalit Kala Akademi, 1959).
57 Jaqueline Tyrwhitt, *Patrick Geddes in India* (London: Lund Humphries, 1947).
58 Memorandum from Jaqueline Tyrwhitt to N. P. Dube, June 23, 1953. TyJ/31/9, RIBA.
59 Tyrwhitt, "Chandigarh," *Royal Architectural Institute of Canada* 32, no. 1: 11–20, 12; and Plane Madras/Bangalore, November 21, 1953. TyJ/31/4, RIBA.
60 Jaqueline Tyrwhitt, "Many Problems in the Evolution of the Ideal Village," *The Statemans Engineering Feature*, n.d. TyJ/39/2, RIBA.
61 Letter from Hinder to Tyrwhitt, January 29, 1954. TyJ/31/9, RIBA.
62 Tyrwhitt Notes. July 14, 1953. TyJ/31/9, RIBA.
63 United Nations Housing & Community Improvement, Memorandum, February 2, 1954. TyJ/29/3, RIBA.
64 Letter from Tyrwhitt to Hinder, March 4, 1954. TyJ/31/9, RIBA.
65 From Tyrwhitt to Hinder, June 10, 1953. TyJ/31/9, RIBA.
66 United Nations, *Social Progress through Community Development* (New York: United Nations Bureau of Social Affairs, 1955), 84–86.
67 Isabel Huacuja Alonso, "Radio, Citizenship, and the 'Sound Standards' of a Newly Independent India," *Public Culture* 31, no. 1 (January 1, 2019): 117–144.
68 Professor Tyrwhitt's Broadcast, January 3, 1954. TyJ/32/1, RIBA.
69 Jaqueline Tyrwhitt, Broadcast Talk to England, January 19, 1954. TyJ/32/1, RIBA.
70 Ford Foundation, Announcement of Interdisciplinary Research and Study Program. Box 204, Folder 26, MM-LAC.
71 For the letter informing Tyrwhitt, see Letter from Sidney Smith to Tyrwhitt, May 29, 1953. TyJ/18/2, RIBA.
72 Letter from McLuhan to Tyrwhitt, July 24, 1953. TyJ/18/2, RIBA.
73 Michael Darroch, "The Toronto School: Cross-Border Encounters, Interdisciplinary Entanglements," in *The International History of Communication*, eds. Peter Simonson and David W. Park (New York: Routledge, 2016), 276–301.
74 Letter from Tyrwhitt to McLuhan, August 20, 1953. TyJ/18/2, RIBA.
75 Darroch, "The Toronto School: Cross-Border Encounters, Interdisciplinary Entanglements"; Michael Darroch, "Bridging Urban and Media Studies: Jaqueline Tyrwhitt and the Explorations Group, 1951–1957," *Canadian Journal of Communication* 33 (2008): 147–169; Reto Geiser, *Giedion and America: Repositioning the History of Modern Architecture* (Zurich: Gta Verlag, 2018), 372–388.
76 Changing Patterns of Man and Society Associated with the New Media of Communication. Box 204, Folder 26, Marshall McLuhan Collection, Library and Archives Canada (MM-LAC).
77 Letter from McLuhan to Tyrwhitt, October 14, 1953. TyJ/18/2, RIBA.
78 Letter from McLuhan to Tyrwhitt, October 29, 1953 and December 8, 1953, TyJ/18/2, RIBA; and Report of the Ford Seminar, 1953–55. Box 204, Folder 26, MM-LAC.
79 Alexander John Watson, *Marginal Man: The Dark Vision of Harold Innis* (Toronto: University of Toronto Press, 2006), 3–25.

80 Harold Adams Innis, *Empire and Communications* (Toronto: Dundurn Press, 2008), 21–32, 138–163; Harold A. Innis, *The Bias of Communication* (Toronto: University of Toronto Press, 1951).
81 Shoshkes, "Jaqueline Tyrwhitt," 116.
82 Shoshkes's account is filled with these incidents. Quotes by Siegfried Giedion, Catherine Bauer, and Ernest Weissmann are found in Shoshkes, 104, 154.
83 At the time Gutkind was working on *International History of City Development*. See Culture & Communications Seminar, "Additions to Library," March 1955. TyJ/17/3, RIBA.
84 Culture & Communications Seminar, 26th Meeting, 1954/55. TyJ/17/3, RIBA.
85 Noted on the 8th Meeting, Culture & Communications Seminar, University of Toronto, November 24, 1954. 3-T-13-1-8, Gta archiv/ETH.
86 Jaqueline Tyrwhitt, "The Moving Eye," *Explorations*, no. 4 (February 1955): 115–119.
87 Marshall McLuhan, *Letters of Marshall McLuhan*, ed. Matie Molinaro, Corrine McLuhan, and William Toye (London: Oxford University Press, 1987), 278.
88 Tyrwhitt, "Creation of the Village Centre (Delhi)," 432.
89 International Federation for Housing and Town Planning, Proceedings of the South East Asia Regional Conference, February 1–7, 1954. TyJ/29, RIBA.
90 See: *Tropical Housing & Planning Monthly Bulletin*, no. 3 (October 1955). Constantinos A. Doxiadis Archives (CADA).
91 Gayatri Chakravorty Spivak, "Cultural Talks in the Hot Peace: Revisiting the 'Global Village,'" in *Cosmopolitics: Thinking and Feeling Beyond the Nation*, eds. Pheng Cheah and Bruce Robbins (Minneapolis: University Of Minnesota Press, 1998), 343.

14

"Ruralizing" Zambia

Doxiadis Associates' systems-based planning and developmentalism in the nonindustrialized South

Petros Phokaides

In the early 1960s, the question of urbanization took firm hold alongside broader debates that continued to be framed by the dilemma of industrialization and agricultural development. In Africa, for example, the United Nations' response to urbanization phenomena exposed a characteristic ambivalence. On the one hand, urbanization was seen as an inevitable trend in modernity, whereby social interaction, communication, and adjustment to social and political institutions could prompt, or so the UN claimed, individuals and local societies to escape "those traditional restrictions that hamper development."[1] On the other hand, other reports stressed the downside of this move from village to town, seen as "expos[ing] rural migrants to considerable mental strain."[2] Consequently, UN-prescribed regional planning, decentralization, and counter-urbanization strategies were as much designed as measures to regulate excessive migration from rural to urban areas in a bid to mitigate the social, cultural, political, and economic impact of that shift.[3]

The ambivalence toward urbanization and urban centers was further informed by a range of responses to Africa's extensive rural populations that highlighted its "revolutionary" potential in contradictory ways. From the mainstream economist Walter Rostow, who believed in Africa's potential to achieve an "agricultural revolution,"[4] to the anti-colonial intellectual Frantz Fanon, who found in Africa's "revolutionary peasantry" the catalytic force for decolonization,[5] rural Africa was routinely positioned as the primary locus of international developmental agendas, planning practices, and postcolonial aspirations. These parallel discourses of the early 1960s allow us to question the conventional but persisting view that links urbanization, along with emblematic urban plans and buildings, with development and nation building and to turn our attention to the crucial role of rural-focused visions in the shaping of Africa's postcolonial development and architectural histories. This chapter further highlights that these discourses and developmental agendas on the rural took fundamentally different forms within various nation-states and were intertwined in complex ways to these nations-states' distinct colonial legacies, patterns of social and racial divisions, and political and economic structures, not to rule out the personalities of postcolonial leaders and patterns of developmental aid and expertise, each of these factors being additionally challenged by the geopolitical dynamics of decolonization. To understand the circumstances under which agendas for "ruralization" emerged and reformulated within particular contexts, this chapter focuses on 1960s–1970s Zambia, during the time when the newly founded country considered the socioeconomic development of rural areas as key to its economic restructuring and nation building.

In the broader histories of development, Zambia has a paradigmatic value. For one, the country was already established as the "largest producer of copper in the developing world,"[6] with an extensive private mining sector that lent the country the additional distinction of being among the most "urbanized" in sub-Saharan Africa. At the same time, the largest part of its African population continued to practice agriculture in near-subsistence levels, remaining physically and symbolically disconnected from the country's wealth and development. This contrast between high population concentrations around mining and related activities and low-density countryside exemplified the uneven impact of extractive capitalism and settler colonialism in Africa that also conditioned Zambia's postcolonial future. Disengaging from this economic pattern, rooted in the country's past as a white settlers' colony in the 1920s, became the focus of national political-economic agendas that turned independent Zambia into a showcase for development discourses formulated within and for the "non-industrialized" South. Drawing on economic theories developed in 1950s Latin America, Zambia's early development planning was focused on import-substitution strategies envisioning the ambitious transformation of rural areas into hubs of productive and consumption activities. In line with these agendas, the country was placed on a distinct path among its neighboring countries, whose rural development was also intrinsically tied to their efforts to establish national sovereignty: while Kenya followed moderate reforms continuing colonial legacies that relied on customary laws in order to administer rural areas, Tanzania completely replaced them, promoting decentralization and direct state control over the land and the population. Zambia, on the other hand, would make attempts to bypass the power of customary authorities by promoting state-led plans for rural settlements. The country's attempts for rural development manifested the aspirations, contradictions, and challenges of postcolonial development, eventually, however, failing to disengage from the monopoly of copper, the "resource curse," as some have put it. Its poor performance in rural areas became the focus of several studies that emphasized an "urban-bias" in states' economic policies, as in other Third World countries, and their adverse effects on agricultural production and rural poverty. These charges of "bias" in state policies offered empirical support to the broader shift in development thinking on a global level from the mid-1970s onwards. The new developmental agendas that unfolded afterward targeted small-scale farmers and the rural "poor" and were promoted also in Zambia as a solution to a debt crisis, making the country a testing ground for another wave of ruralizing agendas in the Global South.

By focusing on the paradigmatic case of Zambia, this chapter attempts to offer critical insights into the complex ties between planning practices and developmental discourses, as well as their links to systems thinking. It will do this by examining the goals and aspirations behind a rural settlement project assigned by the government of Zambia to Doxiadis Associates in 1967 and by investigating the ways in which the firm's planning approach overlapped with various rural-based visions of the development era. The chapter will compare the political rhetoric of the country's president, Kenneth Kaunda, and the planning theories of Constantinos Doxiadis in their varied emphases on rural areas as bearing the potential to shape "human-centered" development policies, presumably against the impact of industrialization and urbanization but more importantly to aid in ideological objectives of social reorganization and integration. The chapter further investigates the way that the economic agenda of the state and its patrons conceptualized rural settlements as critical hubs in the restructuring of Zambia's copper-dependent economy for advancing the expansion of monetary exchanges over the country's agricultural sector. Capitalizing on these agendas, the work of Doxiadis Associates can be seen as advancing claims derived from a systems-based and spatio-economic planning approaches that would overhaul social life and productive patterns within a "restructured" rural landscape. Finally, the chapter demonstrates the manner in which the firm's attempts to shift planning strategies were a response to contestations around rural development as well as broader epistemological shifts that called for more "flexible" and facilitative forms of planning.

"HUMANISM" AS A RURAL-BASED DEVELOPMENT POLICY

"[We] hereby unequivocally declare the birth of the Second Revolution by unanimously adopting the new policy of Humanism enunciated by our beloved leader, a policy which bears a stamp which is neither Eastern or Western, Capitalist nor Communist, but Zambian and our firm belief that all authority springs from Man and as such all authority must be used for the betterment of Man."[7]

For Zambia's first President Kenneth Kaunda, this particular version of "Humanism," a loose philosophical framework shaped by and adopted as the country's official political/ideological program from 1967 onwards, drew inspiration from the rural context and village life, where African culture was thought to be predominantly "man-centered." Egalitarianism, communal effort, and attending the weak and the poor, Kaunda proclaimed, were the foundations of "mutual," "accepting," and "inclusive" rural way of living in "close contact with Nature."[8] As per the official declaration from which the preceding passage is extracted, rural-based social and cultural values would form the "foundations" of a developmental policy tailored to the needs and ideals of Zambia, steering clear of the "individualistic" and the "dehumanizing" effects of both capitalist and communist models.[9] Humanism would thus serve both as a canny strategy to negotiate the pressures of the Cold War and, domestically, as a moral compass to "guide" the newly founded country through the transformations of decolonization and development while appealing to a common heritage to foster national unity.

Immediately after this official declaration, Kaunda's government announced plans to promote rural settlement schemes. Introduced as part of a policy for village regrouping, these schemes were expected to facilitate "the redistribution of people in areas of over-population," and "the aggregation of population in the sparsely populated areas."[10] On April 26, 1967, the government signed an agreement with Doxiadis Associates for the study of sixteen settlements throughout the country (see Figure 14.1). The firm had already established a local office in Zambia since November 1966 and had delivered results in the design and implementation of the industrial development project in Kafue, 40 km south of the capital city, Lusaka. Evidence of the rural project's high priority for both the government and the president himself is borne by the subsequent meeting arranged between Kaunda and Doxiadis. Interrupting a busy traveling schedule, Doxiadis also visited Zambia for the first time, between June 25 and July 3, 1967, during which he eagerly accepted the new assignment, committed the firm to a fast delivery of the study in "half the period originally considered," and aligned his rhetoric to the president's Humanist philosophy.[11] Quite like Kaunda, as

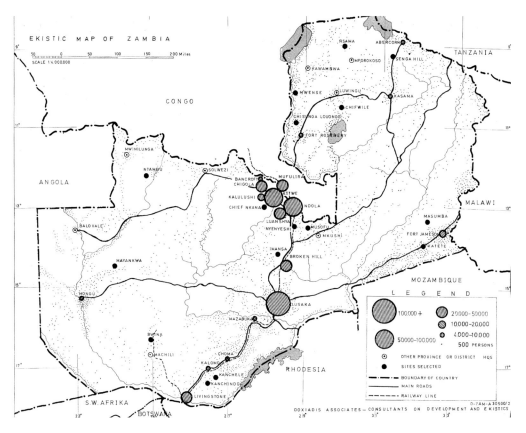

FIGURE 14.1 The rural settlements project involved several "selected sites" across Zambia's countryside.

indeed in the rhetoric of many such postcolonial leaders and experts of the time, Doxiadis's planning discourse also professed to promote "human-centered" development as a response to the social and environmental impacts of industrialized urbanization.[12] Exchanges from that meeting, which were partially disclosed in Doxiadis's internal memos and Kaunda's press interviews, revealed the political demands and aspirations for the rural settlement project while also shedding light on some of the planning assumptions advanced by Doxiadis.

Kaunda's Humanism both emerged from and may be read as an attempt to carve out a niche in the emancipatory Afrocentric visions of sub-Saharan countries, at a moment when decolonization and nation-building processes were being deeply challenged as persistent tribal divides emerged across the continent, accompanied by growing sociopolitical tensions that threatened many of the artificial national borders that had been drawn by erstwhile and extant colonial powers.[13] The brutal civil war in Congo to its north, riven by neocolonial intervention, and the 1966 military overthrow of Kwame Nkrumah's regime in Ghana impacted the independence of Zambia in 1964, founded amid the hostile white minority regimes of Mozambique and Angola, and in particular the 1965 declaration of a white minority government in Southern Rhodesia, to its immediate south. Humanism might thus be seen as a device to subsume tribe by race and to express Zambia's commitment to black majority rule and its attempts to unify the country in the face of segregational efforts aimed at African populations by white rulers, most notably in the case of South African apartheid. Kaunda's call to a common African culture thus drew on precedents like Pan-Africanism, Negritude, and African Socialism and particularly took aim at policies that excluded majority African populations from the continent's socioeconomic development. Privileging Africans/Zambians, defined in terms of their national identity, government policy was thus both a way of circumventing racialized or tribalized identities while at the same time both acknowledging and circumscribing the expert knowledge and economic initiatives offered by Europeans, Asians, and others in the country's efforts for development.[14] The shaping of a common national culture, promoted through Humanism, in Zambia thus primarily reflected the dynamics of tribal rather than racial groupings as well as other forms of ethnic/linguistic politics based in rural regions, which in a sense conditioned the country's geographical imbalances and its fraught domestic politics. "Humanism's" focus on rural areas thus had direct political implications in terms of the Kaundan regime's efforts to consolidate power and the ruling party's legitimacy in the countryside and beyond.

The Kaundan doctrine can thus be understood as Zambia's version of what Mamdani has called the "tripartite agenda of deracialization, detribalization, and economic development."[15] Turning the government's attention to rural societies thus represented an attempt to produce what could be the largest voting bank in the multi-party Zambia. In addition, rural areas could be transformed under this approach into a new economic theater divorced from resource extraction, given the potentially extensive pool of developmental resources in the countryside. Getting access to these resources, however, would mean disrupting the authority of powerful "tribal" groups and customary chiefs whose control over land rights was well established throughout most of Zambia's countryside. In the colonial era, control over the native population had been established on the basis of "indirect rule" by these tribal figures, which formalized the colonial regime as an assemblage of practices of "native" authority. Customary authority thus formed the core of the administrative logic of settler colonies like Zambia. To maintain rural areas as a semi-autonomous, self-regulated sphere, the governing of the countryside was assigned to local chiefs whose key role was to grant land rights to individuals–followers. These institutions were also bound up with gendered divisions of labor, as men mostly worked in the mines and commercial farms, circulating between various "combinations of 'hoe and wage,'"[16] whereas women were more confined to the rural areas "under despotic chieftaincies."[17] The reinforcing of "native" institutions relieved colonial governments from the financial responsibility of improving rural areas infrastructures, as indeed the administrative costs from adjudicating social or legal conflicts—the primary rationale for a state—one effect of which was the perpetuation of these areas at subsistence levels, thus serving as a cheap labor reserve for copper mining, European farming, and migrancy-driven urban servitude. Seen in this context, Humanism was an attempt to reclaim rural areas not only as a symbolic site of African/national heritage but also to negotiate and reform power structures inherited from colonialism and to establish the unifying authority of the central state across urban and rural spaces, as expressed by the official motto: One Nation, One Zambia. While these efforts would never entirely succeed, the Humanism doctrine was inherently responding to social expectations of the postcolonial state as the harbinger and primary agent of decolonization and economic redistribution and as the principal provider of social and economic security of its newly anointed "citizens."

In this respect, the government's rural objectives required maneuvering through its celebration of cultural traditions on the one hand and modernization through social and economic infrastructure on the other. As Kaunda admitted:

> I hesitate to interfere to any great extent with village life as it is today for the very reason that culturally we may be committing suicide—we might—without being aware of it, destroy some of the best things in our national culture. At the same time, to leave our villages as they are today means stagnation and the last may well be worse than the first. We cannot for instance, provide health services, schools, roads, markets and the many other necessities for each and every village throughout Zambia.[18]

The government's program for upgrading rural life would consequently follow a more cautious approach to policies of village regrouping and resettlement, particularly when compared to the much more assertive programs of the Julius Nyerere government in neighboring Tanzania. Proclaimed in the same year as Humanism, Nyerere's famous "Arusha Declaration" had also revealed Tanzania's broad nationalization program and the country's goals of agrarian self-reliance. Under these goals, constructing modern villages *ex novo* would provide the blueprint for a large-scale experiment in the name of socialist transformation with well-criticized effects.[19] In contrast, not only was Kaunda less radical, but his "ruralizing" vision would consciously not portray itself as contradicting Zambia's dependency on copper mining and international capitalism:

> Surely it is not beyond the capacity of man to devise ways and means . . . that would make it possible for us to accommodate the powerful forces in the Western type of economy, as well as preserve the man that is found in the small village unit who is not de-humanized, heart, soul, mind and body.[20]

Indicatively, Kaunda described this "man-centered society" as requiring "very careful planning" and where "[d]evelopment [would] mean changing certain attitudes of our people that stand between them and a fuller life."[21] Humanism, in a word, amount to a normalizing project shaping the interfaces of state development policy and the regulation of social behavior across urban and rural areas.

THE RHETORIC OF "HUMAN-CENTERED" DEVELOPMENT

Doxiadis's planning discourse, too, placed the figure of the human as the centerpiece of a normative project wherein planning would "guide" society through socioeconomic change. In this "man-centered" concept, Doxiadis propounded the idea of a universal subject beyond age, race, ethnicity, religion, class, and gender,[22] devoid of allusions to racial or cultural supremacy, allowing his rhetoric to appeal to both liberal and socialist aspirations of decolonization and First and Third World perspectives. Doxiadis perceived "Man" as a combination of "body, senses, mind and soul,"[23] possessed of life and with predetermined sensory and physical capacities, whose intellectual and spiritual capacities could reach beyond the immediate perceivable scales. In contrast to the Renaissance tradition (e.g., Da Vinci's erect Vitruvian man) as an idealized, static view of the human body, Doxiadis significantly emphasized the sensory and apperceptive aspects of the human, integrated into its environment as a "totality," prehensile, ambulatory, and migratory. In Doxiadis's "humanism," sensory experience was primary, where vision, movement, time-distances, and bodily energy became crucial planning parameters. The human was seen as a crucial component of an interconnected social and built environment.

Manifested in the concept of *Ekistics*, this theoretical/planning framework conceptualized human settlements as a system of five interconnected components: man, society, nature, shells, and networks. By considering man and society as dynamic and adaptable, this *ekistics*-driven approach conceived of the built environment (shells represent buildings of all kinds and networks refer to all infrastructures and communication systems) as a physical setting through which change could be affected both on human societies and nature. The regulation of these effects and their outcomes, Doxiadis presumed, required the development of "rational" and "comprehensive" planning approaches. *Ekistics* lay at the root of Doxiadis's emblematic planning ideas in the 1960s, such as the futuristic vision of Ecumenopolis. Ecumenopolis heralded the "end of traditional villages" on the assumption that in the future rural populations would embrace advanced cultivation techniques while land and settlement patterns would stabilize on a global level.[24] Although these discourses seemed to imply the prominence of the "industrial" and the "urban," Ecumenopolis was rather redefining the "rural," suggesting more generic concepts of spatial organization consisting of decentralized networks of small and middle-sized settlements within productive landscapes and offered as an antidote to an ill-planned and uncontrolled urbanization process.[25] These principles informed Doxiadis Associates' planning practice of the mid-1960s, particularly in Africa.

Doxiadis Associates' plans for rural settlements in Zambia were a significant element in the firm's proposals to accelerate Africa's development at the continental, national, and regional scale.[26] By proposing the transformation of what the firm argued was disorganized and outdated features of existing settlement patterns, the firm envisaged its planning techniques as accelerating the otherwise gradual and millennial transition from "nomadic food-gathering life . . . into the era of agriculture . . . to the urban stage."[27] To do this, the countryside would have be reorganized into a set of concentric scales. The population would resettle into small and middle-sized rural centers: a "village" of 1,000 people; the "rural township" of 2,000 inhabitants as the center for six surrounding villages; and the "market town" of 3,000 inhabitants as the center for six rural townships and the thirty-six surrounding villages.[28] In many ways, this strategy was seen as responding to the government's own objectives for village regrouping and provision of social infrastructure in the countryside. Kaunda thus endorsed Doxiadis's proposals as mirroring his idea of Humanism, in terms of presenting settlement planning as an intensification of the "natural" processes that would inevitably occur in development:

> He recognizes that in Zambia we do not have time to wait for this natural development, so that we have to re-group people somehow into larger units, eventually into smaller towns . . . and then into urban areas. . . . if we learn from him, we should go a long way to meet the demands of Humanism on our society.[29]

Both Doxiadis's and Kaunda's propositions on the transformation of rural Zambia followed their own separate but what they saw as converging postulations: for Doxiadis, the protection of "human"-values in an industrializing/urbanizing world, and for Kaunda, state-led settlement planning as a vehicle for social reorganization and integration beyond rural/urban divides. This convergence thus expressly and doubly mystified and obscured the substantial conflicts over power, representation, and resource usage that underlay these seemingly imperturbable objectives. Doxiadis's reductive view of development as an inevitable and linear process in essence ruled political negotiation and plural strategies off the picture, and in effect covered over the impact of new settlement patterns on social organization and existing institutions. For Kaunda, as we have seen, the promotion of rural development as a unifying political vision was responding to a fragmented social and political landscape. Kaunda's government had been founded in the face of conflict and pressures from multiple political and ideological groups, expressing conflicting interests around the distribution of wealth and the transfer of political, economic, and financial control to Africans. In the copper mines, African workers were demanding wage increases on par with expatriate levels.[30] Wealthy farmers supported opposition parties in favor of commercialized, large tract-based agricultural production.[31] Political rivals within Kaunda's own ruling party criticized him for his alliance with urban and international capital, further arresting the objectives of Zambianization.

SOUTH–SOUTH EXCHANGES AND THE "RESTRUCTURING" OF THE RURAL

The government's rural settlements project can also be seen as an index of Kaundan socialism's engagement with global developmental agendas of the time. Promoted as part of Zambia's First National Development Plan (FNDP), the project reflected key aspects of economic theories and planning practices circulating across the development landscape in the Third World. Following the suggestions of a 1964-Economic Survey organized by the United Nations Economic Commission in Africa (UNECA) and prepared by the British economist Dudley Seers,[32] Zambia's economic planning took aim at the country's extensive dependence on copper, envisaging a move from an export-oriented to an import-substitution economy. In this context, rural areas were seen as a critical component to a process of a broader economic restructuring as sites of both agricultural production and consumption.[33]

In this respect, Zambia's development was modeled differently from the Western or the Soviet-type industrialization model followed by Kwame Nkrumah in Ghana, or the Chinese agrarian model that had inspired Julius Nyerere in Tanzania. Instead, following Seers's guidelines, Zambia would become a testing ground for economic agendas that had emerged in the late 1950s in Latin America. These originated from the work of the Argentinian economist Raúl Prebisch at the UN Economic Commission for Latin America (ECLA), whose core-periphery model understood "underdevelopment" not as a stage in a linear process (as the modernization theories suggested) but rather as the outcome of imperial histories where industrialized countries (the core) developed at the expense of the nonindustrialized (the periphery).[34] The realization that unequal "development" patterns were perpetuated in international trade relations even after the end of colonialism inspired a move away from mainstream models and First/Second World approaches, which, according to Seers, had made economists "unfitted to understand, let alone solve, the problems of non-industrial societies."[35] Having served at ECLA from 1957 to 1961, Seers approached his leading role in surveying Zambia's economy as an opportunity to explore alternatives to mainstream economic aid and planning methods. "[V]isiting economists," he claimed, needed not only to understand a "country's special economic structure" but also to "acquire a 'feel' for local politics."[36] The 1964-Survey in Zambia thus incorporated the government's political aspirations into a planning approach that merged economic and social objectives, such as raising living and employment standards and consumption and literacy levels and claimed to promote the equality "between town and country, rich and poor, European and African."[37]

The fiscal bulwark for these economic agendas, for Seers and the FNDP, would remain the country's extensive copper resources, an "excellent foreign exchange earner," the assumption of a steady flow of earnings being seen as essential for the restructuring of the economy and the development of new sectors. Writing his report just prior to the end of colonial rule, Seers was optimistic that an independent government could take over mining rights back from the mining monopolies that operated "in some respects [as] an enclave" generating massive capital flowing mostly out of the country.[38] Yet the country was bound by a 1950-agreement with United Kingdom, which had fixed copper royalties until 1986.[39] What was left within the country in wages, taxes, and local exchange formed the government's primary revenue, thus making Zambia entirely dependent on fluctuations in the copper value, whose price was ultimately also set by the London Metal Exchange. As a domestic industrial sector did not exist, the country relied all the more on imports, leading to an even greater capital outflow. On this account, the country's economic planning remained invested in the uninterrupted but also growing operation of American and South African mining monopolies, much like the way colonial governments had been in the past.

In this context, the creation of a domestic market and a fairer redistribution of the country's substantial copper revenues occupied centerfield in the country's developmental strategy, bolstered by the rhetoric of restoring the territorial and social imbalances that had aggravated in the 1950s.[40] This ambitious goal, Seers would have us believe, would be better served through the introduction of economic planning methods that closely observed the actual conditions of a nonindustrialized economy that was undergoing "structured change."[41] Criticizing models and methods that had emerged in industrialized economies, such as the Stone-Meade National Accounting System that had been influenced by Keynes's theories,[42] Seers advocated modifying the "input-output system" that had been introduced in the 1950s to map the "complex series of transactions in which actual goods and services are exchanged among real people."[43] This "modified input-output system," Seers claimed, disaggregated economic activities, allowing a closer look into the "fabric" of a country's actual economic structure, as opposed to the "aggregative accounting systems" that had limited application outside of industrialized, socially homogenous, and fully marketized economies.

The "modified" input-output model would not serve as a mere means of analysis: it was seen as an essential tool in the work of economic planning itself. Considered as "highly flexible" to respond even to the lack of economic data in the country, the use of this model aimed primarily to capture the particularities of an export-dependent economy and record subsistence production along with the "formal" agricultural sector, as well as highlight distinct income and consumption patterns of the main racial groups: Europeans and Africans. Rather than accounting only the growth of the main economic sectors—mining and commercial agriculture—this approach was intended to provide a wholistic view, thus allowing the means to supplant the dominance of industry over agriculture and urban populations over rural, but also Europeans over Africans. By shedding light onto the economic activities of the African population, this developmental logic aspired to intensify existing and create new threads of exchanges and economic activities, as an attempt to "weave" the nation together by restoring social and regional desegregations caused by colonial policies.

The economy was thus conceptualized as an aggregate of interactions and effects transmitted via a socioeconomic "fabric." Fraught with determinism and linearity, this economic thinking assumed that an investment in one sector of the economy would not only create growth in that sector but also generate a dispersed set of feedback or complementary effects, producing new demands and new productive activities, in capitalist and noncapitalist (rural) sectors alike. Surpassing what it saw as some of the "biases" of mainstream modernization theories, this logic envisioned development not in terms of a transition from "tradition" to "modernity" but as integrating the rural sector within the national economy. Expanding monetary exchanges and commodity flows and services in and out of rural areas would incorporate them both as a productive sector and as a market into the socioeconomic "fabric" of the nation. The net effect, as expressed in the FNDP, would be the shaping of an "integrated society in which all participate in a monetary exchange economy."[44]

Rural settlements were therefore conceptualized as critical hubs to advance these agendas by facilitating flows and exchanges into and out of these areas, but without the concomitant disruption of customary land tenure systems and existing cultivation methods. The critique of Western, mainstream theories of *homo economicus* also played out in the selection of the main actors to lead these transformations. Rather than privileging supposed self-maximizing actors and "energetic individuals," the stated imperative of maintaining "village community life" led instead to a focus on family-based or cooperative-scale farming.[45] Village-level planning and land distribution on a family basis were seen as the appropriate solution to increase and appropriate agricultural surplus, rather than increasing the percentage of Africans involved in large-scale commercial farming, which continued to be dominated by Europeans. The rural settlements scheme was thus conceived as a form of direct state-led intervention, in terms of providing permanent access to cultivable land and the technical support that would create a rural environment combining farming, trading, socializing, and improved living conditions. Such planned communities, economists believed, could integrate and nurture "radical changes in the social organization of scattered rural populations" and contribute overall to the rural people's "psychological re-orientation towards a monetary economy."[46]

While official developmental agendas only conceptually and propositionally incorporated rural areas into the logic of the monetary economy, it was the work of Doxiadis Associates, and in essence their architectural métier, that expanded these agendas in its positing concrete, empirical links between economic territory and physical terrain. Significant here was the firm's professed emphasis on the extensive survey of local contexts. Its studies comprised extensive "ethnographic" methodologies to capture the complexities of rural life in terms of land use, settlement patterns, cultivation methods, and varieties of architectural expressions with the goal to "to derive the general characteristics of these rural areas . . . and, to propose standards that could be adopted in general,"[47] as opposed to particularities that pertained only to a limited set of instances. The studies also emphasized nonvisual, nonsymbolic aspects as critical parameters to analyze settlement patterns. For example, local cultivation and living patterns were abstracted into spatio-economic forms that would then be recomposed and reassembled in a restructured rural landscape (see Figure 14.2).

This logic prevailed on all scales: from the reorganization of rural settlements and their interconnections, to the rearrangement of land and cultivation patterns, all the way to the design of semi-urban/semi-rural settlement plans. The firm used calculations of spatial distribution of population, cultivation land, and amenities to shape settlement patterns.

"RURALIZING" ZAMBIA

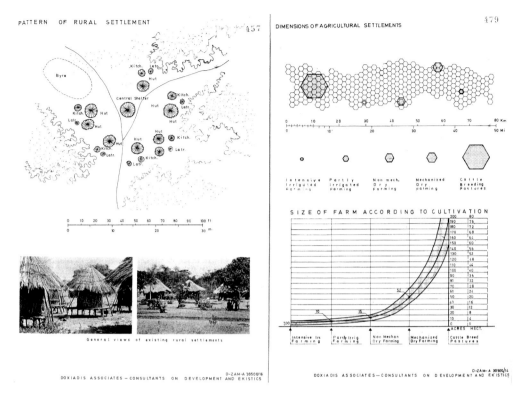

FIGURE 14.2 Pages from Doxiadis Associates' report that demonstrate the firm's methodologies in surveying the Zambian countryside (selected by the author): on the left, the documentation of existing rural settlement patterns and architectural expressions; on the right, the spatio-economic diagrams as an attempt to calculate and turn different cultivation patterns into manageable design parameters.

One key parameter was travel time: the firm estimated walking distances for routine and nonroutine movements across various activities, between dwellings and fields, and between settlements and the local or regional centers where basic and specialized services could be obtained. The goal was to provide better services while at the same time shaping more efficient local production patterns by recalibrating and integrating commuting and local supply chains. As less time and energy was spent in traveling to obtain resources of various kinds, the argument went, more time would be devoted to the most critical activities of farming, socializing, and surplus trading.

Physical and social "stability" were seen as essential to achieve the effects of this form of planning, a conviction shared by modern planners across the spectrum in this period. For Doxiadis Associates, one of the principal obstructions to development were the "fluidity" of Zambian rural settlement patterns, the result of unpredictable and "constant movements over the land in response to ecological demands as well as flooding or kinship pressures."[48] Rather than leave the economy to the vagaries of social or climatic fate, planning would involve the normalization of incoming and outcoming flows, whether in terms of everyday activities, labor patterns, supplies, or services, at the regional as well as settlement levels. Clear zones would be demarcated, each associated by type of activity, circulation, and division of labor. The outcome was a rectilinear settlement with a north–south orientation organized into three zones, with housing on one end, abutting a central zone of social/public amenities. A third zone comprised manufacturing and storage activities, placed along a service road segregated from regional traffic so as to allow "quick transportation of fertilizers, goods and equipment and the smooth outflow of the agricultural production to marketing centers."[49] Maximizing and speeding up local flows was critical not only for raising agricultural productivity and capturing surplus production, but, also, as the firm noted, to allow "information of all kinds referring to agricultural production ... to flow rapidly into the rural settlements."[50] In including spaces for district authorities, police stations, courts, even fire stations, state power would be coterminous with these settlements, facilitating the greater control over customary authorities (see Figure 14.3).

Doxiadis Associates saw these new, permanent settlements as key to internalize new social and economic demands and to foster a new rural consciousness that capitalized on themes of surplus agricultural economy and national rather than "tribal" identity. The demarcation of spheres of activity by function rather than consanguinity—farming fields, public spaces/amenities, and the household—would provide the means to recompose the varied identities of the rural population, highlighting instead a more communitarian identity.[51] In physical terms, for instance, settlement design could create "a sense of cohesion and urbanity" by

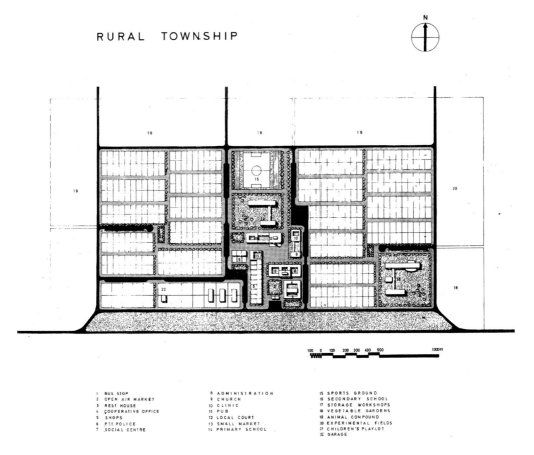

FIGURE 14.3 A model plan for a "rural township" that was conceived as a settlement of 440 × 880 m. and 2,000 inhabitants, as a regional hub offering services for six "villages" and their 6,000 inhabitants.

avoiding continuous linear paths and unobstructed views to the surrounding uninhabited landscape.[52] Likewise, the central zone of social and public infrastructure would promote, presumably, "social interaction and progress within the rural settlement"[53] and without. In contrast to the highly detailed specifications for public spaces and amenities, the plans offered no information on household plots, limiting themselves merely to plot locations, their number, and overall dimension. According to the firm, each plot would offer space for a "small private garden, one or two domestic animals (even if these do not yet exist), and space for a cart or eventually a tractor." The combination of agricultural field and "garden," that is, the mixture of economic activities combining both cash-crop and subsistence agriculture, would thus afford a measure of economic resilience.

The adjustments made to these model plans as part of these projects' realization tend to markedly elide much of the firm's original rationale, exposing how the development of rural areas was guided along significant, yet untenable, state investments over a thirty-year time frame. Despite the optimism expressed by Seers's and Doxiadis Associates' planning outlook in looking to the country's substantial copper reserves as the primary resource for development funding for rural development, other priorities and economic challenges kept the rural economy largely as a subsidized agricultural sector.[54] The country continued to rely on its copper monopoly, while state-directed import-substitution strategies led to the establishment of new industries and manufacturing that largely concentrated on the Zambia's single Kasama-Livingstone rail line, thus further vitiating the prospects of economic redistribution and intensifying existing geographic imbalances. In their failure to expand the domestic market, these strategies further "aggravated the duality"[55] between urban/industrial and rural sectors (see Figure 14.1). Development planning thus oversaw a process where the rural population was significantly weakened in their power against that of the growing urban middle classes and elites. They continued to depend on manually intensive jobs in the cities and in industry and were burdened by the risks of small-scale farming (weather, life patterns, migration) while weathering the impact of frequent changes in direction of state economic policies (new crop policies, subsidies, fertilizers, credit schemes, etc.). The use of unpaid labor, subsistence farming, customary laws, cyclical migration, other sources of income, and broader shifting patterns of labor both within the household and the "peasantry" remained viable strategies for mitigating risks for the urban and industrial elite. As effective development of Zambia's rural areas began to appear less and less feasible by the end of the 1960s, the unsettling effects of rural out-migration generated academic and policy concerns about the nature and extent of state-led interventions in rural economies, in the process triggering new and broad shifts in developmental thinking.

SHIFTS IN SYSTEM-BASED PLANNING AND DEVELOPMENTALISM

As we have seen, the initial goal of creating new rural patterns drew from the convergence of different agendas: Kaunda's "humanist" rhetoric, the structuralist economic logic behind Seers's mission, and Doxiadis Associates' regional and settlement planning approach. All these were part of an attempt to promote social and economic transformations in the name of national development and nation-building. Central in these agendas was an ambivalence toward the change and preservation of local "traditions," which nonetheless legitimized the state as the key agent in defining the country's developmental trajectory. This legitimation in turn sanctioned economic/planning ideas that presumably centered on preserving "human" values at the village or community scale while responding to local specificities such as land patterns, cultural preferences, and even social aspirations. In the case of Seers and Doxiadis Associates, this approach was framed in terms of epistemological claims for comprehensiveness and analytical/planning tools, which, presumably, allowed not only a systematic analysis of local conditions but would generate solutions that promoted socio-economic restructuring from within.

Such claims would amplify the capacities of planning to respond to the particularities of a given context and intervene into complex social processes. For both Seers and Doxiadis, systems thinking provided a framework to understand planning activity in terms of totalities, interrelations, and dynamic processes. Seers would thus render the national economy in the image of a "fabric" woven by the complex interrelations among larger and smaller productive sectors and, in turn, development as the outcome of social and economic "waves" spreading across that fabric. Doxiadis would characterize human settlements as dynamic totalities nested within networks at various scales, arguing for planning as a multi-scalar activity driven by the imperative of "balancing" social and environmental effects in its promotion of specific development goals.[56] Doxiadis's systems thinking was significantly influenced by the spatio-economic theories of Walter Christaller and his Central Place Theory,[57] which was used as a norm against which actual settlement patterns could be measured and, presumably, optimized.[58] Concretized in the idea of Ekistics, Doxiadis Associates' planning methodologies' emphasis on networks and hierarchies were critical to the firm's understanding of rural settlements as regional magnets that could attract population and economic flows into the countryside.

Systems-based developmentalism, where everything could be reduced to scales and networks, allowed its advocates to blur rather than highlight distinctions between modernity and tradition, urban and rural, industry and agriculture, and furthermore between cash-crop and subsistence-based agriculture. Elements of what seemed to define local productive and living patterns were appropriated within an abstract economic logic, systematized, and readjusted to the logics of national developmental planning aspiring to shape an economy in transition. These approaches combined epistemological claims with economic and political priorities to formulate a planning ethos that obscured continuities with late-colonial developmentalism. However, the heavily interventionist rural transformations envisioned by these approaches would run up against competing visions, stemming from factors and factions that reflected both persisting colonial legacies and neocolonial intervention in the country, as well as emerging critiques from social and ecological perspectives. The conflicts and contestations within themes of rural development would reverberate within the government and domestic politics alike, forcing new and important shifts within development discourses and planning as well.

Responding to the inordinate delays in realizing their projects, broadly reflecting the dynamics just identified, Doxiadis Associates would subsequently shift their planning discourse. Seeking to realign themselves with the government's changed priorities and shifting political landscapes, the firm began to deemphasize the economic goals behind the older rural settlements' propositions, couching their intervention now as responding to the government's growing concerns about the social and political upheavals stemming from rural out-migration. The shift to an urbanist rationale underlying rural development was communicated by Doxiadis himself, who underscored how delays in implementing rural development projects would further aggravate the impact "[from the] huge invasion of the urban areas by the rural dwellers."[59] To effectively contain rural–urban migration, as Doxiadis's letters from this time imply, the Zambian government needed to ramp up significant investments in public facilities and infrastructure on a nationwide scale to more extensively penetrate rural territory and rural populations.[60]

This strategy became the focus of Doxiadis Associates' self-funded study titled "Organization of the Countryside,"[61] wherein the firm appropriated the growing criticism of the nature and proposed scale of settlement planning in rural development. Of particular significance here is the 1967-study made by the British geographer George Kay, also commissioned by the government, titled "Social Aspects of Village Regrouping in Zambia."[62] In many ways, Kay's critiques reflected the paradigms of late-colonial expertise. Colonial scientists had discredited excessive, Malthusian, fears that had tied population levels with soil degradation and earlier colonial policies that promoted village regrouping and large settlement schemes on those assumptions.[63] Rather, social/ecological analyses tied to administrative reform rendered rural societies as dependent on complex socio-ecological models in their adaptive relationship to regional and local conditions. By and large, these analyses professed skepticism toward invasive physical planning and especially targeted "major [settlement] schemes" as threating the viability of rural ecological models.[64] Skepticism toward broad-scale interventions in rural areas also began to be expressed within the Zambian government. British officials in the Department of Agriculture, for example, criticized the value of grand gestures in rural development, even as key Zambian officials saw them as running counter to their modernizing ambitions, comparing them with "colonial policies, that aimed to keep the [rural] population in isolation and uncivilized."[65]

In the face of these brewing storms, Doxiadis Associates' study expressly abandoned the idea of creating larger settlements such as the rural "market towns" as a regional center for 50,000 people, curtailing also the initial vision of an artificially imposed hierarchical network of rural communities at different scales. The new study proposed instead a two-level service center called a "Development Unit" whose goal was to serve a surrounding area of 7–10,000 inhabitants (see Figure 14.4). The Development Unit no longer promoted the idea of a compact settlement, as before, but rather comprised a node in social and marketing infrastructures spread through the countryside. This was a decisive shift from the original ambitions of broad relocation and resettlement toward more a "flexible" spatial model adjusted to the existing settlement, population, and land-use patterns. Although the "Units" were based on the same abstract and universal variables combining population sizes, time-distances, and the cultivability of land, the firm's approach shifted from a vision of accelerating rural development and planned communities to a more modest one of gradual social and market-based infrastructural inputs into the countryside.

Regrouping and resettling scattered populations and engendering higher population densities seemed no longer important. Rather, the new approach was premised on the "voluntary" response and imputed interests of rural societies and their gradual adaptation to a new economic system introduced along with educational, health, and commercial services. What was envisioned, eventually, was an indeterminate condition were rural populations would abandon "traditional," "pre-capitalist" structures by becoming adjusted to new consumer and living patterns. Their becoming "productive agents," presumably, would take place not in a top-down fashion and in a less invasive and unsettling way. In this way, these centers, the firm, argued, "[could] survive in all future phases of

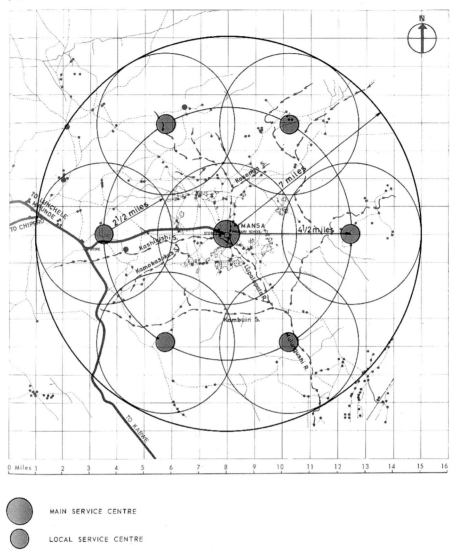

FIGURE 14.4 The abstract model of a "Development Unit" superimposed on existing settlements in rural Zambia.

development . . . irrespectively of how the people are going to settle within them in the next few generations."[66]

As noted previously, Doxiadis Associates' self-funded study very likely saw its efforts to find its way back into shifting governmental attitudes at a time when the preparation for the country's Second National Development Plan was underway. As such, this study was never adopted officially. However, what it did reflect was an emerging paradigm, both within the Zambian government and without, that promoted less intervention and more "flexible" planning approaches in rural areas. It reflected broader epistemological shifts toward greater empirical responsiveness and toward the ground realities of power. In this context, systems thinking was yet again mobilized to serve the new epistemological demands. In 1970, the geographer Akin Mabogunje had pioneered the use of systems theory in the study of intense rural–urban migration in sub-Saharan Africa, described in the terms of "flow phenomena modifying the character of any country."[67] Drawing on metaphors of flows, adopted from physics and mechanics, Mabogunje would explain these processes as constituted by "feedback mechanisms that both reinforce and constrain further migration."[68] Following the major tenets of systems theory, he emphasized "rural-urban migration no longer as a linear, uni-directional, push-and-pull, cause-effect movement but as a circular, interdependent, progressively complex, and self-modifying system in which the effect of changes in one part can be traced through the whole of the system."[69] Such paradigms inevitably cast doubt over planning strategies such as those promoted by Doxiadis Associates, which remained beholden to earlier models of "push–pull" factors driving urban migration, in terms of countering "pull" impulses in the countryside. A more complex approach was required, Mabogunje and others would imply, while still remaining within the functionalist logic of systems theory.

Views expressed by studies such as Kay's exposed factors involving the "high degree of mobility or fluidity [which] is characteristic of all parts of rural Zambia" that resonated better with the new expert and scientific paradigms. David J. Siddle, another British geographer studying Zambia in the 1970s, would also underline how rural societies "[c]ontained within some of their structures are complex adjustment mechanisms and sophisticated calculations of man-environment interaction, from which we could do well to learn."[70] Both geographers seemed to agree that rural areas were zones to be protected and preserved from the impact of far-reaching state-led policies, yet again signaling a paradigm shift in developmental planning. In other words, the assumption of an organized state functioning in full capacity to set up, fund, and manage well-operated settlements was no longer tenable. The priority was no longer to promote the restructuring of rural societies but to promote strategies that engage the ongoing dynamics between rural and urban and the exponential complexities of rural areas, placing an emphasis on the role of individual trajectories, social relations, and networks that spread across space. As the Doxiadis Associates study would also testify, the firm no longer focused on community building, as before, or on enhancing regional and social structures. Rather, planning would target the individual farmer, no longer a cog in the "rural masses" and the "peasantry" but now seen as a self-maximizing agent whose rationales had to be researched and responded to (see Figure 14.5).

The new developmental paradigm expressed in Zambia merged late-colonial scientific legacies with the critiques of the type of global developmentalism promoted by Seers and Doxiadis Associates and fully supported by Kaunda's government for over a decade. These critiques also echoed an ideological turnaround among philanthropic foundations as well as global development agencies such the World Bank,[71] which under Robert McNamara's presidency was shifting its anti-poverty and rural development doctrines, no longer targeting the "masses" but various self-maximizing categories such as small farmers, the "poor," women, and the household.[72] The most direct impact of this shift in Zambia would be felt in a 1975 World Bank *Agriculture and Rural Sector Survey*, which dismissed the utility of "organized resettlements," further underlining that "the principle should be to encourage people to move of their own accord to where they can receive the benefits of Government investments

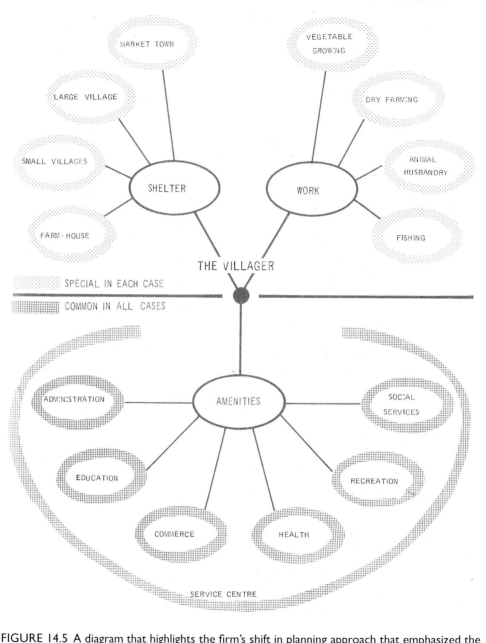

FIGURE 14.5 A diagram that highlights the firm's shift in planning approach that emphasized the needs of the "villager" rather than rural communities.

and commercial facilities."[73] Inaugurating a new regime of austerity aimed at minimizing state intervention in rural areas, the report further highlighted that "[a]lthough planning would be necessary, it should be kept to a minimum and be facilitative."[74] The World Bank's embrace of "facilitative planning" provides us with strong evidence of the broader shift in developmental agendas in Africa and the Third World.[75]

Zambia was, once more, a paradigmatic case study in the new wave of rural developmentalism.[76] New empirical studies found ample evidence for the country's poor performance in rural development, highlighting how the state's interventionist policies in the countryside had in fact favored the growing urban population over the marginalized rural societies.[77] The state's "urban-bias," these studies highlighted, had impeded African countries' comparative advantage—agriculture—while also failing to eradicate rural poverty. The seminal 1981-report *Accelerated Development in Sub-Saharan Africa: An Agenda for Action* generalized the conclusion that 1960s–'70s policies had shown a "bias against agriculture,"[78] a shift that would subsequently inform the so-called Structural Adjustment Programmes of the World Bank and International Monetary Fund in the 1980s–1990s. These program were also enforced on Zambia precisely when the country was seeking to combat its economic crisis after the significant fall of the copper prices by the mid-1970s. The prescription provided involved the elimination of state subsidies, urban wage cuts, and the privatization/sale of state-owned industrial and other companies. According to geographer Deborah Potts, it was on the basis of the discourse of the "urban bias" and the use of data to overemphasize the country's urbanization levels that, under these program, "the living standards of the urban population of Zambia were sacrificed in the supposed interests of an allegedly marginalized rural population desperate for the blessings of a liberalized market."[79] In turn, small-scale farming would be considered the solution to achieve economic growth and eliminate rural poverty, where the environmental and market risks of farming once managed by the state would be distributed through market mechanisms that would bring small-scale farmers into competition with the global market.[80]

CONCLUSIONS

This chapter has sought to challenge dominant perceptions about development in architectural historiography and beyond. It highlights the decisive role that the geopolitical context played in defining development projects within specific nation-states, drawing attention to the ways postcolonial aspirations, exchanges across the "developing" world, and transnational planning, among others, added further nuances to development agendas. Rather than promoting a linear understanding of development history ("from the West to the rest"), this analysis exposes the complex and multidimensional flows of development expertise/discourses and, eventually, "[their] contentious redeployment in particular cultural and historical locations," as anthropologist Akhil Gupta has described it.[81]

Doxiadis Associates' proposals, this chapter has argued, can be seen as responding to various demands emanating from the rural theater as the locus of postcolonial aspirations and dynamics of nation-building; transnational economic agendas; and epistemological contestations around development rooted within the country's colonial legacies and emerging critiques on planning. As such, these proposals also conversed with conflicting conceptualizations of the rural: for one, as a symbolic repository of African cultural values and basis for building a national identity; alternatively, as a pool for underutilized developmental resources; and yet again as a neglected site to be upgraded and reclaimed by state power and market exchanges, and then again as a complex socioecological system to be understood and carefully replanned and remade. By focusing on the firm's attempt to translate these rural-based visions into plans, the chapter ultimately challenged simplistic perceptions of Doxiadis and Doxiadis Associates as modernist "urban" planners, shedding light on rather understudied tactics in the firm's planning approach. To shore up its legitimacy as planners, the firm advanced a range of strategies, often retreating from prior stances to align with new realizations and epistemological paradigms. The emphases in its projects thus went from the reorganization of the population within "stable" community patterns and regional networks to, eventually, the infrastructural modification of the countryside to facilitate incoming and outcoming "flows" of services, state power, capital, labor, and agricultural surplus. These strategies derived from the firm's system-based and spatio-economic planning approach, informing the shaping of developmental expertise beyond merely visual explorations of cultural identity through architectural forms and emblematic urban projects, speaking more acutely to the firm's attempts to set the priorities of development policy itself tied to the governmental reshaping of rural landscapes and reorganization of patterns of everyday life and production.

The chapter also showed how, despite the firm's continued appeals to the government to develop a national strategy for the countryside along the aforementioned priorities, the rural settlement project was caught within various conflicting vectors affecting developmental policies: first, from the country's dependency on copper mining and the import-substitution strategies that aggravated rather than mitigated social, economic, and regional imbalances to conflicting interests around the distribution of wealth and developmental funds; and second, devolving from various epistemological contestations around rural development that reverberated within the government as well as domestic politics. Against this complex and contested landscape, Doxiadis Associates nonetheless maintained its alliance with the government's attempts to address the unsettling effects of rural out-migration in the "urban" context, with various development schemes in the periphery of the capital and in the design of the Master Plan for Lusaka, where parallel histories of "ruralization" unfolded.

In 1970, members of Doxiadis Associates' local office in Zambia repeatedly wrote to the Athens office that "people of Black Africa are not ready for urban living. . . . They do not know how to 'live' the city and use the houses."[82] An outcome of this was Doxiadis's decision to conduct a survey to study users' reactions to the firm's housing project in Kafue, to study the extent of the problem. The local office reported the inhabitants' tendency to extensively use open courtyards instead of indoor spaces for cooking, raising children, or other unprogrammed activities such as storing fuel and raising domestic animals. A principal motive behind the survey was to capture and manage what was seen as "out of place" and did not correspond to the planners' intentions and modernist aesthetics and explore solutions through design. Exposing a form of paternalism that did not acknowledge its colonial and, even, racist undertone—as the previous quote leads us to think—the firm's reports included suggestions for adapting the housing typologies to the users' preferences.[83] Although this was a small episode in the firm's extensive and growing involvement in Zambia's spatial development, it reinforced the realization that local conditions and dynamics needed to be further accounted and managed across urban and rural areas. Attempts to address local dynamics, the changing political priorities and epistemological shifts, as the chapter demonstrated, was central to Doxiadis Associates' strategies to maintain their presence in the changing South. Such episodes shed another light on the complex and understudied histories of "ruralization" within the global project of development and the commensurate processes of expertise that these mobilized, intentionally or unintentionally, transforming both the urban and the rural.

NOTES

1 UN Bureau of Social Affairs, "Positive Aspects of African Urbanization," *Ekistics* 23, no. 135 (1967): 115–117.
2 Economic Commission for Africa, "Recommendations on Urbanization in Africa," *Ekistics* 14, no. 84 (1962): 242.
3 UN Bureau of Social Affairs, "Positive Aspects of African Urbanization," *Ekistics* 23, no. 135 (1967): 115–117.
4 Walter W. Rostow, "African Economies: Lessons of History," *Africa Today* 7, no. 7 (November, 1960): 5–8.
5 Frantz Fanon, *The Wretched of the Earth* (New York: Grove, 2004 [1961]), 76.
6 Stuart J. Barton, *Policy Signals and Market Responses: A 50 Year History of Zambia's Relationship with Foreign Capital* (Basingstoke: Palgrave Macmillan, 2016), 39.
7 Quoted in Stuart J. Barton, *Policy Signals and Market Responses: A 50 Year History of Zambia's Relationship with Foreign Capital* (Basingstoke: Palgrave Macmillan, 2016), 17.
8 Kenneth Kaunda, *Humanism in Zambia and a Guide to Its Implementation*, Part I (Lusaka: Government Printer, 1967).
9 Kenneth D. Kaunda and Colin M. Morris, *A Humanist in Africa: Letters to Colin M. Morris from Kenneth D. Kaunda, President of Zambia* (London: Longmans, 1966), 13.
10 *First National Development Plan 1966–1970*, Republic of Zambia, Office of National Development and Planning (1966), 23.
11 Letter by Skotiniotis, head of Doxiadis Associates' local office, to the Commissioner of Town and Country Planning, July 6, 1967, Archive files 24660, Doxiadis Archives.
12 See also Panayiota Pyla, "Architects as Development Experts: Model Communities in Iraq and Syria," in *Landscapes of Development: The Impact of Modernisation Discourses on the Physical Environment of the Eastern Mediterranean*, ed. P. Pyla (Cambridge: Harvard University Aga Khan Program, 2013), 166–189.
13 Frederick Cooper, *Africa since 1940: The Past of the Present* (Cambridge: Cambridge University Press, 2002).
14 On the issues of race and nationalism with a focus on Tanzania, see Ronald Aminzade, *Race, Nation, and Citizenship in Postcolonial Africa: The Case of Tanzania* (Cambridge: Cambridge University Press, 2013).
15 Mahmood Mamdani, *Citizen and Subject: Contemporary Africa and the Legacy of Late Colonialism* (Princeton, NJ: Princeton University Press, 1996), 287.
16 Henri Bernstein, "Rural Land & Land Conflicts in Sub-Saharan Africa," in *Reclaiming the Land: The Resurgence of Rural Movements in Africa, Asia & Latin America*, eds. Sam Moyo and Paris Yeros (London: Zed Books, 2005), 75.
17 Sam Moyo and Paris Yeros, eds., *Reclaiming the Land: The Resurgence of Rural Movements in Africa, Asia & Latin America* (London: Zed Books, 2005), 34.
18 Kenneth Kaunda, *Humanism in Zambia and A Guide to Its Implementation*, Part I (Lusaka: Government Printer, 1967), 20, 31.
19 By 1972, 15 percent of the rural population had been brought into villages, and by 1976, 91 percent. For a well-known critique on Tanzania's "villagization" schemes see James C. Scott, *Seeing Like a State: How Certain Schemes to Improve the Human Condition Have Failed* (New Haven: Yale University Press, 1998), 223–261.
20 Kenneth Kaunda, *Zambia: Independence and Beyond: The Speeches of Kenneth Kaunda* (London: Nelson, 1966), 32, quoted in James Ferguson, "The Country and the City on the Copperbelt," *Cultural Anthropology* 7, no. 1 (1992): 83.
21 Kenneth Kaunda, *Humanism in Zambia and A Guide to Its Implementation*, Part I (Lusaka: Government Printer, 1967), 8, 22.
22 Doxiadis changed "Man" to the Greek word "Anthropos" as a more universal notion to include "all humans no matter what their sex, age, etc." See Constantinos Doxiadis, "Anthropos," *Ekistics* 37, no. 222 (May 1974): 305.
23 Constantinos Doxiadis, *Ekistics: An Introduction to the Science of Human Settlements* (London: Hutchinson, 1969), 301.
24 Constantinos Doxiadis and John Papaioannou, *Ecumenopolis: The Inevitable City of the Future* (New York: Norton and Company, 1974).
25 Doxiadis highlighted that "[n]ew, dynamic types of settlements interconnecting more and more smaller settlements are the types appropriate to this era." Constantinos Doxiadis, "Ekistics: The Science of Human Settlements," *Science* 170, 3956 (October 1970), 393–404.
26 Petros Phokaides, "De-Tropicalizing Africa: Architecture, Planning and Climate, in the 1950s and 1960s," *Docomomo Journal, Modern Africa: Tropical Architecture* 48 (2013): 76–82.
27 Constantinos Doxiadis et al., "Techniques of Studying Density," *Ekistics* 20, no. 119 (1965): 199–207.
28 "The Development of Rural Townships: A Programme for the Creation and Development of Rural Centres in the Country," October 1968, Archive files 24663, Doxiadis Archives,
29 "President Kaunda Interviewed," *DA Review* 4, no. 40 (April 1968): 15–16.
30 Addressing the mine workers, Kaunda would remind them that their requests for wage increase was a selfish act depriving valuable resources that could be used to develop the rural areas, where their families also lived. See James Ferguson, "The Country and the City on the Copperbelt," *Cultural Anthropology* 7, no. 1 (1992): 84.
31 The African National Congress (ANC), an opposition party, was backed by wealthy farmers. See A. Bowman, "Mass Production or Production by The Masses? Tractors, Cooperatives, and the Politics of Rural Development in Post-Independence Zambia," *Journal of African History* 52 (2011): 214.

32 The request by the government was made in September 1963. The mission started in November and ended in March 1964.
33 *First National Development Plan 1966–1970*, Republic of Zambia, Office of National Development and Planning, 1966, 50.
34 Giblert Rist, *The History of Development: From Western Origins to Global Faith* (London: Zed Books, 2014), 109–123; Cristóbal Kay, "Raúl Prebisch," in *Fifty Key Thinkers on Development*, ed. David Simon (London: Routledge, 2006), 199–205.
35 Dudley Seers, "The Limitations of the Special Case," *Bulletin of the Oxford University Institute of Economics & Statistics* 25, no. 2 (1963): 84.
36 Dudley Seers, "Why Visiting Economists Fail," *Journal of Political Economy* 70, no. 4 (1962): 325–338.
37 Dudley Seers, *Economic Survey Mission on the Economic Development of Zambia, Report of the UN/ECA/FAO* (Ndola: Falcon Press, 1964), 13.
38 Dudley Seers, *Economic Survey Mission on the Economic Development of Zambia, Report of the UN/ECA/FAO* (Ndola: Falcon Press, 1964), 8.
39 Stuart J. Barton, *Policy Signals and Market Responses: A 50 Year History of Zambia's Relationship with Foreign Capital* (Basingstoke: Palgrave Macmillan, 2016), 14–16.
40 The Northern Rhodesia (Zambia) economy suffered from the policies of the Central African Federation, established by the British government in 1953, which also included Southern Rhodesia and Nyasaland.
41 Dudley Seers, "The Use of a Modified Input-Output System for an Economic Program in Zambia," *Institute of Development Studies at the University of Sussex* 50 (1967): 3.
42 Dudley Seers, "The Political Economy of National Accounting," in *Employment, Income Distribution and Development Strategy: Problems of the Developing Countries*, eds. Alec Cairncross and Mohinder Puri (London: Palgrave Macmillan, 1976), 195.
43 Wassily Leontief, "Input-Output Economics," *Scientific American* 185, no. 4 (1951): 15–21.
44 *First National Development Plan 1966–1970*, Republic of Zambia, Office of National Development and Planning (1966), 2.
45 The mission offered two reasons behind this approach: first, the failures of colonial agendas that focused only on individuals, and second, the social convictions that led individuals to share their surplus with less fortunate members of their family. Dudley Seers, *Economic Survey Mission on the Economic Development of Zambia, Report of the UN/ECA/FAO* (Ndola: Falcon Press, 1964), 69.
46 *First National Development Plan 1966–1970*, Republic of Zambia, Office of National Development and Planning (1966), 21.
47 "Rural Townships of Zambia—General Report," December 15, 1967, Archive files 24657, Doxiadis Archives, 2.
48 Ibid., 24.
49 Ibid., 2.
50 Ibid.
51 See the pertinent analysis, M. Ijlal Muzaffar, "Boundary Games: Ecochard, Doxiadis, and the Refugee Housing Projects Under Military Rule in Pakistan, 1953–1959," in *Aggregate, Governing by Design: Architecture, Economy, and Politics in the Twentieth Century*, eds. Arindam Dutta, Timothy Hyde, and Daniel Abramson (Pittsburgh: University of Pittsburgh Press, 2012), 142–199.
52 "Rural Townships of Zambia—General Report," December 15, 1967, Archive files 24657, Doxiadis Archives, 24.
53 Ibid.
54 Antoinette Handley, *Business and the State in Africa: Economic Policy-Making in the Neo-Liberal Era* (Cambridge: Cambridge University Press, 2008), 207–242.
55 Ann Seidman, "The Distorted Growth of Import-Substitution Industry: The Zambian Case," *Journal of Modern African Studies* 12, no. 4 (December 1974): 601–631.
56 For a critique on the different notions of "balance" used by Doxiadis, see Panayiota Pyla, "Planetary Home and Garden: Ekistics and Environmental-Developmental Politics," *Grey Room* 36 (2009): 21.
57 Walter Christaller, *Die zentralen Orte in Suddeutschland* (Jena: Gustav Fischer, 1933); and Walter Christaller, *Central Places in Southern Germany*, trans. Carlisle W. Baskin (Englewood Cliffs, NJ: Prentice-Hall, 1966).
58 For a more detailed analyses of these debates, see Petros Phokaides, "Rural Networks and Planned Communities: Doxiadis Associates' Plans for Rural Settlements in Post-Independence Zambia," *The Journal of Architecture* 23, no. 3 (2018): 471–497.
59 Constantinos Doxiadis, "A Special Program for the Organization of Human Settlements in the Rural Areas of Zambia," March 4, 1969, Archive files 24672, Doxiadis Archive.
60 Expressed in Doxiadis's letters in September 1970, to the Minister for Development and Finance and the Minister of Rural Development. Archive files 24667, Doxiadis Archives.
61 "Zambia: Organization of the Countryside," June 1968, Archive files 24672, Doxiadis Archive.

62 Kay was a professor of geography at the University of Hull, and his research experience in Zambia begun in the late 1950s.
63 Robert Chambers, *Settlement Schemes in Tropical Africa: A Study of Organizations and Development* (London: Routledge, 1969), 30.
64 David J. Siddle, "Rural Development in Zambia: A Spatial Analysis," *The Journal of Modern African Studies* 8, no. 2 (1970): 271–284.
65 Stated in a letter of D. Soteriou from the Lusaka office to central offices in Athens, June 14, 1968, Archive files 24669, Doxiadis Archives.
66 Constantinos Doxiadis, "A Special Program for the Organization of Human Settlements in the Rural Areas of Zambia," March 4, 1969, Archive files 24672, Doxiadis Archive.
67 Akin L. Mabogunje, "Systems Approach to a Theory of Rural-Urban Migration," *Geographical Analysis* 2, no. 1 (1970): 1–18.
68 Ibid.
69 Ibid.
70 David J. Siddle, "Rural Development and Rural Change," in *The Third World Problems and Perspectives*, ed. Alan B. Mountjoy (London: Macmillan Press, 1979), 112–121.
71 For continuities between the World Bank's 1970s agendas and late-colonial projects in Africa, see James Hodge, "British Colonial Expertise, Post-Colonial Careering and the Early History of International Development," *Journal of Modern European History* 8, no. 1 (2010): 24–46.
72 Arturo Escobar, "Planning," in *The Development Dictionary*, ed. Wolfgang Sachs (London and New York: Zed Books, 2010 [1992]), 145–161.
73 World Bank, *Zambia: Agricultural and Rural Sector Survey*, vol. 2, Annex 2 (Washington, DC: World Bank Group, 1975), 7.
74 Ibid.
75 For a critique of the World Bank's focus on small-scale farmers, see Cheryl Payer, "The World Bank and the Small Farmers," *Journal of Peace Research* 16, no. 4 (1979): 293–312.
76 Alastair Fraser, "Introduction: Boom and Bust on the Zambian Copperbelt," in *Zambia, Mining, and Neoliberalism: Boom and Bust on the Globalized Copperbelt*, eds. Alastair Fraser and Miles Larmer (New York, NY: Palgrave Macmillan US, 2011), 10.
77 See, for example, Robert H. Bates, *Markets and States in Tropical Africa: The Political Basis of Agricultural Policies* (Berkeley: University of California Press, 1981).
78 World Bank, *Accelerated Development in Sub-Saharan Africa: An Agenda for Action* (Washington, DC: The World Bank, 1981), 4.
79 Deborah Potts, "Counter-Urbanisation on the Zambian Copperbelt? Interpretations and Implications," *Urban Studies* 42, no. 4 (2005): 583–609.
80 Henri Bernstein, "Rural Land & Land Conflicts in Sub-Saharan Africa," in *Reclaiming the Land: The Resurgence of Rural Movements in Africa, Asia & Latin America*, eds. Sam Moyo and Paris Yeros (London: Zed Books, 2005), 67–101.
81 Akhil Gupta, *Postcolonial Developments: Agriculture in the Making of Modern India* (Durham, NC: Duke University Press, 1998), 15.
82 This letter, sent on January 24, 1970, was part of the personal correspondence between Doxiadis Associates' office manager in Zambia Kostas Kakisopoulos and Constantinos Doxiadis. Archive files 19200, Doxiadis Archives.
83 Report by P. Alexiou on January 26, 1970. Archive files 24680, Doxiadis Archives.

15

Food capital

Fantasies of abundance and Nelson Rockefeller's architectures of development in Venezuela, 1940s–1960s

Fabiola López-Durán

Spanning three decades (1940s–1960s), this is a story of how US oil magnate Nelson A. Rockefeller positioned oil-rich Venezuela to serve as an international pilot project that instrumentalized food production over oil in order to expand capitalism in the Global South. Fearing that Venezuela would follow in the footsteps of Bolivia and Mexico in their 1937 and 1938 embrace of nationalizing oil, Rockefeller masterminded the use of Venezuelan oil camps as laboratories for agricultural production and consumption on a national level. This is also a story of how food production, hygiene practices, and space making became intertwined in Rockefeller's comprehensive development scheme, under the auspices of his oil companies, Standard Oil in the United States and Venezuela—and the governments of both.[1]

We begin at the 1939 World's Fair, which opened in Queens, New York, as a utopian landscape of futuristic and historical buildings, futuramas, dioramas, artificial lagoons, monumental murals, and much more. One of the fair's most celebrated attractions was the Venezuelan Pavilion, an ultramodern glass and steel box that, rather than advertise scientific and technological progress, as do most World's Fair pavilions, showcased Venezuelan rurality and its unique promise of economic development (Figure 15.1).[2] The widely acclaimed pavilion stood as a platform for modernism, agrarianism, and a petrostate moving toward diversification. Architectural journals praised the simplicity of its modernist building, designed by SOM, the young architectural firm founded in Chicago by Louis Skidmore and Nathaniel Owings (later joined by John O. Merrill).[3] The *New York Times* took notice of its "Altar of the Good Neighbor," the country's homage to President Franklin Roosevelt's promotion of nonintervention and hemispheric solidarity.[4] The fair's Official Guide exalted the display of "the two main products of the country—orchids and oil," as well as Francisco Narvaez's sculptures representing other Venezuelan commodities—coffee, cocoa, fruits, pearls, and, again, oil.[5] The *New York Post* memorialized a diorama of a coffee plantation at the center of the pavilion, surrounded by representations of the country's fifty types of coffee and by watercolors depicting workers' daily laboring.[6] International fashion magazines, such as *Harper's Bazaar*, celebrated the traditional costume of rural Venezuela—a colorful skirt and shoulderless white blouse—worn by the pavilion hostess, a stylish peasant outfit

FIGURE 15.1 The Venezuela Pavilion at 1939 New York World's Fair. General view.
Source: Wurts Bros. Museum of the City of New York. X2010.7.1.7636.

that, a few weeks later, *Women's Wear Daily* reported to be tailored by Saks Fifth Avenue and sold to fashion-conscious New Yorkers in its elegant Manhattan department store.[7] The pavilion glamourized Venezuela's rurality, but nothing aroused the press's attention more than the pavilion's promotion of Venezuela's primary selling point as "the only country in the world that has no debts and no taxes."[8]

For Nelson A. Rockefeller, a member of the Board of Directors of Creole Petroleum Corporation in Venezuela (a subsidiary of Standard Oil of New Jersey, and a holding company for Standard Oil Company of Venezuela), the pavilion functioned as an opportunity to capitalize on the nation's countryside and the US strategy of securing political, commercial, and cultural interdependence in the Americas.[9] Convinced that Venezuela was the elemental force for development throughout Latin America, Rockefeller immediately began promoting the diversification of the nation's oil-dependent economy and, by so doing, protected his multi-million dollar investment in Venezuelan oil.[10] By the time the pavilion opened in May 1939, Rockefeller had already begun working toward expanding US economic opportunities in Venezuela. In March, in a conversation with Venezuelan President Eleazar López Contreras in Caracas, he had accepted the challenge of building a new hotel in the capital city to stimulate non-oil businesses.[11] For its design, he chose Wallace K. Harrison, a friend and fellow advocate of modernism.[12] Two months later, Rockefeller's alignment with modernism and development became resoundingly clear. First, he assumed the presidency of the Museum of Modern Art (MoMA), speaking at the inauguration of its six-story modernist building, right after President Roosevelt himself. A few days later, he maneuvered to hold a private reception for US industrialists at the newly built Venezuelan pavilion in Queens.[13] Rockefeller's economic, political, and cultural allegiances had begun to converge.[14]

In fact, these activities were part of a multilayered scheme to create a development corporation in Venezuela that would generate diverse entrepreneurial opportunities—from cement manufacturing to housing to the food industry. In diversifying Venezuela's monoculture of oil, Rockefeller recognized that he had the perfect opportunity to both capitalize on the primitive state of agricultural production in South America and instrumentalize food as an eco-political tool to accomplish his multifaceted agenda. Because hunger overseas was considered a threat to national security, he saw food as an ideal component of US foreign policy, at the very moment when communism was rising and World War II was on the verge of breaking out. In fact, the Point Four Program, the first long-term global US aid program for the "developing world" implemented by President Harry S. Truman in 1949, was inspired by Rockefeller's endeavors in Latin America during the war.[15] In Venezuela, Rockefeller recognized that he could further realize his own techno-scientific agenda by appealing to the desire of Venezuela's government leaders and elites to upgrade its inadequate agricultural technology and, at the same time, exploit the country's obsession with modernization. López Contreras had already made clear that he had no intention of taking radical measures against oil companies but rather sought greater royalties from its petroleum for the nation. At the center of López Contreras and Rockefeller's plans was the transformation of oil wealth into agricultural prosperity, what López Contreras's minister termed "sowing the oil."[16] This metaphor of the "union of oil and agriculture" created an image of "collective fecundity" that masked the profound inequality then germinating throughout the country. In fact, Venezuela's "collective fantasies of progress" ended up promoting a form of modernity based on the advantages of conspicuous consumption—not, of course, available to all.[17]

The Venezuelan pavilion was nothing less than Rockefeller's blueprint and billboard for the development project he would institutionalize in the country after the war. The impact of the pavilion was maximized by creating a dramatic contrast between, on the one hand, the modernist transparency of the building and the interplay of techno-scientific forms and, on the other hand, representations of Venezuelan rural tropicality. Two idiosyncratic panels—one piercing the glass box and the other floating above it—are visible from the building's exterior. Occupying the north side, the first panel depicts an inverted map of the country to convey the pavilion's central message: an art deco figure—Venezuela itself—with a liberated raised arm leads the country and its coveted resources forward—not to the East, as it would have been if not inverted, but to the West, geographically and symbolically; and on top, a declaration of the striking benefit to the United States—this is "a land without debts or taxes." The scene is filled with pictograms of the country's natural wealth: oil, coffee, salt, cattle, copper, coal, cacao, tobacco, gold, iron, sugar, rubber, and more. Together, text and image depict an untapped frontier, framed by an exuberant display of Venezuelan orchids (flown three times a week to New York) on two elongated artificial trees (Figure 15.2).[18] The effect of seeing Venezuelan tropical nature and natural resources *through* a modernist grid, defined by steel supports and glass panels, seems to suggest that the country and its resources could be rationalized and aestheticized, all at once.

FIGURE 15.2 Exhibition panel "Venezuela, Land Without Debts or Taxes." Venezuela Pavilion at 1939 New York World's Fair.

Source: Wurts Bros. Museum of the City of New York. X2010.7.1.7638.

The second panel, decorating the sloped ceiling above the pavilion's entry, displays a 170-foot-long mural by Venezuelan artists Luis Alfredo López Méndez and Miguel Arroyo that depicts Venezuelan fishing and farming folk industries. This panel is, in fact, a faux entrance ramp that recalls the loading ramps of a slaughterhouse.[19] Alongside the mural, an attractive display of a techno-scientific tropical garden features a series of parasols that look like giant ultraviolet lights nourishing exotic orchids under glass globes. This installation resembles another in the back of the pavilion in which a glass cylinder, illuminated by a circular lamp, alludes to the process of extracting oil from Venezuelan reservoirs. Taken together—the ramp gesturing to slaughterhouse technology, the parasols to greenhouse cultivation, and the glass cylinder to oil extraction—all claim a need for intervention in a fecund geography that yearns for development. The whole Venezuelan pavilion was an abstraction of rurality—a stylish warehouse of an underdeveloped geography, a billboard for a rural country unspoiled and ripe for exploitation.

Drawing on a long history of colonial and hygienic practices in the Global South, this story reveals how food production became the template for erasing the region's specificity of land, bodies, and climate to create a supposedly universalized but decidedly US-driven conception of nutrition, leisure, and profit. More specifically, it narrates the ways Rockefeller attempted—through diplomacy, his Venezuelan oil camps, and capital—to create a seamless aesthetic of a sterilized and rationalized rurality centered on food, both in the countryside and in cities. The story traces the three-decade-long transformation of the food industry through the lens of the built environment, from agricultural experiments in the oil camps to gleaming supermarkets strewn across middle-class neighborhoods in Venezuelan cities. To accomplish his mission of transporting a business model and a modernist aesthetic to the Global South, Rockefeller orchestrated an entire system of diversified development, which deflected from the monopolistic oil extraction that served his primary interests. According to this plan, the cultivated soil of the countryside and the architectural marketplaces were an inducement for the government and people of Venezuela to allow US oil companies to continue collecting their soaring oil profits without any threat of expropriation. By capitalizing on the differing jurisdictions of the topsoil and subsoil, Rockefeller managed to establish a compensatory plan that reached its climax in 1947, with the creation of his global company, the International Basic Economy Corporation (IBEC). This private initiative, with its focus on food and housing, targeted Venezuela as its main laboratory. And yet as we shall see, in spite of his success creating a robust network of supermarkets over the next two decades, Rockefeller's master plan was ultimately decimated by violence and widespread dissatisfaction in a country still fighting hunger and inequality.

1940–1946: FROM OIL TO FOOD

In the 1940s, Venezuela was in the midst of a food crisis in which only 50 percent of the food required was being produced.[20] As a result, Venezuela was a clear obstacle to the US strategy to use Latin America's agricultural land and food production capacity to mitigate the food deficit in Europe caused by the war. On May 21, 1946, when former President Herbert Hoover arrived in Caracas, Venezuela had already failed to achieve the food goals set by a bilateral program known as the Food Mission. This mission, part of the InterAmerican Cooperative Food Production Service (SCIPA), had been created three years earlier in May 1943 with the purpose of increasing and diversifying food production in Venezuela as well as training a small number of nationals as technicians to operate the new agricultural stations about to be created.[21] But by 1946, John R. Camp, chief of the mission, admitted that the early growth expectations of the country's agricultural production had been too optimistic and that the mission itself could not resolve the issue because Venezuela had more pressing problems such as the high cost of living, an unbalanced economy, and deficiencies in health and education. So the mission, considered costly, unproductive, and inefficient, was canceled just one week before Hoover's visit.

Yet if the country's food scarcity was disrupting the bilateral relationship between the United States and Venezuela, oil was galvanizing it. Whether a dictatorship or a left-leaning administration, the Venezuelan government favored US oil companies continuing to operate there.[22] In fact, during the Trienio (1945–1948), in which Rómulo Betancourt was installed as provisional president, this symbiotic bond grew stronger, with oil revenues rising and Venezuela becoming a strategic player in the US Cold War agenda. However, this alignment was not without its challenges. When Hoover arrived in Caracas, in a speech at an official dinner, he told the audience that, as a result of the country's failed food mission: "All we ask of Venezuela is to greatly reduce imports during the next 90 days."[23] Betancourt took issue with the US view that Venezuela had hindered plans to mitigate hunger in Europe, insisting the country was chronically experiencing the same kind of famine.[24] This do-not-disturb demand of Venezuela would mark the beginning of the end of the intergovernmental relationship between both countries concerning matters of food.

Yet a different US/Venezuela food chapter was already in the works—one authored by Rockefeller, who saw the situation as a perfect opportunity to create a private and profitable initiative that would, in effect, continue and boost the work of the Food Mission. His first step had actually begun in 1940, when created two institutions through which food was instrumentalized as a developmental strategy: in Venezuela he created the Compañía de Fomento Venezolano, S.A., to initiate a series of non-oil business ventures; and in the United States, he convinced President Roosevelt to invest in Latin America by creating the Office of the Coordinator of Inter-American Affairs (OCIAA) as part of the National Defense Council, and to name him as its director.[25] These projects came at a point when Rockefeller was increasingly concerned that Venezuela would nationalize its oil, as Mexico and Bolivia had done. Moreover, when Venezuela and the United States signed a commercial reciprocity treaty, stipulating that oil export taxes would be cut in half, with Venezuela receiving 90 percent of the import quotas, Rockefeller realized it was critical to reduce the nation's dependence on oil by opening up new areas of economic growth. As a result, the initial action taken by the Compañía de Fomento Venezolano was to build the first modern hotel in Venezuela—the Hotel Avila in Caracas—to stimulate non-oil business transactions, host foreign investors and technocrats, and at the same time, introduce an image of progress.[26] Simultaneously, the OCIAA began deploying agricultural scientists to foster rural modernization in Latin America and, in the coming years, would test several economic diversification programs centered on agriculture and nutrition. In essence, Rockefeller was adopting the strategies of his own foundation to bring technical training, or "technical capacitation," to the "Third World" to develop agriculture and thus mitigate rural poverty. Clearly, Rockefeller had begun to envision a system of development that would expand far beyond the oil fields and the rural lands of Venezuela to the profitable enterprise of food production and the advance of capitalism. Treating Latin America as a test lab and Venezuela as a particularly susceptible territory due to oil dependency, Rockefeller would begin deploying these strategies first in the oil camps, becoming dry runs for new initiatives that shifted the focus from oil to food and from the public to the private sector.

OIL CAMPS AS AGRICULTURAL LABORATORIES

In the Rockefeller family's oil fields—Standard Oil of Venezuela in the East and Lago Petroleum Corporation in the West—the landscape and standard of living was lavish compared to other parts of the country. A faux suburban North American landscape was introduced in the oil camps, scattered across the Venezuelan countryside in strategic locations and featuring repetitive housing surrounded by gardens and complete with "urban services offered at nominal cost, subsidized sometimes at 100%."[27] And this only continued under the Hidrocarburos Law of 1943, which transformed Venezuela into a petrostate by securing 50 percent of oil revenues for the government and forty more years of oil extraction for the oil companies.[28] The law further recognized the subsoil as national property and the state as its landlord, fostering a sustained increase in oil production between 1944 and 1970.[29] Slipping between chthonic laws and visions for the land above, these changes made Rockefeller conceive the oil camps as testing grounds for development projects that he was already planning to launch elsewhere. Thus, the concentrated oil camp communities—already social laboratories promoting a new model of citizen and social and political participation that would have repercussions all over the country—became platforms to test and promote three interrelated schemes: developing the rural to stand at the forefront of modernization; positioning dairy as the nutritional centerpiece of the modern nation; and introducing new hygienic and industrialized sites of consumption (i.e., the precursor of supermarkets) as "an *instantaneous* passage into modern consumer capitalism."[30]

For Rockefeller, Venezuelan rural areas became blank slates onto which he could insert his development strategy. However, he was keenly aware of how modernizing might appear to Venezuelans and that, to circumvent potential objections, he needed a reassuring communication strategy. In a letter to Henry E. Linam, director of Standard Oil of Venezuela, Rockefeller was explicit:

> It seems to me it is becoming increasingly important to convince the Venezuelan people in all walks of life that the Standard Oil Company and American interests in general are not interested solely in coming down to squeeze as many dollars out of the country as possible, but that they have a real concern for the general economic and social welfare of the country.[31]

It was not by chance that, in June 1939, the company launched its trade journal, *El Farol*, which, rather than simply espousing the company's economic agenda, became a platform for linking oil and Venezuelan agriculture with the welfare of the nation.[32] The cover of *El Farol*'s first issue featured a watercolor depiction of the country's rural landscape by artist Tomás Golding, with tropical plants, thatched houses, and local women carrying baskets of food on their heads—a celebration of Venezuelan rurality. Interestingly, the magazine's US version, *The Lamp*, used this same watercolor on its cover; however, if Golding's landscape in the Venezuelan magazine was intended as an expression of national pride, this same artistic rendering was used to promote Venezuela as primitive and thus prime for development in the United States.[33] Moreover, in October of that same year, a similar rural depiction by Golding made the cover of *El Farol*'s fifth issue, but this time the romanticized rural landscape operated in tandem with two avant-garde diagrams on the magazine's back cover: one portrayed the quantity of Venezuela's oil production in 1938, and the other illustrated the worldwide oil quantity for the same period of time. In the lower left corner is a hybrid landscape with palm trees and oil towers standing side by side in a tropical paradise—"a dialectic between landscape and industry" in which agriculture and petroleum coexisted. This juxtaposition is reinforced by the inclusion of a similar, miniature landscape at the center of the Venezuelan pie chart, creating a mise en abîme of a systematized, rationalized, and commodified pastoral landscape (Figure 15.3).[34] So it is clear that Standard Oil of Venezuela conceived the magazine as an opportunity to revisualize the rural as modern—to engineer a new rurality within the oil fields.[35]

Within the oil camps, agricultural activity was touted for its ability to address food shortage in the wake of the Second World War and as a way to prove that the oil industry was working with neighboring communities rather than forsaking them. One of the company's strategies was to spotlight the roads that had been built in regions, otherwise difficult to access, connecting the oil fields and camps to distribution centers. Doing so allowed the oil industry to describe the remote areas as "new fields for a land work force" that would facilitate food distribution to "vast agricultural and livestock regions," even though the

FIGURE 15.3 Standard Oil of Venezuela's magazine *El Farol*, no. 5 (October 1939), front cover painting by Venezuelan artist Tomas Golding, and back cover diagram.

Source: Courtesy of Henry Vicente and Sean Nesselrode.

FOOD CAPITAL 311

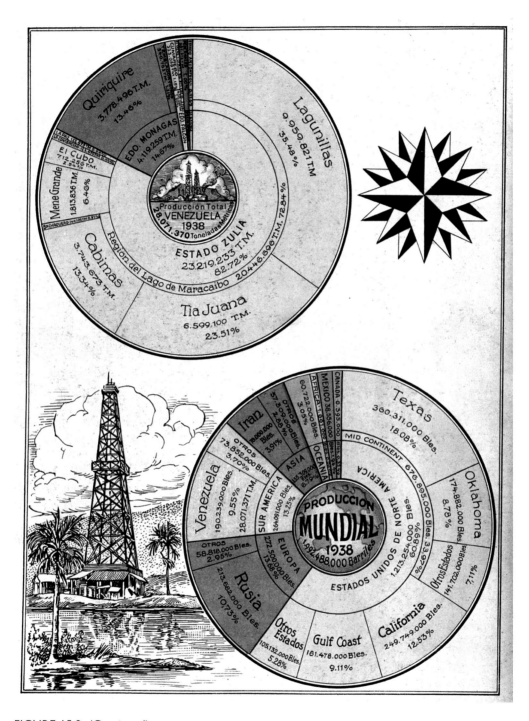

FIGURE 15.3 (Continued)

agricultural population was scarce in oil-producing territories.[36] At the same time, the oil companies sponsored technical experts from the United States to modernize agricultural production and distributed imported vegetable seeds to farmers in the oil camp regions so that food production would be diversified to include vegetables of other latitudes such as carrots, cauliflower, and radishes.

In this Venezuelan 1940s quest, there was no more important food product than milk. Essential to modern nutrition, milk was seen as a solution to mitigate the unhealthy dietary conditions of populations on the verge of famine. Yet at the time, milk was the largest dietary product deficit in the nation—a problem that required not just scaling up production but also updating antiquated milking, packing, and delivery methods. And because of milk's limited shelf life, it was a medium for infectious diseases that called for the instrumentalization of science and modern technology to control nonhuman agents—microbes, bacteria, and the environment itself. It is not surprising that Rockefeller recognized that milk—a product of metabolic labor and one of the most complex entanglements of human agency, animal husbandry, and hygienic and health discourses—was a perfect device for showing that he was carrying out the company's and the Venezuelan government's social responsibility. For over a decade, articles on milk and human nutrition proliferated the pages of *El Farol*. In 1945, an article on farming in the region touted the nutritional importance of milk and the scientific logic of the industry. The article further linked this to Venezuelan history, writing that "since Colonial times" the country had been rooted in farming and hoped to rekindle modern efforts to better the race.[37] Another article announced Standard Oil's first program positioning milk as the nutritional core, and the inauguration of the Caripito Milk Station as a means to undertake "humanitarian work." Through the aesthetics of space, this station became an aseptic laboratory, where bottles looked like test tubes and "poor children and pregnant mothers received a free glass of this precious liquid" after being evaluated by physicians in white robes.[38]

AGRICULTURAL CLUBS AND AGRICULTURAL COLONIES

To further establish Venezuelan oil camps as laboratories for food production and consumption, Standard Oil began incorporating agricultural clubs into its schools to train its residents in modern farming methods as well as establish agricultural colonies in neighboring areas.[39] The Club Agrícola 5V de Venezuela Andrés Bello Creole N° 1, founded in the Andres Bello School of the Caripito camp, one of the most modern and attractive oil camp communities in Venezuela, became a development model. The suburban-styled camp had modern homes and green undulating lawns, scenic roadways, sidewalks with attractive shrubbery, and prominent communal buildings, including a church, a hospital, a commissary, a clubhouse, and the school, with its faux front portico that became a landmark.[40] This "American tropical outpost," as described by a visiting US Navy lieutenant, was "a white camp for foreigners," contrasting the precarious conditions of the rural neighboring villages.[41] Adjacent to the school were plots of land for educational experiments in agriculture. Nearby was a larger farm that complemented the agricultural club's educational activities, where students and farmers from the area learned to harvest vegetables and fruit from orchards lined with citrus trees and avocado plants.

In 1941, Rockefeller's oil companies invested in bonds from the Agricultural and Livestock Bank to further support their agricultural missions, with an eye to marrying the oil and food industries.[42] Previously, in collaboration with the Ministry of Agriculture and Livestock, Standard Oil had helped in the construction of an agricultural colony near the Caripito camp by clearing and flattening the land to create some houses and opening some roads. But in a new agreement with the government, the company would handle everything from conception to construction of an entire agricultural colony, named "the Standard Oil Company of Venezuela Agricultural Colony." When Linam laid off oil company workers due to low wartime sales in 1942, he immediately offered them alternative employment in the burgeoning agricultural colonies, a new comprehensive model of farm labor and food production.[43] Just two months after *El Farol* had published Linam's letter announcing the layoffs, the magazine featured photographs of tractors and crews working on the land to show the progress of the agricultural colony, taking shape in the eastern part of the country. The magazine highlighted the company's "new effort for the benefit of the country's workers and agriculture." These workers, essentially reassigned from oil to agriculture, were now expected to bring the countryside into the oil camps by adopting methods of planting, harvesting, and food production. In so doing, rurality had become central to the discourse on modernization, its "comfortable and hygienic homes, hospitals, schools, churches, sports fields, clubs and now agricultural colonies—all for the welfare of [its] workforce."[44]

Another agricultural colony in the same region, the Agricultural Colony of Monagas, followed a similar model of territorial occupation. Plowing their way through a vast extension of virgin jungle, the colony was almost completed by July of 1943. About 13 miles of road network was built, including a raised bridge over the river Caripe. The blueprint of this development shows that the colony included an aqueduct and water deposit tanks, along with housing for the agricultural technicians as well as for the future colonists.[45] But probably the most important feature of the colony was the "Granja de Demostración" or Demonstration Farm, which, following the Rockefeller tradition, was a kind of "maquette" for the colonists, serving not only as a prototype but as an experimentation zone, occupying a strategic spot within the village, as a central square. By this time, 58 of the 80 plots had been allotted with what the company hoped would achieve a triple goal: to "ease unemployment, foster agriculture and, in doing so, solve the problem of food supplies."[46] In a sense, this was a turning point that demonstrates a more entrenched investment in using food as a primary instrument of development and capitalism.

COMMISSARIES AS A MODEL OF SOCIAL ORGANIZATION

To build on this association of food with capitalism, Standard Oil introduced "commissaries" in the oil camps, precursors to the modern supermarkets. A 1941 article in *El Farol* described the commissary of the Caripito oil camp as a "modern, efficient, and sanitary establishment" that "operates in a large ad-hoc building conveniently situated" and where "executives as well as laborers and their families can visit the establishment any time of day."[47] This ad hoc building was a warehouse, evoking a farm barn or stable, just as the schools had. Its front façade was marked by a pitched roof and, inside, by an open floor plan with products for sale and places designated for storage and refrigeration. For the first time, in 1943, shoppers had direct access to shelves stocked with both local and imported goods. To retrieve something from cold storage, consumers only needed the assistance of a store employee. Another article in *El Farol* published that same year bragged about how expertly the shelves were organized for the sake of practicality, enjoyment, and efficiency. The article goes on to point out that shopping at the commissary was a female chore: "Ladies can look, look again, and choose well-packed articles, which makes the 'shopping excursion' more pleasant."[48] This model, called "El Comisariato" in its hispanized form, was a way for the oil company to promote food shopping as an enjoyable activity while also filling refrigerators with edible goods.

By August 19, 1943, Standard Oil of New Jersey resolved to consolidate all of its interests in Venezuela under one single umbrella organization: the Creole Petroleum Corporation.[49] A year later, Creole had begun presenting commissaries as a social enterprise that would combat the high cost of living in Venezuela.[50] With commissaries in every camp, the company collaborated with the government to determine which products would be considered basic goods, to be sold at the same prices as they had in 1940.[51] By emphasizing the commissaries' social welfare capacity amid the continual escalation of prices, the company believed it was protecting oil camp residents from a crisis in which "the poor had to pay double for beans; the rich had to pay double if they wanted to build a new house."[52] In spite of this crisis, or precisely because of it, the commissaries were considered incredibly successful—as materializations of organization and efficiency, as embodiments of capitalism and pleasure, and as the very bearers of a lifestyle of economic freedom, which soon would be launched by Rockefeller as instruments of US capitalism and Cold War anti-communism in the economic Global South.[53] It is not by chance that, having created a consumer co-op next to the Creole headquarters in the Venezuelan capital, the model of "el comisariato" would be taken to Caracas with its open shelving and "carts with wheels."[54]

1947–1967: THE "PLAN ROCKEFELLER"

The Revolutionary Junta under Betancourt, which had taken control of the country in October 1945, earnestly desired to work with Rockefeller because the food crisis and high cost of living threatened its stability. Betancourt, who for years defied foreign oil companies' extraordinary influence on the Venezuelan economy, nevertheless decided to increase taxes on their revenues and began to talk about the possibility of creating a government-owned oil company and a state refinery. In response, Rockefeller, who was already working toward diversifying the Venezuelan economy, offered foreign oil companies in Venezuela such as Royal Dutch Shell, Gulf Oil, and Socony-Vacuum Oil a different kind of solution to address their economic fears, exacerbated by high taxes and what seemed like the imminent nationalization of oil. His strategy was to create a private international enterprise that could, on the one hand, demonstrate to the government that this new company would be a selfless act in support of the region's development, and on the other hand provide business enticements for the oil companies so they could recover tax money they paid to the government. This double-edged strategy came in the form of the International Basic Economy Corporation (IBEC)—Rockefeller's broad private initiative meant to increase the production and availability of basic goods and services in underdeveloped countries, with its original laboratory in Venezuela and Brazil before expanding to more than thirty other nations.[55]

And yet what Rockefeller did not anticipate in Venezuela was the oil companies' firm rejection of this hemispheric plan—they wanted to concentrate their investment only in Venezuela.[56] As a result, Rockefeller countered with the creation, in May of 1947, of the Venezuelan Basic Economy Corporation (VBEC), a subsidiary of IBEC, with half of the capital from the oil companies and the other half from the Venezuelan government.[57] In handwritten meeting notes, Rockefeller anticipated what VBEC was to stand for: a selection of projects that are "eco[nomically] sound and produce wealth," but also ones that are organized not as charity but rather "to stimulate self-propelled activities."[58] In other words, Rockefeller was sketching a rationale that could balance profit and philanthropy. Thus, after the Second World War ended and his time in public office had come to a conclusion, Rockefeller proposed what was to become his most telling economic initiative in Venezuela, known as the "Plan Rockefeller": the project restarted his ideas and plans drafted before the war to initiate corporate activities that would be co-funded by local capital.[59] Linked to his long-standing interest in solving the Venezuelan food crisis, Rockefeller's plan was very precise: if the government received 50 percent of the oil profits and primarily channeled that into food imports, Rockefeller saw an opportunity to produce the very food that the Venezuelan government needed to import as a way for VBEC (owned by Rockefeller and his partners) to recoup a significant portion of the 50 percent state revenues.[60]

Since the beginning of the century, the Rockefellers had invested in science-driven concepts and practices in Latin American food production, but it was in post-war Venezuela, the largest producer of oil at the time, where Rockefeller launched a system that would prove that food production and food consumption are intertwined.[61] Yet in reality, more than a solution to the country's food crisis, IBEC's operation was constructed to generate capitalistic abundance and to create a countrywide desire for the US system of industrial food production and consumption during the Cold War. At the center of its operations in Venezuela was the countryside and its folk industries—farming and fishing. This went beyond manipulating land and mechanizing agriculture; it also established milk pasteurization plants, the shipping industry, and the massive distribution of food products—all meant to connect the city and the countryside into an integral, productive model. The need to create this model led to the organization of four major VBEC companies: for farming, PACA; for fishing, PESCA; for the production and distribution of milk, INLACA; and for wholesaling, CADA—its greatest success.[62]

The Compania Anonima Distribuidora de Alimentos (CADA) was created in 1948 with the main objective to implement "modern methods of wholesale and retail distribution" in the Venezuelan food market.[63] After a halting start with the creation of small supermarkets called "superettes" and later "minimaxes," neither of which had great acceptance, VBEC opted for the construction of larger-scale supermarkets. Many of these supermarkets expanded into shopping centers. The stores were designed by the company itself—always with an eye to modernist architecture. Replicating the basic metal structures that characterized barns in the countryside as well as the commissaries in the oil camps, the new supermarkets took a very simple typology and gave it a new aim: to contain and embody Venezuelan modernization. The creation through VBEC of the first supermarkets in the country generated changes in Venezuelans' daily lives. TODOS, the first VBEC supermarket, opened in the Bella Vista neighborhood in the city of Maracaibo on December 13, 1949, and was followed by the second in Camoruco, Valencia, on August 6, 1950. By 1956, VBEC had built eight supermarkets in Venezuela, pushing a trend that from the early 1940s to the early 1950s raised the consumption of imported goods by a multiple of twelve.[64] Two decades later, by 1973, VBEC had opened forty-four supermarkets in twenty-one cities around the country, twenty-six of which included soda fountains—a type of restaurant that served milkshakes, sodas, and comfort food in the style of a US diner.

Situated in the emerging Las Mercedes neighborhood of modern Caracas, Supermercado CADA became the most paradigmatic of the VBEC supermarkets, captivating the national collective imagination by emulating the US style of consumerism. Opened on October 20, 1954, this supermarket, also called an automarket, was part of the Centro Comercial Automercado, a shopping center designed by VBEC's US architect Donald Hatch (Figure 15.4). This supermarket acted as a lynchpin in an area that would become the center for much of North American income and interests.[65] The building itself acted as a final marker in the food system—the crown jewel of IBEC's model—intended to bring together the oil and farm industries, the city and the rural. Architecturally, this column-free space, which, as mentioned, recalled the large open spaces of dairy barns and commissaries, marked its reliance on oil wealth. The unsupported wide expanse of the supermarket itself, with its 10,979 square-foot shopping area and 13,993 square feet for storage and office space was made possible by a relatively expensive imported metal structure and metal skin.[66] The walls and ceiling of the supermarket's open space were modulated as geometric grids, almost as if Alejandro Otero, Sophie Taeuber-Arp, and Victor Valera had been invited to leave their mural projects at the Central University of Venezuela to embellish not a site of education and culture but of canned goods, fruits, and vegetables (Figure 15.5).[67] Like the Venezuelan Pavilion at the 1939 New York World's Fair, the store's attempt to infuse the modern with rurality permeated its entire program: traditional Venezuelan music and country dances were performed on its patios and next to the fuente de soda's tropical gardens, while ramps were installed to efficiently connect the store to parked cars—a clone of the automobile-supermarket culture in full swing in North America.[68]

The area where the Centro Comercial Automercado was located became known as one of the oil districts of Caracas.[69] This did not happen in a vacuum. During the decades of the 1940s and 1950s, the oil companies decided to construct their headquarters in the capital city, making their surroundings into enclaves associated with the imagery of modern

FIGURE 15.4 Drawing Centro Comercial Automercado Las Mercedes, Caracas, Venezuela. Architect: Don Hatch.

Source: Rockefeller Center Archive. Collection: 1052 IBEC. Series: 11 (2). Box 24.

FIGURE 15.5 Photo interior Automercado Las Mercedes, Caracas, Venezuela. Architect Don Hatch.
Source: Rockefeller Center Archive. Collection: 1052 IBEC. Series: 11 (2). Box 24.

productivity of the oil corporations and the social and spatial segregation of the oil camps. This Oil District was south of the Guaire river, along a strip that ran from the Los Chaguaramos suburb, where the new Creole Petroleum headquarters was located, to the heart of Las Mercedes district, the residential suburb where most of the executives of the Creole company lived.[70] The architectural iconography associated with its US modern lifestyle that followed is notable. A year before the supermarket opened, the Hotel Intercontinental Tamanaco, which became the most important hotel in Caracas, was built by the American firm Holabird, Root & Burgee in collaboration with Venezuelan engineer Gustavo Guinand; a few years earlier, the first Sears department store in Venezuela opened in Bello Monte (a neighborhood adjacent to Las Mercedes); later, the Venezuelan-American Center and an American School opened in the vicinity of the Centro Comercial Automercado; the first 250-capacity drive-in theater in South America, with a bar, soda fountain, and restaurant, was opened in 1949 in Los Chaguaramos; and the Boy Scouts met in open fields that would later be the grounds of the modernist Hacienda building, designed in 1957 by Diego Carbonell, the architect of the Shell Headquarters in Caracas. In addition, even the most modern gas station in Caracas, designed by Carlos Augusto Gramcko and Jose Lino Vaamonde, was built in 1957, just across the street from the supermarket, with a monumental sculpture by Otero.[71] These were all part of the expanding oil district—imagine the impact of CADA beyond the immediacy of the supermarket itself: the district, the city, and, in turn, the country, grounded in a common physical and ideological matrix of a new lifestyle embedded in the interests and dynamics of the oil corporations. The conceptual scheme of the Venezuelan oil district was apparent not only in its US-style supermarkets, US institutions, department stores, luxury hotels, and entertainment spots; it also correlated with new spatial and urban segregation, identified with the notion of the camp and the suburbs. These oil districts were designed to counteract an anachronic "otherness" present (in the eyes of Rockefeller and CADA) in the nonindustrialized countryside as much as in the non-modernized city.[72] As the oil corporations' headquarters moved in, these oil districts began shifting the city map. Sharing the archetype of the "intensification of modernity," these enclaves demonstrated a plan for territorial occupation that created a suburban circuit with limited contact with the rest of the city.[73]

These development programs as well as the consolidation of the oil districts took place during the dictatorial government of General Marcos Pérez Jiménez, in power between 1948 and 1958—a period marked by a developmentalist quest and backed by what was known as the New National Ideal, a project of the modernization of its physical surroundings in order to achieve "a moral, intellectual and material improvement of the population of the country."[74] According to Perez Jimenez's own words, its goal was "the rational transformation of the physical environment."[75] The New National Ideal was supported by a group of the Armed Forces, the guiding order and leaders of the process, along with a group of non-politicized technocrats. The construction of public infrastructure was an endless whirlwind of building cement road systems and urban buildings. The regime's relationship with the transnational oil companies was generally consensual; they allowed new oil concessions that fostered a "modernizing" model of life, considered desirable. This meant initiatives like IBEC were more than welcome, and the dictatorial regime made sure any form of resistance was eliminated. Furthermore, it was not until 1957, when the dictatorship was in its final stages, that reactions such as the one carried out by the Chamber of Commerce, which had designed "a campaign against the further growth of the IBEC [supermarket] chain," opposed what they considered an attempt of the Rockefeller enterprises to create a monopoly in Venezuela.[76]

The military dictatorship was overthrown on January 23, 1958, and along with the triumph of the Cuban Revolution in January of 1959 would be essential factors to end the relative peace with which the Rockefeller business model had unfolded in Venezuela, embodied by the IBEC. The arrival of Betancourt and the Acción Democrática political party to power by democratic elections, the development of new oil policies, the creation of the Organization of the Petroleum Exporting Countries (OPEC), the agrarian reform, the fight against guerrilla groups maintained during the 1960s, and other factors would propitiate a resistance to any form of US interests in the country, especially in the companies associated with the exploitation of oil resources or with the so-called American way of life, such as IBEC and their supermarkets and shopping centers. In fact, one of the first targets of attack was the paradigmatic Supermercado CADA Las Mercedes, bombed in 1961, with significant damage to property, and bombed again in 1963, the year that CADA reported "record profits."[77] This supermarket-associated violence continued in Venezuela during the 1960s, including the kidnapping of supermarket employees, the hijacking of CADA's trucks, and the shooting and bombing of four other CADA supermarkets.[78] In spite of all this, the middle and upper middle class in Venezuela continued to enjoy the aseptic architecture of the CADA's supermarkets, the well-stocked shelves of imported goods, the sweet fuentes de soda—all those elements that constituted "their induced fantasies of instant modernity."[79]

With IBEC operating as a form of soft developmentalism, intended to secure access to oil, diversify Rockefeller's financial holdings, and bolster Cold War relations, supermarkets became one of the main attractions of modern Venezuela. As a metropolitan asset, they reflected both the considerable US presence in the country and its appropriation by the local middle and upper-middle class, who turned them into a key testimony of the "modernization" of the built environment and Venezuelan society.[80] For Rockefeller, they were the endpoint of an ambitious system of food production, but today it is clear that they represent the failure of IBEC's attempt to balance an extractive oil economy with the promise of agricultural productivity. The lack of rail infrastructure alone made the transportation of edible products from the rural fields to the cities almost impossible, leaving the supermarkets as performative entities of a rural renovation that never took place. The middle-class appetite for imported products kept a market for new goods and even for basic goods from abroad prosperous without increasing or stimulating demand for national products. The supermarkets and fuente de sodas, where they consumed these imports, became outlets for aesthetic pleasure. It is imperative to recognize who was left out of the ranks of food security from the years of the oil bonanza; who was invisible in these projects; who benefited from a productive model that expunged endogenous lands and traditions in favor of a supposedly universalized model of profit, nutrition, and capitalism. As international exporters and the Rockefeller corporation flourished, a contingent, ephemeral phase of Venezuelan modernity, associated with a latent and somewhat fictitious collective imagination, had materialized—not from Venezuela's fertile lands and labor but from abroad.

NOTES

I give my heartfelt thanks to Henry Vicente, who has been my intellectual and archival partner in Venezuela since this project's inception. I am also grateful to Marilyn Levine, Philip Kelleher, and Nikki Moore for their editorial support and Gabriela Gamboa for translating innumerable documents.

1 In March 1937, Bolivia canceled Standard Oil of New Jersey's oil drilling rights and confiscated its facilities; and in March 1938, Mexico expropriated subsoil rights from US and British oil companies, including Standard Oil of New Jersey. In 1939, Rockefeller's oil companies, which operated in Venezuela since 1920, had the most to lose. As a result, Venezuela took political and economic priority in both US oil companies and the US government. Margarita López Maya, *E.E.U.U. en Venezuela: 1945–1948* (Caracas: Universidad Central de Venezuela, 1996), 76.

2 Antonio Ruiz, ed., *Venezuela at the New York World's Fair 1939*, ed. Antonio Ruiz (Caracas: L&S. Ptg., Co., Inc., with Standard Oil of Venezuela, Lago Petroleum Corporation, and Compañía de Petróleo Lago, nd.), Exhibition brochure. I thank Orlando Marín and Gonzalo Tovar for having access to this crucial document.

3 At the 1939 World's Fair, for which Nelson Rockefeller was a charter member, SOM designed nine pavilions, sealing a relationship with Rockefeller that would last over two more decades. The Venezuelan Pavilion was one of Gordon Bunshaft's first projects for SOM. In the late 1940s, SOM would design the oil city of Judibana, Creole Petroleum Corporation's most ambitious project in Venezuela.

4 Russell B. Porter, "Orchid-Decked Venezuela Pavilion Takes Its Place Among Fair Attractions," *New York Times*, May 27, 1939, 9. The Good Neighbor Policy was initiated by US President Roosevelt at the Seventh International Conference of American States in Montevideo, Uruguay, in December 1933.

5 Frank Monaghan, *Official Guide Book of the New York World's Fair, 1939* (New York: Exposition Publications, Inc., 1939).

6 Ibid.

7 Ruiz, *Venezuela at the New York World's Fair 1939*.

8 Ibid.

9 Historically, scholars have not sufficiently differentiated between Creole and Standard Oil of Venezuela (SOV), both subsidiaries of Standard Oil of New Jersey (SONJ). To clarify: from 1920 to 1931, Creole, which operated under the name Creole Syndicate, Inc., acquired SOV. In 1931, Creole not only changed its name to the Creole Petroleum Corporation but ceased all operations, transferring its properties to SOV and becoming a holding company. Until 1943, SOV and other SONJ's subsidiaries took over all field operations. From then until 1976 (when Venezuela nationalized its oil), Creole Petroleum Corporation became the parent company for all SONJ's subsidiaries in Venezuela, becoming the United States' largest overseas investment in a single country. "Creole Petroleum Corporation," *El Farol*, no. 63 (1944): 4–8.

10 In 1936, a few months after Rockefeller first invested in his family's oil business in Venezuela, a new labor law forced oil companies to significantly upgrade workers' living conditions. Rockefeller realized that this was the moment to move beyond the oil camps and its workers to scale up the government's efforts to secure Venezuelan modernity. Darlene Rivas, *Missionary Capitalist: Nelson Rockefeller in Venezuela* (Chapel Hill: University of North Carolina Press, 2002), 26–27.

11 Rockefeller rounded up one-third of the capital for its construction, one-third from several oil companies in Venezuela, and one-third from Venezuelan investors. Ibid., 27.

12 Lorenzo González Casas, "Modernity for Import and Export: The United States' Influence on the Architecture and Urbanism of Caracas," *Colloqui* 11 (Spring 1996): 67–70.

13 Ruiz, *Venezuela at the New York World's Fair 1939*.

14 Niko Vicario, *Hemispheric Integration: Materiality, Mobility, and the Making of Latin American Art* (Oakland: University of California Press, 2020), 123.

15 The Four Point Program was envisioned as a low-budget global mission to fight communism through agriculture and technical assistance. It seems that the idea behind the program originated with Benjamin Hardy, while working for Rockefeller in the Office of Inter-American Affairs (OIAA) in Brazil during World War II. Subsequently, it made its way into President Truman's inaugural address to the country, when Hardy worked as his speechwriter in the White House. Christine Hardy Little, interview by Richard D. McKinzie, 23 February 1973, Harry S. Truman Library (hereafter HSTL), Independence, Missouri, 11–18, www.trumanlibrary.org/oralhist/littlech.htm.

16 Arturo Uslar Pietri, Minister of Education (1939–1941), coined the slogan "sowing the oil" in 1936. Fernando Coronil, *The Magical State: Nature, Money, and Modernity in Venezuela* (Chicago: University of Chicago Press, 1997), 134.

17 Ibid., 5.

18 Ruiz, *Venezuela at the New York World's Fair 1939*.

19 The allusion to Scientific Management—Taylorism—and its systems of productivity, organization, and labor efficiency, which Le Corbusier incorporated into architectural modernism, is here clearly manifested in the adoption of the faux ramp that serves as support for the representation of agriculture and fishery.

20 Wayne Broehl, *United State Business Performance Abroad: The Case Study of International Basic Economic Corporation* (Washington, DC: National Planning Association, 1968), 24.

21 The Food Mission began during the Foreign Affairs Ministers Conference held in Rio de Janeiro, Brazil in January of 1942, with the purpose of fostering inter-American cooperation during the Second World War. López Maya, *E.E.U.U. en Venezuela*, 239–240.

22 Miguel Tinker Salas, "Staying the Course: United States Oil Companies in Venezuela, 1945–1958," *Latin American Perspectives* 32, no. 2 (2005): 147–170.

23 Hoover quoted in "The Ambassador in Venezuela (Corrigan) to the Secretary of State," Caracas, June 18, 1946, in *Foreign Relations of the United States 1946*, vol. XI (Washington, DC: U.S. Government Printing Office, 1969), 1359–1360.

24 Ibid.

25 Rockefeller coordinated the OCIAA from its foundation as the Office for Coordination of Commercial and Cultural Relations Between the American Republics (OCCCRBAR) until December 1944, then Wallace Harrison became the director until President Truman terminated the OIAA on April 10, 1946. Patricio Del Real, "Building a Continent: The Idea of Latin American Architecture in the Early Postwar" (Ph.D. diss., Columbia University, 2012), 150.

26 González Casas, "Modernity for Import and Export," 67–68.

27 Lorenzo González Casas and Orlando Marín, "El transcurrir tras el cercado: ámbito residencial y vida cotidiana en los campamentos petroleros de Venezuela (1940–1975)," *Espacio Abierto* 12, no. 3 (2003): 383.

28 López Maya, *E.E.U.U. en Venezuela*, 105–116.

29 This oil expansion was accompanied by an expansion in oil revenues, and Venezuela became one of the strongest economies in the region during those decades. Ricardo Villasmil, "Venezuela: Public Debate and the Management of Oil Resources and Revenues," in *Public Brainpower: Civil Society and Natural Resource Management*, ed. Indra Overland (London: Palgrave Macmillan, 2017), 358.

30 Shane Hamilton, *Supermarket USA: Food and Power in the Cold War Farms Race* (New Haven: Yale University Press, 2018), 70. For oil camps as social laboratories, see Miguel Tinker Salas, "Cultura, poder y petróleo: Campos petroleros y la construcción de ciudadanía en Venezuela," *Espacio Abierto* 12, no. 3 (2003): 325.

31 Rockefeller's letter to Linam, April 6, 1939, Rockefeller Archive Center RAC, RG3, 4A Folder 1571.
32 *El Farol* magazine was the Venezuelan version of the homonymous magazine *The Lamp*, founded by Standard Oil of New Jersey in 1918.
33 Sean Nesselrode, "The Harvest of Modernity: Art, Oil and Identity in Venezuela" (Ph.D. diss., New York University, 2017), 50–51.
34 Ibid., 55.
35 According to the 1941 National Census results, 76.26% of the active farming population of the country was in the states without oil. Walter Dupouy, "Consideraciones sobre algunos efectos Económicos y Sociales de la Industria del Petróleo en Venezuela," *El Farol* 10, no. 122 (1949): 8.
36 "Progreso Agrícola," *El Farol* 4, no. 39 (1942): 8.
37 "Aspectos Agro-Pecuarios," *El Farol* 6, no. 70 (1945): 23.
38 "Estación de Leche Caripito," *El Farol* 2, no. 24 (1941): 10.
39 Agricultural Clubs began functioning in Venezuela in 1938 as part of a program sponsored by the Ministry of Agriculture and Livestock. "Club Agrícola 5V Andrés Bello Creole No. 1 de Caripito," *El Farol* 6, no. 70 (1945): 1.
40 Tinker Salas, *The Enduring Legacy: Oil, Culture, and Society in Venezuela* (Durham: Duke University Press, 2009), 156.
41 Ibid., 174.
42 "Progreso Agrícola," 11.
43 Letter to workers by Henry E. Linam, *El Farol* 4, no. 40 (1942): 1.
44 "Colonias Agrícolas," *El Farol* 4, no. 42 (1942): 21.
45 "Colonia Agrícola de Caripito," *El Farol* 5, no. 50 (1943): 4.
46 Ibid., 7.
47 "El Comisariato de Caripito," *El Farol* 3, no. 31 (1941): 4.
48 "El Comisariato de Caripito," *El Farol* 4, no. 48 (1943): 9.
49 This was a direct effect of the Hidrocarburos Law of 1943. Between 1945 and 1976, Creole Petroleum Corporation produced more than all the other companies in Venezuela combined. Marco Cupolo, *Petróleo y política en México y Venezuela* (Caracas: Equinoccio Ediciones de la USB, 1997), 90.
50 "La Creole lucha contra el alto costo de la vida," *El Farol* 9, no. 101 (1947): 28.
51 "Labor Social," *El Farol* 6, no. 67 (1944): 18–19.
52 "La Creole lucha contra el alto costo de la vida," 28.
53 Hamilton, *Supermarket USA*, 2–3.
54 "Defendiendo el Presupuesto Familiar," *El Farol* 7, no. 77 (1945): 3.
55 Broehl, *United State Business Performance Abroad*, 12.
56 Ibid., 18–19.
57 VBEC was originally capitalized at $4 million by the Rockefeller family alone. Ibid., 19–23.
58 Nelson Rockefeller's Manuscript. RAC. Rockefeller Family Series AIA-IBEC, 1, 1.
59 González Casas, "Nelson A. Rockefeller y la modernidad venezolana: intercambios, empresas y lugares a mediados del siglo XX," *Petróleo nuestro y ajeno*, ed. Juan José Martín Frechilla y Yolanda Texera Arnal (Caracas: CDCH-UCV, 2005), 183.
60 Rockefeller's oil partners in VBEC were: Creole, Caribbean Petroleum (Royal Dutch Shell), Mene Grande (Gulf Oil), Socony-Vacuum, and the International Association for Economic and Social Development (AIA), a philanthropic organization created by Rockefeller and his family with the goal of raising the living standards of rural populations. Broehl, *United State Business Performance Abroad*, 17–19.
61 Hamilton, *Supermarket USA*, 4.
62 Broehl, *United States Business Performance Abroad*, xvii.
63 VBEC Manuscript. RAC. IBEC Records. Series 2, Nations and Industries, Box 19, Folder 179.
64 "Oil & Caraqueños: Venezuela Boils Over U.S. Import-Cut-Moves," *The Wall Street Journal* (April 17, 1953): 13.
65 "Don Hatch, Architect, Has Joined the Staff of the IBEC Technical Services Corp as Representative in Venezuela," *Architectural Record* (August 1948), 170.
66 Eighty percent of the construction materials as well as the products offered by the supermarket were imported. González Casas, "Nelson A," 201.
67 I refer to Otero's murals in the School of Engineering (1954), Taeuber-Arp's mural in the Psychology Library (1955), and Valera's murals in the School of Law and Political Sciences (1955 and 1956). It is not surprising to find artistic geometric modulations in a building designed by Hatch; he was an art collector and the founder of the Hatch Gallery in Caracas.
68 González Casas, "Nelson A," 201.
69 Henry Vicente, "La arquitectura urbana de las corporaciones petroleras. Conformación de Distritos Petroleros en Caracas durante las décadas de 1940 y 1950," *Espacio Abierto* 12, no. 3 (2003): 391–414.
70 The number of US citizens in the country during the 1950s was the largest in Latin America at that time. John Camp, "Influence of American Private Enterprise in the Venezuelan Economy," November 1954. RAC. Nelson A. Rockefeller Personal Papers. Countries, Series E, 63.

71 Henry Vicente, "Arquitecturas Desplazadas: Rafael Bergamín y las arquitecturas del exilio español en Venezuela" (Ph.D. diss., Universidad Politécnica de Madrid, 2014), 409–410.
72 Henry Vicente, "Distritos Petroleros en CCS," *Prodavinci*, August 8, 2017, http://historico.prodavinci.com/blogs/distritos-petroleros-en-ccs-por-henry-vicente-garrido (accessed July 14, 2020).
73 Ibid.
74 Ocarina Castillo D'Imperio, *Los años del bulldozer. Ideología y Política 1948–1958* (Caracas: Fondo Editorial Tropykos/ Asociación de Profesores UCV / Cendes, 1990), 61.
75 Nesselrode, "The Harvest of Modernity," 108.
76 Hamilton, *Supermarket USA*, 91.
77 Ibid., 92–93.
78 On June 26, 1969, thirteen incendiary bombs exploded simultaneously inside various IBEC supermarkets in Argentina. In 1975–1976, IBEC sold its supermarkets to Latin American investors. In spite of the humanitarian crisis that has affected Venezuela, most of these supermarkets are still functioning. Ibid., 95–96.
79 Lisa Blackmore, *Spectacular Modernity*: *Dictatorship, Space, and Visuality in Venezuela, 1948–1958* (Pittsburgh: University of Pittsburgh Press, 2017), 19.
80 González Casas, "Nelson A," 201–202.

16

The Jewish Agency's open cowsheds
Israeli third way rural design, 1956–1968

Martin Hershenzon

> *We need to see the farmer not as a worker but as a business owner, similar to a factory owner in the city. His income depends, hence, to a large extent on the right management of the factory—that is the agricultural farmstead.*
>
> —Raanan Weitz and Avshalom Rokach, 1963[1]

From 1956 to 1968, architects in the Rural Building Research Center, a unit operating under the Jewish Agency (Israeli rural planning authority) standardized a series of open cowsheds for *moshavim* (cooperative villages) in the context of cooperative settlement planning (see Figure 16.1). The agro-technical improvements this involved, which gradually accommodated growing quantities of milking cows per shed, embodied the shift from diverse to specialized farming in farmsteads. That is to say, whereas under the diverse farming approach of the pre-state rural settlements dairy had been the primary foundation of the Jewish village economy, it now became merely one possible sector of specialization. Dairy modernization in Israel was complicated, however, by its entanglement with issues of territory and human resources in rural development. The shift to specialization was thus not a straightforward story of modernization by way of technological standardization;[2] it involved social and cultural concerns that went beyond instrumental-technological considerations. This chapter examines how the new, postindependence standards emerged from the Israeli state's negotiations with economic, territorial, social, and architectural constraints on its geography of development. Through the example of the open shed—a vehicle on the threshold of rural modernization—we will see that the necessity of addressing these qualifying factors ultimately resulted in a unique, albeit short-lived, vision of architecture in development.

From a macroeconomic perspective, the transition to specialized farming was integral to a shift in the planning imperatives of Israeli authorities roughly from 1950 to 1965. National planners, economists, and agronomists aligned with the Mapai party (the leading Zionist party from 1933 to 1977) implemented, through this transition, a vision of the state as a singular economic entity, thus advancing beyond the proto-national planning objectives that had been salient in the 1937 British Mandate Peel Committee recommendations and up until the beginning of the 1950s. To wit, this involved a focus on increasing the state's absorptive capacities in reference to Jewish immigration and assuring the viability of a Jewish economic market at the level of individual settlements (in collectives, *kibbutzim*, or in

FIGURE 16.1 A Jewish settler, Yechie Aharon, at work in his open cowshed, the Negev, ca. 1960.
Source: Israeli Cattle Breeders Association.

cooperative villages, *moshavim*).[3] The 1950s–1960s move to agricultural specialization was defined instead by a managerial model that characterized late-developing economies in the postwar era. This vision presupposed the establishment of national financial institutions (the State Bank and the Agricultural Bank, among others), a minimized surplus production for domestic consumption, and a general turn to export.[4] As read in the opening quote by Jewish Agency Settlement Department experts Raanan Weitz (1913–1998) and Avshalom Rokach, this shift promoted an intermediate approach for the state's agricultural villages that was located between collectivist and capitalist economies.[5] The terminology shared among Jewish Agency planners at the time situated the Israeli village somewhere between the *kolkhoz* (Soviet collective farm) and the private factory.[6] Cowsheds, as the paradigmatic tool in the making of modern and productive Jewish farmers until roughly the mid-1950s, thus became a site for intense architectural calculations in the aftermath of independence.

The shift to specialization resonated with local and global forms of rural management as its implementation responded to internal and external development challenges in post-independence Israel. Externally, the revision of cooperative planning (henceforth co-op) and of dairy standards appeared in the country's technical-aid programs in Third World countries. These programs have been carried out from 1958 until the present day. They have ranged from instruction in co-op economies and in the management of co-op regional institutions to the survey and planning of rural regions, settlements, and farmsteads.[7] While shed standards were rarely disseminated in this context, these programs defined the setting in which Jewish Agency planners conceived the design for dairy specialization as representative of a national "intermediary way." As much as this way was situated between collectivization and liberalism, within this global development framework, these initiatives stood at the threshold of modernization and presupposed dividing lines between modernized states and the "not yet" modernized.

These divides, in turn, mapped onto the planning experience in Israel. They served planners in describing the relations between the state's metropolitan centers and countryside; additionally, they shaped the portrayal of a gradient of rural forms of settlement as fostering exchanges between internal settings that were, in retrospect, perceived as belonging to the Global North and Global South. Rural planning for dairy specialization posited the pre- and postindependence kibbutzim as a bygone model, in view of their radical collectivization and high degree of accomplished industrialization. Nonetheless, this practice also assessed the kibbutzim as an internal gauge for a sought-after rural modernity in newly founded *moshav ovdim* (workers' cooperative village), and more specifically the *moshav olim* (immigrants village, from now on referred to as moshavim). Together, this set of conditions had sizeable implications for the conception of dairy standards and the architectural knowledge embedded in their production. These paralleled revisionist approaches in Israeli social housing from the early 1960s onwards.[8]

The first section of this chapter discusses the pre-state foundation of cooperative settlement on the basis of diverse farming and the role of dairy farming therein. The second and third sections analyze the revision of cooperative settlement after independence and the institutional setting in which it was embedded. The last section interprets the developmental agenda resulting from this planning revision as it was manifested in the design of open-shed standards.

DAIRY FARMING IN COOPERATIVE SETTLEMENTS DURING THE BRITISH MANDATE FOR PALESTINE

Beginning in 1908, the Jewish National Fund and its chief agronomist Yitzhak Elazari Volcani (1880–1955) promoted the dairy sector as a basis for diverse farming in pre-state Israel and as the major tool for developing modern Jewish agriculture.[9] Volcani's turn to diversify farming relied on colonization models originating in late-nineteenth-century experiments in cooperative settlements in Italy.[10]

Following Volcani's work, rural engineers and architects who worked for the Zionist settlement authorities designed fully enclosed, stone, and reinforced concrete cowshed facilities that derived from German Templers' models. These took on a strategic role as an initial measure in the race for rural development within cooperative villages as they began to form in the early 1910s.[11] The generalization of this model from the early 1920s coincided with the foundation of the *moshav* movement in 1919 by members in the cooperative villages who sought a more moderate model of cooperation than the fully collectivized kibbutz.

This shift to diverse farming also occurred within emerging conditions of conflict with Arab communities in Palestine.[12] Efforts to secure the Jewish economy were reflected in the appreciation of livestock, and the dairy sector in particular, as a source of annual output in contrast to the seasonal fluctuations of field crops. Furthermore, the British Mandate placed various restrictions on Jewish land purchases until the settlement of conflicts with Arab communities were achieved; this led leaders of the cooperative movement to rely on the more compact forms of settlements that Volcani's model enabled relative to those found in the early 1910s communes.[13] Therefore, at the time, cowsheds became one of the major emblems of Jewish labor autonomy and productivity (see Figure 16.2).[14]

FIGURE 16.2 The courtyard of Kibbutz Merhavia, 1946.
Source: Kluger Zoltan. © Government Press Office, Israel, D18–007.

While earlier, through the 1920s and into the 1930s, Volcani's model encompassed both *kibbutz* and *moshav*, it gradually became a more dominant foundation in the latter movement, whose moderate form of cooperation presupposed the relative autonomy of individual family farmsteads.[15] The family was to function as an independent unit of cultivation and consumption that relied on cooperative distribution and purchase.

In the kibbutz movement, while there was some reliance on forms of diverse farming, there was an initial turn to intensification and specialization of production in different agricultural sectors starting in the early 1930s, a result of the movement's collectivized form of labor and production management. Moshavim, the villages under more moderate forms of cooperation, on the other hand, were organized under the Settlement Movement and were predicated upon Volcani's emphasis on dairy production in individually run farmsteads, beginning with the foundation of the movement's first village in 1921 and up until independence.

Thus, from Volcani's tenure through independence and then in the first two decades afterward, two major design trajectories came to define the notion of the shed in development: on the one hand, the economic value of milking cows as an input into national economic frameworks, and on the other, and related to this, villages' social-productive configuration as a constitutive unit of nation-building. Cowshed designs varied substantially in the facilities within kibbutzim from those in the moshavim.[16] These two trends reflect, in the decades following independence, opposing poles in terms of which planners understood the revision of cooperative settlement and dairy specialization within it.

In the kibbutz, collectivized production and labor, beginning in 1912, resulted in different configurations of non-parceled villages and in larger-scope facilities. Village organization relied on a Prussian farm model in which the layout was defined by the work and production quarter; the cowshed in this model was set in an axis relative to a central work court, at the sides of which residential units were organized. The crop fields extended from all sides of this nucleus. With the later specialization of village functions in the 1920s and '30s, collectives continued to be oriented toward the central court, which turned into a social lawn, connecting and separating the social-collective amenities and residential and work areas.

The kibbutz movement's focus on labor and land collectivization enabled the intensification of milk production early on, and by the 1920s, kibbutz cowsheds housed an average of 20–30 milking cows per facility, with the ability to provide dairy output for villages of 120–500 members. Beginning in the 1930s, further intensification of the dairy production in the movement was accompanied by the specialization of structures, such that the housing and milking of cows occurred in separate facilities.[17] By the late 1940s, many kibbutzim had cowsheds that accommodated up to 100–120 milking cows per facility, serving their own members and other communities through the dairy distribution co-op *Tnuva*.[18]

In comparison, the cowsheds of the moshavim, which gained recognition as a distinct phenomenon in 1921 with the village of Nahalal, were smaller and were erected within single-family household plots. In these villages, shared cultural and social amenities were placed at the center; privately owned farmsteads radiated around these in concentric, more or less symmetrical arrangements or were organized orthogonally. Also at the center were the collaborative purchase, distribution, and credit mechanisms related to agricultural production. These settlements were physically compact, with the average farmstead during the 1920s amounting to around 28 dunams. This size allowed a sufficient number of settlers to access the amenities on par with the kibbutzim and justified the investment in these resources while enabling a reduction in taxes. Finally, in all such villages, the cowsheds formed the external limit of the settlement. They were erected as a longitudinal structure parallel to the farmhouses' rear facades and the street front, serving thus also as a protective wall against possible insurgent attacks by the Indigenous Palestinian population.

Given the limitations in parcel size, resources, and labor capacities, the move from diverse farming to dairy specialization was made manifest in several models that came to replace an initial model, which the Jewish Agency rural planners referred to as the "universal cowshed" (*Refet Universalit*, see Figure 16.3).[19] This title denoted a structure that operated on a similar basis as other types of shacks that were imported from several countries, such as Sweden, Finland, Austria, the United States and Canada in the first decade after independence for purposes of temporary, emergency housing in newly founded settlements.[20] Unlike these other shacks, which were primarily made of wood, tin, and canvas, the universal cowsheds were made of silicate bricks or reinforced concrete walls, most likely as a protection from the insurgent attacks that endangered the dairy economy to various degrees until the first years after the 1948 war.[21] Like the later, open and more flexible sheds of the 1950s, the universal cowshed's interior conformed to a rationale of linear organization. Enclosing a space of roughly 2.5 by 3.5 meters, its longer edge was made of an in-situ poured concrete trough serving one to two cows. However, unlike the later sheds, its orientation in the short direction of the plot and the fact that it was composed of solid walls defined it as a finished unit of production. This hampered future extensions and restricted revisions to the production

FIGURE 16.3 A Jewish Agency universal cowshed, ca. 1930s.

Source: Israeli Cattle Breeders Association.

functions of the farmstead more generally. Accordingly, these facilities obstructed the possibilities of specialized agricultural production in the dairy sector.

Along with this limitation, the technical designation as "universal" reflected a basic standard, generalized across many forms of rural development and thus instigating settlement. Discussing the 1950s revision in cooperative planning, Raanan Weitz, who served as the head of the Jewish Agency Settlement Department from the beginning of the 1950s, disclosed the bio-political function of these cowsheds when he described the dairy component in diverse farming as a "universal stamp" (*Khotemet Yesod Aakhat*), a standard that would underscore the viability of Jewish villages and their conquest of new territories.[22] It was in view of this status that these structures formed a component of the initial settlement subsidy-aid that the Jewish Agency provided to settlers to foster the foundation of new moshavim.[23] Settlers' descriptions from the 1920s and onto the 1940s often noted that these sheds were the first symbol of settlement, following land leveling and the arrangement of street and plot lines prior to actual house construction.[24]

These descriptions of cowsheds quietly infiltrated discussions on architecture in the service of welfare institutions from the pre-state to the postindependence period. While not explicitly registered in the architectural historiography of Palestine/Israel, architects' anecdotal descriptions demonstrate how these sheds came to represent the brute economic functionality of building for rural development. As such, these structures took on the discursive role of a *building*, as opposed to *architecture*. *Building* designated, in the interwar period, structures from which all "extraneous" ornament had been removed.[25] While this view directly reflected the Jewish Agency's approach to architecture, other approaches to design attenuated this distinction between function and form. The conceptualization of the cowshed as a building, like other shacks associated with an initial subsistence economy of settlement, also legitimized a more humanistic-aesthetic notion of architectural practice, which positioned itself as a response to the crude necessities of settlement. The co-op ideal of frugality and minimum dwelling to maximum number of settlers was thus translated and sublimated into an architectural form,[26] as seen in the non-ornate, clear-toned and "simple" cubic rural and urban housing and public buildings from the 1930s and '40s. This view of settlement architecture was most sharply argued in the 1940 publication *20 Years of Building*, published by the Federation of Jewish Workers, which summarized two decades of work under cooperative organizations.[27] Hence, architects transformed brute necessity into a symbol of frugality; or, to put it in the terms utilized by philosopher Giorgio Agamben, they transformed bios into a form of life.[28]

In distinction to this emphasis within architectural circles, architects and planners working for the Jewish Agency in the 1950s perceived the universal shed more in terms of the agency's focus on settlement planning and its economy. In this context, they saw the shed as an economic measure that, in its generality and mode of fabrication, was limiting development. They hence came to address the shed relative to the challenges of developmental thinking. The following section delves into the settings in which the agency's post-independence development approach emerged.

THE REVISION OF MOSHAVIM PLANNING AND DAIRY SPECIALIZATION IN THE AFTERMATH OF ISRAELI INDEPENDENCE

As we have seen, the two decades succeeding independence saw Israeli settler authorities contend with a dual shift: from an emphasis on the development of collective (kibbutz) villages to regional cooperative planning that was based on the moshavim model, and in this latter model, from diverse to specialized (industrial) farming.[29] In a practical sense, this meant providing cooperative workers' villages with the tools to operate on a par with the industrial characteristics of both pre-state kibbutzim and capitalist agricultural farms in and outside Israel. At the same time, national economic plans required production, produce-purchase and distribution-related resources to be relocated between clusters of moshavim and the rural region as a whole (e.g. a scheme consisting of multiple villages and a medium-sized town).[30] During this transitory period, the revision of planning standards began to apply the norms of regional planning to address broader social-national challenges.[31]

Postindependence regional cooperative planning served various objectives, and it also provided the general context in which the dairy standard revisions and the related development planning discourse occurred. Planning sought to consolidate and secure national borders, assure a continuous Jewish presence, and limit the future growth of Palestinian settlements between the Gaza strip and Judea and Samaria and along the borders of the latter.[32] Following the establishment of national planning units and a banking system, the state's agricultural planning administrations (the Jewish Agency Settlement Department, the Joint Center for Agricultural Planning, and the Unit for Agricultural Planning in the Israeli Defense Force) also secured and regulated production rates. They treated rural and urban settlements as a single national system of production, surveying and planning their economic flows in units of several years.[33] In pursuit of this national consolidation, they defined quotas dedicated to the reduction of surplus production relative to domestic consumption rates—here the dairy and livestock economy posed significant challenges—and fostered an export economy.[34] These objectives challenged the independence of economic planning, and consequently the autonomy, of pre-state kibbutzim and of moshavim; in so doing, they also advanced a correlation between local and regional planning and national agendas.

Consequently, the purposes of cooperative settlement came to be revised within a broader project of integration and modernization of immigrant populations that were viewed by state authorities as culturally and ethnically inferior.[35] After 1948, the number of Ashkenazi Jews emigrating from European countries fell; instead, Mizrachi Jews from North African and Middle Eastern countries comprised the majority of new immigrants.[36] The plea of Israel's first prime minister, David Ben-Gurion, to settle the rural countryside, which he announced soon after independence, did not sway the pre-state Ashkenazi elites, who were in the majority and settled in the urban centers. The recent immigration of Mizrachi Jews made them an easy target for fulfilling these aims. In 1952, following the reluctance of Ashkenazi members of the kibbutzim movement to integrate recently emigrated Mizrachi Jews, Ben-Gurion revoked his unequivocal support for this movement.[37] This development, together with the other post-independence planning objectives listed earlier, led to a shift in national priorities for settlements: away from full collectivization and toward a more moderate model of cooperation.

Planning authorities sought to address tensions between pre- and postindependence immigrants, Ashkenazi and Mizrachi Jews respectively, by assimilating the latter into the seemingly established Ashkenazi social and cultural fabric, predicated upon Westernized modern values. Moreover, the newly arriving Mizrachi Jews largely originated from rural and urban areas in North Africa and the Middle East, where cooperative movements were not as broadly organized as they were in Eastern and Western Europe. Unlike in Europe, preparation of future Jewish immigrants by such movements for agricultural settlement prior to Israeli independence was rare.[38] Accordingly, settling institutions viewed this group as unprepared to adhere fully to collective rural life and the stern model of the kibbutz.[39] They understood this group's social and cultural integration and labor productivity as contingent on guidance in matters of economic discipline, work, and cooperative ideals, as well as on personal hygiene, and devised different tools and models accordingly. From this vantage point, the cooperative workers village, with the single-family unit as the basis of capital, labor, and social organization, became the dominant planning paradigm; this type of village had been a part of pre-state planning models yet was not previously the prevailing approach. It was based upon the dependence of the individual household on national (leased) lands and the organization of production and consumption between the household unit and the village and region's cooperative mechanisms. Rural planners viewed this village model, which presupposed a nonvoluntary cooperation, as being more propitious for the Mizrachi settlers than the fully cooperative model of the kibbutzim.[40]

The Jewish Agency's planners conceived the dairy standards and the regionally dispersed and interconnected settlements scheme as joint tools for gradual socialization in modern state citizenship. At the level of farmsteads, dairy standards anticipated a tentative professionalization of agricultural labor. At the village level, the independent neighboring units enabled planners to separate (and connect) ethnic groups through semi-autonomous everyday life and work spheres, with the intention of increasing community cohesion and stability.[41]

At the regional level, the planners saw various avenues to encourage gradual socialization: within clusters of villages and interregional service and agricultural production areas and, finally, at work and civic centers in new (mid-sized) towns.[42] As an instrument of socialization of new settlers into a "civilized" and "productive" Israeli society, cooperative regionalism embodied the postindependence welfarist and gradualist metaphor of the melting pot.

This direction in village planning was, however, short-lived. The 1970s saw a large-scale colonization of the Galilee and of the newly occupied West Bank, in which the Jewish Agency moved away from regional cooperative settlement planning. Instead, from the second half of the 1970s, they pushed to substantiate the centrality of the 1950–60s specialized cooperative workers village model with new village models that were designated Industrial Villages (*KAFAT, kfrar taasiati*).[43] This village model referred to purely economic enterprises that were located in proximity to new entirely residential villages (*yeshuv kehilati*, e.g., community settlements that gradually turned into suburban entities) and did not rely on a discourse of cooperation. Turning away from agricultural activities and toward an industrial and postindustrial economy represented the eclipse of the planning revision as outlined through the 1950s and '60s.

DAIRY STANDARDS AT THE CROSSROAD OF INSTITUTIONAL SETTINGS AND PLANNING PARADIGMS

Along with these economic and social pressures, rural planning and dairy standards under the 1950s co-op reform also comprised a practical-theoretical framework involving different efforts to generalize local planning models to serve as technical intermediaries in development.[44] In line with post-World War II global development culture, the agency's planners articulated the Israeli model in terms of a comprehensive planning approach.[45] This conjoined, in local rural settings, issues of physical planning and replanning (design for reuse) and social modernization with a process-based view of agricultural specialization.[46] While rarely disseminated abroad, the agency's dairy facility designs became exemplars of architectural contributions to the state's development model.

A central figure in this transformation was the aforementioned Raanan Weitz. Following in the footsteps of his father, Joseph Weitz, a prominent agronomist, Weitz studied agronomy in Florence in the 1930s. Upon his return to Palestine in 1938, he joined the circle of Mapai and the Jewish Agency Settlement administration.[47] Weitz was not only instrumental in devising—alongside other settlement administrators—the mechanics of regional development in Israel but also became a leading force in promoting its export elsewhere.[48] Israel's transition from the mid-1950s to the mid-1970s can be characterized in terms of a shift from a recipient of development aid to an exporter of development aid. The Jewish Agency's replanning of cooperative workers' villages and its assessment of this process likewise responded to this by elaborating research-based knowledge models that could be transplanted and applied across varied geographies.[49]

As this concerned physical rural planning and design for dairy structures, these efforts to theorize a planning model led to the Jewish Agency's foundation of the Rural Building Research Center and the Center for Research on Settlements. The first was founded in 1956 at the agency's Settlement Department of the northern regions in Haifa. As a subsection of the department's technical bureau, this center was made responsible for surveys and technical provisions preceding settlement planning and the planning of new villages, specifically in view of the improvement of work processes and production facilities standards in single-family farmsteads. Its work involved, initially, the supply of services primarily to moshavim, largely involving the transfer of agro-technical improvements from international rural engineering publications and from pre-state kibbutzim and moshavim. Then, in 1962, the center became affiliated with the Technion Israel Institute of Technology and its new Faculty of Agricultural Engineering.[50] At this point, the Rural Building Research Center expanded its scope to embrace a more global ambition. It was now also responsible for disseminating the Israeli model of cooperative planning by providing technical assistance in regional surveys and pedagogy for Third World countries. This latter orientation also involved a gradual withdrawal by the Rural Building Research Center from its previous mission in the moshavim sector. By the second half of the 1960s, the center's local services concerned villages and farmers that were affiliated with both the moshavim and the kibbutzim movements, as well as Palestinian villages within the Green Line, thus addressing a fuller scope of forms of settlements in Israel.[51] The second applied-research unit, the Center for Research on Settlement, was officially founded in 1962 in Rechovot.[52] Its primary mission concerned the survey and support of new regional development and by extension of moshavim as functioning within regional schemes. It also took equal part in technical aid projects outside of Israel, which resulted in regional surveys, planning, and pedagogy for Third World countries.[53]

Architectural expertise took on a prominent role in the research, planning, and standardization work in these two centers. Correspondingly, as a consequence of the Jewish Agency's broad engagements, architectural knowledge (via models and physical and planning measures) was exchanged among experts—agronomists, geographers, and sociologists—and among settler groups. An example is the work of architect and planner Emmanuel Yalan (1903–1981), who through planning for specialization and dairy farming became institutionally intermingled in a form of negotiation involving technical engineering and social planning.

Yalan began his training at the Architectural Association and graduated from Hessische Baugewerkschule der Technischen Lehranstalten Offenbach am Main in 1926. Upon his return to Palestine, he formed an association with the architect, architectural educator, and military leader Yochanan Ratner, a prominent defender of Neues Bauen in Palestine. Yalan's career took a sharp turn with respect to matters of village planning and livestock facilities design following his winning entry of a plan for the Ta'anach region in the Jezreel Valley in 1950, in a competition organized by the Jewish Agency. His engagement in large-scale planning under the agency's Settlement Department allowed him to become acquainted with the question of planning and the replanning of the family farmstead in moshavim. Economic, infrastructural, and security concerns were seen as constraints defining the size and shape of the family farmstead, constraints that often hampered the use of rural production facilities and the organization of labor.[54] In approaching these new settlements, Yalan observed how individual settlers, who for the most part lacked either the skills or the economic outlook for building, were left to their own devices in shaping their shelters. A discrepancy thus developed between large-scale, hurried planning and the micro-levels of spatial organization and building in rural contexts; to address this, Yalan pushed for the foundation of the Rural Building Research Center—he would direct this until its closure in 1974—and became a member of the Research Center on Settlement. These two institutional involvements enabled Yalan to conceive of multi-scalar interventions relative to the single-family farmstead, the village, and the regional units, a sensibility reflected in Yalan's surveys and designs of dairy standards, which subsequently informed the formulation of the Jewish Agency's comprehensive planning approach.

On a theoretical level, the responses to all these internal challenges drew on two primary applied research pillars—modernization theory and central place theory. While these pillars framed the North/South development rift in a global postwar (or Cold War) development context, in Israel these could also be mapped out on the regional level.[55] Modernization theory prevailed as a form of social thinking in the Jewish Agency Settlement Department and, by extension, defined the preliminary assumptions underlying the work of the Research Center on Settlement. Weitz, as the director of the Research Center on Settlement, translated this vision to the context of rural settlements following Shmuel Eisenstadt (1923–2010), director of the Department of Sociology at the Hebrew University, who was active in introducing North American modernization sociology to the Israeli academic and technocratic scene.[56] Weitz's planning for agricultural specialization sought to gradually involve the participation of new Mizrachi settlers in Israel's economy and society.[57] The physical planning vocabulary of the 1950s and '60s described such participation through a diagrammatic-organizational lens that drew from Central Place Theory.

Central Place Theory became the *lingua franca* of the state's rural and urban planning agencies as early as the 1940s, as manifest from its presence in the first national plan (1948–1953).[58] Specifically, Yalan and in-house geographers in the Research Center on Settlement used the theory to survey and analyze the distribution of various kinds of regional services (educational, cultural, religious amenities, etc.).[59] The theory also undergirded the minimal yet flexible spatial arrangement of rural neighboring units, village clusters, and interregional centers, all with the aim of achieving effective territorial development and social modernization.

Finally, the "optimal" and "operative" livestock "units" that were a feature of Yalan's work between the two centers also reflected the integration of shed design with economic agrotechnical and zootechnical rationales. His designs translated these rationales through the geometric and diagrammatic representation of work processes, the movements of human and animal bodies, and the configuration of facilities as they unfolded in a temporal sequence. These approaches seem to have been in line with functional, *Existenzminimum* reflections that were highly influential in Jewish housing production and at the Technion Architectural Faculty in the 1930s and '40s, where Yalan was an active participant.

The neutral and overtly technical language of planning and design for labor productivity and specialization, based on these various sources, did not address the issue of social modernization directly. Rather, it enabled planners to address a national territory laden with social forces in rather abstract terms. As rural modernization joined territorial and economic features with social and cultural ones, the instrumental approach to design played a more tacit role within development as it came to operate in a broader setting of planning expertise and research.[60]

DAIRY AGRO-TECHNICS IN THE DEVELOPMENT OF THE MOSHAVIM

The process of specialization has not yet occurred in most developing countries, but its time will inevitably come. The job demands a combination of realism and flexibility . . . administrators must view their task in dynamic terms. Their blueprints should design not just a mixed farm, but the kind of mixed farm that can most easily evolve towards an increasing specialization when the time comes.

—Raanan Weitz, "An Ever Changing Farm"[61]

The Rural Building Research Center cowshed standards responded to the ways in which specialization in dairy farming differed from specialization in other sectors. From the late 1950s and into the 1960s, specialization in sectors such as beet sugar, cotton, grain, nuts, and tobacco (sectors that were equally promoted in the moshavim movement) relied on the implementation of irrigated farming. The Jewish Agency planned this shift in parcels of land that were chiefly located outside the individual family farmsteads and independent of any built structures.[62] Distinct from the transition to specialization in these sectors, specialization in dairy farming was pursued in several phases, and the first phase of implementation regarded a replanning of cowshed facilities within the family farmstead.[63] Accordingly, dairy specialization often had to address the restraints of a given parcel size and geometry (an average lot size was 30 dunams, 30–40 meters in width) together with the facilities that were erected therein as part of the settlement's initial foundation phase. This initial phase, which mostly occurred in the first half of the 1950s, was based on a small livestock component, which was housed in the fully enclosed universal shed. The gradual enlargement of cowshed facilities was ideally to be pursued while avoiding the demolition of older structures and allowing for their reuse.

As it involved investment in the erection of buildings, specialization in dairy farming involved a greater economic risk than specialization in other branches of agriculture, resulting in the authorities' pursuit of expert knowledge in agro-technics and their design. The risk associated with dairy farming specialization was also due to the high cost that the purchase of livestock and investment in new equipment and facilities posed for postindependence settlers. The Jewish Agency responded to this issue with a system of scaled, monthly settlement subsidies. It implemented this system between the years of 1956 and 1962, a period in which the agency expected farmers to develop their independent production and cultivation capacities and secure a stable income.[64] The sheds' flexible and phased standards responded thus to the logic of guided credit. Yet in the framework of an intermediary model of cooperation, the flexibility of these standards derived from a broader understanding regarding the need to address contingencies and risks in farmsteads. It was under this logic that the sheds were revised, qualifying the intensification of milk farming in terms of countervailing economic restraints.

Planners thus saw sheds as enabling a dual logic of development; on the one hand, their systematized configuration envisioned a streamlining and an increase in milking ratios, while on the other hand, their flexibility and scalability reflected measures for economic risk control and a response to various types of contingencies. Intensification was manifest in the progression of a series of cowshed models that Yalan designed for the Rural Building Research Center in 1956, 1960, 1961, and 1964. These progressed from the universal cowsheds that had accommodated 1–2 cows to provide space for 5–8, 8–15, and 15–30 cows, respectively. The open shed structure that characterized all these models was predicated upon improved ventilation and the rationalization, phasing, and adaptability of the physical structure and of the labor processes it accommodated. Predominantly, intensification relied on the sheds' linear and extensible organization, as derived from Californian models, which were at the time already fully integrated in Israeli collectives, and on their structural systematization, following English farm models.[65] Against the imperatives of intensification, measures of restraint were imposed by the provisions for flexibility in the facilities' structural system. This system defined relatively independent components or functional strips and allowed various modes of implementation and development. It enabled a flexible arrangement of the sheds' programmatic components and maximal variation in the definition of a farming model, with possible and temporary inclusion of various livestock and modes of functioning (see Figure 16.4).[66] Different technical solutions also

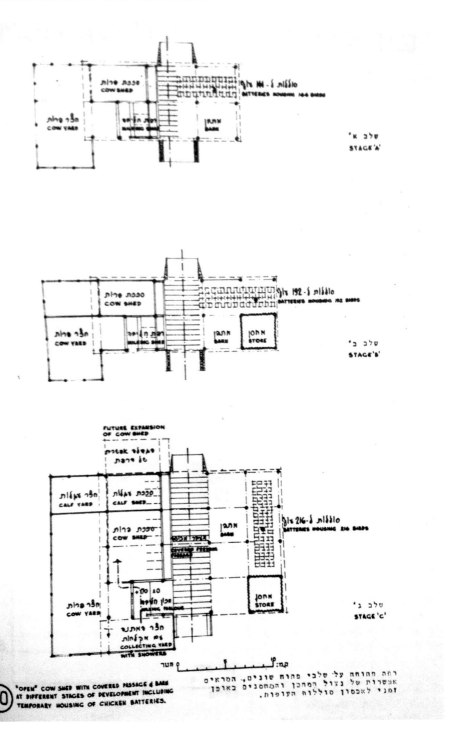

FIGURE 16.4 A theoretical design showing the repurposing of an open shed's sections in three phases.

Source: Emmanuel Yalan, ed., *Private and Cooperative Agricultural Settlement: Physical Planning; International Seminar on Rural Planning* (Haifa: Rural Building Research Bureau, 1961).

advanced the flexibility required by the climate and economy in resources: a demountable, self-built, and extensible trough, which was made of a recycled or prefabricated material; a self-deployable device for a compost collection system under the breeding area, in view of drought conditions; and a demountable roof to simulate a breeding area in natural habitat conditions. In contrast with the sheds that were made to be intensified in advance in pre- and postindependence kibbutzim, these solutions rendered the Jewish Agency's open-shed standards a more flexible device, which could respond to and manage risk, both economic *and* social.

This last point also regarded, albeit via a different kind of calculation, the issue of mechanization and circulation in and outside of the shed. Using the design principles that were characteristic of kibbutzim's farming practices of the 1930s, the new sheds enabled tractor circulation within the facility for the disposal and removal of hay in the breeding area and the distribution of fodder along a longitudinally oriented trough.[67] These practices persisted sporadically in Palestine in moshavim founded in the 1920s. They were not, however, prevalent in the new moshavim established in the 1940s and in the immediate aftermath of independence, where smaller-scale, prefabricated, universal cowsheds were the rule.[68] The Jewish Agency's advancement of these principles aimed to put new moshavim on an even footing with older ones. However, in distinction from the kibbutzim, where tractors were, like other resources, owned and managed on a collective basis, tractor ownership was rare in the new moshavim; there, the scarcity of means at the disposal of settlers precluded the ownership of heavy machinery. Hence, in parallel with the introduction of open cowsheds, the Jewish Agency advanced the establishment of tractor stations, as well as those for other agro-technical equipment, at the center of new cooperative workers village clusters. Managed by the agency on a regional basis, these defined a counterpart to the flexible system of the shed.[69]

The 1956–1964 open sheds' adaptability was informed by principles that were central to postwar functionalist thinking: general flexibility, multi-use, and reuse of existing components and developmentally oriented self-built constructions.[70] Under these headings, the facilities defined at once an organized whole and a kit of semi-independent agro-technical improvements. As also legible through their representation in comparative charts within publications by the Rural Building Research Center, the sheds demonstrated how a union of these principles could negotiate the regional challenges of rural modernization. Indeed, these comparative charts, which reflected on the process of Israeli dairy specialization and village reform from the 1950s through the 1960s, addressed a myriad of issues: the rational and "hygienic" organization of labor and housing, the optimal use and reuse of available resources and adaptation to circumstance, the cultivation of resourcefulness and self-initiative in work organization, and more broadly, the functional distribution of services and infrastructure in view of ideal work flows. These were matters affecting not only the future economic growth of the farmstead but a long-term viability of the rural community. Within the national rural scheme, they corresponded with the ways in which the standardization of sheds was interlaced with the development of a new form of cooperative living and labor. Via the sheds, these publications situated the moshav at a safe and already "modern" distance from pre-state Palestinian villages in Israel, where livestock and habitation were not "hygienically" separated; they also situated it as distinct from the straightforward model of industrial progress that was enabled in kibbutzim (see Figure 16.5). The sheds' systematic flexibility exemplified a developmental, Southern perspective that qualified the facilities'

THE JEWISH AGENCY'S OPEN COWSHEDS 337

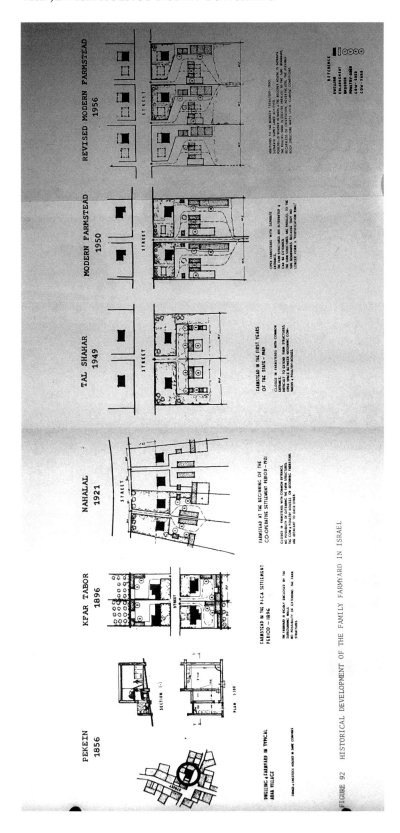

FIGURE 16.5 A chart representing the "Historical Development of the Family Farmyard in Israel."

Source: Emmanuel Yalan, *The Design of Agricultural Settlements: Technological Aspects in Rural Community Development* (Haifa: Jewish Agency and Technion—Israel Institute of Technology Faculty of Agricultural Engineering, 1975).

Northern prospect of progress; they stood for a gradual phasing out of the predominance of the kibbutz—a local model that was representative of early modernization—in favor of a new form of "appropriate" modernization for subjects whose modernity was seen as somewhat challenged. This differentiated modernization was also manifest through the efforts to frame the sheds, and the Israeli moshavim by extension, as a model for international rural initiatives elsewhere.

CONCLUSION

This chapter examined a facet of Israeli development expertise as it emerged in the context of dairy farming facility design under a revision of the state's cooperative planning model. The state's revised model of cooperation—and the place dairy occupied therein—played an ideological role in the configuration of Israeli settler society after independence. This shift would also become influential in the Israeli state's global dissemination of its development expertise. As articulated through architectural design and comprehensive planning, this model was part of a larger, multidisciplinary reflection on agro-technical standards and the organizational deployment of settlements in regional frameworks. The chapter showed how this approach to development was predominantly geared toward managing immigrant populations deemed un-modern by the state. Agricultural planning in Israel echoed, in this case, the general premises of anthropologist James Scott's account of high modernism and geographer Oren Yiftachel's analysis of Israeli development after independence, as an ethnocratic project that, after having dispossessed the Palestinian population of their land, denied land control and an equitable share in national resources to Mizrachi migrant groups.[71]

However, the Israeli concept of differentiated modernization relied also on a flexible and heterogeneous view regarding the development of rural systems. While at the macro level it maintained the variety of forms of rural and urban settlements from the pre-state period, at its micro level, it sought to enable responsiveness to the various populations who occupied and operated these systems and the climatic conditions in which the settlements were situated. In so doing, design for dairy farming represented a form of institutionally embedded architectural practice that was attuned to economic, climatic, and social contingencies and risks.[72]

Thus, while undergirding a problematic history of settlement, internal colonization, and a certain disempowerment of immigrant communities, the history of these sheds also demonstrates the particular kind of agency architects gained in rural development. Their expertise was expressed in their devising a user- and community-oriented vision of economy, resources, and agro-technics. Grounded in expert-based and welfarist rhetoric of development, the flexible dairy standards of the 1950s and '60s produced an open-ended system of large-scale planning and standardization.

In this sense, the Jewish Agency's work manifested countercurrents to Scott and Yiftachel's perspectives on high modernist state planning. These involved the understanding of planning as a tool in community building that was also—to use historian Daniel Immerwahr's notion—"thinking small," that is, envisioning the consolidation of small communities through bottom-to-top dynamics of democratization, an emphasis that was dominant in North American development culture in the 1950s and '60s.[73]

In the case of the Jewish Agency, this occurred as its practice addressed the social makeup of the settlers, their resources and knowledge, and their possible empowerment, despite conflicted predicaments to the contrary.[74] Such counter-threads also corresponded with what Ijlal Muzaffar has recognized as an inherent drive in development thinking, specifically in self-built practices, to make room for alternations to the standards, limitations, and failures in application.[75] The Jewish Agency planners, while overtly technical in their approach to the bio-political management of the Israeli rural south, sought at the same time, with their regionally laden dairy standards, a means to consolidate immigrant communities and gradually coproduce independent modern farmers who would conform, in the long run, to the economic and social standards set by the pre-state settling elites. In this sense, the phasing out of the high modernist kibbutz model corresponded with a gradualist phasing of the settlers into the Israeli society and the standards set by the pre-state elites toward this end. The flexible open cowshed is perhaps the most emblematic form of this parallel process. "User"-responsive and "community"-driven, it provided "lacking" subjects with the crutches putatively necessary for their own self-transformation into productive citizens.

NOTES

1 Raanan Weitz and Avshalom Rokach, *Agriculture and Rural Development in Israel: Projection and Planning* (Rehovot: The Jewish Agency Settlement Department, 1963), 19.
2 Melanie E. DuPuis, *Nature's Perfect Food: How Milk Became America's Drink* (New York: New York University Press, 2002), 129–130.
3 Arieh Krampf, *The Israeli Path to Neoliberalism: The State, Continuity and Change* (London: Routledge, 2018), chap. 5.
4 Ibid., 113 and Raanan Weitz, *The Israeli Village in the Age of Technology* (Tel Aviv: Am Oved, 1967), 63.
5 Raanan Weitz served as the head of the Jewish Agency Settlement Department from 1950 until the 1970s. An agricultural economist, Rokach worked under Weitz at the Research Center on Settlement in Rechovot.
6 The Jewish Agency planners in the 1960s commonly referred to collective villages (kibbutzim) as "big farms," envisioning them as a target of development that assimilated a capitalist logic. Emmanuel Yalan, Jacob Maos, and Lipa Kam, *Rationalization of Farm Parcels in the Cooperative Agricultural Village* [in Hebrew] (Haifa, Rural Building Research Center, 1963).
7 Inbal Aliza Belman and Shachar Zahavi, *The Rise and Fall of Israel's Bilateral Aid Budget 1958–2008* (Tel-Aviv: Tel-Aviv University, the Harold Hartog School of Government and Policy, 2009), 16–23.
8 See experiments in housing typologies carried under architect Artur Glikson in Hadas Shadar, *Avne Ha-binyan shel Ha-shikun Ha-tsiburi: Shishah 'Aśorim shel Beniyah 'Ironit Be-yozmah Tsiburit Be-Yiśra'el* [in Hebrew] (Tel Aviv: Miśrad Ha-binui Veha-shikun, 2018).
9 The Jewish National Fund was the primary land purchase and development organ in Palestine until 1919, when the Federation of Jewish workers was founded. The purchase and distribution cooperatives were *Tnuva*, *Hamashbir*. See Derek Jonathan Penslar, *Zionism and Technocracy: The Engineering of Jewish Settlement in Palestine, 1870–1918* (Bloomington: Indiana University Press, 1991), 111–127; Yaacov Shavit and Dan Gil'adi, "The Cowshed and the Agricultural Economy in Eretz Israel: The Place and Role of the Dairy Farming in the Jewish Settlement Program in Eretz Israel During the Mandate Period," *Catedra* 18 (1981): 178–193.
10 Smadar Sharon, "Import and Translation of the Italian Colonization Model to the Lachish Region," in *Zionism and Empires*, ed. Yehouda Shenhav (Tel Aviv: Van Leer Editing Press & Hakibbutz Hameuchad Publishing House, 2015), 310–311.
11 Together with the Jewish Agency, KAFI (Fund for the Workers of Eretz Israel) was equally significant in developing dairy standards from the 1920s and through the 1930s. See Dori Shlomo, *News from the Past: Chapters in the History of Dairy Cattle Farming in Israel*, vol. 2 (Caesarea: Cattle Breeders Association in Israel, 1996), 121–123.
12 Gershon Shafir, *Land, Labor and the Origins of the Israeli-Palestinian Conflict 1882–1914* (Berkeley: University of California Press, 1996).
13 Avshalom Rokach, "The Land Factor in the Formation of Settlement Patterns," *Karka*, July, 1983, 48–49. See also Michael Chyutin and Bracha Chyutin, *Architecture and Utopia: The Israeli Experiment* (London: Routledge, 2016), 53–56.

14. Ayala Plezental, "'Milky Way': The Dairy Industry in Eretz Israel in the 1930s as a Mirror for German- Jewish Relations," in *Germany and Eretz Israel—Cultural Encounter*, ed. Moshe Zimmerman (Jerusalem: Magnes-Hebrew University, 2004), 133–142; Shavit and Giladi, "The Cowshed and the Agricultural Economy in Eretz Israel,"; Esther Garbinger, "The Cowshed as a Marker of Values," *Motar* 14 (2006): 7–14.
15. Both the collective and cooperative village movements grew out of Eastern European socialist thinking, disseminated by settlers through Zionist youth movements in the course of the second wave of Jewish immigration (1904–1914).
16. Cooperation refers to the variety of cooperative settlement movements, which included primarily collective villages (kibbutzim) and cooperative villages (moshavim). The kibbutz model was based on full cooperation in the use of land, production means, labor, and purchase and distribution of produce; villages in this movement differed along socialist, secular, and religious lines. The moshavim also contained some diversity and included the cooperative workers villages (*moshavei ovdim shitufi*), the smaller movement of cooperative villages (*moshav shitufi*), and, after independence, the immigrant villages (*Moshavei Olim*). These models were based around small-farm-holders, who produced and leased the land on an individual basis and cooperated on issues of produce purchase, distribution, and credit. See Chyutin and Chyutin, *Architecture and Utopia*.
17. Raanan Volcani, "Buildings and Mechanization," *The Economy of Milk and Calve* 12 (1987): 47–49.
18. Weitz, *The Israeli Village in the Age of Technology*, 69; Shmuel Bickels, *The Planning of a Kibbutz Settlement* [in Hebrew] (Hertzelia: the Afro Asian Office, 1961), in Yad Tabenkin Archive, Folder: 15–2–46/5/2 and Freddi Kahana, *Neither Village, Nor City—on the Architecture of the Kibbutz 1910-1990* [in Hebrew] (Ramat-Efal: Yad Ṭabenḳin, 2011).
19. See Uriel Ha'levi, *The History of the Calf for Milk Sector in Israel* [in Hebrew] (Tel Aviv: The Union of the Clave Breeders, 1983), 248–249.
20. Yael Allweil, *Home-Land, Zionism as Housing Regime, 1860–2011* (London: Routledge, 2016), 176–177, 183–184 and Roy Kozlovsky, "Necessity by Design," *Perspecta* 34 (2003): 12.
21. Ha'levi, *The History of the Calf for Milk Sector in Israel*, 352; and Dori Shlomo, *News from the Past: Chapters in the History of Dairy Cattle Farming in Israel*, vol. 3 (Caesarea: Cattle Breeders Association in Israel, 1992), 111–112.
22. Weitz, *The Israeli Village in the Age of Technology*, 65–66.
23. These subsidies were based on several-year programs of amortization, also serving to purchase milking cows, chickens, machinery, and grains. See Smadar Sharon, *'And Thus a Homeland is Conquered': Planning and Settlement in 1950s Lakhish Region* [in Hebrew] (Haifa: Pardes, 2017), 184.
24. Shturman Archive, Ofra Keinan's Papers Collection, Transcripts of settlers' stories in the Jezreel Valley.
25. *Twenty Years of Building, Workers' Settlements, Housing and Public Institutions* [in Hebrew] (Tel Aviv: The General Federation of Jewish Labour in Palestine, 1940), 7–14; Arieh Sharon, *Kibbutz + Bauhaus—An Architect's Way in a New Land* (Stuttgart: Karl Krämer, 1976), 16, 23; see also, Hannes Meyer, "Building," in *Programs and Manifestoes on 20th-Century Architecture*, ed. Ulrich Conrads (Cambridge, MA: MIT Press, 1970), 117–120.
26. *Twenty Years of Building*, 10, 71.
27. Markus Rainer, "On Our Architecture from a Social Standpoint," in *Twenty Years of Building*, 126–127.
28. Giorgio Agamben, *The Highest Poverty* (Stanford, CA: Stanford University Press, 2013), 104.
29. The shift in the advancement of village models in the aftermath of independence is visible in the rise in the number of cooperative workers villages; roughly 260 new moshavim and 100 new kibbutzim were founded in the first fifteen years after independence, whereas prior to independence there were 106 moshavim and 142 kibbutzim. See Emmanuel Yalan, *Private and Cooperative Agricultural Settlement: Physical Planning; International Seminar on Rural Planning* (Haifa: Rural Research Bureau, 1961), 14.
30. Regional surveys in Israel in the 1960s and the early 1970s were conducted by the Settlement Research Center. On regional planning after independence, see also Elisha Efrat, *Ge'ografyah kafrit shel Yi'sra'el* [in Hebrew] (Tel Aviv: Aḥi'asaf, 1994).
31. Weitz and Rokach, *Agriculture and Rural Development in Israel*, 75.
32. Sharon, *'And Thus a Homeland is Conquered,'* 25–26, 95.
33. Weitz and Rokach, *Agriculture and Rural Development in Israel*, 20–24; and Weitz, *The Israeli Village in the Age of Technology*, 19–20.
34. See also Ilan. S. Troen, *Imagining Zion: Dreams, Designs, and Realities in a Century of Jewish Settlement* (New Haven: Yale University Press, 2011), 222; and Weitz, *The Israeli Village in the Age of Technology*, 59.
35. Zvi Zameret, *The Melting Pot in Israel: The Commission of Inquiry Concerning Education in the Immigrant Camps During the Early Years of the State* (Albany: State University of New York Press, 2002); and Sharon, *'And Thus a Homeland is Conquered,'* 214–222.
36. Howard Morley Sachar, *A History of Israel* (New York: A.A. Knopf, 1996), 395–397.
37. Near Henri, *Raḳ shvil kavshu raglay toldot ha-tnuʻah ha-ḳibutsit* [in Hebrew] (Jerusalem: Mosad Biyaliḳ, 2008), chap. 17.
38. Ofra Keinan, *Settlers as Realizers of the Zionist Ideals; the Influence of Immigrants Settlement on the Landscape of the Ta'anakh region, 1948–1967* [in Hebrew] (Unpublished doctoral thesis, Bar Ilan, 1998), 115–116, 122–125.

39 Weitz, *The Israeli Village in the Age of Technology*, 22.
40 Sharon, 'And Thus a Homeland is Conquered,' 97–101, 180–181, 215–216.
41 Raanan Weitz, *From Peasant to Farmer* (New York: Columbia University Press, 1971), 166.
42 Ibid., 52.
43 Dan Handel and Alona Nitzan-Shiftan, "Industrial Complexes, Foreign Expertise and the Imagining of a New Levant," *International Journal of Islamic Architecture* 4, no. 2 (October 1, 2015): 343–364.
44 Shimeon Amir, *Israel's Development Cooperation with Africa, Asia, and Latin America* (New York: Praeger, 1974), 28–29.
45 Michiel Dehaene, "A Conservative Framework for Regional Development: Patrick Abercrombie's Interwar Experiments in Regional Planning," *Journal of Planning Education and Research* 25, no. 2 (2005): 131–148; Ellen Shoshkes, "Jaqueline Tyrwhitt Translates Patrick Geddes for Post World War Two Planning," *Journal of Planning History* 9, no. 2 (2010): 75–94. Other architects and planners who contributed to this approach in Israel were Artur Glikson, Arieh Sharon, and Eliezer Brutzkus.
46 Weitz, *From Peasant to Farmer*, 144.
47 Sharon, 'And Thus a Homeland is Conquered,' 144–145.
48 Avshalom Rokach, "On the Professional Trajectory of Raanan Weitz," in *Hityashvut U-fituaḥ Ezori: Magishim Haverim vVe-talmidim Le-Ra'anan Vaits*, ed. Avraham Rozenman [in Hebrew] *Human Settlement and Regional Development: Presented to Raanan Weitz by his Colleagues and Disciples on the Occasion of his Retirement as Head of the Settlement Department of the Jewish Agency* (Jerusalem: Keter, 1984, Jerusalem: Ham"ul, 1984), 11–16.
49 Leopold Laufer, *Israel and the Developing Countries; New Approaches to Cooperation* (New York: Twentieth Century Fund, 1967), 155, 175–177.
50 *Technion Bulletin*, Autumn 1962. Technion Archive, Publications Collection.
51 Reports on research funding, the Cowshed Archive, Cowshed Facilities. Box 2.
52 Rokach, "On the Professional Trajectory of Raanan Weitz," 14. Laufer, *Israel and the Developing Countries*, 152–153.
53 These included the country now known as Tanzania, as well as Venezuela, Argentina, Brazil, and Burma (now also called Myanmar). In Laufer, *Israel and the Developing Countries*.
54 Jacob Maos, "In Memoriam—Emmanuel Yalan (1903–1981)," *The Transformations of the Moshav. Ofakim in Geography* 59 (2004): 9–11.
55 Oren Yiftachel, *Ethnocracy: Land and Identity Politics in Israel/Palestine* (Philadelphia: University of Pennsylvania Press, 2006); Haim Yacobi, *Israel and Africa: A Genealogy of Moral Geography* (London: Routledge, 2015); and Sharon, 'And Thus a Homeland is Conquered.'
56 Orit Achiob, *Foreigners in Their Homes* [in Hebrew] (Tel Aviv: Ressling, 2010), 99–101.
57 Weitz, *The Israeli Village in the Age of Technology*, 129–130; see also Artur Glikson, *Regional Planning and Development* (Leiden: A.W. Sijthoff, 1955), 9–11. For development studies in postcolonial contexts, see Akhil Gupta, *Postcolonial Developments: Agriculture in the Making of Modern India* (Durham: Duke University Press, 1998), 8–12.
58 Central Place Theory was used in Yalan's plan for the Ta'anach (1953) and by Raanan Weitz's 1954 plan for the Lachish region.
59 Weitz, *The Israeli Village in the Age of Technology*, 88.
60 For a similar case see Timothy Mitchell, *Rule of Experts: Egypt, Techno-Politics, Modernity* (Berkeley: University of California Press, 2012), 51–52.
61 Weitz, *From Peasant to Farmer*, 27–28.
62 Raanan Weitz, "Integrative Planning for Israeli Rural Cooperatives (Moshavim): A New Model," *Israel Journal of Development* 6, no. 2 (1975): 705–723.
63 These phases moved from 5–8, to 8–15, and then 15–30 milking cowsheds. They preceded the Jewish Agency's attempt to erect larger dairy facilities outside the family parcel, beginning in the 1970s. Weitz, Ibid.
64 See Sharon, 'And Thus a Homeland is Conquered.'
65 The importation of Californian models is discussed (without reference to any model in particular) in Volcani, "Buildings and Mechanization." The reference English farm model was a winning entry to the British Association for Planning and Regional Reconstruction competition "New Ideas for Farm Buildings" that was presented in the journal *Farmer and Stock-Breeder* in 1947.
66 Yalan, *Private and Cooperative Agricultural Settlement*.
67 Volcani, "Buildings and Mechanization."
68 Agronomist Ranaan Volcani, who worked in the Volcani Research Center, was key in promoting the construction of the first open-shed systems that he surveyed in California in the late 1930s.
69 Weitz, *The Israeli Village in the Age of Technology*, 88, 111.
70 See *L'Architecture d'aujourd'hui* 22, "Constructions Agricoles" (March 1949): 3–5. For Yalan's functionalist vocabulary, see *The Design of Agricultural Settlements Technological Aspects of Rural Community Development* [in Hebrew] (Jerusalem: Jewish Agency, 1975), 12. On self-help discourse, see Ijlal M. Muzaffar, *The Periphery Within: Modern*

Architecture and the Making of the Third World (Unpublished Doctoral thesis, Massachusetts Institute of Technology, 2007), chap. 2.
71 James Scott, *Seeing Like a State—How Certain Schemes to Improve the Human Condition Have Failed* (Ann Arbor: New Haven Yale University Press, 2008), 89–90 and Yiftachel, *Ethnocracy*, 10.
72 A similar point on development expertise is found in Mitchell, *Rule of Experts*, 37.
73 Daniel Immerwahr, *Thinking Small: The United States and the Lure of Community Development* (Cambridge, MA: Harvard University Press, 2018), 4.
74 See Sharon, 'And Thus a Homeland is Conquered.'
75 Muzaffar, *The Periphery Within*, 41.

17

Floors and ceilings

The architectonics of accumulation in the Green Revolution

Ateya Khorakiwala

In 2012, Punjab suffered from a bumper crop of wheat. That summer, the breadbasket of India, whose agricultural capacity was transformed by the Green Revolution in the 1970s, saw a fifth consecutive year of record wheat harvest. This bounty was the result of a combination of above-normal rainfall, a modest increase in crop cultivation area, and the government's announcement of an increased minimum support price, a floor price, which incentivized farmers to sow more wheat.[1] This increased harvest meant that the government's procurement agencies, overseen by the Food Corporation of India (FCI), struggled to absorb the large quantities of grain that flowed into the market. That July and August, newspapers world over featured images of piles and piles of grain, bursting out of jute bags, spilling into drains, and rotting, unprotected from the rain, in government-owned yards.[2] The reports juxtaposed these images of wasted grain with stories of malnutrition faced by poor Indians across the country. One such article, in the *New York Times*, concluded on the topic of storage, saying that,

> the government is working on temporary solutions to its grain storage problems, putting up new silos and exporting more rice. Still, much of it is likely to keep sitting on the side of the road here in Punjab.
>
> "It's painful to watch," said Gurdeep Singh, a farmer from near Ranwan who recently sold his wheat harvest to the government. "The government is big and powerful. It should be able to put up a shed."[3]

A shed, a plinth, four walls, and a roof, was the site of intersection of state, hunger, power, and waste.

At first glance, Gurdeep Singh's missing shed[4] signals an absence of shelter, a primordial hut, the originary architectural gesture of a refuge, to protect grain from rotting in the sun and rain. However, while the absent architectural object echoes the antediluvian hut that is allegedly the essence of all architecture, it embodies, instead, a modern technique of political economy. The shed sheltered hoarded grain, protecting it for *future* use, and in turn, metaleptically manipulating and protecting the *current* value of grain. This sleight of hand, signaling the future to perform in the present, that transformed the value of the commodity from unpredictable to stable is magical. This magical task was the subject of developmental economics birthed in the 1930s: how could states deploy this sleight of hand at the macroeconomic scale of political economy to *substitute* mature capitalist economies for their tottering and incomplete marketplaces?

Why substitution? In what follows, this chapter argues that substitution provides a formal and analytical theme to understand how development operated, one that goes beyond tropes of the failure of theory and implementation. First, I lay out the critical difference between substitution and fungibility. Next, I demonstrate how substitution provided a critical economic framework to manage inflationary pressure on the price of grain: it gave the state the tools with which to put a floor under and a ceiling over the price of grain. Finally, I conclude that substitution helped sidestep the aporia of development in which structural change remained a perpetually deferred promise.

SUBSTITUTION

What is substitution, and what role did it play in development thought in India between 1950 and 1980? Substitution, in one sense, is a corruption of fungibility; fungible items are exact copies of each other, interchangeable to the extent that their substitution doesn't make sense—a dollar exchanged for a dollar is an uncontaminated transaction, one without meaning. Substitutes, on the other hand, come into the picture when the original is unavailable but the framework demands similitude: a rupee instead of a dollar, *jowar* instead of wheat, *surkhi* instead of cement, or bamboo instead of steel. Substitution presupposed that commodities shared essential attributes, that they had common denominators such that cheap, local versions might fuel a developmental economy as a simulacrum of its capitalist original (see Diana Martinez, Chapter 5 in this volume, on fungibility).[5] At best, this would produce an indigenous modernity; at worst, a mirage of Western capitalism. In either case, far from instantiating structural change, the effect of development policy was to produce a corruption of liberal capitalism in the post-colony. This chapter tells a history of development by investigating the panoply of substitutions encountered in building modern bodies with grain and modern architecture with cement.

The unmanageable agricultural excesses of post-liberalization Punjab are rooted in the history of colonial famines, because the specter of famine spurred the post-1950s industrialization of the countryside, what by the 1970s would be referred to as the Green Revolution. On the discursive front, intellectuals sought to fix famine as a product of a colonial economy, separate from modern democratic political economies. In 1990, Amartya Sen argued that independent India (and democracies in general) had, by and large, avoided the large-scale life-loss that characterized famine.[6] Conversely, Utsa Patnaik, the Marxist historian, noted the paradox of hunger in India, where the poor continue to be malnourished even as the market is awash in calories.[7] This systematic reformulation of data, which refashioned hunger into malnutrition, rewrote the monstrous hunger of an emerging body politic into a domesticated and quantified caloric deficiency that was embedded in an epistemology of postwar demographics.[8] Jenny Edkins writes that although famine calls forth a time before genetic manipulation, large-scale irrigation, and chemical precision, it is patently modern. Famine is not the inadvertent starving of people in the condition of the absence of food but rather a series of political decisions to allow people to starve. Neo-Malthusian theories of famine, she says, depoliticized hunger, framing it instead as a technologized problem of scarcity.[9] In the developmental regime, the materiality of food and shed—which can be indexed by their raw materials, grain and cement—couple body, state, power, and political economy in their role as scarce commodities central to labor and industrialization.

From the 1940s on, India faced continuing shortages of both grain and cement; both these scarce but basic commodities were central to the industrialization agenda set out by the country's planning commission in its five-year plans. Thus, both were often subject to black-marketeering and hoarding, and they found their way onto the schedule of essential commodities.[10] Cement was as necessary for building infrastructure for the state as grain was for building the laboring bodies of its construction workers. As such, the cost of grain indexed the value of labor. But grain and cement share other physical properties that bind them together economically. They are both stable, granular, and fluid; thus, they are stored in silos, where they exert similar dynamic and friction-based bursting forces. The material, physical, and economic similarities of grain (wheat and rice) and cement (Portland) are not a coincidence: their granular and stable forms enabled them to flow through the world and achieve their dominance. This materiality of wheat, rice, and Portland cement prefigures the typology of the shed (more precisely, we should call it the *godown*; also, see Hershenzon on sheds in this volume, Chapter 16).[11] The godown was much more than a mere shelter: it was an apparatus that changed the value of what it stored. It provided a literal and metaphorical (economic) floor under wheat and its price. The godown, by substituting the future for the present, created a space for accumulation during the Green Revolution.

SILOS, PAVILIONS, AND BOOKS: FOOD SUBSTITUTES PEACE

Although it is clear that the Indian state faced alarming food shortages in the 1940s, the statistics around food production from that period are complicated to compute: the country's boundaries were yet in flux, and the available data wasn't consistent. The general trend that intellectuals gleaned from various data that assessed food output is that over the course of the first half of the twentieth century, India had settled into an importing situation with regard to rice and wheat.[12] Development economists in the 1950s looked at the food production data in previous decades and saw a continuous decrease in the per capita availability of commodities with every subsequent year; to them, this data, when inflected by the recent memory of the Bengal Famine, looked like a Malthusian trap that could only be held at bay by importing more grain.

In 1954, under the Eisenhower government, the United States systematized their ad hoc wheat exports through the Agricultural Trade Development and Assistance Act of 1954, better known in India as Public Law 480 (PL480). This law aimed to transfer US agricultural surpluses to food-deficient developing countries, thus appeasing US agriculture lobbies and gaining diplomatic dominance in one fell swoop. Colloquially referred to as the Food for Peace Act in the United States, a gesture of substitution was central to the spirit of the law: food, in exchange for which the Americans expected peace, that is, the curbing of communist revolutions in the East (see Martinez, Chapter 5 in this volume, on Food for Peace and the IRRI). The phrase "food for peace" mimicked Eisenhower's 1953 "Atoms for Peace" speech at the United Nations that attempted to perform a similar sleight of hand, substituting Cold War nuclear research for atomic warfare. What kinds of categories are food and peace that one might be exchanged for the other?[13] Given that hunger is often described as the cause of rioting, is it the case that satiation and revolution are opposing conditions? Are hunger and revolution substitutable forms?

A central feature of PL480 was that the foreign exchange deficient Third World could pay for US grain in local currencies. The US held a reserve of Indian rupees accepted as payment for grain. This reserve of rupees was added to the allocated dollar aid amount, and the total was earmarked for spending as loans and grants to the Indian government and as a fund for running US operations.[14] The rupee amount was credited to and disbursed through the Technical Cooperation Mission (TCM). The TCM had its origins in Harry Truman's point four program, named after a fourth point in his January 1949 inaugural speech where he declared, "Fourth, we must embark on a bold new program for making the benefits of our scientific advances and industrial progress available for improvement and growth of underdeveloped areas."[15] The gist of the fourth point was that the United States could help transfer its technical knowledge to underdeveloped countries. Capital and patents (corporate knowledge) were not part of this deal, only some machines and experts. This was no Marshall Plan aimed at rebuilding Europe; instead, the TCM—structured after the UN's Technical Assistance Administration (TAA)—aimed to send limited industrial technology to support the Indian planning commission's "import substitution" orientated economy.[16] Thus, Americans pledged to help build industry that would produce commodities to substitute imported ones. Given that the US export of grain to India quantitatively overshadowed all other forms of aid, the rupee reserve that TCM had access to was significant. Bureaucracies like the TCM then functioned as an accounting trick by which wheat that was "sold" in rupees could be accounted for as having some value in return, in terms of extending the US's soft power and democratic ideals.

The TCM supported US grain exports by providing agricultural equipment and technology; in 1955 the Eisenhower administration gifted two grain elevators and silos made of prefabricated galvanized iron panels to Nehru's government. The Ministry of Agriculture's Storage Department officials debated where they would locate the two silos for months, eventually settling on the wheat market of Hapur in Uttar Pradesh near Delhi as one of their sites. The Hapur project required the storage department to coordinate with the local authorities to acquire land from farmers, while the engineers of the various Public Works Departments (PWDs) were tasked with designing the reinforced concrete foundations. The ministry shuttled the American construction experts in Delhi to site and back on delayed schedules, bearing the cost of their stays. Even as the project was under construction, in 1957, the regional food director noted Hapur's waning importance as a grain center and questioned the silo's necessity there.[17] Yet the project was inaugurated with much fanfare in 1959 by Uttar Pradesh Governor V. V. Giri and US Ambassador Ellsworth Bunker.[18] The Hapur silo adorned the covers of many official publications for decades to come as a symbol of modern scientific state storage. It still remains in use.

The Hapur silo project offers a gloss on expertise in development: the project memos record, "The specifications and designs of the structures follow the pattern of the Jinjirapool godowns which were drawn up by the experts of this Ministry in consultation with the FAO expert Mr. Harrison."[19] This peculiar formulation, in which "our experts consulted their experts," described the Indian engineers' deferral to American engineers on technologies of grain storage. Since the notion of international expertise implies the transferability of techno-scientific knowledge and thus a standardization and equivalence between "our" expertise and "theirs," the imputation of nonequivalence casts doubts on the entire enterprise of expertise as a form of knowledge. Instead, expertise is derived from mere authority; expertise acted as an effect of itself in that the Americans' expertise came from their being experts.

Another project that absorbed PL480 funds was an American agricultural technology pavilion at the 1959 World Agriculture Fair held in Delhi. The pavilion was added last-minute when the Americans heard rumors that the Soviets and Chinese had plans to put up large, spectacular pavilions (this did not come to pass). The United States Information Agency (USIA) coordinated among the Department of Agriculture, the Atomic Energy Commission, and other various interested departments in putting together the exhibit. The $1.9 million budget was largely made up of rupees from PL480 rupees with a third contributed in dollars from the atomic energy commission.[20] Minoru Yamasaki traveled to India to design the pavilion; he conceptualized an American country fair crossed with an Indian *mela*, calling it the *Amriki Mela*. Inaugurated by President Eisenhower, it featured a merry-go-round, a giant wheel, and an array of golden domes, like piles of wheat, stretching out over the exhibits.[21] This theatrical architectural production circulated bilateral diplomacy and absorbed surplus rupees sitting in India, where the Americans had little else to exchange this currency for. Yamasaki's pavilion was part of an ecosystem of pavilions. These architectural experiments were abundant: an industries fair in Delhi in 1961, a floating pavilion in Madras in 1962, a geodesic dome hosting a *circarama* in Calcutta.[22] The need to spend the excess rupees generated by American foreign policy found home in these peregrine architectural objects; newer mandates to distribute bilateral diplomacy piggy-backed on the older colonial mandate of displaying power through exhibition and exposition design.

The Indian government reserved its dollar fund for importing scientific equipment that was otherwise difficult to acquire over the exchange of experts and books. On the American side, the question of how exactly to spend PL480 funds was left to various agencies, although the US Congress outlined three categories of spending: the exchange of persons, the interchange of laboratory and technical equipment, and the interchange of scientific, technical, and scholarly books.[23] In 1957, the Conference on American Library Resources on Southern Asia met under the aegis of the Library of Congress to discuss the difficulties of acquiring books from South Asia. They formed the Association for Asian Studies, which then made use of "the interchange of Scientific, Technical, and Scholarly Books" mandate to push for a special PL480 fund through which publications from India could make their way back to the United States. The Library of Congress acquired $84,000 and negotiated with the Indian government to procure all government documents that were then deposited in three libraries selected to cover the geographical breadth of the United States: the University of Pennsylvania, the Midwest Inter-Library Center in Chicago, and the University of California at Berkeley.[24] In this convoluted way, India bought surplus wheat from the United States and paid for it in books. The acquisition of books made possible a shift in the study of South Asia. What before World War II was largely the continuation of Sanskrit studies supported by collections owned by libraries now was able to transition to the area studies model that is the legacy of the Cold War. In the 1960s, libraries across the United States began to hire South Asian specialists to acquire and catalog collections beyond government documents.[25]

Thus, the substitutive logic of Food for Peace aggregated within it multiple fungibilities that rhetorically structured Cold War geopolitical relationships. The three interventions here—the silo in Hapur, the *Amriki Mela* in Delhi, and books for US libraries—map a transition in the architectural and spatial relations from the monumental silo type of intervention to the more mobile exhibition information model of design and, finally, to the object of the book that located the shift from the monumental to a networked information state.

BUFFER STOCK ARCHITECTURE: GEOMETRY SUBSTITUTES MASS

While exhibitions, silos, and books absorbed excess local currencies, the grain that produced these surpluses did not always go into the homes and mouths of people. Instead, US grain often went directly into long-term storage toward a buffer stock. Governments built up buffer stocks as an economic technique meant to manage the market price of grain. Buffer stocks consisted of two things—a reserve of grain and a capacity for storage. They operated on the following logic: if grain were scarce, its price would rise, and the food ministry would release stocks from its buffer into the market, bringing the price back down. On the other hand, if there were too much grain in the market, causing the price to fall, the food ministry would absorb it into storage and thus stabilize the falling prices of grain. In this way, the state (theoretically) provided a buffer that, as an effect of its existence, made the speculative hoarding of grain by middlemen a worthless endeavor. Put another way, the state proleptically out-hoarded private hoarders, taking on the role of the benevolent hoarder in an imperfect market. Economist M. L. Dantwala distinguished buffer stocks, writing that while regular stocks evened out intra-seasonal flows, buffer stocks evened out inter-seasonal fluctuations. They were meant to even out bad years with good years.[26] The fallout of the buffer stock policy was the need for godowns to store this buffer in abiotic environments over multiple years. Godowns became crucial as state-owned infrastructure; after all, where do you store so much wheat? The *Times of India* ran articles outlining the scale of the logistical goal: the food department aimed to double current storage capacity between 1960 and 1962 and streamline the distribution of imported grain from the ports to the interior.[27]

The task of creating cheap, durable, fast, replicable storage fell to the civil engineers of the country, as was emphasized by Dhunjisha P. R. Cassad, then president of the Institution of Engineers, in 1958 when giving the presidential address at the institute's annual session. Cassad's broad speech, reprinted in the *Indian Concrete Journal* (*ICJ*), tackled the question of the role of engineers in the planning process,

> The shortage of food grain and their import from different countries of the world has set the Government yet another problem. Their storage has been satisfactorily solved to some extent by the barrel shell type design for grain godowns, . . . [which] has the advantages of better flexibility, better lighting, and the possibility of reducing godown space required per ton of storage. Besides this, the new design is expected to save Rs. 1.8 crores on a planned expenditure of Rs. 22 crores, thus saving a colossal amount of structural steel. Having accepted this new design, the Central Building Research Institute, Roorkee, has started a special course for training engineers in the technique of designing it.[28]

Concrete shell roofs, with their thin cross-sections, came to correspond with economy, efficiency, and flexibility in construction. This was in particular contrast to gravity dams, which harnessed the massiveness of concrete rather than its geometry. Shells substituted geometry for mass. Thus, for Cassad, "the glorious task of securing the country against famine" became a civil engineering project and was conjoined with more the traditional engineering expertise "of increasing the value of [the country's] resources by improved road and rail communications, of harnessing rivers by building dams, of turning material resources into finished products, and of bringing contentment and plenty to our fellowmen." Concrete shell design translated the political economy of famine into an architectural and infrastructural form.[29]

Following Cassad's speech, the *ICJ* published designs and structural solutions for barrel shell structures as designed by engineers and architects. The first article was an analysis of the cost and consumption of steel and concrete in barrel shell construction versus in steel truss construction. Surprisingly, the analysis did not conclude the concrete forms to be hugely beneficial in cost or material use, yet the article recommended concrete shells to address ongoing steel scarcities in India.[30] Regardless of this proselytizing of concrete, the reality remained that steel truss godowns—what the PWD referred to as "conventional godowns"—dominated the genre. Because shells relied on curves, that is on form (expertise) rather than mass (resources), they made for a tantalizing substitution even when it did not directly translate into savings. Tests to check the load-bearing and span capacities of roof shells were routinely conducted in the Roorkee Laboratory in Uttar Pradesh. Doubly curved shells, like other projects undertaken by central government laboratories, aimed to intervene in large-scale problems of material and economic scarcity. By substituting geometry for mass, the double shells were architectural objects that translated financial objectives into formal ones.

One 1959 photo essay simply showcased "Recent Examples of Shell Construction in India." A 1960 snippet reported on a shell roof designed as a catenary curve by the engineering wing of the Calcutta based architecture firm Stein, Chatterjee, and Polk for fertilizer storage that was under construction in Rourkela.[31] Then a 1962 article written by executive engineer L. R. Gupta of the Central Public Works Department (CPWD) outlined the process of designing and building centering and shuttering for the concrete placement for the roof of a series of barrel shell vault godowns built as "as part of the scheme of the Ministry of Food and Agriculture for providing a buffer stock of 3 million tons of food grains during the Third Five-Year Plan."[32] The essay presented designs of centering for concrete vault construction, privileging speed, strength, lightness, and economy of construction. The essay aimed to provide a framework for future projects that could be quickly constructed wherever the Ministry of Food and Agriculture needed the CPWD to build grain storage urgently (see Figure 17.1).

Rather than unique buildings, these storage systems were flexible and replicable and designed to expand with growing food outputs; they were instructions that produced structures when deployed at specific sites. The drawing process was diagrammatic and schematic where plans often consisted of rectangles (warehouses) in polygons (sites) that were the result of computing storage capacities that represented programmatic functions and storage data (see Figure 17.2). Although the diagrams represented physical structures, a certain reversal took place: the buildings themselves tended toward diagrams rather than the other way around. The godowns' plinths acted as the quantifiable units through which the PWD computed the cost of construction and set design standards. The CPWD would release standards every year with plinth area rates, that is, rates for structures categorized by type—warehouse, school, office, and so on—costed by their plinth areas. This procedure of economically determining buildings through typology and plan area came out of a long history of standardizing architectural production in the colony in the attempt to create an army of draftsmen who efficiently reproduced architecture rather than inculcating design knowledge.[33]

CONSTRUCTION OF SHELL ROOFS FOR GRAIN GODOWNS AT NEW DELHI

Fabrication of Centering and Shuttering

by L. R. GUPTA*

Short cylindrical shells of a span of 35 ft and a chord width of 90 ft are being used to roof twelve grain godowns being constructed at the junction of the Delhi-Rewari railway line with the Ring Road in New Delhi. They form part of the scheme of the Ministry of Food and Agriculture for providing a buffer stock of 3 million tons of food grains during the Third Five-Year Plan. The godowns have a total capacity of 50,000 tons and will store wheat and rice. They will be accessible both by rail and by road. The constructing agency is the Central Public Works Department.

TWELVE godowns are being constructed at New Delhi, each consisting of ten short cylindrical shells supported on traverses at 35 ft o.c. The radius of curvature of each shell is 73 ft 6 in, chord width 90 ft 7 in and length 35 ft. Two adjacent shells are continuous over the traverse and are cast monolithic with it. Expansion joints are provided every two shells, *i.e.* at 70 ft o.c. The thickness of the shell varies from 3 in at the crown to 5 ½ in at the springings. Edge beams, 16 in × 10 in, are provided at the edges to account for the edge perturbances.

The traverses (*Fig* 1) are reinforced concrete bowstring girders consisting of bottom tie, top chord, and eight vertical spandrels. They are simply supported on the columns and transfer no moments to them. The simple supports are obtained by means of a hinge in the column reinforcement and a tarfelt sheet 1 in thick, as shown in the figure. The bottom of the tie is 15 ft above the plinth level and the rise of the shell is about 16 ft from the bottom of the shell. Thus the top of the shell is about 31 ft above the plinth level.

Centering

As there are ten shells in one godown, the total number of shells is 120. Initially twelve sets of centering were prepared to finish the work in eighteen months assuming that

A view of a completed godown

one set will be repeated ten times only. However, after casting two godowns, it was found that even twelve sets were inadequate for efficient construction and two more sets of centering were built.

The following points were considered before deciding upon the type of centering :

Ease of erection and dismantling.
Mobility, lightness, and strength.
Capability for being built out of easily available materials.
Capability for being used repeatedly.
Economy.

A mobile steel centering built with telescopic tubes satisfies all the above conditions. But it is not cheap if not used repeatedly and is very heavy also. As every set was to be used only eight times, wooden centering was preferred to steel centering.

The arrangement for the centering is shown in *Fig* 2. Twenty-four frames, 7 ft 4 in × 8 ft, are erected for each shell. Each frame is made of four sal ballies, 6-in dia, cross braced in all directions with 4-in dia ballies and rectangular braces. All joints and connections are made with bolts, nuts and washers so that dismantling may be easy.

The total height of the centering varies from 16 ft at the springings to 31 ft at the crown. Normally sal wood ballies of these lengths are not available, hence each frame was built in two pieces, the first reaching the bottom of the tie and the second resting on the first. The ballies used in the upper piece are 4-in dia and the top bracings follow the curvature of the shell. The frames of both the pieces were separately

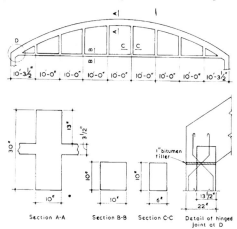

Fig 1 Showing the dimensions of the reinforced concrete bowstring traverses

* Executive Engineer, C.P.W.D.

FIGURE 17.1 A page from an article showing the fabrication of centering and shuttering for government-owned grain godowns in Delhi published in the *Indian Concrete Journal*, December 1962.

Source: Image courtesy the Indian Concrete Journal.

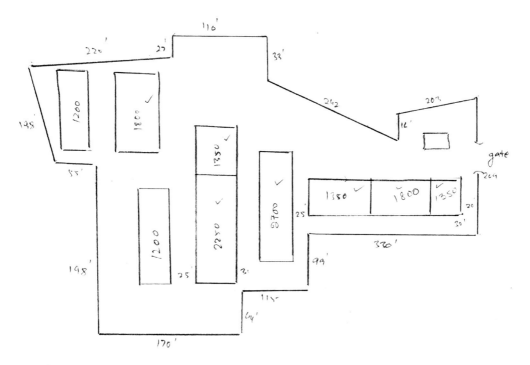

FIGURE 17.2 Representative diagrammatic plan of grain godown layouts and capacities owned by Punjab State Warehousing Corporation.

Source: Image by author.

The delamination of the diagram-like plinth and the shell roof was complementary: the shell was a form without a program, and the diagram-like plinth was a program without a form. Shells roofed any and all granular assemblies: parliament buildings, churches, theaters, warehouses. One of the more iconic shell roof structures built in the 1970s was the hyperbolic paraboloid shell roof designed by Jugal Kishore Chowdhury for the Indian Institute of Technology, Delhi's Convocation Hall. Chowdhury, who returned to India after working with the Tennessee Valley Authority in the United States, spent many years working for different governmental agencies such as the Punjab State Government and the Delhi municipal government. His practice incorporated research done in government laboratories, and Chowdhury experimented with indigenous material substitutes produced by the CBRI on the IIT-D campus.[34] His shell roof married an aesthetic of expertise with a program of storage and assembly and a modern concern for organizing produce and people.

PIPELINE AND BUFFER STOCK: GRAIN SUBSTITUTES MONEY

The work of storing grain belongs to many disciplines, each slicing the task up in a different way. To the structural question, engineers proposed shell structures, and to the administrative one, bureaucrats proposed ceiling and floor prices. Here the political question was how the state would finance these stocks, and on the market aspect, economists theorized how differentiated stocks might behave economically. In August 1969, economists, bureaucrats, administrators, and managers convened together at the Institute for Engineers in Bangalore to present research on buffer stock economics. Dantwala set the stakes of the conference by defining how buffer stocks constituted an economic strategy in which a network of storage presented a countervailing force to the speculative interests of the grain trader.[35] In doing so, he indirectly cited the Bengal Famine of 1943, where speculative hoarding became impossible to curb and legislate against.

The assembly of technocrats held that the economic and logistical management of stocks required new understandings of the commodity of grain and its infrastructure. For instance, if grain were to function like gold (holding value in reserve), the silo and godown were possibly more akin to the vault of a bank than to a granary. Ali Mohammed Khusro, an economist at the Institute for Economic Growth, analogized grain and cash not just metaphorically but also instrumentally:

> The treatment of money stocks in monetary theory provides a good guideline for an analytical treatment of foodgrain stocks. But the analogy only goes so far; foodgrain stock theory has to find its own path beyond a point. Borrowing from an analogous treatment of monetary stocks, foodgrain stocks can be regarded as divisible conceptually though not perhaps operationally, into three types—pipeline stocks, buffer stocks and reserve stocks. These are the counterparts of transaction balances, speculative balances and contingency or precautionary balances of money, and as we shall see, the functional relationships developed in monetary theory would seem to be applicable with some slight difference to the theory and practice of grain inventories.[36]

Khusro used this analogy between stocks, monetary and grain, to modify William Baumol's 1952 formula for how companies could manage cash flows for their day-to-day operations to suit it to grain flows. Ironically, Baumol had derived this formula by treating cash as a kind of inventory, where there were costs to moving it from savings into circulation. In reversing the analogy, Khusro treated the buffer stock as a savings account, pipeline stock as a checking account, and transport costs between the two as transaction costs. The surprising result of his modified equation was that the volume of grain purchased was proportional to the square root of the total volume of required stocks and transportation costs. That is, as the demand for grain increased, the required supply buffer only increased by its square root and, so too, storage capacity. By categorizing grain as pipeline versus buffer stock, economists differentiated the same material grain in economic ways. So even as biologically, grain tended toward becoming a monoculture, economically, it diversified.

To compare grain to cash had an effect of transforming grain itself: the physical commodity of grain had to have lower moisture for more stability; it had to conform to industrial agricultural methods, that is, respond to fertilizer and pesticide and resist breaking down inside harvesting machines and in silos. Grain in the agricultural economy had to transform from being alive to being inert, and its architectural environments responded by tending toward the abiotic as far as they could. To address how grain differed from money, Khusro considered the corporeality of grain in terms of how it was affected during storage in silos and godowns. One enduring debate was the question of whether godowns or silos were better investments. Certainly, both systems were in play at the same time, given the vastness of the food management project, yet the question persisted; the debate hinged on the political economies that flowed from the formal logics of verticality and horizontality.

> While several techniques of storage can be discussed in relation to their costs, the two main techniques prevalent in India are the horizontal godowns and the vertical silos.
>
> The basic difference between the godown and the silo arises from the fact that the godown is a horizontal, land-using and labour-using type while the silo, both because of its vertical layout and the mechanical devices such as conveyor belts, automatic aeration arrangement, etc., is a capital-using but labour-saving and land saving structure.[37]

Khusro concluded that silos worked at ports where land was expensive, whereas godowns worked in the countryside where land was cheap. He used the opportunity to criticize the Ministry's prestige project, the silo at Hapur, arguing that silos made more sense at ports where grain needed to move quickly and where the cost of bagging, transporting, and unbagging grain added to the operational expenses.[38]

Khusro's intervention was conceptualizing godowns as linear rather than volumetric quantities. A volume whose linear dimensions were doubled, he wrote, increased eight times in volume. Thus, lengthening a ship lowered the cost per ton in holding grain, but godowns needed access for stacking, which dictated their planning and cost. Godowns, he surmised, were linear rather than volumetric spaces, that is, the width had to remain fixed for access, but one could, theoretically, infinitely increase the length.[39] Godowns also needed access to railway sidings and roads and space for administrative functions. The Ministry of Food and Agriculture (MoFA) engaged the relevant state governments to acquire land for these functions. The complications stemming from this multiply in the archive, where letters go back and forth between the MoFA, the Finance Ministry, the local officials, and the PWD (see Ginger Nolan in this volume, Chapter 7, on how files move through bureaucracies).

The MoFA would coordinate between the ministries of finance and railways, trying to convince both that land acquisition was really necessary. Land acquisition was a lengthy and tedious process conducted by state-level officials under the instructions of central ministries. Finance would ask for additional evidence before releasing funds. The ministry of railways would write back to finance via food saying, yes, this was necessary and that the curves of the railroad would not work, given the turning radius of trains.[40] In the end, the engineers sent over the diagrams and plans to make their case to the economists, and the money was allocated. This bureaucratic procedure would then be repeated on every site—this "ad hoc" nature of godown and silo building was precisely the blind spot in developmental theory that focused on models and systems. Each silo project was a "model" project in that it hoped to set a precedent for replication and yet, having been installed in an ad hoc way, was necessarily irreproducible.

These difficulties in constructing both godown and silo contextualize the debate choosing between the two. The stakes of this debate on the cost-benefit trade-off of substituting silos for warehouses were higher than they may have first seemed and came to a head in the 1970s: in 1968, Robert McNamara became the director of the World Bank, and he brought with him his military reliance on logistics. McNamara argued that the bank was spending far too little far too cautiously, and they needed to put money out into the developing world if it was to make any difference. Over his tenure of thirteen years, he moved the World Bank from spending US$1 billion in 1968 to $13 billion in 1981. Because of the groundwork laid by USAID and the Rockefeller Foundations, the World Bank became involved in Indian agriculture in its various aspects: irrigation, agricultural credit, water supply, transportation, population, education, and power. In 1971, the World Bank and the Government of India signed their first loan and credit agreement to build silos and godowns across the country, with a large loan from the Swedish government.[41] The agreement consisted of three interventions: (1) the planning, design, and construction of ten silos and ten godowns; (2) the training of silo personnel; and (3) an All-India Grain Storage and Distribution Study. All of this construction was to go toward a reduction in grain loss during storage. The World Bank's interest in tangible projects—particularly infrastructure—meant that silos and godowns became a site for international capital to land in the Third World.

An appraisal report would later note the many delays in construction due to land acquisition issues (a constant refrain), the difficulty in finding engineering consultants, delays in acquiring critical equipment, and the Indian government's bidding process. These roadblocks were compounded by a substantial cost escalation that forced the halving of the project goal: only five of the ten silos were built.[42] Yet the World Bank signed a second wheat storage project agreement with the GOI in 1977. In 1976, the Administrative Staff College of India, Hyderabad, concluded their study as mandated by the World Bank. Balwanth Reddy, citing World War II and the 1943 Bengal Famine as the origin of the GOI's active interventionist food policies, noted that the "Canute-like price conferences of the early years had been replaced by a vast institutional super-structure to shape and implement food policy," a transition that was neither steady nor smooth.[43] Reddy criticized the ad hoc policies of the government, arguing that makeshift price interventions at times of fluctuation and crisis were necessarily ineffective, given the time lag for policies to take effect. Reddy's critique underscored the aporia of development: that its practitioners acted in ad hoc and substitutive ways in the present and promised structural change in the future. Structural change was the continually deferred promissory regime of the postcolonial state.

Nonetheless, one of the key interventions made by the World Bank was mandating that India use the technology of slipform silos and accept international bidders. Where the US gifted silo from the 1950s was made of prefabricated galvanized iron panels, this new transfer of technology promised revolutionary concrete expertise. Slipforming had been around in the concrete literature for some time, yet its technology had not been accessible in India. The cylindrical shape of the silo lent itself to the technique where concreting was performed in one continuous stretch by slipping the ring-shaped formwork upwards, using the set concrete below for support. Slipform construction meant that these vertical structures could be erected with limited amounts of formwork and quick turnaround times. The formwork for the cylinder would be placed on hydraulic jacks, and concrete was poured in. When the concrete inside the formwork was set, the jacks would raise the formwork, using the set concrete below as support to continue the construction of the cylinder. Essays published in the *ICJ* explained how, in silos, the bursting forces exerted by granular material on the walls of the silo determined by the coefficient of friction made vertical seams particularly vulnerable to bursting structural failures that thus needed elimination.[44] Slipforming worked by maintaining a seamless ring of concrete.

The 1971 wheat storage agreement between the World Bank and the GOI noted that the advantage of slipforming was the speed at which projects could be completed.[45] However, the other advantage of slipforming was that the same apparatus could be used to produce multiple structures. These two advantages contradicted each other, in that you would need many devices to slipform multiple structures quickly or lose time if a contractor planned to reuse the equipment. The 1988 project completion report noted that because of these contradictions, slipforming had not been the panacea that they had hoped it was. It had proved hard to find engineers to design and manage the projects given the shortage of expertise in slipforming. Paradoxically, when they did hire engineering consultants, they would often remain underused.[46] Indian engineers pointed out another contradiction, that while slipforming grain silos across the country using the same formwork would be fast and economical, it required standardization and cooperation across different administrative bodies. Given the decentralized nature of agricultural governance, this was the far harder task of the postindependence political project.[47] Slipforming is thus a classic example of the substitution of technological solutions for administrative and bureaucratic problems in the hope that technology might make bureaucracy unnecessary.

By the end of the 1970s, private sector contractors like Gammon and the Engineering Construction Corporation Limited (ECC) were slipforming silos and chimneys all over the country, touting the benefits of speedy construction and quality control (see Figure 17.3).[48] Slipforming eliminated the skilled labor needed for building complex form-work. This method became the standard for the construction of cement silos, chimneys, and various other vertical structures that required seamless volumes in the horizontal plane. Slipforming, like shell technology, also migrated from infrastructure to architecture. In 1973, the cover of the *ICJ* featured an instance of slipform construction in progress, designed by Shirish Patel and contracted to ECC, which had perfected the technique through its industrial slipforming projects over the past two decades (see Figure 17.4). This was Charles Correa's major skyscraper project in Bombay—the Kanchanjunga project—which featured a slipformed structural core around which duplex apartments were cantilevered.

Correa's skyscraper is celebrated for how it resolves the banality of the tall building plan with his theories of climate and domesticity in section. The building is fondly remembered as an artifact of Correa's spatial resolution of the iconic courtyard in the sky, a design intervention that built on his experiments with internal courtyards in his siteless, low-cost, low-income Tube House competition entry for the Gujarat Housing Board, which Joseph Rykwert memorialized as "[demonstrating] an authentic Indian modernity that superseded the condescending orientalism and stale imports of colonialism."[49] But contrary to this dominant reading of Correa's work as an Indian modernism that succeeded in developing a modern Indian vocabulary, his turn to negotiating a floor-ceiling dynamic in the dense real estate landscape of Mumbai is not a continuation from his plinth-roof experiment. Instead, this shift from designing low-income housing to undoing the banality of speculative real-estate towers marked a shift from architecture's social goals to a logic of accumulation in post-developmental, liberalizing India. It underscores a structural and economic parallel between the Indian project of late-to-postmodernist aesthetics and the Green Revolution ideology of accumulation. The Kanchanjunga building thus specifically emerged at the transition from techno-modernism to World Bank capitalism, underwritten by concrete dominance, marking the turn from the developmental model of substitution to a late liberal one of flexibility.

FIGURE 17.3 An advertisement for slipform silo construction by the Engineering Construction Corporation Limited (ECC) in the *Indian Concrete Journal*, 1983.

FIGURE 17.4 The structural core of the Kanchanjunga building under construction, published on the cover of the *Indian Concrete Journal*, November 1973. The twenty-eight-story building, designed by the architect Charles Correa with structural design by Shirish Patel, was contracted out to the Engineering Construction Corporation Limited (ECC).

Source: Photograph by S. Damanlal and image courtesy the *Indian Concrete Journal*.

THE HUT AS PLINTH: GRAIN SUBSTITUTES THE BODY

Gurdeep Singh, the farmer cited at the start of this chapter, had asked for a godown. But in the end, it was neither godown nor silo that absorbed the agricultural surpluses emerging from Green Revolution agricultural surpluses. That problem was resolved by the invention of the Cover and Plinth (CAP) method of storage, which consisted of a plinth as protection from the ground and a low-density polyethylene (LDPE) cover for protection from the rain. The CAP model can be seen as another instantiation of the primitive hut; the question here is whether the comparison is correct, given the technological modernity of fossil-fuel derived plastic, water-proofing concrete additives, and chemical pesticides that made this system functional (see Figure 17.5). Officials referred to this CAP as the "scientific plinth," an attempt to remind critics of the technical nature of the space to inject semantic modernity into what looked like a primitive hut. CAP responded to the need for intra-seasonal flexibility, given that agricultural surpluses spike during the harvest season. In one sense, CAP was the "plinth delaminated from roof as pure diagram/program" taken to its logical conclusion. It provided a universal base of sorts upon which different systems could come to rest. The plinth negotiated a shift from the political economy of substitution (ad hoc interventions) to one of flexibility (delamination of building from program), which coincided with the end of the planning era in the 1970s and the beginning of the opening of the market. It marked

FIGURE 17.5 An ideal example of Cover and Plinth Storage on display at the Food Corporation of India's Hapur Warehouses from 2014. Sacks of wheat are stacked on a plinth and covered with a low-density polyethylene cover with openings (seen on the left part of the covering) for chemical pest control.

Source: Image by author.

the height of the organizational shift that had begun in 1964 where grain pricing and distribution across the country were systematically managed through the Food Corporation of India.

On a more speculative note, the CAP echoes the plastic linings used by people to keep their houses dry in place of the proper architecture of the roof. Mumbai's monsoon conditions mean that concrete, tin, brick, and mortar continually fail to keep water out, and more and more, terraces and roofs are covered with blue plastic. Perhaps someone who worked for the food corporation lived in a home that used plastic sheets to keep water out of their ceilings. Perhaps this spurred the plan to use plastic for temporarily protecting grain when warehouse space ran out. Perhaps the people who implemented these technologies lived in homes protected by LDPE sheets. Perhaps, even as storage is an instrument of macroeconomics, it might also have been a technology emergent from the travails of everyday life.

But to speak of the plinth is to speak of the body, as body and grain are substitutable figures in the caloric economy. To the postcolonial state, securing the body implied securing political legitimacy. Famine, Malthusian or otherwise, hovered as a vague specter to facilitate decision making toward technology, infrastructure, or policy. To protect wheat from rot was to secure the body politic from decay: development theory depended on this transubstantiation between food and body.

Bajaj's news report, cited at the start of this chapter, represented Gurdeep Singh as a native informant and his request for a shed as an innocent query into a straightforward piece of infrastructure, but Singh's citation of the government-built godown indeed reveals him to be a political agent in the long history of the state's deployment of infrastructure toward the management of a monocultural economy. Recently, Jean Drèze pointed out that in separating out the purchase of grain from farmers from its sale to consumers, the Food Corporation accounts for the grain using an accounting delay. The budget allocates a food subsidy that pays for the difference between the ceiling and the floor price of grain. But this value is only accounted for when the grain is released from storage. This delay in recording the money spent helps keep a massive debt from immediately affecting the state's credit ratings on the international market. Drèze says, "In economic terms, releasing excess stocks is costless, and even saves money. But in accounting terms, it is expensive."[50] When grain enters into this network of godowns and silos and plinths, it enters into a biological *and* economic limbo, a stasis, which allows the management of the political economy of food. This is the real work done by infrastructure: not to *shelter* grain but rather to perform the sleight of hand in which it ceases to exist for some time to keep the price of the commodity stable—to create a space for accumulation.

From this perspective, there are times when it makes sense to let excess grain rot, and conversely, times when it makes sense to let people starve. This is the economic calculus that Drèze criticizes the GOI for making during the Covid-19 food distribution failures that took place across India in the summer of 2020. But lest this seem like a morally suspect argument (it is), consider that the real moral failing is that the market is the only method of getting food to people, and thus it is the market that needs to be managed. As long as the market is the primary method of connecting people to food, the cost of the food (to both consumer and government) will be the primary thing to manage. In a political economy where food is exchanged for money, the cost of food is the central variable that is subject to control. The ministry of food and agriculture made it a central priority to manage this price by developing a vast infrastructural network of collection and distribution—in the process, it was able to pay one price to the farmer while selling the grain in the market at an unrelated second price. In this role of the middleman, storage and the models of analysis around storage and flow were new economic situations that the state had to perform and produce.

In the end, we are left with grain, rotting on plinths, exposed to the elements, unable to fulfill its biopolitical function of reaching the bodies of the people it was meant to remake. But ironically, it was also unable to fulfill its economic function of stabilizing the market. Most of the heavy lifting was (and still is) done by the ceiling and floor prices: minimum purchase prices to protect farmers and maximum selling prices to protect consumers, with the difference absorbed by the central and state government ministries. Here, the architectural metaphors of the ceiling and the floor represent an opening up in the market of a space for state intervention and accumulation. The plinths and the piles of rotting grain are indeed the material effects of macroeconomic policy on ground. Food rots not because policy has failed but rather because policy is succeeding. If food prices are grain abstracted to pure exchange value, then the plinth is building pared down to absolute diagram. It is the architectural equivalent of the heterogeneity of the commodity reduced to abstraction for the purposes of making that architecture perform in a post-developmental, liberalizing regime of flexibility, substitution, and exchange.

SUBSTITUTION IN DEVELOPMENT: A CONCLUSION

Development was never meant to be a process of incremental substitution. It was a theory of allocating resources, building capital, and installing an industrial state in a targeted way that stimulated a Rostovian take-off into an advanced mode of production and consumption (see the Introduction of this volume).[51] In substituting the *effects* of development (silos, concrete-technology, etc.) in place of causes (access to capital, advanced industrial production) that would produce prosperity, the postcolonial state has been widely theorized as having failed to implement developmental theory properly. Ironically, the various failures of modernization were, in the 1990s, also attributed to the failure of dogmatic developmental theory.[52] That is, both the theory and its implementation were deemed failures by the emerging neoliberal critics.[53] Yet the power of the idea of development has been unshakeable; it continues to be deployed in electoral politics by both centrist and right governments. To quote Ashish Nandy, "The problem with the idea of development is not its failure. The idea of development has succeeded beyond the dreams of its early partisans who never imagined that they had hit upon something whose day had come."[54]

What accounts for the power of the concept of development that it raises its zombie self in a neoliberal or late liberal world? This chapter suggests that substitution might offer an architectural metaphor that gives form to the ambiguity and slipperiness of the concept of development. Substitution underscores the *aporia* of developmental metapolitics in which structural change is promised but always delayed. The theory and the practice of development were constantly undergoing metaleptic remaking in that its effects were substituted for its cause. Substitution mimics the formal logic of change without a corresponding structural transformation; this formal logic of substitution (the godown) was eventually replaced by the formal logic of flexibility (the plinth), which promised the possibility of abundance without guaranteeing access to this stock.

NOTES

1 Santosh Singh and Allan Mustard, "India: Grain and Feed Annual Report 2012 Grain Report Number IN2026," in *Global Agricultural Information Network* (Washington, DC: USDA Foreign Agricultural Services, February 23, 2012), unpaginated.
2 Vikas Bajaj, "A Failed Food System in India Prompts an Intense Review," *The New York Times*, June 7, 2012, sec. Global Business. www.nytimes.com/2012/06/08/business/global/a-failed-food-system-in-india-prompts-an-intense-review.html.; Nirmala George, AP. "India's Wheat Left to Rot Due to Lack of Storage," *Toronto Star*, May 10, 2012.; Jason Overdorf, "India: Food Rots as People Starve," *PRI*, July 16, 2012, sec. Business, Economics and Jobs, GlobalPost.; Mayank Bhardwaj, "As Crops Rot, Millions Go Hungry in India," *Reuters*, July 1, 2012, https://uk.reuters.com/article/uk-india-wheat/as-crops-rot-millions-go-hungry-in-india-idUKBRE8600KB20120701.
3 Bajaj, "A Failed Food System in India Prompts an Intense Review."
4 Gurdeep Singh likely used the word "godown," which is commonly used to denote a warehouse in South and South East Asia.
5 For a discussion on fungibility, see Ginger Nolan, *Savage Mind to Savage Machine: Racial Science and Twentieth-Century Design* (Minneapolis: University of Minnesota Press, 2021), 105–106.
6 Jean Drèze and Amartya Sen, *Hunger and Public Action* (Oxford: Clarendon Press, 1990), 122.
7 Utsa Patnaik, *The Republic of Hunger and Other Essays* (Gurgaon: Three Essays Collective, 2007), 123–125.
8 On the emergence of the calorie as an all-encompassing quantitative metric of nutrition, see Nick Cullather, *The Hungry World: America's Cold War Battle against Poverty in Asia* (Cambridge, MA: Harvard University Press, 2010), 19–21.
9 Jenny Edkins, *Whose Hunger?: Concepts of Famine, Practices of Aid* (Minneapolis: University of Minnesota Press, 2000), xvi.
10 Essential commodities refer to a mutable list in the schedule of the *Essential Commodities Act of 1955*, which the authors described as a socioeconomic piece of legislation that protected commodities needed for day-to-day life by the common man at reasonable prices. They were classified not simply by their need but also by the propensity to be black-marketed and hoarded; thus, cement occasionally made it into the schedule. See K.B. Asthana, Surendra Malik, and Sarjoo Prasad, *Sarjoo Prasad's Commentaries on Essential Commodities Act, 1955* (Allahabad: Law Publishers, 1992), vii.
11 "Godown," often translated as warehouse, is the word used for storage in South and Southeast Asia, with some evidence that it comes from the Malaysian "*geodong*": Lisa Lim, "Where Did the Word 'Godown' Come from? India, Most Probably via Malay," *South China Morning Post*, June 10, 2017, www.scmp.com/magazines/post-magazine/article/2097479/where-did-word-godown-come-india-most-probably-malay (accessed May 15, 2021).
12 For instance, see S. K. Kelavkar, *Our Food Problem* (Kolhapur: Arya Bhanu Press, 1946).
13 Thomas Keenan, *Fables of Responsibility: Aberrations and Predicaments in Ethics and Politics* (Stanford, CA: Stanford University Press, 1997), 108–114.
14 H. Laxminarayan, "Indo-US Food Agreement and State Trading in Foodgrains," *The Economic and Political Weekly* 12, no. 39 (September 24, 1960): 1441–1447.
15 Concept of the Point Four Program, 1953, Records of US Foreign Assistance Agencies, 1948–1961, Record Group 469; National Archives at College Park, College Park, MD.
16 Vivek Chibber, *Locked in Place: State-Building and Late Industrialization in India* (Princeton, NJ: Princeton University Press, 2003), 32–35.
17 R. K. Sethi, "Construction of Storage Godowns Hapur (50,000 Tons Capacity), Expenditure Sanction," April 25, 1957. Ministry of Food and Agriculture, Department of Storage, F-25(11)/55-SG III. National Archives of India.
18 "Rs. 27-Lakh Grain Silo & Elevator Opened in Hapur," *The Times of India*, March 22, 1959, www.proquest.com/docview/613457284 (accessed April 20, 2021).
19 C. A. Ramakrishnan, "Estimates for the Construction of Storage Godowns at Hapur," June 30, 1956. Ministry of Food and Agriculture, Department of Storage, F-25(11)/55-SGIII. National Archives of India.
20 "Agriculture Fair-US Exhibit World Agriculture Fair," September 17, 1959. RG 306 Entry P 299 Box 2. National Archives, College Park, MD.
21 Minoru Yamasaki, *A Life in Architecture* (Tokyo: Weatherhill, 1979), 59–63.
22 "Circarama: U.S.A.," *American Reporter*, September 6, 1961.
23 TCM Dispatch, "Education Exchange: Proposals for the Use of PL-480 Funds in Connection with the PL-48 (India Wheat Loan) Educational Exchange Program," March 18, 1959. Subject Files 1953–1961, RG 469. National Archives, College Park, MD.
24 Maureen L. P. Patterson, "The South Asian P.L. 480 Library Program, 1962–1968," *The Journal of Asian Studies* 28, no. 4 (1969): 744, https://doi.org/10.2307/2942409.
25 Maureen L. P. Patterson and Louis A. Jacob, "South Asian Area Studies and the Library [with Discussion]," *The Library Quarterly: Information, Community, Policy* 35, no. 4 (1965): 223–238.
26 M. L. Dantwala, "Problems of Buffer Stocks," *Economic and Political Weekly* 4, no. 13 (March 29, 1969): A63–A67, A63.

27 "Grains Storage and Distribution: Brisk Arrangements by Food Department," *The Times of India; New Delhi, India*, May 27, 1960, www.proquest.com/docview/741088538 (accessed April 20, 2021). And "The Times of India" News Service. "Silos to Be Built at Ports: Bulk Wheat Storage New Delhi," *The Times of India*, May 11, 1960, New Delhi edition, www.proquest.com/docview/741096192 (accessed April 20, 2021).

28 Dhunjisha P. R. Cassad, "Institution of Engineers Holds Annual Session at Lucknow; Presidential Address," *Indian Concrete Journal* 32, no. 3 (March 1958): 85.

29 Ibid., 87.

30 K. K. Nambiar, "Editorial: Thin Shell Concrete Roofs for Grain Godowns," *Indian Concrete Journal* 32, no. 1 (January 1958): 1–2.

31 "Shell Catenary Roof for Fertiliser Project," *Indian Concrete Journal* 34, no. 10 (October 1960): 410.

32 L. R. Gupta, "Construction of Shell Roofs for Grain Godowns in New Delhi," *Indian Concrete Journal* 36, no. 12 (December 1962): 438–442.

33 Peter Scriver, *Rationalization, Standardization, and Control in Design: A Cognitive Historical Study of Architectural Design and Planning in the Public Works Department of British India, 1855–1901* (Delft: Publikatieburo Bouwkunde, Technische Universiteit Delft, 1994), 511.

34 "Rigid Pavements Subdiscipline, Surkhi as a Puzzolana, Lime Reactive Surkhi Mortar for Brick Masonry," *Central Road Research Institute Annual Report 1964–65* (1965): 10.

35 M. L. Dantwala, "Summary of Discussions at the Seminar on Foodgrains Buffer Stocks," in *Seminar on Foodgrains Buffer Stocks in India* (Bombay: Indian Society of Agricultural Economics, August 1969), 10.

36 Ali Mohammed Khusro, "Stocks and Storage of Major Foodgrains," *Seminar on Foodgrains Buffer Stocks in India* (Bombay: Indian Society of Agricultural Economics, August 1969), 135.

37 Ibid., 141.

38 Ibid., 142.

39 Ibid., 143.

40 Construction of Godowns Hapur—Railway Siding, Notes, 1956. File SGIII/31/R/56, Department of Storage, Ministry of Food and Agriculture, National Archives of India.

41 *India—Wheat Storage Project (English)* (Washington, DC: World Bank Group, June 15, 1971). i, http://documents.worldbank.org/curated/en/506531468260102494/India-Wheat-Storage-Project (accessed May 15, 2021).

42 *India—Second Foodgrain Storage Project (English)* (Washington, DC: World Bank Group, November 3, 1977), 11, http://documents.worldbank.org/curated/en/391561468033866501/India-Second-Foodgrain-Storage-Project (accessed May 15, 2021).

43 Balwanth Reddy, "Management of Food Policy," *ASCI Journal of Management* 7, no. 1 (September 1977): 49.

44 R. M. Garg, "Maximum Pressures of Granular Materials in Silos: 1," *Indian Concrete Journal* 46, no. 12 (December 1972): 487–493.

45 *India—Wheat Storage Project*, 8–9.

46 "While the Bank at the time of appraisal was convinced of the economic advantages of modern bulk and silo storage, it was quick in dropping this component when problems of timeliness occurred. Since the feasibility of these components was not even tested during the project, one must conclude that the project contributed very little to modernizing grain storage and reducing its cost." *Project Completion Report, Second Foodgrain Storage Project—India* (Washington, DC: World Bank Group, December 30, 1988), viii.

47 Subir K. Sarkar, "How to Achieve Maximum Benefits from Slipform," *Indian Concrete Journal* 53, no. 4 (April 1979): 95.

48 Arun Biswas, "The Vertical Slipform," *Indian Concrete Journal* 50, no. 12 (December 1976): 360.

49 Joseph Rykwert, "Charles Correa Obituary," *The Guardian*, June 19, 2015, www.theguardian.com/artanddesign/2015/jun/19/charles-correa (accessed April 20, 2021).

50 Jean Drèze, "Excess Stocks of the Food Corporation of India Must Be Released to the Poor," *Indian Express*, April 9, 2020, https://indianexpress.com/article/opinion/columns/coronavirus-lockdown-food-for-poor-migrants-mass-exodus-jean-dreze-6353790/ (accessed April 20, 2021).

51 See the work of Walt Whitman Rostow, Paul Rosenstein-Rodan, and Albert Hirschman among others, summarized in the Introduction to this volume, for more detail.

52 For instance, see Terence J. Byres, "Introduction," in *The State, Development Planning and Liberalisation in India* (Delhi and New York: Oxford University Press, 1998).

53 Montek Singh Ahluwalia, "India's 1991 Reforms: A Retrospective Overview," in *India Transformed: Twenty-Five Years of Economic Reforms*, ed. Rakesh Mohan (Washington, DC: Brookings Institution Press, 2018), 47–50.

54 Ashis Nandy, "Development and Violence," in *The Romance of the State: And the Fate of Dissent in the Tropics*, ed. Ashis Nandy (New Delhi: Oxford University Press, 2007), 171.

Part VI

Land

18

Policy regionalism and the limits of translation in land economics

Burak Erdim

The luxury hotels located along the edges of Taksim Square played a particularly important role during the protests against the Gezi Park development proposed in Istanbul in 2013.[1] In many ways the political identity of these businesses became simultaneously defined and complicated by the various functions that they served in relation to the events of that summer. On the one hand, some of these establishments provided a safe harbor to protestors as well as curious onlookers. During periods of calm, hotel lobbies provided different levels of engagement for interested parties. While the ground level lobbies operated as shelters and time-out rooms for wearied activists, the upper level cafes and bars functioned as viewing platforms for others, turning the event into an open spectacle one could view safely or engage at will. In fact, many of the bird's-eye-view photographs and some of the video footage of Gezi were taken from the safety of these luxury sky cafés (Figure 18.1). At the same time, when clashes between the riot police and the protestors escalated, some of the lower level lobbies served as emergency rooms and field hospitals. What protected these safe zones and gave them immunity, paradoxically, was the alliance of the hotel proprietors with the administration and the police. The role and identity of these spaces were therefore ambivalent. They appeared to safeguard the protestors and enthusiasts, helping to broadcast the events, which were otherwise not televised, while they also stood to benefit from the proposed urban transformations.

The dual nature of these spaces revealed a type of informal complicity that ran across the seemingly oppositional forces in Turkish politics and society, complicating any simplistic readings of Gezi events. Viewing the images collected from the sky cafés, many of those who were familiar with the history of Gezi Park pointed to a building that appeared on the northern edges of this site, remarking that "it had all begun with this building." The culprit was clearly the Istanbul Hilton Hotel (1951–54), designed by the well-known American architecture and engineering firm, Skidmore, Owings and Merrill (SOM) in collaboration with the celebrated Turkish architect Sedad Hakkı Eldem (Figure 18.2). However, there was an intentional vagueness in what the pronoun "it" referred to, which paralleled the ambivalence of these spaces. Did "it" refer to the Turkish state's mode of speculative development through the privatization of public land? If so, this practice had once again manifested itself in the current administration's latest scheme to replace Gezi Park with a new shopping center and luxury residences in the form of the Ottoman Military Barracks

DOI: 10.4324/9781003193654-25

FIGURE 18.1 Photograph of Taksim Square and Gezi Park Protests in summer 2013 taken from the sky cafe of Marmara Taksim Hotel.

Source: Courtesy of Ipek Yürekli.

FIGURE 18.2 Aerial view of Taksim Square and Gezi Park showing the recently built Istanbul Hilton Hotel on the upper right corner of the frame, ca. 1955.

that used to be on this site. Or did "it" refer to the series of eight-story apartment buildings that had mushroomed during the 1950s, lining the other side of the Republic Boulevard (*Cumhuriyet Caddesi*) facing the Istanbul Hilton? Or did "it" refer to what was taking place at Gezi and the protests against the autocratic actions of the administration that were taking place on Taksim Square? Regardless of what "it" may have referred to, the events at Taksim appeared simultaneously significant and inconsequential in the shadow of this spatial and political ambivalence. In other words, what had begun in 1950s Istanbul had already shaped the urban landscape to such an extent that the citizens and the city were irreversibly bound to it and to its political economies of housing, construction, and speculative development.

Taksim Square and Gezi Park are two of the primary urban spaces where the various manifestations of Turkish modernity have been staged and contested throughout the history of Ottoman-Turkish modernization. At the same time, the scene that came to life during the Gezi events revealed certain cracks and fissures across the otherwise seemingly tidy oppositional boundaries between the administration's plans and its critics. Not unlike the ambivalence of the hotels and the businesses that surrounded the events, the totality of this urban scene exposed deeper tensions as well as degrees of fluidity across these factions. This essay examines the critical, formative point of this modernity in the aftermath of World War II, when Republic Boulevard (Cumhuriyet Caddesi), its apartments, and the Istanbul Hilton first began to take shape as key components of the modern Turkish city. While the making of the hotel plays a major part in this analysis, it also shows how the apartments and the hotel reflected each other or stared each other down from opposite corners, revealing how the diverging interests and legitimacy battles among the various national and international actors mediated and limited the direct implementation of programs to reform Turkish society, politics, and modernity.

THE ISTANBUL HILTON: THIS IS *NOT* A HOTEL

This essay situates the inception of the Hilton project at Gezi by first examining an extensive but lesser-known report that the American architecture and planning firm Skidmore, Owings and Merrill (SOM) prepared for Turkey in 1951 at the beginning stages of their engagement in the design and construction of the Istanbul Hilton. Also significant in this context is the subsequent visit of Charles Abrams, a New York labor lawyer and United Nations (UN) housing policy expert and lawyer of the New Deal era, on his first overseas mission to advise the Turkish government on issues involving housing finance and the utilization of urban land. What Abrams found in Turkey was that local politics were as much a barrier against regulatory practices in land tenure and speculation as they were in the United States. In fact, local administrators were just as keen as the politicians that Abrams was more familiar with at home in devising the type of development practices that would align most directly with their constituents' interests.

As Annabel Wharton's analysis of the Istanbul Hilton shows, the project provided a paradigm of international cooperation and diplomacy during the early stages of the Cold War, when territorial disputes over the Bosporus emerged as the first and most serious conflict between the United States and the Soviet Union outside of Berlin. As a result, Turkey became the first recipient of postwar aid, along with Greece, under the provisions of the Truman Doctrine and the Marshall Plan.[2] As Wharton describes, the Istanbul Hilton provided a home away from home for American businessmen, diplomats, and early jet setters, while also functioning as a clear sign of American presence to the Soviet tankers navigating the currents of the Bosporus below. At the same time, as Wharton argues, the building also behaved as a machine for viewing and territorializing the city and the region, an ideological function that Conrad Hilton fully utilized to build and popularize his international brand. At the opening ceremony, attended by many American luminaries, Hilton announced, "Each of our hotels is a little America."[3] He meant this "not as a symbol of bristling power, but as a friendly center where men of many nations and of good will may speak the language of peace."[4] In the 1950s, this type of rhetoric and propaganda resonated with both American and non-American travelers and consumers. Within the Turkish context, the Hilton was perceived as the icon of postwar modernity for a whole generation of professionals and consumers alike.

Yet as powerful a symbol as the Hilton had become, it was only the tip of an iceberg and only a morsel of a tremendous international administrative machinery that was put in place in Turkey through the operations of the Marshall Plan between 1948 and 1951. The Hilton Corporation and SOM were only two examples of a number of other American corporations who were collaborating with American agencies on numerous postwar projects of reconstruction, ranging from the creation of transportation and defense networks to projects of resource extraction, power generation, and regional development. Of particular importance was large-scale agricultural irrigation and mechanization projects to build Turkey as a "breadbasket" for Europe. Many of these projects were funded by wartime lend-lease agreements, and the funds often paid for the machinery and the expertise provided by US companies.

Nevertheless, political support in the United States for projects of postwar reconstruction was waning by the beginning of the 1950s, and the Hilton marked the end and the beginning of a new era of international cooperation. The new model would be managed by the UN instead of by the agencies of the United States and would require client nations to obtain their own financing. One of the clearest evidences of this shift was an extensive report that the SOM team prepared for Turkey at the beginning phases of their work on the design of the Hilton. The report, "Construction, Town Planning, and Housing in Turkey," advised the Turkish government on establishing a housing and construction market to build a national economy. The report observed that the construction industry was relatively low-tech and could provide the necessary housing and jobs to absorb the rural migration of farmers displaced by mechanization. In addition, it advocated for a housing finance mechanism to support this industry that would not only provide the basis of a new international aid structure but would also contribute to the socialization of the urbanizing masses through the construction of a participatory economy, not unlike the one begun during the immediate postwar period in the United States. However, as the report showed, much work needed to be done in Turkey in areas such as standardization and regulation of construction technologies through zoning, building codes, and the development of an insurance industry. The country was thus advised to work closely with UN agencies in the establishment of a national planning agency to coordinate housing and construction initiatives at the national and international levels.

Thus, the SOM report reveals another aspect of the Hilton project. Aside from its function as a hotel and a symbol of American power, the building also sought to function as a model of housing and construction planning in Turkey. In this respect, the building spoke more to the concrete-frame apartments that were rising across Cumhuriyet Boulevard than the tankers in the Bosporus. Both the apartments and the Hilton had emerged as products of urban renewal projects that the Democratic Party (DP) administration had initiated. Furthermore, the Hilton project was made possible through the same processes of land appropriation that had paved the way for the boulevards and the apartments. The apartments, in the absence of a housing finance mechanism, had emerged through a series of informal agreements between builders and landowners. Builders would offer a percentage of the flats in the proposed apartment block to the landowner in return for the building rights and would sell the rest of the flats to cover construction and profits. The passage of a flat ownership law (*kat mülkiyeti kanunu*) provided the state sanction for these quasi-official arrangements, which became Turkey's official land tenure and urban development policy in the 1950s. The Hilton project was realized through similarly semiformal arrangements between the Turkish government, the US State Department, and the Hilton Corporation. The DP administration appropriated the land, and because there was no existing finance mechanism, appropriated funds from the Turkish Pension Fund (*Emekli Sandığı*) for the construction of the hotel. The Foreign Operations Administration (FOA) guaranteed these funds to the Pension Fund through a Bank of America loan. Furthermore, the Economic Cooperation Administration (ECA) utilized Marshall Plan funds to purchase, primarily from the United States, materials and equipment not available in Turkey.[5] Procedurally speaking, therefore, this complex web of national and international financing fit perfectly well with the Turkish DP administration's aims. The DP landslide victory over the Republican People's Party (RPP) in 1950 had been won on a platform to build Turkey as "a little America with a millionaire in every district." The hotel served as a symbol of the urban renewal and reconstruction projects that the DP was carrying out in Turkish port cities and especially in Istanbul to position Turkey as an economic hub in the region. However, as Marshall Plan aid came to an end, the SOM report pointed to a different model of development than was signaled at Hilton. As much as the DP had been a willing ally of the United States and interests in the region, they felt that the report undermined this emergent relationship, indicating a turn in US policy. Therefore, as promising as the Hilton project had been for the US–Turkish economic partnership, the SOM report itself marked the beginning of a contentious divide between the Eisenhower and the Menderes administrations.

CHARLES ABRAMS AND LAND ECONOMICS

As a result of the temporary breakdown of the relationship between Turkey and the United States, it would be three years before Turkey invited a UN housing policy expert to follow the key recommendations of the SOM report. Charles Abrams arrived in Ankara in 1954, and he was by all accounts the ideal expert to address the issues that the SOM report had identified in establishing regulatory policies in housing, construction, and planning. At the same time, his approach to housing finance differed significantly from SOM. While the SOM report focused on aligning state policies with the machinations of international finance, Abrams was interested in the creation of equitable housing policies that could benefit the widest possible spectrum of the world population. Two key elements were what set Abrams apart from his contemporaries. First, Abrams did not approach housing as a shortage or as the engine that would drive postwar economies but as the building block of an equitable postwar world system. An example is Abrams's famous roof-loan scheme he developed for Bolivia and Nigeria, which is the origin of current micro-finance mechanisms, providing loans to individuals who could not afford or did not need a full house loan. The partial roof loan was inexpensive and enabled individuals or families to finish a house and protect it properly, allowing the house to gain value and build equity over time. In this way, partial house loans or housing finance created the foundation of what Scott Henderson defined as Abrams's "democratizing ideal."[6] Furthermore, Abrams formulated that the housing issue had to be dealt with at a more fundamental level, through what earlier economists such as Henry George had defined as land economics. These two elements, along with his unequaled knowledge of urban land policies, are what set Abrams apart from other prominent housing policy intellectuals of the New Deal and the postwar period.

Abrams became associated with the United Nations after the publication of his first book, *Revolution in Land* (1939).[7] It was a compilation of lectures Abrams had put together for the courses he taught in the Department of Political Science at the New School for Social Research during the mid-1930s.[8] By this time, Abrams had become a well-known and respected housing advocate in New York. He had played a central role, along with Ira Robbins, in the drafting of the landmark brief that made it legal for housing authorities to construct new housing in American cities. The brief would provide the impetus for the Housing Act of 1937. As the general counsel to the New York City's newest agency, the New York City Housing Authority, in 1934, Abrams became interested in tracing how changing property ownership practices affected the national economy and the political system in the United States.[9]

In *Revolution in Land*, Abrams explained that as industry gradually superseded land as the motor of social and economic organization in the United States, concentrations of wealth and influence began to increase the cost of land and production, especially in urban areas. Further coordination of production policies by private cartels and monopolies to monitor supply and demand pushed prices up, for example in the building materials trade, creating one of the principal causes of the housing problem. This transformation forced the rents to go up, first in newly constructed houses but then also elsewhere, and put them on track to become far out of line with the wages that industry paid to its workers. What Abrams proposed as a *revolution* in land was public intervention of a more integrated and radical nature than what had been accomplished during the New Deal. Consequently, for Abrams, change had to come from inventive and well-designed government policies to reorganize the relationship between land and industry. Abrams defined this proposition as the "middle road."[10] It was not an overnight overthrow of the existing system. Instead, Abrams advocated for the public control over the fluctuations of business practices:

> No matter what the future shape of the world may be, it is already becoming abundantly clear that the use of land must be subjected to an increasing measure of social control. The chaotic conditions of today cannot be permitted to continue if collapse is to be avoided.[11]

Abrams's "middle road" consisted of additional public housing, stronger enforcement of antitrust laws, federal taxation of intangible property, and credit liberalization for housing construction. Although most of these had been a part of the New Deal programs at one time or another, Abrams proposed that in order to succeed properly, these programs needed to be a part of a more comprehensive long-term government plan. Lewis Mumford, who was aware of Abrams's contributions to housing policy in the United States and had become familiar with his book during its writing stages, hailed it with an outstanding review, calling it the most insightful investigation of land economics since Henry George.[12]

ABRAMS AND THE UN-HTCP

During the post-World War II period, when American national identity and modernity became the blueprint for postwar reconstruction, works of intellectuals such as Mumford and Abrams became increasingly influential in determining the shape of American development discourse and foreign policy. Furthermore, Abrams's analysis of the transformation in the United States from an agrarian to an industrial society (Abrams defined this as the passing of a tradition) also became centrally important for development experts and intellectuals of the postwar period. It was within this context that Ernest Weissmann (1903–1985), the Chief of the Housing and Town and Country Planning Section of the United Nations (UN-HTCP), became aware of Abrams's work and asked him to write a report for the UN in 1952 to apply his expertise in US land utilization practices to the international context. Abrams welcomed the challenge, and the resulting report, titled "Urban Land Problems and Policies," marked the beginning of Abrams's influential career as a UN housing and planning expert.[13] Regarding the report, Abrams later noted, "The study sparked my interest in the evolving problems of the less developed nations and widened a focus that until then had been concentrated mainly on the American scene.[14] During the next ten years, Abrams would serve on UN missions in 14 countries including Turkey, Ghana, the Philippines, Pakistan, Nigeria, Ireland, Jamaica, Japan, Singapore, Bolivia, Venezuela, Barbados, Puerto Rico, Jamaica (International Cooperation Administration), and Colombia (Pan-American Union).[15]

What is remarkable about Abrams's initial report is that, even though he was not an academician by training, his analysis of land utilization practices in the United States followed the emerging scholarship on American modernity and national identity during the 1930s. This discourse, which focused on the processes of modernization and democratization, would form the basis of modernization theory and liberalism in postwar America.[16] This curious appearance of the early postulates of modernization theory in Abrams's analysis can be attributed to his teaching appointment in the Department of Political Science at the New School. Although not recognized as one of the key nodes of modernization theory, the New School held an important position in the formation and, later, critiques of modernization theory, with the joining of influential European émigré scholars such as Hannah Arendt to their ranks.[17]

The postulates of modernization theory appear in Abrams's classification of the world into binary categories. For instance, Abrams's emphasis on the differences between the developed and the developing nations in his initial report for the UN formed the basis of his argument.[18] Like many other ideologues of modernization theory, Abrams maintained that both the developed and the developing countries would go through the same phases of development. This was a fundamental point used to validate the universal applicability of modernization theory. Abrams utilized it in order to emphasize the importance of international experts and governance. Abrams held that developing countries would experience the phases of development at a more rapid pace than the developed countries. Building on the ideas he had begun to articulate in *Revolution in Land*, Abrams explained the industrial revolution as a series of four transformations in the report he developed for the UN.[19] First in the process was the maturing of the individual's rights against the state. Second came the deconcentration of land ownership and the break-up of holdings. Third was the decline of land as the dominant form of wealth, giving rise to new forms of intangible property and new uses for land. The fourth phase was the rise of the concept of welfare, in which the desire to advance housing and urban living standards would put regulatory policies in place.[20] For Abrams, a regulatory state and sound policy development were essential to counteracting the effects of the colonization of land during the third phase of the industrial revolution. Abrams argued that developing nations would experience these social and economic transformations "almost simultaneously" as multiple revolutions, making the construction of a sound state apparatus all the more important in developing countries.[21]

Therefore, the conceptualized difference between developing and developed countries served to advance Abrams's argument for the role of international experts and national and international governance. At the same time, he was well aware, through his housing policy struggles in New York, that the welfare revolution, the fourth and a key component of modernization, had not yet been fully implemented in the United States, thus dismantling one of the essentialized differences between developed and developing worlds. Abrams countered this flaw in his argument by subscribing to what Nils Gilman has described as the technocosmopolitan faction of modernization theory.[22] Diminishing the role of a universal or a complete model, the technocosmopolitans held that modernity must be built on the foundations of tradition. Following this approach, Abrams argued that policies developed for one social and political context could not be implemented in another and that differences in national social and economic practices needed to be considered in developing policies responsive to each context.[23] While this approach made perfect sense in terms of Abrams's own experiences in developing housing policies in New York or the United States, it presented a fundamental challenge to the UN. International experts who rarely spent more than two months on a mission simply did not have the time or the expertise to develop policies responsive to each context. Therefore, on the one hand, Abrams's report for the UN had identified the importance of land tenure and housing policy initiatives for the postwar world. On the other hand, it showed that such policies could not be developed through the UN's existing modes of operation.

Following this report, Abrams was asked to chair a multi-day panel on urban land policies and problems in an international seminar organized in 1954, at the invitation of the government of India, by the Technical Assistance Administration of the United Nations.[24] The seminar represented the culmination of a series of activities undertaken by the Economic and Social Council (ECOSOC) of the UN since the beginning of the 1950s regarding issues of housing and community planning. As the Chief of the United Nations Housing and Town and Country Planning Agency, Ernest Weissmann presided over the organization and proceedings of the seminar as the UN Secretariat. Jaqueline Tyrwhitt, professor of town planning at the University of Toronto, served as director. Tyrwhitt conducted the organization of the seminar from the UN-TAA Resident Representative's office in the Council for Industrial and Scientific Research building in New Delhi, India. Aside from the nine international experts appointed by the UN to run the main components of the seminar, the attendees included official delegates from a number of developing countries, representatives of international and governmental organizations, delegates from Indian organizations, businesses, schools of planning, and ministries.[25] Among the presenters, aside from Weissmann and Abrams, there were such well-known names as Constantine Doxiadis, who was working for the Ford Foundation missions in Calcutta and Karachi at the time; Michel Ecochard, CIAM member and the former director of the French Protectorate in Morocco, then serving as TAA advisor to the government of Pakistan on town planning; Maxwell Fry, Jane Drew, and Pierre Jeanerette, in India at the time with Le Corbusier, undertaking the design of Chandigarh; Jacob Crane, assistant to the director of the US Housing and Home Finance Agency; Rafael Pico, the chairman of the Puerto Rico Planning Board; Luis Rivera Santos, the director of Puerto Rico's Social Program; and Frederick J. Adams, professor of town planning at the Massachusetts Institute of Technology (MIT) and the director of the Joint Center at Harvard and MIT.[26] The seminar was organized around three primary sections of paper presentations and discussions, each focusing on a particular topic designated by the organizers.[27] Abrams ran section three, during which he asked each participating country representative to provide brief statements on the various aspects of housing, planning, and building in order to put together comparative data on issues of private property and land tenure.[28]

Therefore, when Abrams arrived in Turkey following the seminar in India on September 6, 1954, he was eager to document the land utilization practices there as well in preparation for his work on Turkey's zoning ordinances, planning matters, and construction finance mechanisms.[29] Upon his arrival in Turkey, Abrams found a number of indicators that showed Turkey had taken steps toward indicative planning recommended by the SOM report and the UN agencies. Reports left by previous UN resident representatives, such as Marshall E. Dimock, as well as the reports of the UN-sponsored teaching staff at the recently established Institute of Public Administration in Turkey and the Middle East (Türkiye ve Orta Doğu Amme İdaresi Enstitüsü; or, TODAIE) were among the first pieces of information that Abrams had access to upon his arrival. However, within a few days of his visit in Ankara, Abrams became aware of a considerable cultural and professional divide between him and his bureaucratic counterparts in Turkey. The fact that many of the ministerial staff did not know English and were not able to translate key documents for Abrams's review made it almost impossible for him to accomplish what he had come to do.[30] Celal Uzer, who was appointed as Abrams's guide and translator, was an exception. Uzer had completed his planning degree in England and was one of the only architects working in the ministry with a degree in planning and a full command of English.[31] Working with Uzer, Abrams identified the documents he needed and sent some of them to the United States in order to get them translated to English.[32] In the meantime, Abrams examined the reports that had been compiled in English by Western experts on housing and planning at the Institute of Public Administration for Turkey and the Middle East and the Ministry of Public Works.

The SOM report was among the documents that Abrams consulted during this period. He realized that this was the report that had paved the way for his mission. At the same time, the copies of this report collecting dust on the ministry shelves had a rather sobering effect on Abrams, especially when he found that Uzer was instructed to take him on a country tour very similar to the one that was taken by the SOM team. Yet Abrams also wanted to see the varying conditions throughout Turkey that the SOM team described in their reports. In his final report for Turkey, Abrams wrote that this trip was taken in two parts, covered 4,000 miles and "enabled me to obtain a fairly comprehensive idea of the country and its conditions."[33] Abrams described

> In the course of the journey, I interviewed twelve provincial Governors, an equal number of mayors and city officials, as well as many private architects, businessmen, directors of factories,

village officials and villagers, and officials of state enterprises. In each case I sought to elicit the nature of the principal problems with which officials were concerned and how they were being tackled.[34]

What one finds here is that Abrams's country survey, which followed the footsteps of the SOM team, differed considerably from other country surveys of his contemporaries. While, for instance, numerous other housing and development experts working elsewhere, such as Michel Ecochard, George Candilis, or Vladimir Bodiansky, approached the countryside to study the everyday life and spaces of its inhabitants, Abrams was primarily interested in observing how effectively policies developed in the nation's capital were carried out in the peripheries. Abrams sought to find how responsive these policies were to the varying conditions across the social and economic variations in the country at large.

In the same way that he had characterized the differences between the developed and the developing regions, Abrams characterized Turkey as "a country of striking contrasts in terrains, customs, occupations, backgrounds, and social and economic conditions," observing that "a visitor who has seen Istanbul, Bursa, Yalova, and Izmir will know little of Tarsus, Amasya, Sivas, or Konya."[35] He added, "Much of the country had been cut off from communication with the rest of the country," especially in the interior and in the smaller towns and provinces. It was in the context of these contrasts that Abrams would first begin to use the term "revolution" to describe the four phases of development he had articulated in his UN report.

However, while trying to assess how he would conceptualize this issue of "striking contrasts" under his broader conceptualizations of development, Abrams began to draft a report for Hayrettin Erkmen, Minister of Labor, based on the documents he had been able to review in existing laws and reports. Abrams's initial report was comprised of a series of observations and recommendation for the revision of the existing national workers' housing cooperative program directed by the Estate and Credit Bank (*Emlak ve Kredi Bankası*). The program that Abrams was examining ran in a very similar way that the construction of the Hilton Hotel was financed. The Turkish Workers Pension Fund provided the funds for the construction of worker's housing cooperatives across the country at low interest rates. Abrams reviewed the tenets of this program and found them to be reasonable and comparable to other similar programs in Finland and Norway. A system that utilizes the pension fund to finance workers' housing may sound unusual or even questionable in today's practice; however, Abrams was aware that this was a widely used mechanism in interwar and postwar Europe not only to provide low-cost housing for the working class but also to grow the pension fund. Such a scheme took the developer or the banker out of the equation and put the generated profits back into the retirement savings of the workers. It was not far from the type of comprehensive funding mechanisms that Abrams would have liked to implement in the United States. In his report for Turkey, Abrams simply identified the loopholes in the existing laws and suggested ways of refining what he otherwise found to be a workable system. However, Abrams found it impossible to meet with upper level officials to discuss the details of his report. As a UN expert, even though Abrams made every effort to understand the workings of the Turkish housing and land tenure practices and to translate and apply his expertise, he had not been able to communicate with his counterparts to implement his recommendations.

ABRAMS MEETS DIKER

Regarding the situation in Turkey, Abrams would later write,

> Certainly the odds were against the success of any mission, for an expert carrying no funds in his portfolio was just another expert. In 1954, he would rarely get to see anyone with the rank of a cabinet minister and was more often assigned to a minor functionary who would spend an occasional hour with him lamenting the predicaments of officialdom.[36]

During his time in the ministry offices, Abrams noted that, "a UN economics mission with three prominent experts, after struggling to make an impact on the government, had packed their belongings and left in despair."[37] Not able to meet with any upper level administrators, Abrams concluded his report and prepared to leave for his next mission in the Gold Coast (now Ghana). It was at this particular juncture of Abrams's mission that Celal Uzer introduced Abrams to Vecdi Diker, an American-trained civil engineer and the former director of the National Department of Highways under the RPP administration. Diker had received his degrees in civil engineering from Columbia University and the University of Missouri during an early wave of scholarships provided by the US government to train future Turkish bureaucrats. Upon his return to Turkey, he took a position with the Department of Roads and Bridges within the Ministry of Public Works in 1937. He quickly rose in rank within the ministry to become the central agent on the Turkish side in the conceptualization of the National Department of Highways.[38] During that work, he experienced how quickly differences of opinion could form between American and Turkish experts on matters ranging from the shape of the highway network to the administration of road crews and maintenance of highway machinery. As a former bureaucrat, he was familiar with the DP's politics of development and the delicate dynamic at the ministry between foreign experts and local bureaucrats. While the American experts arrived with a dual set of assumptions about Turkey and the universal applicability of their expertise, their Turkish counterparts claimed to have a better understanding of local state traditions and modes of operation.[39]

Diker knew that just prior to Abrams's arrival in Turkey, there had been a major breakdown in the operations of the technical assistance machinery that relied on the tri-part cooperation of Turkish, US, and UN agencies. Several reasons led to this contentious atmosphere. First, the Turkish–US economic partnership had come to a screeching halt. US-AID representatives held that the Turkish economy was heading toward a crisis and wanted the DP administration to take a series of precautionary steps before appropriating more aid for Turkey. Similarly, US-AID and ICA officials in Turkey viewed UN experts and projects with great skepticism and rivalry, and this attitude certainly affected Turkish perceptions of the UN as well.[40]

Another reason underlying the DP Administration's disdain for the UN was the United Nations Educational, Scientific, and Cultural Organization's (UNESCO) repeated criticism of the large-scale development projects that the DP government had begun in Istanbul's historic districts such as the Beyazıt Square and the construction of the Palace of Justice. Finding UNESCO's oversight of these projects a liability for their popularity, the DP had declared all UNESCO agents as *persona non grata* in all diplomatic affairs.[41] Furthermore, by the time of Abrams's arrival, Turkish officials were waiting for the UN to deliver on an earlier and, from the DP's point of view, more important project than Abrams's work on housing. In 1951, Turkey, the United Nations Food and Agriculture Organization (UN-FAO) and the International Monetary Fund had signed an agreement for the establishment of a research institute in Turkey in agriculture and related fields of development to benefit Turkey and the larger Mediterranean region.[42] Under this agreement, the Turkish government agreed to provide the necessary resources, such as the facilities and the monetary funds, needed to establish a training and research center to assess and develop economic opportunities in agriculture and related industries in the Mediterranean region.[43] The UN was to provide the initial administrative expertise. However, while the DP administration had been keen to get this project started, the UN had not been forthcoming about initiating the efforts to establish this institute, resulting in further tensions between the DP and the UN agencies.

In addition, the year that Abrams arrived in Ankara, the Turkish government had passed a law allowing Turkish architects and engineers to organize under a union. This legislation had come at the end of a long and arduous battle between these professionals and the Ministry of Public Works. Throughout the history of Ottoman-Turkish modernization from the mid-nineteenth century to the postwar period, the Ministry of Public Works had shown a well-established preference for foreign architects and experts in the design and construction of major public structures, ranging from regional and city plans to buildings. SOM's design and construction of the Istanbul Hilton had in fact figured at the center of these heated debates that boiled over from state and architectural offices and the academies to the pages of contemporary architectural journals. Even though the Hilton filled the imagination of a generation of Turkish professionals, the fact that the commission of such an iconic building project of the 1950s had been awarded to a foreign architectural office also worked to mobilize this group to claim their talents and knowledge as equals to their foreign counterparts. Sedad Hakkı Eldem's assignment to work with SOM as their Turkish counterpart did not ameliorate the debates.

There was yet another factor operating against the favorable perception of foreign experts during the 1950s. Hitherto, the Turkish bureaucratic and professional community had been used to working with a different type of foreign expert who had come to Turkey from Germany and Austria during the 1930s. These experts, most of them political exiles, stayed in Turkey for long periods of time, working as both teachers and professionals in the academies and the ministry offices. By comparison, the UN and US experts did not stay long enough to gain legitimacy in the perceptions of their Turkish counterparts. An editorial essay that appeared in *Mimarlık* as early as 1947 clarify the architectural culture's position on foreign experts. The article maintained that foreign architects and engineers were welcome in Turkey, but only as consultants and educators.[44]

After having heard Abrams's perceptions and considering the state of the technical assistance machinery, Diker made an offer to Abrams that would alter the course of Abrams's mission. Diker suggested that he might be able to arrange a meeting for Abrams with the acting prime minister, Fatin Rüştü Zorlu, if Abrams were to change the scope and content of his mission from policy recommendations to the establishment of a UN-sponsored technical university. Even though this was a significant departure from what Abrams had been assigned to do, Abrams actually found it to be perfectly compatible with his *technocosmopolitan* approach to development. As Abrams had argued, the study of local codes, regulations, and practices required time and the type of expertise that a UN expert did not have. Training and education of local experts who were familiar with local codes and practices as well as international examples could indeed be the answer to the operation of a transnational technical assistance machinery, which in turn could bring about the welfare revolution that Abrams envisioned. Abrams consequently agreed to Diker's proposition in principle, and Diker was able to secure the appointments.

Following meetings with Zorlu, US ambassador to Turkey Avra Warren, and the resident representatives of the Foreign Operations Administration in Turkey, Abrams obtained support for the project and ended up restoring the operations of the technical assistance machinery against all expectations. He now found himself in a position to convince not the client nation but his own agency, the UN-HTCP, of the validity of this shift in the scope and content of his mission. Abrams decided to pitch the idea to Ernest Weissmann as a university that would initially be established as a school of architecture and would provide training in housing and planning. Abrams phrased his letter to Weissmann thus: "any technical recommendations I might make would make no more dent than a mosquito's bill on the hull of a battleship."[45] He explained,

> Ankara itself which hums with civil servants engaged in the nation's development has no technical university in either engineering or architecture so that the city in which policy is made for the whole country . . . is an intellectual desert as far as architectural and planning talent is concerned.[46]

The idea of training and education in housing and community planning would become one of the hallmarks of Abrams's career as an international expert. Later coining the term, "in-pert," Abrams carried the idea, most immediately, to his next mission in Ghana, recommending the establishment of another school there, this time with Otto Koenigsberger and Vladimir Bodiansky.[47]

The truth of the matter was that the idea had in fact emerged in response to the particular professional and political conditions in Turkey and could not be implemented readily in other locations, primarily because the UN sought to limit its direct engagement in establishing schools. In spite of the difficulties involved, the school in Turkey would open its doors in November 1956. It began as a department of architecture and planning but quickly grew into one of Turkey's premier institutions of higher learning as the Middle East Technical University (METU). Abrams later wrote,

> The need for architects and planners was the wedge, but engineering and training in other disciplines were also essential to build the country. A university could be the focus of much needed research. If located in Ankara, it would be oriented toward Asiatic Turkey, as well as Istanbul. It could draw upon the pool of experienced personnel in the nation's capital to help with training. An interchange of ideas between teachers and government officials would benefit both, and the country as a whole. If opened to students throughout the Middle East, the institution could help expand training in other countries as well.[48]

Abrams did not give himself (and Diker) enough credit. The school really became that and something more. By 1969, METU's political consciousness had reached such a level that it became the epicenter of student movements in Turkey. When Robert Komer, the recently appointed US Ambassador to Turkey and the former head of the notorious pacification program in Vietnam (which earned him the nickname, Bob "Blowtorch" Komer), came to visit the METU campus, student protests were so strident that Komer's official coach was turned upside down and burned as he was having lunch in the School's Central Administration Building with METU's legendary president, Kemal Kurdaş. A few years after this event, four METU students would inscribe the word, "D E V R I M", or "Revolution," in mega-size letters onto the poured-in-place beton-brut bleachers of the METU stadium. This inscription, through its multiple meanings, came to define METU's identity, as if to confirm the last of Abrams's four revolutions, the welfare revolution, as an ongoing work in progress, as Abrams had himself envisaged, both in the United States and abroad. Recently, during the annual Spring Festival, METU students and faculty reinscribed "D E V R I M" onto the bleachers as part of a ritual reenacting identity.

So when the observers at Gezi commented that it had all started with the Hilton, they were not entirely inaccurate, especially if the "it" also included the protestors themselves. The Hilton, not unlike the hotels and businesses that surrounded Taksim Square, embodied a complex historical and political identity. As the iconic example of American expansionism, it certainly symbolized the beginnings of state-sanctioned speculative development at both the local and global scales. On the other hand, the international projects that accompanied the Hilton also produced their own critique, as in the case of METU. Abrams's technocosmopolitan approach to instigating the welfare revolution through housing finance and land reform policies at home and abroad had found perhaps its most challenging yet productive reception, ironically within the contentious climate of technical assistance in Turkey. Even though Abrams's policies had little impact on reshaping Turkish cities, METU would yield generations of influential professionals, or to use Abrams's term, "in-perts," with a continuing commitment to the underlying processes of modernization and democratization that played themselves out on and around the spaces of Taksim Square in 2013. During the protests, the METU community stood in solidarity with the protesters in Istanbul, only to find themselves under attack by the fall of that same year. As Gezi events began to subside, the JDP administration turned its attention to the academy and on METU in particular. Melih Gökçek, Ankara's mayor and a member of the JDP, announced plans to resume a highway project that would run through METU's campus, removing approximately 3,000 trees in the process.[49] In response to Gökçek's announcement, METU students and faculty united in protest, in what augured a long season of the JDP's sustained program of punitive actions to frame and discipline the Turkish academy.

NOTES

1. I presented an earlier version of this project under the title "Nation's Domicile: Politics of Housing and Land Economics in the Cold War Frontier" in the Landscapes of Development Symposium organized by Ayala Levin and the Princeton-Mellon Initiative in Architecture, Urbanism, and the Humanities at Princeton University on April 28, 2017.
2. Annabel Jane Wharton, *Building the Cold War: Hilton International Hotels and Modern Architecture* (Chicago: The University of Chicago Press, 2001), 13–38. For Hilton's impact on Turkish architectural culture, see Şevki Vanlı, *Mimariden Konuşmak: Bilinmek İstenmeyen 20. Yüzyıl Türk Mimarlığı: Eleştirel Bakış* [Talking Architecture: The Untold History of Twentieth Century Turkish Architecture: A Critical Perspective] (İstanbul: VMV, 2007). For Hilton's impact on Turkish modernity and domesticity, see Meltem Ö. Gürel, "Consumption of Modern Furniture as a Strategy of Distinction in Turkey," *Journal of Design History* 22, no. 1 (2009): 47–67.
3. Conrad Hilton, *Be My Guest* (Englewood Cliffs, NJ: Prentice-Hall, 1957), 264–266.
4. Ibid.
5. Wharton, *Building the Cold War*, 33. For DP's campaign promise, see Ahmad Feroz, *The Making of Modern Turkey* (London: Routledge, 1993), 103.
6. A. Scott Henderson, *Housing and the Democratic Ideal: The Life and Thought of Charles Abrams* (New York: Columbia University Press, 2000), 5.
7. Charles Abrams, *Revolution in Land* (New York and London: Harper and Brothers, 1939).
8. Ibid., xiii.
9. Henderson, *Housing and the Democratic Ideal*, 62, 89.

10 Ibid., 96.
11 Abrams, *Revolution in Land*, 228.
12 Henderson, *Housing and the Democratic Ideal*, 89. Also see Abrams, *Revolution in Land*, xiii, 4–7.
13 Charles Abrams, "Urban Land Problems and Policies," in *Bulletin on Housing and Town and Country Planning*, no. 7 (New York: United Nations, 1953), 3–58.
14 Charles Abrams, *Man's Struggle for Shelter in an Urbanizing World* (Cambridge, MA: The MIT Press, 1964), v.
15 Ibid.
16 Nils Gilman, *Mandarins of the Future: Modernization Theory in Cold War America* (Baltimore and London: Johns Hopkins University Press, 2003), 16.
17 Nils Gilman examines the Harvard Department of Social Relations, the Committee on Comparative Politics of the Social Science Research Council in New York, and the MIT Center for International Studies as the key nodes in the emergence of modernization theory. Gilman, *Mandarins of the Future*, 4.
18 Abrams, "Urban Land Problems and Policies," 6.
19 Ibid.
20 Ibid.
21 Abrams would begin to refer to these series of transformations as revolutions shortly after his mission to Turkey. He defined the four revolutions as, "a political revolution; a land revolution; an industrial revolution; and a welfare revolution." See United Nations Technical Assistance Programme, *The Need for Training and Education for Housing and Planning* (prepared for the Government of Turkey by Charles Abrams), August 23, 1955, File No. TAA 173/57/018; Report No: TAA/TUR/13), 3. Also see, Abrams, *Man's Struggle for Shelter in an Urbanizing World*, 42–47.
22 Gilman, *Mandarins of the Future*, 9.
23 Abrams, "Urban Land Problems and Policies," 9.
24 United Nations, *Seminar on Housing and Community Improvement in Asia and the Far East, New Delhi, India, 21 January—17 February 1954* (New York: UN Technical Assistance Programme. UN document no. TAA/NS/AFE/1), 1.
25 Burma, Ceylon, Fiji Islands, Hong Kong, India, Indonesia, Iran, Iraq, Japan, Laos, Pakistan, Puerto Rico, Singapore, Thailand, and Vietnam were among the countries represented in the conference. In addition, CIAM, Ford Foundation, Technical Cooperation Mission (USA), International Federation for Housing and Town Planning, World Health Organization, UNESCO, Food and Agriculture Organization, ECAFE, and the International Labour Organization were among the international organizations represented. *Seminar on Housing . . .*, 48–55.
26 M. Ijlal Muzaffar, "The Periphery Within: Modern Architecture and the Making of the Third World" (Ph.D. diss., MIT, 2007), 38–39.
27 For example, thirty-eight separate papers were presented in section 1. A total of seventy-seven papers were presented at the seminar. *Seminar on Housing . . .*, 63–70.
28 Abrams asked each participant to define from among a given list the pressing problems in land tenure. The list included: land speculation; concentration of land ownership; high land costs; difficulty of acquiring land for housing by compulsory purchase; land shortage; difficulty of financing for land development; and a blank space for participants to fill in other aspects. *Seminar on Housing . . .*, 57–62.
29 Abrams's contract defined him as a "housing legislation expert" and described his mission under four headings. United Nations Technical Assistance Administration, "Revised Job Description, TUR-27 (VIII-4) of 8 May 1952," August 12, 1954. See Betty K. Whitelaw, for the Director of Personnel, to Charles Abrams, New York, "Letter of Appointment, (UN/P/131/1/Rev.2, 8 April 1953)," August 5, 1954, 1.
30 Bernard Taper, "Charles Abrams in Turkey," in *The Work of Charles Abrams: Housing and Urban Renewal in the USA and the Third World: A Collection of Papers*, eds. O. H. Koenigsberger, S. Groak, and B. Bernstein (New York: Bergamon, 1980), 47.
31 Ekmel Derya, "Orta Doğu Teknik Üniversitesi Kuruluş Yılları," 4, incomplete manuscript on his memoirs of the establishment of METU, digital word document, personal archive of Baykan Günay, Professor in the Department of Regional and Urban Planning, METU.
32 The documents Abrams sent to the United States included: Public Law 2290, approved June 10, 1933; the typical statute for the Pension Fund Cooperative Housing; the Ottoman Building Code; and digests of Laws No. 1580, 5218, 5228, 5431, 5656 and 3/6739. Charles Abrams to the Minister of Public Works, "Memorandum Re-revision of the Turkish Building Code (October 20, 1954)" (Charles Abrams Papers, Cornell University Library, Reel 25), 1.
33 Abrams Report, 2.
34 Ibid.
35 Ibid., 2–3.
36 Abrams, *Man's Struggle for Shelter in an Urbanizing World*, 202.
37 Ibid.
38 For a recent account of the formation of the National Department of Highways, see Begüm Adalet, *Hotels and Highways: The Construction of Modernization Theory in Cold War Turkey* (Stanford, CA: Stanford University Press, 2018), 85–120.

39 Adalet, *Hotels and Highways*, 91.
40 Abrams was aware of this contentious relationship between US and UN agencies and how that affected the attitudes of client nations. He wrote,

> Official experts from the United States had considerable influence in Turkey thanks to the millions of dollars behind their advice, but UN missions got no cooperation from them either in money or in sympathetic interest. There was in fact a hostility among ICA officials to the idea of a UN-sponsored project that either emanated from or was carried over in the State Department in Washington.
>
> Abrams, Man's Struggle for Shelter in an Urbanizing World, 203

41 Later, DP officials continued to be reluctant allow the UN to shift the project from UN-TAB to UNESCO. Charles Weitz, Madison, WI, to Craig Murphy, Cambridge, Mass., February 11, 2005, email letter transcript in the hand of Craig Murphy. Also see Craig Murphy, *The United Nations Development Programme: A Better Way?* (New York: Cambridge University Press, 2005), 88.
42 Yavuz, 400. Also see *T.C. Resmi Gazete [Official Bulletin of the Turkish Republic]* July 4, 1951, no. 7851, 1561–1562.
43 See the detailed descriptions of the responsibilities of each participating agency in *T.C. Resmi Gazete [Official Bulletin of the Turkish Republic]* July 4, 1951, no. 7851, 1562.
44 *Mimarlık* 4, n. 5–6, 1947, 17. Also see, Gülsüm Baydar, "The Professionalization of the Ottoman-Turkish Architect" (Ph.D. diss., University of California, Berkeley, 1989), 134.
45 Charles Abrams, Ankara, Turkey, to Ernest Weissmann, New York, 2 October 1954, Appendix B of *United Nations Report on . . .*, 1.
46 Ibid.
47 See their report for Ghana, which resulted in the establishment of the School of Architecture and Community Planning in Kwame Nkrumah University of Science and Technology in Kumasi. For Abrams's mission in Ghana, see Charles Abrams, Otto Koenigsberger, and Vladimir Bodiansky, *Housing in the Gold Coast* (New York: United Nations, 1956). For "in-pert," see Abrams, "Aid-Experts and "Inperts," in *Struggle for Shelter in an Urbanizing World*, 89–104.
48 Abrams, *Man's Struggle for Shelter in an Urbanizing World*, 203.
49 The METU Administration made a public announcement opposing the highway project that involved the relocation of 629 conifers and the cutting of 292 pine (çam), 133 ash (dışbudak), 916 wildpear (ahlat), 293 almond (badem), 58 poplar (kavak), and 696 other deciduous trees. See the news release by METU, www.metu.edu.tr/tr/orta-dogu-teknik-universitesi-rektorlugunun-anadolu-bulvarinin-devami-olan-yol-hakkinda-aciklamasi (accessed September 27, 2016).

19

Leisure and geo-economics

The Hilton and other development regimes in the Mediterranean South

Panayiota Pyla

It sounds like the opening line of a joke: "A rich hotelier, a model, and a bishop meet on a Mediterranean island . . . ." Except this actually happened: On February 2, 1967, Conrad Hilton Jr. attended the opening of Nicosia's Hilton Cyprus, the seventy-first hotel opened internationally by Hilton Hotels International Inc.[1] The ribbon was cut by Cyprus president Makarios, who also happened to be Archbishop (see Figure 19.1). Miss Hellas 1966 was a guest of honor, maximizing the event's popular appeal. Other invitees included the financial editor of the London *Times*, Margaret Allen; publisher of *Holiday* magazine, Caskie Stinnett; founder of the Royal Court Theatre Club, Clement Freud; and English actor and singer Lance Percival. Makarios expressed gratitude that his country had obtained part of the "golden chain of Hilton Hotels."[2] Hilton reciprocated with flattery for the island's role in shaping Western roots, claiming "Anything good in America is primarily because of the great heritage of your ancient civilizations. Very few countries reveal richer history and charm than Cyprus."[3] This claim was reinforced by the new building being inaugurated, which elevated the ancient landscape of the island to a key theme. In the hotel's "Copper Bar," the metal believed to have given Cyprus its name in ancient times predominated on tabletops and walls—even the ashtrays were of beaten copper.[4] The hotel's coffee shop, which included a waterfall flowing down a marble wall, was named "Fontana Amorosa" after the area believed to be the ancient birthplace of Aphrodite and which gave Cyprus the fame of being the "island of love."[5]

Parts of the story of Hilton Cyprus politics may be anticipated by those familiar with the published history of the Hiltons.[6] The luxury hotel was an economically and politically desirable endeavor embraced both by Hilton Hotels International Inc. and the Cyprus government. For the American corporation, it was another step toward going international, both to overcome the rising competition from motels in the United States and to further cash in on the Jet Age implications of access to overseas travel.[7] It was, in fact, during the inauguration of Hilton Cyprus that Conrad Hilton announced the merger talks between Hilton International and Trans World Airlines, an alliance that promised to open up new ways of capital escape.[8] Meanwhile, for the US government, Hilton Cyprus was strengthening the Middle East frontier against communism, along with similar hotels in Athens, Tel

FIGURE 19.1 The President of the Republic of Cyprus, Archbishop Makarios, arriving at the Hilton on the hotel's opening day.

Source: Press Information Office, Cyprus.

Aviv, and Istanbul. As for the young Cyprus government and the company that financed the hotel, the "spectacle of glamorous modernity"[9] was a tested means of attracting hard capital, fighting unemployment, and creating the basis for tourism development and economic prosperity.[10] To all parties involved, the Hilton was evidence of Cyprus opening a corridor for American tourists and the country's push for private enterprise, laying healthy foundations for capitalism.

All of this situates Hilton Cyprus in the context of a history of US corporate interests and Cold War politics on the one hand and ties the hotel chain to a local government's eagerness to advance economic growth on the other. Indeed, a brief overview of local and international media around the Hilton Cyprus inauguration confirms this and shows how the Cypriot government's commitment to building a Hilton echoes the cases of Egypt and Turkey, as described in Annabel Wharton's *Building the Cold War*.[11] Yet there is more to the story of the bizarre coming together of Makarios, Conrad Hilton Jr., and Miss Hellas 1966. That encounter speaks to the entwinement of corporate interests with local capital, but it also highlights the need to understand the Hilton against the background of efforts to push tourism as a mode of development that dominated parts of the Global South after the end of colonialism, shaping the aesthetics/architectures of leisure with standardized infrastructural demands (airports, roads, charter flights) and benchmarks for replication (such as the international hotel chain). What follows is an alternative history of Cyprus that helps theorize the ties between tourism and the 1960s era of "high development" by casting the spotlight on the workings of a socioeconomic model of development that guided not only the building of Hilton Cyprus but also the overall tourism boom that Cyprus experienced during that decade. That tourism development model, which was an outcome of systems thinking and given the misleadingly soothing name of "the reconciliation model," shows how tourism was incorporated into development geo-economics that legitimized foreign experts' influence on core institutions in newly decolonized nations. By uncovering the workings of the reconciliation model behind the creation of Hilton Cyprus and by exposing how it became intertwined with Cyprus's complex and particularly ambivalent geopolitical positioning, this chapter interrogates how systems thinking infiltrated notions of tourism and development.

TOURISM AS DEVELOPMENT

Let us begin with the importance tourism was given as a key mode of development in the Global South. The Marshall Plan shaped a model of tourism that had been tested in Southern Europe and was transferred to places like Cyprus. It was, in fact, a "discovery" of the Marshall Plan that many countries of Southern Europe could treat tourism as a commodity through which they could return aid that had been invested in them. The Economic Cooperation Administration (ECA), the administrative body of the Marshall Plan, had identified tourism as "the most invisible earner of dollars" and emphasized tourism promotion programs for countries such as France, Italy, Turkey, and Greece.[12] Tourism was so important for the implementation of the Marshall Plan in Greece that the ECA became uncharacteristically active in promoting negotiations for the Athens Hilton project.[13]

Cyprus did not receive Marshall Plan aid, but it was handed a model of tourism development that had been tested under the auspices of that plan. Development consultants were vigorous in pushing for tourism as a path for national economies that shared the assets of "sun, sand, and sea," a criterion often encountered in tourism expert literature.[14] Tourism development would be advanced through "technical assistance," a proxy system to a Marshall Plan. Tourism was an end goal of a global industrialization process that also secured larger geopolitical claims for the West. Apart from the economics of development and the targets for Cyprus's or Greece's cultural assimilation to a Western lifestyle, what was at stake was also an idea of tourism as a system of stabilization. Countries like Greece and Cyprus (and possibly Turkey and Egypt) were projected onto a regional geography of leisure that would secure the interests of the West in a delicate geopolitical locale such as the Eastern Mediterranean.

In Cyprus, at the receiving end of United Nations technical assistance and economic missions immediately after its independence in 1960, the push for tourism as a means to achieve economic growth and nation-building happened on multiple fronts. The 1961 UN report for Cyprus, written by the American economist and UN consultant Willard Thorp, looked at the country's tourism potential through the optics of Marshall Plan aid and highlighted tourism as a foreign currency magnet. Thorp proposed standardized hotels and predicted the arrival of the Hilton when he vaguely stated,

> It might be helpful to tourism on Cyprus if one new hotel could be part of a foreign chain. This would be of great promotional value, would set a high standard of operation, and would indirectly improve the traffic to the other hotels.[15]

Thorp had served as a US diplomat and engaged with the crafting of the Marshall Plan as Truman's Assistant Secretary of State for Economic Affairs.[16] He was invited by the Cyprus government to make "an independent and objective study of the economic prospects for Cyprus" and to prepare recommendations "towards the acceleration of its economic development." He described tourism as an industry that could be "a major potential foreign exchange earner" that had "not yet been adequately exploited." He called for "long term efforts" to reach tourism markets, underlining that "there is greater economic promise in increasing the number from Western Europe and the United States."[17]

Thorp also suggested the development of the Cyprus Development Bank (CDB), which would finance "self-liquifying facilities for tourism" through support from the International Bank for Reconstruction and Development (IBRD).[18] For costs that could not be self-liquidating such as infrastructure, he suggested securing funds from government sources.[19] In other words, local government would assume the brunt of creating the infrastructure necessary to support tourism and would subsidize the tourism industry, leaving the more profitable initiatives to the private sector. This particular version of "public–private partnership" would be advanced in other aspects of the tourism industry and would also be legitimized by systems thinking.

Another important push for tourism came with Makarios's US visit in 1962. Made soon after he took office, its main goal was to secure support for the country's development plans. And indeed, President Kennedy pledged "continued American interest in the development program of Cyprus."[20] During the visit, Makarios had a half-hour meeting with Conrad Hilton Jr.—evidently, the 1967 Hilton Cyprus inauguration celebration was not the first time the pair met.[21] A few months later, US Vice President Johnson visited Cyprus to announce a joint package of loan provisions from the United States and other Western powers. During his visit, he telegraphed future tourism when he called for a "new industry" to replace mining.[22] Ironically, he also acknowledged the drought problem of Cyprus, but he failed to foresee that tourism and the proliferation of visitor accommodations, hotel gardens, and hotel pools would significantly exacerbate water shortages in the long run.[23]

In early 1963, a few months after the official decision to open a Hilton hotel in Cyprus, the Ministry of Industry and Commerce released a celebratory announcement on the advantages of such an investment, both to entertain reactions against this and also to attract local shareholders for the hotel's owning company. The announcement emphasized that the Hilton's construction would unleash the tourism potential of Cyprus internationally and would promise financial growth and prosperity for every social class.[24] According to the ministry, Hilton's well-established name was strong marketing in and of itself, to the point that the hotel's construction could significantly reduce overall advertising expenses. Hilton Hotels International Inc. would offer a kind of publicity that would be otherwise inconceivable for Cyprus. Already, the argument went, the news of the Hilton agreement led to the inclusion of Cyprus as a new destination for several airlines and travel agencies.[25]

A flood of experts came to Cyprus in the first decade of the Republic, emphasizing the potential of the island to become a major tourist resort in the Mediterranean. Simultaneously, these experts underlined the country's lack of experience and the need for assistance to the state and its institutions. An "export activity" for the South that was particularly appealing as it did not compete with employment patterns in the industrialized North, tourism was advanced through the naturalized universalism of expert knowledge as a world issue, a ground for international cooperation, and a development path for national economies to follow.

The multiple expert documents that reinforced the call for tourism development in Cyprus weave a mesh of influences that promoted tourism policies globally throughout the 1960s. Seeking legitimization from the system that they enacted, these documents were interlinked, either through direct reference of one to the other or by a cause-and-effect chain, according to which reports were commissioned and produced (with the involvement of state agencies) following the advice of other reports. An example: Thorp's UN report on Cyprus called for an "experienced institution" to assist with the creation of the CDB, which would support tourism. The institution selected was Checchi and Company—the US company that had promoted tourism globally from the Caribbean to Southeast Asia with promises of employment and income multipliers.[26] When they shaped their advice for Cyprus, Checchi consultants used Thorp's report as a reference, and they were in line with many of Thorp's provisions.[27] The subsequent report highlighted the importance of tourism for the island's economy.[28] It also rendered tourism as a mode of money transfer, intimately related to labor markets and the mobility of people and capital.[29]

These interdependent documents soon led to the conclusion that the "industrialization" of Cyprus could best happen through tourism. Whereas in 1961, Thorp's report had actually identified agriculture as the key means of development for Cyprus (even as he highlighted the future potential for tourism), by the mid-1960s, turning Cyprus into a leisure hub became a top priority, with tourism development the primary vehicle toward a national imperative to modernize. The creation of luxury resorts, seaside apartments, and the like would surpass agricultural or industrial programs in experts' preferences, and tourism would be declared the quintessential mode of development. In the meantime, CDB charts, which construed people as target groups or income categories, would allow the planner, architect, social scientist, or economist to profess their grasp on social behaviors, cultural disparities, or the workings of global markets. Any variation or disagreement in the proposed plans would only help reinforce the drive for tourism and the primacy of *homo economicus* perspectives. One example: Thorp had proposed standardized hotels, seeing tourism as a foreign currency magnet that could capture tourist flows to the Middle East. Conversely, a year later, French experts counter-proposed the restructuring of Cyprus's coastlines to reshape the country's overall socioeconomic conditions and protect its "unspoilt sites."[30] Even if they outlined different trajectories in crafting tourism, these visions for development professed a grasp on economic and social needs.

FINANCING WITH NO ALTERNATIVES

Just as foreign experts presented tourism as an appropriate industry for Cyprus, they simultaneously made another point: Cyprus had to depend on "her own resources."[31] How exactly would the entire development machine be financed? The "reconciliation model" provided an answer to this conundrum. Outlined in 1963 by David Ernest Apter, the reconciliation model was deemed appropriate for societies with a low degree of centralization of power and a high degree of "secularism."[32] (Apter meant secularism in terms of the values of the society and their willingness to distance themselves from "traditional" behaviors.) Unlike societies with high centralization of power (that is, unlike socialist or welfare states), which could have specific corps of bureaucratic modernizers to coerce society into modernization, societies that followed the reconciliation model would have a government that actively stimulated nongovernmental and local entrepreneurship. In other words, according to this model, modernization depended on particular combinations of state and private enterprise whereby the state would provide robust incentives to "stimulate private entrepreneurship" and "encourage outside investment," and the private sector would compensate for the state's inadequacies in power and institutions.[33] In the process, and in the absence of institutional patterns, the government's policies, resources, and responsibilities were renegotiated, augmented, or curbed, practically on a case-by-case basis.

Apter's reconciliation model emerged out of his analysis of the processes of economic development that had tried to advance the study of the "systemic properties of each national context" so as to distance political science and sociology from empiricism and behaviorism. By analyzing the ties between state, society, and economy, as these were shaped within specific political systems and countries, he was not only trying to make sense of the "unstable" character of new nations but also to examine the failures of these governments to be "effectively institutionalized in relation to the society at large."[34] Apter's abstract framework attempted to devise processes of modernization for any type of relationship between government and society. What he implied was that each political system had different reactions toward development goals and thus a different development profile that, once identified, could lead to the correct prescription. Some societies required "coercion," others "mobilization," and still others "reconciliation."

In a society that fit the characteristics of the reconciliation model, the government had the role to "reconcile diverse interests."[35] As Apter argued, "it mediates, integrates, and above all co-ordinates rather than organizes and mobilizes."[36] Yet he also emphasized the need for "steadfast motives among the top political leaders" and a required "public determination to enforce self-discipline" so as to ensure a fast rate of modernization.[37] Apter's systemic thinking made two big assumptions: first, that national governments are unrelated to society. Second, it confined what he called "politics" (the values and behaviors of societies, their predisposition to reacting to national policies, etc.) within each national context—thus entirely bypassing questions of transnational power dynamics and the politics/agency of the foreign expert. Furthermore, the reconciliation model that referred to societies that had neither strong government structures nor strong traditionalist reactions was a way of subsuming all possible societies into a systemic model—as though to systematize the nonsystemic.

Although Apter had mentioned cursorily some concrete examples of societies, he did not mention Cyprus as a case. However, the head of the Cyprus Tourism Organization (CTO), Antonios Andronikou, nonetheless argued that Cyprus's tourism development fit Apter's reconciliation model.³⁸ Andronikou based this argument on the fact that Cyprus was a pyramidal rather than hierarchical society, with multiple players and decision makers—what Apter had called multiple "accountability groups."³⁹ Although Andronikou did not say it explicitly, the Cyprus Republic fit this model because it could not possibly possess the coercive powers of other society types, not only because of its size and resources but also because of the compromised functioning of the government. Only three years after the island's independence from the British, the Turkish Cypriots pulled out of the country's bi-communal government and withdrew into enclaves, leaving the Greek Cypriots, or 80 percent of the population, in total control of governmental operations. Intercommunal talks began in 1968, but though the talks hinted of optimism for smoother social and economic development, a *coup d'état* in Greece a year earlier complicated things yet again, increasing the threat of Turkey's military intervention on the island.

All this certainly made Cyprus a state with a low degree of centralization of power. Furthermore, what matched Cyprus to Apter's "secular" society was not only the eagerness of the government and entrepreneurs to modernize but also Cyprus's ambivalent geopolitical positioning. Unlike Greece or Turkey, it was not part of NATO, and the Cyprus government carefully avoided defining clear allegiances for either of the Cold War polarities, opting to join the Non-Aligned Movement, with Makarios one of its founding members.⁴⁰ In an effort to sidestep geopolitical influences, the government professed "a policy of equal friendship with all nations" and envisioned Cyprus as a hub for the international flow of capital, ideas, and people, hosting development experts from different countries and with different ideological leanings.⁴¹

For all these complexities, the reconciliation model was particularly appealing to government tourist officials such as Andronikou, as it helped situate tourism development between market capitalism and a planned economy; it helped "systematize" and legitimize what Cyprus was already advancing in tourism development. Andronikou was willing to also admit that Cyprus did not fit all the characteristics of the reconciliation model. This was, after all, the beauty of systems thinking: reality and the specific circumstances of a society did not provide a test for the system but rather enlarged it. What was particularly appealing was the fact that the reconciliation model was also loaded with ethical admonition. What was needed for the societies that fit the reconciliation model were "compromise and rationality" by all parties involved. This was a happy model, where "the pace of growth is never more dramatic than that which the public is prepared to accept, since policy must agree with public desires . . . coercive techniques remain at a minimum."⁴²

The reconciliation model was helping legitimize the discretionary powers of the government and the close ties it was developing with local entrepreneurship. In his speech at Hilton Cyprus's inauguration, Minister of Commerce and Industry Andreas Araouzos echoed the logic of Andronikou when he underlined that government policies for economic development avoided "intensified state control of economic activity" and rather aimed "toward liberating and encouraging the energies and initiative of the private sector."⁴³ He also stressed that this was the spirit of the country's development program, which, in its own words, was "designed to provide an economic environment favorable to private enterprise."⁴⁴ The reconciliation model was systematizing and legitimizing what Thorp had already outlined conceptually: that the financing of tourism development would involve particular combinations of public and private initiatives, especially through the establishment of quasi-private formations like the CDB, which received loans from IBRD with the backing of the government. Through the reconciliation model and its social scientific aura, the state's discretionary authority to invest in the local elite and entrepreneurial class acquired a new validity. It was an all-around convenient path to capitalism, not to mention that it was paving the way for what would come in the future. As though anticipating the "neoliberal There Is No Alternative (TINA)"[45] (which, after the Reagan–Thatcher era, favored market-oriented policies of deregulation even if these were suboptimal for a welfare state), the Cyprus government appeared to have "no alternative" but to heavily support private initiatives. These opportunistic alliances between state legislation, hotel corporations, airline carriers, and international diplomacy were finessed through the spirit of systems.

BIZARRE RECONCILIATIONS

Consider this paradox, highlighted by Wharton in her analysis of the Hiltons around the world:

> Hilton International Corporation, the embodiment of the American entrepreneurial spirit, dependent on state sponsorship.[46]

This entwinement of national governments with private development initiatives was made possible by a type of systems thinking on the development of the South that had legitimized particular ways for the government to provide robust incentives for private enterprise. Hilton Cyprus is a case in point. A manifestation of Apter's reconciliation model, it allowed government to give robust support to private enterprise.

The Hilton corporation had a policy of not taking financial risks, especially in developing countries, and given that no Marshall Plan was available in Cyprus, the corporation expected to receive a financial guarantee from the local government. The Cyprus government was of course positive about the arrival of the Hilton chain, as it considered it a chief priority, comparable to the building of the country's airport, port, and dams. All would be major projects to determine the path of tourism, and as such, they appeared in a 1967 series of government postage stamps dedicated to the country's development program.[47] However, the government had its own ideological restrictions, as it was proudly "operating under the policy of not directly contributing to investment and the finance of projects."[48] Thus, the government initially reached out to private investors to build and furnish the hotel so as to lease it later to Hilton Hotels International Inc. When this failed to attract enough investment, the state stepped in to take the brunt of the risk "to create favorable conditions of security and trust for the private enterprise to invest."[49]

This was the reconciliation model at work. The state created the Cyprus Tourism Development Company Ltd (CTDC) and became its main shareholder, owning half the shares. It also gave more advantages and financial support to this holding company by selling to it—at almost half its market value—land for the hotel.[50] The compromise in the price was clearly stated in the minutes: "Although the market value of the land is estimated by the Department of Lands and Surveys at £144,000, the Government of Cyprus, in pursuance of its policy to promote the tourist development of the Island, have agreed to sell this land to the Company for £80,000 only."[51] The low price meant that the government needed to pay even more cash toward owning half the CTDC shares. In short, the government was compromising land and monetary value to reach the Hilton's budget. Araouzos, in his speech on the opening day of Hilton Cyprus, noted that he was proud of the state's role in incentivizing via land provision, depicting this as an opportunity for the public to collaborate with private enterprise and participate in tourism development.[52] In Apter's terms, Araouzos was describing a tactic of forcing public participation without having to resort to social coercion! Of course, the key detail that remained concealed was that the incentivizing via provision of land was also accompanied by the undervaluing of state land.

The state land provided for the Hilton was in the outskirts of the capital, Nicosia, in a direction toward which the city was already expanding and which was becoming the city's main entrance. Hilton company representative Di Tullio visited Cyprus twice to discuss the location. The hotel was to be built on Nicosia's highest point, on a vast area of government-owned parkland, from which one could observe the entire city as well as the mountains of the northern city of Kyrenia on the one side and the entry point of Nicosia from the southern cities of Limassol and Larnaca from the other (see Figure 19.2).

FIGURE 19.2 Aerial view showing the landscape at the time of the Hilton hotel's completion.

Source: Costas and Rita Severis Foundation—CVAR.

The elevation and scale of the site would enhance the monumentality of the hotel, resonating with the Tel Aviv Hilton, which was isolated in a public park, situated to emphasize its presence as a civic monument.[53] The site's relative detachment from the density of the old city center and its position in the midst of the new and more suburban Nicosia also resonated with American values advanced in many other Hiltons: the building's large porte-cochère and the big parking lot in front of the main entrance celebrated the automobile as the chief means of transportation, while the surrounding greenery, along with the gardens and the swimming pool area among other amenities in the hotel's "backyard," reinforced suburban metaphors, similar to other Hiltons (see Figure 19.3).[54] One also wonders if the fact that the site was opposite the US Embassy had an equal importance, but certainly, during the *coup d'état* and the subsequent Turkish invasion in 1974, Hilton Cyprus became part of an area targeted as American soil, experiencing bombings and the killing of the US ambassador.[55]

FIGURE 19.3 The Hilton Hotel entrance, porte-cochère, and front gardens.

Source: Press Information Office, Cyprus.

To understand the impact of the Cyprus version of the reconciliation model, one must step back and ask: What was the price of the Hilton rubber stamp? The answer is, a great deal, and this was diligently prescribed in the contract that stated that the government of Cyprus would "finance, build, furnish, and equip such a hotel."[56] The Cyprus agreement apparently reproduced the formula employed in Istanbul and Cairo, giving Hilton Hotels International Inc. the full control of the operation and management of the hotel. As was the case in Egypt,

> the Hilton was the managing company. In exchange for its third of the profits, Hilton provided the specifications for construction of a modern deluxe hotel as well as managerial executives and training for local staff. Hilton was responsible for the running costs, but those were repaid from income before profits were calculated. Hilton also linked the hotel to a growing network of travel agencies and a sophisticated reservation apparatus.[57]

By offering its managerial advice and worldwide marketing campaigns, the Hilton corporation was participating in the profits without taking much risk: there was no minimum rent, just a percentage of profits. Additionally, all architect fees and legal expenses, among other early-stage expenditures, were paid by the government, even if Hilton Hotels International Inc. would control and drive the plans and specifications for the design.[58] The Hilton corporation was to recruit and train the initial staff with training programs either in Cyprus or abroad.[59] This agreement appeared to benefit the host country if the local population was in need of educational programs in the tourism industry, as was the case in Cyprus. However, given that the host country would be paying for these training programs and considering the relatively low local salaries, the advantage was on the side of the corporation.[60]

Similar to Istanbul's hotel, the Hilton Cyprus was a building supported and financed by the government, codesigned by Cypriot architects, constructed by Cypriot contractors, and staffed by a considerable percentage of Cypriots, with the Hilton corporation surrounding all this with the aura of a transnational hotel and worldwide marketing campaigns. Such happy partnerships happened in many parts of the world that sought development through tourism, but as John Lea would acknowledge in his analysis of tourism and development in the Third World, "the ability of the parent company to withdraw from this arrangement put it in a controlling position," and this created an "unequal trading relationship."[61]

All in all, that the Hilton enjoyed the personal interest of Cyprus's president and received a robust package of incentives from the government is telling. It also exposes the way of thinking that legitimized the entwinement of the national government with private tourism development initiatives. This reinforced systems thinking while also catering to local political circumstances, particularly in the context of the intercommunal conflict that would break out at the end of 1963. One out of five private investors in the Hilton was a Turkish Cypriot, and this served as proof of the joint participation of both ethnic communities toward the common goal of tourism development.[62] At that time, there were two major hotels in Nicosia: the Ledra Palace Hotel, built in 1948 with the main shareholders being Greek, and the Saray Hotel, a Turkish-owned and -built hotel on Ataturk Square in Nicosia. Built between 1958 and 1962, the Saray represented one of the many acts of economic separatism between Greek and Turkish Cypriots during the turbulent 1960s. Quite often there was a boycott of Greek merchants by Turkish consumers, and vice versa, that rose and fell in intensity with shifts in the political climate. In contrast to all this, Hilton Cyprus and its bi-communal cooperation offered a different narrative against the intercommunal tensions of the previous years and broadcasted the end of conflict in Cyprus. Subsequently, the tourism industry, which was already known to be greatly influenced by conflicts and any type of political tension, could again promise calmness and serenity to the visitor.

That Hilton Cyprus was owned by private citizens not only reinforced intercommunal relationships and local pride, it also put tourism at the forefront of government promises of better things to come. The government continued to invest in tourism in hopes that militarization and conflict would soon cease. Much of the press zealously emphasized life on the island as peaceful. However, by November 1967, a few months after the Hilton Cyprus's opening, Turkey's major intervention overturned these promises. Since armed conflict in 1963 when Turkish Cypriots withdrew into enclaves, and even as tourism development was seemingly moving forward, a slow process of militarization had been unfolding. As *Time* magazine described in 1964, when the glamorous Ledra Palace Hotel was undergoing renovation:

> At Nicosia's Ledra Palace Hotel, a new swimming pool was dedicated with a cocktail party. Not far away, a new Hilton was abuilding. Yet everyone knew that each evening, when the sun fell behind the Troodos Mountains, the smuggling of men and arms into the island resumed, making peace an ugly deception.[63]

The "ugly deception" was also evident in the juxtaposition of articles in local daily newspapers. For example, a celebratory first-page article on the opening of Hilton Cyprus was surrounded by descriptions of an armed conflict in a Turkish Cypriot enclave and rumors of plans for partitioning the island.[64] These were an omen for what would follow: the outbreak of violence that would cause a military response by Turkey, after which the Turkish Cypriot leadership would announce the creation of a separate administration.

BUILDING FINESSE

Raglan Squire, from Britain, was the main architect of Hilton Cyprus, in collaboration with the local office of J+A Philippou. The architects were hired by the Cyprus Cabinet of Ministry, although the contract required that all their drawings be approved by the Hilton's Architectural and Design Department. Squire was not a new figure to the Hilton corporation. Not only did he have an extensive practice in the Middle East,[65] he had completed the Tehran Hilton in 1962 and was designing the Tunis hotel (not to mention that soon after Cyprus he would also become involved with the Hiltons for Bahrain and Jakarta).[66]

Hilton Cyprus was shorter and smaller than its Tehran counterpart but otherwise quite similar. Both were seemingly lifted off the ground with external glass façades and topped with reinforced concrete slabs and a regular grid of box-like balconies. In Nicosia these "Hiltonesque" elements were skillfully adjusted to vaguely connote Cypriot vernacular forms: the massing of the building was to form a T-shaped plan comprised by two blocks that together "surround a typically Cypriot court,"[67] while the balconies would have slightly bent arches, an element widely used in Cyprus's village architecture.[68] Similarly, the extensive use of reinforced concrete as the primary construction material, a characteristic feature of Hilton architecture internationally, was enhanced by the use of local materials such as broken stone, gravel, and galvanized steel.

The allusion to the locale was amplified in the hotel's interior, designed by Maurice Bailey. Following the "Hilton International formula,"[69] indigenous materials and ornamentation based on historical references were interpreted and adeptly applied in the corporation's hotels around the world to increase the experience of the "exotic" for the American tourist and, subsequently, the company's economic profitability. Conrad Hilton had already affirmed the preference of the American tourist toward the ancient landscape of the island during the inauguration ceremony, and this seems to have translated into aesthetic prescriptions, with the hotel's references to copper, Aphrodite, and other aspects of the island's deep past.[70] The hotel's main restaurant, "Commandaria Grill," named after the sweet wine produced in Cyprus by the Crusaders, was designed to remind visitors of Cyprus's medieval period. A wall tapestry illustrated the country's oldest map, steel and brass chandeliers evoked the twelfth century, and wooden ceiling arches complemented the thematic ambience. The medieval atmosphere continued in the "Berengaria Ballroom," where tapestries focused on the marriage of Richard the Lionheart to Berengaria, Princess of Navarre. Elsewhere, the historical decor varied, from the Byzantine murals and mosaics in the lobby to statues of ancient lions copied from originals in the Cyprus Museum embellishing the swimming pool area.

If the reproduction of an ancient past was a marketing tool and part of corporate identity building, then the highly selective character of these historical allusions in the Hilton's interior shouted, loud and clear, about the intense politics of the present. The preference for the medieval and Gothic constituted a particularly diligent avoidance of any neoclassical and Ottoman elements, which were much more disturbing politically, religiously, and economically, given the intercommunal conflict that lasted throughout the construction process. Unlike the Nile and Athens Hiltons, where the medieval past was avoided as it "manifested a disturbing religious and political otherness," in the case of Cyprus, the medieval period was among the less uncomfortable references. It did not quite provide the "stable, transparent deep past" of the Pyramids or the Parthenon, but Cyprus's medieval past appeared less problematic, in comparison to the more recent history that was resonating much more directly with the competing Greek and Turkish nationalisms.[71] Beyond local politics, these controlled hints of locality ultimately reaffirmed the spreading of corporate networks of a globalized tourist culture. With the assurance of Makarios that, indeed, "the hotel forms a part of modern American life and yet it blends so well with the Cyprus scene in an attractive composition,"[72] tourism investments were based on a model where the foreign investment was protected by the state and local political elites of a "developing" country.

GOLDEN ESCAPE

Although it may have been a product of the Cold War, the Hilton Cyprus jump-started a tourism industry that outlived that era. Soon after the hotel's completion, coastal tourism boomed, perhaps faster than expected. Thorp's visions of regional archaeological networks and international business hubs no longer appeared in tune with market behaviors, and beach tourism became the sole emphasis of Cyprus's "tourism product." As the Cyprus Government's Second Five-Year Plan (1967-71) stated,

> The point has already been made that the bulk of the future tourist traffic will be attracted principally to the beaches; and that extensive beach development should, therefore, be the cornerstone of the tourist development policy during the period of the Second Plan.[73]

The emphasis was no longer the American tourist or diplomat visiting the capital and exploring the history of the island but more the leisurely coasts, where conflict would be lighter or in better disguise.[74] The coastal hotels that emerged in the very late 1960s and early 1970s became as important as the Hilton in terms of national development, but their story is different, both in terms of international tourism networks and local politics.

The geographic shift toward the coasts was accompanied by a more confident emphasis on tourism by the government. Officials no longer discussed projected potentialities in tourism and instead unequivocally recognized it as a foreign exchange earner and the best means to achieve "the needs of accelerated growth." As a result, the Second Five-Year Plan was much more open and supportive of the government's potential to "play a more active role in tourist development." The tested formula of providing incentives to private enterprise was now intensified, and the Second Five-Year Plan made it clear that the government had already decided "to undertake itself the development of certain coastal regions with a high tourist potential and go to international tender for the future exploitation of such regions." In addition, the financing of local entrepreneurship was to be augmented with new "low interest long-term loans" and the expressed willingness to offer other "inducements," namely, the duty-free importation of hotel equipment, more infrastructure, and a stated goal to "discourage speculation in land of tourist potential."[75]

Cyprus's Second Five-Year Plan was in tune with international expert advice that called on governments of the Mediterranean and the Caribbean, in particular, to do more than provide infrastructure for tourism and to actively give incentives "to sweeten the pot" for its investors.[76] It is rather telling that in a 1969 report on the Caribbean, expert advice was rather blunt about its requirement for "evidence that governments on the Island are behind tourism." It also asked for "evidence that tourism is not a political issue."[77] At the other end of the world, on the Mediterranean side, the state of Cyprus was doing its best to demonstrate its support for tourism and to distance it from the politics on the ground.

Under this second development plan, the southeastern coastal city of Famagusta, considered to have the highest "tourism potential," was seeing a rapid proliferation of hotel towers that were advancing it into a regional epicenter of a booming tourism industry—so much so that the *Los Angeles Times* called it "A Miami in the Middle East" in 1974.[78] One cannot help but hear echoes of systems thinking in the newspaper's projection of Miami onto this Mediterranean beach, which was used as proof that tourism was helping the underdeveloped South catch up with the industrialized Global North.

The involvement of the government in shaping Famagusta's coastal strip was most pronounced in the creation of the Golden Sands Hotel, which was to be the crown jewel of the city's glamorous beach strip and the biggest hotel complex on the island up to that point. The hotel would be financed by the state itself: no longer a mere supporter of private enterprise, the government was itself turning into such an enterprise. The state was also demonstrating its interest in enhancing the position of Cyprus in the global tourist networks and putting the country on the map of emerging mass tourism. "The tourist-minded Cypriot government," as the *New York Times* called it,[79] was simultaneously creating a direct link to the British tourist market by pursuing partnerships with Cyprus Airways, a subsidiary of British Airways, and with Trust Houses Forte, a British group of hoteliers[80] that was "chasing the sun in its plans for expansion."[81] By integrating accommodation with travel, the government was responding to the demands of emerging tour operators, who had by that time gained great power to channel the global tourist traffic.[82] Host countries did not have much of an option to bypass the tour operators and sell directly to the customer. Direct selling was economically unjustified and ineffective, given that tour operators could lure customers with "packages" that included transportation, accommodation, and food at a much lower price; this, in return, led to increasingly better bargains for the tour operators themselves, because suppliers who opted to become part of such packages ensured full capacity for their business.[83] Along with adjusting to the global demands of mass tourism, the Golden Sands also adapted to the changing circumstances of national development.

Just as the Hiltons had a role in US foreign policy and in "building the Cold War," the construction of the Golden Sands also had a political purpose for the Cyprus government during a period of intracommunal and intercommunal conflict: tourism appeared the best hope for bringing political stabilization, along with economic prosperity. The hotel was created at a time when the stability of the young Cyprus Republic was threatened, both by external powers and by internal turmoil, perhaps more so than the 1968 inauguration of the Hilton. The early 1970s were characterized by civil strife within the Greek-Cypriot community, which had created a formidable intracommunal conflict that was becoming manifest, for example, in the multiple assassination attempts against Makarios. Civil strife emerged in the early 1960s around nationalist/ideological debates, and this conflict, which had already formed the backdrop for the Hilton, intensified even more during the creation of the Golden Sands.

Even if the overall turmoil of the early 1970s was making the increasing influx of tourists appear precarious, the government remained focused and even more determined to enhance the position of Cyprus in the global tourist networks. As evidenced by the active involvement of Makarios in the entire process of the design and construction of the Golden Sands, this project was a high priority on the government's agenda.[84] The government intervened to expropriate land, despite the severe reactions of private owners and complexities of the process, given that the land ownership mosaic of that coastal strip included the church, the state, and private owners, as well as *hali* land ("residue" public land that was not part of the urban areas or utilized as agricultural land). As in the case of the Hilton, the president attended the inauguration of the Golden Sands on May 8, 1974, celebrating the hotel as a "work of economic infrastructure."[85]

Government aspirations for the hotel were reflected in its architecture. The Golden Sands was designed by the British architectural firm Garnett, Cloughley, and Blakemore, whose portfolio already included hotel architecture in diverse contexts outside the UK, such as Guyana, Sri Lanka (Ceylon), and Sardinia, and demonstrated a modernist and universalist ethic that widely appealed to governments of newly independent nations. Collaborating with the aforementioned local firm of J+A Philippou, the project architect, Patrick Garnett, proposed a low-rise and low-density complex that framed open courtyards looking to the sea, attached to a taller and compact central building.[86] The tall tower on the beach strip, which for Garnett alluded to a Miami aesthetic, guaranteed a recognizable tourist landmark that would also help create a corporate identity—something that was already becoming desirable in the hotel industry (see Figure 19.4).[87] The two-story buildings in the complex were a way to seek alternatives to the tower-hotels that already crowded the waterfront of Varosha.[88]

Detached from the city center and the hotel strip—and providing a luxury that constituted another order of magnitude in comparison to most other hotels—the Golden Sands marked a shift toward a new building type that would include not only hotel towers on

FIGURE 19.4 Golden Sands pool area before the hotel's opening.
Source: J+A Philippou Architects Engineers.

the beach but also a larger hotel complex, composed of a wide range of entertainment and recreational facilities: its own arcade of shops, an open-air cinema, piazzas, a theater, and restaurants. Clearly, this new type of hotel, away from the city life, was meant to provide "higher standard facilities which will be mainly for foreign visitors,"[89] and it marked the beginnings of the "all inclusive" logic in the hotel industry that allowed the tourist to entirely bypass any of the realities of the locale. This was doubly convenient since not only was it favored by hoteliers, the all-inclusive logic also created a safe distance between tourism and the political tensions of Cyprus. This was quite palatable both to the government and its tourism consultants, which is perhaps why the design of the Golden Sands did not even attempt the kind of cursory allusions to a local history or vernacular forms that were deployed in the Hilton. The "surroundings" were simply considered in terms of the massing of the complex, with a plateau connecting the topography's altitude differences, from the street level to the beach. Similarly, the buildings were skillfully immersed in the topography, organized along the plateau's levels and the open spaces and courtyards of the complex (see Figure 19.5). The serenity of the compositions of short and tall vertical structures combined on a strip of beach was as far as regional particularity would be considered. The suggestions of a cultural identity that other hotels, including the Hilton, had attempted

FIGURE 19.5 Aerial view showing Golden Sands under construction.

Source: J+A Philippou Architects Engineers.

threatened to have unpredictable repercussions in a conflict-torn island aspiring to become a hub of sun-and-sea tourism.

The Golden Sands had made a new beginning in shaping an aesthetics/architecture of leisure that was tied to standardized infrastructural demands and the resort type that would soon flourish on the coasts of Cyprus, as well as other Mediterranean landscapes. Ultimately, the promises made by the Golden Sands of prosperity and stabilization were thwarted by a *coup d'état* in July 1974, an act supported by the Greek military junta and which ultimately led to an invasion by Turkey and the division of the island along ethnic lines. Tourism's promise may have appeared unfulfilled after the '74 invasion, but that brief period in the early 1970s, and its intense boom, established practices that were picked up in a new wave of tourism in the 1980s that continues to advance as one of the main pillars of Cyprus's economy. The Golden Sands launched a type of tourism development that created an even greater gap between the visitor and the local—and a significant chasm between the sun and sea "product" that the country was exporting and the sociopolitical reality of the country itself. That chasm was the beginning of the predatory character of global tourism.

NOTES

The findings of this essay come, in part, from a research program co-funded by the European Regional Development Fund and the Republic of Cyprus through the Research and Innovation Foundation (Project: INTERNATIONAL/OTHER/0118/0101).

1 "Cyprus Hilton," [in Greek] *Architektoniki Journal* (1968): 93. Local press referred to the hotel as the 70th Hilton. See "Cyprus Hilton Hotel," [in Greek] special issue, *Haravgi*, February 2, 1967.
2 President Opens "Hilton" in Nicosia, February 2, 1967. Cyprus Press and Information Office.
3 "Hilton A Landmark in Cyprus Tourism," [in Greek] *Cyprus Mail*, February 3, 1967, 1; "Makarios Performed Yesterday the Inauguration of the Hilton—Protest by Photojournalists," [in Greek] *Phileleftheros*, February 3, 1967, 6.
4 "Cyprus Hilton," 93; "Cyprus Hilton Hotel."
5 "Cyprus Hilton," 93.
6 Annabel Jane Wharton, *Building the Cold War: Hilton International Hotels and Modern Architecture* (Chicago and London: University of Chicago Press, 2001); Conrad N. Hilton, *Be My Guest* (1957; rep., New York: Fireside, 1984); Lisa Pfueller-Davidson, "Early Twentieth-Century Hotel Architects and the Origins of Standardization," *Journal of Decorative and Propaganda Arts* 25 (2005): 72–103; Stavros Alifragkis and Emilia Athanassiou, "Educating Greece in Modernity: Post-War Tourism and Western Politics," *Journal of Architecture* 18, no. 5 (2013): 699–720.
7 Margaret Allen, "T.W.A.-Hilton Link-Up," *Times*, February 4, 1967, 13.
8 Alexander R. Hammer, "Companies Adding Overseas Hotels—Join US Drive for Greater Share of Travel Dollar," *New York Times*, July 5, 1967, 58.
9 Wharton, *Building the Cold War*, 46. For more published discussions on the geopolitical role of hotels, see also Sara Fregonese and Adam Ramadan, "Hotel Geopolitics: A Research Agenda," *Geopolitics* 20, no. 4 (2015): 793–813; Kenneth Morrison, *Sarajevo's Holiday Inn on the Frontline of Politics and War* (London: Palgrave Macmillan, 2016).
10 "A New Chapter for Cyprus Tourism," [in Greek] *Eleftheria*, January 29, 1967.
11 "The Establishment of a Hilton Hotel in Cyprus Would Variously Benefit Tourism in the Island," [in Greek] *Phileleftheros*, January 13, 1967; "Grounds of Greatest Importance Were Given to the Construction of the Hilton Hotel," [in Greek] *Machi*, January 13, 1967, 8; Peter Braestrup, "Johnson to Warn Cyprus on Reds: Arrives on Way to Greece—Also Will Stress US Ties," *New York Times*, August 31, 1962, 4; Dorothy McCardle, "President Kennedy Pledges Interest in Cyprus," *Washington Post*, June 8, 1962, D1.
12 Statement by Ralph I. Straus to Mission Heads, NARA, RG. 469, entry 968, box 4, quoted in Brian Angus McKenzie, *Remaking France: Americanization, Public Diplomacy, and the Marshall Plan* (New York: Berghahn Books, 2005), 136.
13 Alifragkis and Athanassiou, "Educating Greece in Modernity," 699–720.
14 See, for example, Louis John Turner, *The Golden Hordes: International Tourism and the Pleasure Periphery* (London: Constable, 1975).
15 Willard L. Thorp, *Cyprus: Suggestions for a Development Programme* (New York: United Nations, 1961), 56.
16 Bruce Lambert, "Willard L. Thorp, 92, Economist Who Helped Draft Marshall Plan," *New York Times*, May 11, 1992, D10.
17 Thorp, A-B-4, 53, 55.
18 Ibid., A-C-13.
19 Ibid., A-C-11; Panayiota Pyla and Demetris Venizelos, "Tourism and Leisure Politics: The United Nations Development Agenda in Cyprus," (paper presented at session "The United Nations in the Non-Western World: Norms and Forms of Development Programs" at the 5th International Meeting of EAHN, Tallinn, Estonia, June 13–16, 2018).
20 McCardle, "President Kennedy Pledges Interest in Cyprus," D1.
21 President Opens "Hilton" in Nicosia, February 2, 1967, Cyprus Press and Information Office.
22 Braestrup, "Johnson to Warn Cyprus on Reds," 4.
23 For the problems of water-intensive development in Cyprus, see Panayiota Pyla and Petros Phokaides, "An Island of Dams: Ethnic Conflict and Supra-National Claims in Cyprus," in *Water, Technology and the Nation-State*, eds. F. Menga and E. Swyngedouw (London: Routledge, 2018), 115–130.
24 "Grounds of Greatest Importance," 8; "The Preparation for the Construction of the Hilton in Nicosia Begins," [in Greek] *Phileleftheros*, August 10, 1962, 1.
25 "The Tourism Industry as the Cornerstone for Cyprus's Prosperity," [in Greek] *Phileleftheros*, January 24, 1960.
26 Checchi and Company, Harry G. Clement, and Pacific Area Travel Association, *The Future of Tourism in the Pacific and Far East* (Washington, DC: US Department of Commerce, 1961); D. G. Pearce, *Tourist Development* (New York: Longman, 1989); Dimitri Ioannides, "Tourism Development Agents: The Cypriot Resort Cycle," *Annals of Tourism Research* 19, no. 4 (1992): 711–731.
27 Thorp, A-C-10, A-C-14.
28 Checchi and Company, *Report on the Establishment of a Development Bank in Cyprus* (Washington, DC: AID, Communications Resources Division, 1962).

29 Thorp, appendix C.
30 Eugene Beaudouin, Manuel Baud-Bovy, and Aristea Rita Tzanos, *Cyprus Study of Tourist Development* (Ministry of Commerce and Industry, Republic of Cyprus and Ministry of Foreign Affairs, French Republic, 1962), 7.
31 United Nations Development Programme, *The United Nations Development Programme in Cyprus—1966-1967* (Nicosia: October 1967), 3.
32 David Ernest Apter, "Systems, Processes and the Politics of Economic Development," in *Industrialization and Society*, eds. B. F. Hoselitz and W. E. Moore (Paris and The Hague: UNESCO and Moulton, 1963), 272-339.
33 Antonios Andronikou, "Tourism in Cyprus," in *Tourism—Passport to Development? Perspectives on the Social and Cultural Effects of Tourism in Developing Countries*, ed. Joint UNESCO-World Bank Seminar on the Social and Cultural Impacts of Tourism (New York: Published for the World Bank and UNESCO by Oxford University Press, 1979), 247.
34 Apter, "Systems, Processes and the Politics," 273.
35 Apter, *The Politics of Modernization* (Chicago: University of Chicago Press, 1965), 398.
36 Ibid., 399.
37 Ibid.
38 Andronikou, "Tourism in Cyprus," 247-264.
39 David Ernest Apter, *Choice and the Politics of Allocation* (New Haven: Yale University Press, 1971), 142.
40 Quite active within the movement, Makarios often sought international support from the leaders of Egypt, Yugoslavia, and Ghana to assert the young Cyprus Republic's independence against geopolitical tensions and local threats. See Pyla and Phokaides, "An Island of Dams," 115-130.
41 Address to the House of Representatives for the Announcement of the First Five-Year Programme of Economic Development, Nicosia: Public Information Office, February 26, 1967, Cyprus Press and Information Office; Panayiota Pyla and Petros Phokaides, "Peripheral Hubs and Alternative Modernisations: Designing for Peace and Tourism in Postcolonial Cyprus," in *Proceedings of the 2nd International Meeting of the European Architectural History Network*, eds. Hilde Heynen and Janina Gosseye (Brussels: Contactforum, 2012), 442-445.
42 Quoted in Andronikou, "Tourism in Cyprus," 247.
43 Mr. Araouzos's Speech at the Inauguration of the Hilton Hotel, February 2, 1967, Cyprus Press and Information Office.
44 Ibid.
45 See Regina Queiroz, "Neoliberal TINA: An Ideological and Political Subversion of Liberalism," *Critical Policy Studies* 12, no. 2 (2018): 227–246.
46 Wharton, *Building the Cold War*, 40; Hilton Hotels International Inc. and The Government of the Republic of Cyprus, Lease Agreement Form, May 12, 1962, Planning Bureau of the Republic of Cyprus.
47 Marinos Menelaou, "Cypriot Hotel Industry—A Historical Review," [in Greek] *Tourist Industry Newsletter* (2003).
48 Mr. Araouzos's Speech.
49 Ibid.
50 Cyprus Tourism Development Company Ltd, Board Minutes of the First Meeting—Draft Prospectus, October 3, 1963, Planning Bureau of the Republic of Cyprus.
51 Ibid.
52 Mr. Araouzos's Speech.
53 Wharton, *Building the Cold War*, 128.
54 Ibid., 22.
55 Kate Turner, "Tribute to US Ambassador Killed in 1974," *CyprusMail Online*, August 19, 2014.
56 Hilton Hotels International Inc. and The Government of the Republic of Cyprus, Lease Agreement Form.
57 Wharton, *Building the Cold War*, 45.
58 Hilton Hotels International Inc. and The Government of the Republic of Cyprus, Lease Agreement Form.
59 Ibid. See particularly Article I, Section 4: Training and Pre-Opening Program: Advertising and Promotion.
60 Ibid.
61 John P. Lea, *Tourism and Development in the Third World* (London and New York: Routledge, 1988), 9.
62 Cyprus Tourism Development Company Ltd, Board Minutes of the First Meeting; "RETRO—Nicosia Acquires a Hilton Hotel," [in Greek] *EuroKerdos Magazine* (July 26, 2017).
63 "Cyprus," *Time*, July 24, 1964, 30; quoted in Olga Demetriou, "Grand Ruins: Ledra Palace Hotel and the Rendering of 'Conflict' as Heritage in Cyprus," in *War and Cultural Heritage: Biographies of Place* (Cambridge: Cambridge University Press), 194.
64 "Decisions to Cease-Fire in Kokkina and Nicosia Received in Cyprus," [in Greek] *Haravgi*, February 3, 1967; "Mr. Andreas Papandreou Attacks: Plans for Partitions of the Island," [in Greek] *Haravgi*, February 3, 1967.
65 Tanis Hinchcliffe, "British Architects in the Gulf, 1950–1980," in *Architecture and Globalisation in the Persian Gulf Region*, eds. Murray Fraser and Nasser Golzari (London and New York: Routledge, 2013), 27–29; Raglan Squire, "Architecture in the Middle East," *Architectural Design* 27, no. 3 (March 1957): 72-108.

66 "Raglan Squire," *Sunday Times*, June 9, 2014.
67 "Cyprus Hilton."
68 Ibid.
69 Wharton, *Building the Cold War*, 64.
70 "Makarios Performed Yesterday the Inauguration of the Hilton," 6.
71 Wharton, *Building the Cold War*, 32-68.
72 President Opens "Hilton" in Nicosia.
73 Republic of Cyprus, *The Second Five-Year Plan 1967-1971* (Nicosia: Planning Bureau, 1967), 208, Planning Bureau of the Republic of Cyprus.
74 Panayiota Pyla and Petros Phokaides, "'Dark and Dirty' Histories of Leisure and Architecture: Varosha's Past and Future," *Architectural Theory Review* 24, no. 1 (2020): 27-45.
75 Republic of Cyprus, *The Second Five-Year Plan 1967-1971*, 205–213.
76 Harry G. Clement, *The Future of Tourism in the Eastern Caribbean*, 1969 Report (H. Zinder Associates, 1969), 123.
77 Ibid., 119.
78 Horace Sutton, "Famagusta: A Mini-Miami on Cyprus," *Chicago Tribune*, June 2, 1974.
79 C. Ionnaides, Letter to the Director-General of the Planning Bureau, April 14, 1970, Republic of Cyprus State Archives.
80 Lease Agreement, September 10, 1969, Ministry of Economy 641/72, Republic of Cyprus State Archives.
81 "Trust-Forte Expanding into Mediterranean (London November 3)," *Vaudeville Variety* (Los Angeles) 260, no. 12 (November 4, 1970): 50.
82 "BEA Plan Cyprus Holiday Resort," *Times*, February 9, 1967, 17.
83 Louis Turner, "The International Division of Leisure: Tourism and the Third World," *Annals of Tourism Research* IV, no. 1 (September-October 1976): 253-260.
84 Patrick Garnett, project architect, explained that Makarios "considered this new project as very significant to Cyprus's new image." Garnett's unpublished writings courtesy of Derry Garnett (London).
85 Speech of His Beatitude the President of the Republic, Archbishop Makarios, at the Opening of the "Golden Sands" Hotel in Famagusta, press release, Nicosia, May 8, 1974, Cyprus Press and Information Office.
86 This was reifying an early schematic made by Thorp, who had identified the coastal strip of Famagusta as central to tourism development. See Pyla and Venizelos, "Tourism and Leisure Politics."
87 Patrick B. Garnett, "A View of the Sea," *Interior Design* (August 1977): 437.
88 C. Ioannides, Letter to the Director-General of the Planning Bureau.
89 C. Ioannides, Letter to the Ministry of Interior, Department of Town Planning and Housing, "Famagusta Area Scheme 1—Development of Famagusta Beach Area," April 14, 1970, Republic of Cyprus State Archives.

20

Antiparochì and (its) architects

Greek architectures in failure

Konstantina Kalfa

Antiparochì, the now well-known post-war Greek practice of exchanging land for new apartments on the same land, only began to be described and theorized after it had become an irreversible and colossal problem at the end of the 1970s. Perhaps the most striking evidence of its almost clandestine history up to that point would be its absence from the legal lexicon in previous years. The first explicit reference appears no earlier than the late 1970s, as "a special contract" between a property owner and a building contractor—the emphasis on "special" indicating a certain confoundment within judicial discourse.[1] First conceptualized during the interwar period, this contract, as it were, proliferated rapidly after World War II, and by the early 1950s it permeated a variety of transactions, from land exploitation to construction through cheap methods and rent agreements, in the process standing in the way of consolidated public functions and urban infrastructure. By the late 1970s, antiparochì was the source of all ills: Athens, where the practice first began, and other Greek cities had been densified to unbearable levels, deprived of public outdoor space, and overwhelmed by vehicular traffic, smog, and environmental degradation.

Greek architects and planners began to study antiparochì more seriously as late as the 1980s, as a response to what was described as a "housing crisis" in Greece, manifested both in the failure of services and the steady rise in unaffordable rents. In reflecting on antiparochì, planners and architects insisted on the uniqueness of the Greek case. For them, antiparochì supplied both the rationale and the model for a series of exceptionally Greek issues: the particularities of absolute and differential ground rent in Greece,[2] production relations in the Greek housing industry and their specific modes of capital accumulation, even the very local "wounds" of the economy (i.e., inflation and tax evasion). Gradually, then, antiparochì became the signifier for regional uniqueness, a portmanteau term encompassing the particularities of the traditionally structured, "pre-capitalist" Greek economy and society.[3]

In the context of new shifts in Western architecture and planning, architectural discourse had by then moved away from "universal," systems-based theorization to a new regard for regional and local factors, which criticized the homogenizing mechanisms of modernism. The material product of antiparochì, the *polykatoikia* (the typical middle-rise apartment building popularized through antiparochì), would then provide a symbolic image for countering the multiple failures of modern architecture and planning. Tzonis and Lefevre's as well as Frampton's formulation of "critical regionalism" must be seen as of a piece with

DOI: 10.4324/9781003193654-27

these developments. It is not by chance that they all found the typical qualities of "critical regionalism" in a polykatoikìa, designed by the Greek architectural firm Atelier 66.[4] Frampton first encountered the typical Athenian *polykatoikìes* (plural for polykatoikìa) in 1959, and in his own words, he was left "impressed by the extraordinary continuity and sense of urbanity emanating from this seemingly endless aggregation of five- to seven-story apartment buildings, ingeniously integrated with the existing urban fabric."[5] He publicly expressed his enthusiasm much later, though, a few years after he had used the term "critical regionalism" in his introduction for the 1987 Greek translation of *Modern Architecture: A Critical History*, where he highlighted the polykatoikìa "as a uniquely modern manifestation of urban growth, stemming from the spontaneous evolution of the society, rather than from planned intervention."[6] In further elaborations of this revisionist universe, the common popular polykatoikìa was perceived as a landscape where people literally constructed their own architectural identity. For example, in the 1986 summer issue of the journal *Ekistics*, Greek urbanization was seen as having positive aspects,[7] "providing mechanisms to enable people to create their own spaces," and the polykatoikìa was described as a proof that people could "design without architects and planners."[8] Still today, antiparochì's legacy subsists in this largely visual, iconographic realm, typifying the polykatoikìa as a regional realization of the Corbusian Domino system, combining tradition and modernity, design autonomy and collective value.

Inasmuch as it may be valuable to see the polykatoikìa in this respect, however—that is, as a different strand of architectural modernity—it may be far more important to start interrogating this legacy. What this chapter seeks to do is to get beyond the picturesque and built-form attractions of antiparochì to look at its historical origins as they emerged within the particular political and socioeconomic relations of the post-World War II realm. Much in the story of antiparochì allows considering its history, and indeed the political-economic trajectory of Greek modernization, as commensurate with what in largely Third World contexts would come to be described as "development." Certainly, some of the critical conundrums of development, as both a theory and a system of promulgating export-dependent sectors and priorities (such as tourism for the Mediterranean South) are present in the Greek case, as are the prevalence of large swathes of informal, supposedly "accidental," "para-" developments like antiparochì.

In the postwar era, mass housing became a state priority in developed and "developing" countries alike, straddling multiple arenas of institutional concern and engagement, from wealth creation, consumption patterns, economic and other migration, and land use to infrastructure and construction technology. As such, the domestic economy presented a crux of Cold War ideological propaganda, devolving into party lines that were harped upon by traveling experts, local actors, governments, and institutions alike. The self-propelling nature of antiparochì might appear to be somewhat oblique in the ideological debates on housing, but the growth of small-scale enterprise in the Greek housing sector was hardly natural, or for that matter ideologically neutral. In effect it represents specific responses to an interventionist state that would both benefit from and be undone by antiparochì.

Following this historical line, this chapter particularly assesses how antiparochì evolved in relation to Greek architecture and planning and even as the specific effect of formal devices decided by architects and planners. On the one hand, Greek architects and planners faced the popular scorn for their "inabilities" to lead to organized planning according to the Western models and, at the same time, for their "failure" to understand the dynamics of antiparochì. On the other hand, architects and planners who held key positions, working as governmental officials after the war, such as Constantinos Doxiadis and Prokopis Vassiliadis, would play a key role in the growth of the Greek private housing construction sector. Interestingly, their crucial role would lie less in their actual practice of architecture or planning and more with their entanglement with the surrounding realm of enterprise and politics, of which antiparochì can be understood as a symptom. Of equal significance toward the growth of antiparochì, this chapter suggests, is the story of US involvement during the Greek rural settlement reconstruction (1947–1951), which, intimately linked to emerging Cold War politics, promoted self-sheltering practices and private investments on housing. The effort here, therefore, is to unveil an unwitting history of architecture that asserts architecture as an element in a complex network of mutual co-formations, where aesthetics, politics, ideologies, and social change cannot be segregated.

"FIFTEEN PLOTS AT YOUR DISPOSAL FOR RECONSTRUCTION ON ANTIPAROCHÌ"

In its simplest form, a typical post-war antiparochì involved two parties that agreed to enter into a contract: the landowner, who provided the legal prerequisites to build, and the contractor, who "undert[ook] the obligation of carrying out the works of constructing" a polykatoikìa on a landowner's tract of land, under mutually agreed terms.[9] The contract involved a great degree of risk and speculation, as the contractor committed to realize the building "at his/her own diligence, responsibility and cost," and the landowner trusted the contractor's abilities to do so.[10] It was in fact more of a joint venture—where both parties shared future output and profit—than a simple exchange of goods (land for modern housing): the contractor remained an independent commercial entity who could sell a pre-decided part of the property at market price, while the landowner would end up owning modern apartments with a much higher value than that of the land they stood on, becoming a commercial entity, too, when proceeding to their disposal for sale or rent. This is why the landowner–contractor relationships have been compared to those of a dormant firm: if the two partners had signed a general partnership contract as they ought to (since they both invested capital aiming to profit), they would have to pay startup fees and the relevant taxes. This, however, is not the case with an antiparochì contract, which, "designed" as a vehicle for evading taxation, was "disguised" as a project contract, whereby the landowner was presented as an employer.[11] In effect, antiparochì was woven into the very texture of private enterprise and wealth-holding as a form of (invisible) asset.

Classified ads for antiparochì, which began to appear as early as 1952, testified to its appeal as a business model and to the range of interests contained therein. In such classifieds, apart from landowners declaring their will to have a polykatoikìa erected on their plot, one would increasingly find a certain kind of buyer with a strong interest to invest on real estate using the convenience of the model: "plot wanted for antiparochì"; "attention: declare to me your premises for sale or antiparochì"; "old premise in the centre of Athens wanted for demolition . . . to be paid in cash or in apartments," are some of the typical formulations found in the Greek press during the first postwar decades.[12] Other investors also participated by providing building materials (steel, cement, bricks, window frames) or services (excavations, floor laying, plumbing, steelworks, and plastering) in exchange for one or more apartments in a polykatoikìa.[13]

So ubiquitous and efficient was antiparochì's functioning that it inevitably led public or semi-public organizations, influential public figures, and even ministers to participate. Ads for antiparochì came from the church, banks (the National Bank of Greece being the most enterprising of all), hospitals, the Greek National Tourism Organisation, welfare institutions and bequests, and the Greek State's Monopoly Goods.[14] Emmanuel Kefalogiannis, Deputy Secretary of State for Housing (1958–1961), tasked to formalize the housing policy, was embroiled in a public scandal for two apartments he obtained through antiparochì at the Athens Hilton district (1959).[15] Doxiadis, after having held key positions in the Greek state as the first Undersecretary of State and Director-General of Reconstruction as well as the Coordinator of the Recovery Program under the Marshall Plan (1945–1950), dabbled vigorously in antiparochì, dealing as a land proprietor, building contractor, and even as a consultant for the wealthiest proprietors, including the 1955–1963 Prime Minister Constantinos Karamanlis.[16]

Ironically, a significant percentage of antiparochì ads referred to the practice as "reconstruction." The term invoked high ideals of state intervention and planning after the establishment, in 1945, of the Greek Undersecretariat of Reconstruction (with Doxiadis as its first undersecretary). The Undersecretariat was tasked to carry out the reconstruction of vast war-damages, an effort which, right from birth, assumed control over a wide range of technical, economic, and administrative duties, including the preparation of a broad housing program, training of appropriate staff, procurement of building materials, and the search for possible sources of funding.[17] Greece was not left alone in this effort. Behind the Undersecretariat were US interests driven by the tacit anti-communist war that came to be called the Greek Civil War (1946–1949).[18] The Truman Doctrine, first announced on March 12, 1947, provided the first package of aid and the necessary symbolic impetus spreading the hope that the Undersecretariat's plans could soon be realized.[19] Following the Doctrine, the Marshall Plan for Greece (1948–1952) produced even greater expectations, creating a Higher Reconstruction Council to coordinate and supervise Greek reconstruction.[20]

Next to the US-supported official plans, various disciplines and research bodies began to systematically address the subject, and thus "reconstruction" evolved also into a sort of knowledge field where various, even contrasting, opinions could be expressed. An example is the principal professional association of Greek architects, planners, and engineers, which in its journal, *Technica Chronica*, routinely published experts' articles regarding reconstruction. Another important body was the communist Society for the Pursuit of Science and Reconstruction, led by economist Dimitris Batsis and comprising figures such as the architect Ioannis Despotopoulos, professor of the National Technical University of Athens (famous for his participation in the CIAM IV). According to the society's members, reconstruction should lead to Greece's industrialization, through an organized programming and planning that could open the way for a total reconstitution of the country's outdated value systems.[21] Other analyses, coming from conservative economists, also claimed that reconstruction was not yet accomplished, since no significant progress had been made toward the modernization and, more importantly, the capitalist industrialization of the country.[22]

The fact therefore that antiparochì classifieds (from 1952 and at least for the following decade) used the term "reconstruction" signaled a popular aspiration that antiparochì could be the only possible pathway for reconstruction's fulfillment. In other words, the practice of antiparochì symbolically reinvented reconstruction as a private endeavor and as an eschewal of official planning. Indeed, the political economy of antiparochì grew as an antithesis to the measures undertaken by official planning.[23] The thriving of antiparochì drew on the use of poor (often dangerous) quality of construction materials and techniques, along with the super-exploitation of labor and land. Floor plans eschewed professional inputs and were spontaneously arrived at, in "just twenty minutes" as the saying went.[24] This spontaneity was prescribed of course in the context of formal conservatism, in its prosaic repetition of forms and types (the standardization of the apartment floor plan, the common entrance, the balcony), in order to conform to dominant market trends. And still, these floor plans were but suggestions to the customers, as they could be redesigned at any stage by buyers who had the right to do so, on the basis of the 1929 law that enshrined independence of ownership by floor.[25] If buyers had purchased an apartment off-the-plan, they could nonetheless negotiate with the contractor on what would be most appropriate for their future home. This amounts to a "participatory" logic that would very likely receive little favor from later advocates of participatory design such as Christopher Alexander (see Ginger Nolan, Chapter 7 in this volume). In its own time, however, this modus of antiparochì was distinct in that it laid far from the reality of postwar European reconstruction through welfare housing complexes that involved a highly regulative state and large interventions into urban contexts, secured by the ramping-up of organized industrial production and division of labor. In terms of homemaking, this meant that occupants of large housing complexes would not have any input into their domiciles, whose shapes and patterns were decided by formally recognized professionals, moving into them only after completion.

Apart from being the exact opposite to the European maximal emphasis on regulation and planning at the time, antiparochì was in this respect also the middle-class analog to the era's popular practice of "unauthorized" housing, a semi-squatter form that developed on Athens's and other Greek cities' peri-urban lands. As scholars observed, between the years 1945 and 1975, in terms of the practices used and their relationship to the state, there was a continuum between antiparochì and unauthorized housing. A "continuum [established], not only in view of construction materials and labor markets, but also in terms of the spatial relationship of the areas that were being urbanized through different types of building" as well as "of the social actors connected to them both as constructors and landowners."[26] This continuum exemplified the real convergence of interests among a diverse range of the population with very different economic and social characteristics, bearing new forms of powerful patronage systems that would prove critical in undermining the formal practices of planning espoused by the postwar professional planning elites.

"OUT OF TEN BUILDINGS ONLY ONE IS DESIGNED BY AN ARCHITECT"

Standard accounts in the papers of events such as "demolition of an old two-storey building and the erection of an apartment building in its place" were festive, invoking a shared modernizing sensibility. However, as much as modernization of housing and the city was a shared dream among both the larger population that lived in and benefited from antiparochì and the planning experts, each group had a radically different perspective on the problem, a fact leading to an unresolved tension between professionals and the wider public. On the one hand, architects and planners would distance themselves from what was going on in Athens. In 1949, Kostas Biris, architect and director of Technical Services for the Municipality of Athens until 1965, would maintain that "out of ten buildings only one is designed by an architect . . . the rest are built by the interlopers in the profession."[27] A decade later, things had not changed much. Architect Kostas Kitsikis, NTUA faculty since 1939, otherwise an advocate for polykatoikìa—he produced studies for nearly one hundred of them—had to remind his audience that albeit "all urban anarchies and architectural ugliness are attributed to architects collectively . . . very few of these buildings are built by an architect."[28] On the other hand, professionals were accused exactly for their elitist attitude: as a response to the lack of any "fixed and comprehensive city plan" for urban development, the Greek papers' readership suggested more polykatoikìes through the system of antiparochì.[29] Populist journalists would "wonder which Schools" educated the "inconsolable *esthètes*" who "lament" about old Athens being lost and "for the new constructions that offend the aesthetics of the city . . .; what have they learned to suddenly become superior so that what the nine tenths of Greeks consider as development . . . they see as abuse of aesthetics."[30]

Sticking to their "post-colonial" identification with metropolitan models, these *esthètes* would hardly attempt to articulate an urban theory linked to Greece's local realities. Plans for the reconstruction of the Greek capital and other Greek cities had been formulated as early as 1946, beginning from Kostas Biris's "Reconstruction Plan for the Capital"; yet they were drafted in the spirit of famous schemes elsewhere, like Patrick Abercrombie's Greater London Plan and Lúcio Costa's Brasilia, and they remained unrealized.[31] This failure of implementation through adjustment to local circumstances led, by the 1960s, to the general belief that "Greece d[id] not boast of a proper city planner of prestige and reputation, around whom the self-putative Greek city planners could gather," albeit some quite significant architects and planners were in Greece working on Greek projects.[32] While both antiparochì and the critique against modern architecture and planning in Greece had considerably evolved, planning efforts presented at important venues that had just begun to emerge—such as the two Pan-Hellenic Architectural Conferences, under the telling titles "Town Planning, a National Question" (1961) and "Public Popular Housing-Urban Planning" (1962)—still ignored the existing circumstances in Athens and instead proposed new urbanized centers on new ground. For example, in 1956, the topographer Andreas Sokos proposed the city's center transfer around 7.5 km to the north of the existing city. Similarly, in 1960, Doxiadis proposed the administrative center's transfer even farther away (15 km) to the north; in 1962, Georges Candilis (who having fought under the communist army left Greece to find refuge in France but, beginning in 1958, would draw up a series of plans for Greek cities) suggested its transfer to Faliro, an area close to the port city of Piraeus, while another—extreme—expression of this tendency was Takis Zenetos's techno-social rhizomatic superstructure for an Electronic Urbanism (1959) floating over the ground.

Circumstances regarding experts' "failure" take on greater peculiarity if we consider the case of Constantinos Doxiadis. This is not only because Doxiadis had reached, by the mid-1960s, the peak of his international success and because of his undoubtedly centrobaric role amongst Greek planning authorities during the previous years but also because of Doxiadis's exorbitant self-regard as a real benefactor for the education of Greek architects and planners.[33] Despite all his powers and efforts, Doxiadis's name in Greek circles would become not a synonym for development (as in the Middle East)[34] but of mere ambition. He would be mocked with the nickname "philodoxiadis" (meaning overambitious) and would be called the "gravedigger of Coordination."[35] Even his international career was often discredited: at its very beginning, on 1951, when it came to be known that "UN asked Greece for Mr. Doxiadis intending to use him at an emergency mission to Burma," the sentiment was sarcastic, as "our country suffered greatly from the raids of the Asian tribes. It was time for her to requite!"[36] The target of the reproach, that "Greece d[id] not boast of a proper city planner," was a *vrai protégé* of Doxiadis, Prokopis Vassiliadis. Vassiliadis was first brought into Greek public offices as Doxiadis's employee at the Office of Regional and Town Planning Studies and Research (while still a student at NTUA). Upon Doxiadis's intervention, Vassiliadis was sent to study abroad, at one of the world's best reputed schools for planning of the time, the Department of Civic Design at the University of Liverpool. Despite these professional credentials and experience, as Doxiadis's successor (and frequent proxy in governmental affairs in matters both of development and housing),[37] Vassiliadis was also parodied, caricatured, and mocked.[38]

Overall, the powerful forces nested within antiparochì, to which architects' and planners' gambits for "modernity" might be seen as a reaction, would be the principal reason for the ultimate ineffectiveness of their plans and proposals, based as they were on profound misreadings of the relationship between politics and cities. Abercrombie's Greater London Plan, Candilis, Josic and Woods's Toulouse-Le-Mirail, Doxiadis Associates' intervention in Zambia, the Ford Foundation's mission to Calcutta, indeed a host of high-modernist planning efforts conjured up in the late 1950s and early 1960s would meet the same fate (see Arindam Dutta (Chapter 1) and Petros Phokaides (Chapter 14) in this volume; on planners' reaction to this predicament, see Ayala Levin (Chapter3)). As a self-propelled system responding to housing and urban demands from below, the dynamic proliferation of antiparochì might thus be seen as linked to the corresponding degradation of the state's powers and the status of its officers, in addition to professional elites, in their control over patterns of urbanization.

"WHAT IS OF INTEREST IS TO ACTIVATE BUILDING IN THE COUNTRY"

The complicated relationship between antiparochì and Greek architects' and planners' ideological emphasis on planning is not confined, however, to this antagonistic context. Indeed, from the very inception of the polykatoikìa, during the interwar period, some of the most successful and influential Greek architects had been forwarding the polykatoikìa as a modern-inspired building type for Athens and other cities. Polykatoikìes designed by some of these renowned architects became models for building contractors undertaking antiparochì to imitate. Some architects also saw the formal variations made possible by the polykatoikìa as qualifying the high-handed approaches of modernism, as a way of making modern architecture accessible to the masses. An example is Georges Candilis's suggestion, in keeping with Team X's break with CIAM, of "cheap apartments in polykatoikìes" as a positive urban phenomenon.[39]

It is also a fact that some of the most famous Greek architects had been involved at some point during their careers with antiparochì, as designers for contractors who hoped that through good design they would sell better, or as contractors' collaborators, or even becoming antiparochì contractors themselves. As the system did not allow them any great degree of artistic freedom, these architects have rarely published or spoken of these designs. Thus little is known today about how much of the Athenian "seemingly endless," seemingly anonymous, "aggregation of five- to seven-story apartment buildings" is actually designed by famous Greek architects.[40] But research has so far revealed some quite interesting connections: in Athens, esteemed architects Ioannis Liapis and Ilias Skroubelos built many polykatoikìes as contractors between 1961–1964; "critical regionalists" Dimitris and Suzanna Antonakakis (Atelier 66) worked for at least seven polykatoikìes on antiparochì with four different contractors between 1962–1969; in the early 1970s, Takis Zenetos, whose high-class polykatoikìes were massively imitated, designed a polykatoikìa on antiparochì for the famous contractor of the era, Evaggelos Kouloumbis (President of the Technical Chamber of Greece, 1974–1981, and Minister of Environment, Spatial Planning and Public Works, 1984–1988); Doxiadis built, as an antiparochì contractor, around a dozen polykatoikìes between 1964–1972.[41]

Antiparochì's complicated relations to planning could also be traced in yet another, perhaps more decisive, level, as is the architects' and planners' involvement in drafting the regulations concerning building in postwar Greece. For instance, the importation of the notion of Floor Space Index (FSI, or Floor Area Ration, FAR), a Western and modern planning invention, is of great significance, as it provided a boost to the development of the practice. Given the small size of land properties, antiparochì needed high building coefficients to succeed. The allowance of building coefficients automatically determined the value of the various parcels of land, in a way substituting for the absence of other planning regulations. In that light, the General Building Regulation promulgated in 1955 as a royal decree contains the first Greek translation of FSI, defined as "surface exploitation."[42] While its authors remained anonymous, it is possible that it was Vassiliadis who introduced the concept based on his studies at Liverpool and his subsequent four-year employment in London with the British architect and planner William Holfrod.[43] If in Britain this welfare prototype served as a measure to preserve prewar building densities, its import into Greece would by contract trigger an explosive rise in urban density and overexploitation of urban land.

Even before the import of the FSI concept, a decisive step toward boosting private construction and land speculation was taken by Doxiadis, during his career as Director-General for Reconstruction. Acting in the fiscal field of macroeconomic and political decisions, Doxiadis is responsible for establishing the first set of regulations on urban housing reconstruction, through the KH (28th) decree "On Providing Facilities for Private-Led Reconstruction," effective from 1947 up to 1955 and, in part, up to 1960.[44] In effect, this decree comprised a liberalization of urban regulations, through which the state was (a) resigning from taxation demands of all private property that was to be built; (b) significantly accelerating the process for issuing building permits; (c) easing the process for granting mortgage loans; and (d) releasing new-built properties from existing rent control, thus liberating properties for private exploitation. The provisional and temporary character of the decree, "so that each man hastens to reconstruct," aimed at a boom of private-financed housing construction which was, for the first time, seen as a productive sector of the economy.[45] "What is of interest is to activate building in the country," a stimulus that could create jobs for hundreds of thousands of people and lead to a reactivation of the stagnating building materials industry, not to rule out renewed capital circulation, Doxiadis explained in one of the propaganda articles he anonymously published in the newspaper *To Vima*.[46]

It is striking that these words were written while both in Greece and abroad housing provision was perceived as an unproductive sector for a country's economy.[47] Even half a decade later, in 1952, when economist Kyriakos Varvaressos promoted private housing construction as a key instrument for Greece's development, opponents prevailed, and Varvaressos's report was mothballed.[48] In effect, however, the KH decree, having already been fully applied in the course of the first, most critical postwar years, predetermined the development of the Greek cities, eventually favoring the proliferation of antiparochì. Contemporaneous discussions about the decree directly linked it to the growth of the practice: a 1950 critique noted that those who benefit from the decree are the building contractors whose method is "well known. They negotiate the plot . . . and offer the owner two or more apartments in exchange. . . . Once the permit has been issued by the Office for City Planning, they announce that they are selling apartments waiting to catch a customer."[49] The decree's most fervent supporters, engineers, urban planners, and architects, through their formal professional association (the Technical Chamber of Greece), particularly insisted on its beneficial results for the proliferation of the polykatoikìa type. While the proliferation of antiparochì competed with the high-art claims of the architects, the financial benefits promised by the decree for the profession were indeed quickly realized: because of the decree, it was claimed that by the end of 1952 there were as many as 328 polykatoikìes built, with 5,825 apartments as well as 196 additions of floors with 762 apartments.[50] Doxiadis, writing in 1950, would also argue that: "Greek polykatoikìes are in fact but a sum of detached houses, which are financed by the interested parties for homeownership"—in other words, he, too, would suggest that polykatoikìes were self-financed by families in the ways made possible through antiparochì.[51] "One wonders" he continued, "if those who state that if we stopped this economic movement, investments would be diverted in other directions, really believe their statement," since in reality, "people who place so little money for owner-occupation are not willing to place them in other enterprises which they cannot control by themselves."[52] Indeed, by liberating urban real estate from its constraints, the decree significantly motivated private investments and, in addition to other important economic measures such as the devaluation of the drachma, which would lead to Greece's inclusion in the Bretton Woods Agreement and the IMF (April 1953; on similar developments in South Korea, see Melany Sun-Min Park Chapter 10 in this volume), it eventually led an economic development for the country based on the private house-building sector.[53]

Interestingly, US-led reconstruction activity in Greek rural settlements (1947–1951) also promoted self-housing, and this fact certainly provides the larger framework within which one should understand the prevalence of antiparochì. The theory and practice of aided self-help was first articulated by planner and housing consultant Jacob Crane at the Housing and Home Finance Agency and spread throughout the "developing" world through both US and UN agencies. Crane, who was also one of the first advocates of the idea that housing was basic to economic development, applied for the first-time self-help in Puerto Rico, where he availed himself of the help of his colleague George Reed. Almost immediately after that, Crane, in close collaboration with Doxiadis (at the time, Undersecretary and Director-General of Reconstruction), found a place for Reed in the American Mission for Aid to Greece.[54] In response to the extensive damage inflicted during the German occupation upon the built environment in the Greek countryside, the Greek housing-aid program represented an enormously ambitious experiment for Crane. More than that, the framework of the aid was dictated by the Truman Doctrine, and later the Marshall Plan, with a predisposing goal, firm and undisputed in its intent, to beat back the significant growth of communist influence during the Civil War. As Kwak showed in her transnational history, US housing aid flowed where geopolitical concerns demanded, and the Greek Civil War certainly presented a front of this sort.[55] Characteristically, George Reed's successor as Housing Advisor in Greece, George Speer, stressed the urgency for Greek reconstruction, stating that "if rapid restoration could not be effected, it was possible that the Communists would win the final victory."[56]

Indeed, success in rural Greece was a necessity, and eventually US agencies could tout the Greek self-help rural projects as a great accomplishment, with the prospect of new loyalties gained in the countryside. As communist partisans, from 1947 onwards, left their villages to fight up in the mountains and subsequently fled at the end of the Civil War to socialist countries, Marshall Plan strategists billed the beneficiaries of their programs as victims of communists who had "suffered from the partisans."[57] In the rural areas, therefore, self-sheltering supported by the direct infusion of locally scarce materials and cash to families was linked to a new kind of patronage, and US missions' success was measured in these terms. Could the *laissez-faire* of antiparochì be assessed in the same criteria of success? Perhaps consistency alone should not be a measure of success: as Ethan Kapstein has shown, with regard to land policy, American neocolonial interventions in the Third World can hardly be seen as consistent, adopting in many cases "second-best" or worse options that could often be at cross-purposes with the larger ideological and reformist insistence of "land to the tiller."[58] Indeed, antiparochì, though not directly planned, perfectly served the ideology of self-determination that postwar US foreign politics broadcasted through aided self-help programs around the world as a global mantra. The man who guided Greek rural settlement's reconstruction through self-help, Jacob Crane, would soon have the chance to applaud Greece's housing system, as shaped by the US aid programs in the rural contexts and, in the urban contexts, by the KH decree and the growth of antiparochì.

"THE SATISFACTION OF PARTICIPATING IN THE BUILDING"

In 1955, Crane was instigated by Doxiadis to produce a report for the National Mortgage Bank of Greece proposing a national housing policy. Eight years after the launching of the KH decree, and just four years after the end of US housing aid to the Greek countryside, Crane could observe in his report how all around Greece "the recovery of private home building has been phenomenal."[59] Crane suggested that Greece's policy should maintain and encourage peoples' "satisfaction of participating in the building" and the fact that "they ha[d] the pride and joy of building and owning and living in their own house."[60] This opinion certainly echoed not only his views about aided self-help, as applied in the Greek countryside, but also Doxiadis's KH decree and its insistence on *laissez-faire* ("motivating private initiative in reconstruction will result in . . . reducing the need for state intervention, but will also ensure the contribution of individual financial resources and labor").[61]

Crane's report made it clear that securing Greek families' "own decisions as to what to build, when to build and where to build" did not require a predetermined design or typology, much less any preconceptions as to architecture.[62] Interestingly, the gradual erosion of the status of plans—and by extension planning as a whole (due to the prevalence of antiparochì in Greece)—is the path also followed, from the 1960s onwards, by housing aid programs at the "developing" world, which gradually abandoned "finished" housing projects in favor of free-market operations and a largely hidden governmental role.[63] Antiparochì reflected this liberal capitalist ethos, invoking cultural values of the pride and joy emanating from self-effort without interference from centers of power. This is precisely why in 1963 George Speer could provide a more open definition of self-sheltering that could potentially include the system of antiparochì. According to Speer, housing aid could be provided in "some form" among various possible forms and their "varying combinations."⁶⁴ These forms included the "development of housing policy, programs, legislation and usually the provision of credit" so that families could improve their shelter "through their own efforts."⁶⁵ Consequently, Speer argued, "aided self-help has been found to have a wide range of application," from simple improvements of huts to the construction of modern urban houses.⁶⁶ Since modern urban homes, he continued, are usually "programmed for occupancy by the middle income group" it should be determined whether any (organized, technical) assistance is necessary "other than to insure availability of credit, with reasonable requirements of amortization."⁶⁷

The prevalence of antiparochì was compatible with the blooming up of tourism, promoted since the first postwar years as "the *only* industry which can exist in Greece."⁶⁸ As pointed out in Panayiota Pyla's and Burak Erdim's contributions to this volume (Chapters 19 and 18, respectively), regarding tourism in Greece's abutting nations, Cyprus and Turkey, the kind of development tourism forwarded as a spearhead of economic growth depended on a certain type of state that would provide robust incentives to private local and foreign entrepreneurship in the form of exceptional land gifts, infrastructural support, and customized financial arrangements.⁶⁹ Characteristically, following a significant 1951 report produced by the Marshall Plan's Economic Cooperation Administration Mission to Greece [ECA/G], the Greek state guaranteed Athens Hilton Hotel's (1958–1963) success by all means: particularly by evading restrictions in the General Building Regulation, and even by allowing a building height well over twice the legal maximum of 24 meters. Vassiliadis was one of the three architects who designed the building, and the fact that he served at the time as the architect in charge of the Town Planning Studies Service of the Ministry of Public Works created a public scandal, best caricatured in a splendid 1961 political cartoon by the renowned cartoonist Mentis Mpostantzoglou. Vassiliadis was there depicted as the only one grabbing the whole leg of a lamp roasting on a spit: "could what you have done, Prokopis, be called an offence?" he was asked by a caricatured member of the government.⁷⁰ It is not by chance that all four governmental scandals counted in Mpostantzoglou's caricature were public works. Modernist public works of the era, like Hilton, were meant to advertise Prime Minister Karamanlis's will and ability to bypass procedure, bureaucracy, and law alike to produce the necessary imaginary of development and a touristic iconography for the country.

If the aesthetics of antiparochì presented an unpleasant contrast to this iconography, what was not in contrast were the political, economic, bureaucratic, and legal dynamics that in fact tied together the modernism of the Hilton (and the tourist industry overall) with the domestic housing sector governed by the antiparochì that surrounded it. The professional degradation of architecture and planning that this fact entailed, as architects, planners, and engineers themselves recognized, had less to do with admittedly circumscribed competence of this professional caste but exemplified perhaps what Michel Foucault once termed the "ubuesque" effects of power connoting its absurd maximization at the point of its application—following the proto-surrealist play *Ubu Roi* by Alfred Jarry of 1895, "ubu" being a nonsense word sometimes translated in English as *King Turd*.⁷¹

Given their rush to claim agency in this ubuesque realm, engineers and architects could not but become objects of popular scorn, not just in the eyes of the general populace but also by the ascendant cohorts of economists who would express their derision for engineers making economic decisions.⁷² Paraphrasing Foucault, we could say that "bring[ing] about the exchange of effects of power" between these two roles of technical and economic expertise in the rhetorical service of development necessarily entailed "the disqualification of the figure in whom these institutions are joined together."[73] Engineers, architects, and planners were ridiculed both for doing nothing and doing everything, for failing to plan well and for inserting planning into areas where they had neither skill nor wherewithal, but this entitled floundering around is precisely what turned the techniques of power related to development so effective. The same architectural and planning experts who were involved in official decision making, the drafting of legal and fiscal frameworks, or even designing the plans and buildings associated with Greece's developmental priorities have facilitated the growth of antiparochì—whose control eludes them and in which loss of control they claim a mixture of agency, disgust, and pleasure. These were the experts who comprised the big knowledge-power networks that propounded the virtues of mass housing and touted the futurology of a fully modernized middle-class society, aimed at blunting the prewar antagonisms between the proletariat and the capitalists.

Although the type of sovereign modern states of Western Europe that Foucault had in mind differed essentially from the type of the "developing" states around the postwar world and certainly the type of modern Greek state as here discussed, one is tempted to think that the ubuesque failure presented in antiparochì made architecture and planning in Greece all the more powerful, linking them to unexpectedly expanded fields of agency and expertise heavily entangled with macroeconomic and political behavior. If this was a "failure," it was so only in that it created a wholly alternate apparatus of modern government and biopolitical entitlements, reliant on allegedly bottom-up, impromptu practices and a deployment of systems on which the state's stability would nonetheless rest. Architecture, seemingly expelled from the antiparochì paradigm, would have played a very important role on this form of governance, a role perhaps as central as the one it played in the welfare states of Western Europe.

NOTES

Acknowledgments: Part of the research here presented received funding from the Hellenic Foundation for Research and Innovation (HFRI) and the General Secretariat for Research and Technology (GSRT), under grant agreement No 1693.

1 Charis Patsis, *New Great Greek Encyclopedia with Full Dictionary of the Greek Language*: Volume 7 [in Greek] (Athens: Charis Patsis Publications, 1978–1980), 254.
2 Karl Marx's formulations about ground rent in the third volume of *Das Kapital* were further elaborated for the urban context by Harvey from the mid-1970s onwards (see, for instance, David Harvey, "Class Monopoly Rent, Finance Capital and the Urban Revolution," *Regional Studies* 8, no. 3/4 (1974): 239–255 and "Land Rent and the Transition to the Capitalist Mode of Production," *Antipode* 14, no. 3 (1982): 17–25). Harvey's theories were popular in Greece at the time, and some of the Greek scholars reinterpreted them by sustaining that due to the existence of antiparochì in Greece, land prices did not lead to monopolies or oligopolies (see, for instance: Maria Mantouvalou, "Urban Ground Rent, Prices of Land and Processes of Urban Space Development II: Issues on Space Analysis in Greece" [Greek], *Review of Social Researches* 89/90 (1996): 53–80).
3 Some of the Greek architects and planners who first dealt with antiparochì were: Helen Coromvli, Dimitris Emmanuel, Vilma Hastaoglou, Nicos Kalogirou, Anastasia Kouveli, Lila Leontidou, Thomas Maloutas, Maria Mantouvalou, Emmanuel Marmaras, Nicos Papamichos, Georges Prévélakis, and Yiannis Sarigiannis.
4 Alexander Tzonis and Liane Lefaivre, "The Grid and the Pathway: An Introduction to the Work of Dimitris and Suzana Antonakakis," *Architecture in Greece* 15 (1981): 164–178, 174–175; Kenneth Frampton, "Prospects for a Critical Regionalism," *Perspecta* 20 (1983): 147–162, 162.
5 Kenneth Frampton, foreword to *Builders, Housewives and the Construction of Modern Athens*, ed. Ioanna Theocharopoulou (London: Artifice Books on Architecture, 2018), 6–7.
6 Ibid.
7 Peter S. Allen, "Positive Aspects of Greek Urbanization: The Case of Athens by 1980," *Ekistics* 53, no. 318/319 (1986): 187–194.
8 Carl V. Patton, "The Private Use of Public Space in Greece," *Ekistics* 53, no. 318/319 (1986): 128–136, 135–136.

9 Extract from a typical antiparochì contract.
10 Ibid.
11 Kostas Sophoulis, "The System of Building through Antiparochì: A Mechanism of Huge Tax Evasion" [in Greek], *Economicos Tachidromos* 5, no. 1343 (1980): 9–11.
12 *Ta Nea*, March 25, 1952, 2; May 24, 1952, 4; March 12, 1955, 4. See also: *Macedonia*, February 11, 1962, 15; June 17, 1961, 10.
13 *Macedonia*, June 1, 1961, 6; December 31, 1961, 5; July 20, 1960, 4.
14 *Eleftheria*, August 6, 1957, 4; January 3, 1959, 4; November 25, 1960, 5; November 26, 1964, 2. *Macedonia*, September 6, 1959, 11; October 4, 1959, 6; June 15, 1961, 7; *Macedonia*, October 18, 1961, 6; February 25, 1962, 5; *To Vima*, November 25, 1953, 3.
15 *Macedonia*, March 9, 1961, 3.
16 "Zygos S.A: Signs by C. A. Doxiadis (1968–1972)," file 19182, Doxiadis Archives. See one of the first Zygos ads at *To Vima*, May 28, 1965, 6.
17 Mandatory Law 768/1945 "On the Establishment of the Undersecretariat of Reconstruction" and Mandatory Law 873/1946 "On the Establishment of a State Department Under the Title of Undersecretariat of Reconstruction." During World War II and the Nazi occupation of Greece, Doxiadis and his team at the Office of Regional and Town Planning Studies of the Ministry of Public Works collected information on war damages in Greece, a survey that led to the publication of *The Sacrifices of Greece in the Second World War* (1946). Doxiadis reported that 23.6 percent of prewar building stock was lost, mainly in rural areas, leading to homelessness for some 18 percent of the population. Urban centers were not that damaged, but they faced a vast growth of population: Athens, in particular, grew by 22 percent in 1940–1951 and by 64.8 percent in 1940–1961.
18 Howard Jones, *'A New Kind of War': America's Global Strategy and the Truman Doctrine in Greece* (New York: Oxford University Press, 1997).
19 "Interview with Dr. Constantinos Doxiadis, Minister of Housing and Reconstruction, Greece, 1945–1948, Athens, Greece May 5, 1964 by Philip C. Brooks," *Harry S. Truman Library Independence*, www.trumanlibrary.gov/library/oral-histories/doxiadis.
20 For more on the Truman Doctrine and the Marshall Plan in Greece, see Kyle T. Evered, "The Truman Doctrine in Greece and Turkey: America's Cold War Fusion of Development and Security," *The Arab World Geographer* 13, no. 1 (2010): 50–66; and Nicolaus Mills, *Winning the Peace: The Marshall Plan and America's Coming of Age as a Superpower* (Hoboken, NJ: John Wiley & Sons, 2008), 93–103.
21 Ioannis Despotopoulos, "Reconstruction . . ." [in Greek], *Antaios* 1, no. 1 (1945): 13–14, 13.
22 Alexis Franghiadis, "The Question of Modern Economic Development in Greek Historiography and Its Public Perception during the 20th Century (1907–1990)," *Historein* 17, no. 2 (2018); Andreas Kakridis, "Rebuilding the Future: C. A. Doxiadis and the Greek Reconstruction Effort (1945–1950)," *The Historical Review/La Revue Historique* 10 (2013): 135–160.
23 Ilias Katsikas, "Housing Crisis in Greece: The Political Economy of Antiparochì" [in Greek], *Review of Social Researches* 83 (1991): 48–76; Mantouvalou, "Urban Ground Rent, Land Prices and Processes of Urban Space Development II"; Zacharias Demathas, "Classical and Marxian Ground Rent theories or the Utility of Ground Rent Towards the Understanding of Issues of Greek Political Economy" [in Greek] (Ph.D. diss., Panteion University of Social and Political Sciences, 1998).
24 Athanassios-Marinos Aravantinos (Emeritus Professor of Town Planning at NTUA), unpublished interview to the author, 12/09/2017. Other oral testimonies about antiparochì (including construction workers' point of view) are presented in Stavros Alifragkis and Konstantina Kalfa, "Antiparochì—A Short Introduction," www.youtube.com/watch?v=dvjFiopD9wA.
25 Law 3741/1929 "On Property by Floors." This law was fundamental for the establishment and success of antiparochì.
26 Maria Mantouvalou and Maria Mavridou, "Unauthorized Building: One-Way to a Dead End?" [in Greek], *Bulletin of the Association of Greek Architects* 7 (1993): 78–108.
27 Letter to the director of *Kathimerini* newspaper (11/07/1949), quoted in Manos Biris, *Kostas Elia Biris: A Life Dedicated to the City of Athens* [in Greek] (Athens: Melissa, 2015), 108–109. A very similar observation was made one year earlier by the Greek modernist architect Aggelos Siagas (see: Theocharopoulou, *Builders, Housewives*, 80).
28 Kostas Kitsikis, "Solving the Urban Problem" [in Greek], *Architectoniki* 26 (1961): 3–7, 3.
29 *Eleftheria*, September 21, 1958, 7; *Macedonia*, October 12, 1959, 5. On the popular desire for antiparochì, see Theocharopoulou, *Builders, Housewives*.
30 *To Vima*, June 13, 1956, 4.
31 Other important, unrealized, plans of the first postwar decade were the General Urban Plan of Athens, drafted by the Undersecretariat of Reconstruction in 1947 (set out to regulate traffic axes and classify land uses according to zones as outlined in CIAM's Athens Charter) and the 1954 regulatory plan prepared by Prokopis Vassiliadis and his team at the Housing Service of the Ministry of Public Works, also inspired by Abercrombie's plan and CIAM's zoning principles.
32 *Kathimerini*, June 17, 1962, 6.

33. "Note prepared for Mr Jenks by dr C A Doxiadis, 31/01/1957—C-G 96," file 19248, Doxiadis Archives. Doxiadis led think tanks before and during World War II, first at an authority founded by the Metaxas dictatorship for the centralization of all planning services and later at the Department of Regional and Town Planning (1937–1945).
34. *Middle East Business Digest*, June 25, 1958, 21, quoted in Lefteris Theodosis, "Victory Over Chaos? Constantinos A: Doxiadis and Ekistics, 1945–1975" (Ph.D. diss., Universitat Politècnica de Catalunya, 2015), 98.
35. *Eleftheria*, December 20, 1950, 1.
36. *Eleftheria*, February 24, 1951, 2.
37. "Letter of Doxiadis to Jacob Leslie Crane, 26/10/1956," file 28294, Doxiadis Archives.
38. See Lydia Sapounaki-Drakaki and Eleni Stamatiou, "The Evolution of Public Administration for Space Regulation through Testimonies by the Staff of the Ministry of Public Works during the 1950s and 1960s" [in Greek], in *Town Planning in Greece from 1949 to 1974: Proceedings of the 2nd Conference of the Company for the History of the City and Urbanism* (Volos: University of Thessaly, 2000), 139–150.
39. Georges Candilis, "Cheap Apartments in Polykatoikìas" [in Greek], *Architektoniki* 19 (1960): 92–95.
40. Frampton, foreword to *Builders, Housewives*, 6–7.
41. These facts were revealed through interviewing some of the architects and through archival research, in the context of the ongoing research program "Antiparochi and (its) Architects: Histories of Social Forces, Spatial Politics and the Architectural Profession in Greece, 1929–1974" (National Technical University of Athens, PI: Konstantina Kalfa).
42. Official Greek Government Gazette A 266–30/09/1955.
43. Holford was the principal advisor of the British Ministry of Town and Country Planning, drafting its technical provisions, in 1947, in a ministry handbook which contained the first formulation of Floor Space Index. Emmanuel Marmaras, *Planning London for the Post-War Era 1945–1960* (London: Springer, 2014), 32–33, 153, 166–167. The hypothesis that FSI was transferred to Greece by Vassiliadis was trusted to the author by Marmaras (interview, September 2017). A document kept at Doxiadis Archives seems to confirm this hypothesis, indeed suggesting that Doxiadis too might have been involved in drafting the 1955 Building Regulation: "I [Doxiadis] was pleased to see that there are two colleagues in this committee [for drafting the 1965 Building Regulation] who know our job very well . . . and some other old associates with whom we had made the first efforts for Greece, such as Mr. Spanos, Mr. Vassiliadis and Mr. Vallatas." "Sign to Mr. Dori, 09/02/1965," file 18961, Doxiadis Archives.
44. Official Greek Government Gazette A 184–23/08/1947.
45. Quote from KH decree's Explanatory Memorandum.
46. *To Vima*, August 19, 1947, 1. See also on the KH and the role of Doxiadis: Theodosis, "Victory over Chaos," 56–60. Doxiadis habitually resorted to anonymity in his public advocacy for all of the measures and policies he was promoting in his official capacity, signing off his newspaper articles as a 'Greek Technician,' or 'D'.
47. See Richard Harris and Godwin Arku, "Housing and Economic Development: The Evolution of an Idea since 1945," *Habitat International* 30 (2006): 1007–1017.
48. Kyriakos Varvaressos, *Report on the Greek Economic Problem* [in Greek] (Athens: Savvalas, 2002).
49. Agni Roussopoulou, "Polykatoikies of Luxury or Polykatoikies for the People?" [in Greek], *Nea Oikonomia* 4, no. 9 (1950): 422–425. See also: *Ta Nea*, August 23 and 26, 1950; Dimitrios N. Fountoulis, "The Financial Consequences from the Newly-Built Buildings' Taxation" [in Greek], *Technica Chronica* 47 (1953): 24–27.
50. Pavlos Athanassakis, "Urban Housing, State Policy" [in Greek], *Technica Chronica* 32 (1953): 14–22, 15.
51. *To Vima*, August 24, 1950, 1.
52. Ibid.
53. Dimitris Emmanuel, "The Growth of Speculative Building in Greece: Modes of Housing Production and Socioeconomic Change, 1950–1974" (Ph.D. diss., London School of Economics, 1981), 119, 217–218.
54. For more on the US Housing Aid for Greece's rural settlements' reconstruction: Konstantina Kalfa, *Self-sheltering now! The Invisible Side of American Aid to Greece* [in Greek] (Athens: Futura, 2019); and Konstantina Kalfa, "'Giving to the World a Demonstration': US Housing Aid to Greece, 1947–1951," *Journal of the Society of Architectural Historians* 80, no. 3 (2021): 304–320.
55. Nancy H. Kwak, *A World of Homeowners: American Power and the Politics of Housing Aid* (Chicago: University of Chicago Press, 2015), 50.
56. George Speer, "Aided Self-Help in Housing," in *Study of International Housing*, ed. United States Congress Senate, Committee on Banking and Currency (Washington, DC: U. S. Govt. Print. Off., 1963), 212–217, 213. Speer participated at the Committee being at the time a consultant at the Agency for International Development (USAID).
57. As a high-rank governmental official, Doxiadis also used the term frequently. See for instance: "Plan for a Clearly Articulated Government Program for those Who Suffered from the Partisans, June 5, 1950," file 24395, Doxiadis Archives.
58. Ethan B. Kapstein, *Seeds of Stability: Land Reform and US Foreign Policy* (Cambridge: Cambridge University Press, 2017), 14, 93–132.
59. "National Housing Policy in Greece. Jacob L. Crane, Consultant, May 1955," file 28294, Doxiadis Archives. "National Housing Policy in Greece" was published in Greek, under the same title, in *Technika Chronica* 105/106 (1956): 50–54.

60 Ibid.
61 KH decree's Explanatory Memorandum.
62 "National Housing Policy in Greece."
63 Ijlal Muzaffar, *The Periphery Within: Modern Architecture and the Making of the Third World* (Ph.D. diss., MIT, 2007), 191–205; and Kwak, *A World of Homeowners*, 63 and 74–86.
64 Speer, "Aided Self-Help in Housing," 212.
65 Ibid.
66 Ibid., 213.
67 Ibid., 216.
68 *Kathimerini*, May 24, 1949, 1. For more: Stavros Alifragkis and Emilia Athanassiou, "Educating Greece in Modernity: Post-War Tourism and Western Politics," *The Journal of Architecture* 18, no. 5 (2013): 699–720; and Annabel J. Wharton, *Building the Cold War: Hilton International Hotels and Modern Architecture* (Chicago and London: The University of Chicago Press, 2001), 54–69.
69 Interestingly enough, a system similar to antiparochì grew after the late 1950s in Turkey, too. See Esra Akcan and Sibel Bozdoğan, *Turkey: Modern Architectures in History* (London: Reaktion Books, 2012), 139, 158–164.
70 *Eleftheria*, April 4, 1961, 1. Similar criticisms were expressed in *To Vima*, April 4, 1961, 1.
71 Michel Foucault, *Abnormal: Lectures at the Collège de France 1974–1975* (London and New York: Verso, 2003), 11–14.
72 Best summarized in the famous dispute between Doxiadis and Xenofon Zolotas (economist, three times Governor of the Bank of Greece, Minister of Coordination for the years 1952 and 1974). On June 21, 1949, Zolotas argued: "Let me express my reservations on the economic opinions of engineers, as I will gladly let them express reservations on my understanding of technical matters. . . . Is this an economic program or a coincidental policy?" (*To Vima*). Three days later, Doxiadis, at the time Coordinator of the Recovery Program under the Marshall Plan and Permanent Undersecretary of State at the Ministry of Coordination, replied: "The reconstruction plan is neither economic, nor technical, it is a political plan, and only a synthetic approach can lead us out of this chaos" (*To Vima*, June 24, 1949).
73 Foucault, *Abnormal*, 36.

Index

1939 World's Fair 303; Venezuelan pavilion 303, *304*, 316

Abbott, Andrew 162
Abercrombie, Patrick 406, 407; Greater London Plan 406, 407
Abidjan 72
Abrams, Charles 10, 11, 13, 15, 16, 18, 27, 47, 124–125, 127, 261, 273; in Ghana 47–52, 53, 56, 58; *Man's Struggle for Shelter in an Urbanizing World* 47; *Revolution in Land* (1939) 370, 371; in Singapore 65–67; in Turkey 21, 367, 369–378; "Urban Land Problems and Policies" 371
Accelerated Development in Sub-Saharan Africa: An Agenda for Action (1981) 297
Acción Democrática (Venezuela) 318
accounting systems 287, 346, 359; Stone-Meade National Accounting System 287
Accra 56
action planning 16, 65–66, 68, 70–71, 73, 74–76, 80, 81; action research 70, 74
Adagala, Seth 191
Adams, Frederick J. 261, 373
Addis Ababa 185, 187
Adlai Stevenson Institute of International Affairs 183
Administrative Staff College of India (Hyderabad) 354
adobe 245, 252; *vs.* brick 245
aesthetics 1, 15, 37, 79, 210, 248, 298, 355, 403, 406; of leisure 383, 397; in national formation 15; of scientific neutrality 88, 91–92, 100
African Socialism 283
Agamben, Giorgio 329
Aggarwal, S. N. 267
Aggregate Architectural History Collaborative 15
agrarianism 303
agrarian societies 1, 14, 28, 75, 155, 371
agribusiness 99
Agricultural and Livestock Bank 312
agricultural clubs 312; Club Agrícola 5V de Venezuela Andrés Bello Creole N° 1 312
agricultural colonies 20, 312–313
Agricultural Experiment Stations (AES, USDA) 250; South Dakota 250

Agricultural Free Schools (Mexico) 87, 90, 97, 99–100
agricultural stations 87, 307
Agricultural Trade Development and Assistance Act ("Public Law 480," PL480, 1954) 200, 345–347
agriculture 5, 14, 21, 76, 85–86, 87–88, 106–107, 115, 181, 184, 248, 279, 287, 297, 308, 309, 312, 315, 325, 343, 354, 368, 376, 385; agro-industrialization 87; capitalist 329; demonstration areas 41, 155; and food security 13, 19, 20, 32; modernization of 85, 100, 155; output 20; policy 7, 13, 100, 305; production 7, 70, 79, 280, 286, 290, 303, 304, 307, 312, 328, 331; specialization in 324, 331, 333; subsistence 33, 280, 291, 292; surpluses 20, 85, 200–201, 288, 298, 345, 358
agritecture (Cointeraux) 248
agronomists 9, 17, 87, 308, 323, 325, 331–332; Mexican 85–91
agro-technics 323, 332, 334, 336, 338
Agua Caliente Band, Cahuilla Indians 217, 219–221, 232
Ahmedabad School of Planning 131
aircraft industry 27
Airform Corporation 238
airlines 385, 388
airports 230, 383, 388
Alcock, A. E. S. 244
Alemán Valdés, Miguel 18, 161, 163–164, 167–170; *Comisión de Programa* (Program Commission) 163
Alexander, Christopher 18, 37, 127, 143–158, 405; *The Nature of Order* 148; *Notes on the Synthesis of Form* 150, 152; "pattern language" 133, 143, 148; PREVI competition (Lima) 127
Alexander Construction Company 221
Algeria 2, 27, 129, 132; Kabylia 132; Ministry of Housing 132
Allen, Margaret 381
All-India Grain Storage and Distribution Study 354
All India Radio (AIR) 270
aluminum 59, 109, 110
Álvarez, Augusto H. 85, 89, 94, 95–96, 99, 100, 168
Álvarez and Carral 89, 91, 96
Amazon (rainforest) 3
Ambedkar, B. R. 153
American Colonization Society 250

American Indian Movement 219
"American Indian Point IV Program" 218–219
American Institute of Architects (AIA) 163; Delano-Aldrich Fellowship 163
American Mission for Aid to Greece 409
Amiens 248
ancestors 52, 56–57
Andreú Almazán, Juan 175
Andronikou, Antonios 386–387
Angola 282
Ankara 124, 369, 373, 376, 378
anthropology 8, 43, 71, 137–138, 146, 152, 156–157, 190, 259; cultural 132; structural 40
antibiotics 6, 14
anti-colonial movements 7, 19
antiparochi (Greece) 20–21, 401–412; juridical status of 401; political economy of 404–405; as "special contract" 401
antitrust laws 370
Antonakakis, Dimitris 408
Antonakakis, Suzanna 408
An Tong-hyŏk 201; "3F" policy 201
Aphrodite 381, 393
Apter, David Ernest 386–387, 389; "reconciliation model" 386–387
Araouzos 388–389
architects 10, 13, 161–162, 168, 173, 220, 237, 264, 325, 349, 373, 406, 409; activist 163; *arquitectos planificadores* 167; development 241; fieldwork 146; as *kisulcha* (engineers) 205; legitimacy and status of 20, 123–124, 201, 210; marginalization of 39, 42; relations with other interest groups 10, 17, 20, 40–41, 148, 197, 224; relations with planners 37, 377, 401–403; training of 17, 126, 203, 206, 208
Architectural Association 70, 126, 332; Department of Tropical Architecture 70, 126; Graduate School 130
architecture: *vs.* building 328; debate between the Greys and the Whites 39; as emblematic of development 15; external forces acting on 163; Gothic 393; historiography of 15; medieval 393; "non-architecture" 37; Ottoman 393; as pastoral technology 149, 155, 159; and religion 49; Romanticism in 39; "self-help" 16, 147–148; "semi-architecture" 37; and state-led development 197; "Tropical" 131; vernacular 59, 117, 204, 396
Arenas Betancourt, Rodrigo 171
Arendt, Hannah 371
"*Arkitekturang Filipino*" 106
Aria, Albert T. 96
Art Deco 110, 305
artists 87, 171, 306
Arup 9
ashrams 264, 267, 269
Asian Institute of Technology (AIT, Bangkok) 134
Association for Asian Studies 347
Ataturk Square (Nicosia) 391
Atelier 66 402, 408
Athens 20–21, 381, 383, 401, 403, 405–407; Hilton district 404; Municipality of 405
Athens Center for Ekistics (ACE) 125, 298

Atkinson, Anthony 261
Atlas (company) 113
Atomic Energy Commission (US) 347
Audio-Visual Institute (Dar es Salaam) 190
Augusto Gramcko, Carlos 317
d'Auria, Viviana 16–18
Austin, J. L. 132
Australia 80, 185, 249, 269
Austria 327, 376
automation 217, 221–222, 232; and surplus labor 222
automobiles 316, 390; parking lots 390
Autonomous University of Mexico (UNAM) 96, 167, 170; *Ciudad Universitaria* (CU) 167; "Organic Law" 170
Ávila Camacho, Manuel 87, 88, 161, 163, 167, 175; "National Unity" 161
Ávila Camacho, Maximino 163

Badiou, Alain 5
Bahadur, Joginder 263
Bailey, Maurice 393
balance of payments 41, 201
Bandung 128, 274
Bandung Institute of Technology (BIT) 125; School of Regional and City Planning 125
Bangkok 134, 185, 187
Bangladesh War 27
bankers 9, 10, 374
Bank of America 369
Bank of Korea 209
Bank of Mexico 167
banks 150, 404
Barbados 371
Basic Development Plan (Ford Foundation) 25
Batsis, Dimitris 404
Bauer, Catherine W. 27, 272
Bauhaus 10, 207
Baumol, William 352
Bazerque, Louis 27–28, 37, 42
Beachell, Hank *112*
behaviorism 386
Belgian Congo 127
Belgium 16, 17, 123, 128–129; Ministry of Development Cooperation 128
Bell, Daniel 220
Bell Laboratories 109
Benally, Susue 190; *Navajo Weaver* 190
Bengal famine 345, 352, 354
Ben-Gurion, David 330
Benninger, Christopher C. 131
Berengaria, Princess of Navarre 393
Bertin, Jacques 78
Best, Jorge 171
Betancourt, Rómulo 229, 307, 314, 318
Beyazıt Square 375
"Big Push" model 7, 12, 67
Bilbao Val d'Asua 28, 33
biochemistry 109
biopolitics 1, 5, 10, 15, 16, 113, 182, 187, 191, 218, 328, 339, 360, 412

INDEX

Biris, Kostas 405–406; "Reconstruction Plan for the Capital" 406
Bodiansky, Vladimir 51, 374, 377
body, the 54–56, 58, 269, 284, 344–345, 358–359; as machine 60; as site of biopolitics 16
Bogota 225
Bolivia 20, 118, 303, 369, 371; nationalization of oil production 20, 303, 308
Borlaug, Norman 92, 99
Bosporus 368
Boulding, Kenneth 127
Boumédiène, Houari 132
Bouwcentrum (Rotterdam) 17, 126; "International Course on Building" 126
Bouwcentrum International Education (BIE) 126
Boyer, M. Christine 35
Boy Scouts 317
Brasilia 406
Bretton Woods 3, 85, 88, 129, 259; Agreement 26, 409; conference 3–4, 5; system 3, 5, 6, 9, 16, 31, 41, 200
bribery 145
Brickmaster (Ellson) machine 246
British Airways 394
British Broadcasting Corporation (BBC) 267; Empire Service 270
British Empire 10, 269
British Mandate 323, 325; Peel Committee 323
Broadacre City 13
Brown, Denise Scott 35
Brubaker, William C. 85, 89–98, 100
Brutalism 39, 96, 98, 99; "New" 40
Bucharest 182
Building Material Research Institute (Burma) 245
Bunker, Ellsworth 346
bureaucracy 2, 10, 15, 18, 29, 40, 146–150, 155, 158, 170, 259, 269–270, 346, 355, 411; administrative reform 25; corporate 212; as distributor of government funds 146; folders as element in 143–145, 353; as organizational site of development 2; organization of 18; as sphere of action for architecture 15
bureaucrats 2, 144, 158, 351–352, 375
Burma 28, 245, 406

Cacho, Raúl 168, 171
Caen Hérouville 27, 33
Cairo 391
Calcutta 9, 25, 27–30, 33, 37, 40–43, 347, 349, 373, 407; deindustrialization of 28, 42
Calcutta Metropolitan Planning Office (CMPO) 29; phasing of plan 34
Calcutta Plan 16, 25
Caldeira, Teresa 148
California 146, 149, 334
Caltex 113
Cambridge University 146
Cameron Valley (US) 251
Cameroon 150
Caminos, Horacio 133, 136
Camoruco 315

Camp, John R. 307
campesinos 171
Canada 1, 16, 184, 270, 327
Canadian International Development Agency (CIDA) 184
Candilis, Georges 374, 406, 407
Candilis, Josic, and Woods (CJW) 10, 25, 26, 407
Canguilhem, Georges 60
capital formation 1, 12, 25, 33, 74; rural 19
capitalism 4, 32, 118, 119, 217, 218, 264, 280, 284, 308, 313, 314, 319, 355, 382, 387–388; expansion of 20, 303; industrial 145; liberal 166, 344; state 68, 231
capitalization 6; undercapitalization 6, 7, 19
Caracas 229, 304, 307, 314, 317; Bello Monte 317; Centro Comercial Automercado 316, *316*, *317*; Las Mercedes 316; Los Chaguaramos 317; Oil District 317; Venezuelan-American Center 317
Carbonell, Diego 317
Cárdenas, Lázaro 161, 167, 168
Caripe River 313
Caripito Milk Station 312
Carlson, Eric 242, 244
Caroní River 230
Carpenter, Ted 270, 272; *Explorations* 271
Carral Icaza, Enrique 85, 89, 96, 99, 100
Carrefour 42
Carrió, Manuel Shvartzberg 18–19
Caso, Alfonso 164
Cassad, Dhunjisha P. R. 348–349
caste 71, 152–156, 263, 264, 267; Harijans 152
Castex, Jean 131, 132
Catholicism 128, 166, 168, 172, 175
caudillaje 164
cement 3, 10, 14, 47, 59, 129, 244–245, 269, 318, 344–345, 355, 403; industry 206, 305; Portland 345
Cement and Concrete Organization (India) 267
Center for Environmental Structure 127, 143, 146
Center Interamericano de Vivienda y Planeamiento (CINVA) 240–248; CINVA-RAM 240–248
Central Building Research Institute (CBRI, India) 245, 351
Central Industrial Research Institute (Chungang Kongŏp Yŏn'guso) 206
Central Intelligence Agency (CIA) 183
Central University of Venezuela 316
Centre for Human Settlements (UBC) 126–127
Cerro Bolívar 224, *225*
Chandler, Robert 107–112, *112*, 113
Chang, Jiat-Hwee 126
Chapingo Hacienda 85, 86, 90, *95*, 100; Development Plan *93*; governance of 97; library 91; militarization of 97; organization of 91
Chatterjee, Partha 148–149
Chavez Morado, José 171
Checchi and Company 385
Chenery, Hollis 32
Chermayeff, Serge 207
Chermayeff-Geisman 183
Chiang Kai-shek 28
Chicago 85, 90, 222, 303, 347

Chicago Institute of Design 207
Chimbote (Peru) 225
China 2, 228, 347
Chitrramaja Jagat 99
Chomsky, Noam 8
Chong, Howe Yoon 68
Chonghap Kŏnch'uk 210
chonghap sŏlgye samuso ("comprehensive design office") 210
Chowdhury, Jugal Kishore 351
Christaller, Walter 292; Central Place Theory 292, 333
Ch'ungju Piryo (Ch'ungju Fertilizer Plant) 198, 199, 201–206, 208–209, 212–214; residential quarters 203–204
churches 225, 228, 312, 313, 351
Church of the Holy Cross, Hillcrest Plantation, North Carolina 250
citizenship 19, 239, 241, 330; and integration 19, 330
"city, the" 21, 35; as figure 17; "as housing project" 132–134
Ciudad Guayana (Venezuela) 19, 80, 217–218, 229–232; Avenida Guayana 230; as "laboratory of Third World development" 229
Ciudad Piar 224–225, 228
Clah, Al 190; *Intrepid Shadow* 190
coal 32, 201, 305
Cochran, F. Lee 90
Cocke, John Hartwell 250
"Coco Levy Fund" scandal 117–118
coconuts 106, 110, 114–118; as export commodity 114–115; and Filipino national identity 116; oil 115; products used in war 115
cognitive science 146
Cointeraux, Francois 237, 247–249; *crécize* 248
Cold War 2, 27, 166, 168, 198, 217, 222, 240, 242, 259, 281, 307, 314, 315, 319, 333, 345, 347, 367, 382, 387, 393, 402
Colegio de Arquitectos Mexicanos (CAM) 168–169, 174
Collier, John 218
Colombia 99, 100, 125, 225, 270, 371
Colombian Institute of Agrarian Reform (INCORA) 183
colonialism 50, 108, 119, 137, 283, 286, 355, 383; "corporate" 219; internal 218, 338; settler 217, 219, 232, 280, 283
Columbia University 50, 375
Comintern (Third Communist International) 87
Comisión del Papaloapan (Mexico) 166
command economy *see dirigisme*
Commissariat général du plan de modernisation et d'équipement (France) 26, 41
communication theory 188
communism 5, 27, 28, 67, 107, 114, 168, 240, 242, 252, 281, 305, 345, 381; Greek 406, 409–410; West Bengal 42; *see also* socialism
community centers 154, 261, 263, 265
Compañía de Fomento Venezolano, S.A. 308
computation 146
computers 40, 60; incorporation of into planning 74
Comte, Auguste 9
concrete 14, 60, 88, 91, 99, 208, 325, 346, 348–350, 354–358, 359, 368, 392; as emblem of modernity 269; slipform 354

Concrete Reinforcing Steel Institute's Design Handbook 208
Congo 282
Congrès international d'architecture moderne (CIAM) 33, 228, 259, 261–265, 271, 273, 373, 404, 407
Congreso Panamericano de Arquitectos (Pan-American Congress of Architects) 169
Conjunto Habitacional Unidad Independencia 96
Connecticut 30, 70
Construcción (Mexico) 163
construction 10, 21, 54, 68, 114, 146, 156, 167, 169, 202–203, 206, 210, 221–222, 239, 261, 313, 318, 328, 355, 367, 369, 401, 408; automation in 222; industry 131, 245, 368; informal 21; methods 127, 183, 198, 217, 237, 246, 250, 402, 405; rammed-earth 54, 238, 244, 248, 252; specialization within 209; systems of knowledge 204
consultants 2, 9–10, 13, 26, 40, 67–68, 117, 209, 224, 238, 262, 274, 354–355, 383, 385, 396; consultancy firms 17, 27, 40, 385
Consultative Group for International Agriculture Research (CGIAR) 99
consumption 1, 20, 35, 217, 264, 280, 286–287, 303, 309, 312, 315, 324, 326, 330, 360, 402
contraception 6, 7, 14
Contreras Elizondo, Carlos 163
conversion 157
cooperative planning (co-op) 264, 314, 324, 327, 329, 331
Copernicus 91
copper 280–281, 283–284, 286–287, 291, 297–298, 305, 393
corn 88; hybrid 87; open-pollinated 88–89
Corporación Venezolana de Guayana (CVG) 218, 231
Correa, Charles 355; Kanchanjunga project 355
corruption 51, 59, 107, 113, 117–118, 167
Costa, Lúcio 406
Council for Industrial and Scientific Research (India) 372
counterinsurgency 2
Cover and Plinth (CAP) method 358
Covid-19 359
Crane, Jacob 261, 273, 373, 409–410
Creole Petroleum Corporation 304, 314, 317
crisis 20, 41, 182, 222, 238, 240, 242, 250, 252, 280, 297, 307, 314–315, 354, 375, 401; as governmental figure 182
"critical regionalism" 402
Cuban Revolution 318
Cuicuilco 96
Cullen, Gordon 27
Currie, Lauchlin 183
cybernetics 40, 49
Cyprus 16, 21, 381–389, 392, 397; *coup d'état* (1974) 390; debt 21; Department of Lands and Surveys 388; Famagusta 394; Greek military junta 397; independence 387; invasion by Turkey 390, 397; Kyrenia 389; as "leisure-hub" 385; Larnaca 389; Limassol 389; Ministry of Industry and Commerce 384; Nicosia 380; Second Five-Year Plan (1967-1971) 393–394; US embassy 390; Varosha 395
Cyprus Airways 394

Cyprus Development Bank (CDB) 384, 385
Cyprus Museum 393
Cyprus Tourism Development Company Ltd (CTDC) 388
Cyprus Tourism Organization (CTO) 386

Dag Hammarsjöld Foundation 186
daiku (traditional Japanese carpenters) 203
dairy 19, 309, 316, 323, 324–330, 332–334, 336, 338; laboratories 90; milk 312, 315, 327, 334; standards 325, 330–331, 339
Dakar 72
dams 10, 14, 48, 348, 388
Dantwala, M. L. 348, 352
Dartmouth College 50
data 13, 39, 66, 72, 74, 75–76, 80–81, 158, 188, 252, 287, 344–345, 373; digital collection of 149; relations between plan and 74
Da Vinci, Leonardo 284
Dayal, Din 263
debt 6, 7, 12, 13, 16, 17, 21, 33, 41, 43, 114, 119, 170, 200, 280, 359; "conditionalities" of 41
decolonization 2, 3, 75, 106, 123, 181, 218, 259, 279, 281, 283
deficits 6, 41, 66; foreign exchange 41
deflation 41, 42; *see also* inflation
de Gaulle, Charles 26
Délégation à l'Aménagement du Territoire et à l'Action Régionale (DATAR) 27; organizational diagram of *30*
Delhi 9, 26, 70, 245, 274, 346–347; municipal government 351; *see also* New Delhi
Delrue, Jan 127, *128*
demand 4, 12, 14, 188, 199, 222, 319, 352, 370; and wages 31
democracy 58, 114, 145–146, 188, 344
density (population) 30, 71, 280, 395, 401, 408
Dependency Theory 219; center-periphery (also core-periphery) paradigm 218, 230–232, 286
Desai, Morarji 42
design 150; climatic 131; *vs.* craft 156; criteria 133
Design Methods movement 35
De Somer, Pieter 127
Despotopoulos, Ioannis 404
d'Estaing, Valéry Giscard 41–42
détente 2, 174
Deutsch, Karl 271
"developing nations" (as a figure) 13
development: discourse 1, 3, 14, 16–17, 21, 167–168, 197, 224, 237, 253, 280, 292, 297, 371; indeterminacy in 138; indexes 180; indigenization of 147; of inner cities 223; as narrative *telos* 12, 180, 192; planning 5, 7, 16, 280, 291, 329; public *vs.* private 68; religion in 48; "ruralization" in 280, 298; socialist models of 16; "soft" 319; state-led 198, 212, 280, 288; as substitution 344
development agencies 11, 12, 15, 17, 21, 123, 295
"development market" 17, 27
Development Planning Unit (DPU, London) 17, 126
development theory 1, 2, 13, 359
Dewey, John 9
Díaz, Porfirio 87
Díaz-Ordaz, Gustavo 85, 97–98
dictatorship 87, 307, 318

Diderot, Denis 248; Encyclopedia 248
Dijkgraaf, Cor 130
Diker, Vecdi 375–377
Dimock, Marshall E. 373
dirigisme 10, 26, 27, 32, 42
distribution 18, 31, 79, 113, 146, 217, 221–223, 267, 283, 288, 309, 315, 326, 327, 348, 359–360
doctors 2, 10
doctrine of discovery 217
Domar, Evsey 32
domesticity 3, 355
Doudai, Aryeh 65, 75–76, 78, 79, 81
Doxiadis, Constantinos A. 9, 19, 72, 125, 261, 272, 273–274, 280–282, 284–286, 292–293, 297–298, 372, 403–404, 406–410; Ecumenopolis 285; "Organization of the Countryside" 293; *see also* Ekistics
Doxiadis Associates 19, 281, 285, 288–295, 297–298
Drew, Jane 10, 126, 373
Drèze, Jean 359
Dube, Shri N. P. 263
Dust Bowl 250
Dutta, Arindam 16, 65, 124, 137, 407
dysentery 11

Eames, Ray and Charles 156
earth architecture 237–239, 241–242, 244, 246–250, 252–253; and anti-communism 242
"earth-based technologies" 19
Easterbrook, William Thomas 272
Ecochard, Michel 72, 373–374
École d'Architecture Rurale (Paris) 247, 249
economics 1, 8, 12–13, 19, 51, 352; development 5, 6, 13, 41, 344, 345, 383; formalism in 33, 39; *homo economicus* 288; institutional role of 12–13; Keynesian 31; *laissez faire* 6; land 125, 370–371; liberal 21; macro- 359; as a science 39
economies of scale 7
economists 2–4, 13, 21, 33, 40, 67, 162, 224, 272, 323, 351–352, 353, 370, 404, 411; demand for 12
Edkins, Jenny 344
education 3, 5, 10, 12, 14, 17, 29, 71, 123, 126, 155, 198, 264, 270, 293, 307, 354; adult 186, 270; agricultural 98, 312, 333; asymmetries of 31; literacy 154; planning 125, 377; right to 146; of women 153
Egypt 6, 382, 383, 391; pyramids 393
Eisenhower, Dwight D. 345–347, 369; "Atoms for Peace" speech 345
Ekistics 10, 72, 292; components of 285
Ekistiks 270, 273, 402; *Tropical Housing & Planning Monthly Bulletin* 274
El Batán 85, 98
El Centro Operativo Bancomer 96
Eldem, Sedad Hakki 365, 376
elections 42, 113, 161, 170, 175, 318; in relation to development projects 35
Elías Calles, Plutarco 87
Eller, E.W. 246–247
Ellington, Karl J. and Inez 250; *Modern Pisé-Building* (1924) 250
Ellson Equipment 246

El Niño 113
empiricism 386
employment 4, 7, 32, 74, 232, 313, 385; and productivity 4; standards 287
energy policy 7, 32
Engineering Construction Corporation Limited (ECC) 355
engineers 10, 40, 43, 96, 170, 199, 205, 238–239, 245–247, 263, 269, 325, 346, 348–349, 351–352, 355, 376, 404, 409, 411–412
England 50, 51, 249, 261, 267, 373
Enlightenment 8, 60, 248; ideals 113, 248
Enschede 126–127
entrepreneurs 17, 26, 68, 80, 305, 386, 387–388, 394, 411
environmental policy 7
Erasmus University Rotterdam 126
Erdim, Burak 20–21, 411
Erkmen, Hayrettin 374
Escobar, Arturo 2, 65
Escuela Nacional de Agricultura see National School of Agriculture (Mexico)
Estate and Credit Bank (Emlak ve Kredi Bankası) 374
Estrada, Arturo 171
Ethiopia 185, 186
Ethiopian Nutrition Institute 186
Excélsior 165–168
Existenzminimum 333
experts 7, 9, 11, 18, 27, 49, 73, 123, 137, 210, 240, 253, 312, 412; collaboration between foreign and local 88, 346–347; foreign 10–11, 21, 124, 149, 201, 244, 372, 375–376, 383–386, 402; local 70, 270; planners as 74; training and deployment of 9, 192
Expo 67 (Montreal) 183, 184
export processing zones 117

factories 106, 203
famine 113, 114, 118, 308, 312, 344–345, 348–349, 359; *see also* Bengal famine
Fanon, Frantz 279
farmers 17, 20, 86–89, 111, 114, 118, 155, 200–201, 218, 228, 250, 280, 286, 295, 312, 324, 332, 343, 346, 359
Fatehpur Sikri 272–273
Federal Bureau of Investigation (US) 11
Federation of Jewish Workers 329; *20 Years of Building* 329
feedback (as plan element) 74, 76, 81, 188, 288
Feniger, Neta 259
fertilizer 3, 87, 113, 198, 201–202, 208–209, 290, 291, 349, 352; industry 199, 206, 210
feudalism 14, 151, 155; colonial 145; transition from 218
Fieser, Louis 115
film and television 18, 179, 184, 186, 187–188; cinemas 186; distribution 180; documentary 187; facilities 179; as industry 18; studios 188; technical assistance to countries in 179; television stations 186; training 187
Film News 179, 186
financialization (of societies) 3
financial planning, temporality of 51
Finland 249, 327, 374
Fitzmaurice, Robert 261

Five-Year Plans 12, 26, 31–32, 51, 199; in Cyprus 393–394; in India 33, 263, 345, 349; in South Korea 199, 205
Floor Space Index (FSI, or Floor Area Ration, FAR) 408
Florence 331
Florida 91
Fonds d'Aide at de Coopération 72
Food Corporation of India (FCI) 343, 359
"Food for Peace" 113, 345, 347
food systems 17, 316
Ford Foundation 16, 25–28, 30, 37, 42, 88–91, 96–99, 107–111, 113, 125, 131, 156, 183, 224, 270, 373, 407; "Changing Patterns of Language and Behavior and the New Media of Communication" 270; Educational Facilities Laboratory 88; *Infrastructure Problems of the Cities of Developing Countries* 47
Foucault, Michel 1, 88, 148, 157, 411, 412; *Let mots et les choses* 8; pastoral power 147, 157
Frampton, Kenneth 106, 401–402; "Critical Regionalism" 106, 401
France 16, 26, 29, 41, 131, 247–249, 252, 383; Fifth Republic 27
free trade 26
Freire, Paolo 131
French Revolution 247–248; and citizenship 248; Comité de Salut Public (Committee of Public Safety) 247; Reign of Terror 247
Freud, Clement 381
Friedman, Yona 39, 149
Friedmann, John 230
Fry, Maxwell 10, 126, 373
Fuglesang, Andreas 181, 184–191, 192
Fuller, Buckminster 10, 27; geodesic domes 37, 347
functionalism 162, 295, 334, 336
Funes-Noppen, Cristina *129*
fungibility 8, 115, 158, 217, 344, 347; *vs.* substitution 344
futurism 167

Galbraith, John Kenneth 27
Galilee 331
Galván Reyes, Úrsulo 87
Gammon 355
Gandhi, Mohandas K. (Mahatma) 19, 153, 155, 264, 267, 269
Garcia, Carlos 111
García López, Agustin 170
Gardendale Resettlement Project (Alabama) 251
Garnett, Cloughley, and Blakemore 395
Garnett, Patrick 395
Geddes, Patrick 259, 269, 272
General Electric 109
General Motors Technical Center 106
genetics 8, 109
Geneva 185
Geneva, Utah 222
genocide 2
Gensler 9
geographers 33, 293, 295, 297, 332, 338
George, Henry 370–371
Ghadar Party (India) 87, 99

INDEX

Ghana 6, 16, 42, 47–48, 51, 53, 56, 125, 186, 282, 286, 371, 375, 377; Department of Welfare 56
Giedion, Sigfried 231, 262, 264, 271–272; and monumentality 265; *Space, Time and Architecture* 272
Gilly, David 249; *Bauschule* 249
Gilman, Nils 372
Giri, V. V. 346
Global South 20, 70, 71, 100, 149, 150, 181, 186, 253, 263, 280, 306–307, 314, 325, 383; expansion of capitalism in 20, 303
Goethert, Reinhard 133, 136
Gökçek, Melih 378
gold 17, 305, 352
Golden Sands Hotel (Cyprus) 394–397
Golding, Tomás 309
Gómez, Marte 87–88, 97
González, Manuel 87
Gornov, Vittal 245
Gospel of John 53
governmentality 1, 147, 150, 153, 155, 158, 184; *see also* Foucault, Michel
Graduate School of Ekistics (GSE) 125
Graffunder, Carl 206–208
grain 100, 113, 201, 334, 343–345, 348, 360; hoarding 348, 352; imports 345–346; production 17; stocks 347; storage 19, 20, 265, 343, 349, 351–354, 359; prices 343, 351, 359
Great Depression 3–5, 31, 67, 252
Greece 16, 20, 125, 367, 383, 401; Civil War (1946–1949) 404, 409; *coup d'état* (1959) 387; General Building Regulation (1955) 408, 411; Higher Reconstruction Council 404; housing crisis 401; industrialization of 404; Ministry of Environment, Spatial Planning and Public Works 408; Ministry of Public Works 411; modernization of 402; Monopoly Goods 404; National Tourism Organisation 404; Office of Regional and Town Planning Studies 407; Office for City Planning 409; "On Providing Facilities for Private-Led Reconstruction" 408; Recovery Program 404; rural settlement reconstruction (1947–1951) 403; Technical Chamber 408, 409; Undersecretariat of Reconstruction 404
green belts 27, 66
Greenham, Santiago 168
Green Revolution 86, 92–94, 97–100, 113, 118, 343–345, 355, 358
Greer, Guy 223
Grenoble 247
Gropius, Walter 9
Gross Domestic Product (GDP) 32; Harrod-Domar model of 32, 241; measurement of 32
Guaire river 317
Guerrero, Xavier 87
Guinand, Gustavo 317
Gujarat 143, 147, 156; Bavra 143
Gujarat Housing Board 355
Gulf Oil 314
Gupta, Akhil 297
Gupta, L. R. 349
Gutiérrez, José María 96

Gutkind, Erwin Anton 272
Guyana 395

Habitat: Audio-Visual Program 18, 179–180, 182, 184, 186; "Guidelines for Action" 126; Secretariat 184; The United Nations Conference on Human Settlements 17, 18, 123, 126–129, 179–183, 185–189, 192
Habraken, N. John 132–133
haebang moksu ("liberation carpenters," Korea) 202
Haifa 331
Hamrell, Sven 187–188
Hansen, Alvin H. 222–223
Hanyang University 202
Haq, Mahbub ul 6
Harper's Bazaar 303
Harrar, J. George 107–108, 111
Harrison, Richard 220, 221
Harrison, Wallace K. 304
Harrod, Roy 32
Harvard Graduate School of Design 207
Harvard University 7, 27, 50, 113, 115, 143, 146, 218, 229, 270; Society of Fellows 146
Hatch, Donald 316
Hayek, Friedrich von 10; "Central Planner" 10
Hebrew University 333; Department of Sociology 333
Henderson, Scott 370
hermeneutics 157
Hershenzon, Martin 19, 65, 241, 345
Hessische Baugewerkschule der Technischen Lehranstalten Offenbach am Main 332
Heynen, Hilde 16–18
Hibben, Thomas 251–252
Hilberseimer, Ludwig 13
Hill, Forrest "Frosty" 108
Hilton, Conrad 368, 381, 383, 384, 393
Hilton Corporation 368; Architectural and Design Department 392
Hilton hotels 20–21; Athens 393, 404, 411; Bahrain 392; bombings of 390; Cairo 391; Cyprus 381–383, 384–385, 387–393, 395–396; Hilton Hotels International Inc. 381; "Hilton International formula" 393; Istanbul 21, 365, 367–369, 374, 376, 378; Jakarta 392; Nile 393; Tehran 392; Tel Aviv 390; Tunis 392
Himalayas 4, 28
hind swaraj 264
Hirschman, Albert H. 8, 12, 26, 43
historicism (in architecture) 162
Hodgson Company 238
Holabird, Root & Burgee 317
Holfrod, William 408
Holiday magazine 381
Holland 249
Holy Ghost 52
Hoover, Herbert 307
hospitals 10, 50, 127, 171, 208, 228, 313, 365, 404
Hotel Avila 308
Hotel Intercontinental Tamanaco 317
housing 5, 10–11, 13, 15, 33, 47, 59, 67–68, 123, 126, 131, 137, 146–147, 180, 202, 220, 222, 232, 238–242,

244, 250, 298, 307, 313, 329, 336, 370, 373, 401; as an activity 130; associations 50; clusters 150–151; as a commodity 150; dormitories 90; industry 18, 368–370, 401, 403, 408; low-income 136, 149, 237, 245, 250, 261–262, 267, 270, 355, 405; mass 68, 147, 402, 412; middle class 221; modularization 202; and moralization 231; policy 128, 133–134, 367, 370, 372, 378, 404, 410–411; public 43, 67, 96, 223, 251, 370; "self-help" 16, 129, 149, 252; and "shelter" 123, 182; "unauthorized" 20, 148, 405, 409; workers' 203–204, 230–231, 374

humanitarianism 107, 113, 118, 180, 186
human relations management 71
hunger 17, 113, 305, 307, 343–344, 345–346; in Europe 307; as "malnutrition" 344; as perceived threat to national security 305; *see also* famine
Hunt, Jr., William Dudley 210
Huntington Park, California 222
hygiene 1, 40, 204, 303, 309, 312, 334, 336

IBM 96
Immerwahr, Daniel 338
imperialism 20, 110, 131
India 6, 16, 19, 25, 26–30, 41–42, 65–66, 70–72, 87, 99, 100, 108, 125, 146, 153–157, 186, 228, 244–246, 261–267, 269–273, 343–351, 353–359, 372–373; Central Public Works Department (CPWD) 267, 349; Community Project Administration (CPA) 263, 270; Finance Ministry 353; Five-Year Plans 33; independence 26, 152; Ministry of Agriculture 346; Ministry of Food and Agriculture (MoFA) 349, 353; Ministry of Works, Housing and Supply 263; National Extension Services 263; partition 27, 28; Public Works Departments 245, 263, 264, 267, 270, 346, 349, 353; relations of production in 71; Rourkela 349; Second Development Plan (1956) 71; Third Five-Year Plan 349
Indian Concrete Journal (*ICJ*) 348, *350*, 354, 355, *356*, *357*
Indian Films Division 269
Indian Institute of Technology 351
Indian National Congress 19, 29
indigenous lands 217–219; dispossession of 220–221
indigenous peoples 87, 191, 217–218, 231, 232, 244; "assimilation" of 219; and labor 219; proletarianization of 221; recognition of Tribes 219; relocation of 219; "transition" of 218; tribal termination policies 222; in Venezuela 218
Indonesia 3, 125, 127, 199, 244
industrialization 2, 4, 67, 151, 166, 198, 202, 264, 279, 286, 325, 344–345, 385, 404; deindustrialization 28, 42; export-oriented 17, 115; fully-industrialized economies 32; heavy industry 32; import-substitution 96–97; policy 7; rural 87; semi-industrialized economies 32
inequality 145, 266, 305, 307
infectious diseases 312
inflation 4, 6, 20, 31, 41, 201, 344, 401; predictability of 32–33; *see also* deflation
infrastructure 7, 10, 12, 21, 25, 27, 73, 111, 114, 175, 181, 182, 199, 218, 232, 265, 269, 271, 274, 283–284, 291. 298, 318, 345, 352, 359, 383, 394, 397, 402; administrative 80; civil society 146; distribution 221, 223, 336; education 155; environmental 265; indigenous 217; state buildings 13; transportation 10, 12, 13, 27, 42, 113, 173, 319; urban systems 42, 47; utilities 72

Innis, Harold 271; *Empire and Communications* 271
input-output models 32, 287
Institute for Economic Growth (India) 352
Institute for Engineers (Bangalore) 352
Institute for Housing Studies (Rotterdam) 126
Institute for Planning and Development (IPD) 75
Institute of Public Administration in Turkey and the Middle East (Türkiye ve Orta Doğu Amme İdaresi Enstitüsü, TODAIE) 373
Institute of Social Studies (the Hague) 70
Institutional Revolutionary Party (PRI, Mexico) 97, 161, 167, 170, 174–175
Institution of Engineers (India) 348
Institut National d'Études et de Recherches du Bâtiment (INERBA, National Institute of Studies and Research on Building, Algeria) 132
Instituto de Planificación 170
Instituto Mexicano del Seguro Social (IMSS) 171
Instituto Politécnico Nacional (IPN) 168
integración plástica 171
Inter-American Development Bank (IDB) 11
InterAmerican Cooperative Food Production Service (SCIPA) 307
International Bank for Reconstruction and Development (IBRD) 183, 384, 387
International Basic Economy Corporation (IBEC) 20, 307, 314, 318–319; economic imperialism of 20; *see also* Venezuelan Basic Economy Corporation (VBEC)
International Center for Tropical Agriculture (Colombia) 100
International Communist Party (Mexico) 85
International Cooperation Administration (ICA) 11, 199–201, 204–205, 375
International Development Bank 90
International Exhibition on Low-Cost Housing 261
internationalism 105, 107, 110, 113–114, 117–119, 270, 273
International Labor Organization 265
International Maize and Wheat Improvement Center (CIMMYT) 86, 98–100; funding of 99
International Monetary Fund 5, 114, 118–119, 199, 200, 409; and austerity 114; Structural Adjustment Programs 41, 42
International Potato Center (Peru) 100
International Refugee Organization (IRO, UN) 242
International Rice Research Institute (IRRI, Philippines) 17, 19, 105–114, 116–119, 345
International Style (in architecture) 92, 94
investment 4, 6–7, 18, 31–33, 35, 51, 68, 106, 166, 224, 229–230, 288, 291, 352, 386, 393, 409; criteria for 13; imbalances resulting from 12, 14; in real estate 42
Iraq 16
Ireland 371
irrigation 87, 98, 113, 344, 354, 368
Irving Trust Building 110

INDEX

Israel 16, 19, 50, 65, 73, 76, 244, 269, 323–326, 328–339; Agricultural Bank 324; agricultural policy 324; dominance of Ashkenazi in 330; first national plan (1948–1953) 333; Green Line 332; Industrial Villages (*KAFAT, kfrar taasiati*) 331; Jewish immigration to 323; Joint Center for Agricultural Planning 329; Lakhish region 73, 80; Mapai party 323; Ministry of Foreign Affairs' Division for International Cooperation (Mashav) 75; Nahalal 327; Palestinian insurgency 327; residential villages (*yeshuv kehilati*) 331; settlement economy 329; Settlement Movement 326; State Bank 324
Israeli Defense Force 329; Unit for Agricultural Planning 329
Istanbul 21, 365–367, 369, 374, 377–378, 382, 391; Gezi Park 365; Republic Boulevard (*Cumhuriyet Caddesi*) 367
Italy 131, 238, 325, 383
Ivan Milutinovic-PIM 30–31

Jamaica 242, 246, 371; Agricultural Society 242; Social Welfare Commission 242
Japan 35, 99, 100, 108, 185, 199, 203, 228, 371
J+A Philippou 392, 395
Jarry, Alfred 411; *Ubu Roi* 411, 412
Java 111
Jayakar, Pupul 156
Jeanerette, Pierre 372
Jefferson, Thomas 249
Jenks, Barton P. 238
Jennings, Peter *112*
Jere, Annette 190
Jesus Christ 52–53
Jewish Agency (Israel) 323–324, 327–339; Center for Research on Settlements 331; Settlement Department 324
Jewish National Fund 325
Jews 58; Ashkenazi 330; Mizrachi 330; North African 73
Jezreel Valley (Israel) 332; Ta'anach 332
Joglekar, Krishna Shridhar 263
Johnson, Janet 144
Johnson, Lyndon B. 51, 112, 384
JoongAng Ilbo 210
Jordan Valley project 80
José-Antonio López, Albert 18
Joshua Macy Foundation 49
Joyce, James 259; *Finnegan's Wake* 259
Judea 329
Junglim Architecture Research Institute 197, 198, 209–212, 214; corporate model 212

Kahn, Louis 10, 267
Kalecki, Michal 32
Kalfa, Konstantina 20–21
Kant, Immanuel 40
Kanvinde, Achyut 9
Kapstein, Ethan 410
Karachi 111, 373
Karamanlis, Constantinos 404, 411
Karim, Farhan 18–19, 199, 263
Karinya Mamo tribe (Orinoco) 232

Kashmir 3
Kaunda, Kenneth 19, 280–286, 291, 295; "Humanism" 281
Kay, George 293, 295
Keenleyside, Hugh 9
Kefalogiannis, Emmanuel 404
Kennedy, John F. 51, 384
Kenya 2, 118, 186, 280; Ministry of Information and Broadcasting 191
Keynes, John Maynard 3–5, 12, 51, 275; *General Theory of Employment, Interest and Money* 3, 5
Keynesianism 4–5, 31–32, 33, 175
khadi 264
Khankhoje, Pandurang 87, 89, 99–100
Khorakiwala, Ateya 19–20, 115
Khusro, Ali Mohammed 352–353
kibbutzim 19, 323–327, 329–330, 332, 336–339; central courts 327; contrast with *moshavim* 326 economic activities of 19; Kibbutz Merhavia *326*; Prussian farm model 327
Kigali 129
Kim Chŏng-chŏl 209
Kim Chŏng-sik 198, 202, 208–209
Kim Chŏng-su 207
Kim Hŭich'un 207
Kingsley, J. Donald 242
Kinshasa 72, 127
Kitsikis, Kostas 406
Klong Toey 134, *135*
Kobe, Susumu 66
Koch, Carl 207
Koenigsberger, Otto 10, 16–19, 47–51, 65–75, 78, 80–81, 126, 131, 377; *Infrastructure Problems of the Cities of Developing Countries* 47
Kolkata *see* Calcutta
kolkhoz (collective farm) 324
Komer, Robert 377
Kŏnch'uk (journal) 208
Kŏnch'uk chŏrhak ŭro sŏŭi ŭijangnon (A philosophy of architecture) 197
Konggan 210
Korea Exchange Bank 209
Korean Civil Assistance Command (KCAC) 238
Korean War (1950–1953) 197, 198, 238
Korsmo, Arne 127
Kosygin, Alexei 27
Kouloumbis, Evaggelos 408
Kowalski, Rosemarie Daher 54
Koyré, Alexandre 8
Kristeva, Julia 132
Krugman, Paul 8
Kurdaş, Kemal 377
Kuzosa Architects and Engineers 202, 204, 210
kwahak kisul ("science-technology") 205
Kyŏngsŏng Technical College 202, 206
Kyushu University 203

labor 4, 79, 114, 117, 129, 219–222, 228, 232, 246–247, 264, 267, 291, 298, 313, 327, 330, 333, 355, 385, 405; displacement 221; division of 47, 106, 283, 289; migrant 21, 218, 232; organization of 71, 217, 332, 336; rights 5; value of 345; *see also* surplus labor

laboratories 10, 27, 90–91, 94–96, 98, 109, 118, 179, 349
Labour Party (Britain) 28
Lacan, Jacques 132
Lad Krabang (Thailand) 134
Lago Petroleum Corporation 308
Lagos 70, 191
Laguna de Bay (Philippines) 106
land 19, 219, 221, 231, 252, 263, 280, 283, 307, 312–313, 325, 338, 353, 370, 395, 401, 403, 408, 410; collectivization 327; political economy of 21, 65, 72, 149–151; reclamation 86, 106; redistribution 155, 241, 288, 344; speculation 33, 42, 394, 403, 408; struggles over use of 20; subsoil 308; tenurial systems 21, 42, 71, 87, 155, 288, 308, 367, 369, 373–374; use 68, 81, 182, 201, 228, 288, 293, 370–373, 402; values 29, 42, 353, 370, 388–389
Landcrete machine 238–240, 245
landlords 148, 150, 263, 308
landowners 41, 72, 369, 403, 405
land reform 17, 378
Laski, Harold 9
Laws of the Indies (Spain) 231
Lazo Barreiro, Carlos 18, 161, 163–175; *Pensamiento y Destino de la Ciudad Universitaria de México* 170; *Programa de Gobierno* 165; "Summa Cósmica" 173
Lea, John 391
Le Corbusier 37, 94–95, 267, 373; Domino system 402
Ledra Palace Hotel 391–392
Lee, Dorothy D. 271
Lee, Rohama 179–181
Lefebvre, Henri 33
Le Mirail 16, 25, 27–28, 30, 33, 35–37, 40–43, 407; CJW plan diagram 36; as *zone à urbaniser par priorité* (or ZUP) 28
le Roux, Hannah 126
Leuven 123, 127–129, 132, 137
Levin, Ayana 16, 19, 259, 407
Lewin, Kurt 70
Lewis, W. Arthur 41–42, 241; *Development Planning* 42; *Economic Development with Unlimited Supplies of Labor* (1954) 241; *The Theory of Economic Growth* 41
Lewis, Wyndham 259; *America and Cosmic Man* 259
Liapis, Ioannis 407
liberalism 7, 8, 81, 153, 166, 168, 218–219, 284, 324, 344, 360, 371; economic 5, 21, 79; political 5; rights *vs.* productivity in 8–9
Library of Congress 347 Conference on American Library Resources on Southern Asia 347
liderismo 172
Life Magazine 106
Lilienthal, David 261
Linam, Henry E. 309, 313
Lincoln, Abraham 9
Lindblom, Charles E. 74, 79
linguistics 8, 40
Lino Vaamonde, Jose 317
Literary Digest 250
livestock 305, 309, 325, 330, 332, 334
loans 6–7, 11, 114, 119, 346, 354, 369, 384; housing 60, 369–370, 408; sovereign-backed 6, 31

Loeckx, André 124, 132–133
London 17, 70, 126, 408
London Metal Exchange 287
London School of Economics 2
Loosen, Sebastiaan 17, 18
López Contreras, Eleazar 304
López-Durán, Fabiola 19, 20
López Mateos, Adolfo 175
Los Angeles 221, 222
Los Angeles Times 394
Los Baños 106, 108, 112
lottery 50–51, 53; and the Promised Land 51; religious sanction for 51
Louis XVI 249
Lovanium University (Kinshasa) 127
Luis Sert, José (Josep Lluis Sert) 218, 224–225, 227–231, 271
Luz, Alfredo J. 108–111
L'vov, Nicolay 249
Lyon 247

Mabogunje, Akin 295
Macapagal, Diosdado 113
Madras 347
Mahiga, Joseph 190
Maine, Henry 264
Makarios III 381, *382*, 383–384, 387, 393, 395; US visit 384
Malaya 2, 67
Mamdani, Mahmood 283
Manila 106, 108, 111–112, 115; Polo Club 111
Manila Summit 112
Mañosa, Francisco "Bobby" 106, 116–117
Maracaibo 315; Bella Vista neighborhood 315
Marcos, Ferdinand 107, 112–119; "Edifice Complex" 118
Marcos, Imelda 116
Marin, Louis 88
Mariscal, Federico 168
markets 3–5, 8, 17, 20, 31, 41, 184, 200, 218, 385; "animal spirits" of 31; boom and bust cycles 4; construction of 25; crises 20; labor 385, 405; national 4; real estate 223
Marshall Plan 21, 346, 367–369, 383–384, 388, 404, 409–411; Economic Cooperation Administration Mission to Greece (ECA/G) 411
Martin, Reinhold 109
Martinez, Diana 16–17, 199, 344, 345
Marx, Karl 9, 33, 97
Marxism 2, 28, 168, 218, 231, 344; alienation 147
Mary Magdalen 52
masons 248
Massachusetts Institute of Technology (MIT) 7, 9, 17, 27, 36, 49, 51, 70, 130, 137, 207, 218, 229, 373; Center for Group Dynamics 71; Center for Urban and Regional Studies 123; Kresge auditorium 108
mass psychology 242
mass slaughter 2
master plans 16, 31, 66–68, 70, 72, 73, 75, 229, 298; as genre of document 25–26
Mayer, Albert 27, 65, 70–72, 74, 80, 261, 263–264
McCarthyism 11, 219
McGraw-Hydrocarbon 199, 201–202, 204–205, 209

INDEX

McLuhan, Marshall 19, 184, 259, 262, 270–274; "global village" 259, 270, 272–274; *Gutenberg Galaxy* 273; *Understanding Media* 271
McNamara, Robert 27, 114, 118, 295, 353
Mead, Margaret 73–74
Medellín 225
Medellín, Jorge L. 168
Mediterranean 21, 228, 376, 383, 385, 394, 397, 402
Meière, Hildreth 110
Mekong River Delta 80, 111
Menderes, Adnan 369
Merrill, John O. 303
Mesopotamia 228
Mexicanidad 166
Mexican Revolution 85, 86, 97, 100
Mexico 16–17, 20, 85–89, 92–100, 107, 149, 161–171, 174–175, 185, 303; Alemán government 18; Dirty War 97; First Peoples 96; influence of the military in 161; Ministry of Development 87; nationalization of oil production 20, 303, 308; political economy 162; political society 161; power of executive branch 163; presidency 166; regional authority in 166; *Unidades Regionales* 165; *Zonas Vitales* 165
Mexico City 85, 87–88, 96, 100, 165, 169, 182, 185, 187; Narvarte 171; Pedregal 169
Meza, Manuel 87
Miami 394, 395
Middle East Technical University (METU) 21, 124–125, 377–378; Central Administration Building 377; "D E V R I M" ("Revolution") 378; School of Architecture and Community Planning 124
Middleton, G. F. 269
Midwest Inter-Library Center 347
migration 2, 27, 232, 323, 330, 368, 402; cyclical 291; internal 221–222; rural–urban 66, 67, 75, 79, 224, 228, 279, 291–293, 295, 298
Mill, John Stuart 9
Miller, T. A. H. 250
Mimarlık 376
mining 217, 231, 280, 384; in Cyprus 384; in Venezuela 217, 224, 228; in Zambia 280, 283, 284, 287, 298
Ministry of Finance and Foreign Affairs (France) 41
Minnesota Plan (1958–1974) 204–207, 208
missionaries 16, 48–49, 53–56, 58–59, 155–158
Mission Française d'Urbanisme 72
Mitchell, Mike 190
MIT–Harvard Joint Center of Urban Studies 218, 223, 224, 229–230, 373
mixed economy (as approach to development) 26
model farms 155
model villages 71, 264, 267, 269–270, 273
modernism (architectural) 2, 19, 39, 88, 96, 105, 108, 147, 150, 207, 221, 264, 303, 305, 315, 411; as form 1; "Left Wing" 110; Second 38
modernization 1, 6, 19, 65, 67–68, 132, 152, 164, 229–230, 246, 313, 319, 371, 376, 386, 402, 405; as a project 2; rural 71, 85, 87, 100, 155, 157–158, 308, 323, 333, 334; theory 7, 41, 286, 288, 333, 371–372
Modotti, Tina 87
Moholy-Nagy, Laszlo 207

monetary system 4, 41, 352; global 3–6; role of the state in 5
money 3–4, 12, 32, 118, 145, 184, 209, 271, 359, 385; currency exchange rates 17; devaluation of 41; as form 3–5, 21; as means of economic integration 288; stocks 352–353; supply 31
monopsony 20
monsoons 245, 359
Moore, Nikki 16–17, 107
Moral, Enrique del 96, 167
Moratinos, Almiro P. 163
Moscow 249
Moses, Robert 28
moshavim (cooperative villages) 323–327, 328–332, 333–334, 336, 338; contrast with *kibbutzim* 326; as planning paradigm 330; settlers' descriptions 328
moshav olim (immigrants' village) 325
moshav ovdim (workers' cooperative village) 325
Motor City (Brazil) 225
Mozambique 282
Mpostantzoglou, Mentis 411
multilateralism 4, 11–12, 15
multinational corporations 89, 96, 106, 113–114, 118
Mumbai 274, 355, 359
Mumford, Lewis 370–371
Murray Hill, NJ 109
Museum of Modern Art (MoMA) 305
Muzaffar, Ijlal 16, 259, 339
Mysore 65

Nagel, John 90
Naipaul, V. S. 13
Nairobi 134, 136, 179, 191; Eastleigh 136; Kariobangi 136; Kibera 136
Nandy, Ashis 360
napalm 115; use in Manila 115
Narvaez, Francisco 303
National Agrarian University (Peru) 100
National Bank of Greece 404
National College of Agriculture (Mexico) 87
National Congress of American Indians 219
National Farm Radio Forum (Canada) 270
National Federation of Students in Agricultural and Forest Sciences (Mexico) 97
National Film Board (NFB, Canada) 184, 190; Challenge for Change 190
National Institute of Design (NID, Ahmedabad) 156
nationalism 50, 99, 162, 168, 170–171, 269, 393, 395; economic 166
National League of Agrarian Communities (Mexico) 87
National Mortgage Bank of Greece 410
National School of Agriculture (Colombia) 100
National School of Agriculture (Mexico) 17, 19, 85–89, 92, 95, 98, 100; Administration Building 86; National Institute for Agricultural Investigations 88; satellite campuses 87
National Strike Council (Mexico) 97
National Technical University of Athens (NTUA) 404, 406, 407
NATO (North Atlantic Treaty Organization) 387

"natural cities" 148
Navarro, Aaron 162
NBC Television (Nigeria) 191
Negrí, Ramón P. De 87
Negritude 283
Negroponte, Nicholas 149
Nehru, Jawaharlal 26, 37, 70, 263–264, 267, 273, 346
Neoclassicism (in architecture) 87, 247, 249, 393
neocolonialism 2, 10, 21, 187, 218, 231, 282, 292, 410
neoliberalism 360, 388; "There Is No Alternative (TINA)" 388
neo-Malthusianism 28, 182, 293, 344, 359
neo-Palladianism 249
Nepal 6
Netzahualcoyotl 98
Neues Bauen 332
New Ajena (Ghana) 47, 60
New American Imperial Age 110
New Deal 70, 242, 250–251, 367, 370
New Delhi 27, 29, 261–263, 265, 372; *see also* Delhi
New International Economic Order 181
New School for Social Research 370–371; Department of Political Science 371
New York City 28, 42–43, 67, 100, 305, 370, 372; Housing Act (1937) 370; Housing Authority 370; Queens 303
New York Post 303
New York Times 303, 343, 394
Nigeria 65, 99, 100, 186, 191, 369, 371
Nixon, Richard 17, 41
Nkrumah, Kwame 47, 56, 282, 286
Nolan, Ginger 18, 19, 37, 259, 353, 405
Non-Aligned Movement (NAM) 16, 387
non-governmental organizations (NGOs) 129, 148–149
North American Indian Traveling College 190
North Casper Improvement Association (Wyoming) 251; North Casper Clubhouse 251
Norway 374
Norwegian Institute of Technology (Trondheim) 127
Novoa, Carlos 167
Nyerere, Julius 284, 286; "Arusha Declaration" 284

Oaxaca 87, 166
Oberlander, Peter 125
Obregón, Álvaro 86, 87
Office of Experiment Stations (Mexico) 88
Office of Special Studies (OSS, Mexico) 88–89
Office of the Coordinator of Inter-American Affairs (OCIAA) 308
O'Gorman, Juan 168, 171, 174; *Canto a la Patria* 171
oil 20, 303–309, 312–319; monopolies 307; nationalization of 303, 308, 314
oil camps (Venezuela) 20, 303, 307–309, 312–315, 317; agriculture in 309, 313; as testing grounds 308–309
Old Testament 52
Olinger, Vyola 217
Olmstead, Frederick Law 13
Olusola, Segun 190–191
Ŏ1usola, Segun 1
organicism 36, 39, 79, 106, 117

Organization of Petroleum Exporting Countries (OPEC) 318
orientalism 110, 201, 355
Orinoco Mining Arc (Venezuela) 218, 229, 231; indigenous nations in 218, 231–232
Orinoco Mining Company 224
Otero, Alejandro 316, 318
Ottoman Military Barracks 365
Owings, Nathaniel 303, 365, 367
"Oxbridge" 2
Oxford Polytechnics 130

Pae Ki-hyŏng 202–204; *ondol* 204; *wanja* 204
Pak Chŏng-hyŏn 212
Pak Hak-jae 197, 212, 214; diagram of architectural knowledge 212, *213*
Pakistan 6, 371, 373; Lyallpur 107
Palestine 325, 329, 331, 336, 338; Arab communities 325, 327, 332; Gaza Strip 329
Palmer, Robert 90–91
Palm Springs 18, 217, 219–223, 232; displacement of native Americans 18
Pan-Africanism 283
Panama Canal 224
panchayats 71, 153, 155, 263, 265
Panerai, Philippe 131–132
Pan-Hellenic Architectural Conferences 406
Pani, Alberto J. 168
Pani, Mario 96, 167, 170
Panipat 269
Parahyangan Catholic University (Bandung) 128
Paris 4, 27, 247
Park, Melany Sun-Min 18, 409
Park Chung-hee 199
Parthenon 393
Partido Acción Nacional (PAN, Mexico) 175
Patel, C. B. 244–246
Patel, Shirish 355
patios 217, 227, 228, 230; as architectural form 227, 231
Patnaik, Utsa 344
Patty, Ralph L. 250
Paul I (Tsar) 249
Payne, Geoffrey 130
Peacock, E. E. 80
peasantry 71, 218, 228, 248–249, 279, 291, 295
Peñalosa, Enrique 182–185
Pentecostal Evangelical Church 48, 54
People's Action Party (Singapore) 68, 81
Pepler, Georges 66, 75
Percival, Lance 381
Pérez Jiménez, Marcos 228–229, 318
Pérez Palacios, Augusto 168, 171–173, 174
Perkins + Will 85, 89–91, 96, 98–99
Perón, Juán 165
Perroux, François 230
personajismo 172
Peru 100, 125, 130, 225, 228
petroleum 201, 305, 309
philanthropic foundations 224, 295
Philip II 116

INDEX

Philippine Coconut Authority 115, 118
Philippines 16, 17, 99, 100, 106–117, 371; agricultural development programs 106–107; American colonial period 108; Communist insurgency 107, 114; Congress 114; Corregidor Island 112; decolonization 106; economy 117; export processing zones 117; external debt 114; "Food for Peace Act" 113; industrial elites 114; Islamist insurgency 107, 114; martial law 114; politics of development in 105; *rebolusyon* 116; working class in 114; World Bank loans to 114
Phokaides, Petros 19, 65, 407
Picó, Rafael 261, 373
pied-noirs 27
Piraeus 406; Faliro 406
pisé 247–248
Plain of Jars 111
Plan Chapingo 85, 89, 90–92, 96–98, 100
planning 1, 5, 13, 16–19, 26–33, 39, 41–43, 65–76, 80–81, 88–89, 123–127, 131, 143, 163–167, 181–183, 206, 212, 258, 261, 265, 269, 272, 274, 280–281, 284–289, 291–297, 323–335, 348, 368, 372–373, 377, 401–408, 412; "branch (*vs.* root) approach" 74; bureaucracy 171; co-operative 329–333, 338; curricula 123; economic 33, 123, 199; implementation 16, 72; national 169; paradigms of 66; "participation" in 72; as a profession 66; as teleological aspiration 26; *see also* action planning
Planning Commission (India) 26, 29, 263, 345, 346
Plan Rockefeller (Venezuela) 315
Point IV Program 88, 219, 305, 346
political science 386
polykatoikia 401–403, 406, 407–409
population 1, 28, 280–281, 297, 354, 369; agricultural 75, 181, 248, 279, 285, 290, 293, 312; and demography 25; growth 66–67, 182, 241; policy 7; redistribution of 30, 78, 228, 288; representations of 25
Port Royal grammarians 8
ports 348, 353, 388
positivism 17, 88, 231
Post-Graduate Centre on Human Settlements (PGCHS), Katholieke Universiteit Leuven 17, 123–124, 127–138; student exchanges 127–128; UN-mandated training program 124, 128
post-structuralism 132, 133, 138
Potts, Deborah 297
poverty 7, 107, 112, 245, 252; rural 280, 297, 308; "urban poor" 17, 136
Prebisch, Raúl 286
Preciado, Gil 98
Prieto, Alejandro 96
Primitivism 39
Princeton University 270
Private School of Agriculture (Ciudad Juarez) 87
Privy Council for Scientific and Industrial Research, Building Research Board 250
psychoanalysis 8
public goods 10, 26
Puebla 166
Puerto Ordaz 224–230; "civic center" *227*; site plan *226*

Puerto Rico 371, 409; Planning Board 373; Social Program 373
pulque 98
Punjab 155, 262, 269, 343–344; State Government 351
Punjab State Warehousing Corporation 351
Pusan 239
Pusey, Nathan 27
Pyla, Panayiota 20–21, 411
Pyrene Manufacturing Company 265

Rahman, Habib 9
Rai, Gulshan 263
Raju, S. P. 263
Ramachandran, Arcot 129
Ramirez, Raul 240, 242, 247
Ramírez Vázquez, Pedro 168, 174
Rancière, Jacques 192
Rand Corporation 88
Rangsit 134
Rank, J. Arthur 265
Rao, D. V. 263
Rapoport, Amos 136; Man-Environment Studies 136
Rapson, Ralph 207
Rational Planning Corporation 265
Ratner, Yochanan 332
Raymond, Antonin 207
Reagan, Ronald 388
real estate 42, 67–68, 150, 223, 403, 409; developers 71; industry 68
Rechovot 332
Reddy, Balwanth 354
Reed, George 409
Regional Housing Centre (Delhi) 245
Renan, Ernest 166
rent 391, 401; absolute *vs.* differential 401; control 408
Research and Action Institute (Lucknow) 70
Research Center on Settlement (Israel) 332–333
Rhodesia 4
rice 6, 14, 17, 106, 108, 111–113, 115, 200–201, 343, 345; high-yield 17; hybridization 113; IR8 112; research 17, 107–109, 113; shortages 201
Richardson, Ralph 90
ring city 68, *69*
ring plan 71
ring roads 28, 30, 66
risk 32, 54, 60, 66, 334, 336, 403
Rivas Mercado, Antonio 86, 100
Rivera, Diego 87, 90, 99; *Our Daily Bread* (1928) 100
Rivera, Myra 52–53, 55
Rivera Santos, Luis 373
Robbins, Ira 370
Rockefeller, Nelson E. 20, 303
Rockefeller Foundation 17, 85, 88–91, 97–100, 107–108, 114, 224, 303–309, 312–315, 318–319, 354; Division of Natural Sciences and Agriculture 107; and "international cooperation" 107; Mexican Agriculture Program (MAP) 107
Rodríguez Adame, Julián 88
Rogers, Ernesto 271
Rokach, Avshalom 323, 324

Rome 182
Roorkee 245, 349
Roosevelt, Franklin D. 303, 305, 308
Rosenboim, Or 242
Rossell de la Lama, Guillermo 170–171; *Editorial Espacios* 171
Rosenstein-Rodan, Paul 7
Rossi, Aldo 17, 131, 133–134
Rostow, Walter 7, 21, 55, 279; *Stages of Growth* 51
Row, Arthur T. 37, 42
Roy, B. C. 26–27
Royal Dutch Shell 314
Ruiz Cortines, Adolfo 161, 170, 173–174
Rural Building Research Center (Israel) 19, 323, 331–332, 334, 336
Ruskin, John 9
Russia 249
Ryerson University 271
Rykwert, Joseph 355

Saarinen, Eero 106, 108, 109
Sachlichkeit 39–40
Saigon 111
Saint-Simon, Henri de 9
Salazar Mallén, Rubén 174–175
Salt Lake City (Calcutta) 30
Samaria 329
Samsung 210
San Félix 224, 228–231
Sanskrit 347
Sanz, Moisés 87
SAR 73 132; "tissue analysis" 134
Sarabhai, Gautam 156, 157
Sarabhai, Gita 156
Sarabhai, Mridula 267
Saray Hotel (Nicosia) 391
Sardinia 395
scale 7–9, 21, 52, 133, 146, 150, 212, 230, 264, 284, 292, 378; spatial 49; temporal 47, 49–50
science 40, 95, 98, 108, 115, 162, 197, 205, 312, 315; communities of 90; cybernetics as a 40; economics as a 39; "hard" 108–109, 113; international cooperation in 5
Scott, Felicity D. 18, 252
Scott, James C. 65, 338
Searle, John 132
Sears 317
Second World War *see* World War II
Secretaría de Bienes Nacionales e Inspección Administrativa (Secretariat of National Resources and Administrative Inspection, SNRAI) 164; *Comisión Federal de Planificación* (Federal Commission of Planning) 164; *Comisión Técnica de Arquitectos* (Technical Commission of Architects) 164
Secretaría de Comunicaciones y Obras Públicas (SCOP, Mexico) 161, 163, 170–171, 173–174, 175; administrative reforms 170; *Dirección de Planificación* 170; *Gerencia de Promoción* 171
Secretaría de Comunicaciones y Transportes (SCT, Mexico) 175

Secretaría de la Presidencia 175
Secretaría de Obras Públicas 175
Secretaría de Recursos Hidráulicos (Mexico) 166
"sectoral imbalances" 14
secularism 386
Seers, Dudley 286–287, 291–292, 295
Selva, Rogerio de la 168
semiotics 132, 137
Sen, Amartya 241, 344; *Choice of Techniques: An Aspect of the Theory of Planned Economic Development* (1960) 241
Senegal 118, 186
Seoul 239; City Hall 212
Seoul National University 202, 204, 206–208; Department of Architectural Engineering 206–207
SETAP 72
settlements 3, 10, 15, 17, 19, 73, 123, 127–129, 136–137, 148, 180, 182–183, 250, 285, 288–290, 292, 323, 325, 327, 329, 332, 338, 409; informal 229; as paradigm 132; as site of action 123–124; squatter 130, 181; worker 18
Sevagram (India) 269
Sharon, Arieh 261 [done]
sheds 15, 19, 202, 265, 333–334, 338, 343, 345; cowsheds 323–328, 334, 336, 339; "universal cowsheds" 327, *328*, 334
Shin Kŏnch'uk Culture Research Institute 207
Shirer, Lloyd 48–49, 53–57, 58
Shirer, Margaret 54–56
Shoshkes, Ellen 272
Siddle, David J. 295
Sierra Leone 16, 65, 75–81; Colonial Welfare and Development Act 79; Five Year Plan of Economic and Social Development (1965)75; Freetown 75; rural chiefs 78–79
Sierra Leone National Urbanisation Plan (1965) 76
Singapore 4, 16, 65–70, 72–75, 80–81, 371; 1964 riots 67; achievement of self-rule (1959) 72; British colonial administration of 65, 66, 76; Central Area 67; industrialization of 67; Ministry of National Development 68, 81; Port of Singapore Authority 81; repression of communists in 67; Smart Nation initiative (2014) 81; Urban Renewal and Development Project (1967) 81
Singh, Gurdeep 343, 358–359
Sinha, Subir 155
Situationists 39
Skidmore, Louis 303
Skidmore, Owings and Merrill (SOM) 9, 224, 303, 365, 367–369, 373–374, 376; "Construction, Town Planning, and Housing in Turkey" 368
Skroubelos, Ilias 407
slums 27–28, 37, 42, 127, 134, 136, 220, 222–223; clearance 67–68, 221
socialism 8, 15, 27, 41, 283–284, 286, 386, 410; as developmental model 16, 26
social overhead capital 26, 33
Sociedad de Arquitectos Mexicanos (SAM) 168–169, 174; *Movimiento de Unidad y Renovación* (Movement for Unity and Renovation) 167–168

INDEX

Society for the Pursuit of Science and Reconstruction (Greece) 404
Society of Architectural Historians 15
sociologists 33, 73, 261, 332, 333, 386
Socony-Vacuum Oil 314
Sokos, Andreas 406
sŏlgye ("design") 197, 199, 202, 210, 212–214
Solow, Robert 32
Sonora 92
South Africa 238, 261, 287; apartheid 283
South Korea 16, 18, 197–202, 204–205, 208, 238–241, 409; balance of payments 201; decolonization 202; Five Year Plans 199, 204; industrialization of 18, 199, 201; Illyŏk Kaebal Yŏn'guso (Manpower Research Institute) 205; inflation 201; Japanese colonial rule 198; Ministry of Commerce and Industry 205; Ministry of Finance 209; Ministry of Social Affairs 239; National Housing Authority 239; normalization of relations with Japan 199; North Korean refugees in 240–241; professionalization of architects in 198, 199; Public Law 480 (1954) 200; saengsan 201; Science-Technology Promotion Act (1967) 204; US agricultural imports to 201
Southern Rhodesia 282
sovereignty 1, 2, 5–6, 20, 153, 217, 264, 280; decolonial 219; food 17
Soviet Union 1, 4, 10, 367; *Gosplan* 5; New Economic Policy 1, 5; Soviet Bloc 16
Speer, George 409–411
Spivak, Gayatri C. 274
squatting 127, 130, 181, 229, 405; and "unauthorized housing" 405
Squire, Raglan 392
Sri Lanka (Ceylon) 6, 186, 295, 395
stagflation 41
Standard Oil 113, 303–304, 314
Standard Oil Company (Venezuela) 304, 308–309, 312, 313; *El Farol* 309, 313; *The Lamp* 309
Standard Oil Company of Venezuela Agricultural Colony 313
Stanek, Lukasz 126
statisticians 9, 33, 40
statistics 5, 81, 345
steel 10, 18–19, 96, 203, 217–218, 220–224, 228, 230–232, 344, 349, 392, 403; "as sovereign jurisdiction" 232
Stein, Chatterjee, and Polk 349
Stein, Gertrude 58
Stinnett, Caskie 381
Stockholm 182–183
Stratton, Julius 27
Strong, Maurice 183
structuralism 32, 156–157, 175
students 17, 95–97, 125, 127, 206, 312, 378; campus strikes 97; protest movements 97, 378
subsidies 7, 20, 28, 42, 291, 297, 308, 334, 384
suburbs 28, 143, 224, 227, 308, 317–318, 390
Sudra, Tomasz 137
sugar 305, 334
supermarkets 20, 222, 224, 307, 313, 315–319; bombings of 20, 318; commissaries 314; Supermercado CADA 316

supply chains 10, 28, 299
surplus labor 4, 6, 14, 21, 222, 241–242; absorption of 246; and underemployment 251
surveyors 73
surveys 65, 72–76, 80–81, 185, 286–288, 298, 330–333, 374; accommodation 81; land-use 81
swadeshi 264
Sweden 99, 238, 327, 354; Uppsala 187
Syria 100
systems theory 7–8, 11, 40, 49, 74, 76, 127, 295; position of observer in 49

Taeuber-Arp, Sophie 316
Tahanang Pilipino ("Coconut Palace") 105–106, 116–119
Taiwan 108
Taksim Square 365–367, 378; protests 365, *366*
Tange Kenzo 35; Boston Harbor project 36; Tokyo Bay Plan 36
Tanzania 186, 189, 280, 284, 286
taxes 287, 308, 314, 327, 403; evasion 401; exemptions 99; incentives 7
Team 10 [X] 39, 407
Team 10 Primer 35
Technica Chronica 404
Technical Cooperation Mission (TCM) 346
Technical University of Szczecin (Poland) 126; "International Postgraduate Course of Urban and Regional Planning for Developing Countries" 126
Technion Israel Institute of Technology 332, 333; Faculty of Agricultural Engineering 332
technocracy 17–18, 39, 88, 97, 116, 263
technocrats 14, 27, 70, 113, 118, 167, 205, 217, 220, 229, 231, 253, 308, 318, 352
técnicos 162, 167, 171, 175
Tehran 72, 392; Plan Organization 72
Teige, Karel 13
Tel Aviv 381–382, 390
Tel Quel 132
Templers 325
Tennessee Valley Authority 80, 261, 351
Tenreiro-Degwitz, Jesus 231
Teotihuacan 96
Texcoco 17, 85, 98, 174
Textile Fiber Materials for Industry 208
Thailand 185, 263
Thatcher, Margaret 388
Thijsse, Jacob 261
Thompson, Laura 74
Thorp, Willard 384–385, 387, 393
Time magazine 242, 392
Times (London) 381
Times of India 348
Tiukhill 249
Tlatelolco Square 97
Tnuva 327
Tokyo 125
Torzhok 249
totalitarianism 166, 252
"total planning" 212
Touloumi, Olga 19

Toulouse 16, 25, 27–28, 30, 42–43, 407; regional development plan 25
tourism 20–21, 88, 382–388, 391–397, 402, 411; as development model 383–385; and travel agencies 385
To Vima 408
tractors 87, 291, 313, 336
tradition (*vs.* modernity) 7, 18–19, 59–60, 131, 132, 147, 201, 228, 231, 246–247, 267, 279, 284, 288, 292–293, 319, 386, 401, 402; construction of 19; "folkways" 50; and heritage 71, 281, 283
Trans World Airlines 381
Tropical Study Group (Birmingham) 125
Trotsky, Leon 9
Truman, Harry S. 219, 305, 346, 384; Scientific Research Council 242
Truman Doctrine 367, 404, 409
Trump, Donald 3
Trust Houses Forte 394
Tucker, St. George 250
Tung Song Hong 134
Turkey 16, 21, 118, 124, 367–369, 371, 373–378, 382, 383, 387, 392, 411; Democratic Party (DP) 369; Economic Cooperation Administration (ECA) 369; flat ownership law (*kat mülkiyeti kanunu*) 369; Foreign Operations Administration (FOA) 369; invasion of Cyprus (1974) 397; Ministry of Public Works 373, 375; National Department of Highways 375; Palace of Justice 375; Republican People's Party (RPP) 369
Turkish Pension Fund (*Emekli Sandığı*) 369
Turkish Workers Pension Fund 374
Turner, John F. C. 17, 130–131, 231
Tyrwhitt, Jaqueline 10, 19, 124–125, 259–274, 372; *The Heart of the City* 264; *Patrick Geddes in India* 261

underdevelopment 107, 111, 219, 240, 241, 253, 272, 286, 314, 346
unemployment 4, 28, 67, 221–222, 252, 313, 382
UNESCO (United Nations Educational, Scientific, and Cultural Organization) 186, 265, 270, 272–273, 375
UN-Habitat *see* United Nations Centre for Human Settlements (UNCHS, UN-Habitat)
unions 97, 223
United Kingdom 41, 67, 250, 261, 270, 287
United Nations 5, 11, 67, 88, 99, 124, 200, 238, 259, 279, 345, 367, 370, 383; Bureau of Social Affairs 245; Centre for Housing, Building and Planning (UNCHBP) 66, 126–127; Development Decades 6, 181, 192; General Assembly 183, 238; Regional Housing Centres 244, 245; Special Fund 75; "technical missions" 18
United Nations Centre for Human Settlements (UNCHS, UN-Habitat) 126–129, 137, 146, 149; *Localising Agenda 21* 137
United Nations Civil Assistance Command in Korea (UNCACK) 200
United Nations Conference on the Human Environment (Stockholm) 182; Declaration of Principles 183
United Nations Conference on Trade and Development (UNCTAD) 117–118
United Nations Conference on Women (Mexico City) 182
United Nations Conference on World Food (Rome) 182
United Nations Conference on World Population (Bucharest) 182
United Nations Division of Social Affairs 124; Housing and Town and Country Planning Section 124, 242, 261, 371, 372
United Nations Economic and Security Council 263
United Nations Economic and Social Council 372
United Nations Economic Commission for Asia and the Far East 244, 263
United Nations Economic Commission for Latin America (ECLA) 286
United Nations Economic Commission in Africa (UNECA) 286
United Nations Environment Program (UNEP) 182–184
United Nations Food and Agriculture Organization 265, 346, 375–376
United Nations Institute for Training and Research (UNITAR) 124
United Nations Korean Reconstruction Agency (UNKRA) 199–200, 238–242, 248; Community Development Groups (CDGs) 241; Program Analysis Division 238
United Nations Seminar on Housing and Community Improvement 259, 261, 269
United Nations Seminar on Regional Planning 125
United Nations Technical Assistance Administration (UNTAA) 9, 17, 124, 244, 261; fellowships 125
United States 3, 10, 16; Army 224; Bureau of Indian Affairs 219; as "consumers' republic" 220; debt 17; Federal Works Agency 251; food exports 345; foreign policy 305; housing industry 18; Indian reservation system 218; National Youth Administration 251; Resettlement Administration 251; suburban growth model 224; Works Progress Administration 251
United States Congress 221, 347; Indian Equalization Act (1959) 221; Relocation Act (1956) 222
United States Housing and Home Finance Agency 238, 373, 409
United States Information Agency (USIA) 347
United States Treasury 26, 41
University College London (UCL) 126; Bartlett School 126
University of British Columbia 125–126; Department of Community and Regional Planning 125
University of California, Berkeley 17, 70, 108, 127, 347; Center for Environmental Structure (CES) 127, 146
University of Chicago 183
University of Colorado, Boulder 127
University of Liverpool 407–408; Department of Civic Design 407
University of Minnesota 204, 207; School of Architecture 207
University of Missouri 375
University of Nairobi 134; Housing Research and Development Unit (HRDU) 134
University of North Carolina–Chapel Hill 270
University of Pennsylvania 190; Annenberg School of Communications 190
University of the Philippines College of Agriculture 108
University of Toronto 259–261, 372

INDEX

University of Washington 127
urbanism 127, 148, 163, 217; landscape 137
urbanization 39, 125, 181, 229–230, 279–280, 282, 285, 368, 402, 407; in Sierra Leone 75–76, 78–80; in Zambia 297
urban planning 1, 10, 16, 30, 43, 88, 123, 124, 131, 149, 218, 273, 333, 409
urban-rural linkages 25, 75
urban studies 137
US Agency for International Development (USAID) 11, 91, 113, 115, 354, 375; SPREAD 113
US Department of Agriculture (USDA) 250, 252, 347; Division of Agricultural Engineering 250
US Department of State 28
US Steel 217–225, 228–232; defense contracts 222; Fairless Works 224; Homes division 222; warehouses 222
Uttar Pradesh 70–72, 74, 264, 346, 349; Chandigarh 70, 264, 373; as development model 71; Etawah 264; Hapur 346; Lucknow 70
Uzer, Celal 373, 375

Valera, Victor 316
Vancouver 17, 70, 123, 126, 179–186, 191
van der Rohe, Mies 94
Varvaressos, Kyriakos 408
Vassiliadis, Prokopis 403, 407–408, 411
Venezuela 16, 19–20, 80, 125, 149, 217–218, 224, 225, 229–232, 303–310, 312–319, 371; agrarian reform 318; armed forces 318; Chamber of Commerce 318; Demonstration Farms 313; exports 303; food crisis 307; Food Mission 307; guerrilla groups 318; Hidrocarburos Law (1943) 308; middle class 319; middle-class neighborhoods 307; Ministry of Agriculture and Livestock 313; Monagas 313; National Defense Council 308; National Guard 228; New National Ideal 318; as petrostate 303, 304, 308; political parties 218; Revolutionary Junta 314; Spanish colonial rule 231; treaties with US 308; Triento (1945–1948) 307; unbalanced economy 307; War of Independence 231
Venezuelan Basic Economy Corporation (VBEC) 314–316; Compania Anonima Distribuidora de Alimentos (CADA) 315
Veracruz 166
Vernon, Raymond 175
Verschure, Han 124, 127–128
Victor Gruen Associates 221
Vietnam 2, 28, 113, 377; South 112
Vietnam War 113, 377
village design 19, 150
Virginia 250, 251; Company 50
Virilio, Paul 252
Volcani, Yitzhak Elazari 325–326
Volta River Valley (Ghana) 47–49, 53; Project Area 48
Voorhees, Walker, Foley, and Smith (VWFS) 109

Wachsmann, Conrad 9
Wakeman, Rosemary 42
Waldheim, Kurt 183
Walker, Ralph 109–110

Warao tribe (Orinoco) 218, 232
Warren, Avra 377
Washington, Bushrod 250
Washington, DC 5, 41, 183
Washington State Agriculture College 99
Washington University Law Review 41
Weaver, Warren 107–108
Weber, Max 51, 147; "traditional" *vs.* "rational" authority 147
Wee, H. Koon 67
Weiner, Myron 27
Weiner, Norbert 49; *see also* cybernetics
Weiss, Lynn 56–57, 58
Weissmann, Ernest 124–125, 242, 244, 246, 261, 263, 272, 371, 372, 377; *Manual for Supervising Self-Help Home Construction with Stabilized Earth Blocks* 246
Weitz, Joseph 331
Weitz, Raanan 73, 80, 324, 328, 331, 333
welfare 31, 74, 309, 314, 328, 338, 372, 378, 388, 405, 408
Wellhausen, Edwin 98
Welton Becket and Associates 210–212; organizational chart *211*; *Total Design: Architecture of Welton Becket and Associates* (1972) 210
West Bank 331
West Bengal 27; election of Marxist government 28, 42; government of *29*
West Bengal Public Works Department 9
West Germany 238
Wexler, Donald 220, 221, 222
Wexler & Harrison 220, 221, 223, 232; Development House *223*
Wharton, Annabel 367–368, 383, 388; *Building the Cold War* 383
wheat 14, 89, 92, 98, 200–201, 343–348, 354, 359; Norin 10 92; shuttle breeding 92; "Trigo/Wheat" 94
Whittlesey, Julian H. 27, 28, 37, 42
Whole Earth catalogue 253
Wiener, Paul Lester 218, 224–225, 228, 229–231
Wilbur Smith and Associates 31
Williams College 50
Williams-Ellis, Clough 250; *Cottage Building in Cob, Pisé, Chalk & Clay: A Renaissance* (1919) 250
Wilson, Harold 41
women 18, 47, 59–60, 272, 283, 295; as figure of nature 57; "purity" of 153
Women's Wear Daily 304
Woods, Shadrach 33, 35, 37, 41, 43
World Agriculture Fair (Delhi, 1959) 347
World Bank 5, 27, 88, 114–115, 117–119, 123, 181, 183, 295–297, 353–354, 355; *Agriculture and Rural Sector Survey* (1975) 295; "facilitative planning" 296; Permanent Advisory Panel on Agriculture and Rural Development 183; structural adjustment loans 118
World Health Organization (WHO) 108, 265
World War I 115, 250
World War II 1, 2, 12, 25, 28, 35, 70, 88–89, 96, 112, 115, 181, 217–219, 222, 224, 242, 263, 305, 309, 315, 347, 354, 367, 401
Worth, Sol 190
Wright, Frank Lloyd 13, 106, 116
Wright, Richard 56–58

Xalapa Mexican Communist Party 87

Yalan, Emmanuel 332–334
Yamasaki, Minoru 347; *Amriki Mela* 347
Yiftachel, Oren 338
Yi Sang-hŏn 206, 212–214
Yi Sŏng-ch'ul 202
Young Men's Christian Association (YMCA) 155
Yugoslavia 16, 30
Yun Chŏng-sŏp 207

Zambia 16, 19, 186, 280–291, 293–298, 407; agreement with the United Kingdom on copper mining 287; British colonial rule 283; Department of Agriculture 293; "Development Units" 293, *294*; economic crisis, 1970s 297; First National Development Plan (FNDP) 286; foreign mining monopolies 287; import-substitution strategy 280, 291; "indirect rule" in 283; Kafue 281; Kasama-Livingstone rail line 291; Lusaka 281; "One Nation, One Zambia" 283; rural settlement schemes 281, 288; Second National Development Plan 294; "tribal" administration 283; village reorganization 285; "Zambianization" 286
zamindari system 155, 263
Zapata, Emiliano 17, 97, 99
Zenetos, Takis 406, 408; Electronic Urbanism (1959) 406
Zionism 323, 325
zoning regulations 21, 27, 368, 373
Zorlu, Fatin Rüştü 376–377
Zúñiga, Francisco 171